D0984619

A SHORT HISTORY OF THE FAR EAST

THE MACMILLAN COMPANY
NEW YORK · BOSTON · CHICAGO · DALLAS
ATLANTA · SAN FRANCISCO

MACMILLAN AND CO., LIMITED
LONDON · BOMBAY · CALCUTTA · MADRAS
MELBOURNE

THE MACMILLAN COMPANY
OF CANADA, LIMITED
TORONTO

A SHORT HISTORY OF THE FAR EAST

BY KENNETH SCOTT LATOURETTE

STERLING PROFESSOR OF MISSIONS AND ORIENTAL HISTORY AND FELLOW OF BERKELEY COLLEGE IN YALE UNIVERSITY

REVISED EDITION

New York THE MACMILLAN COMPANY

First Printing

PRINTED IN THE UNITED STATES OF AMERICA

TO WILLIAM TRUFANT FOSTER

To whom both this book
and the author are
deeply indebted

PREFACE

THE PURPOSE of this book is to provide an introduction to the contemporary Far East. The readers whom the author has in mind are thoughtful, educated Americans who have no previous contact with the region and who desire such a survey as will give them background for an understanding of the peoples, the cultures, and the current problems of that area. It is hoped that the book will be of use to two types of constituencies. One is composed of the somewhat hypothetical "general readers," those who wish such a knowledge of the lands on the east shores of Asia as will enable them to read intelligently the newspaper dispatches and the magazine articles that pass by them in endless and often bewildering procession. The other is college and university teachers and students who desire a textbook for a general course on the Far East.

The volume is primarily designed for Americans. It therefore devotes a somewhat larger proportion of its pages to relations between the United States and Far Eastern peoples than it would had the entire English-reading public been in mind.

However, the book is in no sense intended as a work of propaganda in which the case for the policies and actions of the United States is set forth and defended. Nor is there any thought of presenting in favorable light those peoples with whom most Americans are for the moment in sympathy or of providing justification for the enmities which the majority of Americans cherish. The book is based upon the conviction that the American public will best be served by as objective and dispassionate a treatment as the author can achieve.

Underlying the volume is the assumption that the present can be understood only through a knowledge of the past. The story, therefore, is made to begin with the dawn of recorded history. Approximately half of the space is devoted to the pre-nineteenth century course of events and to the cultures of the region before the changes wrought by the coming in force of the Occident. Always in that narrative, however, the objective of elucidating the contemporary scene is kept in mind. Men, events, and movements that have contributed to the Far East of today are stressed, and from time to time the fashion in which these are still potent is pointed out.

In the treatment of the subject, history is thought of as including more than past politics. Because so much of public interest is focused on political events and the relations between governments, the larger proportion of our space is devoted to this side of the story. However, other phases of human activity and achievements may prove quite as significant as the political. Frequently, too, the political cannot be explained without taking into account other aspects of culture. For instance, Japan's activities upon the neighboring continent remain unintelligible without some comprehension of the economic situation and of the religious history and presuppositions of the Japanese. Moreover, the basic structure of China's culture, including the political theories and organization of the land, rests upon philosophical convictions inherited from a remote past. We must, therefore, cover all phases of the history of man's thinking and acting in the region we denominate the Far East.

By the Far East we mean the eastern portions of Asia and the adjacent islands. The land which is largest in population and the most influential is China. Next in population, and recently outstanding in political power, is Japan. To these two countries the major part of our attention must be devoted. Also included are regions which in whole or in part have at one time or another been included in the Chinese imperial system and some of which have lately partially or entirely been under the control of Japan—Korea (or, to give it the name the Japanese prefer, Chosen), Formosa (Taiwan to the Chinese and Japanese), Manchuria (from 1932 into 1945, in Japanese terminology, but not so officially recognized by most of the rest of the world, Manchukuo), Mongolia, Sinkiang (Chinese Turkestan), Tibet, Annam, and Tongking. Also within the Far East are the Russian possessions in Eastern Asia, Cambodia, Cochin-China, Laos, the Malay Peninsula, Siam (or Thailand), the Philippine Islands, and the East Indies. To these, lesser sections of our pages will be devoted. We must, too, say something of India and occasionally mention Ceylon and Burma, not because they are in the Far East but because through geographic propinquity and, in the case of India, because of cultural influence, they have entered into the Far Eastern story. Yet we must confine our consideration of these last three lands chiefly to the events and the movements through which they have affected the countries properly included in the Far East.

Indeed, at the outset we must disabuse ourselves of one of the commonest misconceptions of Occidentals, that the Orient is a unity. We speak of the Occident and the Orient. By the Occident we mean peoples which have a common heritage. The Occident embraces most of Europe and those nations in America, Australasia, and South Africa who are Europeans by physical and cultural descent. Although it displays great variety, it finds a unity in its Greek, Roman, and Jewish-Christian antecedents. Perhaps because the Occident designates a cultural entity, the common assumption is that the Orient is also a unit. Nothing could be further from the truth. The Orient means merely those sections of the Euro-Asiatic continent, with the adjoining islands and with the related portion of North Africa, which are not included in the Western European tradition. They embrace the major part of Euro-Asia. Indeed, Europe is simply a large peninsula of that land mass. The only unity in the Orient is that it is not the Occident. To be sure, the peoples of the Orient have influenced one another, but they have also influenced the Occident. Indeed, the Occident is largely a development from the Western Orient. Yet among the major cultures of the Orient as great differences in history, background, and outlook exist as separate the Occident from the Orient. Between the civilizations of India and China, for instance, in spite of the contributions of the former to the latter, fully as wide a gulf yawns as between those of India and Europe.

Although affected by other civilizations of Euro-Asia, particularly by those which geographically lie closest to it, and although, like Europe, displaying within itself varieties, the Far East has been and still remains an entity. Geographically and culturally it has been and is as much apart from the rest of Asia and of the world as is Europe. As we have said, until the latter half of the nineteenth century China was the dominant feature of the Far East. It presented, and, indeed, still presents, the largest unit of population. It was the chief empire. It shaped its neighbors. The Japanese, next to the Chinese the most numerous people of the Far East, derived civilization chiefly from China, and their culture is a variant of that of China. Culturally as well as geographically the Far East belongs together.

The very term, the Far East, is part of the clue to our story. It is of Occidental mintage. To Occidentals it designates the part of the Orient which is most remote from them. The distance is not only geographical but also cultural. Until the latter part of the nineteenth century, fewer contacts and less interchange existed between Western European and Far Eastern peoples than between the Occident and any other of the civilized folk of Asia. In the latter part of the nineteenth and in the twentieth century, the Occident came in augmented power to the Far East. The revolutionary disturbances wrought by that impact have been among the most extensive ever experienced by any major group of mankind. They are by no means concluded. They constitute a large portion of our narrative.

The Far East as a term has still further import. While it was coined by Western peoples, it has a counterpart in the Far East itself. Nippon, in its more familiar form, Japan, means the land where the sun rises, or, to give it a free and euphonious translation, the Land of the Rising Sun. To the Japanese this has peculiar significance. They have regarded their Emperor as descending from the Sun Goddess and having a divine origin and mission. In the expansion of Japanese power on the continent of Asia and in the island world of the Far East, which was one of the most striking features of world history of the past half century and more, they saw steps toward the fulfillment of that destiny. In employing the term Far East, it need scarcely be added, we are not intending to endorse the Japanese claim. An alternative designation might be Eastern Asia. This, however, is not as inclusive as the Far East. The latter embraces island groups not strictly in the former. The Far East is, therefore, the title we employ.

A word needs to be said concerning the organization of the book. First, as is proper, is a chapter on geography. This is succeeded by a long section, approximately half of the book, describing India and the Far East before the revolutionary impact of the Occident. This section has first a chapter on India before the nineteenth century, to serve as an introduction to the bearing of that country and its culture upon the Far East. Then follow chapters which describe the history and culture of the Far East before the time when, in the nineteenth century, the Westerner came in force and inaugurated the sweeping changes of the past two generations. After that is a section, also nearly half the volume, in which we enter upon a somewhat more detailed account of the Far East since these changes began.

To each chapter two bibliographies are appended. The first is brief and is made up only of such books as should be in the library of every moderate-sized city and of every college and university. The second is longer, and includes books that should be in the libraries of all the larger cities and of the major universities. Very few books in languages other than English are given. A large list of these might be included, but to the average American general reader and undergraduate, because of linguistic handicaps, they would be of little use. Nor have many references to magazine articles been made. For Japan an excellent selected brief bibliography is H. Borton, S. Elisséeff, E. O. Reischauer, *A Selected List of Books and Articles on Japan in English, French, and German* (Washington, 1940). For China fuller bibliographies, but still selected, will be found in K. S. Latourette, *The Chinese. Their History and Culture* (New York, 3d edition, revised 1945). For the Far East in general the best bibliography is R. J. Kerner, *Northeastern Asia. A Selected Bibliography* (Berkeley, 1939).

In a sense, this is a thrice-told tale. For thirty-seven years the author has been narrating all or part of it annually to successive relays of students. In previous books on China and Japan, he has covered most of it. Yet all this may bring a certain advantage. To the author, at least, the story has never become trite. To have lived with it for a generation and to have presented it again and again should enable one to separate the essential from the nonessential and to give vividness to the outstanding features. Long meditation and familiarity, moreover, should have given birth to insight. As to whether the author has made the most of these advantages the reader must be the judge.

The author is indebted to many for assistance in the preparation of this volume. He recalls with gratitude his introduction to the Far East by instructors in his student years at Yale; his immersion in the life of the Far East and the Chinese language through his period on the teaching staff of Yale in China; the opportunity for giving instruction in the Far East afforded by Reed College, Denison University, and Yale University; the students who by the stimulus of their presence and their questions have aided his thinking and the organization of the material; the labors of the specialists without whose compilations of sources and whose writings this book would have been impossible; the kindness of William Trufant Foster, who first made possible the offering of the course, in Reed College, in the years 1914–1916; the unvarying courtesy and helpfulness of the staffs of the libraries of Yale University; and the skillful typing of the manuscript and the suggestions as to style by Mrs. Charles T. Lincoln. To all of these this volume must in large part be attributed.

TABLE OF CONTENTS

A SHORT HISTORY OF THE FAR EAST

Chapter I. THE GEOGRAPHIC SETTING

THE HISTORY AND PRESENT PROBLEMS of the Far East have been profoundly influenced by the geographic setting. This seems a banality and it should be. Yet it is sometimes forgotten. We must not only begin our account by a brief description of the geography of the region, but again and again we must revert to the bearing of the physical environment upon events.

General Features

At the outset, we must remind ourselves of certain general features of the Far East which influence the whole.

First of all is the pre-nineteenth century remoteness of the Far East from other great centers of civilization. The Far East, as the very name indicates, is at the extreme eastern edge of the Euro-Asiatic Continent. On this land mass and its closely associated northern shore of Africa was until the sixteenth century practically all of the advanced civilization of mankind. The only exceptions of consequence were the ancient cultures of Mexico, Central America, and Peru, and these were separated from the civilizations of the remainder of the human race by vast and almost untraversed stretches of ocean and by the forbidding route through eastern Siberia, the Bering Strait, and the northwest coast of America. Not until the close of the fifteenth century did Western Europeans, by the development of new sea routes, begin to overcome the barriers that separated them from the Far East, and not until the nineteenth and twentieth centuries did Westerners come in such force that the major peoples of the Far East radically reconstructed their cultures to meet the menace.

Incidentally we must note a fact of primary importance in our story: it was the Occident and not the Far East which bridged the distance separating the two extremities of Euro-Asia. The fact of the Occidental initiative is of basic significance in the recent history of the Far East, as it is for every other cultural area of the globe. The reason or reasons for the initiative, if they can but be determined, are of even greater import. To both the fact and the causes back of the fact we must recur in a later stage of our narrative.

The remoteness of the Far East from other major cultural areas was accentuated by formidable land barriers. Between the Far East and one of the nearest of its civilized neighbors, India, rose the highest of mountain ranges, The Himalayas and the Pamirs, and the greatest elevated plateau on the globe, Tibet. Some contact was established by sea, but that had been in spite of the intervening, southward-jutting large promontory on which Burma, Siam, and Indo-China are situated, which culminates in the Malay Peninsula, and which lengthens by hundreds of miles the voyage between India and the Far East. Between the Far East and the majority of the cultures of Central and Western Asia stretched desert and semidesert regions. From very distant, probably from prehistoric, times trade and travel, taking advantage of mountain passes and oases, existed across what is variously known as Chinese Turkestan and Sinkiang. By these routes influences entered from India, from Central Asia, and even from more western lands. Yet the distances were great and the roads were difficult.

A second general feature arises from the barriers interposed by nature—isolation. The Far East was long more nearly cut off from other areas and peoples having high civilizations than have been any other major centers of culture except those in the Americas before the time of Columbus. It developed, therefore, with fewer contributions from the outside than did any other section in Europe, Asia, and North Africa. Because of the geographic obstacles, moreover, the resulting changes in civilization, particularly in China, were the more revolutionary when once the intervening seas and land were overcome by invaders from the Occident. In spite of the achievements made possible by the mechanical devices of the past few generations, distances have not yet been annihilated. The Far East is still remote from the Occident, even the American Occident. Because of the protection afforded by the great intervening reaches of sea and land, Japan, equipped with the machines of the West, became formidable, quite out of proportion to her intrinsic strength, to the armies, navies, and air forces of the Occident. Were China similarly armed, it is doubtful whether even a united Occident could impose its will upon her. For similar reasons of geography, the Occident need have slight fear of effective attack from the Far East. The possibility of a Far Eastern conquest of the world or of any important part of the Occident, a fear harbored by some alarmists in the West and a hope lately cherished by a few extreme chauvinists in Japan, is so slight as to be negligible. Geography has made the Far East the Far East. It still makes it so.

A third general geographic characteristic of the Far East is the sufficiency of its natural resources for the maintenance of high preindustrial cultures, and, compared with the Occident, the paucity of natural foundations for an elaborate industrialized civilization of the modern type. For a preindustrial culture the natural provision was almost lavish. This was particularly true of the largest Far Eastern unit, China. To a lesser degree it was true of Japan, and, with some qualifications, of some of the other portions of the region. Fertile valleys and plains, some extensive, some small, in the aggregate provided food adequate for a teeming population and sufficient cotton, silk, and other fibers to clothe it. Enough timber was grown for fuel and housing. Over much of the area climate was favorable. Iron, copper, gold, and silver were mined in quantities equal to the needs of a nonmachine age.

For an industrial civilization of the type developed in the Occident in the nineteenth and twentieth centuries the Far East is poorly supplied with some minerals and sadly deficient in several others. It has sufficient tin, tungsten, and antimony. In the East Indies, in Burma, and possibly in some other sections fairly extensive reservoirs of petroleum exist. Yet the two chief countries, Japan and China, are woefully lacking in petroleum. Coal, while by no means wanting, is not nearly so abundant as in the Occident, and in iron, so necessary to modern industry, the deposits in the Far East are notably scanty. With modern means of transport, in a peaceable world with low tariff barriers and few trade restrictions, these deficiencies would not prove particularly grave, for the Far East has abundant supplies of various materials important in world trade which it could exchange with other parts of the globe for what it needs. In tin, antimony, rubber, copra, hemp, quinine, sugar, tea, and silk, it provides important portions of the world's supply. In Japan and China an industrious and numerous population is an ample source of labor for an immense factory development. However, in a world subject to wars and with nationalistically accentuated barriers to international trade, the Far East is at a disadvantage.

From these general features of the geography of the Far East, we must now turn to a more detailed survey, country by country.

China Proper

First of all we must speak of China. This is partly because the Chinese Empire which we see on most of our maps and which, as a legal fiction and to a large extent in fact, is still in existence, is the most extensive of the Far Eastern countries. It is also, and this is more important, because the Chinese are by far the most numerous of the peoples of the Far East. Indeed, they constitute about two-thirds of the population of that region. As we suggested in the preface, it is also because the Chinese were long dominant both politically and culturally. The Far East has been traditionally the area of Chinese culture. Obviously this culture prevailed in China itself. It also influenced practically all the other nations and tribes of the Far East, and the largest of these, the Japanese, had as their traditional culture a variant of that of China which had been imported and adapted to their own genius and needs.

The Chinese Empire is divided into two parts. The first is China Proper. China Proper is the historic China. Here the vast majority of the Chinese live. The second consists of the outlying dependencies. These, proceeding from south and west to the north and east, are Tibet, Sinkiang (literally, the New Dominion) or Chinese Turkestan, Mongolia, and Manchuria. Several of these have periodically been ruled from China. In all of them some Chinese are found. In one of them, Manchuria, the overwhelming majority of the population is now Chinese.

It is not an accident that China Proper has been the home of the dominant culture of the Far East. Of all the areas of that region, it is the best equipped by nature for that role. It presents the largest alluvial plains, the most extensive fertile valleys, ease of communication between its various parts, and a favoring climate—a combination of conditions unparalleled elsewhere in the Far East.

The main strength of China Proper has been and continues to be in the valleys of two great streams, the Yellow River (Huang Ho)[1]

[1] In the romanization of Chinese names for English usage, what is commonly known as a modified form of the Wade system is generally employed. The chief differences from the ordinary English pronunciation are as follows. *A,* as in the word *Yang,* or *Yangtze,* is like *a* in *father; i,* as in *hsi,* is like *e* in *she,* and, indeed, *hsi* is approximately *she; hai,* as in *Shanghai,* is like the English *high; ei* as in *wei,* is like the English *ei* in *weigh; ua,* as in *huang,* is much like the English *wa* as in *was* and

and the Yangtze River. Both have their rise in the great mountains and plateaus to the west which constitute the backbone of Asia. From this same mass of highlands issue the chief rivers of India, Burma, Siam, and of Indo-China. As in China, the valleys of these drainage systems from the roof of the continent afford support to dense populations and are centers of culture.

The Yellow River takes its name from the color of its waters. This is due to the heavy load of sediment carried by the stream. This in turn is derived in part from a type of soil, the loess, which is widely distributed in the northern part of China Proper. The loess, which the Chinese call by a name which means "yellow earth," is of wind-blown origin. It is a very fine silt, of yellowish-brown color, originally deposited by the wind, but in places reworked by water. It blankets much of the land in North China, often to the depth of many scores of feet. It erodes easily. The main river of North China, the Huang Ho, is heavily laden with it and with soils of somewhat similar properties but of different origin. With this sediment the Yellow River has built up a huge alluvial plain on either side of the Shantung promontory. The loess is very fertile, and it is not surprising that on the plains in which it is a large constituent were most of the main centers of China's earliest civilization and that on these plains today much of the most densely settled portions of the country are to be found. To be sure, parts of these plains are rendered infertile by alkali, salt, and sand. However, in general their soil invites agriculture. Because the Yellow River carries so much silt, on the sluggish margins of its lower courses it builds up its banks higher than the plain. That means that in time its bed also becomes higher than the adjacent country. The process is accentuated by the dikes man builds to safeguard his fields from floods. In time of flood, the river often breaks these banks, natural and artificial, and seeks a lower level. Disastrous

is sometimes written *hwang; ê*, as in *fêng*, is close to the English *u* as in *slung; u*, as in *Hunan* and *Hupeh*, resembles the English *oo* in *hoop; ü*, as in *Hsü*, approximates the German *ü; t*, as in *Shantung*, is much like the English *d; t'*, as in *t'ung*, is near the English *t; ch*, as in *chang*, is close to the English *j; ch'*, as in *ch'ang*, is near to the English *ch; p*, as in *pu*, is close to the English *b; p'*, as in *p'u*, is not far from the English *p; k*, as in *Kansu*, is like the English *g* as in *go; k'*, as in *K'ang*, is like the English *k* as in *kind; hs*, as in *hsi*, is akin to the English *sh*. To the beginner, this sounds very confusing. It is complicated by the fact that in common English and American spellings a few of the prominent geographic names have become fully anglicized. Thus we say *Peking*, giving all the letters their ordinary English sounds (*Pē-kĭng'*), rather than the more correct *Peiching*. However, with a little close attention, even the tyro may readily acquire a reasonably accurate pronunciation of the main Chinese names.

inundations have followed. The Huang Ho has found its outlet to the sea, now south, now north, of the Shantung promontory. Each change has entailed untold suffering and death.

Into the Yellow River some tributaries enter. Of these the most important in history is the Wei, which joins the main stream about where the latter turns sharply to the east from its long southward bend. In the valley of the Wei more than one dynasty has had its capital.

The Yangtze, with a volume of water much larger than that of the Yellow River, has also built up a large alluvial plain near its mouth. Into it flow more major tributaries than into the northern stream. Each of these has a valley of its own. Through part of its western reaches, the Yangtze drains the huge province of Szechwan. The heart of this province is what for a generation or so foreigners have called the Red Basin, from the color of prevailing sandstones and shales. Well watered, fertile, and with a salubrious climate, it is one of the most populous sections of China. Indeed, Szechwan contains more people than any other of China's provinces.

Lesser river systems also add to the cultivable land of China. Between the Huang Ho and the Yangtze flows the Huai. Fully as much as its larger neighbors, it is subject to disastrous floods, and also like them it has an extensive alluvial plain. Its inundations are accentuated by the fact that its lower course has been usurped by the Huang Ho and it has been forced to discharge its waters into shallow lakes. In the south is the West River (Hsi Kiang), near whose mouth is the southern metropolis, Canton, and on whose delta and lower courses is another center of teeming population. Smaller streams, but still important, drain the mountainous coastal regions from Hangchow and Ningpo southward. On them flourish cities, and on the slopes of their valleys, usually steep and made arable by man-created terraces, human settlement is often crowded.

Between these valleys in which are the chief centers of population and of civilization, the mountains and hills are usually not so high as to offer serious impediments to communication and to political unity. Mountains and hills there are, many of them imposing. Physically much of China Proper is rugged. Spurs from the great mountains and plateaus of Central Asia extend eastward, in places to the coast. Along the coast, in Shantung and from Hangchow southward, are independent ranges. Much of western China is rugged. The province of Yünnan is a moderately high plateau bounded by mountains. Szechwan is nearly cut off from the rest of China by mountains to the north, east, and south, and on its western borders rise the huge ranges of Tibet. Shansi and Kansu in the north, Kweichow and Kwangsi in the south, are predominantly mountainous. Yet none of these mountain systems within China Proper have been of a nature to estop migration and commerce. Across them are numerous passes. Even the barrier between Szechwan and central and eastern China has been overcome by the Yangtze, and through the magnificent but perilous gorges cut by its waters extensive river traffic has been and is maintained.

THE CLIMATE

In general the climate of China Proper is favorable to civilization. By far the larger part of the country lies within the temperate zone. The Tropic of Cancer crosses China only a few miles north of Canton. Within the tropics, therefore, are only relatively small portions of China Proper. It is the temperate zone in which most of China falls which seems the best fitted for the development of human culture.

Important for its climate is the position of China Proper on the continent of Euro-Asia. To the north and west lie great interior land masses, and to the east and south vast oceans. In the spring and summer, roughly from March to October, because of the northward course of the sun and because land changes its temperature more quickly than water, the air over the interior of Asia is hotter than that over the oceans and the prevailing course of the wind is from south to north. As the sun moves southward, the air over the interior of the continent becomes cooler than that over the oceans, and from October to March the chief winds are from north to south. This means that the rains, due as they mainly are to precipitation of moisture borne inland from the sea, come mostly in the spring and summer, at a time when they are of most benefit to the growing crops. This also is responsible for the fact that the heaviest rainfall is on the south coast. As the moisture-laden currents of air move northward, they more and more are deprived of their water and the rainfall declines. In the north and west of China, therefore, are semiarid regions. This means, too, severe winters. The north winds of the winter bring low temperatures. The north of China Proper has cold, dry winters. In the middle and lower Yangtze Valley, in about the latitude of Florida, the winters are accompanied by a penetrating chill and usually some snow and ice. Ice forms occasionally even in Canton, one of the few places at sea level within the tropics where this phenomenon is to be found.

The monsoonal character of China's climate, to give it a name more usually applied to India, is modified by many factors. Local topography has its effect. What weather forecasters know as cyclonic and anticyclonic storms move eastward and cross to Japan and pass over to the Pacific. They are akin to those with which we are familiar in North America and Western Europe and which are responsible for the pulse of weather which repeats itself about every week in the fashion that even the man on the street notices. It is this cyclonic variation which is held responsible for the stimulus to the human mechanism that favors the emergence of a high civilization. It is not so marked in China as in Western Europe and in parts of the United States, but it is present and may help to account for the advanced culture of the Chinese. From the sea on the southeast of China come typhoons, chiefly in the summer. They resemble the West Indian hurricanes. Like the latter, they are most violent over the oceans and along the coasts and quickly lose their strength as they move inland. Because of these several circumstances the monsoons are a less pronounced feature of the climate in China than in India.

China Proper is fairly well endowed with the useful minerals. The extent of these has not been fully determined. However, we seem to know roughly what China possesses. In coal China Proper is well supplied. Her known reserves are thought to give her third rank among the countries of the world, with only the United States and Canada ahead of her. However, she is far behind these two lands. China has more coal than has any other nation in the Far East. Her coal, indeed, has been part of the temptation which has lured Japan. Some coal is to be found in almost every province. The overwhelming percentage of it is in the northeastern provinces of Shansi, Shensi, Hopei, and Honan. Important also, although far behind this other region, is the west and southwest, notably Szechwan. Petroleum, so important in twentieth century mechanical civilization, seems to be largely lacking in China. The considerable sums which have been spent in its search have failed to disclose extensive deposits, and the geologic structure is such that it seems unlikely that any large ones have been overlooked. Iron ore is widely distributed in China and in quantities quite sufficient for a preindustrial civilization. However, the known deposits are entirely inadequate for the demands of an industrial age. If China were ever to become highly industrialized, most of her iron would have to be obtained from foreign sources. Like iron, copper is found in many places and in amounts which sufficed for earlier needs, but evidence is lacking of extensive reserves. China has a fair amount of tin. Of antimony and tungsten, both of them important in modern industry, she appears to have the largest deposits in the world. Certainly, she has recently provided the overwhelming proportion of the world's output of these metals. While China has long been a major consumer of silver, she is poor in silver ore. So, too, deposits of gold are not known to be large. Modest reserves of lead, zinc, manganese, and mercury have had some importance. While, then, for an earlier age China's mineral resources enabled her to be relatively self-sufficient, only in coal are they adequate for an extensive development of industry of a modern type.

THE CHIEF SUBDIVISIONS

China Proper presents a great variety in topography, natural resources, and climate. Nature has divided it into several sections.

The first of these, the chief center of China's oldest culture and still one of the most densely populated sections, is the North China plain. It is mainly the result of the millenniums of deposition of sediment by the Yellow River.

North and west of the North China plain, as a second section, are the highlands of the provinces of Honan, Shansi, Shensi, and Kansu. The lower slopes are usually covered with loess. The upper slopes often rise into rugged and in places lofty peaks and ridges. In them streams have cut valleys, some of them favorable to the cultivator.

The China made up of these two regions is the area where wheat, millet, kaoliang (a kind of sorghum, resembling somewhat the American broom corn, growing from ten to twelve feet high, and whose grain, about the size of a small pea, is used for food for man and beast), rather than the rice of the south, are the chief grains, with barley and corn as minor ones, and with the soy bean as an important adjunct.

Between the valleys of the Yellow and Huai Rivers on the north and the Yangtze River on the south is a third section, mountainous. The mountains are an eastward-stretching tongue from the great ranges and highlands to the west, and especially of that K'un Lun system which forms the northern rampart of Tibet. In the western part of China Proper this dividing mountain belt attains heights of more than ten thousand feet. Toward the east it tapers downward until it disappears under the alluvial plains of the Yellow, Huai, and Yangtze rivers. Southward, beginning with its southern slopes, the prevailing grain of China Proper is the familiar rice thought of by most of us as the characteristic food of the Chinese.

East of the Yellow River plain, and dividing it into two portions through which the Yellow River has alternately emptied, is a fourth section, the rugged mountain mass that constitutes the eastern part of the province of Shantung. Most of its rocks are old, geologically speaking. It is largely denuded of its forests. It thrusts into the sea bold headlands which here and there recede to make such harbors as Weihaiwei and Kiaochow. Its most famous peak is T'ai Shan, slightly over five thousand feet high, the sacred mountain *par excellence* of China.

South of the Yellow and Huai rivers, the Yangtze River has built up what may be called a fifth section, an alluvial plain which on the north merges with those of its northern neighbors. Along the eastern sections of this composite plain the Chinese constructed centuries ago and at various periods the Grand Canal. Parts of the Grand Canal have now fallen into disrepair and are no longer in use, but in its heyday this great waterway stretched from near Peking in the north to Hangchow in the south, crossing the Yangtze at Chinkiang. The alluvial plain of the Yangtze is among the most intensely cultivated and densely populated portions of the earth's surface. On it are some of China's largest cities, among them notably Shanghai, the great modern port which owes its size and importance to the sea-borne commerce of the past two generations.

West of this alluvial plain is a sixth section of China, the central part of the Yangtze Valley, stretching to the eastern limit of the Yangtze gorges. Into the Yangtze from this region enter tributary streams, each with its own valley. From the north the chief tributary is the Han. At the mouth of the Han are the three cities which together constitute the metropolis of central China. They are collectively known as Wuhan and are Hankow, Hanyang (on the down-river and up-river sides of the Han, respectively), and Wuchang (opposite the mouth of the Han). On the south are two lakes, the P'o-yang and the T'ung-t'ing, each draining into the Yangtze and each with tributaries. To the north of this part of the Yangtze Valley the boundary is outlined by the mountains of which we spoke a moment ago. To the south are also hills and mountains. They are cut up into many valleys, most of them fertile.

We have already mentioned a seventh section, the Yangtze Valley west of the gorges, with its most highly cultivated center, the Red Basin of Szechwan.

South of Szechwan is an eighth section, a mountainous tableland, a lower continuation of the great western mountain mass of Tibet. Administratively the Chinese have divided it into the two provinces of Kweichow and Yünnan. The Chinese have not yet fully occupied it. In the hills especially are non-Chinese tribes which the Chinese have not assimilated in blood, language, or culture. The plateau of Yünnan connects with the coast in Indo-China through a French-built railway.

From Hangchow and Ningpo southward along the coast of China is a ninth section. Here the shore is rugged. It is indented with estuaries and bays and studded with islands. It is backed by mountains from which flow seaward numerous streams, most of them too swift for navigation. Here and there are plains, the majority of them small, and much of the cultivation is on hillsides which have been terraced through a great expenditure of human labor. That kind of coast invites navigation. On it were most of the chief pre-nineteenth century ports and on it today are some of the great centers of foreign trade—notably Canton and Victoria (usually called Hongkong, from the island on which it is situated). From it have gone most of China's overseas emigrants, including those who have come to the United States. Partly because of the topography, broken by hills and mountains into many small districts, linguistically it presents great variety. This is the region of dialects. The great majority of the Chinese, beginning with the Yangtze Valley and extending northward to the limits of their settlement, speak forms of what foreigners usually term *mandarin*. From Shanghai and Soochow, however, on the alluvial plain of the Yangtze, southward along the coast, is an area of many local dialects. Although basically Chinese, most of them are reciprocally unintelligible, so that a Chinese speaking one of them cannot understand a Chinese speaking another of them. Only in late years, largely by government action through the schools, has a common form of *mandarin*, as the national speech, been spreading among the educated as the *lingua franca*. The dialectical variety is partly the result of racial diversity. Here in prehistoric centuries dwelt peoples who differed from the Chinese of the north in culture and speech and probably in blood. Only slowly were they conquered and assimilated. Here, too, at various times came immigrants from the Yangtze Valley and the north. Some of these, notably the Hakkas, partly preserved peculiarities in speech and customs. In the hills of Kwangsi, in the extreme south, are non-Chinese tribes which, like those of Yünnan and Kweichow, continue quite distinct from the Chinese.

South of the extreme southern corner of the coast of China Proper is the island of Hainan. It is within the tropics and is mountainous. While Chinese have come in and are numerous, non-Chinese tribesmen form a prior and important element of the population.

GEOGRAPHY AND HISTORY

From this rapid survey of the topography and climate of China Proper, some of the main effects of geography upon Chinese history must be fairly obvious.

First of all, China Proper is fitted by nature to be the home of a numerous, fairly unified, self-contained people. It is approximately half the size of the United States without Alaska, and about twice as large as the United States east of the Mississippi River. It has an extensive supply of rich, alluvial lands and, especially in the loess region, fertile uplands. It is well watered. Some of it is semiarid, but in very little of it is the rainfall so slight that agriculture is impossible. Through its heart runs the Yangtze, one of the great rivers of the world. Together with its tributaries, that stream affords navigable access to a large part of the land. The climate is, on the whole, favorable. The mineral resources are sufficient for a high culture of a pre-industrial type. The climate is, in general, friendly to civilization. The internal barriers of mountain and hill are not sufficiently formidable, even in days before the railway and the telegraph, to prevent the establishment of a political administration for the whole. The natural resources are so extensive and so well balanced that there was little need to supplement them by foreign commerce. The land was big enough to absorb practically all the energies of the Chinese.

In the second place, certain qualifications of this generalization must be noted. China Proper was so large and the internal barriers of mountain and stream, while not insuperable, were in places so marked that local peculiarities of customs and language came into existence and the political unification of the land was a major achievement. Only the energy and genius of its people could have accomplished the remarkable political and cultural unity that the old China displayed. In the face of no greater internal obstacles, Western Europe never attained so great a degree of cultural integration and never has been all brought together under one empire. The cohesion of the larger area of the United States was made possible chiefly by the timely invention of rapid means of communication such as the old China did not know.

Moreover, although China Proper was formerly self-contained, by the beginning of the twentieth century it was ceasing to be so. Population had multiplied beyond the ability of the land to afford it adequate support, and it was spilling over into Manchuria, Inner Mongolia, and, where that was permitted, to neighboring lands and islands on the south and east. Mineral resources, while sufficient for a pre-industrial era, had grave deficiencies which made impossible an extensive self-contained industrial development of a modern kind. By the first half of the twentieth century the Chinese were outgrowing the land which had once been adequate for their needs.

The Outlying Dependencies of China

On the land borders of China Proper are vast areas, together much larger in square miles (although with a decidedly more sparse population) than the traditional China. On maps printed as late as the 1930's these were still included with China Proper under the designation "the Chinese Empire." With important exceptions, which we are to note in a moment, they are and have been overwhelmingly non-Chinese in blood and culture. Most of them were conquered partly from the imperial ambition of China's rulers and partly from a desire to guard China Proper from invasion. They were pushed to their widest extent by the great Manchu Emperors of the eighteenth century and were held until, as the Empire began to disintegrate under the less able rulers of the nineteenth century and under the weakness that followed the Revolution and the establishment of the Republic in the twentieth century, they regained their independence or were torn away one by one.

At its widest extent the Chinese Empire, or, as some would prefer to call it, the Manchu Empire, embraced Burma, Annam, the Indian border state of Nepal, Tibet, Sinkiang (literally, the New Dominion), Mongolia, Manchuria, and Korea, as well as China Proper. Burma, Annam, Nepal, and Korea were really autonomous states which recognized the suzerainty of China but in whose internal administration Peking interfered little if at all. Of them, when they concern our story, we are to say something later. The other lands, however, were somewhat more closely supervised by Peking (although on some of them this supervision always sat rather lightly and at times disappeared) and here demand consideration.

TIBET

Tibet is a vast plateau, between a half and two-thirds as large as China Proper and three-fourths of it over ten thousand feet high. It is the most extensive lofty area in the world. On the south it is cut off from India by The Himalayas and prodigious canyons of streams such as the Brahmaputra, the Indus, and the Sutlej. To the southwest are the Pamirs and the Karakoram mountain systems. On its northern border are the K'un Lun and the Altyn Tagh and Nan Shan ranges, whose highest peaks reach twenty thousand feet and more. It is separated from China Proper in the east by great mountains, one of them soaring to twenty-five thousand feet, and in the south by the deep gorges through which the Yangtze, the Mekong, and the Salween and their tributaries cut their way from the highlands to lower levels. In some portions of the plateau and in the valleys agriculture is carried on. In other places human life is supported by flocks and herds. Much of the plateau is too desolate even for nomads. The mineral resources are very imperfectly known. The native population is dominated by Lamaistic Buddhism with its monasteries, and the chief rulers are heads of leading monasteries, notably the Dalai Lama at Lhasa. Over much of Tibet, particularly that farthest from China Proper, the Chinese have exercised little or no control. Of late years Outer Tibet, with its chief center at Lhasa, has been more within the British than the Chinese sphere, although China still claims suzerainty. Portions nearer to China, however, have been more under Chinese influence. A few years ago (1928) the portion next to Szechwan was marked out by the Chinese as the province of Hsik'ang, and the second south and west of Kansu as the province of Ch'inghai, or Kokonor. Even here the Chinese are in the minority, and their political control is by no means constant or universally recognized.

SINKIANG

In contrast with the high plateau of Tibet, Sinkiang (sometimes known as Chinese Turkestan) is much lower. It is the corridor through which run the caravan roads which for untold centuries were the overland trade routes between China on the one hand and Central Asia and the West on the other. It is divided into two parts by the T'ien Shan range. To the south of the T'ien Shan is the basin of the

Tarim River, a stream that drains eastward from the mountains separating Sinkiang from the Russian portions of Central Asia into the Lob Nor. North of the T'ien Shan is the Dzungarian basin. Much of the region, particularly south of the T'ien Shan, is desert, an extension of the Gobi, but here and there are oases. These oases, as is to be expected, are largely in belts near the foot of the barrier and dividing mountain ranges, for the latter catch much of what precipitation forms and from them drain streams. The middle slopes of the T'ien Shan have forests. Just below the mountains is usually an arid piedmont belt of gravels, then the section in which are the oases, and beyond this the desert into which the streams disappear. Dzungaria is slightly less arid than the Tarim basin. From the northwestern corner of China Proper the traditional caravan route leads westward, following oases. Later it divides, one fork going north and the other south of the T'ien Shan. Part of the population of Sinkiang is nomadic, living off herds which follow the pastures. The other is settled in the oases. Since Sinkiang is a corridor, it contains a mixture of many races, descendants of the peoples who from time to time have entered it. Islam is strong. Such Chinese as are there are chiefly in the infrequent towns and cities. Because of the vast time distances, for the caravan journey across Sinkiang from east to west requires weeks, during the periods of Chinese domination, which over the past two thousand years have lasted intermittently for centuries, the control from the capital of China has usually been weak and has had to be delegated to governors and generals who have been granted much discretion. After a revival of Chinese rule in the second half of the last century by a remarkable series of military campaigns, Chinese authority has tended to decline, supplanted often by that of native rulers. A few years ago Russian influence began to grow, particularly, as is to be expected, in the western part of Sinkiang. In the 1940's Chinese were again in the ascendant.

MONGOLIA

East and north of Sinkiang and north of China Proper lies Mongolia. Parts of it are continuous with portions of Sinkiang, and in places the political division is highly artificial. All of Mongolia is semi-arid or desert. Its southern and central sections are a tableland, not so elevated as Tibet, but much of it from three thousand to four thousand feet high. To the north and northwest are mountains in which the rainfall is slightly higher than in the center. There pasture is more plentiful and some timber is found. Politically this is Outer Mongolia, with its capital at Urga, now called Ulan Bator. Chinese influence has only infrequently been strong, and such few Chinese as lived there were merchants and officials. For several years, while nominally Chinese suzerainty continued, Russia was dominant. In 1945, at Russian instance, China recognized the independence of Outer Mongolia.

South of Outer Mongolia are desert regions, chiefly embraced in the Gobi, the Ordos, and the Alashan. Much of the desert is a rolling country of rock and gravel across which an automobile can be driven in almost any direction.

Next to China Proper is Inner Mongolia. Here are marginal lands, where in good years the rainfall is sufficient for a precarious agriculture. Of late decades, partly because of the pressure of population from the south and partly from policy of state, Chinese settlement has pressed in. Chinese, indeed, now form the large majority of the population. The Chinese are farmers, not nomads, and do not engage in pastoral pursuits. In a fashion reminiscent of the experience of part of the West of the United States, in the climatic cycles of better rainfall they push forward the limits of cultivated land. In times of lessening rainfall, they are forced to fall back. Also as in part of the American West, their farming breaks up the sod, and in times of drought the wind denudes the soil. Administratively, under the Republic the Chinese have endeavored to incorporate Inner Mongolia into China Proper. To this end they have divided it into the four provinces of Jehol, Chahar, Suiyüan, and Ninghsia. The Japanese, after their occupation in the 1930's, attempted to weaken the Chinese by playing off the Mongols against them and giving the latter proportionately a larger share in the government.

Across the Gobi from Outer Mongolia are caravan routes that debouch in cities on the border between China Proper and Inner Mongolia. Most of these cities are now connected by rail with Peking and so with the coast.

Outside of Inner Mongolia, the prevailing population of Mongolia is, as the name indicates, Mongol. Much of it, because of the scanty rainfall and the enforced dependence upon herds, is nomadic. It is, accordingly, sparse.

Religiously, Lamaistic Buddhism prevails, and the monasteries (or lamasaries) are often centers of such permanent settlement as exists.

MANCHURIA

East of Mongolia and northeast of China Proper is Manchuria or, for a time, Manchukuo. Which name should be used was recently a moot question of significance. Under Japanese encouragement and surveillance, a state, Manchukuo, was set up in 1932 that embraced the three provinces into which the Chinese divided Manchuria and also incorporated the former Inner Mongolian province of Jehol. Yet only Japan, a few other governments, and the Vatican accorded the state recognition, and the downfall of Japan brought the regime to an abrupt end. Officially to the large majority of the governments of the world, the area remained Manchuria and an integral part of China.

Topographically Manchuria is somewhat like a trough or, perhaps better, an irregular bowl. In its center is a plain. The plain averages about a thousand feet above sea level and so is not nearly so high as the adjoining one of Mongolia. It is broadest in the center of the country. In its southern end it is narrow. It is the result of folding of the earth's crust and erosion, and not, as are the plains of the north and east of China Proper, the product of deposition of the sediment of streams. On the west, north, and east the plain is bounded by mountains. On the east are several ranges, some of them well wooded, one of the main sources of timber in the Far East. The southernmost portions of these eastern mountains are akin geologically to the mountains of Shantung. Like the latter, they jut into the sea and, with the latter, dominate the approach by water to North China. Their tip, the Liaotung Peninsula, is, accordingly, of great commercial and strategic importance. On the north are the Little Khingan Mountains, and on the west the Great Khingan. Toward the south, the Great Khingan fade out and the main plain of Manchuria rises gently to the higher plain of Mongolia. The Little Khingan and the Great Khingan are forested, although with somewhat different kinds of trees than the mountains to the east. The chief plain of Manchuria is very fertile. It has a severe climate. Its winters are long and cold and its summers short and hot. Fortunately most of its precipitation is in the late spring and the summer, at the time when it is of most use to the growing crops.

Manchuria is fairly well supplied with minerals. Like China Proper, its iron reserves are not great compared with those of the United States and Western Europe, but it has extensive deposits of coal. It seems to lack petroleum, but it has huge quantities of oil shale which, if economical processes of distillation could be devised, would prove of great importance.

Until the latter part of the nineteenth century, Manchuria was relatively unpeopled. From it various Tungusic folk had invaded China. The latest of these had been the Manchus. However, comparatively few Chinese had moved in. Beginning in the latter part of the nineteenth century, and swelling to a flood of several hundred thousand a year in the 1920's, millions of Chinese entered the land and became permanent settlers. They now form the overwhelming majority of the population and have reduced to cultivation most of the better favored sections of the great plain. A good many Mongols are found in some of the western portions of Manchuria, and in the area next to the Korean border several hundreds of thousands of Koreans have settled.

Until nearly the close of the nineteenth century, Manchuria was one of the most promising undeveloped portions of the Far East. The last decade of the nineteenth century and the twentieth century have witnessed the rapid utilization of its resources, partly, earlier, by the Russians, and latterly more extensively by the Chinese and the Japanese. Thanks to the Russians, the Chinese, and the Japanese, but especially to the Japanese, Manchuria is better supplied with railways than is China Proper. These have facilitated its development.

EFFECTS OF THE OUTLYING DEPENDENCIES ON CHINA

The effects of the outlying dependencies upon China Proper and so upon the Far East have been important.

First of all, these regions have constituted a barrier between the Chinese on the one hand and the civilized peoples of India and of Central and Western Asia and Europe on the other. Because of them, China and most of the rest of the Far East have until very modern times been comparatively isolated. Not until the advent of the steamship and the railway was the importance of these barriers lessened. Even now they have not been overcome. Rail communication with Western Asia and Europe is by only one road, the Trans-Siberian. It is more because the oceans have been conquered by the steamship than because the land barriers have been negated that the Far East has been brought into the main currents of world development. These barriers still tend to shut the Far East off by land. They do not prevent commerce, but they make difficult extensive armed invasion from the

West. As long as the West possessed superior mechanical equipment, as it did in the nineteenth and the first part of the twentieth centuries, it might impose its will in the Far East. When once Far Eastern peoples acquired that equipment, as did the Japanese, the obstacles presented by these vast borders, added to those of the sea, made successful armed action by the Occident in the Far East most difficult.

A second effect of the outlying dependencies has been that they were the source of most of the invasions that have troubled China Proper. Until the modern age, indeed, and the coming of the Westerner in force, the only incursions of importance that did not come from these regions were those of the Japanese. These, while troublesome, were infrequent and until the present century did not seriously menace the independence of China. From the contiguous border regions, however, China was repeatedly conquered in whole or in part. Huns and Turks of several kinds from the northwest, Khitan and Chin Tatars from the northeast, Mongols from the north, and, last of all, the Manchus from the northeast came in successive waves.

A third effect followed from the second. The defense of China had to be directed landward, not seaward. China's eyes were turned inland. It was against the menace from the north and the northwest that the Chinese erected the most extensive frontier fortifications in the history of the world, the Great Wall. From the sea at Shanhaikuan, northeast of Peking, it stretches westward along the northern marches into Kansu, about twelve hundred and fifty miles as the crow flies, and, with all its windings, probably over fifteen hundred miles. In several places it is double and even triple. In some sections only an earthen parapet, in others it is a substantial barrier of rubble faced with brick or stone, reinforced by towers and, on its outward side, by a moat. Some of the more powerful Emperors were not content with the passive defense of the wall, but forestalled attack by carrying their conquests into the homes of the invaders and made themselves masters of part or all of the borderlands.

From the standpoint of defense, a navy was unimportant. Only once in her history, in the early part of the fifteenth century, did China have a formidable fleet, and that was for the purpose of overseas adventures, and not against an aggressive foe. It is not strange that, with this tradition, China fell an easy victim to Occidental attacks from the sea and that when, in the twentieth century, the Japanese invasion came, no considerable effort was made to meet the enemy before they landed or to threaten their sea communications.

A fourth effect of these borderlands was to enhance the Chinese feeling of superiority. Because of them and of the ocean to the east, until the last century the Chinese had no intimate contact with any people equal to themselves in culture. The harsh climate and the forbidding topography of the boundary lands kept their populations below the level of the civilization of the fertile valleys and more salubrious climate of China Proper. From time to time these "barbarians" might overrun part or all of China, but usually they paid their victims the flattery of imitation and conformed to their culture in whole or in part. Even the Japanese, next to the Chinese the most numerous people in the Far East, adopted and adapted the culture of the Chinese. It is not strange, therefore, that deeply ingrained in the Chinese mind has been a calm assumption of superiority. Nor is it remarkable that with this quiet but basic conviction the Chinese should have delayed so long in accepting Western culture. The Japanese, who had the tradition of adopting what seemed to them useful in the civilization of foreigners, began a generation earlier than the Chinese the reorganization of their national life to take advantage of the machines and the learning of the Occident. When the Chinese finally realized that the only way to save their political autonomy was to sacrifice their cultural independence, the collapse of the old culture was, accordingly, more complete than it was in Japan. Their reorganization was, moreover, begun too late to save themselves from deep humiliation at the hands of the Japanese, who had forestalled them in the adjustment. These vast borderlands of China Proper contain the clue to much of China's pride and of China's sorrow.

Eastern Siberia

To the north of the Chinese Empire is a region which until the sixteenth century was a kind of no-man's-land. In some respects it is a continuation of Manchuria. At present it is separated from the latter by the Amur River and by a northward-flowing tributary, the Ussuri, but until the middle of the nineteenth century the political boundary was not there, but on the northern watershed of the Amur. The great central mountain backbone of Asia runs northeasterly from Afghanistan. North of Mongolia and Manchuria it leaves a narrowing corner between itself and the eastern sea. It is this corner which is Eastern Siberia. So far north that it suffers from long winters and short, intense summers, its valleys and plains can never support an agriculture sufficient for a large population. Its climate is not unlike that of

Labrador, with which it shares approximately the same parallels of latitude. It has, however, more fertile soil and probably larger mineral resources than the latter. Separated from western Siberia by mountains and substantial distances, it is difficult of defense for the Russians. On its plains and in some of its valleys grain and sugar beets are raised. Along its shores are tempting fisheries. Its forests are extensive. While none but the Russians know its mineral resources, and these may not have been explored by them at all fully, it is possible that it has large deposits of coal and of iron, the latter particularly attractive to Far Eastern peoples whose stores of that essential metal are all too meager. Certainly the Island of Sakhalin, which is regarded as Russian and as part of eastern Siberia, has petroleum, and petroleum is peculiarly lacking in China and Japan. Latterly industrial development and settlement have been rapid. Moreover, the chief harbor, Vladivostok, as a submarine and air base menaces Japan at especially vulnerable points, her commerce and her inflammable cities. It is not strange, therefore, that the most aggressive of modern Far Eastern peoples, the Japanese, have laid covetous eyes upon the region. Nor is it remarkable that the Russians have bent every effort to develop and defend it.

Japan Proper

Next in the Far East to the Chinese in numerical strength are the Japanese. Moreover, during the seventy years and especially during the fifty years before 1945, they were the most rapidly expanding people of the Far East. In increase in wealth, in territory, in commerce, and as an active factor in international affairs they excelled all others in East Asia.

The Japanese Empire as it existed in the fore part of 1945 was, like the Chinese Empire, made up of areas in which the Japanese were in the overwhelming majority and of areas which had been conquered and in which they were in the minority.

We turn first of all to Japan Proper, to the islands which the Japanese think of as home and in which they are in the majority. These islands are very numerous. They extend in a fringe from Hokkaido, just north of the Main Island to not far north of Formosa in the south. Formosa, as we are soon to see, and other islands that were part of the Empire but not of Japan Proper, carried Japan's possessions farther south. The chief islands are the Main Island, Honshu, which accounts for the major part of the area of Japan Proper, Kyushu and

Shikoku, off the southwest coast of the Main Island, and Yezo, more commonly known as Hokkaido or the Hokkaido (the Hokkaido, it must be said, is an administrative term which embraced both Yezo and the Kurile Islands, but in common parlance it is usually synonymous with the northern island of Yezo). North and east of Kyushu and largely between Shikoku and the Main Island is the Inland Sea, studded with little islands and famed for its beauty.

Even of Japan Proper some of the islands have only recently been fully integrated into the administration of the Empire and have not yet been completely assimilated by the Japanese. The Ryukyu Islands, south of Kyushu, long recognized a dual suzerainty, on the one hand of Japanese feudal overlords in Kyushu, and on the other of China. Not until the latter half of the last century did the Japanese put an end to the Chinese connection. The Kuriles were not brought fully under the administration of Japan until the second half of the last century. While containing some Japanese, the Hokkaido was not really occupied by them until that same period. Even now it is something of a frontier land and has remnants of aborigines, the Ainu. After 1945 the Kuriles were occupied by Russia.

In area Japan Proper is much smaller than China. It contains about a tenth as many square miles as does China Proper. It is slightly smaller than the State of California.

Moreover, Japan Proper is in many respects much poorer than China Proper in natural resources. Even in proportion to its size it is not so well off in arable land. Geologically Japan Proper is part of the crumpled eastern edge of Euro-Asia. It is mountainous, with many volcanoes, some extinct and some active. It is subject to frequent and sometimes disastrous earthquakes. Only about a fifth of its surface can possibly be cultivated and of this almost all has been brought under tillage. No great alluvial plains exist comparable to those of China. Valleys are small and the farmer has had to obtain many of his fields by terracing the hillsides. In proportion to its size, Japan Proper is fairly well supplied with coal, but, unlike China, it has almost no anthracite. In iron ore it is even poorer than China. It has very little petroleum. The only mineral which is produced in excess of normal peace-time needs is copper. Like China Proper, it is well equipped for the preindustrial age in which it lived until the latter part of the last century, but even more than China it is handicapped in the industrialization into which it has been lured.

Yet the present prominence of Japan is not a miracle. Back of it lie assets which have equipped Japan for her recent hegemony in the Far East.

First of all is the Japanese people themselves. Of them we are to say so much in subsequent chapters that we need not elaborate the point here. We must, however, note that the ability, the initiative, the perseverance, the industry, and the self-confidence of the Japanese are leading factors in the part the nation has played in recent history.

Next must be mentioned the geographic position of Japan Proper. Like the British Isles at the other end of Euro-Asia, the Japanese islands command the approach to the adjacent coast. Even more extensively than the British Isles curtain the west coast of Europe, Japan curtains the east coast of Asia. As in the case of Britain, nearness to the continent has meant that Japan has been responsive to cultural currents on the mainland. Yet the straits that separate Japan from the continent are broader than those which divide England from France and Belgium. For climatic and topographical reasons the main centers of culture and population in Japan are on the opposite side of the islands from the continent and not, as in Great Britain, on the same side. Until very recent times, therefore, Japan has been more nearly isolated from the continent than was Great Britain. While the latter has several times been conquered from the continent in whole or in part, never in historic times has an invader obtained full sovereignty of a square foot of Japanese soil. Nor, until the last decade of the last century, were the Japanese as active in continental affairs as the English have been since the Norman conquest. To be sure, over long periods the Japanese controlled southern portions of Korea, the nearest part of the mainland, and once they aspired to the conquest of China. During one era they repeatedly raided the coasts of China. However, not until improved means of communication came through contact with the Occident did the Japanese begin to have a role on the neighboring continent at all comparable with that which the English have long had in Western Europe.

We must also note the fashion in which Japan's insular position has invited commerce. In the twentieth century Japanese shipping has been seen on all the seven seas. Yet this, too, is a recent development. It was not Japanese but Occidental inventiveness which created the type of ship on which modern Japanese commerce has been carried, and it was on machines of the kind first developed in the West that the Japanese have manufactured the goods for these ships to convey. This, however, does not argue a congenital inferiority of

Japanese to Occidentals. The reasons for the invention of modern machines in the West rather than in the Far East are obscure. They are by no means necessarily to be found in a native superiority of one people over another. Moreover, to adopt and adapt them when they were invented, as the Japanese have most successfully and skillfully done, has required imagination, ability, and resolution. Once these machines were invented and introduced, Japan's insular position, combined with nearness to the continent, furthered commerce and industry.

A fourth asset of Japan Proper has been climate. Japan Proper lies entirely within the temperate zone. All of it is well watered. It shares the monsoonal climate of China Proper, but in even more modified forms. Its mountains give it a very complicated topography and this results in marked local variations. In its southern half, the Main Island runs mainly from west to east, and in its northern half from south to north. In general, too, the Main Island has two ranges of mountains, one on the west and one on the east, with a series of valleys between. In the central part of the island, where the turn to the north is made, this valley is filled with volcanoes, among them Fujiyama. In the south and west the valley becomes the Inland Sea. On the west coast the precipitation is fairly extensive, with marked snowfalls in winter. The heaviest annual rainfall, however, as might be expected, is on the south coast, where it may exceed eighty inches a year. On or near the south coast were the main centers of culture of the old Japan. Since the climate on this south coast is salubrious and without severe winters, it encouraged habits of living and styles of architecture which the Japanese carried with them elsewhere but which have been unsuited to more rigorous climes.

A fifth asset of Japan has been its natural beauty. Its mountains, its forests, its flowers, its lakes, its swift rivers, and its Inland Sea studded with picturesque islands have made it physically one of the most charming lands in the world. It may be that this is in part responsible for the highly developed aesthetic sense of the Japanese and for some of their artistic achievements.

We must, moreover, remark that in other ways the geography of Japan has helped to determine the course of Japanese history and the nature of Japanese culture. The fact that the mountains and islands have divided the land into so many districts furthered the particularism and the feudalism of the old Japan. Yet the insular character of the country with a certain compactness in the chief islands tended toward intense national consciousness and pride and to solidarity. The clans and the patriotism of Japan are no accident.

It must also be said that the climate and the insular character of Japan Proper have helped to determine the diet of the people. Rice is the staple grain, and fish, caught chiefly in the waters about the islands, constitute an important element in the food supply.

The Outlying Dependencies of the Japanese Empire

Japan Proper became the heart of an empire. Between the 1860's and 1943 Japan achieved a remarkable expansion. The story of that expansion we are to narrate in later chapters. Here we must note the lands into which the expansion took the Japanese and say a little about their physical characteristics. From north to south, they were the southern half of Sakhalin, or Karafuto as the Japanese call it; Manchuria, or Manchukuo; Korea, or, again to use the Japanese name, Chosen; certain parts of Inner Mongolia and of China Proper; Formosa, called by Japanese and Chinese Taiwan; and island groups to the south of Japan Proper, including the Bonin, the Marianna, the Caroline, the Marshall, and the Spratly Islands, and, after December 1941, much of Southeastern Asia and the East Indies.

Karafuto was acquired from Russia in 1905 and is valuable chiefly for its timber and its fisheries. In the northern part of the island, under Russian rule, is a petroleum field which for some years Japanese worked under lease.

Of Manchukuo we have already spoken. In theory it was an independent state, bound to Japan by a close military alliance and by economic ties, and in which Japan's possessions were limited to leaseholds in the Liaotung Peninsula and to the South Manchurian Railway and its zone. In practice the Japanese were in control through the Kwantung army and through advisers in all governmental bureaus.

Chosen, or Korea, is, as a glance at the map will show, a peninsula. As a peninsula, for long centuries it was able to have an independent or a semi-independent life of its own. However, it has both profited and suffered from being near to states with much larger areas —China, Japan, and, in the latter part of the nineteenth and the first part of the twentieth centuries, Russia. Chosen profited by this proximity, because it was from China that it received most of its pre-twentieth century culture. It suffered, for again and again it has been invaded by these larger and hence more powerful neighbors. Repeatedly it was conquered in part or in whole from China. More than once the Japanese invaded it and for long periods held territory in its south. In the latter part of the nineteenth century it acquired peculiar strategic importance because of its command of the sea approach to North China, Manchuria, eastern Siberia, and part of Japan. Neither China, Japan, nor Russia could be entirely happy to have it in the possession of either of the others, or of some other power. Japan fought two wars to secure her interests in it, the first with China and the second with Russia. After the second war, in 1905, Japan's possession was undisputed except by the Koreans themselves. A little later (1910) Chosen was fully annexed by Japan and until 1945 was an integral part of the Japanese Empire.

Chosen is a mountainous land. Its main range lies nearer the east than the west coast. In consequence, the major streams, the chief valleys, and most of the cultivated land are on the western slopes of the peninsula. A larger proportion of the soil is under cultivation than in Japan. Rice and barley are the chief grains. The climate is more nearly like that of North China than of Japan. Unfortunately for the future of industrial development in Chosen, the mountains are largely deficient in the needed minerals. Some coal and iron are found, but not in quantities adequate for an extensive growth of manufactures. Gold has been mined. Large parts of the mountains were reforested under Japanese supervision, and in the north are vast virgin stands of timber. If the land is ever to be anything other than predominantly agricultural, however, it must be through the importation of most of the necessary raw materials.

The sections of China Proper and of Inner Mongolia under Japanese domination have been covered in earlier paragraphs. The story of how that control came to be is recounted later in our narrative.

The Bonin Islands, a group south and east of Japan Proper, with an area of less than fifty square miles, were acquired in the last quarter of the nineteenth century for their strategic value in the defense of Japan's shores.

Formosa (Taiwan) came into the possession of the Japanese as the result of a war with China in 1894–1895. Before that time and since the second half of the seventeenth century, it had been part of the Chinese Empire. As a consequence, the large majority of the population is Chinese by ancestry, the descendants of immigrants from the neighboring coast provinces of China Proper. Crowded back into the hills are the aborigines, a small percentage of the population, many of them still in a most backward state of culture.

Formosa has a backbone of mountains, some of them very lofty. As in Chosen, the chief range is nearer the east than the west coast. As a result, on the east coast are some magnificent sea cliffs plunging abruptly to great ocean depths, while on the west coast is a broad plain subsiding gently into the relatively shallow sea which divides the island from the mainland. Formosa has a little coal and petroleum, but its chief economic resources are in its fields and its forests. It was the major producer of sugar for the Japanese Empire, and from it comes much of the world's camphor. It also exports rice.

By her possession of Formosa, Japan was brought another stage southward, for the southernmost cape of Formosa is only a few miles north of the northernmost point in the Philippines.

In the present century Japan advanced still farther to the south. As an outcome of World War I, Japan was given a mandate to the former German islands north of the Equator—the Marianna, Caroline, and Marshall groups. These small clusters have very little commercial or direct economic value. Their area is small and their native population neither numerous nor vigorous. They possess, however, strategic importance both for fleets and for aircraft. The Spratly Islands, mere dots in the sea between Borneo, the Philippines, and Indo-China, taken by Japan as an incident of her hostilities with China which began in 1937, are even more purely strategic and of use chiefly as a possible landing place for airplanes or as bases for submarines. Of the acquisitions subsequent to December 1941, we are to say more in later chapters.

The Philippine Islands

South of Formosa lie the Philippine Islands. Like the Japanese Islands, they are part of the crumpled edge of the continental platform of Asia. They are, therefore, mountainous and contain many volcanoes, active and extinct. They number more than three thousand. The largest, together embracing more than two-thirds of the land surface, are Luzon and Mindanao. The total land area of the Philippines is somewhat more than two-thirds that of Japan Proper. The Philippines lie entirely in the tropics. In the western part a sharp distinction exists between the wet and the dry season. The eastern coasts are humid with a heavy rainfall throughout the year. Typhoons are numerous and destructive. In between is a transitional zone, and throughout the islands the climate and rainfall are modified by the varied topography. Rice and corn are the chief grains. Coconut palms, sugar, and manila hemp are sources of important exports. The Philippines contain some coal, fairly large deposits of iron (but a deficiency in coal militates against smelting), a number of the rarer metals used in modern industry, such as chromium and manganese, and a good deal of gold. Their petroleum resources have not been adequately explored. Their population is predominantly of Malay peoples, divided into various tribes and languages, but there are sprinklings of other stocks—Chinese, Japanese, Spanish, American, and, in the hills, negritos. The population is much less dense than in Japan Proper and China Proper.

French Indo-China

On the map is seen, south of China Proper, an area labeled French Indo-China. The name is a rough designation of the cultural history and composition of the region. In earlier centuries Indian settlers and culture entered from the south and left their imprint upon the land. At several times, some of them protracted, northern portions were part of the Chinese Empire. Chinese culture is, accordingly, influential. Today Chinese form an important element in the population, particularly in the south. Beginning in the seventeenth century, the French began to acquire a foothold in the country. First came missionaries; then, in the last quarter of the eighteenth century, French political influence began. In the nineteenth century this was extended until what now appears on the map as French was brought under the Tricolor. Over some of the region France has had a protectorate. Part was fully annexed to France. Of the Japanese occupation in the 1940's and of movements away from France we are to speak later.

The area, which on most maps appears in one color and seems compact, is varied topographically, racially, and politically. In the north is Tongking, comprising principally the basin of the Red River, a stream which rises in Yünnan. As might be expected, the basin and especially the alluvial plain of the Red River are very fertile. Tongking is separated from China Proper by mountains. South of Tongking is Annam, although the latter has at times politically included the former and today theoretically has suzerainty over it. Annam is bounded on the west by a range of mountains which is a southward-projecting spur from the Yünnan massif. Across these mountains high passes give access from Annam to the regions on the west. Spurs from the range reach eastward and divide the coastal strip of Annam into a number of separate basins. As is to be expected, it is in Annam and Tongking that Chinese influence has been strongest. Institutions and language have been shaped or modified by it. West of this range is the valley of the Mekong, one of the great rivers that cut their way down from the central mass of mountains and plateaus on which Tibet is situated. In the lower part of the Mekong, Indian influence was long potent. On the delta of the Mekong is Cochin-China, low-lying and fertile, an exporter of rice. North of Cochin-China is Cambodia, a saucer-shaped basin, also fertile. North of Cambodia is Laos, a tangle of forested hills and plateaus, the least developed portion of French Indo-China. As might be surmised from this varied topography, racially and linguistically French Indo-China is a patchwork and has no unity. The area has valuable minerals—coal, tin, zinc, chromium, antimony, tungsten, manganese, iron, and phosphate rock.

Thailand (Siam)

West of French Indo-China is Thailand or, as it is better known, Siam. The most fertile part is in the lower portion of the valley of the Menam. It is a great producer of rice. Here, too, is the center of political power and of culture. The north is mountainous. It has valuable forests. The eastern portion of the country is a huge shallow basin encircled by hills and handicapped by poor soil and an adverse climate. In the rainy season it is largely swamps and in the dry season an arid waste. In the south, Thailand politically stretches into the Malay Peninsula. The Chinese are numerous in the lower and fertile part of the Menam Valley and have had an important share in the economic life of the land and in shaping some of the institutions. However, the dominant people, whom we think of loosely as the Siamese *par excellence*, are of Thai stock, their religion is Buddhism, and, accordingly, the chief elements in their culture are of Indian provenance. The land has owed its continued independence to the fact that it lies between British and French possessions and has been allowed to exist as a buffer state between the two. The Japanese occupation of the 1940's was an important stage in the land's history.

Burma

It is debatable whether Burma should be included in the Far East. Under British rule it was for years administratively a part of India. Many Indians have come into the country, and, as in Thailand, the dominant culture has Buddhism as its religion and so has been profoundly molded by India. However, on the north Burma is bounded by China Proper, its peoples are mainly Tibetan-Mongoloid by race, for a time under the last dynasty of China it was once under the suzerainty of Peking, for centuries an overland trade route has led across its borders into China, and during World War II a highway was constructed across the border to accommodate automobiles and a railway from China to Burma has been talked of. Burma loomed very prominently in the Japanese imperialistic adventure.

Topographically Burma is predominantly mountainous. Its most intensely cultivated portions and the main center of its culture are, however, in the valley and the delta of the Irrawaddy, a stream which, like the Huang Ho, the Yangtze, and the Mekong, rises in the great highlands of Central Asia. Between the two major rivers is the valley of a third, but smaller one, the Sittang. Many different peoples and tribes are found in Burma. In the valleys are the civilized Burmese, Buddhist in religion. In the mountains which flank the valleys are many groups, presenting a variety of languages and traditions, and generally on a lower stage of culture. Burma is predominantly agricultural, but it has extensive oil deposits which were developed under British rule.

The Malay Peninsula

The Malay Peninsula is chiefly a backbone of mountains, with a central core which, geologically speaking, is fairly old. It has a heavy rainfall, an average of about a hundred inches a year. Its climate is hot and humid. It is, therefore, clothed with tropical forests except where man has made clearings for his plantations.

Historically the Malay Peninsula has owed its importance to the fact that it lies across the main sea route from Southern and Western Asia and from Europe to the Far East. Politically it has been subject successively to the various peoples who have controlled that route. Within the last millennium it has been dominated first by the Arabs, then by the Portuguese, next by the Dutch, and eventually by the British. The Japanese conquered the area in 1942. Racially the peninsula was formerly overwhelmingly Malay, but latterly Chinese have flooded in and have become about as numerous as the Malays. Tens of thousands of Indians have also entered, mainly as laborers. The chief religion is Islam, a heritage from the prolonged contact with the Arabs. In late years the Malay Peninsula has been notable not only for its continued importance on a route to the Far East, but also as a major source of rubber and tin and of some iron. The first two are of great significance in the world market and the third to a Far East which is deficient in iron ore.

The East Indies

Southeast of Asia stretches a huge archipelago. It is only the fringe of the Far East, but because of its geographic location it has a part in the Far Eastern situation and place for it must be found in our survey. Politically the larger portion of the East Indies has belonged to the Dutch, but the British have had sections and there are remnants of the Portuguese colonial empire. The Japanese occupation began in 1942 and lasted until 1945.

In dimensions the East Indies are of vast extent. It is, for example, farther from the western to the eastern end of the Netherlands East Indies than it is from San Francisco to New York.

The chief islands are Sumatra, Java, Borneo, and New Guinea. Java, while the smallest of the four, has more than half of the population of the East Indies. It is one of the most densely settled sections of the earth's surface, a crowding which has come in consequence of a phenomenal increase in the population in the nineteenth and twentieth centuries.

The East Indies are mountainous and include many volcanoes, active and extinct. The soils are very fertile where they are composed of disintegrated volcanic ash.

The diversity of tongues and tribes is great, but the prevailing stock and language are Malay. Here, as in so much of southeastern Asia, many Chinese have come, and, as usual, form an enterprising and industrious element.

The East Indies are important in world commerce as a source of sugar, tea, and coffee, and especially of quinine (of which they are the world's main producer), of petroleum, and of rubber. Earlier they were chiefly valuable to the Occident for their spices, and it was for these that Arabs, Portuguese, and Dutch came one after the other to the islands. All these peoples and the Hindus who preceded them have left cultural deposits.

Summary

This, then, is the geographic setting of our story. In the Far East is about a third of the population of the world. In it are peoples who for centuries have been highly civilized. In it, too, are minorities of primitive culture. Most of that population lives within the temperate zone. The region possesses vast resources in fertile land, and, while it is not so well supplied with coal, iron, and petroleum as is the Occident, it is a chief source of some of the products—notably rubber and tin—which are indispensable to modern civilization. The history of the region and the events of the present are of major significance to the human race.

BIBLIOGRAPHY

For Brief Reference

G. B. Cressey, *Asia's Lands and Peoples* (New York, 1944).
L. D. Stamp, *Asia. An Economic and Regional Geography* (New York, 1929).

For More Extended Study

H. Foster Bain, *Ores and Industry in the Far East* (New York, 1933).
J. Barnes (editor), *Empire in the Pacific* (New York, 1934).
C. Bell, *Tibet, Past and Present* (Oxford, 1924).
R. C. Chapman, *Across Mongolian Plains* (London, 1921).
G. B. Cressey, *China's Geographic Foundations. A Survey of the Land and Its People* (New York, 1934).
É. R. Huc, *Travels in Tartary, Thibet and China, 1844–1846* (London, 1928).
E. Huntington, *West of the Pacific* (New York, 1925).
O. Lattimore, *The Desert Road to Turkestan* (London, 1921).
O. Lattimore, *Inner Asian Frontiers of China* (London, 1940).
W. H. Mallory, *China, Land of Famine* (New York, 1926).
The Japan Year Book (Tokyo, 1905 *ff*.).
D. C. Worcester, *The Philippines, Past and Present* (New York, 1921).

PRE-OCCIDENTAL SOUTH AND EAST ASIA

Chapter II. PRE-BRITISH INDIA

India to the beginning of the British territorial conquest. Geography; history; culture

As a second chapter, and also still by way of introduction to the Far East, we must give a brief account of India. As geography both furnishes the stage for Far Eastern history and conditions it, so India has had a profound effect upon Far Eastern lands. Upon most Far Eastern peoples that effect has been cultural and with religion, mainly Buddhism, as the vehicle. In what we call Indo-China and in the East Indies commerce, colonization, and even conquest by Indian peoples were known. In China and Japan conquest was completely absent and direct commerce was either nonexistent or inconsiderable. Yet through Buddhism and the philosophy, art, and literature which came with it, India left its stamp more or less deeply upon almost every civilized people of the Far East. Until the advent of the Westerner in force in the nineteenth century, no other foreign culture made so transforming an impression upon the Far East as a whole as did that of India.

Moreover, beginning with the sixteenth century, Western Europeans began impinging upon India as well as upon the Far East. In the course of time, Western imperialism accomplished a more complete political subjugation of India than of the Far East. The progress of the Occidental advance in the Far East was closely connected with that in India. Since the stories are so interrelated, recognition of India, its history and culture, must be included in any comprehensive account of the Far East. This is the more imperative because of the ignorance of most Westerners, and particularly Americans, of India. India is not embraced in the Far East. It will, therefore, be passed over much more briefly than will China and Japan. However, for an understanding of the Far East we must preface our narrative with a summary of India before the beginning of the British conquest, a process which began not far from the middle of the eighteenth century, and later we must insert a chapter narrating events in India after the beginning of that conquest. In our survey of India, we shall have in mind the bearing of what we are to say upon the Far East. That survey will, therefore, be proportioned with this purpose to the fore and will be viewed in a somewhat different perspective than if we were centering our attention upon India.

Geographic Setting

Geographically India is mainly a peninsula jutting southward from the land mass of Euro-Asia. In this it resembles Europe, which is also a peninsula of Euro-Asia. While it is only about two-fifths the size of Europe, with an area of slightly over a million and a half square miles, topographically, linguistically, and racially it is about as varied as is Europe. It is really a subcontinent. Until very recently India, unlike Japan, could not be called a nation. In contrast with China, it could not even be termed an empire. Politically it has never been fully united. The British brought more of it together under one rule than ever had been done before. Yet even at the height of British power, small fragments remained under Portugal and France. Moreover, the British did not erase all the political lines that existed before their rule was established. Numbers of what were termed "native states" remained. Each of these preserved its own princes and institutions. Over them the British *raj* exercised the functions of the paramount power. India, like Europe, presents a certain community of culture, but not so markedly as does China Proper. Until very lately it has been more nearly a continent or a subcontinent than a country.

What gives India its geographic distinctiveness and makes it topographically an entity is its boundaries. On the north, northeast, and northwest it is separated from the rest of Asia by mountains. The barriers between it and the remainder of Euro-Asia are much more formidable than those between Europe and Asia or even than those between China and the rest of Asia. On the north is the loftiest mountain system on earth, The Himalayas, buttressed by the great plateau of Tibet. On the northeast are other ranges, pushing southward from the core of Asia, which make land passage to the adjoining Burma extremely difficult. On the northwest are still other mountain chains, not impassable but forbidding. In all these mountain walls man has found weak points which he has used for trails. In the northwest particularly are passes through which men have regularly made their way. It was by these that most of the great migrations entered and that the conquests of India by the land routes were effected. Yet on the northwest where the mountains afford less adequate protection there is a further obstacle of desert. It is only by closely restricted routes that the invasion of India by land-conducted forces is physically possible. The seas that flank the western and eastern sides of the triangle which is India have also been a barrier. Across them from time immemorial have come merchants. Some settlements have been made, and now and again footholds have been conquered on the coast by the seafarers. However, good natural harbors are few. Not until improved seamanship and naval construction overcame the ocean was India seriously threatened from it. The most nearly complete conquest of India, that by the British, was from the sea, but was not until the eighteenth and nineteenth centuries. Within these protecting boundaries India achieved a certain degree of unity.

Yet never perfectly. The interior physical features of India, like those of Europe, have made for diversity of language, culture, and political power which until the application of the physical inventions developed in the Occident in the nineteenth century subdivided India. In the great mountains of the north are many valleys, several of which constitute regions in themselves. South of these mountains is what is sometimes called the Indo-Gangetic Plain. It is made up largely of the detritus borne by the rivers draining the vast barrier mountain systems, much as China Proper is substantially indebted to the valleys of the streams that flow eastward from this roof of the world. On the extreme east is what in its main reaches is called the Brahmaputra. The upper portion of the valley of the Brahmaputra south of The Himalayas is embraced in what politically is known as Assam. The chief river system of the Indo-Gangetic Plain is that of the Ganges. The Ganges and the Brahmaputra unite to build up the extraordinarily fertile Bengal with its huge delta. Bengal is one of the most densely peopled portions of the earth. On the Hoogly, one of the branches through which the waters of the Ganges make their way across the delta to the Bay of Bengal, sprawls what is now India's largest city and leading port, Calcutta, the second city in the British Commonwealth. The western section of the Indo-Gangetic Plain has the Indus River as its principal stream. The northwestern part of the plain is made up of the fanlike Punjab, drained by the Indus and its tributaries. On the west the Indo-Gangetic Plain tends to be arid and in places desert, in contrast with the heavily be-rained eastern portions.

South of the Indo-Gangetic Plain lies the peninsula proper. Mountains, the chief of them the Vindhya range, form the boundary between the two sections. The central part of the peninsula is the Deccan, a plateau that slopes gently eastward from the Western Ghats, a long range of hills rising abruptly from the western shore. It is separated from the east coast by the more subdued Eastern Ghats. Near the south of the peninsula the Western and Eastern Ghats come together in rolling downs of approximately seven thousand feet elevation, with peaks which attain a height of about nine thousand feet. Much of the Deccan is made up of denuded ancient rocks and is relatively sterile. Here, too, are vast flows of lava. However, a portion has soil which is extremely fertile. The west coast of the peninsula has a few good harbors. Here from early times came merchants from Arabia, Persia, and more western lands. The Malabar Coast was long particularly inviting.

The main physical divisions of India are in turn subdivided by natural features. Great diversities in physiography make for variety in the racial, cultural, and political structure.

Climate

The climate of India is partly determined by the fact that the peninsular portion of the land lies in the tropics. Even the north is in the subtropics. The peninsula knows no cold season, only a cooler time of the year. The northwest has burning heat in the summer and frosts in the winter.

Important for India climate, too, is the monsoon. This is due in some degree to the factors we noticed in connection with China. In the summer, the great interior of Asia heats up more quickly than the southern oceans, and the prevailing air currents are from the south. Moving inland from the sea, these carry the moisture with them. As the monsoon strikes the various hills and mountains it drops its water. The amount of rainfall is largely dependent upon the configuration of the land. In some areas it is very sparse. In others it is very heavy. In the winter, since the land cools more quickly than the water, the winds are predominantly from the north and are usually dry. If for some reason the monsoon fails, drought ensues, often followed, until the British developed measures to fight it effectively, by famine.

This, the traditional account of the monsoon, needs modification, for The Himalaya barrier is so formidable that it arrests many of the air masses as they move to and from the interior of Asia. The Indian monsoons are largely in the nature of trade winds whose course is affected by the surface of the subcontinent.

Natural Resources

India's greatest natural resources are her soil and climate. Much of the former is poor, but much also is rich. Through soil and climate India has been and remains primarily agricultural. The overwhelming majority of her population have, from time immemorial, made their living from the land. Rice is the major grain, with wheat predominant in the northwest and sorghums, mainly jowar, also of importance. From the land came, too, the spices and the cotton which for many centuries were the attraction to foreign trade. Fine cottons were long a major article of commerce. Calico took its name from the port of Calicut, on the Malabar Coast. Jute, a coarse fiber used for burlap and gunny sacks, is a main export. India is said to have about half the world's cattle. Hindus hold the cow sacred and do not take its life. Millions of useless beasts compete for the subsistence needed by working cattle and by men. Diamonds were once among the exports, and gold was extensively mined. As assets in the present industrial age, India possesses some coal and rich deposits of iron. The coal reserves are estimated as only a fourth or a third of those of China, but an iron belt in the northeast is thought to be the largest in Asia, with the possible exception of the Soviet Union.

Racial Composition

Racially India is mixed. Moreover, fusion has not proceeded so far as in China. Intermixture there has been, but, thanks in no small degree to caste, a feature of Indian life to which we are to recur a little later, lines between races are somewhat less blurred than in many countries.

The racial variety is paralleled by cultural diversity. India's population has ranged and still ranges from aboriginal tribes of primitive culture to highly civilized peoples.

Racial diversity has been furthered by the attraction of India to invaders. The rich plains and valleys have had an agelong lure for the peoples of the less hospitable interior and to seafaring folk from overseas. The great migrations have come over the northwest passes. Through these convenient breaches in India's mountain barriers, wave after wave swept down into the Punjab, each driving its predecessors south or submerging them. The Vindhya ranges have opposed something of an obstacle to mass movements into the peninsula, but on either flank the Vindhyas can be turned, and again and again the northern invasions have not spent themselves until they have added their deposit to the mixture in the Deccan, its bounding hills, and the coastal plains.

The main racial groups of India have been counted as seven in number. First are the Dravidians. These are dark, almost black peoples, below medium stature. They are the prevailing type in most of the peninsula. It may be that they were once predominant in all of India, but were supplanted in parts of the north by later invaders. Their source is by no means certain. Whether, like most of the others, they came by the northwest passes we do not know. Nor are we sure that they were the earliest inhabitants of India. There are primitive tribes who seem related, at least in speech, to peoples who in neolithic times were widely spread in Southern Asia and who are represented from Madagascar on the west to Easter Island in the eastern Pacific. There are other folk who may be descendants of pre-Dravidians.

A second group are the Indo-Aryans. Linguistically and presumably in blood they are akin to the ancient Persians and to many of the peoples of Europe, including the Greeks and the Latins. Tall, fair, long-headed, dark of eye, and with much hair on the face, they are at present most nearly in their pure form in the northwest, in Kashmir and the Punjab. They seem to have come into India in successive migrations through the northwest passes. Precisely when they arrived we do not know. It was certainly as early as the second millennium before Christ and it may have been long before then.

Third are the Turko-Iranians. These, too, are most numerous in the northwest, west of the Indus, in Baluchistan, and in the northwestern part of the Punjab. They appear to have arisen from a mixture of Turkish and Persian peoples.

Fourth are the Scytho-Dravidians. They are most numerous east of the Indus and in the northwestern part of the peninsula.

Fifth are the Aryo-Dravidians, a prevailing type east of the Punjab and in the mid-Ganges Valley, in the present political subdivisions called the United Provinces and Bihar. Supposedly they originated through the colonization of the region, previously inhabited by Dravidians, by Indo-Aryan invaders.

Sixth is the Mongoloid type. It prevails in Assam, in The Himalayas, and on the southern fringes of The Himalayas, and is found in the Punjab and Kashmir. Difficult though the natural barriers are between India on the one hand and Tibet and China on the other, Tibeto-Chinese peoples have been filtering through for untold centuries.

The seventh group, the Mongolo-Dravidian, a mixture, as the name indicates, of the Mongoloid immigrants with the Dravidians, is prominent, as the Bengali type, in Bengal and the adjoining Orissa.

Within these major groupings are many subdivisions, and between some intermixing has occurred.

The Dawn of History

The orderly clarification of the past of India is peculiarly difficult. The Indians have not been historically minded. They have no such mass of carefully compiled and conserved historical records as we are to find in China. Moreover, the multiplicity of states and empires and the absence of political unity have conspired to make the task of the historian arduous.

Archeology has disclosed ancient ruins in the Indus Valley of a civilization of the third and fourth millennia before Christ, which was fairly advanced, with cities, wells, bathrooms, and elaborate drainage systems, and which seems to have had kinship to some of the early culture of Mesopotamia. Remains of stone age man make it clear that that stage of civilization was known in both north and south India. In the north this was followed by an age of copper. Then came iron.

The Indo-Aryan Invasions and Culture

Of major importance for India were the Indo-Aryan invasions. As we have suggested, scholars are not agreed as to when these occurred, nor do they know their precise geographic origin or their duration. From the Indo-Aryans, however, came the standard classical literature of India and many of the institutions and ideas that have characterized and still characterize Indian culture.

Our earliest clear glimpses of the Indo-Aryans are derived from a collection of hymns, the Rig-Veda. These hymns are of various dates, but in general they depict the Indo-Aryans as already settled in northwest India. As seen in them, the Indo-Aryans were partly a pastoral people, using milk and butter, and partly cultivators of the soil. While eating meat, they also employed for food vegetables, grains, and fruits. Their organization was patriarchal and by tribes. Already, apparently, there were the beginnings of the later caste structure. The four main caste divisions of latter days were foreshadowed—the Brahman, or priestly, the Kshatriya, noble or warrior, the Vaishya, or commoner, and the Sudra, slave or of the non-Aryan subdued stock. The Indo-Aryans were metal-using, but whether copper, bronze, or iron we do not know. They valued gold for ornaments. They had armor, fought from chariots, and employed the bow. They warred with one another and with the aborigines. They made much of religion, but regarded the gods as benevolent rather than sinister and as beings from whom favors might be obtained through gifts and the proper ceremonies. The language of the Rig-Veda, as of others of the classical books of the Indo-Aryans, was Sanskrit.

As time passed, developments in Indo-Aryan culture occurred. To the Rig-Veda were added three other Vedas, likewise collections of hymns. Then there were Brahmanas, prose compositions of theological and ritual content, and the numerous Upanishads, prose philosophic treatises. The writing of the many documents embraced under these designations extended over several centuries. From the simple beginnings reflected in the Rig-Veda, caste showed a process of continuation, elaboration, and subdivision which began to give it the prominence it has held to this day. Sacrifices and religious ritual became more complex. From the pre-Aryan population was taken over much of the existing village system and system of taxation.

Some spread of this Aryan culture was witnessed, part of the process which gave it the dominance it later enjoyed. There was also absorption of non-Aryan culture.

The Rise of Buddhism

Not far from the sixth century before Christ a great outburst of religious life occurred. Precise dates elude us. There is even doubt as to the exact century. Probably the religious awakening was not confined to a single hundred years but was in progress over several generations. As a result of the surge in the religious tide a number of philosophical schools arose, some of them clearly new religions. They seem to have been at once outgrowths from the current religion which had the Brahmans for its priests and teachers and protests against it. Of these are Jainism and Buddhism, which have survived to our day. Jainism appears to have had no direct effect upon the Far East, and its following in India was and is a small minority. In contrast, Buddhism attained large dimensions in India and made a profound and enduring impression upon the peoples of the Far East. Later it all but disappeared in the land of its birth, but it survives in the Far East as a potent, although in several countries, including China, as a decadent force. It is interesting that it is through religion that India has exerted most of its influence outside its own borders. Also of significance for the Far East is the fact that, except in a few smaller areas, it was not what became the prevailing faith of India, Brahmanism, or, to give its better known designation, Hinduism, but Buddhism, through which India made its impression on other lands.

Here is not the place for a detailed account of Buddhism. However, so important has that religion been for the Far East that a brief summary, even though necessarily superficial, is essential to our story. Buddhism had as its originator a scion of an aristocratic family of north India. His dates are uncertain, but what seem to be the most probable ones make him approximately a contemporary of Confucius, that is, of the sixth and fifth centuries before Christ. He is commonly known by a title, the Buddha, which means "the Enlightened." As a young man he became deeply concerned over the problems of life and was depressed by the presence of suffering. Accepting as true the transmigration of souls, then as now a current Indian conception, he set out to discover a way of escape from it. It was a dreary and horrible fate to which the beliefs of his time condemned not only man but all living creatures. All were bound to the wheel of life. All, from the gods down, were subject to the endless succession of birth and rebirth. Since to exist was to suffer, it is no wonder that sensitive spirits (and of these there were many besides him who became the Buddha) were seeking deliverance from this agonizing fate. The future Buddha tried all the ways recommended by the teachers whom he knew and proved them futile. Finally, when, in despair, he was sitting in meditation under a tree, the answer flashed upon him. Satisfied that he had found salvation, through a long life he taught it to all who would listen. He must have been a commanding figure. Dignified, serenely confident in the truth of his message, full of tender pity for struggling and suffering humanity, a superb teacher, he attracted a large following and lived long enough to impress his message indelibly upon a numerous body of disciples.

With an admirable sense for pedagogy, the Buddha put his precepts into numerical categories. He spoke of what were to him four basic truths—(1) life and suffering are inseparable; (2) the cause of suffering is desire; (3) to be rid of suffering one must escape desire; (4) escape from desire can be achieved through following the eightfold path. This eightfold path included right views (embracing a comprehension of what life really is, always in flux and with no abiding entity called the soul), right aspirations, right meditation, and right action. The end of the path was *nirvana*. This involved the extinction of desire and so of pain, and release from the tragic sequence of birth and rebirth. In a sense, it was good news that the Buddha proclaimed—that it was possible to achieve escape from life with its intolerable burden of suffering.

After the death of the Buddha, his teachings were perpetuated, but were developed in two different directions. One, self-styled Mahayana, or "the Greater Vehicle," professed to foresee the salvation, in the Buddhist sense, of all living beings. It made much of the *bodhisattva*, one who, with *nirvana* within his grasp, postpones entrance into it until, partly through his instrumentality, all living beings have been saved. The Buddha had not taught prayer and worship, for he believed that the gods, like men, were caught in the sequence of transmigration and could not assist in the escape from it. However, both prayer and worship made their way back into Mahayana. Mahayana did not esteem the Buddha as being a god, but it regarded him as possessing attributes of divinity and as having embodied eternal, all-pervading wisdom. It thought of him, too, as one of a long procession of Buddhas. Hinayana, "the Lesser Vehicle," so-called derisively by the Mahayanists, taught that each must work out his own salvation and that the Mahayanists' dream of universal salvation through the aid of *bodhisattvas* is illusory. Hinayana held up as the ideal the *arhat*, he who has found enlightenment for himself.

In this summary of Buddhism we have run chronologically ahead of our story. Buddhism achieved widespread popularity in India, but not suddenly. Its victory was gradual and its decline was also a matter of centuries.

The Macedonian Invasion

In the fourth century before Christ occurred an invasion which had momentous consequences for India and especially for Buddhism and for some of the phases of the expansion of that religion. The immediate incident was brief. Militarily it was little more than an incursion. However, the events to which it was a prelude were prolonged and the effects upon culture profound.

In the course of his triumphant career Alexander the Great, of Macedon, made himself master of Persia. This achievement led him into India, for the Punjab had long been under Persian influence and part of it had been conquered by the Persians. Late in 327 or early in 326 B.C., Alexander came down from the northwest, although through precisely which pass or passes is uncertain. He reduced to submission numbers of the tribes and petty states then found in the extreme western and northwestern portions of India. In a battle famous in the annals of his wars, Alexander's cavalry overwhelmed an Indian army whose center was made up of elephants. In 325 B.C., after having been in India only about a year and a half and on its confines perhaps three and a half years, Alexander began his westward march. Presumably he believed that he had permanently incorporated his Indian conquests into his empire, for he founded cities and left in them garrisons of Greeks. However, when the magic of his power was shattered by his early death (323 B.C.), his Indian possessions broke away. Although late in the fourth century one of the inheritors of Alexander's power, Seleucus Nicator, led an army into northwestern India, he did not succeed in establishing his rule in that country.

Short though Macedonian and Greek rule in India was, Alexander's exploits had amazing consequences. In Central Asia north of the Punjab, Alexander established colonies. From these centers, Hellenistic civilization in more or less garbled form was perpetuated for centuries. Here, and particularly in Gandhara, on the northwestern fringes of India, the expanding Buddhism came in contact with Hellenized art. Here eventually arose a Buddhist art displaying the influence of Hellenism. Much of the Buddhism that penetrated to the Far East came by the Central Asiatic routes. It therefore carried with it in its painting and sculpture clear evidence of its contacts with Hellenism. Moreover, following Alexander came an extension of Greek colonies and commerce in Western Asia. Greeks and Greek trade reached India. In succeeding centuries commerce, direct and indirect, between India and the eastern shores of the Mediterranean multiplied. Knowledge of India came to the Mediterranean world, and some knowledge of that world reached India. A Greek visitor reported favorably on the wide use of irrigation and the fact that the soil bore two crops a year.

The Maurya Empire

Among the sequels of Alexander's exploits in India was the rise of an empire one of whose monarchs greatly aided the propagation of Buddhism.

Late in the fourth century, and possibly because he had profited from the example of Alexander, an Indian, Chandragupta, made himself master of most of the Indo-Gangetic plain and extended his rule into the highlands in the northwest. Seleucus Nicator found him so firmly entrenched that he deemed it wise to enter into friendly alliance with him. It is from Megasthenes, a Seleucid envoy at the court of Chandragupta, that we gain some of our information of the realm.

It was the third monarch of the Maurya dynasty, Asoka, who became the most famous of the line. In his day the Maurya domains stretched into the peninsula far south of the Vindhya Mountains. About a decade after he ascended the throne, Asoka became a convert to Buddhism. He is said to have been moved to that step by a revulsion from the slaughter and suffering entailed in a campaign of conquest in the south. He became an ardent advocate of his new faith. He visited and made donations to Brahmans, ascetics, and the aged, he had wells dug and trees planted by the roadsides, he provided medical aid for men and animals, and he distributed useful plants. Much of this he did not only in his own territories but also in adjacent states. In accordance with the Buddhist regard for life, he restricted the slaughter of animals. He exhorted his subjects to be kind and considerate within their families and toward their slaves, servants, and neighbors. He asked for tolerance among the several religions. He had his officials instruct his subjects in the moral law. He encouraged charitable gifts and endowments. He erected Buddhist shrines and monuments. He himself became a lay disciple and then a monk. He kept himself accessible to his subjects and officials for the administration of justice and the conduct of public affairs. Most of this information is derived from inscriptions which he himself had placed in enduring form in various parts of his domains. He is said to have sent Buddhist missionaries to other countries. Obviously this active support by the most powerful ruler of the India of his day must have made for the growth of Buddhism both at home and abroad.

After Asoka's death the Maurya Empire entered upon swift decay. The contribution to Buddhism, however, and through it to the Far East, was enduring.

Five Centuries of Division Punctuated by Invasions

We need not pause long on the events in the five centuries and more following the collapse of the Maurya Empire. As was to be expected there were recurring invasions from the northwest. Before the close of the first century before Christ the last of the Greek states in the Punjab had disappeared. We hear of Scyths, of various tribes, who from the second century before Christ moved into the northwest and left large permanent deposits in the Indian racial structure. It was possibly they who overwhelmed the Greek states in Central Asia. There came, too, conquerors from Parthia. In the first century after Christ a people whom the Chinese had known founded a state in the northwest, under the Kushan dynasty, which was the nursery of much of the Hellenistic Buddhist art of which we spoke a few paragraphs above. It was the espousal of the Kushan rulers which contributed to the growth and expansion of Mahayana Buddhism. In other parts of India various states and ruling houses governed more or less limited sections of the country. Because of the unsatisfactory condition of Indian historical records, often, indeed, a complete absence of them, and the consequent dependence of the modern scholar upon scanty archeological remains, at best fragmentary, most of these kingdoms and principalities and even the mightiest of their monarchs are but dimly seen in the shadows of the past.

The Gupta Empire

In the forepart of the fourth century after Christ a ruling house, the Gupta, established an empire which embraced much of India and lasted for over two centuries, until about A.D. 535. Like the Maurya Empire, it had its seat in the Ganges Valley. Interestingly enough, its first ruler bore the name of Chandragupta. Like the Maurya, the Gupta Empire embraced most of the Indo-Gangetic Plain and extended south into the Deccan. Under the Gupta, as under Asoka, Buddhism flourished. Under the Gupta the arts of peace prospered. In architecture, sculpture, painting, poetry, and drama the period was noteworthy. It was one of the most brilliant in the history of India. Indian artists were developing a style which, while indebted to the Hellenistic tradition, was clearly indigenous. Its greatest surviving examples prove that it ranks among the outstanding æsthetic achievements of mankind. It left its stamp on later India and, carried to the Far East through Buddhism, had pronounced effects upon the art of that region. Commerce flourished and embassies were sent to foreign courts, among them three to Rome.

In the records of their journeys, Chinese Buddhist pilgrims, the most famous of them Fa Hsien, whom we are to meet two chapters below, have left us vivid accounts of India under the Gupta. The sacred sites of their faith and monasteries with their libraries and scholars were the great attraction to these pious devotees, but incidentally they were much impressed with the magnificence and the novelty of the scenes about them. While Buddhism appeared prosperous, Hinduism (or Brahmanism) was gaining. The process was under way by which Hinduism assimilated much of Buddhism and so eliminated from India Proper that offshoot and protest which had become a rival.

The Hun Invasions

What proved a fatal blow to the Gupta Empire was dealt by a fresh invasion through the northwest passes, that of a branch of the Huns. For centuries the Huns had had their home in Central Asia. As we are to see in subsequent chapters, they were long a chronic menace to the northwest borders of China. Their contribution to the chaotic years which marked the dissolution of the Roman Empire in the West is well remembered in the history of the Occident. Not far from the middle of the fifth century after Christ what were known as the White Huns made their way into the Punjab. In this first incursion they were defeated by the Gupta forces, but toward the close of the fifth century they returned to the attack, overwhelmed the Gupta armies, and until the second half of the sixth century remained a power to be reckoned with in the northwest.

Accompanying the White Huns were a people who as the ancestors of the Rajputs made a permanent contribution to the Indian scene. The Rajputs became a congeries of warlike clans who won acceptance in the Hindu caste system and by holding the key to the passage from the Punjab into the Ganges Valley long occupied a strategic place in the kaleidoscope of Indian history.

The Coming of Islam

In the seventh century of the Christian era came the meteoric rise of Islam. Islam was born in the visions of an Arab camel driver, and before the close of its first century Arab arms, inspired by it, had made it politically dominant from the Pyrenees, along the southern and western littoral of the Mediterranean, through Persia, to the very borders of India. Recommended by the prestige of its military successes, Islam was adopted by people after people in that reservoir of invasions, Central Asia. Beginning with the eighth century, all the peoples who entered India as conquerors by way of the northwest were Moslems. In the course of the next thousand years they mastered most of north India and extended their power southward into the Deccan. Millions of Indians accepted Islam. The Prophet and his faith became one of the outstanding political, social, and religious factors of India. Yet only a minority, even though a substantial minority, of the population of India became Moslems. The demise of the decrepit Buddhism of India was hastened by the destruction wrought by the Moslem invaders, but Hinduism survived as the religion of the vast majority.

The story of the Moslem invasions is long and complicated, for the Crescent was borne by more than one people and conqueror. Here there is space only for the briefest mention of some of the more important figures and events.

By the beginning of the eighth century after Christ, Islam was on the northwestern borders of India. For a time in the eighth and ninth centuries the Abbasid Caliphs, Arabs, whose capital was at Baghdad, in Mesopotamia, included part of northwestern India in their domains. In the ninth and tenth centuries, there were Moslem states, independent of Baghdad, in the northwest.

Not far from A.D. 1000, Mahmud, of Turkish stock, ruler of Ghazni, a state which embraced the modern Afghanistan and some adjacent territories, invaded northwest India. From that year until 1026 Mahmud made repeated expeditions into India, gathering booty, as a pious Moslem destroying images and with them much of Hindu art, and incorporating part of the northwest into his realms.

After the death of Mahmud, a line of rulers, probably of Persian stock, with their center at Ghur, also in the modern Afghanistan, made themselves masters of a large proportion of the realms of Ghazni. In 1175 one of these monarchs, Mohammed of Ghur, began a succession of conquering expeditions into India. By the time of his death, in A.D. 1206, the Moslems were masters of most of the Indo-Gangetic Plain.

Mohammed's viceroy in India, who has been called the real founder of Moslem dominion in India, was a Turk, once a slave, Qutb-ud-din Aibak. Mohammed gave Aibak a free rein. It was to Aibak that most of Mohammed's Indian conquests must be attributed. On Mohammed's death, Aibak assumed the title of Sultan. He was the first of a line of rulers, by no means all of his blood, who reigned from Delhi. They were called the Slave dynasty, because their earlier members were Turkish slaves who through native ability and the favor of their masters rose to supreme power. The territory controlled by the Delhi monarchs included all the Indo-Gangetic Plain and even extended slightly south of the Vindhyas. In the fighting that established the realm, great damage was done to the surviving examples of Hindu and Buddhist art, and Buddhism especially suffered. Yet Hinduism was tolerated and the Moslem rulers utilized Hindus in their army and had Hindu princes and landowners as vassals.

In the thirteenth and fourteenth centuries the Mongols, who were building a huge empire which stretched from Korea and the China Sea into Russia and Mesopotamia, repeatedly invaded India through the northwest passes. At the outset they were not Moslems, but they did not at that time acquire enduring territorial possessions in India, nor did they seriously retard the extension of Moslem rule in that land.

Other lines of rulers succeeded the Slave dynasty on the throne at Delhi. Like their predecessors, they were of Turkish blood. Under some of these monarchs Moslem arms were carried triumphantly into the Deccan and even as far south as Madura. For a time in the first half of the fourteenth century almost all of India, excepting the extreme south and two or three other areas, was governed directly or indirectly from Delhi. Mohammed, of the Tughluq dynasty, a brilliant but erratic prince of contradictory characteristics who dreamed of subduing the world, in the first part of his reign (1325–1351) actually governed most of India. Because so large a portion of his domains was in the peninsula, he built a new capital in the northern part of the Deccan, presumably as a more central location. Before his death, however, the Deccan had slipped from his grasp. Various portions of the Delhi Empire became independent, some of them under Hindu princes.

In 1398, when the Delhi Empire was in decay, Tamerlane, or Timur the Lame, the famous conqueror of Mongol descent and an ardent Moslem, led his armies into India by way of the northwest. He captured and sacked Delhi and, although he was in India only a few months, until March 1399, his forces are declared to have wrought more destruction to life and property than any other one of the many invasions. Northern India was left in great confusion, and it was half a century before an Afghan succeeded in reestablishing a sultanate at Delhi. Even then only a portion of the domains of the greatest of the earlier Delhi dynasties was brought under its rule. Not all the Indo-Gangetic Plain submitted to it.

Although in the fifteenth century the Delhi Empire was sadly shrunken, most of India was still under Moslem overlords. Here and there, notably in the southern part of the peninsula, were states with Hindu princes. Moreover, Hindus constituted then, as now, the overwhelming majority of the population. The tradition had been established, however, that those who held the political power in India should be predominantly of the Moslem minority. These Moslems were of several races. Most of the governing aristocracy were the descendants of invaders who had entered by way of the northwest passes. Yet with some exceptions they had now been domiciled in India for many generations and deemed themselves as much Indian as the Hindus. They owed their position to their superiority in the field of battle. The tradition of military prowess and of mastery of the government had been so solidly established that it was to have important consequences as late as the twentieth century.

The Mogul Dynasty

The Mongols at the height of their Asiatic conquests and their descendant, the great Tamerlane, had raided India but had not established their rule there in any enduring fashion. In the sixteenth century princes in the line of Tamerlane and so of Mongol blood succeeded in bringing most of India under their control. Although the original Mongols had not been Moslems, these conquerors, like Tamerlane, were followers of the Prophet. Their empire was the last of those to be set up by Moslem invaders from the northwest.

This latest of Moslem Indian empires is known by the name of Mogul or Mughul, from the Persian name for Mongol. It had as its founder Babur. Tamerlane's vast realm had broken up soon after his death, but some of its fragments remained in the hands of members of his family. Babur was born in 1483 and at the tender age of eleven succeeded his father as head of the kingdom of Farghana, in Central Asia. At twenty-one he made himself master of Kabul, in the modern Afghanistan, on one of the best roads to India. He had ambitions in Turkestan, but he was balked in these and turned to the India which lay, wealthy and weak, so invitingly accessible from his mountain eyrie. He may have hoped that conquests in India would give him the means to achieve his hopes in Turkestan. In 1505 he made his first raid through the Khyber Pass. Another followed in 1507. It was not, however, until his capture of Lahore in 1524 that his Indian career really began. Between that event and his death, in 1530, he laid the foundations for the Indian empire of his line. Intensely active in mind and body, like many of his family given to bouts of drunkenness but in spite of this trait a devout adherent of a faith, Islam, which forbade the use of intoxicants, fearless in battle, an able general who was said to be one of the first in Asia to appreciate the value of artillery, Babur began the erection of a domain which under his family was to become more extensive than any created in India until that of the British. He eliminated the Afghan sultanate of Delhi and by doing so fell heir to the state which more than any other continued the tradition of dominant power.

Babur, dying in middle life, was succeeded by his eldest son, Humayun. Humayun ruled until his death in 1556. He proved less competent than his father. Although courageous and showing endurance in adversity, he was careless, at times was lacking in decision, and was a victim of self-indulgence which could not resist the enervating Indian environment. On his death he left to his son and heir, Akbar, a most difficult situation.

Akbar proved more than equal to the challenge bequeathed him by his dissolute father. Indeed, he became one of the outstanding monarchs of history. At the time of his accession, Akbar was only thirteen years of age. Due to his father's unwisdom, his actual inheritance was confined to the Punjab. He reigned until 1605, or for nearly half a century. In his long rule Akbar enlarged the precarious domains he inherited, until they embraced all of the Indo-Gangetic Plain and reached into the modern Afghanistan and Baluchistan and south of the Vindhya Mountains into the northwestern portion of the Deccan.

Akbar was memorable not so much for his conquests, for his realm was not so extensive as that of some others who have reigned in India, as for his administrative and religious measures. He endeavored so to organize his empire as to centralize it and to rule it through a graded civil service and an officialdom whose members were paid stated salaries, rather than, as theretofore, through those who were recompensed in land or by the right to collect taxes. He sought to systematize taxation and to bring about the adoption of uniform weights and measures. He reformed the currency. Akbar was a religious innovator. He seems to have been sincerely religious and deeply interested in the various faiths of the world. Presumably, too, as a statesman, he was distressed by the religious differences among his subjects which made difficult the achievement of a unified empire. Although reared a Moslem, he long stood for tolerance. He made himself familiar with the teachings of various religions, including Christianity. He removed the tax traditionally levied by Moslem rulers upon their non-Moslem subjects. He took into his harem several Hindu princesses. Eventually he became less tolerant toward Islam than toward the other standard faiths of India and in time seems to have abandoned that religion. Indeed, he devised a new religion in which he sought to incorporate what appealed to him as the desirable elements of the various existing cults. Apparently he hoped to obtain its adoption and thus to do away with the religious divisions in his empire. However, he won few adherents to his syncretistic invention.

Akbar was followed by a son who took the name of Jahangir (Holder of the World). In contrast with his father, who in spite of an active mind was illiterate, Jahangir left behind him personally written or directed memoirs of his reign. He knew Persian literature and was fastidious in it and in artistic matters. He displayed, too, fairly wide intellectual interests. He believed the daily public administration of justice to be one of his royal duties and was faithful in its discharge. However, he was addicted to strong drink and opium, and that in spite of his nominal adherence to Islam. He was not so able or vigorous a monarch as Akbar.

On his death (1627), Jahangir was succeeded by his son, Shah Jahan. Shah Jahan is best remembered by the modern age as responsible for the Taj Mahal, one of the most beautiful monuments in the world, which he had erected at Agra, his new capital, as a mausoleum for his favorite wife. He also had built other notable structures, among them the pearl mosque in Delhi and a new city with a huge palace at that historic seat of Moslem power. He proved a more orderly ruler than his father, and he was diligent and businesslike in his conduct of affairs of state. He was a more loyal Moslem than his father and grandfather had been, but he preserved a certain degree of tolerance toward other faiths.

Shah Jahan was followed in 1658 by a son, Aurangzeb. Aurangzeb attained the throne by deposing and imprisoning Shah Jahan and killing his brothers. In him the Mogul dynasty reached its acme and began its sharp decline. He reigned until his death, in 1707, or for almost precisely the same length of time that the other great monarch of the dynasty, Akbar, had held the throne. Aurangzeb professed to have acted against his father because of the latter's incompetence and sloth and to be the instrument of God for moral reform and good government. Shah Jahan lived until 1666, a captive in his palace in

Agra, bitter against his rebellious son and devoting his time largely to religion. Aurangzeb was undoubtedly able and, in addition, in contrast with Akbar, a fanatical adherent of Islam. He was a man of an abounding physical energy which he preserved until extreme old age, for he died in his ninetieth year and retained to the end all his faculties except his hearing. He was a lover of books and knew Persian poetry and Moslem sacred literature. In his personal life he was austere, free from vice, and faithful in marriage. He gave minute and unflagging attention to the administration of his realm. He had great personal courage, a cold, clear mind, complete self-confidence, distrust of others, but, on occasion, tact and sagacity. As a military leader he was marked by quickness in grasping a situation, rapidity of movement, and careful coordination of his forces. Aurangzeb was an inveterate traveler through his growing realms, and roads were of the essence of his imperial structure.

During the first half of his reign, Aurangzeb added to his territories in the north. Part of Tibet acknowledged his suzerainty, and he conquered footholds in Assam. He maintained his rule among the restless Afghans by force and by setting tribe against tribe. He sought to elevate the morals of his realm by prohibiting strong drink, the voluntary burning of Hindu widows (*suttee*), and the castration of boys for sale as eunuchs, by discouraging gambling, and by commanding all courtesans and dancing girls to marry or emigrate. He reduced taxes and abolished illegal exactions.

Aurangzeb's undoing came largely from the excess of his virtues. His attention to detail led to the centralizing of too much of the administration in his own hands. Capable though he was, no one man could handle directly all the minutiae of the government of a large empire. He sought to curb what to him was unorthodoxy in Islamic circles. His zeal for Islam had about it the sincerity of conviction, but it led him to measures that antagonized the majority of his subjects and brought upon him costly rebellions.

Particularly disastrous were the measures against the Sikhs and the Hindus. The Sikh religion had arisen through Baba Nanak (1469–1538), who denounced caste and idolatry and preached the worship of one God. Under the direction of its series of heads, *Gurus*, the spiritual successors of Nanak, the majority branch of the Sikh community gradually was knit together and began to develop military power. In his religious zeal, Aurangzeb ordered the destruction of the Sikh temples and seized and killed the ninth of the *Gurus*. These measures led the tenth and last of the *Gurus* to hasten the militarization of the Sikhs as irreconcilable enemies of Aurangzeb and Islam. They became a formidable fighting brotherhood which plagued the Emperor.

Moreover, Aurangzeb revived the restrictions of Islamic law against unbelievers, including particularly Hindus. The tax on unbelievers was reimposed, wherever possible Hindus were replaced by Moslems as collectors of revenue, a discriminatory impost was levied on Hindu merchants, and various inducements were held out to attract converts to Islam. Numbers of Hindu temples were destroyed.

By these actions Aurangzeb alienated the majority of his subjects. By them he stirred up the opposition of powerful Rajput princes who had been a bulwark of his predecessors against attack from the northwest. Aurangzeb's anti-Hindu measures also made more difficult his attempt to control the Mahrattas. The Mahrattas, Hindus of low caste sharing a common language, were being welded into a fighting confederacy by one of their number, Sivaji, who died in 1680. In spite of the loss of its leader and the prolonged effort of Aurangzeb to subdue it, the Mahratta Confederacy continued and in 1707 was the dominant force in the Deccan.

In his long wars against the Mahrattas and with other enemies, Aurangzeb spent much of the latter half of his reign in the Deccan. During his prolonged absence from the north, administration in the Indo-Gangetic Plain deteriorated. At first the Mogul armies were fairly successful in the Deccan and the south. Aurangzeb's domains were pushed farther southward than were those of the predecessors of his line. However, in his old age the Mahrattas proved too much for him. The indomitable old man fought on until his death, but his realms were slipping from him.

Aurangzeb's successors were unable to revive the glory of their house. A severe blow was dealt what remained by a Persian invasion, led by Nadir Shah, which sacked Delhi in 1739. Fragments of the empire broke away into independence, notable among them being Hyderabad, whose head, once viceroy to the Moguls in the Deccan, bearing the title of Nizam, founded a state which continued into 1949, the largest of those which preserved their separate existence under British rule. By the close of the eighteenth century the Mogul domains had shrunk to a mere fragment of their former extent and the grandeur of the house, jealously guarded by the feeble holders of the name, to a mere shadow of its erstwhile dignity. In 1857 the last of the puppet Emperors was banished by the British to Burma.

We have given so much attention to the story of the Moguls because it is an accompaniment to the beginning of the European period of India's history and so to present times. It was in these years that modern India had its inception.

The Coming of the European

On the eve of the advent of Mogul power came the beginning of those invasions from Europe which in the course of the next four centuries were to bring all of India into political subjection.

This conquest was without precedent. All of India was now constrained to acknowledge the rule of one or another of the European powers, and no invader or congeries of invaders had hitherto quite attained that goal. Moreover, this invasion came not from the northwest and the land, the avenue of the other major foreign conquerors, but by the sea.

Western Europeans were not the first to journey by sea to India. For centuries the ocean had been a highway. Greeks and Romans had carried on a brisk trade with Indian ports. Persian merchants had come and founded communities which continued to cherish their ancestral Zoroastrianism even after it had been all but extinguished at home. Their descendants were called Parsees. Nestorian Christians had arrived, probably from Mesopotamia or southern Arabia, and from them had sprung churches in southern India. For centuries before A.D. 1500 most of the seaborne trade, especially its westward part, was in the hands of Arabs. For a time, chiefly at the beginning of the fifteenth century, Chinese shared in the commerce from India eastward.

Western Europeans reached India at least as early as the thirteenth century. They were there as well in the fourteenth and from time to time in the fifteenth century. Some of them came as merchants. Others were missionaries. They were not numerous and made but a slight impression upon India.

Late in the fifteenth century began that irruption of Europeans which eventually was to have such momentous consequences upon India and the Far East. It was part of the expansion by which Europeans, chiefly Western Europeans, became dominant throughout the globe.

Accepted though it now is as a fact of history as well as present experience, this expansion is nevertheless amazing. Europe is a peninsula of Euro-Asia, as is India. Until the latter part of the fifteenth century the peoples on its western coasts played a relatively minor part in the world scene. To be sure, its southern coasts had been important. For a few centuries beginning with Alexander the Greeks had been prominent in Western Asia and part of Central Asia. Their commerce and their culture had affected the peoples bordering the Mediterranean and, as we saw a few pages back, had made themselves felt, usually in a minor way, in India, Central Asia, and even the Far East. Yet the Alexandrian empire was not so extensive as the slightly later and much less ephemeral Han dynasty of China, and until the modern age when, as a constituent of Western European culture, it had world-wide effects, the influence of Greece was less far-reaching geographically than that of India or of China. The Romans had built a huge empire, but it was no larger than the contemporary Han Empire of China. The Italians of the thirteenth and fourteenth centuries as churchmen or merchants traveled over as great distances as any people of their time, but their immediate effect upon civilization was not of such widespread potency as was that of the Arabs of their day or as had been that of Indians a few centuries earlier. In the European middle ages, Western Europe did not occupy nearly as prominent a part in the world as a whole as did India or China. Yet beginning with the latter part of the fifteenth century Western Europeans suddenly began a series of explorations and conquests which within less than a hundred years carried them around the world and won for them footholds on each of the non-European continents. In the nineteenth and twentieth centuries that expansion was accelerated. Its effect was revolutionary upon every non-European culture. Its impact upon India and the Far East and the repercussions from it will be the theme of about half of this volume, so important is it for an understanding of the current Far East. Commonplace though the coming of the Occident now appears to us to be, seen against the background of the long centuries of the history of the race, it is recent. To one with any imagination it never ceases to be thrilling, and at times terrifying.

Into the underlying causes of the expansion of Western European peoples we must not attempt to go. This is not because they are unimportant. They are of the utmost significance. Upon a correct understanding of them are probably dependent the correct answers to such basic queries as the future of the power and impact of the

Occident, whether the West is to be a continuing or a transient phenomenon in the culture of India and the Far East, and the ultimate effects upon India and the Far East of the Occidental invasion. We are refusing to explore causes largely because we are not sure of them, or at least of their proportionate strength. Quite obviously geographic position, race, climate, religion, and economics are all factors, but no agreement exists among scholars as to what weight shall be given to each. Any discussion of them, therefore, would be tantalizing and inconclusive.

Although we are not certain of the precise combination of factors that produced the expansion of Europe, we can trace the course of that expansion and can note the most striking results. That we must do, first for India and later for the various lands and peoples of the Far East.

In the present chapter we will recount the beginnings of the coming of the European to India and will carry the story down to the time when, about the middle of the eighteenth century, European, in this case British, territorial conquest began on a large scale and with it the effects of European culture began to be extensive and profound. In a later chapter we will bring the narrative down to the current scene. This roughly corresponds to the program for the book as a whole, for about half our space is to be devoted to the pre-nineteenth century history, before the Occident became of primary importance in the Far East, and the second half is to be concerned with the heightened incursion of the West in the nineteenth and twentieth centuries and the developments that ensued in the Far East.

The Portuguese Era

The coming of Western Europeans to India was led by the Portuguese. Since the first quarter of the fifteenth century the Portuguese had been nosing their way southward along the west shore of Africa. After nearly a century of preparation in which Portuguese ships voyaged farther and farther south, in July 1497, three small ships sailed from Lisbon under Vasco da Gama and in May 1498, having rounded the Cape of Good Hope, cast anchor off a small village a few miles north of Calicut on the southwest coast of India.

The primary purpose of the expedition, as of the subsequent Portuguese enterprise, was commercial. By going directly to India and the Far East, the Portuguese wished to obtain a monopoly of the profitable trade which had heretofore been in the hands of the Moslem

Arabs with Italians as middlemen between the Arabs and Western Europe.

In 1500 a second and larger Portuguese expedition, led by Cabral, reached Calicut. In 1502 Vasco da Gama commanded another, still larger, fleet to India. A trading post, or factory, was established at Cochin, south of Calicut, at what proved to be a better harbor under more friendly rule.

In 1505, the better to conserve Portuguese interests and the more effectively to drive the Arabs out of the Indian Ocean and the Arabian Sea, a viceroy, Almeida, was appointed for India. Before the decade was out, Almeida was followed by Albuquerque. Under these able men vigorous action was taken against the Arabs. Albuquerque took Socotra, off the mouth of the Red Sea, as a vantage point against the Arabs. In India he deemed Goa strategic. He captured it and to this day it remains in Portuguese hands, now as it has been since 1530 the capital of Portuguese India. He also took Malacca, as a strategic point on the Malay Peninsula from which to command the sea route to the East Indies and the Far East. He vainly attempted the capture of Aden, near the southern entrance to the Red Sea, but succeeded in asserting Portuguese suzerainty over Ormuz, near the mouth of the Persian Gulf.

Albuquerque's policy was followed, in general, by his successors. The Portuguese made no attempt at extensive conquest in India. They were content to be a sea power and thus to profit by the trade between India and the Far East on the one hand and Europe on the other. To assure their control of the seas, they took and fortified strategic posts, among them several ports in India and Ceylon.

The Portuguese essayed no large migration to India. Portugal was too small and too distant a land to make that possible even had it been desired. Albuquerque encouraged his men to take Indian wives. From regular and irregular unions a mixed population arose in the Portuguese possessions claiming to be Portuguese but actually partly of Indian blood.

Although Portugal's ambition in India and the Far East was primarily commercial, the desire to propagate Roman Catholic Christianity also entered. This was especially the case after the great revival in the first half of the sixteenth century which Protestants often call the Counter Reformation but which is more accurately termed the Catholic Reformation. Missionaries, notably of the young Society of Jesus, went to the various Portuguese possessions. A hierarchy was created under the immediate direction of the Archbishop of Goa and under the control of the Portuguese crown. Most famous of all the churchmen was the pioneer of the Jesuits in the East, the Navarrese Francis Xavier. He sailed for India in 1541. In the little more than a decade between his arrival and his tragic death (1552) in a vain endeavor to introduce his faith to China, Xavier covered part of the coast of India and Ceylon, spent some time in the East Indies, and led the initial group of his society to Japan.

Roman Catholic missions in India were confined largely but not entirely to the restricted Portuguese possessions. In these footholds the population became Christian. For a time, at first at the invitation of Akbar, Jesuits were at the Mogul capital, but they made few converts.

By the middle of the sixteenth century Portuguese power in India had reached its peak. The Portuguese continued, but were less and less prominent in India's foreign trade. In time the ports that remained in their hands became quiescent backwaters, little touched by the main currents of India's life and commerce.

The Dutch in India

The Mogul Emperors were content to be a land power. They did not seriously contest the Portuguese dominion on the seas. The Portuguese acquired most of their Indian territories before the Mogul rule was well established. In obtaining possession they had to contend merely with Hindu princes in the south and local Moslem princes in the north. Had they been faced with the necessity of wresting ports from the great Mogul monarchs they might have fared less well.

The first major threat to the Portuguese after the destruction of the Arab sea power came from the Dutch.

The Netherlands had long contained cities which were centers of commerce, but while they were part of the Spanish Empire their merchants were not free to engage directly in the Indian or Far Eastern trade. When in the course of the second half of the sixteenth century the northern Netherlands achieved their independence from Spain, these restrictions ceased to bind them, and they were the more emboldened to challenge Portugal when in 1581 that land came (until 1640) under the ruling house of Spain.

In 1595 the first Dutch boats to round the Cape of Good Hope sailed from home. At the outset the Dutch attacked the Portuguese in the East Indies rather than India. In 1602 free competition between various groups of Dutch merchants was terminated through the formation of the United Company to which the Dutch government gave the monopoly of trade between the Cape of Good Hope and the Straits of Magellan, together with the authority to make war, conclude treaties, and acquire territory.

The center of Dutch power was established in the East Indies and remained there. Here was the chief source of the pepper and spices which were the most desired prizes of the Eastern trade. India was subsidiary.

Yet in the first half of the seventeenth century the Dutch acquired factories in India, for they desired Indian goods to exchange for East Indian products. In the first quarter of the seventeenth century the Dutch acquired footholds at a number of places on the Indian coast. Before the close of that century they had driven the Portuguese out of their strongholds on the Malabar (southwest) Coast and had supplanted them in Ceylon.

However, Aurangzeb's conquests in the south in the last quarter of the seventeenth century dealt the Dutch trade on the Coromandel (southeast) Coast a blow from which it never fully recovered. On the Malabar Coast and in Ceylon the expense of the military and naval forces that the Dutch deemed it necessary to maintain often exceeded the profits of the commerce of that region. In some other parts of India, Dutch commerce showed a gain.

French Beginnings

More tardily than the Dutch, the French sought a share in the trade of India and the Far East. In the third quarter of the seventeenth century, at the instance of Colbert, Louis XIV's great minister, a French East India Company was organized. For a variety of reasons, among them preoccupation with European affairs, the French did not achieve the prominence in the trade of India attained by the Portuguese, the Dutch, and the English. However, they obtained a few territorial footholds, chief among them being Pondichery on the Coromandel Coast. These they were able to retain. Moreover, in the eighteenth century they were for a time formidable opponents of the rising English power.

Other Europeans (Aside from the English)

Still other Europeans made a bid for the trade of India. In 1616 the Danish East India Company was organized, and in the seventeenth and eighteenth centuries it was succeeded by others under

Danish auspices. A settlement was effected at Tranquebar, on the southeast coast, and, later, at Serampore, on the Hoogly, near the present Calcutta. These were held, in spite of temporary capture by the English during the Napoleonic Wars, until their purchase by the English in 1845.

In 1713 what remained of the Spanish Netherlands (approximately the later Belgium) after the independence of the northern provinces became the property of Austria. In 1723 the merchants of Flanders obtained from the Hapsburg Emperor a charter for what was usually known as the Ostend Company. Factories were established in India, but bitter British opposition eventually terminated the enterprise.

There were also Swedish, Austrian, and Prussian companies, largely for China, but they did not attain significant dimensions.

English Beginnings

It was the English rather than the Portuguese, the Dutch, the French, or the various other European peoples who became the leading power in India.

In 1600, two years before the formation of the United Company of the Dutch, there was organized "The Governor and Company of Merchants of London Trading into the East Indies." It was given for fifteen years the monopoly of English commerce between the Cape of Good Hope and the Straits of Magellan. Partly because of changing governments at home, this English East India Company experienced vicissitudes. In 1698 a rival, "The English Company Trading to the East Indies," was chartered. In 1702 an agreement was reached for the amalgamation of the two concerns and "The United Company of Merchants of England Trading to the East Indies" became the official title of the fusion. The name, the English East India Company, by which the British enterprise is usually known, is a convenient but not a precise designation for more than one incorporation and a varied history.

Like the Dutch and French companies, the English East India Company was concerned with all of the vast territory east of the Cape of Good Hope. In its early years it engaged in commerce in the East Indies and for a time made common cause with the Dutch against the Portuguese. However, friction with the Dutch was inevitable. Before long the English all but abandoned the East Indies to their Dutch rivals. They remained active in China, but most of their energies were devoted to India.

Early in the seventeenth century the English established factories at a number of points in India. For a period their main headquarters were at Surat, north of the present Bombay, and clearly within what the Portuguese had deemed their sphere of influence. Hostilities arose between the English and the Portuguese, and in 1622 the English aided the Persians in driving the Portuguese out of Ormuz. The Portuguese were beset by so many foes, including the redoubtable Dutch, that before many years they deemed it best to make their peace with the English and thus to be rid of at least one enemy. In 1635 a truce was agreed upon, a treaty was entered into in 1642, and in 1654 the Portuguese granted to the English the right to trade with all Portuguese possessions in the East except Macao. Indeed, Portuguese and English united against the Dutch. From 1652 to 1654 the English and the Dutch were at war. In 1661, by the treaty through which Charles II married Catherine of Braganza, of the ruling house in Portugal, the English guaranteed the Portuguese holdings in the East against the Dutch, and the island of Bombay, off the west coast of India, was made part of the bride's dowry.

Before many years Charles II gave to the East India Company a perpetual lease on Bombay. Here the Company proceeded to build what eventually became its main base on the west coast. After two unsatisfactory ventures in factories on the east coast, in 1639 permission was obtained from a local ruler to erect a post at the little town of Madras. Here the British constructed Fort St. George, and from 1641 Madras was the British headquarters on the Coromandel Coast. In Bengal, the outlet for the profitable trade of the wealthy Ganges Valley, various factories were established, and toward the end of the seventeenth century what proved to be a permanent settlement was made at what came to be called Calcutta. Here Fort William was erected. By the year 1700, then, the English had a number of factories, or trading posts, in India. Of these the chief were at Bombay on the west coast, Madras on the Coromandel Coast, and Calcutta in Bengal. These three centers became the seats of what were termed presidencies and continued to be the main headquarters of British activities in India.

By the year 1700 the English began the acquisition of territory, even though limited to the immediate environs of their factories. This procedure seemed to them necessary if they were to maintain their commerce with India. The Portuguese had set the precedent and the Dutch had followed it. Moreover, this appeared essential in view of the chronic wars which racked India, and in defense against the arbitrary exactions of local princes. The Europeans felt that they must be able to hold their own by armed force against rivals of other Occidental powers, against pirates, often from Europe, and against Indian belligerents. At the outset this policy was purely ancillary to the commercial purposes of the East India Company. Out of it, however, arose the strange anomaly by which a corporation formed for the purpose of trade conquered India and became the instrument through which for many years the English ruled the land. Not until the 1850's was the paradox resolved by the abolition of the East India Company's regime and the substitution of direct control by the Crown.

The story of this development leads directly to the India of today and so must be reserved for a later chapter.

The Culture of Old India

From the chronological account of the development of India we must turn to the culture of India on the eve of the British conquest. That conquest was to be followed by momentous changes in Indian life. If we are to understand these and the India of our day we must know something of the civilization of India as it was when it began to be subjected to the revolutionary pressure from the Occident.

Religion

Even from the brief survey contained in the preceding pages of this chapter it must be apparent that an outstanding feature of India's culture has been religion. It was through religion that the peoples of India made their chief contributions to other lands, notably to those of the Far East. Of commerce outside their borders the Indians had some which they carried on directly through their own traders. Of settlement and conquest there was a little. Commerce by Indians, settlement, and conquest had to do with only minority sections of the Far East—in the southeast and the East Indies. Through religion, however, India influenced, and influenced profoundly, all the civilized Far East. Upon the Far East, indeed, India's religious effect was much greater than upon any other portion of the globe. Although it was known in the West and made contributions to the Occident, Indian religion spread eastward much more than it did westward.

The preponderance of religion in the effect of India upon her neighbors was not an accident. It arose out of the nature of Indian culture. It was in religion and philosophy, and especially in religion, rather than in government or even in art or literature that Indian civilization registered its most notable achievements.

In this India was in striking contrast with the Far East. China, the major country of the Far East in culture and influence, gave birth to philosophies which had in them religious elements. However, its bent was social and political rather than religious. It was in the development of a system of imperial government closely related to a structure of society that China was outstanding. To be sure, this political organization was based upon a philosophy, but the philosophy under which unification was first achieved was not the one that prevailed during most of the history of the imperial system. It was the government which enforced a particular philosophy as much as it was a philosophy which created the government. In contrast, India gave birth to no enduring empire or major system of government. China was primarily this-worldly. India was predominantly other-worldly. Japan, next to China in its historic prominence in the Far East, gave birth to only one religion, Shinto, and that was of a primitive type and was closely bound up with a theory of the state and subordinated to it. Its major distinctive achievement was even more clearly political than was that of India.

To the religious nature of Indian civilization is probably related another characteristic. After the fall of the Gupta dynasty, in the sixth century, all the major empires built in India were the work of invaders. Kingdoms and confederacies arose created by those from a long Indian lineage, but from the sixth century onward the only realms that embraced most of India were the work of foreign conquerors and their immediate descendants. Nor did any of the empires built by foreign conquerors enjoy a permanent existence. Under the influence of the Indian environment, each in time passed—even including the British, once seemingly all-powerful and only recently liquidated.

The bearing of this fact upon India's future must be obvious. It is yet to be demonstrated that the Indians can maintain a unified, independent state embracing all of India. Under the direction of conquerors they have served as officials, often with great distinction. Not for more than a thousand years have they built an empire. In spite of the recently achieved independence, their record is far less encouraging than is that of the Chinese. In the course of the last thousand years the Chinese have more than half the time been ruled by foreign dynasties, but that rule has been through a state organization originally created by the Chinese and has operated through an officialdom which has usually been overwhelmingly Chinese. Moreover, twice in the last six centuries the Chinese have ousted a foreign dynasty and after the earlier of these victories were unified under a native house for over three hundred years. Usually, too, the conquering dynasty adopted Chinese culture, including the prevailing philosophy, and claimed to be a legitimate enforcer of Chinese traditions. In contrast, the foreign builders of empire in India were of different religions from that of the majority of their subjects and remained so. From the eleventh to the eighteenth century they were Moslems. The English have professedly been Christians. Whether this fact means that the Indians can never achieve or maintain, unaided, a unified, independent government, the historian ought not to say. He must content himself with recording what has happened and call attention to the question which emerges from that fact, so important for the nationalistic India of the present, and so unpleasant to those who cherish its aspirations.

HINDUISM

In the middle of the eighteenth century, as now, the religion of the large majority of Indians was Hinduism. Hinduism is so multiform that in the brief space we can here devote to it we ought not to attempt a comprehensive description. We can simply present a few of its features. In it were many elements. The most ancient of its sacred writings were the product of the early Indo-Aryans. The Brahmans, the priestly class of the Indo-Aryans, retained their ranking position in it. Often it is called Brahmanism. Into it came contributions from the non-Aryans of India, notably from the Dravidians. Hinduism proved to have great powers of absorption. Gods were taken into its pantheon from many different sources or identified with an existing god by a convenient doctrine of incarnation which made it possible for one divinity to assume various forms. Partly through this capacity of Hinduism for assimilation, Buddhism was eventually largely eliminated from the land of its birth and persisted only on the borders or among immigrants.

Prominent in Hinduism was the belief in the transmigration of souls (metempsychosis). The doctrine made for fellowship in all animal life, for in rebirth one did not necessarily reappear in human guise. *Karma* was associated with transmigration. It was the sum of an individual's action in all his previous existences and determined his fate in his next incarnation. In his present existence he might modify his *karma* for good or for ill, but he could not escape from it.

The cow was sacred. The leading gods of the Hindu pantheon were Brahma, Vishnu, and Siva. Related to Siva was his spouse, known under various names, including that of Kali. Vishnu had two chief avatars or incarnations, Rama and Krishna.

Of the immense literature of Hinduism, the most revered were the Vedas, the Brahmanas, and the Upanishads, which we have already mentioned, the two great epics, the Mahabharata and the Ramayana, the Puranas, and the Tantras. One hears, too, of the rules of social ethics contained in the ancient code of Manu and of that model expression of mysticism, the Bhagavad-Gita.

The Ganges was esteemed a sacred river. There were many holy sites, prominent among them being the city of Benares with its shrines.

There was a popular Hinduism, with much of what to the Westerner was crass superstition and gross immorality. There was also the Hinduism of the erudite and the lofty-souled, with subtle and profound philosophy and cultivated mysticism. No sharp line separated the two. Between them were many gradations.

Hinduism had many sects. It contained different religious outlooks—animism, polytheism, atheism, pantheism, and theism.

Prominent in Hinduism, and even outside Hinduism, were the holy men, ascetics, who forswore the world, mortified their flesh, and strove for the sanctity of the spirit. Many of these were filled with pride and morally were a detriment to society. Others were sincere.

Pilgrimages, with a tinge of asceticism about them, were a frequent occupation of the rank and file of Hindus and combined, as religious pilgrimages of all faiths usually have done, the lure of travel and of religious experience and merit.

Hinduism was both tolerant and intolerant. It could incorporate almost any belief or system that was willing to be absorbed, but it was adamant against any religion that, like Christianity or Islam, claimed to be the final and complete revelation of the divine.

With all its seeming inclusiveness, Hinduism was primarily a racial and regional, not a world religion. Here and there it was planted beyond the borders of India, chiefly in Indo-China and the East Indies. In very few places outside of India, and they small, such as the island of Bali, east of Java, did it persist into the twentieth century. It never was so actively missionary as was Buddhism, Christianity, or Islam. It did not even move as extensively out of India as did Confucianism out of China. Confucianism became much more continuously potent in Korea, Japan, and Annam than did Hinduism among any major people outside of India.

ISLAM

Next to Hinduism in numerical strength in India was Islam. In the twentieth century it claimed about one-fifth of the population as compared with the two-thirds who were counted as Hindus. As can be readily discerned from the historical sketch embraced in this chapter, it was introduced by invaders and conquerors from the northwest and, to a much less extent, by Arab merchants by way of the sea. Its adherents were either these invaders and their descendants or converts and their descendants. Most of the converts were from the lower social strata. Because it had entered so largely by way of conquerors from Central Asia, Islam was relatively strongest in the northwest, in the Punjab. Moslems were, however, numerous throughout most of the Indo-Gangetic Plain and were found even as far south as the Deccan.

Between Hindus and Moslems was a chronic even though sometimes latent antagonism. The Moslems had long been accustomed to rule. For centuries before the British conquest theirs had been the main empires of India. They were also in power in many of the smaller states. They despised the Hindus as idolators and heathen. Educated Hindus held Moslems in contempt, especially since many of the latter were illiterate. There were, moreover, some powerful Hindu states. This deep religious gulf made Indian unity difficult. In the twentieth century, in the days when nationalism was a rising movement, it was a chronic thorn in the flesh of Indian patriots.

Although Islam brought enhanced religious division to India, it also made positive contributions. Among these were notable architectural monuments in a distinctive style and the composition of histories. Moreover, it was because of the Moslem Moguls that Hindustani forged to the front among the languages of modern India. Since it was the vernacular in and around the Mogul capital, Delhi, the Mogul supremacy gave it wide currency. To contacts with Moslem peoples, too, was due the development of Urdu, a language with a Hindustani base to which were added many Persian words.

RELIGIOUS MINORITIES

A number of religions, numerical minorities, added to the religious picture. Zoroastrianism was represented by the small but wealthy groups of Parsees, in the cities. The Sikh faith was, as we have noted, of relatively recent Indian origin. Its adherents had become an important military power. There were animists, primitive tribes, usually in the hills, who had not yet been culturally absorbed into the prevailing Hinduism and Islam. Christianity had long been present. Tradition ascribed its first propagation in India to Thomas, one of the Twelve Apostles. For centuries its history is obscure. It seems to have been present before the end of the third century, but the confusion in the early records of southern Arabia with what we now call India makes this somewhat uncertain. Inscriptions which cannot be dated positively, but one of which may be as early as the seventh century, point to a Persian connection, for they are in Middle Persian. In the thirteenth and fourteenth centuries European travelers found long-established Christian communities in southern India. At the time of the advent of the Portuguese, in the fifteenth and sixteenth centuries, there were strong Christian communities in the south owning ecclesiastical allegiance to the Nestorian Patriarch in Mesopotamia. The Portuguese brought Roman Catholic Christianity. In the Portuguese possessions most of the population became adherents of that faith, and zealous missionaries carried it outside the Portuguese boundaries, but with only slight numerical success. Many of the Nestorian or "Syrian" Christians became Roman Catholics. Before the middle of the eighteenth century Protestantism had been introduced by the Dutch, Danes, Germans, and English, but was still not so strong as the other two main divisions of Christianity. Although Buddhism had disappeared from its old strongholds in India, it persisted on the northern borders of India and in Ceylon. The Jains continued. Some of these minorities were vigorous, but in the year 1800, even more than now, Hinduism and Islam were the main religions of India.

Caste

Peculiar to India and an integral and pervasive feature of its social structure was the institution of caste. No complete agreement exists among scholars as to how caste came to be. In it were undoubtedly occupational elements. The Brahmans were the priests, the Kshatriyas the nobles or warriors, and the Vaishyas were commoners or husbandmen. These three were, supposedly, of Indo-Aryan stock. A fourth major group, the Sudras, were non-Aryans, presumably conquered by the Indo-Aryan invaders. Into caste, therefore, from very early times the element of color and race entered. These four continued to be and still are the main caste divisions. Occupationally the distinctions between them did not remain hard and fast. For instance, by no means all the Brahmans were priests. Yet as classifications the four persisted. Many subdivisions added to the complexity of the caste picture. Some of the caste groupings were occupational. Caste determined the range within which one might or might not marry. It also regulated the degree and kind of social intercourse between castes, including those with whom one might eat.

A continuing feature was the so-called outcastes. These were perhaps a fifth of the population. Some kinds of contact with them brought ceremonial defilement to members of the castes, and they were poverty-stricken and on the lowest rungs of the social ladder. Often they were the scavengers who performed the more menial tasks of society—sweeping, removing the offal, and working in leather (to work in leather, from the hide of the sacred cow, was forbidden to the caste Hindu). Even among the outcastes groupings existed which had all the binding character of caste.

Caste was primarily a phenomenon of Hinduism. Indeed, one of the distinctive marks of that religion was the honor paid to the Brahman. However, it penetrated non-Hindu groups. Theoretically Islam, Sikhism, and Christianity was each a brotherhood which knew no caste divisions within its borders. In practice, however, each became a kind of caste. Within Christian communities, made up of converts or of the descendants of fairly recent converts, pre-Christian caste differences were sometimes not obliterated. Europeans tended to be a separate caste. Caste was so much a part of Indian society and thought that it tended to invade the groups which in theory opposed it.

The Family

Prominent in India as in so many other lands was the family. Its control over its members was strong. Marriage was usually early. Women were subordinate to men, but mothers often exercised a strong influence over their children.

The Village

Important, too, in India's life was the village community. India was primarily an agricultural country. That means that the vast majority of its population lived by tilling the soil and by closely associated industries. This rural population was scattered in thousands of villages. Each village was largely a unit by itself. Its different occupational and caste groups lived together, with tasks and perquisites prescribed by custom. The villagers engaged not only in the cultivation of the soil, but also, especially in months in which work on the fields was not pressing, in various industries, among them spinning and weaving. Handicrafts, therefore, had a large place in village life. Each village was, in the main, self-governing and self-regulating. Its local assembly, the *panchayat*, was made up of the more prominent men, especially the village landowners. To it were taken for discussion and decision matters of village concern.

Government

Government in India was personal rather than by a continuing structure. We have already noted the absence of the latter. The former was the counterpart. Because there was no enduring framework such as existed in China and Japan, kingdoms and empires were founded by individuals and were dependent upon them. To be sure, any form of government relies for its efficiency and even its endurance upon those who run it, and especially upon those at the top. The personal factor is always important. Yet in numbers of lands in the Occident and in Japan and China the machinery of government has gone on, even under incompetent rulers, and in China the main structure survived the demise of dynasty after dynasty and for two thousand years was modified only in details. In India, on the other hand, there was no continuity in the centralized administration from dynasty to dynasty and from kingdom to kingdom. Now and then an oligarchy held power, but even that headed up in an individual monarch. The village, family, and caste structure survived the rise and fall of empires and kingdoms, but the larger political units were built up by and depended upon individuals. This made for a kaleidoscopic political scene. The British, too, capitalized on it when in the second half of the nineteenth century they made their Queen Empress and following her their Kings Emperors of India. Indian loyalty could then be directed toward a person.

Economic Life

The economic life of India was characterized by extremes of riches and poverty. The land had some of the wealthiest men on earth. It also sheltered vast masses of abject and festering poverty. For these depressed classes war or the failure of the monsoon meant famine and pestilence. Rice was the staple food, but meat seldom appeared on the farmer's menu.

The wide range in the economic status of the Indians was due to no one factor. Caste was partly responsible. The political tradition of states founded by conquest and personally ruled through absolute monarchs was another. The very wealthy were usually the kings and emperors, their favorite officials, and the nobles. Land tenure had much to do with it. In a land so predominantly agricultural, land-owning was one way of amassing property. There were landholders who bled the cultivators of the soil. Some forms of taxation enabled the tax collector to extract all that he could from the cultivator and to acquire at least a modest fortune. Debt was chronic for the villager and, judged by modern standards, interest rates were high. Marriages and the price of the accompanying dowry were a frequent source of debt. The endless subdivision of land through inheritance led to such small tracts that agriculture was handicapped. The use of liquor and narcotics was impoverishing. Whatever the causes, the poverty of the masses and the wealth of the few were features of India's life, and remain so today.

India was a reservoir into which poured gold and silver. Even approximately accurate statistics of foreign commerce are lacking before the very modern period, but it seems probable that during much of India's history she had what is usually termed a favorable balance of trade, that is, she sold more commodities than she bought. Although India was primarily agricultural, she had many handicrafts. In the days before the industrial revolution made Europe a source of cheap textiles, India's cloth was an important item of export. In payment of the balance against them, foreigners brought the precious metals. In the sixteenth and seventeenth centuries the silver of America which found its way to Europe through the Spaniards was available for the growing Occidental commerce with India. Much of the silver and gold thus obtained was kept in the form of jewelry. Much was hoarded.

Language and Literature

In language, as in race and the political scene, India presented great variety. The number of languages was said to be about one hundred fifty, but there were, as well, many dialectical subdivisions. These many languages were of about twenty linguistic families. The majority of the people spoke tongues with an Indo-Aryan base. A substantial minority, a majority in the south, spoke Dravidian tongues. The speech of a still smaller minority, in the northeast, was of the Tibeto-Burman family.

The standard literature was chiefly religious and philosophical. The outstanding poetry was either frankly religious or shot through and through with religion. Yet some literature was secular.

Art

In the aesthetic side of her life, India was rich. She had a music all her own which, although different from that of the Occident, in its best forms appeals strongly to the discerning among Occidental musicians. Often it was improvised for particular occasions and was meant to fit the mood of the player or of a situation.

Architecture was varied. Much of it was religious and was the outgrowth of Buddhism, Jainism, and Hinduism. With the disappearance of Buddhism except on the borders, the architectural expressions of that faith survived only as ruins. The Jains, being a small community, were not outstanding in their architectural contributions. Hinduism created a multiform and extensive architecture. It varied with the era and with the district. In the south, as was to be expected, it was largely Dravidian. In the north it later showed the effects of Moslem examples. Islam added enormously to Indian architecture. It eschewed the animal and human forms which were so prominent in Hindu sculpture. In contrast with the elaborate ornateness of much of Hindu architecture, it tended to simplicity. It made much of the arch and the dome. It was characterized by dignity and grandeur, and, in some of its examples, by grace. Many of the mosques, tombs, palaces, and fortresses it created were and are monumental.

Summary

Indian culture, of which the preceding paragraphs are a greatly curtailed and quite inadequate summary, was unique, rich, and varied. Into it came contributions from many peoples and civilizations, mostly from Western and Central Asia. It gave much to the Far East, chiefly through Buddhism, to a less extent through Hinduism, and through the literature, philosophy, folklore, and art for which these faiths were vehicles. Indeed, through religion and its associated gifts India shaped the east and south of Asia more widely than did the greatest indigenous cultural force in the Far East, China.

By the close of the fifteenth century the flow of Indian culture to the Far East had all but ceased. However, the earlier contacts had left abiding impressions and remained an integral part of Far Eastern life. Yet Far Eastern civilization was basically very different from that of India. It, too, was unique and varied. In some of the lands and islands of southeastern Asia and the East Indies Indian culture was predominant. However, the leading peoples of the Far East subordinated the importations from India to the genius of their own traditions. By the sixteenth century, indeed, India and its culture were a waning factor in the Far East. Hinduism was on the way out, displaced by Buddhism and beginning to be supplanted by Islam through contacts with the Arab traders. In China, Korea, and Japan, notably in China, Buddhism, the main purveyor of Indian influence, was declining. In China it had been in decay since about the eighth or the ninth century of the Christian era. It was stronger in Japan and did not so soon begin to wane. It continued dominant in the religious life of Tibet, Mongolia, Siam, and Burma. India and the Far East had always been distinct from each other. At the beginning of the nineteenth century they were becoming even more so.

BIBLIOGRAPHY

For Brief Reference

T. W. Holderness, *The Peoples and Problems of India* (New York, 1912).
V. A. Smith, *The Oxford History of India* (Oxford, 1920).

For More Extended Study

The Cambridge History of India (Cambridge, Vols. 1, 3–6, 1922–1937).
S. Das Gupta, *A History of Indian Philosophy* (Cambridge University Press, 3 vols., 1922–1940).
Charles Eliot, *Hinduism and Buddhism* (London, 3 vols., 1921).
S. Lane-Poole, *Babar* (Oxford, 1909).
C. B. Malleson, *Akbar and the Rise of the Mughal Empire* (Oxford, 1908).
R. Mookerji, *Asoka* (London, 1928).
W. H. Moreland, *From Akbar to Aurangzeb. A Study in Indian Economic History* (London, 1923).
W. H. Moreland, *India at the Death of Akbar. An Economic Study* (London, 1920).

J. B. Pratt, *India and Its Faiths* (Boston, 1915).
H. G. Rawlinson, *Intercourse between India and the Western World from the Earliest Times to the Fall of Rome* (Cambridge, 1916).
H. G. Rawlinson, *Indian Historical Studies* (London, 1913).
H. G. Rawlinson, *India. A Short Cultural History* (London, 1937).
T. W. Rhys Davids, *Buddhist India* (New York, 1903).
G. Slater, *The Dravidian Element in Indian Culture* (London, 1924).
V. A. Smith, *Early History of India Including Alexander's Campaigns* (Oxford, 1914).
V. A. Smith, *Akbar. The Great Mogul Emperor* (Oxford, 1917).
V. A. Smith, *Asoka. The Buddhist Emperor of India* (Oxford, 1909).
H. Morse Stephens, *Albuquerque* (Oxford, 1897).
E. Senart, *Caste in India. The Facts and the System* (London, 1930).
W. W. Tarn, *The Greeks in Bactria and India* (Cambridge, 1938).

Chapter III. ANCIENT CHINA

Through the formation of the Empire (to A.D. 200)

IN OUR SURVEY of the history of the Far East proper we start with China. This is because, as we have repeatedly suggested, the Chinese are the most numerous of the Far Eastern peoples, and until the present century their culture has been dominant in that portion of the world.

Every Chinese is born at least thirty-five hundred years old. The ideas, customs, and institutions that shape him and his fellows come down from a remote antiquity. More than any other people, the Chinese have a long continuous history unbroken by major cultural revolutions. Contributions have come in from abroad, notably Buddhism in the early centuries of the Christian era, bringing various concomitants in art, philosophy, and folklore. Always, however, the prevailing strains in Chinese culture have been indigenous. Not until our own day has there come, in consequence of the impact of the Occident, a thoroughgoing remaking of Chinese culture. Even now, in many respects the changes are superficial. Many of the basic institutions survive, and, except possibly among a minority, the fundamental presuppositions and attitudes of mind are altered but slightly if at all. If, then, one is to understand the China of today, and with it the Far East, he must know the story of the development of China's past and the growth of the structure of the Chinese mind and of Chinese life.

Beginnings

As is true of most peoples, the Chinese have traditional or mythical accounts of the beginnings of their history. Among other rulers, they tell of one who taught his people to produce fire by boring one piece of wood with another; of another who taught his subjects to fish with nets and to rear domestic animals; of still another who instructed his people in agriculture and medicine; and of the Yellow

Emperor (Huang Ti) who is credited with instituting official historiographers, with erecting an observatory, with inventing building bricks, and with correcting the calendar. Much is said, too, of the model Emperors Yao, Shun, and Yü. Yü is said to have drained away the waters of a great flood.

How much, if any, truth lies back of these stories we do not know. It is, however, important that, when these accounts took the shape in which we know them, it was accepted as axiomatic that there must be one ruler at the head of Chinese society. Something akin to the imperial institution was regarded as so normal a part of life that it was believed to have existed from the dawn of civilization. Presumably, therefore, much of later conventional thought was read back into the past and myths were recast in conformity with it.

Verifiable facts of the early stages of China's growth are beginning to accumulate, thanks largely to recent archaeology and scholarship. They are as yet insufficient to tell us positively of the origins of the Chinese and their culture. Experts are still conjecturing and debating. We are not sure how long human beings have been in China. We do not know whether Chinese culture at the outset was native-born or whether it was an immigrant. If it was indigenous, we do not know to what extent if at all outside influences impinged upon it and modified it.

On some facts we are clear. They are established parts of the puzzle, but other parts doubtless exist and we cannot piece together the whole with any degree of satisfaction until more of them are found.

First of all, it is certain that when we obtain our initial glimpses of them, the Chinese and their culture were in the northern part of China Proper, on the North China plain and adjacent highlands and valleys. Here were the seats of the first dynasties. Here lived China's earliest scholars, and here are the chief surviving specimens of early art.

Second, skeletal remains of a very primitive form of man have been discovered near Peking and have been carefully and scientifically studied. Some features about them lead to the hypothesis that this Peking man was among the ancestors of the present Chinese, but that is as yet unproved. We do know that Peking man used crude stone implements.

Third, evidences of paleolithic man have been identified in North China underneath the loess, indicating a great antiquity.

Fourth, in the north (in southern Manchuria, in Kansu, as far west as Kokonor, in Shantung, and notably in Honan) remains have been found of neolithic cultures. The neolithic cultures are of at least three types. Between one of them and present China some continuity is established, chiefly in certain kinds of implements and utensils. This neolithic culture included the manufacture of pottery. Some of this was painted and is reminiscent of what is known in Western and Central Asia in neolithic times. Some is of a black type of fine texture, rivaled in delicacy and refinement only by the best in China's later history. Millet was raised, possibly introduced from or through India.

Fifth, in the north, notably at one site on the North China plain, extensive relics have come to light of a rich bronze-age culture. This was of the Shang, the second of the traditional dynasties of commonly accepted Chinese history. It is of the kind which presupposes a long preliminary development. It seems to have been later in appearing than bronze in Western Asia, and the knowledge of the metal may, therefore, have been an importation. However, we do not know outside of China bronze techniques and designs or forms of writing to which those of the Shang are clearly akin.

Sixth, North China, where most of these remains have been found, is where the overland trade routes through the present Sinkiang debouch.

Seventh, in Central and Western Asia from which these roads lead, very early cultures existed, earlier, as we suggested, than any of an equally advanced stage of which we know in China.

Eighth, in other parts of China Proper than the north remnants of early cultures are coming to light. Some of these, among them that which produced the black pottery, seem continuous with those of the north.

On the meaning of these facts about the origins of Chinese culture, as we have said, we ought not yet to be dogmatic. Many Occidental scholars have been inclined to surmise that much of China's earliest culture entered from the west, by way of the known overland trade routes, but others have guessed a southern provenance, and some have inclined to a belief in a native origin, with possible modifications from the outside.

Chinese writers of the first millennium before Christ stressed Yao, Shun, and Yü, but present scholarship is inclined to regard these alleged rulers as mythical, although possibly with a nucleus of fact, idealized and elaborated in an attempt to provide the sanction of antiquity for political and moral precepts of later thinkers. We do not know of any literary records, even in edited form, that antedate the Shang.

Traditional Chinese history tells us of a dynasty, claimed to be the first, which immediately preceded the Shang. To this it gives the name of Hsia. It is said to have been founded by Yü and to have come to an end after about four and a half centuries through the depravity of its last ruler. An outraged country, so the story goes, rose against it, led by one who founded the second dynasty, the Shang.

We do not certainly know, however, whether Yao, Shun, and Yü ever lived, nor have we clear proof of the existence of Hsia. Much less are we warranted in ascribing even approximate dates.

The Shang Dynasty

When we come to the Shang (also known as the Yin), we are on the solid ground of facts established by archaeology. Remains of this era have been discovered, notably in a capital of the Shang on the northern border of Honan. Here are found bronze weapons, sacrificial vessels, and chariots. The technique of casting the bronze was as skillful as any that has ever been developed. The vigorous designs show high artistic sense and ability. Tamped earth was used for the foundations of houses, much as it is employed in that region today. A beautiful hard pottery was produced by means of the potter's wheel. A highly developed writing was in use. Most of the examples of this are found inscribed on bone by sharp instruments for purposes of divination, but conclusive evidence exists that writing was also done with a brush. Probably books existed, written on bamboo slips, as in the next period. The characters used in Shang writing are the lineal ancestors of characters on the present-day Chinese page. In Shang times they were so highly sophisticated that they seem to presuppose a long preliminary development.

Society had class stratifications. Judged by modern standards, much of cruelty existed in this Shang culture. Human sacrifices were extensive. Apparently many of them were of prisoners of war. Horses, sheep, goats, pigs, cattle, dogs, and probably water buffaloes were domesticated, and we know of sacrifices of some of these animals. As today in that region, wheat and millet were grown. For a medium of exchange, cowry shells were employed.

From the oracle bones have been identified a large proportion of those names of rulers which have been handed down in the cherished records of the far past as Shang monarchs. However, we are not sure who the Shang were or whether their culture sprang from the soil or entered from abroad. Nor do we know what relation it bore to the neolithic cultures whose remains are found in North China. There were other rulers of other groups in the time of the Shang, but whether any of them acknowledged the overlordship of the Shang we are not sure. We are not clear, in other words, whether the Shang princes should be called monarchs of China or whether the North China plain and the adjacent lands contained other ruling lines which considered themselves on an equality with the Shang. That war was fairly chronic we know. It may have been to defend and extend the borders of what we might begin to call China. The traditional dates of the Shang are 1765 to 1122 before Christ, but these may be in error by several centuries. Presumably, however, the Shang belongs to the second millennium before Christ, an era in which the civilizations of Egypt and of the Tigris-Euphrates Valley were already old. While probably later than those of Western and Central Asia and the Nile, and possibly to some degree indebted to them, Shang culture appears to have been primarily a local development.

The Founding of the Chou

For what the Chinese term their third dynasty, that of the Chou, our information is much more extensive. From that period a number of books have come down to us, their texts edited again and again and in part corrupt, but some of them authentic in their main features. The traditional dates are 1122 to about 256 before Christ. The dynasty is the longest in Chinese history.

The Chou first governed a state which had its center in the Wei Valley, that tributary of the Yellow River which enters the latter not far from the great bend from a southward to an eastward course. They were, therefore, from the western frontiers of the China of the time. The conventional account tells of a tyrant on the Shang throne whom the Chou, in righteous indignation, overthrew and followed with their own ruling line. The suspicion is voiced that this story was fabricated, or at least modified, by the Chou to justify the forcible conquest by their ancestors. It would be the kind of narrative told at ceremonies in honor of the founders of the house. The account gives indication that when it acquired its present form a sense of right and wrong in public affairs existed which demanded that the transition from one dynasty to another be on moral grounds. Already the

Chinese were insisting on what became a continuing feature of their political theory, that the monarch must govern righteously and that if he failed to do so rebellion against him was justified and he could be replaced by another who would rule according to moral principles.

The Chou seem to have brought no sudden break in the cultural history of China. Probably at the outset they were not so highly civilized as the Shang. Certainly their culture was somewhat different. Whether this means that they were of a different race or tribe from the Shang or simply a different family from the same racial group and owed their crudity to residence away from the main centers of culture and on the frontier we do not know. If the former, they at least adopted and continued much of the culture of their victims. Indeed, they had contact with it before their successful conquest. One hypothesis is that from the Shang came the scholars who tutored the rude Chou in the arts of civilization. Certainly the traditional genealogy of the most famous thinker and teacher of the Chou period, Confucius, traces the lineage of the sage to the Shang. Certainly, too, the Chou cherished some of the art forms of the Shang, although in the technique of manufacture they showed deterioration. They also used the literary vehicle of the Shang.

The Chou: Political

Under the many centuries of the Chou period, a number of important developments occurred in China.

First of all, the territory ruled by the Chinese expanded. At the outset of the period, the Chinese state and its culture were probably confined chiefly to the North China Plain, the valley of the Wei, and some of the fringing mountains, particularly in the modern Shantung. By the close of the Chou era Chinese rule and civilization had permeated far into the highlands of the present Shansi and Shensi, into Szechwan, and especially into the Yangtze Valley east of the gorges. In all these areas it met other peoples. To the Chinese, these folk were barbarians, but all of them had cultures of their own and some of these, although different, may have been almost if not quite as far advanced as that of the Chinese. Contact with other peoples modified Chinese culture, but it seems not to have changed its basic concepts.

A second development in the Chou period was the weakening of the central authority and the division of China into many states. The Chou monarchs (whose title was *Wang*) continued to have a certain preeminence. They possessed ritual functions which none of the other princes were supposed to perform. Yet more and more their actual authority waned. The real power was in the heads of the various states.

These states were bound together by the tie of a common culture. For more than two centuries most of them were associated in a league whose head received investiture from the Chou *Wang* and which held assemblies at stated intervals—a kind of league of nations. Warfare, which was fairly chronic, was regulated and restricted by custom. In theory war was not for the extinction of the enemy (an attitude which has come down to the present and weakened China in her struggle with Japan), but was for the punishment of the wicked. Relations between higher and subordinate princes existed that bore resemblances to the later European feudalism, although the parallel is not exact.

In the third place, as the centuries passed, warfare became intensified and ended in the victory of one of the contending states and the setting up of an empire which, while having its roots in the past, was a new creation. In the course of the expansion of Chinese culture, great states arose on the frontier which were only partly Chinese in outlook and institutions. The chief rivals eventually became Ch'in, in that Wei Valley in which the Chou had their rise, and Ch'u, in the Yangtze Valley. In a sense it was a conflict between two empires and two closely related but somewhat different cultures. In the fierceness of the struggle, much of the old China disappeared. The league of states dissolved; feudalism tended to disintegrate; the rules of polite warfare gave way to the ruthless elimination of the weak by the strong. In the middle of the third century before Christ, Ch'in triumphed over its rivals. It appropriated the remaining territory and the symbols of authority of the last Chou *Wang*. With the assistance of an able minister, its prince still further extended the territory ruled by the Chinese and set up a new type of regime for all China which, with important modifications, became the skeleton of the structure of the Chinese Empire.

In the fourth place, this warfare and this seeming anarchy in the later centuries of the Chou did not mean a decline in culture. Indeed, remarkable advances were achieved. Art flourished, with bronze vessels and implements which continued, with modifications, the traditions of the Shang. Population probably increased. Commerce prospered and merchants rose to prominence. Metal coinage supplanted cowry shells as money. Presumably, in spite of the destruction of war, wealth multiplied. Iron now began to compete formidably with the hitherto dominant bronze. Jade was valued as a semiprecious stone. The seven-day week appeared, possibly an importation from Western Asia. The ox-drawn plow came in, probably also from Western Asia, and worked changes in agriculture. There were contacts, seemingly indirect, with India.

Literature was produced. The books that the Chinese of later centuries regarded as classical and venerated as authoritative took form. Prominent among them is the *Shu Ching*, or *Classic of History*. This is made up of a number of historical documents of varying ages and by many different hands. Prominent, too, is the *Ch'un Ch'iu*, or *Spring and Autumn* (*Annals*). It is based upon the terse and official annals of one of the feudal states, that of Lu in the present Shantung, the birthplace of some of China's greatest thinkers. Traditionally attached to the *Ch'un Ch'iu* as a commentary is the *Tso Chuan*. It is really of independent origin or origins, made up of one or more histories and at least in part probably as old as the second century before Christ. Another history is a book whose title is freely translated as the *Bamboo Annals*, thus termed because the copy discovered in the third century after Christ and from which existing texts are descended was written on bamboo. A collection originating with the professional diviners is the *I Ching*, or *Classic of Change*. An anthology of ancient Chinese poems is the *Shih Ching*, or *Classic of Poetry*. Most of the poems came certainly from the Chou, though some are said to have come from the Shang. Compilations were made of the rituals that had so large a place in the highly formalized life of the period. The most venerated are the *Li Chi*, or *Record of Rites*, which was not given its present form until a later dynasty, and the *I Li* and *Chou Li*. The dates of both the latter are uncertain and are placed by some scholars in a period after the Chou. The *Chou Li* sets forth a Utopian plan for the organization of the state. Other works have survived which are assigned to the Chou but which we do not here have the space or time even to name. Of some of them, the works of the philosophers, we shall speak incidentally in the ensuing paragraphs. Even the titles which we have listed in staccato fashion in this paragraph will seem confusing to the uninitiated. They are, however, basic to China's literature and culture. They have been studied by successive generations of scholars and have been fundamental in Chinese customs and institutions.

The Philosophic Schools of the Chou

From the standpoint of its influence upon later and present-day China and the subsequent Far East, the most important development in culture under the Chou was the emergence of schools of thought.

This intellectual activity was stimulated and furthered by the political divisions and struggles of the time. Earnest souls arose who wished to save China from the strife and the exploitation of the weak by the strong which so characterized the age. For the most part the philosophers were scholars whose primary concern was not pure speculation but society and politics. The majority of them either were actually engaged in government as officials and ministers of the princes of the various states or desired to be so employed. Many of them traveled about seeking appointment. At the courts of the various princes they debated with one another. The division of the land into many states made impossible the enforcement of the tenets of any one school or any one philosopher over China as a whole. The political fissiparousness encouraged freedom of thought and discussion. The intellectual ferment thus stimulated led to the most creative period in the history of the Chinese mind. Never again did the Chinese grapple with such originality and profundity, and in such diverse fashions, with the problems of society and the related problems of the universe.

The common problem to which these various schools addressed themselves was the salvation of society. What is the ideal human society and how can it best be attained? Inevitably, as they wrestled with these issues, the philosopher-statesmen were compelled to consider other questions. What is the nature of man? Is man inherently good or evil, or is he at birth neither? If good, then a worthy example and the minimum of force are what are required if that nature is to build an ideal society. If bad, then force and forceful education will be demanded. If neither, then education and probably some force will be needed.

In any event, the assumption was that mankind is divided into two groups, the rulers and the ruled. This arose from the aristocratic nature of current Chinese society. On the one hand were the upper classes, who included the scholars, and on the other the lower classes who tilled the soil and who provided the economic basis for the entire structure.

The thinkers of the time were keen enough to discern that, if men are to give an answer to the question of what will save society, they must ascertain the nature of the universe in which man finds himself. Is the universe friendly or unfriendly to man, or is it indifferent? Does it reward the good and punish the evil or is it morally blind and neutral? Is the universe such that man can, at least in part, determine his own future, or is the future of man and of individual men fixed beforehand by unyielding and undeviating fate?

While the primary problem which haunted the thinkers of the Chou was the salvation of society, these other queries would not down, but kept pressing for answers—as, indeed, would have to be the case if the initial problem were to be successfully solved.

Many were not content with the salvation of society as a whole. They wished to know the fate of the individual. They endeavored to find a way of deliverance from the death which seems to be the lot of all men and a road to blissful personal immortality.

These two questions, the salvation of society and a happy immortality for the individual, have continued to engage the Chinese mind from that time to the present. For the Chinese neither problem has been theoretical. In their outlook, the Chinese have been preeminently practical. On the second issue many have been agnostic. For the majority of thinkers the primary question in most later periods as in the Chou was the first, the salvation of society. This still is true of most of China's intelligentsia and statesmen.

We must note another feature of the thought of the Chou which also persisted, the seeking for authority in the past. No matter how radical or new the philosophy might be, its formulators endeavored to find for it a precedent. Antiquity was held to have contained great men whose acts and words were basic. They were variously interpreted and were adduced to support quite opposing convictions, but a Chou thinker usually felt it necessary to bolster his position by an appeal to the past. The chief exceptions to this attitude were the Legalists, whom we are to describe in a few moments. They held that institutions must be adapted to changing conditions and must not be bound by the past. Even they, however, appealed to history.

By Chinese intellectuals of the twentieth century, with their self-conscious departure from the past, this reliance upon the authority of antiquity was challenged, and the writings of the time were fearlessly scrutinized for authenticity and authorship. Even for these rebels, however, the literature ascribed to the Chou and the pre-Chou period has held a peculiar fascination.

Presumably absorption in social issues was not a new development. The very admiration for antiquity argues for it a past. It may well be that the main patterns of the Chinese mind which existed in the Chou and are still with us go back to the Shang and even to remoter times.

What eventually became the dominant school of thought had and has continued to have as its chief figure one whose name is best familiar to the West in its latinized form, Confucius. The sage was born in the state of Lu, probably in 551 B.C., and lived to pass his threescore years and ten, the date usually given for his death being 479 B.C. The traditional account of his life declares him to have been the son of an aged father of Shang descent and a young mother and reports that, left fatherless in infancy, he was reared in poverty by his mother. He was early fascinated by scholarship, ceremonies, and the records of the past and became so proficient in them that he soon attracted students. He is said to have held office in his native state, rising to be its chief minister (although that is questioned), but in middle age, supposedly in protest against the conduct of his prince, he retired into private life. For several years he traveled with his disciples from state to state, hoping that some prince would adopt his theory of government and appoint him to carry it into effect. Such hopes proved illusory, and in his old age he returned to Lu, continued to study and teach, and there died and was buried. What purports to be his grave is still guarded by those to whom is attributed lineal descent from him. Nowhere else on earth is there a tomb for which the claim is made of such prolonged filial guardianship.

Confucius, like the majority of the other philosophers of the Chou, was chiefly concerned with the achievement of an ideal society. Himself an official during part of his life, he thought of this as obtainable through the state and through the governing classes. Interested as he was in the past, he is reported to have declared himself as being a transmitter and not a creator. Like all who seek to understand and hand on the past, however, he interpreted, even though not necessarily deliberately or consciously, what had gone before him. He believed that the sages of antiquity had striven for an ideal society by setting a worthy example. He would, therefore, have the ruling classes cultivate in themselves high moral character. If their conduct were righteous the masses would follow it and all would be well. A ruler should govern by his virtue. Moreover, Confucius made much of ceremonies. In the orderly and reverent perpetuation of sacrifices and other ritual that had come down from antiquity he saw an indispensable means for the conservation of civilization.

On some questions Confucius seems not to have expressed himself clearly. It is not certain, for instance, whether he believed man to be by nature good or bad. On some issues he was reticent. Among these was life after death.

However, Confucius firmly believed that the universe is on the side of righteousness. He seemed to be convinced that governing the universe is a personal Being on whom man can rely, who protects the good and who will not allow worthy teaching to be forgotten.

Confucius sought to embody what he taught. High-minded, conscientious, studious, he endeavored to be the kind of man that he desired all members of the governing class to be.

The precepts and sayings of Confucius were recorded and preserved by admiring disciples. They are chiefly in the *Lun Yü*, or *Analects*. They were written down from memory. Some of them are clearly inexact. Even in the others we cannot be sure that we have the exact words of Confucius. Yet presumably they are close enough to the original to enable us to know the main outlines of the master's thought.

For more than a century after his passing no outstanding figure arose in the school which continued the tradition of Confucius. Then came another man of the first rank. We of the Occident best know him also under a latinized form of his Chinese designation, Mencius. Like Confucius, Mencius was a native of the state of Lu. His traditional dates are 373–288 before Christ. Even more than Confucius, he was deeply indebted, so it is said, to his mother for his early training and his introduction to a life of scholarship. Like Confucius, his chief interest was in encouraging worthy government, and he spent much of his life teaching and wandering from state to state catechizing rulers and seeking one who would put his principles into practice. In his teaching, Mencius maintained fully as much as Confucius that if the rulers set a good example those whom they governed would respond and society would be ideal. He went beyond Confucius and contended emphatically that man is by nature good. This, indeed, seems to have been a logical corollary of his insistence that if princes were virtuous their subjects would, without constraint, follow them. He seemed to set less store by ceremonies than did Confucius. He also appeared to justify rebellion against a prince who was persistently unjust, for he held that Heaven, seeing and hearing as the people heard and saw, would withdraw its sanction from one against whom the governed persistently complained. He was, however, no democrat, but accepted the existing distinction between the rulers and the ruled.

An outstanding figure who is often reckoned as in the Confucian succession was Hsün K'uang, more usually called Hsün Tzŭ. Hsün Tzŭ was probably a younger contemporary of Mencius, but he lived on into an age in which the mounting disorder and conflict with their disintegrating effect on the old order seem to have become more pronounced than in the times of his two great predecessors. Like Confucius and Mencius, he strove for good government. In contrast with Mencius, perhaps because of the effect upon him of the growing anarchy, he insisted that man is by nature evil. He was, however, sufficiently optimistic to believe that man is indefinitely improvable. That improvement he would seek to bring about through educating men to self-effort and the acquisition of right habits, through the civilizing effect of the traditional ritual connected with religion, through music, through the perpetuation of worthy customs, through the example of righteous princes, and through laws. He deprecated war and declared that a prince could win the allegiance of the people of a bellicose rival state by the attraction of his character and of good administration without resorting to arms. He glorified the state and wished it to enforce the right kind of education. Like Confucius and Mencius, he was convinced that the universe is on the side of righteousness, but he believed it to be governed by impersonal, unvarying law. The prayers and ceremonies of men, he held, are therefore quite unavailing to alter the course of events. He decried divination and derided the practice of fortune-telling by the reading of the physiognomy. The maintenance of the customary religious ritual, which, as we have said, he encouraged, he regarded as having value merely for its effect upon the people and not because of any influence upon divine beings. The existence of gods and spirits was to him absurd.

Besides Confucianism, the only other school of the Chou period to have a continuing existence to the present was Taoism. Traditionally, the founder of Taoism is given as Lao Tzŭ, who is said to have been an older contemporary of Confucius and the keeper of the archives at the Chou court. Since, however, his earliest known biography is a brief affair appearing in a history written about four or five centuries after the supposed date of his death, it may well be that Lao Tzŭ was a fictitious character invented by Taoists in their debates with Confucianists, for he is represented by them as having interviews with Confucius in which the latter is invariably discomfited. If he ever lived, we know practically nothing about him, and even his century is highly uncertain.

The outstanding classic of the huge literature which through the centuries has been created by Taoism is the *Tao Tê Ching*. The *Tao Tê Ching* is a small book whose authorship is attributed to Lao Tzŭ. It is clearly the product of the Taoist school, but who were its author or authors or what the date or dates of its composition we do not know.

The *Tao Tê Ching* is not so much concerned with problems of the state and society as are the writings of Confucius and his great successors. However, it has something to say of them. It speaks much of the *Tao*, although in its course it discouragingly declares that those who know do not speak and that those who speak do not know. By the *Tao* it seems to mean the Unknown and Unknowable which it thinks of as underlying, permeating, and controlling the universe. Man is to find his fullest life in conforming to this *Tao*. The way of the *Tao* is *wu wei*, a phrase which it is difficult to put precisely into a word. It is sometimes translated, although not quite accurately, as "inaction" or "doing nothing." It is more nearly "doing everything by doing nothing," or doing nothing that does not conform to the *Tao*. As applied to society and the state, *wu wei* means *laissez faire*, the minimum of organization and of regulation. The ideal society, so the *Tao Tê Ching* declares, is one in which villages are near enough to one another to hear the cocks in the neighboring villages crowing in the morning but in which the villagers have no desire to know the owners of the cocks. This would mean no commerce or trade. Laws, elaborate codes of ethics, and ceremonies were anathema, for they only encouraged men to violate them. Wealth was not prized, for it tempts men to theft. Politically, the Taoist theory was the absence of government. In its attitude toward ethics, statecraft, ritual, and economic life, Taoism was opposed to Confucianism.

The greatest author of the Taoist school in the Chou dynasty of whose historicity we can be sure was Chuang Tzŭ. He wrote with charm and vividness.

Another strain existed in Taoism, intertwined with the philosophic. How early it was there we do not know. It may have been present from the beginning or it may even have antedated the other. It dealt in magic. In contrast with Confucianism, which had little or nothing to say of personal immortality beyond the ceremonies in honor of the ancestors, it was a channel through which its devotees strove to achieve the endless continuation of their personal existence. Many Taoists sought an elixir of life. Many, too, endeavored to find means for the transmutation of metals. This strain certainly existed by the end of the Chou and it may have arisen much before that time.

A third school of the Chou, and one which for centuries enjoyed great popularity, arose out of the teaching of Mo Ti, or Mo Tzŭ. Mo Ti was probably a native of that small state of Lu from which came Confucius and Mencius. His dates are uncertain, but he seems to have flourished between these two fellow-countrymen. Certainly his teachings were popular in the time of Mencius, for the latter felt called upon to combat them. The clue to Mo Ti is to be found partly in his warm religious convictions and partly in his reliance upon reason. He believed the universe to be governed by a Being who loves men. For this Being the term he most frequently employed was the more personal one, *Shang Ti,* which had come down from the past rather than the less personal one, also of marked antiquity and in general use, *T'ien.* Since this Being loves all men, men ought to love one another. He would extend this love, not merely to one's family, but also to all men. He opposed aggressive war, and would go to great sacrifices to prevent it. Defensive war he allowed, and he himself was skilled in the art of fortification. In contrast with much of the skepticism of his day, he believed profoundly in the existence of spirits and argued stoutly for it. Yet he protested against elaborate funerals. The extensive ceremonies and even the music so dear to the Confucianists were anathema to him. He encouraged only those customs and activities which seemed to him useful for men. He wished to regulate consumption and to confine production to what he deemed the necessities. In contrast with the determinism of many of his contemporaries, he insisted that men had freedom of will and could perfect themselves by their own efforts.

The followers of Mo Ti tended to divide into two branches. One of these emphasized his religious beliefs. Its members lived simply, worked hard, and abstained from elaborate funerals and ceremonies. The other specialized in logic and argument. Because of their addiction to debating and their emphasis upon terms, they are often called sophists or dialecticians.

Another school, and one displaying several variations, was the Legalists. This had a rapid growth in the later years of the Chou when the old China was breaking down and ruthless war was increasingly the order of the day. Its adherents believed that society was not to be saved, as the Confucianists taught, by the moral influence of the rulers. A stern age required more drastic measures. These were to be found in the enforcement of codes of law, impartially and firmly administered. Laws were to be changed from time to time to meet altered circumstances. Strangely enough, for with their closely regulated state the Legalists seemed at the opposite poles from it, the school owed a certain debt to Taoism. It held that laws must conform to the *Tao*, the controlling principle of the universe, and had authority to the degree to which they are so adjusted. Taoists and Legalists agreed, too, on simplicity and ignorance as the proper state of the common people. Codes of law were not unfamiliar to the Chinese, even as early as the Chou. The Legalists, however, stressed them. As a kindred policy, they wished to strengthen the hands of the prince. They would have the state, under the direction of the prince, actively control more phases of collective life. Some Legalists emphasized agriculture and wished to make each state self-sufficient. Others advocated encouragement to commerce to add to the wealth of the state. They stood for the socialization of capital and a governmental monopoly of commerce. In the intense struggle for power which characterized the later years of the Chou, the Legalists sought to enable any state which would employ them to act as a unit and under the direction of its prince to concentrate all its resources on the elimination of its rivals.

These four were not all the schools, but they were the main ones of the Chou. The others need not detain us. Indeed, we need not take time even to mention them. Perhaps we should note one philosopher who seems not to have founded a school, but whose teachings had wide currency in the days of Mencius. Yang Chu, of the fourth century before Christ, was both a skeptic and a pessimist. He thought of life as full of woe. The great sages of antiquity revered by the Confucianists he regarded as fools, for they spent themselves in painful labors for society and never knew a day of happiness. The historic villains were wiser, for, although neglecting the state, they gave themselves to their pleasures. In the grave all are equal. Therefore, Yang Chu held, each should take life as it comes, enduring it and trying to make the most of it for himself, and not concerning himself with the supposed welfare of others.

For the intellectuals, the Chou must have been a stirring time in which to live. Scholar-statesmen of the various schools argued with one another. Mind rubbed against mind. Debate, comparative freedom of thought and expression, and daring ideas were the order of the day. The very divisions and struggles between the states proved stimulating. If scholars of any school were persecuted in one state, they could flee to another. Indeed, a rival prince might welcome them in the hope that they would enable him to tip the scales in his favor.

The Triumph of Ch'in

When Ch'in eliminated its rivals and took the symbols of power from the last of the feeble Chou *Wang*, it opened a new age for China. The prince of Ch'in deliberately set about the inauguration of a new order. He called himself Shih Huang Ti, the First Emperor. Scorning the title *Wang* that had been associated with the *rois fainéants* of the Chou and which he himself had borne when he was head of only one of the states of China, he combined two titles *Huang* and *Ti*, from mythical antiquity, and prefixed them with *Shih*, "first."

The state of Ch'in had been built on the principles of the Legalist school. It was to this that Ch'in in part owed its success. The entire realm which Ch'in now held was, accordingly, reorganized on the basis which had worked so well in the conquering principality. The system of separate states governed by hereditary rulers was abolished. With it went that Chinese equivalent of feudalism which characterized the Chou period. In place of the old forms of government an appointive bureaucracy was installed, centering in the Emperor and controlled by him. The realm was divided into thirty-six (later forty) provinces, and each of these in turn into *hsien*, or prefectures, of differing sizes. Over every province and prefecture was placed a member of the bureaucracy.

The imperial residence of the Ch'in was in its hereditary seat, in the valley of the Wei. Here, not far from the present Hsianfu, was the capital city. To this the wealthy and powerful of the realm were required to move. Thus they could be better kept under surveillance. Presumably, too, they would add dignity and prestige to the city and so to the imperial regime. Across the river from the main body of the city a vast palace was built.

The cumbrous forms of writing in current use were simplified, one system was substituted for the variant types, and the new system was made compulsory throughout the Empire. Attempts, too, were put forth to render uniform the weights and measures and to standardize implements and gauges of wagons. This would help to unify the economic life of the country and promote internal trade and communication. Revolt was discouraged by the requirement that the weapons belonging to the feudal lords be confiscated and melted down into huge bells and statues. One body of law was to run current throughout the Empire. The system of private ownership of land by the peasants, which had prevailed in Ch'in, was extended to the entire country.

Since the Empire was built on Legalist principles, the effort was made to give this school dominance and to stifle the free discussion among the rivals that had characterized the Chou. It was probably for this reason that a famous step was taken, the burning of many of the classical books, including the *Classic of History* and the *Classic of Poetry*, the writings containing the discussions of the various philosophers, and, with the exception of that of Ch'in, the histories of the several feudal states. The memory of the past with its many political divisions was, so far as possible, to be wiped out and references to it forbidden. The loss was not so great as has been sometimes said, for copies in the imperial archives were exempted, and books on medicine, divination, and agriculture were spared. Moreover, some copies were hidden, and the prodigious memories of Chinese scholars carried over the texts of the more famous until, when conditions permitted, they were once more committed to writing.

How much of this organization of the Empire was the work of Shih Huang Ti and how much of his great minister, Li Ssŭ, we do not know. Both seem to have had a share. Shih Huang Ti was subject to many of the superstitions of his time. He gave willing and fearful heed to the teachings of popular Taoism. He dreaded death and did not wish to hear of it or of funerals. He encouraged the search for the elixir which, so it was believed, would insure immortality. He sought to make himself a divine being and, possibly for this purpose and to hide himself mysteriously from his people, is said to have attempted to conceal the particular portion of his huge rambling collection of palaces in which he was residing at any particular moment. Yet these beliefs were not inconsistent with enormous energy and they may not have been in conflict with an acute organizing and administrative intelligence.

Whosever the achievement was, whether that of Shih Huang Ti or of Li Ssŭ, it was one of the most important in the history of the

Far East. The large area into which the Chinese and their culture had spread during the Chou was welded together under one centralized administrative system. That system was based upon one officially supported political, social, and economic theory. Cultural unity was, therefore, made an essential concomitant of political unity. The succeeding dynasty was, as we are to see, to make important changes in the details of the system of the Ch'in. A modified Confucianism was to be substituted for Legalism as the basis of the state and of society. Yet the central contributions of the Ch'in were to persist. A bureaucracy whose members were appointed and supervised by a central authority and which conformed to a particular school of social and political thought was to continue as a permanent part of the life of China.

The achievement was not only of major importance in the history of the Far East. It is also unique in the history of the world. Through this centralized administration based upon one accepted political and social theory, in spite of occasional disunion, China Proper has been kept together for over two thousand years. Never in human experience has so extensive an area with so large a population been held together culturally and politically over so long a period of time. Even foreign conquerors have found it advisable to conform and to rule through the traditional principles. This unity was maintained, moreover, without the assistance of modern means of communication. Time-distances were huge, fully as great as those in the Roman Empire or in Western Europe before the nineteenth century. Yet, in spite of periods of division, China Proper remained one, and from time to time parts of the fringing countries were conquered and controlled. But for the political achievement of the Ch'in and their successors, China Proper might well have been divided into a number of states, as was the somewhat equivalent area of India until the coming of the British *raj* and as Western Europe has been. Had this been the case, the history of the Far East would have been very different. There would have been no dominant empire, overshadowing all other states of the region. Probably more cultural variety would have developed. Possibly Japan would not have been so impressed by the culture of the continent and would not have been so extensively Sinicized. It is entirely fitting that our word China, as a designation of a thus unified empire, should be derived historically from Ch'in, the dynasty whose rulers first applied to so much of the land the principles on which the subsequent realm rested.

Although much of the credit for the political unification of China must go to Shih Huang Ti and Li Ssŭ, their achievement would have been impossible without the contributions of others. The conception of one emperor for all civilized mankind did not originate with them. Before them were the many social and political theorists and statesmen-scholars who wrestled with the problems of China's unity and of political and social regeneration. From these came the schools of thought used by the Ch'in and the successors of the Ch'in. The very system which Shih Huang Ti and Li Ssŭ applied to the whole of China was an extension of what had been put into practice in the state of Ch'in before their time, particularly by one of the Legalists in the fourth century before Christ. The Chinese Empire was the outcome of a long evolution. The contributions of Shih Huang Ti and Li Ssŭ were the imagination and the resolution to take advantage of the past and the ruthlessness which swept aside the hindering diversities and separatist institutions.

Shih Huang Ti not only unified the China that had existed at the time of his birth. He also added extensively to the territories controlled by the Chinese. He extended his dominions to include the coast south of the Yangtze as far as the delta of the Red River, in the later Tongking. Into part of this region he compelled the emigration of colonists from the older sections of China. Probably he thus wished to promote their assimilation. His realm embraced much of the present Hunan, Kweichow and Szechwan, and he enforced migration into the last-named area. In the northwest he is said to have carried his conquests as far as the present Lanchow. A prince who ruled in a portion of what is now Korea acknowledged his overlordship. However, the center of Chinese power and culture continued to be, as in the past, in the lower part of the valley of the Yellow River and in the valley of the Wei. The rest of the Empire was frontier and was regarded as barbarous or semibarbarous.

On the northern marches, as a defense against invasions of the non-Chinese peoples who were so chronic a menace, Shih Huang Ti constructed fortresses and barriers, portions of the Great Wall. Frontier walls had existed before Shih Huang Ti, and succeeding dynasties also labored on the border defenses. The Great Wall was not an original idea with him, nor is much if any of that impressive structure as it exists today his work. Yet he gave a great impetus to what became a tradition in Chinese military strategy.

The Ch'in dynasty was not of long duration. Shih Huang Ti

died in 210 B.C., on one of the many journeys he made through his realms. Through intrigue in which Li Ssŭ had a part, an inexperienced son of the great Emperor was placed on the throne. This weakling was soon dominated by a crafty palace eunuch. Some of the strongest men who had helped to make Shih Huang Ti's reign notable were eliminated. Thus the commander-in-chief of the armies guarding the frontier was ordered to commit suicide, and Li Ssŭ was first imprisoned and then executed. Rebellion broke out. Resentment against the stern destruction of the old order, the strict laws, and the heavy burdens of taxation and forced labor entailed by the wars and public works of Shih Huang Ti had long been smoldering. Now that the men who had created the realm were removed, it broke out into open conflagration. The eunuch did away with the incompetent Emperor and was himself killed by the grandson of Shih Huang Ti whom he elevated to power. Rebels plundered the capital and gave to the flames the great palace of Shih Huang Ti. In this destruction, incidentally, was lost much of the literature which had come down from the Chou and which had been preserved in the imperial archives. The rule of Ch'in was ended.

The Earlier or Western Han (*207* B.C.–A.D. *8*)

The welter of civil strife which succeeded the downfall of the Ch'in did not entirely destroy the work of Shih Huang Ti and Li Ssŭ. After a brief period of disorder a new ruling line was established upon the vacant throne, and much of the essential administrative machinery of the Ch'in was eventually restored, although in modified forms.

The founder of the new dynasty was not from the old princely houses. The wars which had inaugurated the Ch'in and, perhaps, the enervating effect of hereditary power had done their work too well. It was new men who came forward, men who could force their way to the top in the rough and tumble of the times. To be sure, in the initial stages of the struggle, scions of the old aristocracy were prominent, but those who were eventually victorious were of humble stock. The successful contestant was Liu Chi, later called Liu Pang (Liu being his family name). He is also known by his dynastic title, Kao Tsu. Although after he rose to power an elaborate genealogy was devised for him to trace his descent from ancient rulers, Liu Pang began life in humble fashion. He was at first a farmer, then a village official, and then head of a group who turned bandit in the distresses of the times. He was a creditable but not a great general, for he lost some of the battles he fought against his rivals. He was, however, a good politician and a shrewd judge of men. He was both energetic and adaptable, and was able to attract and hold men of native ability. Most of his leading colleagues were commoners, underneath whose rough surface he discerned promise and whom he bound to himself. In his personal habits and his vocabulary (which he could use in fluent billingsgate) Liu Pang remained of the common folk, even after he ascended the throne. He was fond of his cups and of women, but he did not allow these to warp his judgment or to deflect him from his purposes. After he had conquered most of his rivals, he was proposed by his followers as Emperor and, following the triple refusal which etiquette demanded, ascended the throne. The date was February 28, 202 B.C., but the inception of the dynasty is customarily reckoned from 207 B.C., when the last ruler of the Ch'in surrendered.

The new dynasty was denominated the Han. With a break in the first century after Christ, it survived into the third century. The dynasty before this break is known as the Ch'ien (Earlier) or Western Han (because its capital was in the west, in the Wei Valley), and after the break as the Hou (Later) or Eastern Han (because its capital was moved eastward). In this period of over four centuries, the task of unification begun by the Ch'in was carried further. Han gave permanence to the Empire. Only in details and in the elaboration of principles did later dynasties alter what came down to them from it.

Much was carried over by the Han from the Ch'in. The capital of the Empire was placed by the Western Han at Ch'angan, in the plain of the Wei and not far from the capital of Shih Huang Ti. Administration through an appointive bureaucracy was retained. For a time, to be sure, the Han experimented with the hereditary principle in regional administration. Liu Pang, for instance, divided his realms into sections over each of which he placed either a member of his family or one of his military commanders who had been of marked assistance. He continued, however, the administrative divisions of the Ch'in and the government of them through an official hierarchy appointed by the Emperor. Moreover, when, in time, these hereditary principalities proved a menace to the central authority, their power (in reigns subsequent to that of Liu Pang) was restricted and they were divided and subdivided in such fashion as to weaken them. Feudal particularism to the extent to which it had existed under the

Chou was never revived and such of it as existed was progressively curbed.

In several important ways, however, the Han modified what had come to it from the Ch'in. Liu Pang had been carried to the throne in part on a wave of reaction against the Ch'in and was wise enough not to revive features of the former regime that had aroused the more severe protests. The stringent laws of the Ch'in were repealed or modified. Taxes were lightened. The absolute autocracy of the Ch'in was relaxed. Liu Pang felt that he had come into power through the assistance of his chief subordinates and that they must be consulted before important decisions were made. In practice, he limited the power of the Emperor by seeking advice and acting only on the suggestion of others.

Most important of all the innovations, the Han adopted as the basis of the state, not the Legalism of the Ch'in, but Confucianism. This did not come all at once. Liu Pang was a rude man of the people and of the camp who had dislike and contempt for the elaborate etiquette and, to him, pompous and fussy formality of the Confucian scholars. However, one of Liu Pang's brothers had studied with Confucian teachers. Then, too, when Liu Pang scornfully declared, in response to quotations from the *Classic of History* and the *Classic of Poetry*, that he had won the Empire on horseback and did not need to bother with these hoary books, the rebuked scholar had the courage to tell him that although he had won the realm on horseback, that did not ensure his ability to rule it from horseback. Probably, too, Liu Pang saw that Confucianism was more popular with the masses at large than were the rival schools. He and his successors, therefore, increasingly adopted Confucianism as the basis of the state. It was a Confucian empire which they handed down to their descendants. So firmly was Confucianism established that it remained the school enforced by the state until the collapse of the Empire in the twentieth century. Political unity was obtained partly by the appointive bureaucracy inherited from the Ch'in and partly through the persistent inculcation of cultural unity with Confucianism as the norm.

The rival schools did not disappear at once. For many years they persisted. Stirring debates, for instance, took place between the adherents of Legalism and of Confucianism over policies of state. Taoism proved very popular with many throughout the Han and, although greatly altered, has endured to our own day.

Moreover, the rivals left their imprint upon the victor and upon the Chinese state. It was a modified Confucianism which triumphed. Han Confucianism had something of Mo Ti, for it was more positively theistic than either Confucius of Mencius had been, stressing the beneficent rule of Heaven in the affairs of men and making much of a belief in spirits. The bureaucracy and the continuation and formation of codes of law (albeit more lenient than those of the Ch'in) seem to have reflected in part Legalist influence. Taoism, with its *laissez faire*, appears to have left its mark, certainly for a time. Then, too, as a growth within Confucianism, came the beginnings of a cult of Confucius, the precursor of the temples and rites in honor of the sage and of his leading exponents.

To the Han, too, are usually traced the beginnings of what later became one of the outstanding features of the Chinese educational and state system, the recruiting of members of the bureaucracy through civil service examinations. This was a logical outgrowth of the administrative official hierarchy taken over from the Ch'in. If officials were to be appointed on the basis of worth rather than of birth, some method of selection must be devised. For a time, appointments were made on the basis of the recommendations of regional officials who were instructed to seek out the best men. Gradually, however, tests were developed for ascertaining the more promising. Eventually, although not until later dynasties, these were based entirely upon the classics revered by Confucianism. In general, however, even under the Han, the examinations were in accord with the Confucian principle that the realm must be governed by the most worthy. Through this bureaucracy and the principle of recruiting it through civil service examinations, and through the adoption of Confucianism as the basis of the state, the general method of unifying the Empire inaugurated by the Ch'in was continued. Even though Confucianism was substituted for Legalism, the essential features of the Ch'in survived—a bureaucracy appointed and controlled by the Emperor and one political and social philosophy, rather than many, as the basis of the realm.

In a work of this scope, an enumeration of the monarchs who came after Liu Pang would be both unnecessary and confusing. We must, however, pause to speak of the reign in which the Earlier Han reached its zenith, that of Wu Ti ("the Martial Emperor"), or, to distinguish it from the Wu Tis of other dynasties, Han Wu Ti. The dates of Han Wu Ti were 140 to 87 B.C. It was the longest reign of the dynasty and one of the most famous in the annals of China.

The reign deserved the title of martial, for one of the outstanding features of its half century was foreign conquests. Chinese territory was extended on the west, north, and south.

On the west, frequent wars were waged against the Hsiung Nu. The Hsiung Nu were probably akin to the Turks and were either the Huns who appear in European history a few centuries later or were related to them. The Hsiung Nu were a horse-using, semi-nomadic folk who were attempting to press into the fertile lands of China. The reign of Han Wu Ti did not see them finally crushed, but it witnessed the reduction of their power. Imperial generals pushed the Han borders westward to include most of what is now Kansu, and the Great Wall was extended. Moreover, in part with the purpose of encircling the Hsiung Nu and coming at them from their western frontiers, the Chinese daringly extended their enterprise to the far west, into Central Asia—even into what is now Russian territory. An envoy, Chang Ch'ien, was dispatched to find allies against the Hsiung Nu. Thanks to him, what appear to have been China's first direct contacts with Central Asia were established. He introduced alfalfa and the cultivated grape. Following him, and by an extraordinary military feat, Chinese arms were carried successfully into the valley of the Jaxartes, west of the present Sinkiang. On this westward expansion, the Chinese must have come upon the fringes of the Occident, for, as we saw in the last chapter, in the wake of the easternmost campaigns of Alexander the Great states had been established in parts of Central Asia in which Greek influence was strong.

In the northeast, under Han Wu Ti, Chinese authority was carried into what are now the southern part of Manchuria and the northern portions of Korea. Here a state had been established whose name, under its Japanese pronunciation, Chosen, is now the designation which has been applied to the entire peninsula. This state was annexed to the Han domains. Chinese settlers moved in, a wealthy Chinese colony was established near the former capital, and Chinese culture penetrated to the region. Indeed, important excavations in the present century have disclosed rich remains of Han culture in the vicinity of the colony.

The Han Wu Ti reign renewed the extension of Chinese rule into some portions of the south coast to which it had first come under the Ch'in and carried Chinese authority beyond what had been the Ch'in frontiers. From the present Chêkiang southward along the coast into Annam, regions which had been forced to acknowledge the Ch'in and which had broken away after the death of Shih Huang Ti were once more subdued. The island of Hainan was brought within the sphere of Han influence. Colonization by Chinese, especially in the Canton area, on the fertile lower reaches of the West River, proceeded rapidly. Petty states in what are now Kweichow and Yünnan were reduced to submission. Not all of this southern area was as yet fully assimilated, but the rule of the north was extended into it.

Under Han Wu Ti, then, practically all of what is now China Proper was under the imperial sway, and Chinese arms had been carried effectively westward beyond the Tarim River basin and northeastward into the later Manchuria and Korea.

The Han Wu Ti period witnessed internal achievements. One of China's greatest historians, Ssŭ-ma Ch'ien, flourished. The son of a court astrologer, in his youth he memorized the texts of antiquity which later provided him much of his source material. He traveled extensively through the Empire. He succeeded his father in the latter's post. It is possible that some of his *magnum opus* was written by his father. This work, the *Shih Chi*, or *Historical Records*, covers the history of China from the beginning to the author's own day. It inaugurated a famous series of official histories, for it was continued by the *Ch'ien Han Shu*, or *History of the Earlier Han Dynasty*, and this in turn was followed by a succession of dynastic histories which come down to the end of the Empire, in 1912. In its size and range of material Ssŭ-ma Ch'ien's work is much more ample than the Greek and Roman histories. Moreover, it often incorporates with slight changes earlier books and documents and thus becomes a boon to the modern Occidental historian, with his passion for the sources.

During the Han Wu Ti reign interesting economic measures were adopted. Commerce was regulated by the state, by purchase of leading staples when they were cheap and their sale when prices rose. Coinage was taken away from various magnates and confined to the imperial administration. A government monopoly of salt and iron was maintained. Great irrigation works were constructed, and flood control of the Yellow River, a perennial problem, was furthered. The power of the surviving hereditary princes was curtailed, and additional steps were taken for the preparation and selection of competent members of the appointive officialdom, through which administration was increasingly carried on.

The achievements of the reign were not without their counterbalancing penalties. Taxes were increased and fresh sources of revenue were sought. The currency was debased, as surviving examples of the coinage vividly indicate. There was much discontent.

In spite of its costs, the reign of Han Wu Ti was not followed by the sharp and disastrous reaction that brought ruin to Ch'in after the regime of Shih Huang Ti. The dynasty went on. Most of the conquests were retained, and in the west Chinese power continued to advance.

Wang Mang

About a century after Han Wu Ti, the line of Liu Pang was clearly declining and appeared to be about to lose the mandate of Heaven. One of the most interesting figures in Chinese history, Wang Mang, attempted to inaugurate a new dynasty.

Wang Mang was of a family which had provided an Empress. Through this favoring circumstance, it virtually controlled the Empire during the reign of the Emperor who was born of this union. Scholarly, ambitious, unscrupulous, a patron of learning, living with comparative frugality and distributing much of his enormous income among needy friends and followers, Wang Mang won a large entourage and became both popular and powerful. The realm was controlled through puppet Emperors, and in A.D. 8 Wang Mang deposed the last of these and assumed the throne.

Wang Mang called the dynasty he sought to establish Hsin, or New, and brought in many innovations. He nationalized the land, thus annihilating the huge landed estates which had arisen, and he abolished slavery. He ordered the division of the land into equal tracts and its distribution among the cultivators. To the imperial monopolies of salt, iron, and coinage he added those of wine and mines. He sought to protect the farmers against the merchants by having the state fix prices. He provided for state loans, without interest, to those in need of funds for funerals and sacrifices and for the advance of capital at moderate rates of interest for productive purposes. He stimulated the study of the Confucian classics and greatly honored Confucius. He has been accused of altering some of the ancient books to make them support his theories, but the charge is not usually regarded as proved, except for some portions of the texts. Apparently by these changes Wang Mang hoped to bring in a happier and better society and to be remembered as one of the ideal monarchs.

Wang Mang ruled as Emperor for about fifteen years (A.D. 8–23).

In that time he brought ruin to himself and his house and embarrassment to the Empire. Changes as drastic as those he attempted to enforce could not but arouse opposition. The propertied and powerful were embittered. Although the repeal after three years of the law against the sale of land was designed to mollify them, they were quite unreconciled. Several of the outposts of the Empire in the northwest and in Tongking broke away from his rule. Brigands, some of them known as the Red Eyebrows, became annoying. The Liu family, from which had been drawn the rulers of the deposed Han, were still influential and were in active war against him whom they deemed a usurper. Old and discredited, Wang Mang was killed in his capital, Ch'angan. The Liu line was restored. Wang Mang became a memory, execrated by orthodox scholars, but an interesting, even if an extreme example of the belief, so characteristic of the Chinese political tradition, that a ruling line is justified or condemned according to its success or failure in promoting the well-being of the masses.

The Later Han (A.D. *23–220*)

The Han, thus brought back into power, continued for about two centuries longer. The capital was moved eastward, to Loyang, in the present province of Honan, but, while that was nearer the ancient centers of classical China, it was still far enough west to permit of the control of the western marches. None of the reigns of the renewed dynasty was as brilliant as that of Han Wu Ti. Toward the end of the second century the quality of the monarchs deteriorated and the baleful influence of eunuchs and the intrigues of women in the palace increased the weakness. However, the Later Han produced some able monarchs. Thanks in part to them, the total span of the Han, even after the interruption by Wang Mang is deducted, was longer than that of any authentic dynasty except the Shang and the Chou. Moreover, the Shang dates are uncertain, in neither Shang nor Chou was the ruling line an imperial dynasty in the same sense as those which began with the Ch'in, and neither ruled over territory approaching in extensiveness the domains of the Han.

Under part of the Later Han the territories of China were restored to approximately the extent that they had attained under Han Wu Ti. In some directions Chinese power was being extended. Chinese arms were again carried to the western border of the Tarim basin, and diplomatic contacts were established with princes still farther west. A more or less shadowy suzerainty was gained over the peoples of Mongolia and western Manchuria. The Hsiung Nu, weakened, were for a time less of a menace. The delta of the Red River and most of what is now Annam were conquered.

Over some of the occupied areas the process of assimilation to Chinese culture progressed further than under the Earlier Han. Thus the cultural and administrative penetration to the south prepared the way for the future Annamite state and culture.

The Later Han was contemporary with the palmy days of the Roman Empire. In the first and second centuries after Christ the two greatest empires on earth were that in the west ruled by the Caesars and that in the east ruled by the Han. Some of the military exploits which established the Han rule on its far borders are fully the equal of those which built the Roman domain.

Under the Han the Chinese were much more successful in establishing an enduring fabric of empire than were the Romans under the Caesars. In the west the Roman Empire disintegrated. In the Byzantine Empire its eastern fragment survived into the fifteenth century, and in the Holy Roman Empire a professed continuation of its western portion endured into the early part of the nineteenth century. In laws and institutions and in the Roman Catholic Church its contributions are still visible. Yet as an empire the second century saw its apex, and with the close of the second century a decline set in which proved permanent. In contrast, the fabric of the Confucian empire built by the Han endured into the twentieth century. As we are to see, it had periods of weakness, but it attained its widest territorial extent as recently as the eighteenth century. Only within the present century has the cultural structure which constituted its basis disintegrated. What has carried over from that great past is still more potent than anything—except the Roman Catholic Church—which the world has inherited from the seven hills by the Tiber.

As we have suggested, the basis of this continuing Chinese unity was Confucianism. Even more than the Earlier Han, the Later Han emphasized that school of thought and made it the foundation of the state and of society. Under the Later Han sacrifices in honor of Confucius were for the first time compulsory in all the schools in the larger cities. Standard texts of the Confucian classics were officially established. For a time the leaders of the Confucian school formed a kind of ruling clique which was knit together by the intermarriage of their children. Confucian writings were the chief basis of the curriculum in the schools that prepared men for the service of the state. Thus a unified society was ensured on the basis of an officially supported social and political philosophy.

This espousal of Confucianism discouraged intellectual originality and weakened or obliterated rival schools. The vigorous debates and the throbbing intellectual activity of the Chou declined and disappeared. They were not immediately quenched. However, as Confucianism was more and more sponsored by the state, the road to official preferment and so to what ambitious men most desire—wealth, power, and prestige—lay through its advocacy. Intellectual variety and advance slowed down. China tended to become a static society, bound by one set of ideas. Change and progress were sacrificed to unity and stability.

Yet one other school of the Chou survived, Taoism. As it developed, Taoism became not so much a social philosophy as a means of attaining personal immortality and controlling spirits to the advantage of the individual or the family. Since Confucianism was primarily a social philosophy, the two could exist side by side with the minimum of conflict. To be sure, in the closing decades of the Later Han, Taoists established a sect which rebelled and for a time maintained an independent state in the present Szechwan and Shensi, but this was exceptional. Taoism was often sponsored by members of the imperial family and did not normally come into sharp competition with Confucianism.

Han scholarship, diverted from free speculation, found vent in collecting and editing the literature of the past. We owe largely to Han scholars the preservation of such works of the Chou period as have survived. Paper was invented, probably in the Later Han, and presumably this new material, perishable though it was, aided in the multiplication and dissemination of books.

In some other directions the culture of the Han showed achievement. Sun dials and water clocks, with precise divisions of time, were employed in measuring time. The observation of sun spots was known. A primitive seismograph was invented. Paper came into fairly general use. Improved methods of agriculture were introduced or developed.

Enlarged contacts with the outside world were established. The prosperity of the Han attracted merchants from other countries. The permanent incorporation into the Empire of the south coast, with its many harbors, must have encouraged ocean-borne commerce by way of the Straits of Malacca and the Indian Ocean. Land conquests in the Tarim Basin facilitated trade along that natural track of the caravan routes. Central Asia become more of a reality to the Chinese.

Trade was maintained with the Roman Empire. Silk from China became a familiar material for fine fabrics in the Mediterranean world. In return, China received glass, jade, horses, precious stones, ivory, tortoise shell, and some fine cloths. Art designs entered from Central Asia. China was being modified, even though slightly, by the outside world. This was not the first time that non-Chinese cultures had contributed to the civilization of the Chinese. Now, however, we begin to know a little more certainly some of the influences which entered.

The Coming of Buddhism

What ultimately proved to be the most potent of the importations until the advent of the Occident in force in the past half century was Buddhism. Just when Buddhism entered China we do not know. Nor do we know by what route it first arrived. The traditional story which tells of its coming during the reign of the second Emperor of the Later Han and by the overland route from Central Asia is false, for we know that it was already in China at the date set by the tale. It may have come overland and it may have been brought by way of the sea.

Through Buddhism the Chinese were put in touch with the life and thought of India. In civilization the two lands were probably not far from the same age. In outlook they were poles apart. The Chinese were historically minded, kept elaborate records of their past, and sought in antiquity support for their various philosophies. The Indians were not historically minded. The dominant purpose in most of China's schools of thought, including notably the one which became dominant under the Han, Confucianism, was the realization upon this earth of an ideal society. Much was made of honors to ancestors and the majority believed the dead to live on, but the emphasis was this-worldly. To be sure, through Taoism many sought to attain personal immortality, but Taoism, while persistent, when compared with Confucianism was a subordinate strain in Chinese life. By the third century before Christ China, as we have seen, attained political unity. This was followed by cultural unity and by an assimilation which made China Proper largely racially and linquistically one. In India, in contrast, the major emphasis was on the life beyond the present and upon ensuring a happy future, not for society, but for the individual. In India a fundamental conception, quite alien to the Chinese, was the transmigration of souls. Physical death was believed to usher one into another stage of existence from which in turn one would move into still another stage.

The Chinese were basically optimistic. In the main they believed life to be good and the universe friendly. The Indians were pessimistic. They assumed it to be an axiom that life is not worth living. So long as an individual continues to live, no matter in what form, that individual will suffer. To the Indian, therefore, salvation was the escape from the endless succession of birth and rebirth. India, moreover, never achieved political unity until that was forced on it by the British in the nineteenth century. Until the British made it so, India was never an empire. India was nearer to the other centers of civilization than was China and while on the land side, like China, it was partially protected by mountains, it was frequently invaded. Alien cultures achieved larger footholds in it than in China. India did not arrive as nearly to linguistic or racial assimilation and uniformity as did China. India had caste, to a degree not known in any other land, and this China was as far from having as any numerous people has ever been. It was this quite different world, fully as alien as is the modern Occident from the traditional China, that Buddhism opened to the Chinese.

Both Mahayana and Hinayana Buddhism were carried to China. Mahayana is sometimes called Northern Buddhism, for it developed principally in the north of India. From there it spread to Central Asia. Through the contacts which the Chinese had with that region, it penetrated to China Proper by way of the overland trade routes. Hinayana is often termed Southern Buddhism, for it has been strongest in Southern Asia. From Southern Asia it was carried by sea to China. Of the two great branches of Buddhism, Mahayana was the more prominent in the Middle Kingdom.

It is from the Later Han that we first have certain knowledge of Buddhism in China. At first it seems to have been welcomed by some of the Taoists. Indeed, it appeared to many to be a kind of Taoism. Like the latter, it professed to make possible the salvation of the individual beyond this present life.

However, Buddhism did not become particularly strong under the Han. Perhaps this was because Confucianism, supported by the government, was too deeply entrenched. For its greatest growth it was to wait until the centuries after the Han. Then the realm was divided and Confucianism, weakened by the disunion, could not offer as effective resistance as when it was supported by the inclusive Han.

Han Art

In art, the Han period, taken as a whole, showed distinctive developments. Some of these had begun under the Ch'in and probably earlier. Bronzes were still popular, but on many of them appeared designs which were less stiff and conventional than those which we associate with the Chou and the Shang. More lifelike portrayals of living objects appeared. So, too, in the carvings on stone, animals, birds, and men are depicted in vigorous action, some of them with such vivid realism that they gave us insight into the life and the beliefs of the time. Pottery representations of houses, animals, and men were buried in graves, presumably in the attempt to supply the dead with the comforts of life. Glass and lacquer objects have been found, dating from Han times, and many mirrors. Part of this Han art was of indigenous development. Part was influenced by contacts with the outside world.

Summary

At the beginning of the third century after Christ, China and its civilization had developed most of the main aspects which were to characterize them down into the twentieth century. Some additions were to be made. Several of the institutions in existence at the end of the second century were to be amplified. However, the Chinese Empire had come into being, China Proper had for the most part been occupied, even though parts of it had not yet been assimilated, the written characters had, in general, acquired their present form, and the ideals which henceforward were to govern the land had been formulated and accepted.

When we first catch glimpses of it, in the second millennium before Christ, Chinese culture existed in what later was North China, on the great alluvial plain of that region and in the adjoining Shantung. It already wrote with characters some of which are the ancestors of ones employed today. It used bronze and had a remarkably skillful technique for casting it. Probably it was already an old culture. It may possibly have been of indigenous origin. Certainly man had been present in North China millenniums before it. This bronze culture was associated with the ruling state of Shang.

The Shang were overthrown by the Chou, at a date traditionally set in the twelfth century before Christ. For nearly nine centuries the Chou were to be the unifying center of China. That China included many states held together more or less loosely by the suzerainty of the Chou and by the consciousness of a community of culture. In that culture local variations existed. There was much freedom of discussion. The Chinese mind was active and was hammering out, through lively debate and under the pressure of what it regarded as alarming disorder, ideals and methods of thinking which were to prevail down to our own day. Indeed, they are still with us. No one can understand the China, or the Japan, Korea, and Annam, of the twentieth century without some knowledge of the intellectual history of the Chou. The chief interests of this intellectual activity were social and political. Thinkers were often also statesmen and were eager to help create an ideal society. An essential ingredient of that society they believed to be morality, although they differed as to what that morality should be and as to how it should be achieved. Under the Chou this Chinese culture was spreading. Peoples and states in the Yangtze Valley were being brought within its orbit. What to the scholar-statesmen who were creating the various schools of thought seemed anarchy and increasing disorder proved to be the growing pains of a larger and richer China.

Near the middle of the third century before Christ, the prolonged internal warfare which troubled the closing generations of the Chou was temporarily ended by the triumph of one of the states, Ch'in, over its rivals. The administrative system and the political philosophy which the rulers of Ch'in had adopted were applied to the whole of China. What now for the first time can be called the Chinese Empire came into being.

Political ineptitude on the part of the immediate successors of the First Emperor (Shih Huang Ti) under whose leadership the Ch'in dynasty was founded led to the speedy end of the Ch'in. However, the Ch'in achievement proved permanent. After a brief period of civil strife, a man emerged from obscurity and placed his family on the throne. The Han dynasty began and with an interruption which divided it into almost equal parts endured for over four centuries.

Under the Han the main outlines of the continuing Empire were seen and became so commonly accepted that the Chinese henceforth regarded them as a part of normal human society. Indeed, in spite of the revolutionary changes brought by the impact of the Occident in the present century, some of the most important of them still exist. The idea of a bureaucracy, appointed and controlled by one central authority, was taken over from the Ch'in. In place of the Legalism into which the Ch'in had sought to regiment the Empire, Confucianism became the accepted philosophy. Even under the Republic of our day this appointive bureaucracy persists and although Confucianism as a cult enforced by the state has vanished, the attitudes of mind inculcated by Confucianism continue dominant. The Ch'in and the Han became memories, but the imperial structure they created and the cultural unity they fostered survived. They were largely responsible for the China which we know today and helped also to mold much of the rest of the Far East.

BIBLIOGRAPHY

For Brief Reference

K. S. Latourette, *The Chinese, Their History and Culture* (New York, 1945), Chapters II and III.

For More Extended Study

ON THE BEGINNINGS OF CHINESE

H. G. Creel, *The Birth of China* (London, 1936).
O. Lattimore, *Inner Asian Frontiers of China* (London, 1940).

ON THE CHOU PERIOD

O. Franke, *Geschichte des chinesischen Reiches*, Vol. I (Berlin and Leipzig, 1930), Parts 1 and 2.
O. Lattimore, *Inner Asian Frontiers of China* (London, 1940).
H. Maspero, *La Chine Antique* (Paris, 1927).
For translations of several of the standard works of the Chou, see J. Legge, *The Chinese Classics* (5 vols., revised, Oxford, London, 1893, 1895), and J. Legge, in vols. 3, 16, 27, 28 of *The Sacred Books of the East* (Oxford, 1879, 1882, 1885).

ON THE PHILOSOPHIC SCHOOLS OF THE CHOU

H. H. Dubs, *Hsüntze, the Moulder of Ancient Confucianism* (London, 1927).
H. H. Dubs, *The Works of Hsüntze* (London, 1928).
J. J. L. Duyvendak, *The Book of Lord Shang. A Classic of the Chinese School of Law* (London, 1928).
A. Forké, *Yang Chou's Garden of Pleasure* (London, 1912).
Y. L. Fung, *History of Chinese Philosophy*, translated by D. Bodde (Peiping, 1937).
E. R. Hughes, *Chinese Philosophy in Classical Times* (London, 1942).
J. Legge, *The Texts of Taoism* (Vols. 39 and 40 of *The Sacred Books of the East*, Oxford, 1891) contains translations of the *Tao Tê Ching* and Chuang Tzŭ.
Translations of the *Analects* and of Mencius by J. Legge in *The Chinese Classics*.
H. G. Creel, *Confucius, the Man and the Myth* (New York, 1949)

Y. P. Mei, *The Ethical and Political Works of Motse, Translated from the Original Chinese Text* (London, 1929).
W. E. Soothill, *The Analects of Confucius* (Yokohama, 1910). The translation, without the Chinese text or the notes, has been reprinted (Oxford, 1937).
A. Waley, *The Way and Its Power* (London, 1934) has a translation and interpretation of the *Tao Tê Ching*, with an excellent introduction.
A. Waley, *The Analects of Confucius* (New York, 1939).

ON THE CH'IN DYNASTY

D. Bodde, *China's First Unifier. A Study of the Ch'in Dynasty as Seen in the Life of Li Ssŭ* (Leiden, 1938).
E. Chavannes, *Les Mémoires Historiques de Se-ma Ts'ien* (5 vols., Paris, 1895–1905).
O. Franke, *Geschichte des chinesischen Reiches*, Vol. I (Berlin and Leipzig, 1930), pp. 223–267.
O. Lattimore, *Inner Asian Frontiers of China* (London, 1940).

ON THE HAN DYNASTY

T. F. Carter, *The Invention of Printing in China and its Spread Westward* (New York, 1931).
M. P. Charlesworth, *Trade-Routes and Commerce of the Roman Empire* (Cambridge, 1924).
C. Eliot, *Hinduism and Buddhism, An Historical Sketch* (3 vols., London, 1931).
O. Franke, *Geschichte des chinesischen Reiches,* Vol. I (Berlin and Leipzig, 1930), pp. 268–431.
E. M. Gale, *Discourses on Salt and Iron: A Debate on State Control of Commerce and Industry in Ancient China, Chapters I–XIX. Translated from the Chinese of Huan K'uan with Introduction and Text* (Leiden, 1931).
R. Grousset, *China* (New York, 1934), Chapter I. Especially valuable on art.
C. Hentze, *Chinese Tomb Figures* (London, 1928).
F. Hirth, *China and the Roman Orient* (Shanghai, 1885).
G. F. Hudson, *Europe and China: A Survey of their Relations from the Earliest Times to 1800* (London, 1931).
O. Lattimore, *Inner Asian Frontiers of China* (London, 1940).
B. Laufer, *Sino-Iranica, Chinese Contributions to the History of Civilization in Ancient Iran, with Special Reference to the History of Cultivated Plants and Products* (Chicago, 1919).
Pan Ku, *The History of the Former Han Dynasty, by Pan Ku, a Critical Translation with Annotations,* by H. H. Dubs (2 vols., Baltimore, 1938, 1944).
J. J. Shryock, *The Origin and Development of the State Cult of Confucius* (New York, 1932).
O. Sirén, *A History of Early Chinese Art* (4 vols., London, 1929–1930).
A. Stein, *On Ancient Central Asian Tracks: A Brief Narrative of Three Expeditions in Innermost Asia and Northwestern China* (London, 1933).
N. L. Swan, *Pan Chao: The Foremost Woman of China* (New York, 1932).

ON ART OF THE THIRD CENTURY B.C.

W. C. White, *Tomb Tile Pictures of Ancient China. An Archaeological Study of Pottery Tiles from Tombs of Western Honan, Dating about the Third Century B.C.* (Toronto, 1939).

Chapter IV. IMPERIAL CHINA

From the end of the Han Dynasty to the early part of the nineteenth century

TO THE CASUAL NOVICE reading Chinese history for the first time, the period from the fall of the Han to the advent of the Westerner in force in the nineteenth century often seems a dreary waste of strange names which are impossible to remember and which have little or no significance. Dynasty succeeds dynasty with but little apparent change except in nomenclature. The impression given by an initial reading of the history of China is that when once the Chinese Empire was formed by the Ch'in and the Han nothing much that was new was accomplished. Some dynasties were stronger and longer lived than others, occasionally China was conquered in whole or in part by one or another of the peoples who were constantly pressing against the northern defenses, but on first acquaintance little that was really new or significant appears to have taken place.

In a certain sense, this impression has much to warrant it. As we have said, in its main outlines the machinery of government under which the Empire was ruled until our own day was developed under the Ch'in and the Han. Certain features were expanded and details were added or dropped, but administratively and in its fundamental ideals the state continued essentially as it had been shaped by the Ch'in and the Han on the basis of conceptions inherited from the Chou. One ruling line would lose its vigor and be supplanted by a successful warrior who would place his family on the throne. That family would hold on for a time and then, after a generation or two or perhaps after two or three centuries, would in turn deteriorate and be displaced by another. The Ch'in and the Han had carried China Proper roughly to its natural frontiers, and succeeding dynasties simply witnessed the filling by the Chinese of the territory then staked out. Under especially powerful dynasties, the borders of the Empire were extended into the encircling countries, but not until the thirteenth and again in the seventeenth and eighteenth centuries were imperial boundaries much beyond those which the Han had from time to time held. The larger expansion in the thirteenth, seventeenth, and eighteenth centuries was accomplished not primarily by the Chinese but by foreign conquerors ruling as Chinese Emperors. The invaders who subdued China brought in nothing that wrought fundamental alterations in Chinese life. Usually, although not always, they themselves succumbed to Chinese culture and ruled through existing political machinery. Not until the twentieth century did aliens work radical changes in the basic patterns of Chinese life. No such violent breaks in the stream of history occurred as Occidental history has known. The familiar categories of ancient, medieval, and modern do not fit China. The idea of progress which has characterized so much of Occidental thought in the past century and a half or more has been lacking in China. If the Westerner were to complain that Chinese history shows no progress, the cultured Chinese might, bewildered or surprised, declare that it is not in the nature of history to do so.

Yet, while the changes are not so marked as in the Occident, Chinese history is by no means a dull repetition. Even after the Han it contains major periods, each of which has its special characteristics. Alterations were made and some innovations were witnessed, although not in such striking fashion as in the Occident.

To this story we must now address ourselves. We will treat it by major periods, stressing the distinctive features of each. Most of these periods take their name from a dynasty, for it is under the pulse of dynasties that Chinese history moves.

Division and Invasion

Following the downfall of the Han, a prolonged period of political division and weakness ensued. For more than three and a half centuries China knew no great unifying imperial line such as she had had under the Han. With slight and brief exceptions, what we would term China shrank to China Proper and did not fully occupy that natural domain. Invaders from the north, ever pressing toward the fertile and wealthy valleys to the south, took advantage of the weakness and conquered much of the country. They established ruling lines which had varying durations and which governed smaller or larger sections of the north.

Into the details of these nearly four centuries we must not go. In a book with the purpose ours professes. the understanding of the present Far East, they are unessential and the many names would prove confusing. We must, however, mention some of the main features of the era.

First we must note again what we have already remarked, the division of the realm into several different states. For a time after the fall of the Later Han, these were three in number, and the period of their existence (A.D. 221–265) is known as that of the Three Kingdoms. The warfare between them has for centuries been celebrated in popular tale and on the stage, and one of the most famous of China's historical novels, *The Romance of the Three Kingdoms*, has it as its theme. For a brief period after the Three Kingdoms, China was unified under one ruling line, but soon division reappeared. Part of the era is known to the Chinese as that of the Northern and Southern Dynasties. In the Yangtze Valley were states ruled by Chinese. In the north were states most of which were headed by invaders. Sometimes, too, the Chinese use for the period the term the Six Dynasties, by which they mean the six principalities which successively had their capital at Nanking between the downfall of the Han and the reunification of China in A.D. 589.

Second, we must elaborate a little on the invaders from the north who, as we have said, were one of the outstanding characteristics of the centuries. These peoples were not all of one race. The Hsiung Nu, who had constituted a problem for the Ch'in and the Han, established themselves in a part of the north and for a time had a strong state. Of the racial affiliations of several of the groups we are uncertain. Some seem to have been Mongols, or of one of the strains which entered into the Mongols. Others may have been Turks. At least one group was certainly Turkish.

In the third place, the invasions did not mean the erasure of Chinese culture. Most of the conquerors adopted, some slowly, others quickly, the civilization of their subjects. Indeed, one of the most powerful and longest lived of the foreign ruling lines eventually proscribed their own language and costume, insisted upon conforming to Chinese speech, dress, family names, and court ceremonial, and encouraged intermarriage with the Chinese. This helped to strengthen the conviction we have heard voiced so often in these late years of Japanese invasion, that ultimately the Chinese absorb their conquerors. That, as we are to see later, has not always been true, and even if it had been uniformly the case in the past, under the altered conditions of our day it might not repeat itself in the future. Yet the experience of the past has had much to do with shaping Chinese attitudes toward recent events.

In the fourth place, not only did Chinese culture persist in the north, but it also was strengthened in the Yangtze Valley. War and invasion helped to stimulate migrations of Chinese from the north southward, into territories ruled by Chinese. Now, for the first time, the center of Chinese culture shifted from the north into the Yangtze Valley. Moreover, population in the Yangtze Valley seems to have increased. Great aristocratic families arose which intermarried with one another and sought to keep a monopoly on the public offices. Naturally, they tended to conserve traditional Chinese culture and their example was potent. Developments in native culture continued, some of them without a serious break. For example, the tomb figurines in pottery which appeared in the Han were elaborated and improved.

As a fifth feature of these years, it is also important that the dream of a united, comprehensive Empire did not die. Even under the Chou the conception had been inculcated that all civilized mankind should have but one ruler. The Ch'in and the Han had translated that ideal into concrete form. So firmly had the idea been implanted that even the centuries of disunion did not eradicate it. So thoroughly, too, had the Ch'in and the Han done their work that the general principles of the administrative system evolved by them continued. The political unity which subsequent dynasties achieved was facilitated by this perseverance of the earlier tradition.

A sixth feature of these years of political division was the comparative fluidity of Chinese culture. Even though the main outlines of Chinese institutions persisted, the absence of a strong, united administration based upon the historical heritage of the past could not but lower the resistance to changes and to the influx of new ideas. We now read of the use of coal for fuel. The strangers who invaded the north might pride themselves on ruling as Chinese Emperors according to Chinese traditions, but they could not entirely divorce themselves from their own past. As the Chinese moved southward into the Yangtze Valley, they very probably were modified by the new environment and may have taken over something from the pre-Chinese cultures of that region. Foreign commerce persisted across the land routes, and the growth of Chinese power in the south must have encouraged the coming of foreign merchants to the ports whose development the indented coast line favored. The knowledge of outside countries on the south, southwest, and west increased. With foreign trade foreign goods and some foreign ideas entered. The drinking of tea was introduced. The beverage first became common in the south and did not become general in the north until sometime between the eighth and the tenth century. The wheelbarrow and the waterwheel were in use, presumably at first as importations. We now hear for the first time of dice and sedan chairs.

As the seventh feature of the age, we must speak of the growth of Buddhism. Of all the alterations wrought in these centuries of division, the rapid spread of Buddhism was the most spectacular. Buddhist missionaries arrived, some by way of the sea, through the ports in the south, and some from Central Asia via the overland trade routes. Several of the non-Chinese rulers were particularly friendly to the foreign religion. Chinese were permitted to take the Buddhist vows and thousands entered Buddhist monasteries. Buddhist writings were translated into Chinese. Chinese devotees traveled as pilgrims to the sacred sites in India, some of them brought back Buddhist sacred books, and all must have returned with tales of foreign lands and of highly civilized peoples which could not but expand the horizons of their fellow countrymen. The most famous of these pilgrims was Fa Hsien. He went overland to India, following one of the caravan roads in the Tarim Basin, and returned by way of Ceylon and the sea route, bringing Buddhist scriptures with him. Buddhism now became part of the warp and woof of Chinese life.

Buddhism was the vehicle for foreign influences. From it new terms entered into the Chinese language, mainly from Sanskrit. Buddhist missionaries, in their study of Chinese, originated a phonetic analysis which aided Chinese philology. Indian chants enriched Chinese music. The practice of medicine was enlarged. Especially did Buddhism prove the channel for new contributions in art. Buddhism brought in *bodhisattvas* and *arhats*. Its pictures and statues had developed under the influence of several artistic traditions. Among them were Greek, Graeco-Roman, Persian, and Indian of more than one period. To those of us from the Occident, the Greek influence in Buddhist art is particularly interesting. It entered through the great wave of Hellenism that swept eastward in the wake of the armies of Alexander the Great. In some Buddhist statues in China and even in Japan it is so obvious as to be apparent to the veriest amateur. In others it has been so altered that it is discernible only to those who know the history of the development of a particular convention. Buddhist themes and iconography were a great stimulus to the

Chinese. Some of the best of Chinese painting was done under the inspiration of Buddhism.

A number of schools of Buddhism emerged in China. Most of these professed to trace their origin to Indian antecedents, but some were purely the product of the reaction of the Chinese mind and spirit to the stimulus of Buddhism, and all showed the modifying influence of the Chinese tradition. As under the Chou the Chinese mind had concerned itself with the problem of achieving an ideal society and several schools had come into being, so now the Chinese were fascinated by the themes presented by Buddhism.

One of the major schools of Chinese Buddhism was what the Chinese call *Ch'an,* and what the Japanese (for it spread to Japan and had great effect there) term *Zen. Ch'an* insisted that salvation, or enlightenment, is attained not primarily by good works, asceticism, ceremonial, or the study of books, but by sudden illumination. It made much of meditation and in Japan was associated with an arduous discipline.

The *T'ien T'ai* school took its name from a mountain in Chêkiang, where was the center in which the founder taught. It said that salvation is to be achieved by a combination of meditation, ritual, moral discipline, insight, and the study of books. It emphasized one of the Buddhist writings, the Lotus Sutra, and tended to a pantheistic monism. It showed, too, the influence of Taoism.

The Pure Land school proclaimed salvation as obtainable by simple faith. The object of this faith was Amida or Amitabha, who was one of the Buddhas with which Mahayana peopled the universe. Those who call upon Amida in faith, so this school declared, are admitted on death into the Western Paradise. Obviously, since it did not entail the specialized discipline demanded by the other schools, but could be followed by lay folk, Pure Land Buddhism had a great popular appeal.

Under the influence of Buddhism, the native Chinese Taoism was profoundly altered. It built temples, collected its writings into forms paralleling the Buddhist scriptures, talked of Heaven and Hell, and elaborated a pantheon which clearly showed the stimulus of the Indian faith. It continued to be popular, pursued its search for the transmutation of metals and the elixir of life, and enlarged its literature.

It is interesting that while China was passing through these centuries of division, the Western world was having a somewhat similar experience. The Roman Empire was collapsing as had the Han in China. Barbarians were establishing kingdoms on what had been the soil of Rome as was being done in the former domains of the Han. Indeed, the Huns, kinsfolk of the Hsiung Nu who were so tragically known in China, were prominent in the Occident. A new religion, Christianity, was being adopted, much as Buddhism was entering China. Between the Occident and China, however, marked differences existed. The collapse in China was not so marked as in Western Europe. The old was more persistent. The break with the past was not so great. Christianity worked more revolutionary changes than did Buddhism. The new Europe which emerged after the Dark Ages was far more different from the Gaeco-Roman world than was China after the division from the China of the Han.

Yet, although these centuries did not mark as sharp a break in China as in Europe, they were the era in which Chinese culture was more nearly fluid than it was to be until the twentieth century. More than in any age until our own, China was being shaped by a foreign culture. The results might have been more striking had Buddhism, the vehicle of that culture, been more aggressive in the political and social aspects of life. Since it emphasized retreat from the world it did not displace Confucianism, with the latter's positive affirmations and this-worldly emphasis. The main fabric of Chinese life was less affected than in the twentieth century.

The Sui (A.D. *589–618*)

As the division and civil strife in the closing centuries of the Chou period were terminated by two dynasties which unified the country, one of them brief and the other long, so the centuries of disunion that followed the Han were ended by two dynasties, the first of which, the Sui, lasted for less than a generation, and the second of which, the T'ang, had a life of nearly three centuries.

The Sui dynasty, which ruled the Empire from A.D. 589 to 618, had only two reigns which really can be called such. It introduced no revolutionary changes comparable to those made by its counterpart, the Ch'in, eight centuries before. It unified the Empire. It wrought modifications in the administrative system which, in spite of the divisions of the preceding centuries, had been handed down from the Ch'in and the Han. It greatly strengthened the civil service examinations and did much to give them the form they were to preserve for more than a thousand years. While its power was confined chiefly to China Proper, it exercised authority over what are now Tongking and a section of Annam and took part in the politics of Central Asia. It augmented the walls along the northern marches. It developed a series of canals to connect the north with the Yangtze Valley. This latter was not an entirely new project, but the Sui added to it and gave it more importance in welding the realm together commercially and politically. The second Emperor of the Sui, Yang Ti, is a figure who, somewhat like Ch'in Shih Huang Ti, has both fascinated and called forth the execrations of orthodox historians. He was a man of volcanic energy, great ability, and ambitious projects who, in his later years, met with misfortune and came to a violent end (618). The puppets who were set up in his place scarcely counted and quickly disappeared, one by violent death and the other by abdication.

The T'ang (A.D. *618–907*)

The Sui was succeeded by the T'ang dynasty. The real creator and the greatest figure of the T'ang was Li Shih-min, who is better known as T'ai Tsung or T'ang T'ai Tsung and who reigned as the second Emperor of his house. His father was the first Emperor, but he greatly assisted his sire in winning the throne and it was he who gave the dynasty the impulse which largely accounted for its brilliance and its long tenure of power. The capital was fixed at Ch'ang-an, in the valley of the Wei, not far from where the Ch'in and the Earlier Han had had their seats. Here in time a great city emerged, one which may in its heyday have been the largest and most populous in the world.

The T'ang reached its apex of splendor and power under an Emperor variously termed Hsüan Tsung and Ming Huang who ruled from 712 to 756. It was then that the dynasty possessed its widest territorial extent. It was then, too, that the greatest poets and the most distinguished painter of China flourished. China vied with the Moslem Arab Empire in the distinction of being the richest and most powerful state on the globe. Compared with it, the empire of Charlemagne of the same century was small and semibarbarous. Its splendor drew and dazzled all the Far East. It was then, as we are to see a little later, that Chinese culture poured into Japan, continuing revolutionary transformations in that realm which had begun under Chinese influence shortly before the advent of the T'ang.

It was, moreover, in the later years of Ming Huang that the decline began which eventually brought the dynasty to an end. That decline is associated with one of the most famous beauties of China, Yang Kuei-fei. Yang Kuei-fei had been the wife of a son of Ming Huang, but in 738 the infatuated Emperor took her to be one of his own concubines. She encouraged him in a life of magnificent luxury and gaiety. As he entered old age Ming Huang was unable to give the vigorous attention to the affairs of state that he had once done. A serious rebellion broke out. Ming Huang fled from his capital and the imperial troops demanded and received the life of Yang Kuei-fei as a cause of the disasters that had come upon the realm. The rebellion was suppressed, but the aged Ming Huang abdicated in favor of one of his sons. The dynasty retained its hold on the throne until A.D. 907, but its authority and grandeur were never restored to the peak of the earlier years of Ming Huang.

Several features of China under the T'ang made the dynasty stand out as a distinct period in the annals of the Empire.

First of all, the Empire attained an even greater area than it had under the Han. The T'ang domains embraced almost all of China Proper and extended southward into Indo-China. In the northeast they included parts of Manchuria and Mongolia. It was westward that they had their greatest extension. Chinese suzerainty was acknowledged by the peoples of the Tarim Valley, that basin stretching westerly toward the heart of Central Asia. At more than one time it was also accepted by important centers across the mountains from the Tarim, in Transoxiana. Here Chinese diplomacy came into conflict with the advancing borders of the young Moslem Arab Empire. Some of the Tibetans were constrained to acknowledge the power of the T'ang. By one of the most noteworthy military achievements of history, Chinese arms were carried across the Pamirs into the upper reaches of the Indus. Not even the Han had been so mighty in the west.

A second feature of the T'ang followed out of this first, many contacts with other peoples and cultures. The huge territorial extent of the Empire brought non-Chinese peoples into its fold or entailed diplomatic and commercial relations with them. The wealth of the realm attracted merchants and others who came in gainful pursuits. Glazed earthenware tomb figures from graves of the T'ang period make vivid what we learn from literary sources. In them we see the features of Jews, Arabs, Persians, Tartars, Syrians, and Greeks, with all of whom the Chinese artist must have been familiar. Probably foreign commerce attained larger proportions than at any previous time. While the overland routes to the west were in the possession of the T'ang, commerce along them would be reasonably secure and would flourish. Merchants came by way of the sea to the ports of the south coast. So numerous were they that on one occasion in the later years of the dynasty they looted the leading port, Canton, perhaps in retaliation for Chinese exactions. We hear, too, that a Moslem was appointed by the Chinese to supervise his fellow believers according to the law of Islam, a principle akin to the extraterritoriality which in the nineteenth century was adopted for foreigners in China.

Adherents of foreign religions entered China. Manichaeanism, once widespread in Asia, North Africa, and Southern Europe, was present, largely because many of the Uighurs, a Turkish folk who were prominent in China's west, adhered to it. Islam, which came into being in Sui and early T'ang times, appeared. Zoroastrianism was brought by merchants and by refugees from Persia (for during the T'ang period the Moslem Arabs overthrew the Zoroastrian Sassanid line in Persia). From the T'ang, moreover, we obtain the first authentic evidence of the presence of Christianity in China. Nestorian, Jacobite, and Greek Orthodox forms of the faith were represented among the peoples with whom the T'ang was in touch. Of these Nestorianism had the widest following and, so far as we know, it was only Nestorianism which entered China.

None of these contacts wrought as great changes in Chinese culture as had Buddhism in the period of division after the Han. None of the newly introduced religions made the deep impression upon China that Buddhism had done. Their adherents were mostly foreigners and their Chinese converts seem not to have been very numerous. Manichaeanism lived on into the seventeenth century. Moslems later constituted a substantial minority, but the strength of the Moslem community dates from later dynasties. Zoroastrianism completely disappeared—in contrast with its endurance in India among the wealthy Parsees. Christianity died out, to be renewed a few centuries later.

Even Buddhism began a slow decline which has continued to our own day. To be sure, in the early years of the T'ang it was vigorous. Pilgrims still journeyed to the Buddhist sacred sites in India. The stream of missionaries persisted. Buddhism was favored by some of the rulers, among them a powerful but infamous Empress in the first century of the dynasty. New schools of Buddhism appeared, always an indication of vitality in a religion. Among them was *Chên-yen*

("True Word") which the Japanese term *Shingon.* Buddhist themes were still important in Chinese art. Yet by the close of the T'ang Buddhism was waning. Partly because of the decay of Buddhism in India, the stream of missionaries and pilgrims dwindled. In the latter part of the dynasty several of the Emperors were opposed to Buddhism and we hear of imperial edicts which sought to prevent the further entrance of Chinese into the ranks of the monks and which commanded the destruction of Buddhist temples and the return of monks and nuns to secular life.

A reason for the decay of Buddhism was a third feature of the T'ang, the revival of Confucianism. This was associated with the strong administration of the T'ang. The T'ang made no sweeping innovations in the machinery of government that had come down from the Han through the intervening dynasties. They were, however, strong enough to enforce it over all of the territories in which the Chinese were the predominant elements of the population. It was only with the weakening of T'ang power in the later years of Ming Huang that the centralized control from the capital began to be relaxed. This administration meant the appointment and control of officials from the capital. A large proportion of the officials were recruited through civil service examinations. These examinations were still further developed under the T'ang. While the Confucian classics were not so exclusively the subject matter as they were to be under some later dynasties, they were important. They were, therefore, prominent in the curriculum of the schools. Moreover, the Emperor T'ai Tsung required the erection in every *chou* and *hsien* (administrative divisions of the realm) a temple to Confucius and commanded that sacrifices be offered in them by scholars and government officials. In these temples were placed the names of distinguished worthies of the Confucian school. All of this meant the strengthening of Confucianism and, as a consequence, the weakening of rival cults. It is not surprising that some of the outstanding Confucian scholars of the T'ang were vigorous in their opposition to Buddhism. A state built upon Confucianism might permit rivals, but it would also from time to time place restrictions upon them if they threatened to become too powerful.

A fourth feature of the T'ang was the appearance of some of the greatest of Chinese poetry. Indeed, Li Po and Tu Fu, both of the T'ang, are said to be the outstanding poets of all Chinese literature. They were contemporaries and did much of their writing during the brilliant period of Ming Huang. Both were for a time in the circle of genius that gathered about the court. Li Po was always something of a wanderer and had many matrimonial ventures. He was, too, fond of his cups. He knew and loved both the haunts of men and the solitary mountain and stream. His poems were not labored, but were largely spontaneous, and are still read and enjoyed for their lyric beauty, their daring originality of style, their mastery of words, their skill in handling older poetic forms, and their successful departures from literary conventions. Li Po lifted himself and his readers into a dream world on an ecstasy of form and rhythm. Tu Fu was more of a realist. His life was marked by much disappointment and anguish, and in a troubled period in his mature years some of his children died of starvation. All this reflected itself in his writings. He depicted suffering in very moving fashion.

A fifth characteristic of the T'ang was its art. What some consider China's greatest painting was produced in this period. Probably the outstanding painter of the dynasty and possibly of all China's artistic history was Wu Tao-hsüan (also known as Wu Tao Tzŭ and Wu Tao-yüan). Like Li Po and Tu Fu, he was one of the adornments of the court of Ming Huang. The themes of Chinese painting were partly Buddhist and Taoist. The vivid life in Buddhism during the most glorious years of the dynasty accounts for at least some of the artistic achievement. Landscapes were popular subjects and we hear of a famous painter of horses. Porcelain became important as an artistic medium, although we can be by no means sure that it originated then. It was the product of a long evolution, and a hard ware which resembles it had been produced centuries before.

A sixth development under the T'ang was printing. Just when this revolutionary device first developed we do not know. It may have been as early as the Sui dynasty. From the T'ang, however, comes our earliest example of a printed book. It is a Buddhist sutra and it may well be that printing was a gift of Buddhism to the world, the result of the attempt to make widely available the literature of that faith. This first printing was by wood blocks, not by movable type. Indeed, the best printing in China has always been by the wood block, akin to the woodcut, on which the desired text has been affixed by pasting the inscribed page face down upon it, and then carving it in such fashion that the characters are left, raised, ready to make the impression. Movable type and other methods were devised in China, but it was by the wood block that the finest work was done.

It was a great epoch in the cultural history of mankind, the T'ang dynasty. In many ways it resembled the Han. In the territory occupied it did not differ greatly from the latter. In its administrative system it continued the general principles of the Han and the Sui, although it modified and added to them. Yet it possessed distinctive features. It had more intimate contact with more different peoples from distant parts than did the Han. It left a deeper impress upon the cultures of its Far Eastern neighbors. Buddhism was much more prominent. In literature the Han had been distinguished for its recovery and editing of the Chou classics and for its prose style. The T'ang was famous for its poetry. It knew, too, what seems to have been the beginning of prose fiction in the vernacular. In art, painting was more outstanding than under the Han and the style in sculpture and in ceramics was distinctive. The T'ang was an age in itself, different from both its predecessors and its successors.

The Five Dynasties (A.D. *907–960*)

For a half century after the T'ang no ruling line succeeded in mastering all of the Empire. Orthodox historians, who insist that there can be only one legitimate ruler of the Empire at any one time, trace a succession of five short dynasties from 907 to 960. As a matter of fact, while the center of their power was in the region in which had been the traditional seats of China's earlier dynasties, none of them ruled all of China Proper, and their authority was disputed by families who set up states in other parts of the country. In the north, invaders of Mongol tongue, the Khitan, the nucleus of whose domains was in Manchuria and Mongolia, assumed a dynastic title.

In this half century, however, anarchic though political conditions at first sight appear to have been, culture by no means disappeared. For instance, printing was further developed, and a revised text of the Classics, prepared by an official commission, was reproduced by this method. Painting continued. The way was prepared for some of the outstanding features of the succeeding period.

The Sung (A.D. *960–1279*)

The period of the Five Dynasties was brought to an end by a general who succeeded in placing his family so firmly on the throne that it remained there, under the dynastic title of Sung, slightly longer than the T'ang had done. The little more than three centuries of the Sung also form a distinct epoch in China's history and culture.

As the builders of an empire the Sung were far behind the Ch'in, the Han, the Sui, and the T'ang. The Sung never ruled quite all of China Proper. Nor was their authority recognized in the borderlands as had been that of their great predecessors. All through their history they were forced to share with aliens the rule of those whom we should call the Chinese. These aliens came in from the north, the direction against which China's defenses had faced since at least the Chou. One group was the Khitan, who had planted themselves in the north in the declining years of the T'ang and during the Five Dynasties. In the northwest a people speaking a Tibeto-Burman tongue, but who had adopted something of Chinese culture, founded a state. In the twelfth century a people from northern Manchuria, called by the Chinese the Juchên, displaced the Khitan. At first the Sung welcomed them as allies against the Khitan, but they proved even more of a menace than had the latter. They founded a dynasty which they called by the name Chin. They captured the Sung capital, the present K'aifêng, and the Sung were forced to move their seat of government southward until it found prolonged lodgment in the present Hangchow. After this move the Sung are known as the Southern Sung (A.D. 1127–1279).

In the latter part of the twelfth century a fresh menace appeared from the north—the Mongols, led by Temuchin, better known by his later title, Jenghiz Khan, the "Universal Emperor." Jenghiz Khan was one of the world's greatest conquerors. He began his life as the son of a chief of a confederation of some of the Mongol tribes. After his father's death, he fought his way to the headship formerly held by his sire. He then conquered several of his neighbors, among them a Turkish tribe whose ruler had once been his overlord. Other peoples in what are now Mongolia and Sinkiang were forced to recognize his suzerainty. Supported by this assemblage of hardy peoples, he directed his energies against the states in the north of China Proper. He also turned his arms westward, into the regions east of the Caspian. He died in 1227, but the onward sweep of his armies continued under his sons. For a time the Sung allied themselves with the Mongols against the non-Chinese states in the north, but when these latter were erased, the Mongols were not content with the north, but pressed southward against their quondam confederates.

Although the Mongol Empire stretched westward into Mesopotamia and Europe, the most stubborn opposition it met in lands that it eventually subdued was from the Sung. It was not until 1279, in the days when a grandson of Jenghiz Khan, Khubilai Khan, headed the Mongols, that the latter finally succeeded in eliminating them. For the first time in its history, all of China Proper fell into the hands of a foreign invader. The political weakness of the Sung and the eventual prostration before the alien marked the dynasty off from its great predecessors—the T'ang, the Han, the Ch'in, and even the Chou.

CULTURE UNDER THE SUNG

Political weakness did not mean cultural decay. The Sung period is one of the most brilliant in achievements in civilization in the history of China. Here it possessed distinct characteristics. To be sure, it represented not a break with the past but a development from it. It preserved, with modifications, the administrative machinery, the laws, and the civil service examinations which it inherited from earlier dynasties. Confucianism remained the basic philosophy upon which the state and society were built. Yet the Sung era possessed features that gave it a character of its own.

For one thing, the center of Chinese culture now moved to the south, chiefly to the lower part of the Yangtze Valley and adjoining districts. This migration had begun in the period of division after the Han, but the Sui and the T'ang had kept their capitals in the north, and in China, as in many other lands, culture tended to follow the capital. With the occupation of the north by foreign invaders during so much of the Sung, and especially after the removal of the imperial residence to the south, art, literature, and scholarship followed. The north did not permanently lose its traditional cultural supremacy, but for a time it did so.

The Sung was noted for aesthetic refinement. The printing which had come down from the Han and the Five Dynasties was developed, and some of the Sung editions that have survived are exquisite examples of the printer's art.

Porcelain became popular. The numerous examples of the Sung wares that have reached us are notable for their good taste, their studied simplicity, and the skill of their manufacture. As a rule, one or two colors were employed on a given object. The many-colored ornate designs of later periods were to wait for the taste of subsequent generations. Glazes of several different colors were employed, some of them delicate and others of them rich. A light green, often spoken of as celadon, was much used. Many pieces of porcelain, too, were pure white. Crackle-glaze was frequent. The porcelain was made at many centers, some of them private, some of them under imperial supervision. The famous works at Ching-tê-chên, which have persisted to our own day, take their name from a reign period of the Sung in the first decade of the eleventh century.

Painting was highly developed. Many different themes were treated—flowers, birds, animals, *buddhas* and *bodhisattvas*. However, the Sung is remembered chiefly for its landscapes. These are as beautiful as any which have ever come from the brush of the painter. It was probably the earliest great landscape painting in the history of the world. All art has in it much of the subjective. Even photographs reflect something of the one who takes them. Yet Chinese landscapes especially show the influence of the soul of the painter. The painter sought not an exact reproduction of the landscape as it appeared to the untutored eye. Rather he steeped himself in it and endeavored to convey the impression it had made upon him.

SUNG NEO-CONFUCIANISM

The Sung, too, was remembered for its philosophy. This was chiefly a reinterpretation of Confucianism. The time was one of great intellectual activity and discussion. Several schools emerged. However, they did not concern themselves, as had most of creative thought between the Han and the T'ang and in the early years of the T'ang, with the imported Buddhism, but with the native Confucianism. Buddhism, while still potent, was waning. The result was what is often called Neo-Confucianism. The antecedents of the Confucian revival go back to the T'ang. The main development, however, was during the Sung. The thinkers who produced what later became the orthodox form of this Sung Confucianism were molded not only by the Confucian writings which had come down to them from the Chou through the Han, but also by Taoism and Buddhism.

The outstanding figure of this dominant school was Chu Hsi (1130–1200). Chu Hsi was not its originator. Behind him were a number of creative minds. His was rather the gift of synthesis, clarity of thought, and an attractive literary style. He was the son of an official and spent much of his life in the service of the state. He obtained, however, a great deal of leisure for study and writing, some of it through sinecure posts and some when, through the pressure of enemies at court, he was out of office.

The Neo-Confucian system as it issued from the pen of Chu Hsi had in it much of the older Confucianism, something of Buddhism and Taoism, and also, as was inevitable, contributions from Chu Hsi and his immediate predecessors. From Buddhism came the practice of meditation and, especially from Ch'an Buddhism, the conception of sudden enlightenment. From Taoism was derived a belief in a Principle which underlies the universe and which enters into nature in its various aspects and into individual minds. The basic writings were those revered by the Confucian school, but some portions were singled out for special attention and much was made of a few phrases. An orderly, systematized garb was offered for the universe, a cosmology into which mankind and all of which man was aware were fitted. Some of this was probably implicit in the sayings attributed to Confucius, but apparently that sage had not been interested in elaborating any coherent explanation of the universe.

The school of Chu Hsi was by no means the only one developed under the Sung. Eventually, however, it was accepted as standard. Right up to the collapse of the Confucian Empire in the twentieth century it continued to be esteemed as orthodox Confucianism.

SUNG SOCIAL EXPERIMENTATION

The Sung was also famous for its social experimentation. The name to which this is attached is Wang An-shih (1021–1086). Wang An-shih was a practical statesman who wished to remove flagrant economic and social ills and to put the realm on a better footing to deal successfully with its foreign foes. He elaborated a program which had in it features that we of the Occident associate with socialism. Indeed, when, in the twentieth century, there was a strong swing in China toward communism, some Chinese declared that China would never accept that ideology, for it had had its experience with it under the Sung and after experimentation and long and acrimonious discussion had finally rejected it.

The main features of Wang An-shih's plan included (1) a commission to draft a budget for the state and thus to effect savings; (2) a state monopoly of commerce, the surplus above taxes and the needs of each district to be purchased by the government and either to be held in depots for local needs or to be transported elsewhere and sold in places of dearth; (3) loans by the state to farmers in the growing season to assist in the planting and harvesting of crops; (4) the division of land into equal portions and the annual reappraisal for purposes of taxation, thus to avoid the exemption of some of the soil from taxation and to ensure the equitable distribution of the land tax; (5) the taxation of all property, both real estate and movable; (6) the abolition of the conscription of labor by the government (an impost which bore especially heavily on the poor) and in place of it labor on state works paid by the proceeds of a graduated tax based upon the division of property holders into groups according to their wealth; (7) military reorganization, with a form of compulsory service; (8) a device for recruiting the cavalry needed in the defense of the frontier; and (9) a reorganization of the civil service examinations to render them more effective as tests of the candidates' ability to deal with practical problems of government. It is interesting that in the 1930's an American Secretary of Agriculture made a careful study of Wang An-shih to assist him in his own program and took over from him the phrase an "ever normal granary."

Wang An-shih was not as much an innovator as a first reading of these measures might indicate. Some of his proposals resemble those advocated and inaugurated by the Legalists centuries before. Several are akin to those of Wang Mang, between the Earlier and the Later Han. Some probably represented practices with a long precedent behind them.

However, Wang An-shih met with bitter opposition. His program was adopted in whole or in part for periods which varied from a few months to several years in length. The struggle went on after his death. The dissensions over it may have been one of the causes of the weakness of the Sung. As a whole it did not find a permanent place in the policy of the state. Yet whether because of his advocacy or in spite of it, some features, in modified form, such as the storing of tribute grain in government granaries and its release in times of dearth, were in use down into the twentieth century.

OTHER SUNG ACHIEVEMENTS

In other ways, in addition to philosophy and political science, the Sung was a period of literary activity. Much poetry was produced, and if the best of it did not quite reach the heights of the great masters of the T'ang, it is deemed among the best that China has produced. Some of it displayed originality in style. One of the outstanding Sung poets wrote as an avocation in a busy official life. Another was a recluse for whom Taoism held a fascination. Still another ended his life as a Buddhist monk. Works of botany, mathematics, medicine, and astronomy were produced. Vernacular fiction continued to be composed. Collections of extracts from works of earlier periods were made—a form of literary labor which has been very popular in China. Histories were compiled, some of them of all China, and some early representatives of a voluminous portion of China's literature, accounts of particular cities and administrative divisions. One of the most famous histories of China was written, a history which became the basis of other works. In literature the Sung displayed genius of no mean order and of wide variety.

The Yüan (A.D. *1279–1368*)

The Mongol conquest constituted an interruption in the development of China's culture. For nearly a century all China was ruled by aliens. Although the Mongol monarchs reigned as Chinese Emperors and carried over much of the earlier administrative machinery, and although rapid growth occurred in two features of Chinese life which we are to note in a moment, in general the contact with foreigners which the Mongols brought resulted in no such fructifying influences as had come with Buddhism during a previous period of alien domination.

Under the Mongols, China became a part of the largest land empire which up to that time the world had seen. Khubilai was Grand Khan of a realm that stretched from what is now European Russia, Persia, and Mesopotamia in the west to the China Sea on the east, and from the outer boundaries of Mongolia in the north into Indo-China in the south. From his capital at Cambaluc, whose site is partly identical with the present Peking, he reigned over a larger area than had acknowledged the Caesars, the Caliphs, Han Wu Ti, or Ming Huang. His envoys penetrated farther than ever Chinese representatives had gone.

Yet over much of this territory Khubilai's control was little more than nominal. Time-distances were too great to permit it to be knit closely together. In Western Asia descendants of Jenghiz Khan acknowledged the suzerainty of Khubilai, but went their way without much dependence upon him.

Moreover, the reign of Khubilai, brilliant though it was, saw the Mongol rule reach its apex. Some of the expeditions dispatched by Khubilai either met complete failure or won dubious victories whose sequel was little better than defeat. Twice Khubilai directed expeditions against Japan, but each time with disaster. On both occasions a storm joined with the Japanese in discomfiting the attackers. The Japanese record of never having been successfully invaded in historic times was kept clear. The successive armies sent against Annam were usually victorious on the open field, but they fell victim to the twin foes of disease and climate, and on a third attempt were so decimated that they were overwhelmed by the defenders. So, too, the citadel of the Chams, in Indo-China, was captured, but the quarry escaped to the hills. Mongol armies penetrated into Burma. They there established Mongol suzerainty, but this was exercised mainly through local chiefs. The initial successes won by an armada dispatched against Java were followed by enforced retirement. The design against the Liu Ch'iu (Ryukyu) Islands was also frustrated. The Mongol tide had reached its high-water mark and even before Khubilai's death had begun to recede.

Khubilai and his successors strove to rule through existing Chinese institutions. They were tolerant religiously and racially. They employed Chinese and also brought into office in the Middle Kingdom men from their Central Asiatic domains. They are regarded as Chinese Emperors and their line is listed officially as a dynasty under the name of Yüan.

Yet the Mongols did not win so prolonged a tenure as did the next conquering aliens, the Manchus. After the grandson who followed Khubilai on the throne, the line speedily lost in vigor, revolts broke out, and a man of humble origin, who had been orphaned as a boy and had sought refuge in a Buddhist monastery, led a force which expelled the foreigners and in 1368 placed his own family, of native Chinese stock, on the throne.

FOREIGN CONTACTS UNDER THE MONGOLS

The most prominent feature of the Mongol period, aside from the Mongol rule, was the wide variety of foreigners who came to China. Since China was a part, and the most populous and wealthiest part, of a huge empire, thousands from other sections entered the land. Some of these were brought in as soldiers or officials. Others were merchants. Never before had the Chinese seen such a wide variety of aliens. Arabs and Persians were present in large numbers and one Arab from North Africa recorded his travels in a book which can be read today.

Those who traversed the longest distances were merchants and missionaries from Western Europe. For the first time, the Far West of Euro-Asia touched the Far East. Now arrived the vanguard of those peoples who in the nineteenth and twentieth centuries were to work for such revolutionary changes, not only in China, but also in all the Far East. Some traversed the overland routes. Others came or went by sea.

The most famous of the merchants from Europe was Marco Polo. He arrived with his father and uncle, from Venice, for a time held office under Khubilai, and owes his fame not so much to his achievements in China as to the account of his travels which he left behind him after his return to Europe and which, widely read, stirred the imagination of Westerners. However, many in Venice and Genoa also made the round trip. It was the period when the Crusades and the growing commerce of Italian cities brought many Western Europeans to the Near East. From there, numbers pushed on to China. There they saw cities which seemed, at least to Marco Polo, to be the largest and the wealthiest in the world.

The missionaries were Franciscans, for the rise of the Mongol power coincided with the birth of that order and with the widely flung missions established by the enthusiasm of the young and devoted band of Brothers Minor. Two made the round trip to the earlier Mongol capital, Karakorum, in the present Outer Mongolia, as diplomatic envoys from the West. Later ones attempted, and not without results, to plant their faith in China.

With these aliens came the strengthening of foreign religions. Islam now became more prominent, largely through immigrants of that faith, and henceforward was a permanent feature of Chinese life. Christianity was reintroduced. Christianity, so far as we know, died out in China Proper toward the end of the T'ang. However, in the form of Nestorianism it continued to exist on the borders, among non-Chinese peoples in what are now Sinkiang and Mongolia. Many Christians were drawn into the Mongol Empire. Indeed, the mother of Khubilai was from a Turkish tribe in which were Christians. Numbers of them followed the Mongols into China. We know, too, of a body of Christian troops from the Caucasus and of Armenian Christians. We hear, moreover, of two Nestorian Christian youths, non-Chinese, from the north of China, who journeyed westward. One of them was made Patriarch of the Nestorians, with his seat at Baghdad, and the other, a native of Cambaluc, went to Western Europe, as far as Paris and Bordeaux, on a diplomatic mission for the Mongols. It was the first time, so far as we are aware, that anyone from China had reached the western shore of the Euro-Asiatic continent. As we have seen, Roman Catholic missionaries penetrated to China. We have no proof that many converts from among the Chinese themselves were made by either Nestorians or Roman Catholics. The Christian communities seem to have been predominantly non-Chinese. It is not surprising, therefore, that when, after the collapse of Mongol rule, the non-Chinese who had depended upon the Mongol regime largely withdrew, Christianity once more vanished from the Middle Kingdom.

CULTURAL CHANGES IN MONGOL TIMES

Chinese culture as a whole underwent no basic changes under the Mongols. The Mongols ruled largely through Chinese institutions. Movement and color and the portrayal of scenes from everyday life became more prominent in painting. Persian influences were obvious in some forms of art, including ceramics. The many contacts with outside cultures made contributions to Chinese life. Sorghum was introduced and added an important crop. Cotton was now first cultivated on a wide scale. A few new vegetables appeared. We hear of the abacus, later widely used.

In two phases of Chinese culture, the drama and the novel, the Mongol period witnessed a sudden flowering. Both the drama and the novel had long been present. Now they developed very rapidly and achieved a prominence that they had not heretofore known. Why this should have been so we do not know. We can simply record the fact.

The Ming (A.D. *1368–1644*)

The dynasty founded by the former humble inmate of a Buddhist monastery took the name of Ming, which may be translated as "brilliant" or "glorious." In a certain sense this title was deserved. The Empire was fairly prosperous. It may have been the most populous of its day. Under the third Emperor of the line, whom we best know by the title of his reign period, Yung Lo, naval expeditions were dispatched to Cambodia, Cochin-China, Siam, Sumatra, Java, India, and Ceylon. A prince in Ceylon who gave offense was taken prisoner and transported to China, and for a generation or so at least part of the island is said to have paid tribute to the Ming. Never had Chinese suzerainty been carried so far abroad by the sea.

The era was one of building. Nanking, "the Southern Capital," was given a great city wall. Peking, "the Northern Capital," was erected on a site which in part coincided with the Mongol Cambaluc. Its massive walls, vast palaces, and impressive temples, which for grandeur made the city unrivaled among the capitals of the world of its time and which so impress the visitor of today, were chiefly the work of the Ming. The succeeding dynasty simply kept them in repair and modified them. The Great Wall on the north was augmented. The Grand Canal, connecting the north with the Yangtze Valley, was improved. The literary and artistic output was voluminous, and much of it showed a high degree of technical skill.

However, in brilliance and genius the Ming by no means equaled the Chou, the Han, the T'ang, and the Sung. Their domains did not attain the extent of those of the Han and the T'ang. They did not rule Sinkiang, as had the other two. The impressiveness of the vast fortifications which they renewed or constructed on the north were evidence that they were on the defensive, and that they could not once for all remove the menace of the continued attacks by the Mongols by subduing the enemy in his own domains. During much of the course of the dynasty, the coast of China suffered from repeated raids by the Japanese. The sea power which early in the dynasty had given such promise was not developed sufficiently to curb them. The Japanese then, as in our own day, had no cause to fear the Chinese on the water. While populous, China was not so powerful as the empire that the Ottoman Turks were building during the early years of the Ming, nor did it approach in territorial extent the vast domains over which the Russians and the Spaniards were extending their authority in the latter half of the Ming period. No longer, as under the Han and the T'ang, could China be called one of the two mightiest empires of the day.

The literary labors of the period were prodigious in bulk. Indeed, a vast compilation of excerpts and entire works assembled in the reign of that third Emperor under whom the dynasty reached its zenith was so huge that even the imperial treasury found the cost of printing so appalling that it was allowed to remain in manuscript. Yet not nearly as much original genius was displayed as in some previous eras. Poetry was not so notable as under the T'ang and the Sung.

No such originality in philosophic thought was manifested as that which produced the schools of the Chou, or which gave birth to or developed the various forms of Buddhism in the period of division between the Han and the Sui and under the T'ang, or which created the Neo-Confucianism of the Sung. The most famous of the philosophers of the period was Wang Yang-ming (c. 1472–1528). He was not content, as were most of the scholars of his day, to accumulate and repeat, parrotlike, the learning of the past, but struggled to find for himself an answer to the vexing basic questions of life. He found unsatisfying the Confucianism of Chu Hsi which contemporary scholarship accepted as orthodox. The answer flashed upon him through a gleam of sudden enlightenment. Yet in this illumination and in the answer which came to him there was not so much originality as a reproduction of the experience of the Ch'an school of Buddhism, and his writings, even with such degree of novelty as they possessed, had far greater popularity in Japan than in China.

In political organization and thought the Ming were content to develop past traditions. Their code of laws was a modification of those of their predecessors. Their administrative machinery was in the main that which had been inherited from the Ch'in and the Han through the T'ang. They continued and stressed the civil service examinations, but made them far more stereotyped than before. In the form that the Ming gave them, they became a straitjacket in which the Chinese mind was bound until our own day. No such vigorous debate over political and economic theory engaged the attention of scholars and statesmen as under the Chou, the Han, and the Sung. No innovator so pointedly and dramatically challenged the established order as had Wang Mang and Wang An-shih. The Confucian state as formulated in the Chou and the Han was being worked out to a logical conclusion. A society in which one interpretation of one school of thought was being enforced by the state could have little room for diversity and originality.

So, too, in art. Nothing much that was new was appearing. Porcelain was utilized with more perfection of technique than previously. Intricate designs in several colors were ingeniously applied. Painting was popular and was elaborated with great technical skill and attention to detail. One has the impression, however, that in art as elsewhere the China of the Ming lacked the spark of genius.

WERE THE CHINESE LOSING THEIR VIGOR?

Why the China of the Ming was so much less aggressive than the China of the Ch'in, the Han, and the T'ang, and why it had so much less of intellectual originality than some of its great predecessors we do not know. We are perplexed and perturbed by the further fact to which we are to come in a moment that at the close of the Ming China fell once more into the hands of aliens and that this period of foreign rule lasted far longer than any other in the history of the country.

In other words, as the stream of Chinese history moved onward, the Chinese did fewer new things, showed less of ability to create, and for increasingly long periods were politically under the dominion of foreigners. In numbers and wealth they probably increased. Certainly in the Ming dynasty China was as prosperous as during the Sung and the T'ang, and under the succeeding dynasty the population became several times larger than ever before.

Does all this indicate that the Chinese were declining in ability to rule themselves and to think? If so, are not the disorders of the twentieth century symptoms of a further and fatal decay?

If to both these questions the answer must be affirmative, the outlook for China is very grave. In that case, the Chinese, if they are to go on as a people, can do so only by appropriating the ideas which their own ancestors and other peoples have created and under the political governance of aliens. Any attempts, by them or well-wishers, to reinvigorate them and ensure their cultural renewal and political independence are foredoomed.

The answers to these questions are of primary importance not only for China but also for all the Far East, including especially the Japanese. They are likewise of large significance to the rest of the world. It is part of the tantalizing and perhaps bitter challenge of our times that we do not certainly know the answers. We can guess at them, but we cannot prove them beyond peradventure or debate. Yet the entire world, including the Chinese, must act as if they knew the answers.

We must remind ourselves that though our posing of the questions seems to admit of only a gloomy outlook, this is by no means the only possible outcome. It may well be that the cause of the phenomenon is to be found in the thoroughgoing and prolonged application of the principles on which the unity of China was based by the Han and its successors, the inculcation of a community of culture through a particular type of government. It is possible that with the profound alteration of those principles which the present century has witnessed, the Chinese spirit, liberated, and stimulated by contacts with other cultures, will once more become creative and also succeed in setting up a virile, independent national existence. It is a practical testing of that hypothesis which our generation is witnessing.

To the queries which we have here attempted to formulate we must return at a later time.

MING CONTACTS WITH EUROPEANS

Before leaving the Ming we must call attention to one other feature of the period. It was under the Ming that a renewal occurred of the contacts between Europeans and Chinese which in the twentieth century were to break down the straitjacket in which the Chinese had increasingly confined themselves and which were to bring to the Chinese spirit fresh impulses and opportunity to demonstrate to itself and to the world that it was not hopelessly decadent.

The contacts between Europe and China established under the Mongols had come to an end with the breakup of that empire and the establishment of a native line on the throne of China. Europe, however, had not forgotten them. Particularly had the account by Marco Polo kept their memory alive. With the close of the fifteenth and the beginning of the sixteenth century the expansion of Western European peoples renewed them. They were never again to lapse, but were, rather, to increase, and were to work the most basic revolution in China which that land has ever known.

One of the very familiar facts of history is this renewed expansion of European peoples. In its influence upon mankind it is also one of the most important. The Spaniards pushing westward and the Portuguese pushing southward and eastward between them carried European commerce and culture around the globe and brought a large proportion of the earth's surface under their political control. Not far from the same time the Russians traveled eastward across the sparsely settled reaches of Northern Asia and on into Alaska and extended the Russian flag over these vast areas. The Dutch, the English, and the French followed the Spaniards and the Portuguese and in time became important agents of the Occident.

For the purposes of our story, it is important to remind ourselves that the lure of the Far East was potent as a cause of the discoveries of both the Spaniards and the Portuguese. Just how far the hope of reaching the Far East was the purpose of Columbus on his first voyage is debated by specialists. Undoubtedly, however, the Far East was in his mind during at least part of his later explorations. The attraction of the Far East proved so strong that it drew the Spaniards across the

Pacific to the Philippines. One of the purposes of the Portuguese in seeking the sea route to the Indies was to make direct contact with the sources of the spices which were so important in the Eastern commerce of the time. The Spice Islands were in the East Indies, and the Portuguese were, therefore, not satisfied until they had reached them. Again and again explorers attempted to find sea routes past the barrier placed by the Americas between Europe and the Far East. The many efforts to discover a northwest passage and Magellan's successful voyage around South America were among the results.

Since the Far East was such a magnet to the doughty European adventurers of the fifteenth, sixteenth, and seventeenth centuries, it is not strange that mariners from the Occident made their way to China in Ming times. The Portuguese were the first to come in force. In 1511 they took possession of Malacca. Very soon afterward, probably in 1514, they reached China. To the Chinese they proved lawless and troublesome. They were expelled from the mainland and set up a temporary trading center on an island off the estuary of the West River. In the latter half of the sixteenth century they effected a permanent settlement at Macao, on a peninsula on a large island not far from Canton, and there they have remained to this day. Long before the end of the Ming the Spaniards had conquered the major part of the Philippines and from there were coming to China. The Dutch were not so prominent as some of the other trading powers, but shortly before the downfall of the Ming they also arrived. The English, who were to be the leading power in battering down the doors of China in the nineteenth century, arrived only a very little while before the Ming gave way to the Manchus.

Under the Ming, the impact of the Occident had two phases, commercial and religious. Commerce was entirely on the south coast, chiefly through Macao and Canton. It was the means, now and under the next dynasty, of introducing and popularizing food plants from the Americas, among them maize, the peanut, and the sweet potato. The tobacco plant was also brought in and became widespread.

The religious impact was made both from the coast and in the interior. After the expulsion of the Mongols, Christianity died out a second time from China Proper. Indeed, in contrast with its persistence on the periphery between the T'ang and the Yüan, Christianity now disappeared from all the lands that bordered on China Proper. In the latter part of the Ming it was reintroduced by Roman Catholics from Europe. The European age of discoveries coincided with a great religious awakening in Western Europe. In Roman Catholic circles this gave rise to the most extensive missionary enterprise which Christianity had thus far produced. Roman Catholic missionaries proclaimed their message over much of the Americas, along the shores of Africa, on the southern coasts of Asia, and in many of the islands and most of the countries of the Far East. The large majority of the missionaries were members of religious orders—Franciscans, Dominicans, Augustinians, Jesuits, and a number of smaller groups. The Jesuits, of a society which was brought into being in the revival of the sixteenth century, were particularly prominent. Their great pioneer in Southern and Eastern Asia, Francis Xavier, was the first to make a serious attempt to renew the faith in China. In a vain effort to enter China, he died off the south coast late in 1552. Xavier was followed by others of his society. These entered by way of Portuguese Macao. Their chief figure under the Ming was an Italian, Matthew Ricci. Ricci won the friendship of Chinese officials. His knowledge of mathematics and astronomy was greater than any in the China of his day, he made himself a respectable scholar in Chinese literature, and he tactfully sought to find points of similarity between Christianity and classical Chinese concepts and terms and to permit to Christians the important rites in modified form in honor of ancestors and of Confucius. Thus he commended himself and the faith he represented to the educated class who ruled the Empire. He succeeded in establishing his residence in Peking and opened the way for other members of his society. Members of other orders also entered, some of them Spaniards, by way of the Philippines. In the last days of the Ming, when the Ming forces had been driven into the south, several members of the imperial family were baptized. However, through the Empire as a whole only a few converts had been made. Neither through commerce nor through Christianity did the Occident have much effect upon Ming China.

The Ch'ing to the First Yielding to the Occident (1644–1838)

The Ming were forced to go the way of their predecessors by a fresh wave of conquerors from the north, the Manchus. The Manchus, as may be guessed from their name, were from what we traditionally know as Manchuria. The Manchus were a Tungusic people, related to the Juchên, whom we have met as invaders of China during Sung times. At the dawn of the sixteenth century they were living in what are now the central and northern portions of Manchuria. In the latter part of the sixteenth and in the early part of the seventeenth century, they were welded into an effective fighting force. They took Mukden from the Ming and moved their capital there. Numbers of Mongols accepted their rule, some from force and others voluntarily.

The Manchus attempted to extend their domains south of the Great Wall. About the middle of the seventeenth century their opportunity came. In China Proper a rebellion fomented by famine and heavy taxation broke out against the declining Ming. The leader of the revolt captured Peking, and the Ming Emperor hanged himself as the city fell (1644). The Manchus joined forces with one of the Ming generals, marched on Peking, and seized it. The rebel forces were scattered and their leader disappeared.

Although the year (1644) in which the last of the Ming to reign in Peking came to his unhappy end is reckoned as the transition to the Ch'ing dynasty (as the line is called which the Manchus set up), the conquest was neither quickly nor easily accomplished. Not until 1662 did the last Ming claimant to the throne perish. The Ming adherents retreated, fighting, until they were driven to the extreme southwestern border of China. The Manchu victory had been assisted by divisions among the Chinese and by aid from Chinese generals and armies. Indeed, without this it might not have been accomplished.

Even more than the Mongols, the Manchus ruled as Chinese Emperors and through Chinese officials and Chinese institutions. Each of the chief bureaus and departments at the capital had a Chinese as well as a Manchu head. The traditional bureaucracy was continued along with the examinations through which the membership of civil service was recruited. With some modifications, the Ming code of laws was kept.

Yet the Manchus attempted to preserve their identity and to rule as conquerors. They maintained some of their own customs and dress. They kept garrisons in several of the strategic points and chief cities. As a precaution against his building up a seditious following among his kinsfolk and fellow provincials, they did not permit an official to serve in his native province. They moved officials fairly frequently, probably to prevent a man through long tenure from gathering a powerful local clientele. They had a system of checks by leading provincial officials on one another. Special messengers were sent from time to time to observe local developments and report back to the capital. Not all of these measures were invented by the Manchus, nor were they all adopted at once. Early in their rule the Manchus encountered a rebellion of some of the Chinese who had assisted them and who had been given high posts in the south. The uprising was so formidable that the Manchus sought to safeguard themselves against another like it. Moreover, as a badge of loyalty the Manchus required the Chinese men to adopt the Manchu fashion of wearing the hair, the shaved forehead and the queue. While the Manchus took over much of Chinese culture, they attempted to keep themselves on top.

The long duration of Manchu power was made possible largely by able reigns in the forepart of the dynasty. The two most notable of these each lasted for more than half a century. Together, with a brief, rather colorless reign which came between them, they spanned more than a century and a quarter.

The first of the two great Manchu Emperors was the second to have his capital in Peking. He is best known by the title of his reign, K'ang Hsi. The K'ang Hsi Emperor ruled from 1661 to 1722. He was thus a contemporary of such notable monarchs as Louis XIV of France, Peter the Great of Russia, and the fanatically Moslem Aurangzeb of the Mogul line in India. He was probably fully the equal in ability of any of them. His realm was more extensive than that of any except possibly Peter the Great and it was probably the most populous and wealthy on the face of the globe.

The other long reign is that which goes by the title of Ch'ien Lung. The Ch'ien Lung Emperor was a grandson of the K'ang Hsi Emperor and was on the throne from 1736 to 1796. In the latter year he abdicated, but he continued to dominate the state until his death, in 1799. He, too, was able, probably as much so as the two outstanding European monarchs of his day, Frederick the Great of Prussia and Catherine of Russia. Under him the Ch'ing reached their zenith and began to decline. In his later years internal unrest and corruption in high places gave warning that Heaven might withdraw its mandate from his house. None who came after him equaled himself or his grandfather. They were all mediocrities or worse. Yet the dynasty went on and was not deposed until 1912. By that time the Far East had been thrust into the new era which we are to treat in the later portions of our narrative.

It was during the K'ang Hsi and Ch'ien Lung periods that the realm ruled by the Ch'ing reached its widest extent. Indeed, no previous dynasty had boasted such broad domains. Manchuria was retained, and the northern limits were fixed at the northern watershed of the Amur, far beyond where they now are. Some of the Mongols, as we have seen, had been associated with the Manchus in the conquest of China. The rest of the Mongols were now brought into subjection to the Ch'ing. The Tarim Basin was conquered and administratively organized, with adjoining territory on the north, as Sinkiang, "the New Dominion." Tibet was subdued and the Manchu authority was pressed southward into Nepal. Burma was invaded and was compelled to send periodical tribute. Annam was under the suzerainty of the Ch'ing. Formosa was made a part of the Empire. The Liu Ch'iu (Ryukyu) Islands were claimed as vassals and sent tribute. Korea recognized the overlordship of Peking. Much of the relationship between the Ch'ing court and the vassal states was unlike anything existing in the Occident. It had commercial aspects. Indeed, the "tribute" was largely offset by compensating return "gifts" which had resemblances to trade. Yet the connection of suzerain and vassal was political as well as economic. It was a vast empire which the great monarchs of the Ch'ing transmitted to their unworthy successors.

Under the firm but benevolent rule of the K'ang Hsi and Ch'ien Lung Emperors, moreover, China Proper became more populous than ever before. Accurate census figures have never been obtainable for China. However, it seems clear that in the eighteenth century the population more than doubled. By the time that the Ch'ien Lung Emperor abdicated, it was probably more than three hundred millions. Never before had there been anywhere on the earth so populous an empire. The vast increase was due in part to the peace and order maintained by these two monarchs. It may also have been possible by the food plants which, as we saw a few paragraphs above, were brought in from the Americas. Certainly deforestation and the terracing of the hillsides were greatly increased in the seventeenth and eighteenth centuries.

In culture the Ch'ing period was largely a continuation of the Ming.

An enormous amount of literature was issued. In sheer bulk more printed books existed in China than in all the rest of the world. Much of the new production was pedestrian, the product of uninspired even though painstaking labor. Great compilations of existing literature were made, what we somewhat loosely but not quite accurately term encyclopedias. One of the most famous of the dictionaries of the language was put together and is designated by the name of K'ang Hsi.

Yet there was some originality. The Chinese genius was by no means moribund. Novels continued to be written, among them what are probably some of the greatest ever composed in China. One of the best known bears a title which is often translated as *The Dream of the Red Chamber.* Moreover, a most interesting and original school of historical scholarship appeared. Its members were in rebellion against the officially orthodox Sung philosophy. This was in part because they were distressed by the weakness of the Chinese before the alien conquerors and were inclined to find the cause in the type of thought which controlled the state. They believed the difficulty to be not with Confucianism but with its interpretation. They sought, therefore, to go back to the texts of the ancient books as they had come down to them from the Sung and to reach, if possible, the originals. The earliest texts which they had any hope of obtaining were in the forms in which they had been edited by the Han scholars. They endeavored, accordingly, to restore the Han texts. As a result their school is known as *The Han Learning.* They reached some startling conclusions and, quite independently of Western influence, worked out methods for determining the validity of a text which are not unlike those employed by the best Occidental scholarship. The Chinese mind still had daring and vigor.

In art, much activity and skill were displayed. There were many painters, but their work did not attain the heights of the great masters of the T'ang and the Sung. Beautiful porcelain was produced. Vast quantities issued from the potteries at Ching-tê-chên. The best examples are justly famous for technical skill and color. Yet in art no such creative and original genius was present as in earlier times.

The Occidentals Persist

The contacts with Europeans which the Ming had witnessed continued. Westerners persisted in coming by both sea and land. By the sea came Portuguese, Spaniards, Dutch, French, English, and a few Italians and Germans. Toward the end of the period, beginning in 1784, after their war of independence from Great Britain, Americans arrived from the new United States. By land came Russians. As under the Ming, some of the Occidentals sought China for purposes of commerce and some as Christian missionaries.

Commerce was carried on under embarrassing restrictions. Economically the Empire was practically self-sufficient. An imperial document declared loftily and quite accurately that China did not need the goods of Europe. Until opium began to be imported in quantity, not many decades before the wars of the mid-nineteenth century, Westerners were hard put to it to find merchandise which the Chinese would take in exchange for the products that the Occident wished from China. To balance their account they imported silver. Sea-borne commerce was compelled to come chiefly through Canton. There the foreigners were confined to a small district, the "Factories," on the waterfront outside the city wall. In the off-season they were supposed to reside in Macao, the little foothold near by still held by the Portuguese. During much of the period a group of Chinese merchants, the *Co-hong*, had an official monopoly of the trade. The Chinese did not dream of receiving resident ambassadors at Peking or of diplomatic intercourse on the basis of equality. The Russians were permitted to maintain a mission at Peking, made up largely of ecclesiastics, which formed a channel for such negotiations as were needed for the trickle of overland trade between the two empires. The Russian territorial advance was successfully resisted by force of arms. Several treaties, the first of them signed in 1689, at Nerchinsk, defined the boundary and regulated the intercourse between the two realms.

Attempts were made to obtain better facilities for trade and diplomacy. In 1793 and again in 1816 embassies from Great Britain reached Peking, the first headed by the Earl of Macartney and the second by Lord Amherst, but in each instance they were treated as bearers of gifts from a tributary state and their major requests were denied. A Dutch embassy in 1795 and a Russian one in 1806 met with no better success. The Manchu Emperors took the traditional Chinese attitude and regarded themselves as the supreme rulers of mankind and all others as barbarians and subordinate. When, in the nineteenth century, European peoples became more powerful and better able to back up their requests by force, an open and violent clash was inevitable.

Christian missions were still predominantly Roman Catholic. Additional missionaries came and penetrated to all of the provinces. For a time in the latter part of the seventeenth century they enjoyed a slight degree of popularity. In Peking Jesuits had charge of the imperial calendar and observatory and proved useful in negotiations with the Russians. The K'ang Hsi Emperor, with his inquiring mind, found interesting what they told him of European learning. In 1692 he issued what in effect was an edict of toleration. At the dawn of the eighteenth century the number of Roman Catholic Christians in the Empire was probably more than two hundred thousand.

However, the eighteenth century proved difficult. A prolonged controversy among the missionaries over what were known as the Rites divided the foreign staff, which was never numerous, and weakened its morale. The issue was the legitimacy of accommodations to Chinese culture such as Ricci had advocated. After prolonged deliberation, Rome decided against them. This antagonized the K'ang Hsi Emperor, who had come out in favor of them. The century was marked by increasing persecution, due in part to the fear of the Manchus of all possible sources of sedition and rebellion. Portugal and Spain, which had been important as supporters of missions, were waning powers. The Society of Jesus, which had supplied more missionaries than any other body, was dissolved by the Pope (1773). The skepticism of eighteenth-century Europe undercut missionary enthusiasm, and the French Revolution and the ensuing Napoleonic wars meant diminished support and fewer recruits from Europe.

At the beginning of the nineteenth century Roman Catholic missions had lost ground. The Russian Orthodox Church was represented by a few ecclesiastics in Peking and by the descendants of a small group of prisoners taken in a clash between the Russians and Manchus in the latter part of the seventeenth century, but no converts were made. The first Protestant missionary entered China Proper in 1807, but until after the wars between China and Great Britain, Protestant Christianity made almost no impression on the Empire. Chinese culture was still too solidly intact and was too closely integrated with Confucianism to permit Christianity much growth.

China in Europe

In the eighteenth century China had more effect upon European culture than the Occident had upon China. For a time China was idealized and things Chinese were popular. The intellectuals of the Enlightenment thought that they saw in China an embodiment of their dreams—a realm ruled by philosophers and by reason—and in Confucianism a "natural religion" akin to their Deism, with a reverent regard for a Supreme Being whom man had discovered and who had not, as Christians declared, revealed Himself uniquely and supremely in Jesus of Nazareth. Chinese art and art objects were in vogue. Gardens, pagodas, and pavilions in Chinese style were built by those who could afford them. Many flowers and plants were introduced from China. Tea, incense, lacquer, Chinese colors, the Chinese style of painting, and sedan chairs were fashionable. Wallpapers came in, some of them imported from China, and others in imitation of those of Chinese manufacture. Porcelain was highly prized, some of it brought directly from China and some of it, because of the Chinese example, produced in Europe.

All of this was superficial. The basic patterns of Western life were not altered. Yet Europeans were more ready to grant that China had a civilization which was worthy of respect and to pay it the flattery of imitation than were the Chinese to copy Europe. At best the Europeans were to the Chinese amusing barbarians whose mathematics and astronomy were useful and whose painting and architecture were diverting. The Chinese had no inkling that these strangers from the West were soon to level the barriers raised against them and to bring revolution which would shake the very foundations of civilization as the Chinese had known it and usher in a completely new era in the history of the Empire and of the Far East.

Summary

The political and social structure and the basic attitudes toward life which emerged from the creative minds of the Shang, the Chou, the Ch'in, and the Han periods went on from the third into the nineteenth century without fundamental alterations. Again and again China was invaded. From time to time it was conquered in whole or in part. Indeed, in the latter of the nearly two millenniums which elapsed between the heyday of the Han and the revolution wrought by the Occident, alien domination increased. Some cultural importations entered and brought modifications to Chinese life. Of these the most influential was Buddhism. Buddhism not only became prominent as a cult and introduced new conceptions of philosophy, of life and death, and of spiritual beings, but it also served as a vehicle for new forms of art. Yet in their essence and main outlines China and Chinese culture entered the nineteenth century much the same as they had entered the third century. Dynasty had followed dynasty, some long and ruling all of China Proper, and some short and having control over only a part of the Chinese. Modifications were made, so that each major dynasty and period had characteristics which marked it off from its predecessors and successors. However, a Chinese who had entered into a Rip Van Winkle sleep in the Later Han and had awakened in the declining years of the Ch'ing would have felt more nearly at home than would a Western European who had gone to sleep in the fourteenth century and roused to find himself in the nineteenth century. The Chinese would have had his great surprise had he been restored to consciousness in the second quarter of the twentieth century.

BIBLIOGRAPHY

For Brief Reference

K. S. Latourette, *The Chinese, Their History and Culture* (New York, 1945), Chapters IV, V, VI, VII, VIII, IX.

For More Extended Study

ON THE BARBARIAN INVASIONS BETWEEN THE HAN AND THE SUI

O. Lattimore, *Inner Asian Frontiers of China* (London, 1940).
W. M. McGovern, *The Early Empires of Central Asia* (Chapel Hill, 1939).
E. H. Parker, *A Thousand Years of the Tartars* (London, 1924).

ON THE FURTHER INTRODUCTION AND DEVELOPMENT OF BUDDHISM

C. Eliot, *Hinduism and Buddhism* (London, 1921).
J. Legge, *A Record of Buddhistic Kingdoms, Being an Account by the Chinese Monk Fa Hien of His Travels in India and Ceylon* (A.D. *399–414*) *in Search of the Buddhistic Books of Discipline, translated and annotated with a Corean Recension of the Chinese Text* (Oxford, 1886).
K. L. Reichelt, *Truth and Tradition in Chinese Buddhism* (Shanghai, 1927).

ON THE SUI AND THE T'ANG

W. Barthold, *Turkestan down to the Mongol Invasion* (London, 1928).
C. P. Fitzgerald, *Son of Heaven, A Biography of Li Shih-min, founder of the T'ang Dynasty* (Cambridge, 1933).
H. A. R. Gibb, *The Arab Conquests in Central Asia* (London, 1923).
A. von Le Coq, *Buried Treasures of Chinese Turkestan* (London, 1928).
A. Stein, *On Ancient Central-Asian Tracks: A Brief Narrative of Three Expeditions in Innermost Asia and Northwestern China* (London, 1933).
A. Stein, *Serindia* (Oxford, 1921).

ON FOREIGN COMMERCE UNDER THE T'ANG

F. Hirth and W. W. Rockhill, *Chau Ju-Kua* (St. Petersburg, 1912).
A. Stein, *Innermost Asia* (Oxford, 1928).

ON BUDDHIST PILGRIMS UNDER THE T'ANG

S. Beal, *The Life of Hiuen-Tsiang by the Shaman Hwui Li* (London, 1911).
S. Beal, *Si-Yu-Ki. Buddhistic Records of the Western World. Translated from the Chinese of Hiuen Tsiang* (A.D. *629*) (London, 1906).

ON THE BEGINNING OF PRINTING

T. F. Carter, *The Invention of Printing in China and Its Spread Westward* (New York, 1931).

ON THE INTRODUCTION OF FOREIGN RELIGIONS OTHER THAN BUDDHISM

J. Foster, *The Church of the T'ang Dynasty* (London, 1939).
A. V. W. Jackson, *Researches in Manichæism* (New York, 1932).
K. S. Latourette, *A History of Christian Missions in China* (New York and London, 1929).
A. C. Moule, *Christians in China before the Year 1550* (London, 1930).

ON WANG AN-SHIH

H. R. Williamson, *Wang An Shih* (London, 1935, 1937).

ON THE SUNG NEO-CONFUCIANISM

J. P. Bruce, *Chu Hsi and His Masters* (London, 1923).
J. P. Bruce, *The Philosophy of Human Nature by Chu Hsi* (London, 1922).

ON THE MONGOL CONQUEST

H. H. Howorth, *History of the Mongols from the Ninth to the Nineteenth Century* (London, 1876–1888).

ON CONTACTS WITH EUROPEANS UNDER THE MONGOLS

E. Bretschneider, *Medieval Researches from Eastern Asiatic Sources* (London, 1910).
W. W. Rockhill, *The Journey of William of Rubruck to the Eastern Parts of the World, 1253–55* (London, 1900).
H. Yule, *Cathay and the Way Thither* (new edition by H. Cordier, London, 1913–1916).
H. Yule, *The Book of Ser Marco Polo* (new edition by H. Cordier, 1921).

ON WANG YANG-MING

F. G. Henke, *The Philosophy of Wang Yang-ming* (London, 1916).

ON THE MANCHU BEGINNINGS

F. Michael, *The Origin of Manchu Rule in China* (Baltimore, 1942).

ON ART AND ARCHITECTURE

C. Hentze, *Chinese Tomb Figures* (London, 1928).
R. L. Hobson and A. L. Hetherington, *The Art of the Chinese Potter from the Han Dynasty to the End of the Ming* (London, 1923).
O. Sirén, *Chinese Sculptures from the Fifth and the Fourteenth Century* (London, 1925).
A. Waley, *An Introduction to the Study of Chinese Painting* (London, 1923).

ON POETRY

F. Ayscough, *Tu Fu. The Autobiography of a Chinese Poet Arranged from his Poems and Translated* (Boston, 1929).
W. Bynner and Kiang Kang-hu, *The Jade Mountain. A Chinese Anthology.*

Being Three Hundred Poems of the T'ang Dynasty 618–906 (New York, 1929).
A. Waley, *A Hundred and Seventy Chinese Poems* (New York, 1909).

ON CONTACTS WITH EUROPE UNDER THE MING AND THE CH'ING

G. F. Hudson, *Europe and China: A Survey of Their Relations from the Earliest Times to 1800* (London, 1931).
K. S. Latourette, *The History of Early Relations between the United States and China 1784–1844* (New Haven, 1917).
H. B. Morse, *The International Relations of the Chinese Empire* (Vol. I, New York, 1910).
H. B. Morse, *The Chronicles of the East India Company Trading to China 1635–1834* (Cambridge and Oxford, 1926, 1929).
A. Reichwein, *China and Europe: Intellectual and Artistic Contacts in the Eighteenth Century* (New York, 1925).

ON ONE FOREIGN CONQUEROR UNDER THE SUNG, BUT WITH IMPLICATIONS FOR ALL FOREIGN CONQUESTS OF CHINA

K. A. Wittfogel and Fêng Chia-shêng, *History of Chinese Society. Liao (907–1125)* (Philadelphia, 1949).

Chapter V. CHINESE CIVILIZATION

The Chinese and their culture on the eve of the changes wrought by the Occident

AFTER THIS HISTORICAL SURVEY of the development of China up to the beginning of the revolutionary contacts with the Occident, and before passing on to a description of these events, we will do well to try to form a picture of the Chinese and their culture on the eve of the great changes. What were the characteristics of the Chinese and what were their institutions which were to be so profoundly altered? Obviously much of the old China has passed over into the new, and the new cannot be understood without some comprehension of the old from which it is sprung.

The World-Embracing Ideal of Chinese Culture

First of all, it is important to note that the old China was an empire rather than a state. To the Chinese and their rulers, the word China did not exist and to them it would have been meaningless. They sometimes used a term which we translate "the Middle Kingdom." To them there could be only one legitimate ruler for all civilized mankind. All others were rightly subordinate to him and should acknowledge his suzerainty. From this standpoint, there could not, as in Europe, be diplomatic relations between equal states, each of them sovereign. When, in the nineteenth century, Europeans insisted upon intercourse with China on the basis of equality, the Chinese were at first amused and then scandalized and indignant. Centuries of training had bred in them the conviction that all other rulers should be tributary to the Son of Heaven.

The tie which bound this world-embracing empire together, so the Chinese were taught to believe, was as much cultural as political. As there could be only one legitimate ruler to whom all mankind must be subject, so there could be only one culture that fully deserved to be called civilized. Other cultures might have worth, but ultimately they were more or less barbarous. There could be only one civilization, and that was the civilization of the Middle Kingdom. Beginning with the Han, the ideal of civilization was held to be Confucian. The Confucian interpretation of civilization was adopted and inculcated as the norm. Others might be tolerated, but if they seriously threatened the Confucian institutions and foundations of society they were to be curbed and, perhaps, exterminated as a threat to the highest values.

Since the bond of the Empire was cultural and since the Empire should include all civilized mankind, racial distinctions were not so marked as in most other parts of the world. The Chinese did not have so strong a sense of being of different blood from non-Chinese as twentieth-century conceptions of race and nation later led them to develop. They were proud of being "the sons of Han" or "the men of T'ang," but if a people fully adopted Chinese culture no great distinction was perceived between them and those who earlier had been governed by that culture.

This helps to account for the comparative contentment of Chinese under alien rulers. If, as was usually the case, these invading conquerors adopted the culture of their subjects and governed through the accustomed machinery and by traditional Confucian principles, they were accepted as legitimate Emperors. Few of the non-Chinese dynasties completely made this identification. This probably in part accounts for such restiveness as the Chinese showed under their rule. For instance, so long as they were dominant, the Manchus, while they accepted much of the Chinese culture and prided themselves on being experts in it and posed as its patrons, never completely abandoned their distinctive ancestral ways.

The fact that the tie was cultural rather than racial helps to account for the remarkable homogeneity of the Chinese. Many different ethnic strains have gone to make up the people whom we call the Chinese. Presumably in the Chou and probably, earlier, in the Shang, the bearers of Chinese culture were not a single race. As Chinese culture moved southward it encountered differing cultures and, almost certainly, divergent stocks. The many invaders from the north and west brought in more variety. In contrast with India, where caste and religion have tended to keep apart the racial strata, in China assimilation made great progress. That assimilation has not been complete. Today the discerning observer can notice differences even among those who are Chinese in language and customs, and in many parts of China Proper there are groups who preserve not only their racial but also their linguistic and cultural identity. Still, nowhere else on the globe is there so numerous a people who are so nearly homogeneous as are the Chinese.

This homogeneity is due not merely to a common cultural tie, but also to the particular kind of culture which constitutes that tie. Something in the Chinese tradition has recognized as civilized those who conform to certain ethical standards and social customs. It was the fitting into Confucian patterns of conduct and of family and community life rather than blood kinship or ancestry which labeled one as civilized and as Chinese.

The Political Structure

The instrument through which the Empire was held together and cultural unity was achieved was the government.

At the head of the government was the Emperor. In theory, as we have said, he was the ruler of all mankind. As there was only one sun in the heavens so there was only one Emperor on earth. In theory, too, he held his position through the mandate of Heaven and ruled by his "virtue." That "virtue" had ethical content. It also implied adequate force.

In practice, as we have seen, each dynasty was founded by a successful warrior who seized the throne through the rough and tumble of civil strife and passed it on to his descendants. Usually, too, somewhere in the early course of the dynasty was an unusually able monarch under whom that particular ruling house reached its apex. Then would follow a more or less prolonged period of decline. The dominant family would succumb before the baleful influence of the court with its luxury, the intrigues of its eunuchs and its women, and its remoteness from the everyday life of the people. Misgovernment or weakness would give rise to rebellions, never far below the surface. In time a rebel or a foreign invader would upset the ruling line, place himself on the throne, and thus demonstrate by his prowess that he had in turn been given the mandate of Heaven.

Underneath the Emperor was a bureaucracy, appointed from the capital and responsible to it. Important in it were ministries in the capital itself which headed various branches of the state. Among these, under the Ch'ing, were the Board of Civil Office, the Board of Revenue, the Board of Ceremonies, the Board of War, and the Board of Punishments (or better, the Board of Law). There were also a consorate, whose business it was to watch and, if necessary, criticize officials, up to and including the Emperor himself; an Office of Transmission which opened, recorded, and transmitted memorials on routine matters; and a Grand Court of Revision which exercised a general supervision over the administration of the criminal law. Above these, under the Manchus, was the Grand Council, or Council of State, which usually met every morning in the presence of the sovereign to discuss the most important items of public business. In theory above the Grand Council was a body created by the Ming, the Grand Secretariat (more literally, Inner Cabinet or Hall), but under the Ch'ing it was left with functions which were almost nominal, somewhat like the modern Privy Council in England, with much honor and little work.

For administrative purposes China Proper was divided into provinces. These varied in number, but during most of the nineteenth century totaled eighteen. Indeed, one of the designations of China Proper was "the Eighteen Provinces." The leading officers in each province were usually (to employ a rather loose translation of their titles) a Viceroy or a Governor (generally a Viceroy was over two provinces), a Treasurer, a Judge, a Salt Comptroller (salt was a state monopoly), and a Grain Intendant (for a large proportion of the taxes was paid in grain).

The provinces were in turn divided into smaller units to facilitate local administration. Of these the one which came most closely in touch with the people was the *hsien*, roughly corresponding to a township or precinct. The official who headed it had a combination of functions—those of judge, head of the police, collector of taxes, officiator at various religious observances, and other administrative duties.

The bureaucracy was divided into two wings, civil and military. Of these the civil was the more highly esteemed. Both were recruited through competitive examinations. Back of the examinations was the principle that offices should be filled on the basis of worth and not of birth. To have allowed birth to be the determining factor, as the Chinese early discovered, would have resulted in splitting the realm into hereditary principalities and would have made effective unity impossible.

Of the two sets of examinations the more highly regarded was that leading into the civil service. It was grueling in the extreme. The main tests were three in number. As a rule, a man was eligible for office only if he had passed successively and successfully all three. In each, especially the lower ones, only a small percentage of the contestants could be awarded the coveted degrees. That meant that many thousand more went through the educational process of preparing for them than ultimately held office. In the last few centuries of the examinations the emphasis was upon the Confucian classics. Since most of the formal education in China Proper was to prepare aspirants, since, except for members of a few despised occupations, anyone might enroll as a candidate, regardless of birth, and since tens of thousands entered into the elementary stages of the course for every one who attained the third degree, a wide diffusion of the common body of standard Confucian literature was assured. The prestige which attached to the scholar also gave currency to the ideals for which the *literati* stood. The bureaucracy and the civil service examinations, therefore, were an unrivaled means of furthering cultural unity.

The price China paid for this cultural unity was, as we have suggested, heavy. More and more through the centuries the civil service examinations and the education leading to them became stereotyped. They stressed memory, literary style, and conformity to established standards. Originality of thought was discouraged. The Chinese mind, thus shackled, created progressively less that was new. Indeed, the desire to produce novelties was looked at askance. The ideal was to conform to the ways of the ancient sages and not to seek fresh paths.

The ideals of Chinese government were shaped by the schools that had arisen during the Chou. Confucianism was dominant, but both Legalism and Taoism had left their imprint.

To Legalism are probably ascribable the codes of law. Each dynasty promulgated its own code, but as a rule it took over that of its predecessor and contented itself with modifications in it. The codes dealt primarily with what we in the Occident call criminal matters; what we know as civil law was not prominent. From Legalism, too, may have been derived the state granaries in which the tribute grain was stored in such fashion that it could be issued to equalize prices, particularly in times of scarcity.

From Taoism may have come reinforcement to one of the features of Chinese government—the slight control exercised by the central government. Some control there was, but the ideal appears to have been to have as little interference as possible from the imperial bureaucracy.

To this the Confucian ideal contributed. Confucianism, which, after all, was dominant, held that government should be by the moral example of the rulers and not by crude force. If, therefore, the Emperor, his ministers, and the bureaucracy were worthy in their lives, all would go well. If disasters overtook the Empire, the Emperor, in official proclamation, might blame himself and his lack of worth. While on occasion force was used, and used drastically, officials believed it to be a last resort. The preference was for persuasion and reason. Official proclamations employed the tone of argument as much as command. In the Ch'ing dynasty some sententious maxims of the K'ang Hsi Emperor were expanded into homilies in the vernacular, and as the Sacred Edict were read officially to the people throughout the Empire at stated intervals. The Sacred Edict embodied Confucian morality. It appealed to the good sense of the listeners and had little to say of penalties enforced by the courts.

Probably in accordance with the Confucian and Taoist tradition, and possibly because of some lingering traces of the school of Mo Ti, military methods and the army were looked down upon. In contrast with Europe and with Japan, where a large proportion of the aristocracy has traditionally been tied closely to military occupations, socially the civil official and the scholar far outranked the soldier. Fighting was, in theory, beneath the dignity of a gentleman.

In practice these ideals were far from being observed. Officials were often notoriously corrupt. Office and literary degrees were sometimes purchased. Official moral exhortations were hypocritical devices which deceived only the simple. Chinese history has in it as much fighting as do the annals of the Occident. Again and again the Empire has been wasted by war. Indeed, pacifism has not had as much practical effectiveness in China as in the West. Some of the most popular tales purveyed by the professional storyteller and the theater and elaborated on the pages of the most widely read romances reek with bloodshed and glorify the exploits of the soldier. Every dynasty was founded by a successful warrior.

Yet the ideals have been there and have not been without their influence. The system produced many characters of great nobility and unswerving integrity. In their private as in their public relations the Chinese have relied strongly upon reason and have felt that they must give excuses for the use of force. The sage, who was the ideal extolled by Confucianism, was wise, learned, cultivated, and, above all, moral. He might on occasion resort to arms, but his greatest triumphs were those of reason and peace.

Actually the major part of social control was exercised not by the central government and its officers, but by local, self-governing units—the family, the village with its elders, and the guilds. The imperial machinery brought cohesion to the entire structure, but it interfered as little as possible in the affairs of the individual and the units which made up the community.

The imperial structure, on the whole, performed the tasks designed for it extremely well. It held together China Proper, a vast area measured in pre-nineteenth century time-distances. It was too decentralized to hold at bay a powerful, well-organized, aggressive invader. This fact helps to account for the frequent conquest of China in whole or in part. It also contributed to the weakness of China before the Occident and Japan in the nineteenth and twentieth centuries.

The Chinese Family

Fully as important as the state was the family. Of the five relationships of which the prevailing ethics spoke—prince and minister, father and son, husband and wife, elder brother and younger brother, friend and friend—three had to do with the family and only one with the state. This was a rough approximation to the situation in actual practice. Most men and women felt their primary loyalty to be to their family. If a man defrauded the state to benefit his family his dishonesty was popularly condoned. Nepotism was not so much a sin as a virtue. The family had functions which in the modern West are commonly assumed by the state. It educated its youth, cared for its unemployed, disciplined its erring members, and supported its aged. In turn, the state held the family accountable for the misdeeds of its members. In many instances prosperous families lived together in huge aggregations in a village or a series of courtyards, controlled by the elders or a grandfather or grandmother.

The family included not only the living, but also the dead. Those who were well-to-do kept elaborate family records. Many had ancestral halls in which tablets to deceased members were preserved and honored, and in which meetings of the family were held. Ceremonies in honor of the ancestors were regularly maintained. Tablets to deceased parents and to the ancestors were part of the equipment of every respectable home.

Filial piety was a major duty. Parents were to be cherished while living and revered when dead. Any conduct which would bring them sorrow or discredit was to be eschewed. A frequently quoted story, probably apocryphal but true to the spirit of the Chinese, tells of an aged father punishing a son, himself somewhat advanced in years, by beating him. When the latter wailed under the chastisement, the father inquired whether he were hurting him more than usual. The son replied that he was weeping because the blows were feebler than on earlier occasions and, therefore, he was heartbroken at the thought of soon losing his parent.

The individual was of far less importance than the family. The individual member was to make his earnings available to his less fortunate relatives. By that same token, he knew that he himself, if overtaken by ill fortune, could always be sure of a bowl of rice in his family village. Marriage was primarily not for the happiness of those who entered into that relationship, but for the purpose of continuing the family line. No sin was greater than that of dying without leaving male issue to revere the memory of one's ancestors. Marriage was, accordingly, a family affair. It was arranged by the elders. Frequently the young couple did not see each other until the close of the marriage ceremony. Marriages, births, and other important events were formally announced to the ancestors.

Since descent was by the male line, boys were more highly valued than girls. To obtain succession, adoption of a son might be resorted to. Women were in an inferior position. The handicap was increased by a custom of long standing, the binding of the feet of women. The practice had no religious significance or sanction, and some groups, the Manchus for instance, did not conform to it. Yet it was held that if a girl were to obtain a desirable husband her feet must be bound. This involved the painful and sometimes dangerous cramping of the toes and was a restriction to freedom of movement and healthy exercise. However, while women were held in less regard than men, they were not without honor. A mother was revered by her sons, and a mother-in-law and a grandmother, particularly if she were a widow, had much influence in the home. Moreover, if she had force of character a woman could dominate her husband. Then, too, monogamy was the rule. If he were able to support them, a husband might take a concubine or concubines, either to satisfy his fancy or to provide him with a male heir if his wife failed to do so. A wife might even take the initiative in providing a concubine for her husband to obtain for him a son. Yet the wife far outranked the concubine and often it was felt necessary to apologize for the latter. Woman's lot in China, then, was not so servile as in some other lands. It is not entirely surprising that in the twentieth century women took a prominent part in the new order.

Economic Life

Until the unprecedented increase of population under the Manchus, China Proper had ample room for all the Chinese. From time to time wars had brought a reduction. Floods and drought often wrought disaster on a large scale. Pestilence took its toll. The death rate, especially of infants, was high. Until the nineteenth and twentieth centuries China could scarcely be called overcrowded.

The Chinese economy could support a large population. It was diversified. The Chinese were industrious and intelligent.

AGRICULTURE

The chief occupation, as was natural, was agriculture. Probably eighty per cent of the population were either directly engaged in it or were in occupations closely allied with it. The Chinese displayed marked skill in agriculture. They cultivated a wide variety of plants for food, clothing, and shelter. Some of these were indigenous. Many had been introduced from other lands. Even before the nineteenth century some had entered from so distant a region as the Americas. In the north the leading grains were wheat, millet, and kaoliang. In the Yangtze Valley and the south the major grain crop was rice, although in some places wheat was also grown. Rice was of many varieties. Tea was grown and cured for the prevailing beverage. Beans were a major crop, and provided one of the chief sources of protein. From vegetable oil came fats. Cotton was the chief material for clothing, but silk of various kinds had been used for centuries for finer materials, and grass-cloths were woven from several vegetable fibers. The bamboo was employed for a number of purposes—including building material, coarse clothing, and, in the form of young sprouts, for food. Fruits, nuts, and root crops of many kinds were grown. The Chinese seem never to have used milk, butter, or cheese. Thus they saved, probably without deliberate intent, the waste that comes from passing the vegetable products through the animal before obtaining the benefit of the soil. From very early times pork was a food. Some goat meat and mutton were eaten. Chickens entered into the menu, both with their flesh and their eggs. Ducks and geese were reared. The fisherman helped to stock the table. The sea, the lakes, and the rivers were sources of fish, and the thrifty farmer planted fish in his irrigating ponds. Some wool was utilized, especially in the north. The Chinese were adept in conserving the fertility of the soil. They employed leguminous plants in the rotation of crops. They made use of compost. They returned to the fields human excreta instead of wasting it as does much of the modern Occident. They anticipated by many centuries some of the methods of modern scientific agriculture in the West. The Chinese, too, had a crude kind of forestry. In parts of the country they planted trees to be reaped in the future as a profitable crop.

Yet the Chinese utilization of the land had grave defects. The hills were denuded of their forests, and often even grass roots were dug up for fuel. Rains, therefore, robbed the hillsides of their fertile soil and in some places made the plains unfruitful with the detritus. In seed selection the Chinese were weak. The modern West was far in advance of them in fighting the diseases that beset plants and animals. The enormous expenditure of human labor and the comparatively little use of animals in cultivating the soil and the lack of labor-saving machinery probably made for poverty. Much land was allowed to go untilled, both in uplands and in marshy or periodically flooded lowlands, which could have been reclaimed by proper methods. As farmers the Chinese, while skilled, were by no means impeccable. Ruinous interest rates also burdened the cultivator.

INDUSTRY

While agriculture employed the large majority of the population, millions were engaged in industry. The average farmer did not provide much of a market for the manufacturer, for his house and house furnishings were simple and largely made by himself, and his clothing was not elaborate. However, in so large a population those in comfortable circumstances were in the aggregate a considerable number, and the land abounded in towns and cities. Industry was in the handicraft stage. The factory system and labor-saving machinery such as the nineteenth- and twentieth-century Occident knew were in the future. Industry and commerce were organized in guilds. There were guilds for various crafts and, also, those in a large city from another city or province might have a guild for mutual assistance and protection. Some of the guilds were very powerful.

COMMERCE

Commerce, too, was extensive. Traditionally the merchant was below the scholar and farmer in the social scale. No such powerful mercantile class developed as in medieval and modern Europe. The largest fortunes were seldom those accumulated in trade. Yet merchants were numerous, and, as we have said, they were organized into guilds. In many villages fairs were held at regular intervals and to them came traders and farmers.

CURRENCY AND BANKING

China has tried many forms of currency. She early knew the use and the dangers of paper money and even earlier had had experience with debased coinage. At the dawn of the nineteenth century the prevailing coin, indeed the only one then minted in China, was of copper—the "cash," round and with a hole in the center to facilitate stringing and so carrying and counting. Larger sums were represented either by the foreign silver dollars which had begun to come in from Spanish America or, much more usually, by silver ingots which were weighed and tested for fineness in each transaction.

Banking was represented by "cash shops" (whose business it was to carry on exchange between "cash" and silver and between one unit of weight and another), by pawnshops, by merchants who dealt incidentally in bills of exchange, and by institutions which received deposits, made loans, and bought and sold drafts. In the nineteenth century bankers of this latter type were largely from the province of Shansi.

TRANSPORTATION

Commerce was dependent upon means of transportation. Often these were very imperfect. Rivers, especially the Yangtze and its major tributaries, fortunately afforded access to much of the country and were plied by different kinds of craft. Rivers were supplemented by canals, notably the Grand Canal. In the north the roads were of the sort that could be traversed by carts and wheelbarrows. Donkeys were also employed and, for trade with Mongolia, camels. In the Yangtze Valley and the south the typical road could be used only by the wheelbarrow or the coolie, who transported freight by means of a carrying-pole balanced on his shoulders. Travel was either on foot, by horseback, or in a sedan chair. All transportation was slow, and land transportation was also costly. Conditions were probably no worse than in the Occident before the advent of the steamship and the railroad, but time-distances were vast and even internal commerce was handicapped.

MINING

The Chinese did not engage extensively in mining. However, they utilized by simple processes the widely scattered deposits of iron. They early began to burn the coal with which parts of the country were so well supplied. They made use of copper and a little gold and silver.

THE BASIC ECONOMIC PROBLEM

As we saw in the last chapter, by the dawn of the nineteenth century population was multiplying rapidly. We can only surmise the reasons for the increase. Whatever the causes, China Proper was, for the first time, becoming crowded. The Chinese were beginning to spill over its borders. They were occupying Formosa and the southern part of Manchuria. Before long they would be moving overseas. The basic economic problem was the support of population. This was becoming acute in a fresh fashion.

Religion

In their religious life the Chinese presented a number of characteristics.

They were eclectic. The average Chinese did not think of himself as an adherent of any one religion to the exclusion of others. He observed ceremonies that had come down from a remote past. He paid reverence to his ancestors. He praised Confucian ethics. He might have in his home images or pictures of both Taoist and Buddhist divinities. Many a household contained evidence that it honored the three major religions of the land. In a funeral all three faiths might be represented. To be sure, a minority were thoroughgoing adherents of a particular religion. Many scholars held to Confucianism with scorn for all other cults. Numbers of ordinary folk were exclusively devoted to Taoism. Buddhist monks and nuns and lay adherents of some of the vegetarian groups were purely or nearly purely Buddhist. Christians and Moslems religiously kept themselves apart. Yet the vast majority of Chinese sought the advantages of more than one religion and popular folklore bore traces of several religious traditions.

The Chinese, too, were fairly tolerant. Theirs was the tolerance of skepticism. To them all religions might be equally true and equally false and they were prepared to seek whatever advantage might accrue from all or any of them. Yet the tolerance was by no means thoroughgoing. If a religion was believed to threaten the basic structure of Chinese society or morals as defined by Confucianism, the state would curtail it, and mobs, stirred up by the scholars and winked at by officialdom, might take violent action against it. More than once nation-wide efforts forced Buddhist monks back into secular life. Persecutions of Christians were frequent, and from time to time wars which were purely religious were waged against Moslems.

Like most peoples, the Chinese were both this-worldly and other-worldly. They thought of religion as useful to the degree to which it brought them advantages here and now, such as prosperity, health, and sons. They were also other-worldly, and sought through religion a blissful existence after death for themselves and members of their families.

In general, in their outlook the Chinese were optimistic. They were inclined to believe the universe friendly to the righteous.

They were also ethical. Confucianism, Taoism, and Buddhism all inculcated high standards of conduct. Righteous living was demanded by all faiths.

The religious life of China had many components. First was the stream that had come down continuously from very early times. Confucianism, the philosophy which since the Han had enjoyed the support of the state, was, as we have seen, conservative. It prized and inculcated the ceremonies of antiquity. The *Book of Rites*, one of the classics revered by Confucianism, went back in part to the Chou period and was influential in fixing the procedure at funerals and on some other formal occasions. Of course the ceremonies did not persist unaltered. In time both additions and subtractions were made. Yet a great deal that was ancient endured, and much of the general spirit and attitude of antiquity persisted. So the Chinese stressed ceremonies in honor of their ancestors. They spoke of *T'ien*, or "Heaven," as a supreme, personal power, and associated it with another term that had come down from the remote past, *Shang Ti*, "the Supreme Ruler." The Emperor offered a number of sacrifices, either in person or by proxy. The most solemn and impressive of these was on the Altar of Heaven at the winter solstice. Officials in the various provinces and other administrative divisions of the realm were supposed also to participate on certain occasions, among them at sacrifices to the spirits of the rivers and mountains in the locality, to the gods of the soil and the grain at the time of the spring planting, and in the temple of the City God. Ceremonial honors to ancestors were a part of the routine of every well-regulated family, whether official or private.

Closely akin to this contribution from antiquity was a great deal of popular religion. There was an official pantheon to which admission was by imperial decree and in which promotion and demotion were also by act of the Emperor. Most of the members of this pantheon were honored by the populace. Many deities arose through popular initiative. Numbers of them had purely local cults. Thus to some hero or a popular official a temple might be erected and prayers offered. The spirits of the mighty dead were believed to be capable of assisting those who called on them. To the popular mind, moreover, spirits, good and bad, were everywhere. Particularly must men be on their guard against the evil spirits, *kuei*. *Kuei* were the cause of disease and of many another misfortune. They might be in leaves, in trees, in animals, or wander about in ethereal form. Against them amulets and charms of various kinds were devised. Ritual acts were performed to expel them or to guard against them.

Closely intertwined with popular polytheism and animism was a belief in the *yin* and the *yang*. The *yin* was the female principle in the universe, and was associated with evil and darkness. The *yang* was the male element, related to righteousness, health, light, and warmth. *Yin* and *yang* were held to be continually interacting. For man's happiness *yang* must be strengthened and *yin* weakened. *Kuei* were full of *yin*, and to expel them aid must be sought of *yang*. The sun was full of *yang*. It was, indeed, the *t'ai yang*, the "great *yang*." The rooster, who greeted with his crowing the rising sun, was on the *yang* side. So was the peach which by its early blooming signaled the march of the sun northward in the spring. Through these and other agencies the Chinese strove to fortify themselves with *yang* to ward off the *yin*.

The *yin* and *yang* were dominant elements in a kind of pseudoscience, *fêng shui*, wind and water. According to *fêng shui*, the habitations of the living and the dead must be located in places in which the *yang* was as robust as possible and the *yin* absent or weak. Otherwise misfortune would ensue. To fix places for houses and especially for graves and to devise methods for improving the *fêng shui* of a city, a house, or a tomb, supposed experts were consulted.

Confucianism, which enjoyed the support of the state, was perpetuated largely by the scholars, or *literati*, who had been trained in the Confucian Classics. The *literati* were the product of the educational system which prepared for the civil service examinations maintained by the government. Long before the nineteenth century dawned, a cult in honor of Confucius and the chief exponents of his school had developed. In every province and *hsien* and in Peking itself, as well as in some schools, a Confucian temple was erected. In this temple the place of honor was held by a tablet or, in rare instances, a statue of Confucius, and ranked on either side were tablets to the leading disciples of the sage and to the chief exponents of the school through the centuries. At stated intervals ceremonies were performed in these temples. Twice a month an official visit was supposedly paid to each shrine. The teachings of Confucianism were strongly ethical. They emphasized the family and made for rational moderation. Nourished in them, the Chinese spirit frowned on novelty and excesses and applauded reasonableness.

Taoism, the other of the native cults that persisted throughout China, had been much influenced by Buddhism. Probably in imitation of the latter, it had temples, a pantheon, a priesthood with its distinctive garb, a canon of revered writings, and heavens and hells. Many of its professionals made their livelihood by participating in various ceremonies in behalf of the dead and the living and in preparing charms against the *kuei*. The professional Taoists had a kind of national organization, very loosely knit, headed by one whom foreigners inaccurately styled the Taoist Pope. He claimed descent from a Taoist worthy of the Han dynasty. Among the Taoists were anchorites and recluses who sought immortality through the ways prescribed by Taoist books. The regimen included disciplined breathing, meditation, and diet. Some Taoist celibates lived in monastic communities. In the nineteenth century the cult seemed very decayed. In general, Taoism encouraged the Chinese to esteem quietism, to distrust aggression, and to think of the visible as veiling the eternal.

By the nineteenth century, Buddhism had long passed its heyday. No longer did missionaries come from India and Central Asia. No more Chinese pilgrims made their way back to the Indian shrines of the faith. Japanese Buddhists did not, as under the T'ang, look to China as to the spring from which fresh life issued. Japanese Buddhism, indeed, was far more vigorous than that of China. It had been many centuries since Chinese Buddhism had had sufficient vitality to produce a new major school. Most of the schools which had once existed had disappeared, or had merged through a tolerance in which indifference and ignorance were the chief factors. Not only in China but everywhere else in the world Buddhism had passed its zenith.

Yet Buddhism was still prominent in the life of China and its dependencies and was far from dead. In Mongolia and Tibet Lamaistic Buddhism dominated not only the religious but also the intellectual and much of the social, political, and economic life. In China Proper Buddhism had much more vitality than had organized Taoism. Its strength varied in different sections, but it was to be found in almost every locality.

Buddhism centered, as was natural, in monasteries. The monasteries usually were placed in sites noted for their beauty—on a mountaintop or in a mountain glen, along a rugged hill or at the foot of some mountain. Often they were surrounded by ample grounds in which groves of trees were allowed to grow unmolested by the economic hunger for wood which stripped most of the hillsides of China. They were supported chiefly by endowments of cultivated land and by fees for religious services rendered to the laity. The monastic communities were mainly of men. Those of women were in the small minority. The membership was recruited partly by purchase from poor families who were glad to assure extra sons a livelihood in return for a small grant of money, partly by vagabonds who sought security and support, partly by criminals who found there a haven from justice, and partly by earnest spirits to whom Buddhism appealed as possibly having the answer to the haunting riddle of existence. Once admitted as novices, the prospective monks were given a training in their faith and in their religious duties. Ordination followed. By it, for Chinese Buddhism was overwhelmingly Mahayana, the monk undertook the role of a *bodhisattva.* That is, he was to seek salvation not only for himself but also for others and was to foreswear its full attainment until he had helped to make it possible for all living beings. His duties consisted in taking part in the services of the community, in helping in the routine of its material life (in the preparation of food and the upkeep of the buildings), and in assisting in ceremonies for the laity outside the monastic walls. The morale of the monasteries varied greatly. In some a vigorous and intelligent abbot kept it on a high level. In others the moral precepts of Buddhism were disobeyed and ignorance of Buddhist tenets was rife. In general, Buddhist monks were held in contempt by the laity, partly because, being celibates, they had not performed their filial duty of bringing into the world offspring to carry on the family line. Yet they were also feared as having power over the mysterious forces that surround man not only here but hereafter.

The laity were touched by Buddhism at various points and in differing degrees. Some were very devout. Among these women were more numerous than men. Others were quite indifferent. Often the most devout, a very small minority, were members of religious societies. Numbers of these, in the effort not to take life, were vegetarian. Some met periodically to read Buddhist sacred books. Several of the popular festivals were either of Buddhist origin or showed Buddhist influence. Into popular beliefs had come conceptions of reincarnation and heavens and hells which were of Buddhist provenance. Buddhism had many sacred sites, chiefly mountains. To these thousands of the laity made pilgrimages. The pilgrimages ostensibly had religious objectives, but, as was natural, also appealed as an excuse for travel. In many homes were Buddhist shrines.

Confucianism, Taoism, and Buddhism were the major organized religions, but there were others. Christianity had three times been introduced into China. Twice it had disappeared, but, as we have seen, after its third entrance, in the sixteenth century, it had persisted. In the nineteenth and twentieth centuries it was to have a phenomenal growth. Islam had been continuously present since at least the Mongol period and was numerically much stronger than Christianity. Moslems were the descendants partly of foreign immigrants and partly of converts. Many of them were non-Chinese in appearance. They lived a life somewhat apart from that of other Chinese. They tended, too, to specialize in certain occupations, notably those connected with travel—to be in charge of inns, and to provide and drive horses and camels. They were in all of the provinces of China, but they were strongest in Yünnan and in the northwest. Yet even Moslems showed the power of China to assimilate. Usually they had no minarets to advertise the existence of their mosques and no public call to prayer. A few Jews had kept a separate existence in China for centuries, but the last strong Jewish community, that in K'aifêng, disintegrated in the nineteenth century. China had many small religious societies, some of which were secret and many of which were syncretic in their beliefs—a composite of Confucianism, Buddhism, and Taoism, and occasionally with ingredients from Islam and, later, from Christianity.

Art

Few peoples have been as creative artistically as the Chinese. In a number of fields they have produced distinctive forms of a very high order. By the beginning of the nineteenth century they had passed their great period of artistic creativity. They were repeating, in an uninspired way, the forms that had been developed in past epochs. This sterility, however, must not blind us to the remarkable achievements of earlier generations.

We have seen that at the very dawn of history, in the first "dynasty" of whose existence we have certain proof, the Shang, the Chinese had shown marked skill in working bronze. In the technique of casting bronze the Shang have never been excelled anywhere and the vigorous designs which they used compel our admiration. With their respect for antiquity, the Chinese have ever since held bronze art objects in high regard. They have prized examples which have come down from ancient times and they have continued to produce bronzes, some of them in archaic designs.

In painting, as we have seen, the Chinese have been unsurpassed. The materials and conventions of their painters differed from those of the West, but even Occidentals who have had no training in them find much of charm. Chinese painting had kinship with calligraphy. The same brush pen was used for both. Much was made of the strokes executed with this pen. The strokes, indeed, furnished the foundation of the picture. The subjects treated were of wide variety. Figures and scenes revered by Taoists and Buddhists were favorite themes. Under the inspiration of these religions, particularly of Buddhism, some of the world's greatest painting was executed. Horses were frequent subjects, especially in some periods. Flowers and birds were pictured minutely and with marked taste and skill. Landscapes were favorites. Chinese painters delighted in scenes in which water and rugged mountain could be joined. The mountains were often depicted as partially covered by cloud or fog. In many a landscape man was introduced, but usually in such fashion as to give the impression of his insignificance in a scene which inspired him to awe or impelled him to contemplation. Court scenes were also depicted, but seldom in the greatest examples of the painter's brush. In portrait painting the Chinese did not attain to such excellence as in some other fields.

The Chinese method of achieving perspective—of giving the illusion of three dimensions on a two-dimensional surface—has differed from that of the Occident. In the Occident perspective has been attained by lights and shadows and by lines. The object or landscape is depicted as viewed from a particular point. The Chinese artist did not intend his landscape to be thought of as seen from one point, but from several angles or from a height. The sense of flatness was guarded against and the impression of distance was given by colors, and, in landscapes, by introducing the mists and clouds which in nature are prevalent in the Yangtze Valley and the south. Some painters were also poets. Painting and poetry were in practice more closely related than in the West.

Calligraphy was, as we have suggested, a fine art. The outstanding experts in it were as famous as the great painters. The Chinese characters with their lines written with the brush pen lent themselves to fine writing. Honorary arches, shop signs, and tablets over city gates and in government offices offered abundant opportunity for the practice of the art. Scrolls which gave examples of the calligrapher's skill and which were produced in pairs designed to match each other were favorite forms of gifts.

In ceramics the Chinese have been rightly famous. Porcelain has been so widely used by them that the Occident has thought of it as "china" or "chinaware." We have seen something of its development and of the forms given it in various dynasties. In several other kinds of ceramics the Chinese have also been noteworthy. Some of the earthenware figures buried in graves have been both realistic and beautiful. The ornate tiles which are prominent on roofs have been characteristic of Chinese architecture.

The Chinese have produced beautiful lacquer. At least as early as the Han they were making lacquered objects. They were skilled in the use of enamels—in cloisonné (in which the enamel is placed in pattern outlined by thin metal strips upon the surface to be treated), in champlevé (in which the enamel is placed in incised patterns), and in spreading the enamel with a brush upon metal or porcelain before heating the whole. The Chinese have been adept at carving glass.

A favorite semiprecious stone more highly prized by the Chinese than by any other people has been jade. In Chou and Han times it was quarried in China Proper, but as domestic sources were exhausted it was imported from Turkestan, Yünnan, and Burma. It was employed for many purposes—in worship, in jewelry, for amulets, as an aid to immortality, for insignia of authority, and for recording important documents.

Sculpture has been widely used. Although the names of sculptors were not transmitted with as much honor as were those of painters or calligraphers, some really great sculpture has come down to us. The vivid scenes, some of them of everyday life and some from mythology, engraved in Han tombs abound in grace and vigor. Under the inspiration of Buddhism beautiful figures of *buddhas* and *bodhisattvas* were produced, notably in the period of division which followed the Han (one of the northern dynasties of that era, the Wei, has given its name to a distinct style of sculpture), in the T'ang, and in the Sung. Portrait sculpture, like portrait painting, while not absent, was not so prominent as in the Occident. Some of the sculpture showed grace, some the calm repose of Buddhism, and some of it a wild, robust fierceness in which action seemed to break through the materials of the artist.

In architecture the Chinese were noteworthy. Partly because wood was so extensively used in buildings and partly because of the wars which have swept the land, not many examples of early architecture have come down to us. However, the China of the nineteenth and twentieth centuries abounded in structures of many kinds, many of which had been erected in the Ming and some few of which were from earlier dynasties.

We know from paintings and from tomb sculptures that architecture had a long development and that at least as early as the Han it had acquired most of the main characteristics which it possessed in later periods. It was marked by balance and a sense of proportion. It made much use of the enclosing wall, of the courtyard, and of the roof. Its roofs were of tile, had broad eaves, and were supported by pillars, sometimes of stone but usually of wood. The walls did not support the roof, but were fitted in between the pillars to keep out the weather. The open timbers over the columns on which the roof rested were often highly decorated. The pillars were on platforms, usually of brick or stone. These were ascended by steps and sometimes were surrounded by ornamented balustrades. The Chinese were not afraid of the use of rich and striking colors on their buildings and employed them with taste and discrimination.

The total effect of the greatest of Chinese architecture was that of repose, balance, and massive power. It comported with a great enduring civilization. Yet it was designed to fit in with the natural surroundings and not to contest with them or to overpower them. Most houses were of only one or two stories. Only the towers of city walls and pagodas reached a much greater height. Even the pagodas were often designed to aid the *fêng shui.* They seemed to be a part of the environment provided by nature and to supplement and crown it. In China man erected no Tower of Babel by which to mount to heaven and show himself equal with the gods.

City walls, bridges, temples, pagodas, and palaces give the most prominent examples of the skill of the architect. Some of the walls are among the greatest monumental structures ever erected by man. Every city had its wall, and the largest of them were more formidable than any of which we know elsewhere. They usually had a core of rubble faced with brick and, sometimes, trimmed with stone. We have had occasion again and again to mention the Great Wall which guarded the northern frontier and which was longer than even the frontier fortifications constructed by modern machinery in Europe. Beside it the Roman border walls were almost insignificant.

Peking, in spite of the fact that its grandeur has departed, is still in many respects the most impressive capital in the world. As it now stands, in its main outlines it is a contribution of the Ming, but the general plan and the conceptions it embodies go back to much earlier dynasties—certainly to the T'ang and probably to the Han and the Ch'in. It was designed as the seat of an Empire which, as we have reminded ourselves, was conceived as rightfully embracing all mankind. Its massive city wall, punctuated systematically by storied towers, in its rectangular enclosure embraced a vast area of many square miles. Its regularly spaced gates opened upon broad, straight avenues. One of these ran from the main south gate to the inner city which contained the imperial palace. The entrance to this "Forbidden City" was impressive—a gate flanked by great walls. Beyond were vast courtyards bounded by walls and colonnades which led to the great pavilion in which was the imperial throne. The city with its walls and its streets was built to give a fitting setting for the presence of the Emperor who by the mandate of Heaven ruled all men.

The Chinese made much use of gardens. Behind the blank walls which the city dwellings of the rich and powerful offered to the street were courtyards and gardens. Many of these gardens appear to the Westerner grotesque. Their attempts to reproduce nature with its lakes, streams, and mountains at times seem overdone. Yet some of them were spacious and gave the sense of repose and proportion which is one of the charms of Chinese architecture. The Summer Palace near Peking, constructed in the latter part of the nineteenth century in the Chinese tradition, gives the impression of a vast landscape with water, hill, and wood, in which the bridges, walls, and buildings of man are subordinate to nature.

Language

So different is the Chinese language from anything which we know in the Occident that it is difficult and perhaps impossible to convey in a few words an account of it which will be at once accurate, comprehensive, and intelligible. Yet so important is the Chinese language, both in China and in Japan, that the attempt must be made.

First we must endeavor to say something of the spoken language. It had many dialects. Several of these were reciprocally unintelligible. For instance, a Chinese knowing only Cantonese could not make himself understood orally to another Chinese speaking only the language of Foochow or Tientsin. Most of these striking dialectical differences were on the coast from the Yangtze southward. The large majority of the Chinese spoke what the foreigner called mandarin. Within mandarin, dialectical differences also existed. Northern mandarin differed from southern mandarin, and some local patois was almost as difficult for the outsider as were the dialects of the south coast. Yet with a standard mandarin one could understand and be understood throughout the north and most of the valley of the Yangtze and its tributaries. The vast majority of the Chinese spoke —and speak—one kind or another of mandarin.

While possessing many dialects, some of them reciprocally unintelligible, basically all spoken Chinese had a common and striking family likeness. It was almost without inflections to indicate case or tense. It had no derivative words, such as *teach-er* and *coward-ice* formed by affixing syllables. The number of separate syllables, or vocables, was very limited. This would seem to lead to confusion. The confusion was avoided by several devices. Chinese was a tonal language. This meant that each vocable could be spoken in any one of several tones. In Peking mandarin these were four in number. In southern mandarin they were five. In Cantonese they were nine. Then, sometimes, two vocables with the same or approximately the same meaning were combined. So *k'an* and *chien*, each meaning "to see," were used together as *k'an chien*. Context, too, and the order of words in the sentence aided in avoiding ambiguity. A descriptive word might be prefixed or added. Thus *hu*, "tiger," was *lao hu*, "old tiger," and *shih*, "stone," was *shih t'ou*, "stonehead." Some words were practically compounds. Thus "electricity" is *tien ch'i*, "breath of lightning." There are, too, what the foreigner calls classifiers. Just as we say "a strip of paper" or "a chunk of wood," so the Chinese say *i ko jên*, *i* being "one," *ko* being the classifier, and *jên*, "man." By the use of compounds, terms could readily be coined to designate new ideas or objects. This spoken tongue was in the nineteenth century, and still is, the native speech of more people than any other that has ever been used by men.

The Chinese method of writing is, so far as we know, an indigenous creation. The Chinese written language is in use not only in China, but also in Korea and Japan. With modifications which we are to note in their appropriate places in a later chapter, it has been taken over by the Japanese to write their own tongue.

The writing is by means of characters. Some of these characters were originally pictures of objects. Thus 月, "moon," was once [illegible], a representation of a partially darkened disk of that orb. 馬, at one time [illegible], seems intended for a horse with his mane, tail, and legs. 門 shows the posts and two leaves of the gate for which it stands. Some characters were attempts to portray ideas. Thus 中 is obviously "middle" or "center," and 三 "three." 明, "bright" or "brilliant," is made by combining the characters for "sun" and "moon." The majority of characters appear to have come into being as a kind of phonetic writing. With the paucity of vocables, a number of objects or ideas would have the same sound in the spoken language. Thus there are several words with quite different meanings which are pronounced *fang*. There is a symbol of ancient lineage 方, meaning "square," and now called *fang*. When the *fang* meaning "to ask" is written, before 方 is prefixed 言, meaning "words," and 訪 is obtained, still called *fang*. A kind of wood called *fang* is represented by 枋, which is composed of 方 prefixed by 木, which means a tree (in an early form [illegible] in which the branches and roots of a tree can be discerned). *Fang*, "kettle," was written 鈁 in which 金, meaning "metal," was placed before 方. 糸, meaning "silk," helps to show that 紡, also pronounced fang, is "spin." However, in not all composite characters is the modern pronunciation so clearly indicated as in these various characters called *fang*.

It must be clear that these characters appeal to the eye rather than to the ear. Differing pronunciations may be given them without altering their meaning. This facilitated their adoption by the Japanese, whose language is basically quite different from Chinese. Thus 山,

meaning "mountain" (in an early form, presumably a picture of one), is called in modern mandarin *shan* and in Japanese *yama* or, a Chinese derivative, *san*.

The larger proportion of Chinese literature has been in what we may term the classical style. Whether this ever reproduced any form of the spoken language we do not know. Probably, under the Chou or Shang, it approximated to the vernacular. Even now it closely resembles the spoken language in structure. It has, too, influenced the latter through contributions of quotations, words, and phrases. Yet this literary or classical style differs so markedly from the vernacular that even the educated cannot understand an unfamiliar passage when they merely hear it read. It appeals to the eye rather than to the ear. Some of its auxiliary words differ from the speech of every day. Especially is it more condensed. It uses fewer words than the vernacular. To write or read the literary style, then, required special training. So difficult is it and so time-consuming that it has reduced literacy and has tended to make of reading and writing a privilege of the comparative few. Yet it has the advantage of being understood by all the educated, no matter what their local vernacular, and thus has helped to bind the Empire together and to make available to the present the writings of earlier dynasties.

The written character could be employed to write the vernacular. At least as far back as the T'ang a vernacular literature existed. The learned might affect to despise it, but some of them wrote anonymously in it. We are to see that one of the revolutionary changes of the present century has been a more extensive use of a literary style which is close to the vernacular.

Literature

Through the written character a vast literature was produced. The early fabrication of paper had aided in its dissemination, and the invention of printing, centuries earlier than in Europe, still further assisted in its multiplication. In bulk Chinese literature at the outset of the nineteenth century probably surpassed that of all the rest of the world.

This literature covered a wide range. The Chinese were historically minded, and a large proportion of their books were histories. Some of these embraced all the Empire from the beginning. Others were for special periods, dynasties, or phases of the past. Many were for particular localities. The Chinese wrote extensively on government, for they were, as we have seen, politically and socially minded. They compiled many dictionaries. They were fond of assembling works into composite collections. Many of these we designate as encyclopedias, for some of them compassed all of Chinese learning and others a specialized range of subjects, such as the origin and history of family names. They are made up, however, not of articles written specifically for them, but of extracts, long and short, from existing works. Many commentaries were composed on the great works of the past. Much energy, too, was expended in obtaining correct texts of the revered books of antiquity. The religions and philosophies of the land, notably the most prominent, Confucianism, Taoism, and Buddhism, gave rise to vast literatures. Philosophy, closely related to religion as it is, was extensively represented. With the Chinese, philosophy was not put into ordered systems as it was by the Greeks and, under Greek influence, by the Occident in general. It was not logical in the Western sense. It was, however, voluminous, and much of it was very penetrating. Poetry was popular and was produced in every dynasty. Fiction, most of it in the vernacular, has been written and read for centuries. Some works of fiction attained considerable bulk. There were many essays, numbers of them having literary criticism as their subject.

In one branch of literature the Chinese, as compared with the modern West, were weak. They had little or no science. Medicine called forth voluminous works. Agriculture was well represented. However, the Chinese were backward in mathematics and in most branches of what we call natural science. With all their this-worldliness and practical-mindedness they did not develop the scientific method. Why this should have been we do not know. Various hypotheses have been offered. Whatever the explanation, the fact remains. For the scientific outlook and for the knowledge accumulated by science, the Chinese were to wait until their contact with the modern Occident. The Chinese tradition was not for the mastery of nature but for accommodation to it. In this the Chinese were markedly in contrast with the modern Occident.

Education

In no other land or culture has the scholar been so honored as in pre-twentieth century China. In no other have the rewards of scholarship been so great. To those who ranked high in the civil service examinations the road was open to any of the chief positions in the state except that of Emperor and those reserved for the imperial family and to the Manchus. Success in the examinations reflected glory not only on the candidate's family but also upon his city. According to the Confucian theory on which China was organized, the scholar was to exemplify the ideals on which society was based. To a great extent in practice the Empire was governed through scholars—or at least through men who had had scholarly training. The prominence of the scholar has persisted into our own day. The student is privileged and honored. He views manual labor with disdain. He has repeatedly been active in politics.

The education by which the scholars were produced was prolonged and exacting. It began with the memorization of huge quantities of the literature regarded by the Confucian school as standard. In the most elementary stages, a little of this was in the nature of textbooks and simple compendiums of Confucian ideals and Chinese history and learning. More of it was the classical writings, such as the *Lun Yü* (the *Analects*, containing many of the sayings attributed to Confucius). This involved a prodigious feat of memory, for in literary style and in content most of the material was beyond the comprehension of children. The explanations and comments given by the teachers were often as difficult as the texts. Yet the process gave to the best minds a storehouse of the ideals of the Confucian school and familiarity with standard examples of literary style. Practice, too, was obtained in composition according to accepted canons. The education discouraged originality of thought, but it ensured the perpetuation of ideals on which Chinese culture had been formed.

The state interested itself in the schools through which this education was obtained. Dynasty after dynasty had a system of schools which it supervised and to which it gave subsidies. Under the Ch'ing (the Manchus) the central administration concerned itself chiefly with the higher reaches of education. Elementary instruction was left largely to private initiative. Primary schools were maintained by villages through subscription or by clans. In well-to-do families tutors might be employed. The chief control of the state was exercised through the civil service examinations. These were the goal of the schools, and the intense competition they engendered helped to keep up to standard the processes of instruction. Those who had received the first degree were expected to continue their studies and to be subject to official supervision. Some schools in which advanced work was done were provided by the state government. Since it was to the interest of the Confucian state to have a constant stream of trained men flowing into its bureaucracy, the government kept a close eye on the educational process.

Not all of the formal education was in preparation for the civil service examinations. There were examinations, less highly esteemed than the former, for entrance into army posts, and some preparation for these had to be obtained. Buddhist monasteries imparted to their novices the knowledge expected of monks. Training was given in the better homes to the girls for their vocation of wifehood and motherhood. A few girls had a literary education—although, of course, they could not make use of it in office-holding. Still, the bulk of the formal education was for the preparation of members of the civil bureaucracy.

The emphasis on the civil service meant that the rewards of education were open only to a small minority, for the membership of the bureaucracy was a very small percentage of the population. Even when one includes clerks of various kinds, the number was not large. Scholars disappointed in the examinations might eke out a precarious livelihood as teachers. Yet teaching did not afford employment to all needy scholars, as for every one who achieved the coveted higher degrees and appointment to office, several thousand began the education which it was hoped would lead to this goal. However, although the vast majority of the boys who entered upon the arduous road did not pursue it, and of those who persevered only a small minority met with success, the very numbers who made the beginning and the esteem in which scholarship was held ensured the wide dissemination of a modicum of learning. The educational system, faulty though we may adjudge it to have been as a stimulus to the human mind and to creative thought, achieved phenomenal success in knitting the Chinese together as a cultural whole. Sayings from the Confucian classics found their way into current speech. The scholar set the ideals for the local community and conducted many of the ceremonies by which life was regulated. While its immediate impact was upon the minority, no other educational system through so many years has so successfully molded to its ideals so numerous a people.

Recreation and Amusement

The Chinese obtained diversion and amusement in a variety of ways. There were ages in which they engaged in vigorous physical sports, such as polo and hunting. Under the Manchus, however, the scholars looked askance at such violent activity as undignified. The exacting discipline of the school left little leisure for play. Many a scholar was stoop shouldered, flabby muscled, and tubercular. A slow walk was the extent of the exertions of most of them.

Yet recreation there was. This was partly in the prodigious banquets which were essential to many formal occasions and major business transactions. It was partly in games of chance. At these the Chinese were very skilled. Some of it was in the literary pursuit of capping verses, some in completing quotations. The professional storyteller gave amusement to many at the ubiquitous tea shops or at fairs. Jugglers and acrobats were unusually skillful. The Chinese, too, were and are extremely fond of the theater. Professional actors were traditionally placed very low in the social scale, but this did not prevent Chinese from patronizing and enjoying their performances. What the theater lacked in scenery it made up in elaborate costumes. It had its peculiar conventions. A house did not appear on the stage, but the audience was trained to know that by certain gestures the actor indicated that he was entering a door. Other gestures showed the actor mounting a horse. A special facial makeup was reserved for a villain. An actor with a wand tipped with white horsetail hair was known to represent a supernatural being. Much of the dialogue or monologue was in a high falsetto. The conventions were so different from those of the Occident that for the average Westerner they were first amusing and then boring. However, to those trained to appreciate them, they could give evidence of consummate skill.

Holidays broke the monotony of the year. The Jewish Christian week with its recurring day of rest was not observed—although Moslems had their Friday. However, festivals were fairly frequent. The New Year was the great occasion of the year. Debts were supposed to be settled before it dawned. It was marked by feasting, formal calls, family reunions, and honors to ancestors. For three or four days all but the most necessary work stopped. Theoretically it carried on until the Feast of Lanterns, on the fifteenth day of the first month. At Ch'ing Ming, in the spring, the dead were commemorated by cleaning and repairing graves and by offerings before the ancestral tablets and on the tombs. The Dragon Boat festival seems originally to have been associated with the summer solstice. The festival of the weaver maid and the herdsman and the feast of departed spirits came in the summer. The harvest festival was sometimes called the moon's birthday. The ninth day of the ninth month was a time for excursions and picnics to the top of a hill or to the city wall.

The winter solstice was the occasion for the last great day of the year.

Fortunately the Chinese have had a keen sense of humor. What for many of them has been the hard and grinding routine of the unremitting toil required to keep body and soul together has been lightened by a sense of the ludicrous and by an eye for the comic.

Group Action

In China the isolated individual has been at a disadvantage. Individualism as we have had it in much of the post-Renaissance Occident is all but unknown. The Chinese act by groups and find protection and support in association. The chief of these groups has been the family. Merchants and artisans have had their guilds. Secret societies have flourished. Because of their esoteric character, their activities have not been fully known, but they have probably played a larger part in Chinese life than do the numerous fraternal organizations in the United States. Sometimes the tie which has bound them together has been in part religious. Some have been active in politics, and on more than one occasion a troublesome rebellion has arisen through one or another of them.

The Chinese, too, have been adepts at organized boycotts. In their controversies with foreign powers in the twentieth century they have repeatedly resorted to this method with striking effect. Here is no recent innovation. For generations the Chinese have been employing this device in their internal affairs. Repeatedly it has been invoked against unpopular acts of officials. Of course it is organized and has its leaders, but in a sense it is a democratic way of expressing the will of the public or of a section of the public. Public opinion voicing itself through group action has been potent.

So much have the Chinese been accustomed to act in groups and mobs that individuals who will stand out against the mass have been much rarer than in the Occident. They have not been lacking, but they have been less numerous and they have not been so high esteemed.

Allied to group action has been the Chinese capacity for compromise. If individuals are successfully to cooperate, no one must be intransigent. Each must be willing to yield something of his own desires for the sake of peace. This sometimes seemed to be synonymous with weakness in adhering to moral principle, but it was the price that the Chinese had learned to pay for harmony among the many persons and social groups who had, whether they liked it or not, to live together.

Social Conventions

To the average Westerner, the Chinese have been amusing and incomprehensible. Many of their traditional customs are the opposite of those of the Occident and, accordingly, seem bizarre. In the old China the men wore skirts and long gowns and the women baggy trousers. At banquets what we think of as dessert came first and rice concluded the meal. Men in greeting one another shook their own hands, not the hands of the other (a much more sanitary proceeding than that of the West, be it said). The place of honor was on the left, not on the right. In meeting on the streets gentlemen removed their spectacles and not their hats. White and not black was the color of mourning. Food was lifted to the mouth with chopsticks and not with forks. A knife was not employed on the table. After childhood, the sexes did not mix socially in respectable society. These, and an almost endless number of other contrasts, seemed to place the Chinese in another world and to baffle any attempt to understand them.

Moreover, "face" has seemed to be a feature peculiar to the Far Orient and particularly to the Chinese. Appearances must be saved. A committee is forced to resign. The action is taken quietly, behind the scenes. Then, after the decision has been reached, a public meeting is staged. The members who have been forced out tender their resignations. The chairman of the meeting, who has been chiefly instrumental in bringing about the change, more than once politely urges them to reconsider their action and remain in office. The offenders as politely decline and are adamant in their determination. At last, with a great show of reluctance, their resignations are accepted. No one is deceived. Every one knows what lies back of the courtesies. Yet the "face" of the expelled members has been saved. A servant has been stealing sugar from his master's larder. The master calls him in, but, instead of accusing him, hints that some one from the outside may have been slipping in and taking it and suggests that the servant keep careful watch. The servant goes out of the room and in a few moments returns and makes the counter suggestion that a particular door which opens on a passage which leads to the street has been habitually left unlocked and begs to suggest that it be henceforth fastened to keep out pilferers. He knows and he knows that his master knows that thieving could not have occurred through this door and that he is being rebuked. However, he has not been directly accused, his "face" has been saved, and, on the whole a satisfactory servant, he remains on. The sugar no longer vanishes. In a multiplicity of ways "face" has been important in relations of Chinese with one another. "Face" makes for compromise. It is deemed unfair and cruel to cause another, even an enemy, a complete loss of "face." If an opponent is pushed too hard he may commit suicide, possibly on his antagonist's doorstep. Thereby his own "face" will be saved and public opinion will hold the unyielding party to the conflict responsible for the death. If at all possible, some adjustment of difficulties must be permitted which will allow each to "save his face."

Naturally Chinese have brought their conceptions of "face" into their relations with foreigners and with foreign governments. Foreigners, bewildered, have seen in it something peculiarly "Oriental" and have felt that because of it the Chinese dwell in a world apart. Before the inscrutable mask, the "poker face," which the Chinese can so successfully assume, or before the bland and smiling politeness and even the genial affability which the cultivated Chinese may employ, the puzzled foreigner is baffled. He suspects the sinister. The Chinese seem to come at a question indirectly and to be evasive. They are surprised that the foreigner does not understand the hints whose meaning to them is so clear, and are offended by what is to them the Westerner's crude bluntness and directness.

The Chinese appear to the Westerner to have a penchant for "squeeze." To be sure, the myth has arisen that the Chinese merchant is more honest than other folk and that his word is as good as his bond. In their dealings with one another the Chinese themselves do not cherish this illusion. They insist upon guarantors for all their fellows to whom they entrust business. From the lowliest coolie to the highest official it has been customary to take something from one's employer beyond the stipulated wage or salary. The servant takes it from his master and the official from his subordinates or from the public revenues which pass through his hands. To the foreigner this seems dishonest, but the Chinese does not object to it unless it passes beyond what seems to him reasonable.

However, the Chinese are basically not so different from the Westerner as the surface indications would proclaim. No one can deny that the social conventions of the old China were unlike those of the West or that, in spite of the changes of the past few decades, many of them are still different. Moreover, without a knowledge of these conventions the foreigner would continue to find the Chinese an enigma. Yet fundamentally the Chinese are like the rest of the human race. It is the conventions that differ. When once a knowledge of these is obtained, much of the strangeness of the Chinese vanishes. The Chinese individual has had essentially the same emotions, the same urges, the same reactions as the individual Occidental. In dress, table manners, and the methods of formal greetings they may have been as remote from each other as the poles, but back of the mannerisms has lain the same desire to be civilized and to act in an orderly way. "Face" has been found as much in the Occident as in China. Indeed, as we are to see in later chapters, one of the important causes of some of the wars between China and Occidental peoples in the nineteenth century was the fashion in which the latter believed their dignity (their "face") to have been disregarded or deliberately flouted by the Chinese. When once the motives back of the conventions of the Chinese and Westerners are recognized as being substantially the same, the conventions themselves become understandable.

Chinese Characteristics

With all their basic similarities to the rest of mankind, Chinese appear to have some characteristics peculiar to them. They seem to have in them something of a difference in physical heredity. Chinese men appear to have what to the Westerner is a certain degree of femininity. This does not mean that they cannot be as brave and as resolute as any Westerner, for again and again they have displayed both qualities. However, they seem to have a sensitivity and a delicacy which the West often thinks of as feminine. The keen sense of humor, the perceptions of the feelings of others, the almost instinctive reading of character, often disconcertingly accurate, seem to go with this quality. However, the moment one names it, he thinks of the many Chinese who do not seem to possess it. He recalls many individuals who have been stolid, obtuse, and slow. Not all Chinese are the same, and generalizations are dangerous.

Summary

To attempt to describe in a short chapter a civilization as old and as complex as that of the Chinese is little short of preposterous. Every one of the above paragraphs cries for amplification, many need qualifying, and scores of additional paragraphs would be required to give a picture which is anywhere nearly complete.

Yet the foregoing pages may have their value. They may succeed in conveying some hint of the richness of Chinese culture and of the notable achievement of the human spirit which that culture has presented. They may, too, help to make vivid some of the outstanding features of the old China.

It may assist, moreover, those who come to the reading of this volume with little previous knowledge of the Far East if we essay, in summary, an enumeration of the main features of the civilization whose separate phases we have endeavored to set down.

First of all, we must remind ourselves that Chinese culture was old. It may not have possessed the antiquity of that of the Occident. What we call Western civilization has sources in ancient Egypt, Mesopotamia, and Palestine. For these, stages have been discovered which are millenniums older than the first Chinese state of which we have sure evidence, the Shang. Yet this stream of Occidental civilization has suffered great breaks and has again and again been profoundly altered. The civilization with which the Chinese entered the twentieth century had had a longer, fairly continuous development uninterrupted by revolutionary changes and less modified by its contacts with other cultures than any other in the contemporary world.

In the second place, we must recall that in this civilization less and less that was new was appearing. The price paid for continuity from antiquity was a progressive sterility. The Chinese multiplied in numbers and their total wealth increased, but more and more they were repeating, in uninspired fashion, the cultural forms of their ancestors. Originality had by no means vanished. Even under the latest dynasty it gave indications of its presence. But, so far as its visible expressions gave evidence of its existence, it was declining. In government, in art, and in literature men were simply elaborating the details of systems and ideals whose main features had been brought into being centuries before.

In the third place, we must repeat what we said at the outset of this chapter, that a fundamental principle of Chinese culture was that it was normal civilization and that of right it embraced all mankind. In principle and in the minds of its exponents, Chinese culture was world-embracing: it was civilization. All cultures which did not conform to it were barbarous.

A fourth feature was allied to this other, a pride, a sense of superiority over all other people and cultures. This was not so much a conscious conviction, to be argued for, as it was an inbred quality.

Chinese scholars had so long been sure that the Empire and the culture it embodied were supreme and that all outside their pale were barbarians, that denial seemed to them stupidity or barbarism or both. This attitude helps to explain the long, stubborn resistance to the Occident which we are to recount in later chapters. In it is to be found a major reason for the delay in adopting the machines of the Occident which gave Japan her great advantage in the fourth and fifth decades of the present century. The Japanese were just as proud as the Chinese, but they had had the tradition of learning from their neighbors. Their pride was coupled with an unacknowledged sense of inferiority. They had so long been conscious of the greatness of Chinese civilization and, in their desire not to seem backward, had so repeatedly gone to school to it, that, when once they were convinced of the might of the nineteenth century Occident, they quickly reorganized their life to meet it. In this adaptation they were a generation ahead of the Chinese. Yet the inbred quiet confidence of the Chinese in the essential superiority of their heritage was of the greatest advantage in the maintenance of Chinese morale in the twentieth century war with Japan. The Chinese were assured that ultimately they must win.

A fifth feature was a kind of sophistication. The Chinese were conscious of having lived a long time as a race and of being heirs of a great culture. They were smilingly skeptical of progress. They had seen so many philosophies and religions offer, with positive conviction, contradictory views, that they were dubious about the finality of any of them. They had a kind of agnosticism. Yet many were troubled by the unsolved mysteries of life and the majority were confident that the universe is on the side of righteousness.

A sixth feature is one which we have repeatedly noticed—this-worldliness. While the Chinese were behind no people in their reverence for the dead and in ceremonial honors for ancestors, and while through Buddhism and Taoism they had painted for them vivid pictures of life after death, they were very much interested in this life. They were continually striving to realize an ideal society here and now.

A seventh feature which we have also stressed was the dominance of Confucianism. Chinese civilization was primarily based upon the ideals which we associate with the name of Confucius and which had their leading exponent in that sage.

The chief bulwarks of this Confucianism were what we may

mention as the eighth and ninth features of Chinese civilization, the state with its Emperor and its bureaucracy (the latter recruited through competitive examinations and steeped in Confucian traditions), and the family. Both of these were major social achievements.

A tenth feature was the distinctive art and literature of the Chinese. While showing the effect of contributions from other cultures, these were primarily the creation of the Chinese and *sui generis*. Chinese painting, architecture, porcelain, poetry, and prose, the Chinese language both spoken and written, the paper and printing by which literature was disseminated, and the dominant philosophy have been creations of the Chinese themselves.

It was a culture with these features which entered the nineteenth century. The transformation wrought in it by the impact of the Occident is one of the major events in the history not only of the Far East but also of mankind. To it we must devote large portions of the later chapters of this book. While much of the old China described in this chapter has disappeared, what is probably the larger part has survived. The attitudes of mind bred in the Chinese by their cultural past endure and condition present action and events.

The great questions presented to herself and the world by China are the ones to which we referred in the last chapter: Why was it that the creativity of the Chinese has slowed down in recent centuries, especially since the Sung? Why for over half of the nearly ten centuries since the advent of the Sung has China been ruled in whole or in part by aliens? Are these two questions related? Obviously upon the correct answers to these queries depends much of the future of China and the Far East. With them is bound up as well the welfare of much of the rest of the world. They are of prime significance to the United States, particularly in view of the responsibilities in the Far East which that country has assumed in the twentieth century. If the Chinese cannot defend and govern themselves, the efforts of the United States to protect the territorial integrity and the political independence of China are foredoomed. It is as yet too soon to know with assurance the answers. These can come only through the crucible of the remaining decades of the twentieth century. However, the clue to the mystery seems to be in the nature of Confucianism and in the fact that for nearly two millenniums China was constricted by her system of government within the strait jacket of that one school of philosophy. In the twentieth century, as we are to see in later sections of this volume, that strait jacket was broken. For a time chaos ensued.

Only slowly and painfully have the Chinese been making their adjustment to the new conditions. If the hypothesis we have suggested is correct, the presumption is that, freed from their traditional shackles, the Chinese will prove again to be creative and to be capable of maintaining an orderly, independent existence.

BIBLIOGRAPHY

For Brief Reference

K. S. Latourette, *The Chinese: Their History and Culture* (New York, 1945), Volume II.

For More Extended Study

IN GENERAL

S. Couling, *The Encyclopædia Sinica* (London, 1917).

ON THE RACIAL COMPOSITION OF THE CHINESE

L. H. D. Buxton, *China. The Land and the People* (Oxford, 1929), Chapter 3.
Chi Li, *The Formation of the Chinese People* (Cambridge, 1928).
S. M. Shirokogoroff, *Anthropology of Northern China* (Shanghai, 1923).
S. M. Shirokogoroff, *Anthropology of Eastern China and Kwangtung Province* (Shanghai, 1925).

ON THE POLITICAL ORGANIZATION

H. S. Brunnert and V. V. Hagelstrom, *Present Day Political Organization of China* (Shanghai, 1912), translated from the Russian edition of 1910.
Pao Chao Hsieh, *The Government of China (1644–1911)* (Baltimore, 1925).
Han Liang Huang, *The Land Tax in China* (New York, 1918).
D. H. Kulp, *Country Life in South China. The Sociology of Familism. Vol. I. Phenix Village, Kwangtung, China* (New York, 1925).
Y. K. Leong and L. K. Tao, *Village and Town Life in China* (London, 1915).
Chuan Shih Li, *Central and Local Finance in China* (New York, 1922).
W. D. Mayers, *The Chinese Government. A Manual of Chinese Titles, Categorically Arranged and Explained* (Shanghai, 1878).
H. B. Morse, *The Trade and Administration of the Chinese Empire* (London and New York, 1908).
W. S. A. Pott, *Chinese Political Philosophy* (New Y rk, 1925).

THE FAMILY

Pearl S. Buck, *The Good Earth* (New York, 1931).
Lady Hosie, *Two Gentlemen of China* (London, 1924).
Fei Hsiao-tung, *Peasant Life in China* (New York, 1939).
E. T. C. Werner, *China of the Chinese* (London and New York, 1919).

ECONOMIC LIFE

J. L. Buck, *Land Utilization in China* (Chicago, 1937).
J. L. Buck, *Chinese Farm Economy* (Shanghai and Chicago, 1930).
J. S. Burgess, *The Guilds of Peking* (New York, 1928).

L. H. D. Buxton, *China. The Land and the People* (Oxford, 1929).
G. B. Cressey, *China's Geographic Foundations* (New York and London, 1934).
J. Edkins, *Chinese Currency* (Shanghai, 1901).
S. D. Gamble, *Peking. A Social Survey* (New York, 1921).
F. H. King, *Farmers of Forty Centuries* (Madison, Wis., 1911).
Mabel Ping-hua Lee, *The Economic History of China, with Especial Reference to Agriculture* (New York, 1921).
W. H. Mallory, *China: Land of Famine* (New York, 1926).
H. B. Morse, *The Trade and Administration of the Chinese Empire* (London and New York, 1908).
H. B. Morse, *The Guilds of China* (London, 1909).
S. R. Wagel, *Chinese Currency and Banking* (Shanghai, 1915).

RELIGION AND PHILOSOPHY

H. G. Creel, *Confucius, the Man and the Myth* (New York, 1949).
H. Dore, translated by H. Kennelly, *Researches into Chinese Superstitions* (Shanghai, 1914, *et. seq.*).
C. Eliot, *Hinduism and Buddhism* (London, 1921).
Fung Yu-lan, *A Short History of Chinese Philosophy* (New York, 1948).
J. J. M. de Groot, *The Religious System of China, Its Ancient Forms, Evolution, History, and Present Aspect* (Leyden, 1892–1901).
J. J. M. de Groot, *Sectarianism and Religious Persecution in China* (Amsterdam, 1903, 1904).
C. H. Hamilton, *Buddhism in India, Ceylon, China and Japan. A Reading Guide* (Chicago, 1931).
E. D. Harvey, *The Mind of China* (New Haven, 1933).
L. Hodous, *Folkways in China* (London, 1929).
L. Hodous, *Buddhism and Buddhists in China* (New York, 1924).
E. R. Hughes and K. Hughes, *Religion in China* (New York, 1950).
K. S. Latourette, *A History of Christian Missions in China* (New York, 1929).
J. Legge, *The Religions of China* (London, 1881).
J. B. Pratt, *The Pilgrimage of Buddhism* (New York, 1928).
K. L. Reichelt, *Truth and Tradition in Chinese Buddhism* (Shanghai, 1930).
J. K. Shryock, *The Origin and Development of the State Cult of Confucius* (New York, 1932).
J. K. Shryock, *The Temples of Anking and Their Cults. A Study of Modern Chinese Religion* (Paris, 1931).
A. Waley, *Three Ways of Thought in Ancient China* (London, 1939).

ART

L. Ashton, *Introduction to the Study of Chinese Sculpture* (London, 1924).
L. Binyon, *Painting in the Far East* (London, 1908).
D. Carter, *Four Thousand Years of China's Art* (New York, 1948).
E. F. Fenollosa, *Epochs of Chinese and Japanese Art* (London, 1912).
R. Groussėt, *The Civilizations of the East. China* (New York, 1934), translated from the French by C. A. Phillips.
C. Hentze, *Chinese Tomb Figures* (London, 1928).
A. L. Hetherington, *The Early Ceramic Wares of China* (London, 1925).
R. L. Hobson and A. L. Hetherington, *The Art of the Chinese Potter from the Han Dynasty to the End of the Ming* (London, 1923).
R. L. Hobson, *Chinese Pottery and Porcelain* (New York and London, 1915).

R. L. Hobson, *The Wares of the Ming Dynasty* (London, 1923).
R. L. Hobson, *The Later Ceramic Wares of China* (London, 1922).
B. Laufer, *Jade* (Chicago, 1912).
O. Sirén, *A History of Early Chinese Art* (London, 1929, 1930).
O. Sirén, *Chinese Architecture*, in *The Encyclopædia Britannica*, 14th edition, Vol. V, pp. 556–565.
O. Sirén, *The Walls and Gates of Peking* (London, 1924).
O. Sirén, *The Imperial Palaces of Peking* (Paris, 1926).
O. Sirén, *Chinese Sculpture*, in *The Encyclopædia Britannica*, 14th edition, Vol. V, pp. 579–588.
O. Sirén, *Chinese Sculpture from the Fifth to the Fourteenth Century* (London, 1925).
E. F. Strange, *Chinese Lacquer* (London, 1926).
A. Waley, *An Introduction to the Study of Chinese Painting* (London, 1923).

LANGUAGE

H. G. Creel, *Literary Chinese by the Inductive Method*, Vols. I and II (Chicago, 1938, 1939).
B. Karlgren, *Sound and Symbol in Chinese* (London, 1923).
G. A. Kennedy, *Chinese Reading for Beginners* and *Key to Chinese Reading for Beginners* (Yale University, 1939).

LITERATURE

F. Ayschough and A. Lowell, *Fir-Flower Tablets. Poems* (Boston, 1921).
W. Bynner and Kiang Kang-hu, *The Jade Mountain. A Chinese Anthology: Being Three Hundred Poems of the T'ang Dynasty, 618–906* (New York, 1929).
C. S. Gardner, *Chinese Traditional Historiography* (Cambridge, 1938).
H. A. Giles, *Strange Stories from a Chinese Studio* (London, 1880).
E. B. Howell, *The Restitution of the Bride and Other Stories from the Chinese* (London, 1926).
Tsao Hsüeh-chin and Kao Ngoh, *Dream of the Red Chamber Translated and Adapted from the Chinese by Chi-chen Wang* (London, 1929).
A. Waley, *A Hundred and Seventy Chinese Poems* (London, 1923).
A. Wylie, *Notes on Chinese Literature* (Shanghai, 1902).

RECREATION AND AMUSEMENTS

L. C. Arlington, *The Chinese Drama from the Earliest Times until Today* (Shanghai, 1930).
L. Hodous, *Folkways in China* (London, 1929).

SECRET SOCIETIES

J. S. M. Ward and W. G. Sterling, *The Hung Society, or the Society of Heaven and Earth* (London, 1925).

SOCIAL CONVENTIONS

W. G. Walshe, "*Ways that are Dark*": *Some Chapters on Chinese Etiquette and Social Procedure* (Shanghai, 1906).

CHINESE CHARACTERISTICS

A. H. Smith, *Chinese Characteristics* (New York, 1894).

Chapter VI. THE DEVELOPMENT OF JAPAN

Japan before the changes wrought by the coming of the Occident from the beginning to the advent of Commodore Perry (1853)

THE SECOND MOST NUMEROUS PEOPLE of the Far East and, in the twentieth century, the most aggressive, are the Japanese. To say that they are second in size does not mean that they are a small nation. Even at the dawn of the nineteenth century, before the growth in population of the past two generations, there were probably more of them than of that other active insular people at the other end of the Euro-Asiatic Continent, the British. At present they continue to outnumber the British and are not far from the size of the most numerous of Western European peoples, the Germans. From the standpoint of the census as well as of commerce, industry, and empire building, the Japanese have been one of the great powers.

Origins

The origins of the Japanese, like those of many other peoples, are to some degree shrouded in obscurity. We are clear that they are a mixed people. We know that amalgamation began at a very early time. We are aware of some of the elements which have entered into the resulting nation. Other elements, however, are at least partly conjectural, and we cannot be sure of the precise proportions in which the various contributory streams have mingled to constitute the present Japanese. The Ainu, a hairy folk sometimes classified as proto-Caucasian, who survive in the Hokkaido, seem formerly to have been scattered over most or all of the islands. Whether as they were conquered they were exterminated or were partly assimilated into the present Japanese is in dispute. Probably the latter is the correct answer. As might be readily guessed from a glance at the map, the Korean Peninsula, separated only by a strait from the islands, was undoubtedly a highway for immigration. Groups related to the Mongols and the Tungus of the present Mongolia and Manchuria made the passage, probably in neolithic times. It is usually supposed, too. that other settlers who came in from the south were related to the Malays, themselves a mixed race, and to the prehistoric or early historic peoples of south China. The favoring southward-stretching chain of islands and the oceanic Black Stream sweeping up from the south presumably facilitated this movement. In historic times came Koreans and Chinese, but as minorities. While the Japanese are as self-consciously a nation and a people as any folk on earth, physical diversities still exist among them. These have at least a social background but may also perpetuate differences in strains of immigration.

The Land of the Gods

As with so many other peoples, the story of the beginnings of the Japanese is enshrined in myths and legends. These, however, are of unusual importance for an understanding of the present-day scene, because they have been officially taught and have helped to shape the attitudes of the Japanese with whom the world now has to do.

We hear of the god Izanagi and the goddess Izanami, from whose union were born the islands of Japan. Indeed, according to this mythology, all objects, both animate and inanimate, are the offspring of the gods. We read of the Sun Goddess, Amaterasu-Omikami, born as Izanagi washed his left eye, and of many other deity. The Sun Goddess, outraged by the conduct of a brother, retired to a cave, leaving the world darkened, and only by subtlety did the other gods lure her forth. Later the Sun Goddess sent to earth to rule it her grandchild, Ninigi-no-Mikoto. He descended to the island of Kyushu, bearing with him a jewel, a sword, and a mirror which had been given him by his grandmother. A great-grandson of Ninigi-no-Mikoto was Jimmu Tenno, the first Emperor of Japan.

There is much more to these myths and legends than this brief summary. Modern scholars have thought that back of them may have been memories of actual historical events and have endeavored to discover what these latter might be.

The stories were not put into their accepted written form until early in the eighth century of our era, after Chinese influence had entered and efforts had been put forth to make the imperial institution correspond to what the Japanese had seen in China. Presumably in the process they were distorted to include some of the then popular Chinese ideas and to give the sanction of antiquity to the position of the imperial family.

In their effect upon the Japanese of the twentieth century these narratives were as important as though they were sober and accurate history. They reinforced in the Japanese a firm belief in the supernatural origin and divine nature of their nation. They strengthened the conviction that the Emperor was divine, ruling not only by the commission of the Sun Goddess but also by virtue of actual descent from her. To this day the most sacred emblems of the imperial power are the jewel, the sword, and the mirror. These myths and legends, thus accepted, have helped to make the imperial institution the center of coherence of the Japanese state and of Japanese society.

Pre-Chinese Japan

What the actual beginnings of the history of Japan were we do not know. Writing was probably unknown until sometime early in the Christian era. The Chinese characters, the form of writing employed, were not officially adopted in Japan until late in the fourth or early in the fifth century. It was only with the end of the fifth century that dates begin to be fairly reliable and that native chronicles commence to be fairly dependable. Presumably until that time records of matters of state were kept irregularly if at all. Chinese histories tell us something of early contacts between the Middle Kingdom and Japan. The myths and legends can be made to yield a nucleus of fact, although over details there is much debate. Archaeology contributes something. Out of these and other evidence an outline of the early past can be reconstructed which, as might be expected, increases in definiteness as the centuries progress.

Not far from the beginning of the Christian era two centers of culture existed in Japan. One was at Izumo, on the southwest part of the main island, opposite Korea. Presumably its population was derived from the near-by continent and its culture from that continent by way of Korea. The other was at Yamato, on the peninsula of the main island south of the present Nara and Kyoto. Here was the nucleus of the later centralized government of Japan. This nucleus is said to have been founded by conquerors from Kyushu who, led by Jimmu Tenno, made their way along the eastern shore of that island and then along the Inland Sea until they established themselves in Yamato. If this is correct, there must have existed on Kyushu an earlier center of culture. Its racial composition is uncertain, but it may have been derived in part from peoples from the south, possibly from the south of the later China or from islands, and in part from migrants from the continent by way of Korea. The Yamato state early was iron-using, a skill which its founders seem to have had, along with the employment of stone implements, before leaving Kyushu.

This early Japan was not a highly centralized monarchy. It was composed of a good many ruling family groups or what we may term, rather loosely, clans. Each was made up of households which claimed a common ancestor, worshipped a common god, and were under a common chieftain. Each clan had its own lands. The imperial family was the leading clan and had as its head him who, reading back into these times the later importance which he did not then possess, we term Emperor. The imperial line has continued to the present and constitutes the oldest ruling house now in existence, and probably has reigned longer than any other family in human history. The Emperor enjoyed a certain amount of preeminence, ruling the country through the heads of the other clans. The members of these clans were what might be termed the aristocracy, for then as throughout history the Japanese social structure was stratified in hereditary layers and was not the relatively fluid society which that of China eventually became. Attached to each clan and usually socially inferior to it were occupational groups which we may denominate guilds and corporations. Membership was hereditary, and the position and trade of the members were determined by those of their fathers. Usually the occupational groups were subordinate to the clans, but some of them achieved an independent status and became as important as the latter. Below the clans and occupational groups were slaves.

The culture of the Yamato state had advanced beyond the primitive stage of civilization. Then as now rice was the principal grain food, and the raising of rice was basic to agriculture. The presence of the occupational groups shows a somewhat diversified economy. Houses were built, although they were not elaborate. Hunting and fishing were engaged in. Cloth and pottery were made. Jewelry was extensively used. The religion of the land was the predecessor of the present Shinto. To the early Japanese all objects, whether animals, plants, mountains, lakes, islands, rivers, the sun, or the moon, were deemed to have life. The word *kami*, usually translated "god," was not closely defined and embraced a great variety of objects and beings. Yet certain of the gods were regarded as more powerful than others and as worthy of special honor. Before contact with China ancestor worship seems not to have been present, and although each clan thought of itself as descended from a god, that god was not necessarily a deified ancestor. There was no elaborate or profound philosophy or theology. Purity was required in worship, but that was not so much ethical as ceremonial. The sense of sin was not pronounced. Religion was more a matter of thankfulness than of fear. It consisted largely in ceremonies. No elaborate priesthood existed and while there were professional priests, these were few, and priestly ceremonies were performed largely by those who varied that function with other occupations. While modified by later developments and by contacts with other faiths, much of this primitive religion with its ideas and customs survives today.

This early Japanese state with its center in Yamato was not large. Gradually, however, it extended its borders. That was done mainly by conquests and at the expense of peoples who were regarded as barbarians. Contacts, too, were made with the continent through Korea. Territorial footholds were acquired on the southern tip of that peninsula. We hear especially of an Empress Jingo, presumably of the second half of the fourth century, who reduced part of Korea to submission. Then as now Japan was warlike and rejoiced in military exploits.

Early Contacts with China

It was to be expected that this small but growing state in the Japanese islands would be brought into contact with the great Empire on the continent. As China became unified and extended its borders under the Ch'in and the Han dynasties it and the Japanese would become aware of each other. This would be facilitated by the Han, for that dynasty ruled for a much longer period than did the Ch'in and for years a wealthy Chinese colony existed in Korea and the Han governed part of that peninsula. Chinese culture was carried to the southern tip of Korea. From Korea its influence penetrated to Japan. If our interpretation of Chinese records is correct, Japanese made their way to Han China, some of them as official envoys to the Han court. They would, of course, carry back with them something of Chinese culture.

In the long period of political division that intervened between the breakup of the Han dynasty and the reunification of China under the Sui and the T'ang, intercourse with Japan was irregular. From time to time, however, Japanese reached China. Some of them came as official envoys to the courts of the states which during this era of disunion embraced larger or smaller portions of China. Moreover, increasingly Chinese and Koreans who had been in touch with Chinese culture came to Japan. Some of these were refugees from the wars that swept China and Korea. Some were sent by one or another of the states into which Korea was divided to seek the support of the Yamato state in the wars with their neighbors. Artisans, farmers, merchants, and scholars arrived. Some of them settled permanently in Japan. Buddhism had been making great progress in China in the centuries which followed the Han and had penetrated to Korea. It is not strange that a faith which was achieving popularity in lands to which the Japanese looked for culture should make its way to the island kingdom. The time usually set for that event is the sixth century. Not at once, however, did Buddhism win a large following.

Transformation Through China

In the latter part of the sixth and in the first part of the seventh centuries China was united under the Sui and the T'ang and greatly increased in wealth and prestige. Under the T'ang, as we saw in Chapter IV, the Chinese Empire reached a new height of power and culture. The T'ang capital at Ch'angan became the largest city in the Far East. All who visited it must have been dazzled by its size and its splendor.

It was natural that in the time of the Sui and the T'ang, Chinese culture should rapidly increase its influx to Japan. Nor is it remarkable that the Japanese adopted much of it and gradually adapted it to their own purposes. Japanese went to China in fairly large numbers. Some accompanied the official embassies which were sent to the Chinese court. Others were engaged in the growing commerce with China. Many remained for years as students. Returning, all brought back something of what they had learned and became centers of its propagation. Chinese came to Japan for a variety of reasons. Many were merchants. Some were scholars and artists. All were teachers of their native culture, some formally and others informally and incidentally. Koreans were also active, whether as merchants, sea captains, sailors, or permanent settlers, as purveyors of the civilization that had come to them from China.

The transformation of Japan by Chinese culture was one of the two greatest revolutions which that land has experienced. Indeed, it was more thoroughgoing than has been the second of the two, that produced by the impact of the Occident in the nineteenth and twentieth centuries. In a very real sense it prepared the way for the latter.

The Japanese, having become accustomed through their long contacts with China to take over and apply to their own purposes what impressed them as desirable in a foreign culture, found it easier than did the Chinese, who had never remade their culture on a foreign model but had been teachers rather than learners, to reorientate themselves to the culture which pressed in on the Far East from the modern Occident. As with the revolution induced by contact with the West, so with the earlier one which accompanied the influx of Chinese culture, the transition was initiated and engineered by members of the ruling classes. It did not come, as did that in China in the twentieth century, by an irruption from below, but by direction from above. This was of basic importance. It meant the perseverance of the old upper classes and of much of the basic structure of Japanese life. While changes seemed and were revolutionary, they did not completely sweep aside the past. No sudden or sharp break occurred. The new was made to subserve the old. In time it greatly altered the old, but much of the latter persisted. The imperial house and some of the other ancient clans continued. The position of the imperial clan was modified, and of the other clans some disappeared and others rose to power. Much that was new was added. Yet a great deal of the old continued and the revolution was not so sweeping as a superficial view might have led one to expect. This was also to be the case in the nineteenth and twentieth centuries.

No logical order seems to exist in the changes wrought by Chinese culture. All aspects of life were affected and, in general, simultaneously. When, as in the following paragraphs, the different phases of culture are separated out, it must be understood that this is purely for convenience and not because one set of alterations was finished before another was begun.

We must remember, moreover, that the changes were not a matter of years or even of decades but of centuries. Contacts with China had been in progress before the T'ang for almost twice as long a period as has elapsed between the coming of Columbus to America and the present time. They continued without a break from the T'ang into our own day. At times the flow of Chinese influences into Japan was more rapid than at others. When, in the nineteenth century, Japan turned her eyes to the Occident and China began to fall a victim to the West it almost ceased. Yet since the rise of the Han dynasty Japan has been intensely sensitive to what has been transpiring in China and during most of these centuries has been a learner rather than a teacher.

In language and literature the introduction of Chinese gave Japan a medium for writing and enriched the land with the vast and varied products of the Chinese mind. At the outset and, indeed, for centuries, the Chinese written language and the works in it were limited to the Chinese immigrants and to a small, aristocratic Japanese circle. At first Chinese came in as a purely foreign language. Basically the Chinese and Japanese tongues were unrelated and in many ways were in striking contrast. Japanese had long sentences, was almost without accentuation, and was poor in vocabulary. Chinese had short concise sentences, was tonal, had several sounds that the Japanese found difficulty in pronouncing, and possessed a rich vocabulary. To learn Chinese was as much of an effort for the Japanese as it is for present-day Americans. To use the Chinese characters to write Japanese was as much a *tour de force* as it would be to write English through them.

Two methods of transcribing Japanese by Chinese characters were devised. One was to take Chinese characters, regardless of their meaning, which had the same or somewhere nearly the same pronunciation as the Japanese syllables, and use them to transcribe Japanese phonetically. The other was to utilize the Chinese characters which had the same meaning as the Japanese words. In the latter case either the Chinese or the Japanese pronunciation might be given to the ideas represented by the character. Both methods were employed.

One trouble with the first method was the lack of agreement as to which Chinese character should be adopted for a particular Japanese syllable. At first great confusion existed, and only gradually, and then imperfectly, was uniformity achieved with the use of one particular symbol for a particular sound. Then, too, different pronunciations of the Chinese characters were imported, depending upon the time at which contact was had with China and the part of China with which contact was established, for while the characters themselves were the same from age to age and throughout the Empire, the phonetic values given them varied with the dialect and with the period. Thus to a single character was given in Japanese more than one sound, the two or more attempts to carry over the Chinese pronunciation and the equivalent Japanese word.

All this placed upon the Japanese intelligentsia a heavy burden from which to this day they have not escaped. Could they have invented or imported an alphabet their intellectual task would have been immeasurably lightened.

With the language came the introduction of the Japanese to Chinese literature. The Chinese classics, including the writings of Confucius, were brought in and studied. Works on divination entered, and Chinese methods of divination superseded the older, perhaps indigenous ones which had long been employed. Chinese histories were known. Chinese poets, including some of the great masters of the T'ang, then in the freshness of their charm, were prized.

For many years this utilization of Chinese language and literature was confined to a very small proportion of the population of Japan, largely court circles and the aristocracy. Not until much later did it make its way extensively into the middle and lower strata of society.

Gradually the Japanese ceased to be parasitic students of Chinese. They began writing their own literature. Poems were composed, some of them apparently showing the influence of old native folk songs. Histories were written incorporating indigenous myths and traditions but showing the effects of imported Chinese ideas. Notable were the *Kojiki* (Record of Ancient Things), compiled in 712, and the *Nihon-shoki* or *Nihongi* (Chronicles of Japan), written in 720, our chief written sources for the early history of Japan. Laws were compiled. Romances appeared, among them the extraordinary *Genji Monogatari*, one of the world's great books, written by a court lady, Murasaki Shikibu, in the first part of the eleventh century.

Eventually, and by slow stages, the Japanese began creating, from the adaptation and simplification of Chinese characters, phonetic systems for writing Japanese, the ancestors of the phonetic representation of Japanese syllables which later came into extensive use. Unfortunately no scheme of phonetic writing ever freed the Japanese from the awkward and heavy incubus of the Chinese character. The use of that character and of the Chinese language kept the Japanese in touch with the movements of thought in the greatest cultural center of the Far East. Yet it also proved a handicap, stifling indigenous creativeness, lengthening the educative process, and crippling the Japanese mind.

Through religion and the ethics and social ideals which entered with it the civilization of the continent exercised a profound influence on Japan. With the Chinese classics came, inevitably, something of Confucianism. While Confucian religious and philosophical ideas never attained quite the position in Japan which they held in China, they were influential. The honors to ancestors inculcated by Confucianism had important repercussions. The Confucian ideals of the family and of filial piety bore fruit. The belief in *T'ien*, or Heaven, entered, and worship of Heaven by monarchs and commoners developed. Taoism made contributions, partly in the form of magical practices, but never became the important distinct cult that it did in China.

Buddhism Arrives

As a formal cult Buddhism became much more prominent than either Confucianism or Taoism and relatively was far more outstanding in Japan than in China. All the reasons for this difference are not entirely clear, but some seem fairly obvious. The period in which Japan was coming into close touch with China was that of the heyday of Buddhism in the Middle Kingdom. In the period of disunion between the Han and the Sui, it will be remembered, Buddhism had a very rapid growth in China and under the T'ang reached the apex of its popularity and vigor in that Empire. It was natural that it should make a profound impression upon the Japanese, then importing as they were the civilization of China. Then, too, Confucianism was not tied up intimately with the development of Japan as it was with China, and Taoism did not have the footing of an indigenous faith. In Japan neither could offer the resistance to Buddhism that they could in their native habitat. What might have happened had they possessed the same standing in Japan that they enjoyed in China may be conjectured from the persistence of Japan's indigenous religion, Shinto. Although Shinto was much weaker philosophically and structurally than was Confucianism and even Taoism in China, it survived as a potent force in Japan and, while modified by Buddhism, was probably no more affected than were Confucianism and Taoism in China.

The precise date when Buddhism made its way to Japan we do not know. It seems first to have been brought by aliens, Chinese or Koreans. In the sixth century one of the states of Korea sent to Japan an image of Buddha, some of the Buddhist scriptures, or *sutras*, and Buddhist monks. In the same century there came, also from Korea, more *sutras*, makers of Buddhist images, images themselves, monks, and a temple architect. The Japanese ruling house did not at first take a decided stand either for or against the new faith. The issue provoked a struggle between some of the leading families. On the one hand, two who were then powerful but whose names need not be a charge on our memory and one of whom owed its position largely to the fact that it was in charge of the Shinto rites at the court and in the chief shrines, bitterly opposed Buddhism. On the other hand were the Soga, who championed the new faith seemingly as a means of enhancing their own position and displacing their rivals. The Soga won and their victory gave a great impulse to Buddhism. At the end of the sixth and at the beginning of the seventh centuries Shotoku Taishi, prince of the imperial line and one of the most influential men in the entire history of Japan, gave Buddhism his support. Teachers came from the continent, at first largely from Korea, and temples and priests and nuns multiplied. Later, in the T'ang period, numbers of Japanese went to China to study Buddhism at its leading centers in that country. Both the main schools of Buddhism, Hinayana and Mayahana, gained fairly early entrance, and several of the schools or sects which were prominent in China were represented.

In the seventh and eighth centuries Buddhism made remarkably rapid progress in Japan. Its chief stronghold was among the upper classes, but Buddhist missionaries, both Japanese and foreign, spread it widely through the country. Great temples and monasteries were built and huge statues of the Buddha were erected. Buddhist monasteries became richly endowed with lands and embellished with costly gifts. Outside the aristocratic court circles the Buddhist monks were almost the only possessors of learning. Like the Christian monks in medieval Europe, they helped to spread both material and spiritual culture and to care for the underprivileged members of society. In the provinces their monasteries became civilizing centers. They promoted the building of dikes, bridges, and roads. They inaugurated orphanages, infirmaries, and other charitable institutions.

Shinto offered little effective opposition. Buddhism was a religion with a much more mature philosophy, a much deeper insight into the mysteries of life and of the universe, and was the vehicle of a higher civilization. As usually happens when a more advanced faith connected with a more powerful culture comes in contact with a primitive religion, Shinto yielded ground without a serious struggle.

However, unlike many other religions under similar circumstances, Shinto did not disappear nor was it absorbed by its rival. It continued its separate course as a distinct cult. To be sure, Buddhist priests frequently took part in Shinto rites and a *modus vivendi* was evolved in which the Shinto deities were esteemed phases of the beings revered by Buddhism. This long threatened the assimilation of the native cult to the powerful alien. However, Shinto never quite lost its existence and eventually was revived.

The Coming of Continental Art

The Japanese proved unusually receptive to the art and architecture of the continent. Much of this came in connection with Buddhism. The images, paintings, frescoes, and temples associated so intimately with Buddhism as to be almost inseparable from it gained quick and wide popularity. The Japanese seem early to have had a sensitive appreciation of beauty, and Buddhist art wakened in them whatever of this was latent. Buddhist art came to Japan by way of China and that cultural satellite of China, Korea. Much of it, therefore, was Chinese. Yet the many traditions by which Buddhist art had been affected in its pilgrimage to China—Indian of several periods, Persian, Hellenic, and Graeco-Roman—also crossed to Japan as integral parts of the whole.

Chinese secular art also entered. For instance, the capitals which the Japanese constructed under the impulse of continental example, first Nara and then the later Kyoto, at the outset known as Heian-kyo, "the capital of peace and tranquility," had as their models the T'ang capital, Ch'angan, with its regular form and rectangular arrangement of streets.

Chinese costumes and ceremonies had their influence upon the Japanese.

As in other phases of culture, the Japanese did not remain blind or slavish imitators. They early began making adaptations of what they received. Before long, distinctive touches and modifications were being given to the foreign styles. While in art Japanese civilization was obviously a child of that of China, the variations in it from its Chinese parentage often bore the evidence of genius.

Political Changes

Some of the most spectacular and far-reaching changes brought by contact with China were in the structure of the state.

In the China of the Sui and the T'ang the Japanese came in touch with a government in many ways fundamentally different from their own. Theirs was a small state, a nation, ruled by aristocratic families recruited on the basis of heredity and with one family having an acknowledged priority over the others but not dominating them. That family had held this position since the dawn of history. There had been only one dynasty. China was an empire embracing a vast stretch of territory and united by a culture inculcated through a system of education and a structure of government. The theory on which it was built was Confucian. At the head was an Emperor, presumed to be ruling by his virtue. In practice each dynasty was founded by a successful warrior and the throne went by heredity until the line by losing its vigor sacrificed the mandate of Heaven and was forcibly ejected by another. This Emperor, however, governed through a bureaucracy which was recruited not on the basis of birth but of worth. That worth was tested by competitive examinations. Intrigue, influence, and bribery in part determined appointment to office, and certain families by tradition and the hereditary atmosphere of culture gave to their scions an advantage in the preparation for the examinations. In general, however, Chinese society was fairly fluid, offering opportunity for ability to come to the top.

The effort was made to reproduce this system in Japan. One of its great exponents was the prince Shotoku Taishi (died 621 or 622) whom we met in connection with the introduction of Buddhism. He was Crown Prince and later Regent. He was a student of the Confucian classics as well as of Buddhism and a warm, although not an indiscriminate, admirer of foreign culture. Somewhat after the Confucian spirit of exhortation and ethical instruction of the ruled by the rulers, he issued what has been variously termed a constitution and a set of laws. It was in part moral maxims applied to government and social relations and in part principles and a framework of state. It had in it both Confucian and Buddhist ideas. There were others besides Shotoku Taishi, some of them also of the imperial clan, who had a share in transplanting the Chinese political system to China.

In the change the position of the Emperor was exalted above the kind of primacy which had once been his. The Soga family, who had controlled the imperial house and who for a time sought to displace it by their own, were forced out of power (A.D. 645). An edict issued in 646 gave to the period 645–650 the name Taikwa, Great Reform, and if carried out would have revolutionized both the political and the economic structure of Japan. Other edicts and measures of the seventh and eighth centuries, including codes of laws, contributed to the framework of the change. A bureaucracy was set up. The territory of the nation was to be divided into provinces, the provinces into districts, and the districts into townships. Civil service examinations were introduced. The agricultural land was to be apportioned among the farmers in allotments varying with the size of the family. From time to time it was to be redistributed to ensure equalization as the population changed. A new system of taxation was adopted.

In general, the coming of Chinese political institutions made for the exaltation of the position of the Emperor, the centralization of authority under the crown, the partial end of the old patriarchalism, and a uniform law promulgated from above and applicable to all subjects. The nation was divided, according to the Chinese theory, into two classes, the rulers and the ruled. The latter were to support the former and were not to concern themselves with matters of government.

Never was the Chinese system literally reproduced. From the outset concessions had to be made to the great families. The imperial family had the continuation of the headship of the state as a permanent possession and not, as in China, on the basis of its "virtue." The position of the Emperor was enhanced. He continued, in theory, a visible or incarnate god, owing his throne to divine descent from the Sun Goddess. He was given the added authority that was associated with the Chinese Emperor. The higher offices of the central administration usually went to scions of the most powerful clans and some of the local offices became hereditary in the more influential local families. The examinations were not thrown open to all who cared to apply, as in China, but were restricted to a narrow aristocratic group. The leading Shinto shrines with their priesthood and numbers of the Buddhist monasteries and their monks were accorded special privileges. The support of the majority of the most influential elements was thus ensured for the new type of government, but at the cost of some essential features of the Chinese model. The system preserved the aristocratic nature of Japanese society, based upon birth, in contrast with China, with its recruiting of the ruling classes by worth proved through competition.

Even though modified to take account of Japanese conditions, the imported Chinese political system eventually largely broke down. In place of it developed a feudalism with a dual form of government peculiar to Japan, part of it centering about the Emperor and an evolution from the pre-Chinese and Chinese stages, and the other, which did the actual administering of the state, a military structure. To this important development we must revert more in detail after sketching the chronological sequence of the next few centuries.

The Fujiwara Come to Power

One phase, and an early one, in the modification of what had been imported from China was the acquisition of much of the real power by the Fujiwara family.

The Fujiwara had as their founder one of the great men of Japan, Kamatari, a son of one of the older prominent families. Interestingly enough, this family had been one which, because the chief priests of Shinto were drawn from it as a hereditary right, had opposed the introduction of Buddhism. Now the tables were turned. Against the Soga, who had employed Buddhism to further their interests, arose from their ancient enemy a supporter of the Chinese political system. A pioneer in introducing a phase of continental culture was ousted through one who, at least ostensibly, was aiding in bringing in another feature of that culture. Kamatari championed Chinese culture and the political changes associated with it. He used this advocacy to assist in the overthrow of the Soga. It was not the last time that the leadership of a clan reversed its attitude toward the introduction of a foreign culture and utilized this reversal to further its own interests. We are to see the same phenomenon paralleled in the nineteenth century when the great Western feudatories, from being opponents of intercourse with the Occident who used that recalcitrancy to embarrass the family then in charge of the state, became converts to the necessity of making their peace with the Westerner.

The demotion of the Soga did not mean the restoration of full control to an absolute sovereign. It meant that the Soga were replaced by Kamatari. Kamatari became dominant. After him the Fujiwara, the family which looked back to him as their founder, continued his power. In the course of the next several generations they increased it and for centuries held their favored position.

The Fujiwara achieved this leadership not by forcing off the throne the descendants of Jimmu Tenno and making of themselves a new imperial dynasty. Rather they aided in exalting the nominal authority of the Emperor and exercised their power through their control of the monarchs. They saw to it that enough of the chief offices of state were held by members of their family to ensure their dominance. They insisted that men of the imperial line marry Fujiwara women and took care that the Emperors were sons of Fujiwara mothers. The Fujiwara men took advantage of their position as members of the Empresses' family to dominate the state. This had precedent in China, although it does not necessarily follow that the Fujiwara looked to that precedent for support. During the Emperor's minority a Fujiwara was Regent (*Sessho*), and after he attained his majority a Fujiwara became Dictator (*Kwampaku* or *Kampaku*).

In the position of the Soga and the failure of that family to gain the imperial title and in the place achieved by the Fujiwara there was a marked departure from the Chinese system. In the latter in theory the Emperor ruled not by right of birth but by his "virtue," and in practice one family after another held the imperial throne. The most aggressive aspired to the throne and, if they proved forceful and able enough, succeeded in grasping it. In Japan the imperial dynasty was never deposed. The individual members who occupied the throne were often handled very roughly. Many were compelled to retire or to abdicate, and now and then one was disposed of in more violent fashion. However, the family itself went on and the supreme authority was vested in one of its members. Never was there a change of dynasty. Yet the real power was exercised by whoever was able to seize it.

This, as we shall see again and again in the course of our story, has been characteristic of Japan, not only of the imperial institution but also in some other aspects of the nation's life. Much has been made of continuing the nominal authority in the family which has held it, but the actual rule has been exercised, in the name of the legitimate holder, by the one who has had the skill to grasp it. For the possession of this real power bitter struggles have been waged.

This Japanese method has made for a kind of stability combined with flexibility which is akin to another feature we have earlier noticed, the espousal by the aristocracy of the changes necessary to the assimilation of foreign culture, the engineering of revolutions from the top rather than from the bottom.

In accordance with this principle of continuity the Fujiwara continued to be prominent in the life of Japan. Later, as we shall see, the active administration passed out of their hands. Their aristocratic prestige was preserved, however, and in the present century the family has been represented in some of the most influential positions in the state.

Nara

In 710, in pursuance of a decision made a few years before, the capital was moved to Nara. Up to then the imperial residence and with it the capital had been changed very often. This transiency had been from a variety of reasons, and was made possible by the modest construction of the imperial palace from such perishable materials that a new one could be erected for the new sovereign more readily than the old one could be repaired. Now something more permanent was built and the capital remained there during the greater part of the eighth century.

Nara was laid out with the T'ang capital at Ch'angan as a model. With the magnificent Ch'angan as an ideal, it was built on generous lines. In it in the course of the next two generations there were erected temples, palaces, and buildings for the offices of state. Some of these were very large. The great hall of the chief imperial Buddhist temple was enormous. Its present successor, although smaller than the original, is said to be the largest wooden structure under one roof in the entire world. The huge metal Buddha for which it is the setting was a prodigious undertaking. Nara became the center of a brilliant and luxurious society, reveling in the culture that was flowing in from the continent. Art flourished. Some of the surviving examples indicate skill and exquisite taste.

Throughout the country there was also much building. By imperial decree a temple and a pagoda were to be erected in each province. Buddhism was prospering. It had the position of a state religion. It possessed a hierarchy whose leading positions were filled by imperial appointment. In addition to the temples constructed under imperial order, many others were rising. Some of this was from religious enthusiasm. Some was to obtain exemption of lands from taxation.

The area under cultivation was increasing. Apparently population was growing. Certainly the portion of the islands controlled by the Japanese state was being enlarged. Economically that state was based mainly upon rice. In the Nara period new land was being brought under rice culture. The frontier was being pushed northward on the main island. All Kyushu seems finally to have been occupied, and settlers were moving still farther south into the Ryukyu Islands. The standard of living was improving for the upper classes.

Yet this Nara era, so brilliant in many ways and marked by an increase in wealth for the nation as a whole, more and more suffered from economic and political maladjustment. Nara with its costly buildings and its even more extravagant aristocracy meant an ominous advance in expense. The officialdom planned on the Chinese model proved costly. What could be borne by a great empire was onerous for the relatively small Japan of the time. Taxes mounted and the load proved crushing for the lower classes. The peasant cultivators were ground down by imposts and by hard compulsory labor under the guise of military service. Many of those with influence succeeded in gaining tax exemption for their lands. This, naturally, augmented the burden for those who were not so exempt. The unsound economic structure of the state contributed to a social and a political revolution which went on for several centuries and which ultimately issued in important innovations.

Heian

Late in the eighth century the capital was moved to Heian-kyo, or, to give it the briefer name by which it is usually known, really an adjective, Heian. It is also called Kyoto. The original decision had been to place the new capital on a site a few miles from Heian, but after a decade of construction, when the buildings on this location were nearing completion, a change of plans brought about the fixing of the capital at Heian-kyo. We do not know why either transfer was made, although different conjectures have been ventured. Heian-kyo was approximately on the site of the present Kyoto, but most of the present city lies east of what was meant to be the central avenue of the original city. For Heian-kyo as for Nara the model was the T'ang capital, Ch'angan. Although by this time the T'ang dynasty had begun the slow decline which brought it to its end, Ch'ang-an was still the most imposing city which the Japanese knew and it is not surprising that they took it as a guide. Although Heian-kyo was considerably smaller than Ch'ang-an, in the ninth century it was one of the larger cities of the world.

Heian-kyo, even more than Nara before it, became the habitat of an aristocratic, refined, luxurious, sophisticated culture. This culture was confined chiefly to the upper classes. Not for three centuries or more did it spread at all notably to the provinces nor did provincial centers become important cultural rivals to the capital.

As was to be expected, Heian culture was based largely upon Chinese models, but was given Japanese modifications and additions.

Etiquette was stressed, originally with T'ang precedents in mind. Indeed, the days, especially of the Emperors, were burdened with elaborate ceremonies. There was much of amorous intrigue, also according to studied rule. Verse-making was a popular avocation and contests in it were part of the life of court circles. Japanese poetry as well as that of Chinese prototypes flourished. Romances were written, the most notable of them being the *Genji Monogatari*, which we have already mentioned, famous not only for its style but also for its picture of Heian society. In accordance with Chinese precedent, calligraphy was prized. Penmanship became as much a fine art as painting or sculpture. In the luxury of the court and the aristocracy, a large amount of attention was paid to the fine arts. Painting flourished. Buddhist subjects were familiar and popular, but there was also a secular art. There was landscape painting, as was natural in view of the emphasis placed upon it in the dynasty in China, the Sung, which began about two generations after the removal of the capital to Heian. There was sculpture, much of it in wood. Beautiful buildings were erected, some of them palaces and some temples. Gardens were elaborated and pains were often taken to give temples a beautiful natural setting. In the latter part of the period pictured scrolls, later to enjoy a marked development, had their beginning. Much of the art is characterized by a certain femininity. This was to be expected in circles as refined as those of Kyoto and as given to intrigue and as removed from the rough and tumble of life. As in China, there was a keen sense of the fleeting nature of life, of the sadness of the falling leaf and the fading flower, an undercurrent of melancholy, but in Kyoto the robustness of Chinese art was toned down, and some of the starker features of what came from the continent were not reproduced or were given milder forms. There was little profound philosophy or agonized and determined grappling with the problem of evil.

Buddhism continued popular. Buddhist temples and monasteries multiplied, partly out of religious conviction and partly because of the tax exemption given by the state to temple lands. To the schools or sects of Buddhism present in the Nara period, six in number and all derived from the continent, were added others, also based upon continental originals. T'ien T'ai, which we have already mentioned in connection with its origin in China, was made the basis for the *Tendai* school. The founder was Saicho, better known by his posthumous designation, Dengyo Daishi. He studied T'ien T'ai at its mother monastery in China. However, he did not reproduce it blindly but added to it other elements. From his monastery on Mt. Hiyei, outside of Kyoto, he found it easy to keep in touch with the court and enjoyed marked influence there. Another school, this time not of Chinese but of Indian creation, but coming to Japan by way of China, was the True Word, in Chinese *Chên-yen*, in Japanese *Shingon*. It was a late development from Buddhism. Pantheistic, it declared that the one spirit manifests itself in many emanations and forms, and claimed that it had an esoteric, "true word," doctrine revealed to initiates only after a long and grueling novitiate. It stressed magic formulas, spells, ritual, and incantations. Baptism became in it an important rite. Its Japanese founder was a contemporary of Dengyo Daishi, Kukai, usually known by his canonical title, Kobo Daishi. He, too, studied in China, and there had the benefit of instruction by priests from Kashmir and southern India. Pure Land (in Chinese *Ch'ing T'u*) Buddhism did not begin in Japan as a formal school (*Jodo*) until the twelfth century, but much of the teaching it embodied had come in more than two centuries before that time. Its reliance upon simple faith in Amida Buddha for entrance after death into the Western Paradise, the Pure Land, had a wide popular appeal. All Japanese Buddhist schools felt the effect and adopted some features of the Amida cult.

The popularity and growth of Buddhism did not prevent moral practices repugnant to the faith. As the Heian period went on, much sexual laxity was seen, both in aristocratic circles and in the Buddhist monasteries themselves. Moreover, in the mounting political disorder of which we are to speak in a moment, numbers of the Buddhist monasteries, probably originally in self-protection, recruited armed bands and engaged in the fighting which more and more became common.

The Rise of Feudalism

The removal of the court to Heian-kyo did not prevent the progress of a political evolution which had already begun while the imperial residence was at Nara. The structure of the state built after the Chinese pattern failed to meet the needs of the Japanese situation and there arose a military feudalism through which most of the actual government was carried on. In true Japanese fashion, the old was not entirely supplanted. The Emperor was still the sacrosanct fountain of honors and authority. The court nobility continued, an aristocratic, cultured circle, with great social prestige. In fact, however, administration, national and local, was through a feudal structure which was growing up without any one person planning it. Not until the twelfth century did a political genius give it a comprehensive form.

From the very beginning the seeds of decay were in the form of government which had been inspired by Chinese example. The traditions in China and Japan were so different that the kind of government which had arisen in the one after centuries of experience, much of it painful, could scarcely be taken over successfully. To be sure, the copying had not been blind. Compromises had been made, as we have seen, with the aristocratic tradition of Japan. The leading offices had been reserved for the members of the more powerful families and competition in the civil service examinations had been restricted chiefly to those of noble blood.

To a large degree, however, these very concessions to the Japanese background were the cause of the downfall of the imported system. The more influential of the aristocracy obtained for their estates exemption from taxation. Many had their holdings declared to be private and not public land and so not subject to the periodical redistributions of the public domain among the cultivators. Numbers, too, while possessing the titles and the emoluments of offices whose duties should have taken them to the provinces, remained in the capital, but sent substitutes one of whose duties it was to remit to them as much wealth as possible. Special inducements had to be offered to the aristocracy to persuade them to assume posts that required residence away from the capital. Then, too, influential officials and prominent members of the imperial family were granted the right to bestow some of the provincial offices upon those whom they chose and, in return, received part of the perquisites of the posts.

The privately owned lands which were not subject to periodical redistribution constituted *sho* or *shoen*. These were akin to the manors of European feudalism. The owners of the *shoen* sought to gain for them exemption from taxes. This they largely succeeded in doing. They also endeavored to win for them exemption from control or visitation by officials of the imperial government. Those *shoen* which had these rights became in fact independent *imperia in imperio*.

The *shoen* had their rise in a number of ways. Some were lands which in the great reforms by which the Chinese system had been introduced had never been incorporated into public property. Many belonged to temples, shrines, or monasteries and because of their status of grants in perpetuity by the state and their exemption from taxation were no longer under the direct control of the government. Others grew out of awards of lands for special services, and although not all of these were in perpetuity many which were supposed to return to the state at the end of a specified time in practice did not do so. Large numbers came into being from the reclamation of lands hitherto uncultivated. In the expansion of territory and the growth of population of these years, the amount of waste ground brought into rice fields was very considerable. Much nonarable land, in the form of pasture or forest, and which was not taxable, was appropriated by private individuals.

The *shoen* grew like snowballs under what in European feudalism was termed commendation. Commendation took various forms, but in essence it was the surrender by its owner of taxable land to the possessor of a tax-free estate. In return the original proprietor retained the use of the land but paid a proportion of the income to the commendee. This led to a very complicated set of relationships, for to be sure of retaining their privileges less powerful owners of *shoen* commended their holdings to more powerful ones and they in turn to still more influential institutions or personages.

Shoen were frequently subdivided through the practice of benefices. Benefice was the grant by the holder of a tax-free estate of rights or privileges attached to a piece of land, such as part of its produce or of the labor of men attached to it, for a given return.

Efforts were made from time to time to restrict the growth of *shoen*, for the increase in their number and area meant the reduction of the imperial revenues and of the direct authority of the imperial administration. So many powerful personages and institutions benefited by them, however, that attempts to force the return of the *shoen* to the imperial jurisdiction and fiscal system usually proved futile. The proportion of the realm embraced in them rose and with that rise the effective authority of the Heian court declined.

The decay of the Chinese-imported imperial system was further evidenced by the prominence of piracy and brigandage and by costly wars against the Ainu. In some sections piracy and brigandage became common. Although the Ainu were in time defeated and the borders of the realm were pushed northward in the main island at their expense, corruption and inefficiency in the Japanese armies greatly delayed the achievement and the costs placed an additional burden upon the treasury and added to the tax load.

The Fujiwara Continue

The exercise of his prerogatives by the Emperor was further curtailed by the continuing dominance in the capital of the Fujiwara and by the custom of brief reigns and early abdications. At the close of the ninth, the beginning of the tenth, and in the latter part of the eleventh centuries vigorous sovereigns made temporarily successful attempts to curb the Fujiwara. Yet that family continued powerful. Indeed, their heyday was in the second half of the tenth and the first half of the eleventh centuries, after one of the most aggressive of these efforts against them. As earlier, the Fujiwara married their daughters to the Emperors, and as soon as an heir was born to one of these ladies and became old enough to beget sons he was in turn mated with a Fujiwara. If this heir had sons, his father was persuaded to abdicate in his favor. Thus the throne was filled by a succession of boys or inexperienced young men, the sons of Fujiwara mothers and under the control of their maternal relatives. So onerous were the ritual duties and the requirements of the court etiquette upon the reigning monarchs that the latter were generally not unwilling to retire.

Some of the more vigorous of the abdicated monarchs sought to use their freedom to dominate their successors and contested with the Fujiwara the exercise of the power behind the throne. Thus through the tradition that he who reigned was not the real ruler but a puppet, the structure of administration acquired additional complications.

The Fujiwara almost never presented a united front. There were intrigues and conflicts among them for the leadership of the family. The family itself developed many branches, and some of these became bitter rivals.

Although the dignity of the Emperor was still intact and the social position of the court nobility remained high, the real power was slipping from Heian and was being decentralized. It was coming to reside actually in feudal lords.

The weakening of the capital and the development of feudalism did not mean that Japan was in decay. On the contrary, the area occupied by the Japanese was expanding. That expansion was mainly eastward and northward on the main island. Here was the chief frontier. Moreover, the population and presumably the wealth of the country were growing. That wealth was increasingly in the feudal *shoen*. Luxurious and sophisticated Heian with its aristocratic culture might be the center of nominal authority, but the economic resources of the land were progressively passing out of its hands.

The Rise of the Military Class

Associated with the decentralization of power, the proven futility of the administration system associated with the adoption of Chinese institutions, the expansion of Japanese territory, and the rise of feudalism with its *shoen*, there came the development of a military class. In the breakdown of the imported Chinese system some kind of armed force was required by landowners and officials for defense and aggression against one another and the robbers and pirates and for carrying on the wars with the Ainu. Accordingly private armies of varying sizes came into being. As was to be expected, these were especially strong in the provinces. New families gradually came to the fore, based upon the land and strengthened by their armed retainers. The clan or family tradition, so strong in Japan from the earliest times, persisted in them and took on forms adapted to the needs of the times. The most prominent of these families provided the *daimyo*, the "great names," of this new feudal and military aristocracy. Their armed retainers became the *samurai*, "those who serve," a warrior caste. The new military class exalted as virtues loyalty to the clan and the lord, physical courage, and contempt of death. The sword became its badge and symbol. As such and as an effective weapon the sword was accorded marked attention. Much skill and artistic taste went into its manufacture. In time it represented a distinct form of art.

Taira and Minamoto

The two leading groups of the military clans or families were the Taira and the Minamoto. Both claimed descent from scions of the imperial family, princes of the imperial blood for whom there had been no future in crowded Heian and for whom provision had been made in lands and offices in the provinces. There were several major branches of the Minamoto, each with the son of an Emperor for an ancestor.

No unity existed between these military families. On the contrary, feuds were chronic. For a time the Fujiwara were able to play off one family against another and so to retain power. Because of the divisions among the military, the *kuge* (court nobles), although more and more impotent in arms, were able to hold on to at least some of their privileges.

At the close of the eleventh and in the twelfth century the feebleness of the imperial court and the *kuge* could no longer be concealed. Armed priests of rival temples, Buddhist and Shinto, fought in the streets of Heian. The forces of the Taira and the Minamoto had to be called in to preserve order. The situation was complicated and Kyoto weakened by the efforts of an unusually strong Emperor who happened not to have one of the Fujiwara for a mother to curb the power of that family, by dissensions among the Fujiwara, and by ill feeling between the Emperor and the cloistered or retired Emperor.

In the second half of the twelfth century came a period of civil strife in which the chief rivals were the Taira and the Minamoto. The story of the struggle, with its battles, its generals, and its military heroes, is classical in Japan and its prominent names are household words. The details are far too numerous and confusing to be incorporated in a narrative which, like this, must be a summary. Only the barest outline can be given.

In the first stage of the conflict the Taira, under their great leader, Kiyomori, were victorious. Yoshitomo, the outstanding figure among the Minamoto, was killed and practically all other members of that family who seemed to give promise of seriously contesting the power of the Taira were put out of the way. A few escaped, among whom were two who later revived Minamoto power, Yoritomo and Yoshitsune, sons of Yoshitomo by different mothers. Yoritomo was spared because of his charm and self-possession and until he reached maturity lived in exile under Taira surveillance. Yoshitsune together with two full brothers was allowed to live and was placed in a monastery to be reared for the priesthood because his mother, of dazzling beauty, was desired by Kiyomori and as a price exacted the lives of her sons. Kiyomori now dominated Kyoto. He was given high office and even outranked the Fujiwara. One of his daughters was married to the Emperor and in time her child, the grandson of Kiyomori, became Emperor.

However, the father's death, in 1181, gave the Minamoto the opportunity again to raise their heads. Indeed, the year before, 1180, Yoritomo had already reared the standard of revolt. Yoritomo was a man of unusual ability. Dauntless in war, cold-hearted and courteous, cheerful in adversity and, as the event later proved, gifted in intrigue, ruthless in attaining his ends, and possessed of unusual gifts of organization, he became one of the leading figures in Japanese history. Others of the Minamoto joined him.

In 1183 the Taira fled westward from Kyoto, carrying with them the infant Emperor in whose veins flowed their blood. A cloistered Emperor came to the capital supported by the Minamoto and assumed charge. It was not Yoritomo who was in Kyoto, however, but a cousin. Yoritomo was in the east, mastering provinces and organizing his administration. He and the cousin fell out and the latter was defeated and slain. The cloistered Emperor gave his support to Yoritomo. Yoshitsune, who cooperated with Yoritomo, although only in his twenties, proved a consummate general. He moved westward into the traditional strongholds of the Taira and defeated them not only on land but also on the water, their special element. In the great naval battle where the Taira were finally overwhelmed the young Emperor perished, drowned in the sea into which, when all was lost, one of the court ladies plunged with him in her arms. Yoritomo was jealous of his brilliant brother, ordered his execution, and had him pursued. After adventurous wanderings, Yoshitsune, defeated and trapped, killed his wife and children and in good Japanese style committed suicide. Not long after the death of Yoshitsune Yoritomo overwhelmed his other remaining serious rival, one of the wealthy branches of the Fujiwara.

The Shogunate (Bakufu)

Yoritomo now set about the task of organizing his victory and giving it permanence. In doing so he devised for Japan a form of government which, with important modifications and additions, endured until the second half of the nineteenth century.

Yoritomo probably did not think of himself as a revolutionist. He did not seek to supplant the imperial house or its court. Both continued as the nominal source of authority and of dignities. His characteristic title, the one which was usually that of the head of the arm of the government which he elaborated, was *Sei-i-tai-Shogun*, "Barbarian-Subduing-General," or, as it is abbreviated, *Shogun*. It was bestowed upon him in 1192, a date which is generally reckoned as that of the beginning of the Shogunate. It was not a new title nor was it created especially for him. It had been known as early as the latter part of the eighth century. It was not assumed by him in his own name but was awarded him by the cloistered Emperor who had endorsed him. From time to time he sought the sanction of Kyoto for various items of his policy. The Fujiwara were not eliminated, and some of the members of that family were continued in the possession of their estates. He did not disturb the principles of the feudalism which he found in existence. He was simply endeavoring to make secure and to extend his own power.

The title of *Shogun* gave Yoritomo the legal control of all the military forces of the land. It was these and the feudal structure with which they were associated which he organized in such fashion as to ensure the continuation of his power. The administration to which he gave form was known as the *Bakufu*, which may be translated as Army Headquarters or Camp Office. It is usually termed in English the Shogunate. He placed his residence and the center of his administrative system at Kamakura, in the east, presumably because in this region most of his own estates lay and the majority of his dependable vassals and friends lived. The Minamoto had lands and allies throughout much of Japan, but it was in the east that their strength was greatest. It may be, too, that Yoritomo wished by this step to keep his regime uncontaminated by the enervating luxury of the over-refined Kyoto. His was an administration by vigorous warriors and they, or their descendants, might well succumb to the Kyoto traditions if they were exposed to them.

At Kamakura Yoritomo brought into being machinery for his central government. This was in three divisions—military, administrative, and judicial. His courts developed careful judicial procedures and appeared eager to see that justice, as that word was understood in the military circles of the time, was even-handed. Outside of Kamakura Yoritomo created an officialdom which was dependent on him. In provinces where it seemed wise he appointed a Constable or Protector (*shugo*). This official was a military governor in charge of military and police matters. To a very large number of private and public domains Yoritomo assigned stewards (*jito*) who, supported by the necessary armed forces, were to levy taxes for military purposes upon all cultivated land. This step ignored the traditional tax exemption of the *shoen* and, accordingly, aroused much opposition. However, Yoritomo carried it through. He had himself named Constable General and Steward General and as the holder of these posts was in control of the new administrative system. In time the offices of Constable and Steward became hereditary. From the former came several of the most important lords of the later feudalism and from the latter some of the lesser gentry.

This new military system of offices did not supplant the old structure of government. The civil governors and the various other civil officials whose creation dated back to the introduction of the Chinese system continued. They, too, had become hereditary and could not be abolished, even had Yoritomo so desired, without great and possibly insuperable opposition. The imperial institution was preserved. The imperial judiciary heading up in Kyoto still dealt with civil and ecclesiastical disputes: the jurisdiction of the courts of the *Bakufu* was not all-inclusive. Moreover, a large number of estates were not brought under the Stewards (*jito*) or subjected to the military tax. Presumably Yoritomo did not feel himself strong enough or believe it necessary to extend the new structure to all the realm.

However, the new inevitably weakened the old. The families through whose members most of the clerkships in Kyoto were filled and through whom most of the actual work of imperial administration had been performed tended to move to Kamakura to find employment with the *Bakufu*. This largely stripped Kyoto of those trained in government and left there only the *fainéant* aristocracy, or *kuge*, who had inherited the titles of offices but had delegated the work to others. Kyoto retained its prestige and the aristocracy who held the old civil offices in theory outranked in social position the new military aristocracy, but in practice the power was passing to the latter.

Here again is an example of a fairly constant feature of Japanese life. What in reality was a revolution was effected while the forms of that which preceded it were largely preserved. Those who had proved their capacity by seizing the actual power constituted the real government and ruled either through old titles given in practice a new meaning or through new offices created to fill a felt need. Yet the old structure was allowed a nominal existence and retained some of its functions and prerogatives and the imperial house remained the fount of honor and dignity. The tradition permitted enough flexibility to meet fresh conditions, yet did not make a clean sweep of the past. We are to see this repeated again and again, even in our own day.

In this feature of their history the Japanese resemble the English. Both peoples, while from time to time disturbed by civil strife and experiencing marked changes in their political institutions, have had a reverence for the past and have preserved many outward forms which might seem anachronisms were it not for the fact that they still, with somewhat altered functions, prove useful.

The triumph of the military over the civil authorities also has continuing significance. From now on the warrior class were the actual rulers of the country. In their hands was the power. In this Japan turned its back upon the Chinese example. In spite of much reverence for Chinese culture and responsiveness to new currents of thought and art in the Middle Kingdom, the Japanese have had a political structure and a social tradition differing basically from those of the Middle Kingdom. This has made it very difficult for the two peoples sympathetically to understand each other. In its tradition of being ruled by an hereditary landed aristocracy honoring military prowess and with a feudal background Japan has been much more nearly akin to Western Europe than to China. Here is one of the reasons why the Japanese adjusted themselves so readily to Western civilization in the nineteenth and twentieth centuries and why the Chinese were much slower to do so. Here, too, is a source of the recent power of the army in the government.

Hojo Supremacy

The family of Yoritomo did not long hold the actual power. Yoritomo died in 1199 as the result of a fall from a horse. His descendants, while for a short time retaining the title of *Shogun*, became as much impotent puppets as were the Emperors in Kyoto. The actual power passed into the hands of the Hojo. The Hojo were a family in which Yoritomo had found support in the days of his struggle against the Taira. He married the Lady Masa, the daughter of a Hojo. His father-in-law, Hojo Tokimasa, proved an astute adviser and may have had much to do with the creation of the Shogunate as a continuing institution. Tokimasa became the head of the council of regency which was set up to supervise the administration of the son of Yoritomo. This son proved singularly incompetent and from a quarrel arising out of a struggle over the appointment of his heir was forced by his Hojo mother, the masterful Lady Masa, into early retirement. His eleven-year-old younger brother was thereupon made *Shogun* and Tokimasa became sole Regent. Before many years, as the result of an unsuccessful intrigue to transfer the title of *Shogun* from this son to another of Minamoto stock, a son-in-law of Tokimasa, the Lady Masa compelled her father, Tokimasa, to go into retirement and placed his son in the post of Regent. Since the latter was also a Hojo the power remained in the hands of that family.

The newly organized *Bakufu* did not escape serious challenge. Not many years after the death of Yoritomo a cloistered Emperor,

Toba II, sought to overthrow it and came too near to success for the comfort of the Kamakura officials. Toba II displayed much more energy and ability than most of the descendants of the Sun Goddess. He was a master in aristocratic physical sports and an adept in the literary occupations, including verse-making, popular in court circles. He had been placed on the throne at the age of four. When yet in his youth, apparently making up his mind that he could thus have both more power and more leisure, following well-established precedent, he abdicated in favor of a son. As retired Emperor he began plotting against the *Bakufu.* He gradually accumulated armed forces and obtained support of some of the monastic establishments with their armed contingents, no mean military asset. In 1221 he sought by a lightning *coup d'état* to overthrow the Hojo Regent. Kamakura proved too prompt and too strong for him. The Lady Masa and some of Yoritomo's advisers were still active and were not to be trifled with. The Regent soon made himself master of Kyoto, Toba II was banished to an island, the Emperor and two of his brothers were exiled, and another son of Toba II, also now an ex-Emperor, was removed elsewhere for safekeeping. Here was a spectacular but by no means isolated instance of vigorous dealing with the holders of the imperial title by those who held or who sought the reality of power. The imperial institution did not suffer, but if those who chanced to be the bearers of the imperial title proved too obdurate in seeking their own way methods were found for rendering them innocuous. This precedent, it may be added, has not been forgotten in the recent politics of Japan.

The abortive challenge of Toba II redounded, as the event proved, to the advantage of the *Bakufu.* The estates of many of those who had taken the part of Toba II were seized and were parceled out among the loyal vassals of the *Shogun.* Kyoto and the imperial court were placed more closely and effectively than before under the surveillance of Kamakura. The *Bakufu* was not abolished, but was reinforced.

The actual direction of the *Bakufu* long remained in the hands of the Hojo. That family produced an unusual succession of able men for the post of Regent. The office of *Shogun* was preserved, as the nominal head of the military regime. The direct line of Yoritomo early died out. To give the position dignity and to ensure the necessary prestige to the *Bakufu,* the post was filled from members of the Fujiwara family with its unimpeachable aristocratic name. In later years it was given to highly placed members of the imperial family. Always, however, in accordance with the tradition which the Fujiwara themselves had had so large a part in creating in their days of power in Kyoto, the *Shogun* was a puppet. If, on approaching maturity, he gave evidence of independence, he was forced to abdicate.

For many years the *Bakufu*, under its Hojo Regents, gave Japan a remarkably able and efficient government. Justice was, in general, even-handed. The code of law which was used as a basis for the decisions of judges was an evolution from the house law of the Minamoto family. It took cognizance of the actual conditions of feudalism and was grounded in practical experience. It was not, as had been early imperial codes, an importation from China with adaptations to Japan. While confined to matters which came under the *Bakufu* and not in theory applicable to civil officials and monasteries, in time this code of Kamakura constituted much of the common law of the country. In addition to its scrupulous administration of justice, the Kamakura *Bakufu* was careful to supervise the members of the bureaucracy whom it set up throughout the country. Inspectors investigated the acts of the Constables and Stewards and efforts were made to adjust taxation fairly to the capacity to pay. Through the secrecy of its debates, the council of state over which the Regent presided preserved outward unanimity in its decisions. This had obvious advantages. Moreover, the leaders of the *Bakufu* attempted to preserve the stern simplicity and physical hardihood which they felt should characterize the life of the warrior.

As time passed, the Kamakura regime decayed. Court nobles came from Kyoto and brought with them the luxurious and effeminate manners of that ancient capital. In spite of sumptuary legislation, the scale of living rose. Weakness set in. In 1333 the Hojo regency was brought to an end in acute civil strife and Kamakura was destroyed. This story, however, we must reserve for a later paragraph. We must first say something of changes in culture in what is known as the Kamakura period when, first under Yoritomo and then under the Hojo, that city was the center of the *Bakufu* and so of the real political life of Japan.

Kamakura Culture

The Kamakura period was marked by a series of striking developments in Japanese Buddhism. More than at any previous time Buddhism became popular, was given distinctively Japanese forms, and became the property of the masses and of the military class. Buddhism, as we have seen, owed its introduction to Japan to the upper aristocracy. Its first great strongholds were in the capital. In the course of time it spread to the provinces and long before the Kamakura period it had begun to penetrate the lower social strata. However, in the thirteenth century it made rapid strides among the rank and file of the population and adapted itself to their needs.

One feature of this spread among the ordinary Japanese was the development of Amidist schools. The preaching of salvation by faith in Amida which had begun earlier and which had found lodgment in most of the schools which had made their way to Japan now crystallized and was intensified in distinct schools. Pure Land, or Ch'ing Tu, as it was known in China, in Japan became paralleled by Jodo. It was Honen Shonin (1133–1212) who gave form to it and preached it among high and low. In spite of bitter opposition from the older schools, an opposition motivated more by economic than by religious rivalry, Jodo made rapid headway.

From Jodo came other schools. Of these the most famous was Jodo Shinshu, or True School of Jodo. Its founder was Shinran (1173–1262), a younger contemporary of Honen Shonin. Both men were learned and could write profoundly in abstruse philosophical language, but both could also speak the language of the streets and make their message plain to the simple. Shinran declared that since one wholehearted invocation of Amida was sufficient to ensure entrance into the Western Paradise, there was no need for the faithful to practice asceticism, to delve deeply into philosophy, or to engage in elaborate ceremonies. They should live as members of ordinary society, behaving decently. Accordingly the Shin priests married and dressed in lay garb. They were to be teachers rather than monks. Both Jodo and Shinshu were preached to the masses by popular evangelists.

A third new school bore the name of its originator, Nichiren. In some ways Nichiren (1222–1282) was unique and the most individual of the founders of Japanese Buddhist schools. Like Honen Shonin and Shinran he had scholarship in things Buddhistic and could give philosophical reasons for his tenets. Like them, too, he expounded a simple way of salvation and preached it to both men and women and to high and low. Salvation he found in the Lotus Scripture and for the rank and file stressed the utterance of the name of this sacred book as the one essential in religious faith. He was aggressive and highly intolerant of other Buddhist schools. A patriot, he had the welfare of Japan at heart. He was aware of the social and political evils of the day and foresaw that they must lead to growing disorder. Regarding himself as uniquely commissioned, he declared that the only way of avoiding national disaster was to give heed to him and accept the truth as he preached it. So vehemently outspoken and uncompromising was he that he met much opposition and, indeed, narrowly escaped execution on the charge of treason. He could, however, be kind and even tender to the humble and won a following in which were some of the warrior class. The school which he founded was ardently missionary and thrived in spite of persecution. It still exists, with a constituency running into the millions.

Ch'an, or, as it was known in Japan, Zen Buddhism flourished. Zen had long been known in Japan and had had influence. Now, however, it gained footing as a separate school. It appealed particularly to the warriors. Its belittlement of dogma, its declaration that enlightenment came as a sudden inner experience, its rigorous self-discipline, its austerity, and its studied simplicity appealed to the *samurai*. It did much to help form the ideals of that class.

In the realm of art and architecture the Kamakura period was marked by various developments. There was much temple building, some of it the renewal of structures destroyed in the wars which introduced the *Bakufu* and some for the embellishment of the city of Kamakura. A ceremonial tea-drinking began in connection with Zen Buddhism. It became a kind of ritual. Porcelain, some of it of extreme beauty, was being produced in Sung China, which partly overlapped the Kamakura period. It was not strange that it stimulated the Japanese aesthetic sense to emulate it. The father of Japanese porcelain went to China to study the art. Ceremonial tea-drinking, which needed pottery, promoted the manufacture of porcelain. There was a good deal of sculpture. Painting flourished. Sung landscapes had an effect. The picture scrolls, begun earlier, multiplied, and the extant specimens give vivid portrayals of the life of the times. Artistic skill was lavished on the armor and the swords of the warriors. This was to be anticipated in an era in which that class was prominent.

In general literature the Kamakura age made no remarkable contributions. Many legal documents of the time survive. A national written language arose. Yet the era was not one of literary creativeness. It is most noted for its political achievement in the *Bakufu* and for its religious developments. The other distinctive features were largely ancillary.

The Mongol Invasions

The Japan of Yoritomo and the Hojo Regents was not immediately affected in any profound fashion by the cultural brilliance of the contemporary Sung dynasty. Sung philosophy eventually made an impression, but that was largely later. Sung art had its admirers and inspired the Japanese genius to emulate some of its forms. Yet China of the Sung did not work such revolutionary changes as the China of the T'ang had done.

However, the Mongol invasion which overthrew the Sung extended to Japan and became a major event in Japanese history. Twice, in 1274 and 1281, the Mongols attempted to conquer Japan. On the first occasion the attacking expedition was launched from that most convenient continental point of approach, the southern tip of Korea. On the second occasion a large force came directly from China and another, smaller, by way of Korea. The Mongols were a land, not a sea power. They were compelled to use Chinese and Korean ships and sailors, and the considerable contingents of Mongols who embarked on these flotillas had no aptitude for naval warfare. The Japanese had ample warning and made preparations, especially against the second and more formidable onslaught. They fought bravely. Yet each time the Mongols effected a landing on Kyushu, the only foe until the year 1945 in times of which we have record to gain even a temporary footing on any of the major islands of Japan. It was geography and natural forces fully as much as Japanese valor which brought about the repulse of the invaders. The Japanese were then not particularly competent on the sea and could not sally forth to beat off the attackers. On each occasion a storm came to the aid of the defenders and wrought such havoc in the Mongol fleets that they were constrained to withdraw. Her geographic position then, as throughout her history and down into the present day, gave to Japan her chief security.

Kamakura Collapses

The Mongol invasions probably hastened the fall of the Hojo and an interruption in the *Bakufu*.

Before the invasions decay had already set in at Kamakura. Justice was no longer promptly administered. Luxury was sapping the vitality of the Kamakura lords. The Mongol invasions brought a heavy strain on public finances. Hampered by this load and by the impoverishment of the country, the *Bakufu* was called upon to reward its vassals who had responded to its appeal for aid in the defense of the country. Dissatisfaction multiplied.

The final blow which overthrew the Kamakura *Bakufu* came from Kyoto. Disputes had arisen over the succession to the imperial throne. These were accentuated by the provision, through the will of an earlier monarch, that the imperial title was to go alternately to the descendants of his two sons, thus creating junior and senior lines. The Hojo Regents interfered in the contests which arose. In doing so they ran afoul of the Emperor Daigo II (Go-Daigo). Daigo II had ascended the throne as a mature man and had energy and imagination. In the succeeding struggle numbers of the military, including some of the vassals and supposed supporters of the *Bakufu*, came to his aid. Among these was Ashikaga Takauji, of Minamoto blood, whose family had intermarried with the Hojo. For a time Takauji was one of the chief commanders of the forces of the *Bakufu*. However, in 1333 he suddenly went over, with his troops, to the side of Daigo II. This and the revolt of many in eastern Japan in the vicinity of Kamakura led to the thorough defeat of the *Bakufu*. Kamakura itself was captured (July 1333) and given to the flames. In spite of brief and futile attempts to revive it, Hojo supremacy had come to its end.

The Ashikaga

The victorious Daigo II wished to be monarch in fact as well as name. The court nobles (*kuge*) thought that the opportunity had come to resume the power that had been their ancestors' before the rise of the military class and the formation of the *Bakufu*. For a time a civilian government with court nobles in the chief posts was established at Kyoto. The military were relegated to subordinate positions.

However, the overthrow of the Hojo did not mean the collapse of the military. It had been brought about chiefly by military lords who had revolted against Hojo rule. The *kuge* had neither the resources nor the competence to govern the country. The military came out on top, and the outstanding figure among them, Ashikaga Takauji, reestablished the Shogunate.

This revival of the Shogunate was accomplished through the support by Takauji of a member of the senior branch on the throne (1336) in opposition to Daigo II, who was of the junior branch. Takauji was named *Shogun* (1338).

There now ensued more than a generation of civil strife. Daigo II and his supporters did not accept Takauji's protégé. Daigo II was forced to flee. Two lines of Emperors came into being, the southern, representing the junior line, and the northern, springing from the senior line. The latter had possession of Kyoto and the endorsement of the Ashikaga. Not until 1392 was unity regained. The period (1336–1392) is known to Japanese historians as that of the Northern and Southern Dynasties. While ostensibly waged over the question of the succession to the throne, the wars were in reality chiefly contests between the feudal lords for lands and vassals and of the Ashikaga for supremacy. Some families changed sides more than once to promote their own interests. In the conflict the authority and machinery of the central government, both imperial and of the *Bakufu*, were greatly weakened. The prestige of the imperial house declined. The great feudal lords, notably those having the position of *shugo*, tended to become autonomous. This condition was not quickly remedied when unity in the imperial line was restored but continued down into the sixteenth century.

The Ashikaga did not revive the headquarters of the *Bakufu* at Kamakura. The office of *Shogun* was long kept in their family, and the *Bakufu* and much of the machinery created for it by Yoritomo and his advisers were continued. The *Bakufu* had attained legitimacy and was considered the normal organization for military feudalism. However, the center of the *Bakufu* was now moved to Kyoto and was set up in the Muromachi quarter. The period, therefore, from 1392 to 1573 is known by the name of Muromachi. From its vantage point in Kyoto the Ashikaga *Bakufu* controlled the imperial court more effectively than the Kamakura *Bakufu* had been able to do. In the capital the military were supreme. Yet in the provinces the local authorities were inclined to pay scant heed to the Muromachi administration. The courts of the Ashikaga did not have the respect which those of Kamakura had commanded. In maintaining order and justice the Ashikaga regime was notoriously feeble. Moreover, as formerly in Kamakura so now in Kyoto, the *Shogun* became a mere puppet. The real authority was exercised by other officials of the *Bakufu*.

Muromachi Culture

In the course of the long civil wars between the supporters of the Northern and Southern Dynasties the court nobles (*kuge*) perforce mixed with the military nobility and in the process took on some of the manners of the latter. By bringing together in Kyoto the imperial court and the center of the *Bakufu* the warrior class was compelled to rub shoulders with the *kuge* and acquired more and more of the customs of the latter. At first the warrior might express contempt for the effeminate court noble but later he paid him the sincere flattery of at least partial imitation. There took place, accordingly, a fusion of the cultures of the two classes. Kyoto became a scene of luxury and ostentation.

In the competition, the *kuge* lost in wealth. Their estates had largely been seized by members of the military class, and they themselves were impoverished. Something of their former social position clung to them, but they fell in the economic scale. Even the Emperors became impecunious. We hear, for instance, that the body of one Emperor remained unburied for six weeks because there was no money for the funeral.

The decline of the *kuge* and the spread of culture to the warrior class had the advantage of making for a wider dissemination of some of the arts of civilization. These, formerly largely confined to the narrow circles of the Kyoto court and the monasteries, now became the property of a larger proportion of the population and flourished in more places. The very weakness of the *Bakufu* and the resulting decentralization of authority reenforced the trend, for the households of the more powerful of the various local magnates became centers of wealth and refinement. Towns, too, grew in importance and some of them achieved a certain degree of autonomy. Many of the widely scattered monastic establishments were sanctuaries of the arts and of literature. In spite of recurring civil strife which sometimes brought violence to its streets and destruction to its buildings, Kyoto with its luxurious court, now of the *Shogun* instead of the Emperor, continued to be the outstanding headquarters of culture. It was, however, no longer so nearly the exclusive possessor of it as it had once been.

One of the greatest agencies for nourishing and spreading culture was Zen Buddhism. As we have seen, Zen was popular with the military class. Since the latter was now dominant, it was to be expected that Zen would flourish. To be sure, some of the other schools of Buddhism also prospered. Jodo was widespread and the followers of Nichiren had a stormy but not unsuccessful course. Yet, especially in the first part of the Muromachi period, Zen monks were particularly prominent. They were political as well as religious advisers of leading members of the ruling warrior class. While Zen did not entirely lose its earlier simplicity and austerity, it gave rise to huge buildings for its monasteries. In some of these Chinese classical learning was cherished. The Ashikaga, indeed, encouraged this learning. Chinese poetry was emulated. Historiography had an unusual flowering. Zen monks conducted schools in which reading, writing, and simple ethics were taught to many in the lower walks of life.

In spite of the popularity of Zen Buddhism, religious movements arose which were not specifically connected with it. Shinto went on, partly through continuing to make its peace in syncretistic fashion with Buddhism. Indeed, the low ebb of the fortunes of the imperial house in which the cult of the Sun Goddess might be supposed to share seems to have stimulated the native cult. The priests of the great Shinto shrines at Ise, unable to rely as heretofore upon imperial benefactions, turned to popular associations for financial support.

Among the Muromachi developments in the aesthetic realm were painting with the Sung and Yüan masters as models and inspiration; the continuation of architecture with care to set buildings in carefully designed settings of landscapes and gardens; a further growth of the tea ceremony; and the creation of *No*, an indigenous drama with the accompaniment of music which was probably the outgrowth of mimetic dances.

In literature Chinese poetry for a time was in vogue. Histories were written. Chinese philosophy was studied. Chu Hsi, who was becoming in China the standard commentator on the Confucian classics, had his disciples.

In spite of the great debt to Buddhism of the refinements in Japanese culture, the Muromachi period saw a secularizing trend. Architecture, painting, and literature took on secular forms.

In the face of the civil disorder of the period and, indeed, partly because of the decentralization of power and the growth of local autonomy which went with it, both domestic and foreign trade flourished. Commerce with China grew. This was largely in the hands of Zen monks. The Ashikaga sent embassies to China and even, to the annoyance of later patriots, acknowledged a kind of vassalage to the Ming dynasty. Commercial cities arose with merchants and moneylenders and with guilds. An urban class came into being and acquired special privileges. Notable were the cities near the present Kobe and Osaka through which much of the commerce to Kyoto and its neighborhood was conducted. Some of the provincial magnates encouraged foreign trade. Japanese fared forth upon the sea as in no previous time. Many of them were freebooters who plagued the coasts of China and Korea. Others were merchants. Japanese made their way not only to China and Korea, but also to southeastern Asia. Toward the latter part of the period came the first direct contact with European merchants and missionaries—part of a phase of Japanese history of which we must speak more a little later. Imported Chinese copper coins had extensive use as currency.

Various social changes in addition to those we have already mentioned marked the Muromachi period. The family as against the larger clan became more significant. Women were more subordinate to men than they had been in the Heian and Kamakura eras. Something akin to primogeniture developed as a guide to inheritance. It was not precisely primogeniture, for a younger son might be picked for the heir in preference to the eldest and frequently the family line was perpetuated by adoption rather than by birth. The peasants had always borne the weight of the economic burden. Working interminably and heavily taxed, they were chronically poor and repeatedly suffered from famine. In this era they occasionally asserted themselves in violent but usually futile revolts.

The Three Who Brought Peace

During the sixteenth century the weakness of the Ashikaga increased and with it came an augmentation of civil strife. The disintegration of the established order gave opportunity for the emergence of new leaders from obscure families. Three of these by their successive careers restored order, and the last established a regime which was to endure into the second half of the nineteenth century and was to give Japan more profound peace than any she had known. The three men were Oda Nobunaga, Toyotomi Hideyoshi, and Tokugawa Ieyasu, or, to give them the briefer names by which they are most conveniently known, Nobunaga, Hideyoshi, and Ieyasu.

Nobunaga (1534–1582) began life as the son of an obscure feudal lord and built his fortunes upon the foundations laid by his father. He was courageous, as must be anyone who would prosper in those turbulent times, and proved to be a very able general. By his prowess he attracted the attention of a reigning Emperor who was seeking the support of the military arm. With imperial commission he restored order in Kyoto. He did not presume to have himself appointed *Shogun* but contented himself with dominating the figurehead member of the Ashikaga family who was the titular possessor of that office. The last of the Ashikaga to hold that post, it may be added, did not die until 1597, some years after the demise of Nobunaga.

Nobunaga's leading lieutenants were Hideyoshi and Ieyasu. Hideyoshi was of plebeian stock, the son of a common soldier. He was one of the few Japanese of nonaristocratic lineage to achieve a leading position in the administration of the government. He was short of stature and is said to have had a face like an ape. Ieyasu was of Minamoto blood but of what before him had been a relatively unimportant branch of that extensive wing of the Japanese military aristocracy. Of robust physique, fearless, shrewd, and a good judge of men, Ieyasu proved to be one of the outstanding makers of Japan.

Aided by these two, Nobunaga became master of most of the Empire. His strength was in the vicinity of the capital. He sent Hideyoshi to reduce the west and at his suggestion Ieyasu built up a center in the east and north, making his headquarters at Yedo, not far from Kamakura with its traditions of the early days of the *Bakufu.* He himself directed much of his energies to the destruction of the military power of the Buddhist clergy. As from several centuries past, Buddhist monasteries were among the great landholders. Some had become the equivalent of secular lords. Their armed forces often dominated their neighborhoods, and those on Mt. Hiyei were a chronic menace to Kyoto. Had they been coordinated by a common administration under one ecclesiastical head they might conceivably have controlled the country. Nobunaga set himself to break them. In this he was markedly successful. However, before he could complete the reduction of the Empire, he was surprised by one of his enemies and perished.

By his promptitude and astuteness Hideyoshi succeeded to the power of Nobunaga. Self-reliant and of boundless energy, he was a skillful general, but he was even abler in the diplomatic handling of men. After the death of his chief some of his associates, including Ieyasu, as well as his enemies were a threat, but he came to terms with Ieyasu and either subdued or conciliated the others. The entire Empire was subject to him. True to Japanese tradition, he did not seek to sweep away past institutions or to put aside the imperial house. Indeed, he felt himself honored by imperial appointment and his highest titular post was that of *Kwampaku,* or Dictator, which, as we have seen, was the office through which the proud Fujiwara had anciently dominated the land.

Hideyoshi Invades the Continent

Having united Japan, Hideyoshi set himself to conquests on the continent. His motives were probably complex. Undoubtedly personal ambition and the desire for further glory were prominent. It may be, too, that he sought to forestall the renewal of domestic strife by directing to foreign enterprises the energies of the military class, now unoccupied at home.

What Hideyoshi dreamed of was nothing less than the reduction of China, the largest empire of which he had anything approaching intimate knowledge. China was then under the Ming dynasty. That line was showing signs of decrepitude, but it was yet to have more than half a century of life and was still formidable. By geographic necessity, the road to China must lie through Korea. Hideyoshi demanded of the Korean monarch passage through the latter's domains. He was met with a refusal and found himself compelled to reduce that realm as a preliminary to the larger enterprise. After careful preparation, in 1592 a huge army was ferried across the intervening strait to southern Korea, the scene of Japanese holdings in earlier ages. The Japanese forces fought their way northward, some of them to the northeastern frontier of Korea. They wiped out the small army which the Chinese sent against them. However, the Japanese were weak on the sea, and their communications were made precarious by daring Korean craft. On land they were harassed by guerrillas. Hideyoshi, finding the undertaking more difficult than he had anticipated, withdrew most of his forces, and Chinese envoys came to arrange a peace. Hideyoshi, enraged at the letter from the Ming Emperor which proposed to invest him, in accord with the Chinese theory of relations with other states, with the dignity of a vassal prince, sent the envoys home. Later he dispatched another army to Korea, but his death (1598) led to its recall.

So ended what was the most ambitious Japanese enterprise for continental expansion before the nineteenth century. It was a foreshadowing of nineteenth and twentieth century undertakings. It was not merely the logic of geography which led the Japanese empire-builders of the modern era to begin their continental conquests in Korea. There were also long history and precedent for their approach.

The Triumph of the Tokugawa

Hideyoshi had hoped to pass on his power to his son, Hideyori, but this heir was only five years old at the time of his father's death. Hideyoshi had appointed a board, of which Ieyasu was a member, to act as regents. This arrangement did not prevent strife. An appeal was made to arms. In 1600 at the decisive battle of Sekigahara Ieyasu was victorious. He was now master of Japan. Hideyori was allowed to retain his father's estates, but dissatisfaction and intrigues led to further fighting. The recalcitrants gathered around Hideyori, and it was not until 1615 that Ieyasu, by reducing Hideyori's stronghold at Osaka, won full security for his rule.

Ieyasu had himself appointed *Shogun* (1603). This began a tenure of that office by members of his family, the Tokugawa, which was to last until 1867. Ieyasu did not revolutionize the forms of government. He preserved the imperial house and the *kuge*, the old court nobility. He worked through the inherited feudalism and the *Bakufu*. Yet through the modifications and additions made by him and his immediate successors, Hidetada (*Shogun* 1616–1622) and Yemitsu (*Shogun* 1622–1651), Japan was given a longer period of peace than it had ever known. His was a remarkable political achievement.

The more important features of the system by which the Tokugawa so successfully perpetuated their power are fairly quickly summarized. They established their complete control over the imperial house. The Emperors and their court were accorded a sufficient revenue to enable them to maintain a modest dignity, but they were given no land. No one was permitted to approach the Emperor except through channels prescribed by the *Bakufu*. Appointments to court office could be only through the approval of the *Bakufu*. The Emperor was sacrosanct, but he was allowed no active part in the administration of the country and his functions were ceremonial. By stressing his divine character, the Tokugawa removed the Emperor further from his people and from effective participation in government. The capital of the *Shogun* was established at Yedo and this city became the real center of government.

Here a huge castle was built for the *Shogun*. Here the feudal lords (*daimyo*) were required to spend portions of each year in residence, and when they were absent in their fiefs they were expected to leave in Yedo their wives and members of their family as hostages. They could thus be kept under watch. The *daimyo* were also constrained to undertake public works at their own expense. By this device a feudal lord whose wealth appeared to be making him dangerous could be taxed into relative impotence.

Various checks and balances were devised. Officers of the *Bakufu* were maintained whose duty it was to act as spies, or, more euphemistically, censors, on those who might give trouble. The vassals of whose loyalty the Tokugawa felt most nearly assured were placed in the central and eastern provinces as a safeguard to Kyoto and Yedo. Soon after the battle of Sekigahara the feudatories were required to take a written oath of loyalty. A feudal lord of whose fidelity the Tokugawa were uncertain would have a loyal vassal placed on an estate near him. Vassals who seemed trustworthy were also given holdings which commanded the main towns and strategic points on the chief highways. The building and repair of feudal castles were strictly limited. The beginnings of autonomy which some of the cities had gained under the Ashikaga were reduced and the more important urban centers were supervised directly by officials of the *Bakufu.* Travelers were closely scrutinized at convenient barriers along the principal roads. Nobunaga and Hideyoshi had destroyed the military power of the Buddhist monasteries. The Tokugawa took care that this should not be revived. Buddhist establishments were not so potent as they had been in previous centuries. The study of Confucianism was encouraged, and of the Confucian virtues loyalty was stressed. So far as they could do so, the Tokugawa took every precaution against rebellion and the disturbance of the peace and of their own supremacy. More than at any previous time Japan was regimented under autocratic direction.

European Contacts

One feature of the sixteenth and seventeenth centuries which proved of major importance was the coming of the European. So far as we know, in the first period of European journeyings to the Far East, the thirteenth and fourteenth centuries, no Westerner reached Japan. Marco Polo heard of the country but he did not go there. However, what he told of it was one of the attractions which lured the European explorers of the fifteenth and sixteenth centuries across the seas. Inevitably as European merchants and missionaries multiplied in the Far East they endeavored to gain entrance to Japan.

As might be expected, the first to arrive were the Portuguese. It was about 1542, although the date is not clearly established, that they made their initial landing in Japan. Toward the end of the century came the Spaniards. Not long after the Spaniards the Dutch and the English arrived. Voyaging as they did from the south, through the Straits of Malacca or by way of the East Indies or the Philippines, the Europeans found their chief marts on the island of Kyushu, especially at Nagasaki. The local feudal lords welcomed them, for the trade promised to be lucrative.

Following the merchants came Roman Catholic missionaries, representatives of the enterprise which was then carrying that form of the Christian faith around the world. The first in Japan was the Jesuit pioneer in the south and east of Asia, Francis Xavier. Accompanied by three Japanese and three fellow Jesuits he landed in 1549. He made a few converts and went as far as Kyoto. He was soon away, to prepare for the attempt to enter China which brought about his sad death off the south coast of that Empire in 1552. He had, however, laid the foundations for the work of his society in Japan. Other Jesuits followed. After some years came Franciscans, Dominicans, and Augustinians from the Philippines, for in the sixteenth century these islands were being conquered by the Spaniards, largely as an ecclesiastical outpost in the Far East. Estimates of the number of Japanese converts vary and at best can be only approximations to the facts. It seems clear, however, that several scores of thousands were baptized. Early in the seventeenth century probably a larger percentage of the population were professing Christians than after the extensive missionary efforts in the nineteenth and twentieth centuries.

Why Christianity enjoyed this rapid growth is not entirely clear. Yet some reasons seem fairly obvious. Nobunaga was friendly, and at the outset Hideyoshi and Ieyasu were not antagonistic. Some of the southern *daimyo* apparently hoped by favoring the missionaries to gain a larger share in the lucrative foreign trade. The novelty of the new faith may have appealed to some, for ever since the introduction of Chinese culture there had been Japanese who responded eagerly to the latest importations from abroad. Possibly some high-minded spirits were distressed by the degradation of Buddhism through the worldly warrior monks of the time and welcomed what seemed to them a purer religion. The devotion and ability of the missionaries could not have been without an effect. Whatever the reasons, for a time Christianity made rapid headway. Men prominent in feudal circles as well as many of the more humble espoused the faith.

The Closing of the Doors

To this rapid growth of Christianity came a series of reverses which led to the proscription of the faith and ultimately to the closing of the doors of Japan to the Occident until only a little crack remained ajar.

The sources of the action against Christianity and the foreigner appear to have been purely political. Hideyoshi, who began the persecution, and the Tokugawa, who continued and intensified it, were engaged in the unification and pacification of Japan. To them Christianity eventually seemed to be a source of domestic dissension and a possible instrument of foreign aggression. The zeal of the missionaries and their converts in endeavoring, when they gained influence, to stamp out rival religions, and the dissensions among the religious orders and between Spaniards and Portuguese, appeared to be complicating the problem of bringing order to the nation. Moreover, various factors contributed to the fear that Western nations, especially Spain, were seeking to use missionaries as advance agents of conquest. The fate of the Philippines and stories from Europe seemed to give confirmation to this apprehension.

In 1587 Hideyoshi came out with an edict which declared that Japan was the land of the gods and could not permit a religion which denounced its deities. He ordered the missionaries to leave the country. Some years later he followed this with active persecution which was cut short by his death. Ieyasu was at first tolerant and even friendly. Like many of the Japanese of his time, moreover, he was eager for foreign trade. Japanese had gone abroad in numbers to China, southeastern Asia, the East Indies, and the Philippines. Ieyasu even sought to open direct trade with Mexico, or New Spain as it was then called. However, in 1612 he also began placing restrictions on the Christians. These were followed up and intensified by his successors. As missionaries sought to evade the orders for their deportation and others persisted in coming in spite of the command that they keep out, and as many Christians refused to obey the government's commands to abjure their faith, sterner measures were adopted. Numbers of Christians were put to death, some by means which brought excruciating and prolonged suffering. When, in 1637 and 1638, Christianity appeared to be the exciting cause of an armed revolt, the *Bakufu* felt its worst fears confirmed, and still more drastic steps were taken.

Even before this rebellion, presumably to eliminate various possible sources of infection, Japanese had been forbidden to go abroad, Japanese returning to their native land were ordered put to death, and commerce with the Philippines had been prohibited. Now Portuguese ships were also placed under the ban. For a time English trade continued, but that was eventually stopped. Of Europeans only the Dutch were permitted to continue. They were confined to a small island, Deshima, in the harbor of Nagasaki, and were closely regulated and kept under minute watch to make sure that no emblems of the abhorred religion gained circulation through them. Commerce with China could be carried on only through authorized subjects of that land, and care was taken that no Chinese translations of Christian books were imported. Edict boards against Christianity were posted throughout the country. All Japanese were required to register as members of one of the various schools of Buddhism. Even as late as the second half of the eighteenth century the inhabitants of Nagasaki, as a suspected center, were compelled to tread annually on a representation of Christ as proof of their innocence of the proscribed faith.

In spite of the measures taken to terminate it, this intercourse with the Occident left some enduring deposits. Firearms entered with it and were widely adopted. The castles erected by Hideyoshi, the Tokugawa, and the great feudal lords, in their bastions, stone walls, and moats showed the influence of European fortifications. Some Portuguese words crept into the language. In the mountains of Kyushu remnants of the Christian communities secretly preserved their faith and clandestinely transmitted it to their descendants, until, in the nineteenth century, it was once more brought to light. Moreover, through the Dutch some knowledge of the West and of its learning kept seeping in, especially of medicine. Through Dutch contacts dictionaries were compiled, some mechanical objects were acquired, and information concerning European politics entered.

In the main, however, Japan was now sealed against the Occident and remained so, far more effectively than any other major land in the Far East, until the middle of the nineteenth century.

Tokugawa Culture

A Japan kept aloof from the outside world and with an internal administration designed for the peaceful preservation of the *status quo* did not mean an unmodified Japan. In some ways Japan was stagnant. Certainly there was not the pulsating new life it had known in the centuries in which Chinese culture was being first introduced and feudalism and the military class were developing. In this respect, however, Japan was but paralleling the China of the time. Yet Japan was experiencing changes.

One marked feature of the Tokugawa era was the growth of some of the cities, notably of Yedo. Since Yedo was the seat of the *Bakufu* and since *daimyo* were required to maintain residences there and themselves to live there part of each year, Yedo became the largest city in the Empire. *Samurai* followed in the trains of the *daimyo*. Merchants, artisans, servants, and various hangers-on multiplied to minister to the dominant class. As a result, at the beginning of the nineteenth century Yedo had a population of over a million. This made it among the half dozen largest cities of the world of that day.

With the growth of cities and the achievement of internal peace came an increase in the merchant class. Its members catered to the *daimyo* and their retainers as well as to the lower social strata. Believing that larger advantage would accrue through participation in trade than through an impecunious gentility, some of the aristocracy sacrificed their social standing to engage in commercial pursuits. Thus the Mitsui family, which in the nineteenth and twentieth centuries became one of the major financial powers of the Empire, claimed to trace its lineage back to the Fujiwara, but first rose to prominence in the Tokugawa era as merchants and financiers. The wealth of the merchant class mounted. If socially its members were below those of the military, they had the satisfaction of holding many of the latter in the bondage of debt, and some made their way into the charmed circle by purchasing adoption.

With the rising prominence of the towns and the merchants came a money economy instead of the old one based upon rice. This worked to the advantage of the merchants and against the military, for the incomes of the latter were traditionally drawn from the land and its produce.

During the latter half or more of the Tokugawa regime the population of the country was about stationary. In the seventeenth and down into the first quarter of the eighteenth century it seems to have registered a slight increase, but through most of the eighteenth and until past the middle of the nineteenth century it remained not far from thirty millions. This pause in growth must probably be ascribed to the widespread practice of abortion and infanticide and to famine and pestilence. It seems to have been associated with very adverse conditions in the largest class of the population, the tillers of the soil. The lot of the peasant had long been hard. Under the Tokugawa it remained difficult and may even have become worse. The exactions of landlords were severe and the burden of taxation and of the growing financial embarrassment of the military aristocracy was ultimately largely passed on to the tillers of the soil. Peasants' revolts punctuated the chronic suffering. The agrarian difficulties of the twentieth century were no novel phenomenon but had their roots in the past.

In religion and philosophy the Tokugawa era saw stagnation in Buddhist life and the increased popularity of Confucianism.

The lassitude of Buddhism appears to have been due to several factors. Nobunaga and Hideyoshi had curbed the power of the militant Buddhist monks, presumably as part of their effort to abolish the internal disorder of the realm. They were, naturally, not friendly to the religion represented by these disturbers of the peace. The Tokugawa, also intent on domestic quiet, would take no chances through the recovery of independence and the revival of truculence by the religious houses. They insisted upon closely regulating Buddhist activities. Moreover, in China and Korea, and, indeed, on the continent in general, Buddhism had long since passed its zenith. While Buddhism remained stronger in Japan than in either China or Korea, a people as sensitive as the Japanese to cultural currents in the neighboring Middle Kingdom could not be expected to retain their full enthusiasm for a religion which was losing its grip upon the Chinese. However, it was patronized by Ieyasu and most of his successors, members of the rising merchant class enriched many of its shrines, and its literary labors and preaching were extensive.

The study of Confucianism was officially encouraged by the Tokugawa and became popular. As was to be expected, Chu Hsi, whose interpretations of Confucianism were standard in the China of the time, was also esteemed in Japan as authoritative. Wang Yang-ming, who had arisen in China in the Ming dynasty, under the Japanese name of *O Yo-mei* won a following among the ever responsive islanders. Since Wang Yang-ming had favored intuitive judgment and independence of mind, his Japanese disciples were regarded with suspicion by the Tokugawa *Bakufu*, intent as it was upon regimentation.

Bushido, the code of the *samurai*, was being elaborated. Like the corresponding chivalry of Europe, it attained its apparent flowering after the knightly class with which it was associated had begun to decay and the society which brought it into existence was passing.

In the realm of the aesthetic the Tokugawa era reflected the conditions of the age. Buddhism and religious subjects were less a force in art than they had once been. The studied restraint associated with Zen Buddhism was passing. Architecture became ornate and even florid, as is still only too vividly seen in the gorgeous but overdone mausoleums of the Tokugawa at Nikko. Painters depicted realistically the passing scene of everyday life which they saw about them. The color prints, so prized by some Western collectors, shared in this characteristic. The *No* drama and the tea ceremony continued, but in an anemic fashion. The theater was frequented by the rank and file, and puppet shows with their skillfully constructed and manipulated manikins had a marked development. Courtesans and actors became popular, and the Yoshiwara district with its commercialized although highly regulated amusements and prostitution became a prominent feature of Yedo life. Art was ceasing to be exclusively for the cultivated aristocracy and was for those who made up the heterogeneous population of the cities.

The very success of the Tokugawa brought about their decay. With that decrepitude came also the undermining of the entire system of the *Bakufu* and the beginning of the disintegration of the class out of whom the *Bakufu* was constructed. Prolonged peace, the striking achievement of the Tokugawa, meant the decline of the military. The disorder that had brought them into existence and the chronic fighting on which they had been nourished were now in the past. The military virtues were still extolled and swords were decorated and kept sharp. Yet the *raison d'être* for the class had passed. *Daimyo* and *samurai* were deeply in debt to the merchants who flourished in the towns made possible by the profound peace. *Ronin*, masterless (or unemployed) *samurai*, became a familiar feature of the times. They had drifted away from positions whose incomes were insufficient to support them and were at once a rowdy element and one which appealed to the sentimental side of a nation where deeds of arms were honored but as a rule had become possible only for the lawless. The study of Confucianism fostered by the Tokugawa made the educated increasingly familiar with Chinese political theory. This theory taught loyalty to the Emperor but knew neither *Shogun* nor *Bakufu*. Peace gave leisure for the study of the nation's history. Out of this sprang a revived interest in Shinto with its emphasis upon the divine origin and authority of the imperial house and a vivid knowledge of a past in which there had been no *Shogun* and the imperial court had been supreme. By a strange irony of fate this study of history had one of its strongholds in the home of a branch of the Tokugawa family. There were plots to depose the Tokugawa and to restore the Emperor to power. In the west some of the *daimyo* whose families had never been entirely happy over the rule of the Tokugawa kept aloof from the full impact of the forces which were undercutting the Tokugawa regime. They were not so deeply in debt as were many of those more closely affiliated with Yedo and were better able to maintain the frugality and discipline traditionally associated with the military class.

The way was being prepared for the overthrow of feudalism and the emergence to power of the western fiefs.

As in China the Confucian theory had become stereotyped in an order which increasingly discouraged cultural change and bred stagnation, so in Japan the military feudalism and the organization of the state and of society which had become integrated with it had about reached their term. In both countries the scene was ripe for revolutionary change. In the Middle Kingdom the Manchus were clearly about to forfeit the mandate of Heaven. In Japan the Tokugawa were somnolent. In both lands, however, it was not just the ruling house which was becoming nerveless. In each the entire structure of the state and even of society had about run its course. Presumably, had the Occident with its quite different civilization not forced itself upon the Far East when it did, no such profound cultural revolutions would have occurred in either China or Japan as marked the nineteenth and twentieth centuries. The Manchus would have been driven out, but only to give place to another dynasty. The Tokugawa would have been deprived of their power, but it may be that another family would have tried to continue the *Bakufu.* As it was, the irruption of the Occident in the nineteenth century found both Empires ripe for change.

All unconsciously, the Tokugawa were preparing Japan for participation in the modern age with its stern competition with strong nation-states. They were knitting Japan into a unity such as that land had never before known. They were regimenting Japan in such fashion that it was becoming accustomed to a centralized control by the government of all phases of the nation's life. Moreover, the military spirit was far from dead. The tradition was there, firmly imbedded in the life and thought of the Empire. Military feudalism survived as it had not in Europe. Militarism was to be a feature of the Japan of the nineteenth and twentieth centuries. There were, too, those who dreamed of imperial expansion. Isolation was breeding an intense and ambitious nationalism.

BIBLIOGRAPHY

For Brief Reference

G. B. Sansom, *Japan: A Short Cultural History* (New York, 1943).

For More Extended Study

K. Asakawa, *The Early Institutional Life of Japan: A Study of the Reform of 645 A.D.* (Tokyo, 1903).

K. Asakawa, *Documents of Iriki* (New Haven, 1929).

H. Borton, *Peasant Uprisings in Japan in the Tokugawa Period*, in *Transactions of the Asiatic Society of Japan*, 2d series, Vol. XVI.

H. Borton, S. Elisséeff, E. O. Reischauer, *A Selected List of Books and Articles on Japan in English, French, and German* (Washington, 1940).

B. H. Chamberlain, "*Ko-ji-ki,*" . . . "*Records of Ancient Matters*" (Tokyo, 1906).

W. Dening, *The Life of Toyotomi Hideyoshi* (Tokyo, 1906).

G. Droppers, *The Population of Japan in the Tokugawa Period*, in *Transactions of the Asiatic Society of Japan*, Vol. XXII.

G. M. Fisher, *Kumazawa Banzan. His Life and Ideals*, in *Transactions of the Asiatic Society of Japan*, 2nd series, Vol. XVI.

G. M. Fisher (translator), *Da Gaku Wakumon by Kumazawa Banzan*, in *Transactions of the Asiatic Society of Japan*, 2d series, Vol. XVI.

J. H. Gubbins, *Some Features of Tokugawa Administration*, in *Transactions of the Asiatic Society of Japan*, Vol. L.

K. Hara, *An Introduction to the History of Japan* (New York, 1920).

E. Honjo, *The Social and Economic History of Japan* (Tokyo, 1935).

Y. S. Kuno, *Japanese Expansion on the Asiatic Continent* (Vols. I and II, Berkeley, 1937, 1940).

A. Lloyd, *Historical Development of the Shu Shi Philosophy in Japan*, in *Transactions of the Asiatic Society of Japan*, Vol. XXXIV, Part 4.

Lady Murasaki, *The Tale of Genji*, translated by A. Waley (5 vols., London and Boston).

J. Morris, *Makers of Japan* (Chicago, 1906).

J. Murdoch, *A History of Japan* (3 vols., Kobe and London, 1903–1926).

Nihongi, translated by W. G. Aston (2 vols., London, 1896), in *Transactions and Proceedings of the Japan Society*, London, Supplement I.

C. J. Purnell, *The Log Book of Will M. Adams, 1614–1619, in Transactions and Proceedings of the Japan Society*, London, Vol. XIII.

R. K. and J. Reischauer, *Early Japanese History* (*c. 40* B.C.–A.D. *1167*) (2 Parts, Princeton, 1937).

A. L. Sadler, *The Maker of Modern Japan: The Life of Tokugawa Ieyasu* (London, 1937).

G. B. Sansom, *Early Japanese Law and Administration*, in *Transactions of the Asiatic Society of Japan*, 2d series, Vols. IX, XI.

J. Saris, *The Voyage of Captain John Saris to Japan, 1613* (London, 1913).

Neil Skene Smith, *Materials on Japanese Social and Economic History: Tokugawa Japan*, in *Transactions of the Asiatic Society of Japan*, 2d series, Vol. XIV.

Neil Skene Smith, *An Introduction to Some Japanese Economic Writings of the 18th Century*, in *Transactions of the Asiatic Society of Japan*, 2d series, Vol. XI.

Y. Takekoshi, *The Economic Aspects of the History of the Civilization of Japan* (3 vols., London, 1930).

T. Tsuchiya, *An Economic History of Japan*, in *Transactions of the Asiatic Society of Japan*, 2d series, Vol. XV.

Chapter VII. OLD JAPAN

The culture of Japan on the eve of the changes wrought by the coming of the Occident

FROM THE CHRONOLOGICAL ACCOUNT of the development of the Japanese to the time of the renewed irruption of the Occident, we must turn, as we did for the Chinese, to a description of the culture of the land as it was on the eve of the great changes which began about the middle of the nineteenth century.

It is so axiomatic as to be a banality to say that present-day Japan is a continuation of the old Japan. Yet it needs emphasizing. To the casual observer from the West, especially to one who has come to Japan by way of India and China and has visited only the large cities, Japan has seemed so thoroughly transformed by its contacts with the Occident that a complete gulf is assumed to exist between the old and the new. This is almost the exact opposite of the truth. It is less than a hundred years since Commodore Perry ended the Tokugawa seclusion. That time has not been sufficient for the elimination of the institutions and still less the basic attitudes of a people as tenacious of their inheritance as are the Japanese. Behind the facade of Western dress, buildings, factories, electric lights, railways, and automobiles the pre-Perry Japan lingers. It not only lingers, it is still potent. If we are to understand the Japanese with whom we have to do today, we must pause to discover the characteristics of their great-grandparents. For this the sketch of the history of Japan has been a necessary introduction.

Teachability

One of the basic features of the Japanese which the preceding chapter must have disclosed has been a willingness which amounts to eagerness to learn from foreigners, an extraordinary responsiveness to life and thought in neighboring civilized nations. We have seen how ardently the Japanese craved the tuition of China, and how Chinese institutions were adopted and adapted. The Japanese were not content with going to school to the Chinese once for all. They kept in touch with changing currents in thought and art in the huge Empire and opened channels for them to their own country. One reason for the Tokugawa severance of intercourse with the Occident was the popularity of things Western, and especially of Christianity. The rapidity with which the Japanese were adopting what had come from abroad accounted for the vigor of the measures taken to stamp out what the Shogunate believed dangerous.

That characteristic we are to see prominent in the Japan of the past two or three generations. The Japanese, convinced that they must take account of the powerful culture which in the nineteenth century renewed its invasion of the Far East, went to school to it, as they had been doing to the Chinese for over a thousand years. They responded quickly to the changes in the Occidental climate of opinion. When democracy was prospering in the West, it found enthusiastic advocates in Japan. When, in the 1920's, war was unpopular and aggression taboo, Japan seemed to conform. In the 1930's and 1940's, with the swing of the pendulum toward totalitarianism and militarism, Japan also moved in that direction. After 1945 the Japanese were impressed by the conquering democracy of the United States, but a minority, influenced by Russia, were Communists. .

In this the Japanese were quite different from the Chinese. The latter, being convinced of the superiority of their own unaltered culture, were a generation later than the Japanese in setting themselves wholeheartedly to learn from the Occident. Possessing the advantage of this leeway, the Japanese became equipped with the machines and methods of the West much earlier than the Chinese and were able to defeat the latter on the field of battle and for a time in the 1930's and 1940's to conquer much of the soil of China.

Basic Conservatism

In apparent contradiction of this eager teachability was another trait of the Japanese. While going to school to others and being responsive to climates of opinion in the world they knew, the Japanese did not abandon their old institutions and attitudes, but adapted what they acquired to the existing pattern of their life. Their indigenous culture displayed amazing vitality.

This was true in the centuries when the Japanese were learning from the Chinese. The theory of government introduced from China insisted that the Emperor reigned by his virtue and looked complacently upon repeated changes in dynasties, holding that these came when a family by its misdeeds had forfeited the mandate of Heaven. The Japanese used the imported system to reenforce the position of the Emperor. They would not contemplate any change of dynasty. The imperial line which was sprung from the Sun Goddess, having existed from the beginning, must, so they assumed, go on to the end of time. The Chinese political theory called for the recruiting of officialdom by free competition in civil service examinations. The Japanese went through the motions of adopting the system, but restricted participation to the scions of the aristocracy. Japan remained under the rule of hereditary orders rather than under the administration of a scholar class entrance to which was through demonstrated merit. Instances of this tenacity in their own ways and of the fashion in which imported phases of culture were adapted to what already existed might be multiplied.

This combination of teachableness and holding to inherited ways arose in part, as did the conservatism of the Chinese, from pride of race and culture. The Japanese were so fearful of being considered uncivilized and backward that they wished to respond to what the more powerful and advanced peoples about them were doing. Yet they were so convinced of the rightness of their own ways that they made what they introduced ancillary to their own culture.

There followed three corollaries. In the first place, in spite of all they had learned from the Chinese, the Japanese remained quite distinct from these neighbors. The two peoples were as different in their attitudes and traditions as though they lived on opposite sides of the globe. To employ a European parallel, the contrast between the two peoples was even greater than that between the French and the English. The very resemblances, since they seemed to make for a community of culture but were largely superficial, heightened the friction. Using the same written characters and reading the Chinese classics, the Japanese believed that they understood the Chinese. Actually they did not. The assumption contributed to the tragedy of the twentieth century relations between the two peoples. The Chinese exalted the scholar, the Japanese the soldier. The Japanese were aristocratic, with carefully graded classes which were kept conscientiously apart. Through their later history the Chinese were largely without an hereditary aristocracy. Their social stratification was less rigid and it was easier for an individual to pass from one group to another than in Japan.

In the second place, the Japanese never really conformed to Western political patterns. For a time late in the nineteenth and early in the twentieth centuries they appeared in the way of becoming a democracy. They even adopted some of the Western machinery of democracy—a representative, bicameral parliament and universal manhood suffrage. Then, when Russia went Communist, many Japanese seemed to favor that system. A little later, when Fascism and National Socialism appeared to be supplanting democracy in Europe, Japan gave evidence of becoming totalitarian. Actually she was never democratic, Communistic, or totalitarian in the Occidental senses of those terms. Some phases of these systems she either toyed with or actually adopted, but always she adapted them to the genius of her own past.

In the third place, the revolution brought by the coming of the West was not so thoroughgoing in any phase of Japanese life as surface indications would have led one to believe. The basic ideologies and institutions of the land were only slightly altered. Fundamental change was slow.

The unwillingness of the Japanese to abandon what had once been a feature of their civilization is seen both in native and in imported elements in their culture. As we saw in the preceding chapter, the Japanese were reluctant to abolish a political institution, even when it had apparently outlived its usefulness or had passed into the hands of incompetent heirs. They preserved the imperial house, although for centuries the bearers of the imperial insignia participated only nominally in the actual conduct of affairs of state. The court nobility, or *kuge*, retained their social position even when the titles they bore were the only vestiges of the power they once exercised. The Fujiwara, for instance, were accorded the prestige of a great name after their dominant place in administration had been lost. Shinto was never fully supplanted by the imported religions. Buddhism displayed more continuing vigor in Japan than in China or Korea. All the thoroughgoing measures taken by the Tokugawa to stamp out Christianity were only partially successful. The faith survived, although in secret, loyally conserved by generation after generation of the descendants of the original converts.

The reluctance of the Japanese fully to abandon the past while eagerly adopting coveted elements of foreign cultures made for an important characteristic of what appeared to be the striking cultural revolution which attended the introduction of Western civilization in the nineteenth century. Much less of the old was swept aside than in China. The revolution was directed largely by the ruling classes. The old families continued their direction of affairs. As between these families there were reshufflings of place and power. The head of the Tokugawa was still a person of importance. The imperial house went on, with slightly but not radically altered functions. In the realm of economics, where the changes were particularly striking, what became the outstanding leader in the new capitalistic enterprises, the Mitsui family, traced its lineage to the Fujiwara and under the Tokugawa had begun its career in trade and finance. Japan entered the circle of Western intellectual life. She availed herself of Western science. She adopted and adapted Western methods of education. Yet she continued the use of the expressive but cumbersome Chinese characters. The children in her modern schools probably spent two or three years longer in acquiring the basic tools of literacy than if the Chinese ideographs had been abandoned for a simple phonetic form of writing. The immediate shock of the contact with the West was eased by the combination of the two traits of teachability and conservatism, but conservatism entailed problems.

Are the Japanese Creative?

How far, if at all, were the Japanese creative? Did the eagerness to learn from foreigners combine with the unwillingness to abandon the cherished past to discourage the Japanese from making fresh contributions to culture?

At first sight the answer would appear to be a negative. The Japanese adopted religions from abroad—Buddhism, Confucianism, and Christianity—but the only religion born on Japanese soil was Shinto, and Shinto never escaped from an atavistic primitivism. Most of the sects of Buddhism that flourished in Japan were imported. The Japanese produced beautiful architecture, paintings, and ceramics, but the forms which these took were not fresh creations, but adaptations and developments of traditions and schools which came from the continent. The Japanese appeared to be skillful in copying and adapting, but not in making important new beginnings.

On more careful investigation, however, this reply is seen to have only partial truth. To be sure, the Japanese displayed marked capacity for taking over much from alien civilizations. Yet some important features of their culture were of their own construction, were unique, and proved a decided asset. This was especially marked in their political life. To that we now turn.

The Emperor

Nowhere else in human history has there been an institution quite comparable with that of the Emperor of Japan. Here is a reigning family which goes back with a continuous history of rule to the dim beginning of the recorded course of the nation's life. Amid the many vicissitudes which have beset Japan, the Emperor has been the center of unity. Once, to be sure, there was a division with a conflict over legitimacy extending over about half a century. That, however, was exceptional, and the tradition of unity was so strong that the breach was healed. Individual Emperors might be forced to retire, but the institution continued. It obtained enhanced dignity from the descent from the Sun Goddess and the divine commission which were traditionally ascribed to it.

In the stormy period that followed the advent of the Westerner and in the tempests in which Japan was involved in the 1930's and 1940's, the imperial institution was peculiarly an asset. Sharp dissent between the various factions might have brought internal anarchy, but the Emperor, in theory standing above partisan strife and a center and symbol of loyalty to which all professed unqualified allegiance, ensured the nation from splitting apart.

The imperial institution and the beliefs and affections clustering about it cannot be ascribed to any one individual. It is the creation of generations. It is a distinct achievement of the Japanese genius.

Legitimacy and Power

The persistence of the imperial institution was made possible by another feature of political life that was the creation of the Japanese genius. The Japanese were reluctant to abolish an institution or to remove the name of power from a family which had once exercised it, but found ways of placing the actual administration in the hands of the most forceful and, presumably, the most competent. Authority was nominally continued in the family which had originally held it, but in practice it was exercised by whoever could grasp it. Ability to govern is not always transmitted by heredity. Strong fathers are succeeded by weakling sons. Families go to seed or fluctuate in their production of the qualities required of those who govern. In most lands the incompetent inheritors of a great name are swept out by the competent. That has not been unknown in Japan. For instance, Ieyasu crushed Hideyori, the son and heir of the great Hideyoshi.

Yet there was so much of the opposite as to constitute a strong tradition. The Fujiwara on coming into control of the state did not place themselves on the throne, but contented themselves with continuing that dignity in the existing imperial line, and ostensibly based their position upon authority obtained from the Emperor. When the military nobility became the most potent element in the state, they did not sweep aside the effete *kuge*, the court nobility who had preceded them in the seats of the mighty, but permitted them to retain their titles and social position. The head of the military hierarchy, the *Shogun*, sought his post from imperial appointment. If an Emperor displayed too much disposition to act independently, the effort was made to force him into retirement, but another member of the imperial house was put in his place. The *Shogun* did not attempt to supplant the Emperor. When the line of Yoritomo no longer provided competent incumbents of the office of *Shogun*, that position was not abolished, but the Hojo, in whose hands was the actual administration, saw to it that it was filled by men whom they could dominate. Under the Tokugawa some of the lines of *daimyo* produced incompetents, but the latter retained the outer trappings of authority while the real power was exercised by a retainer. Instances might be multiplied of the operation of this principle. It became part of the Japanese mental and social heritage. It did not prevent revolt or violent revolution, but it minimized the sweeping destruction of revolution and favored orderly change. Change there must be, but here was a method which eased its pains and prevented a sharp break with the past.

In this the Japanese were not unique as in their imperial tradition. Other peoples have known orderly transition. The English especially have been noted for it. In England office after office, institution after institution, and form after form have been conserved when the conditions out of which they arose have passed. However, the Japanese developed their tradition quite independently of any knowledge of English practice and were even more thoroughgoing in its application.

A corollary of this feature of Japanese political life must be noted. If an Emperor attempted to assert himself too prominently ways were found to force him out of office. The Emperor was the fountain of authority, but he must exercise his power through subordinates and he must not too obviously direct them or interfere with them. Such influence as he exerted on public policies he must exercise *in camera*. In this, too, his position has been not unlike that of the later British monarchs.

The Military Tradition

Out of the political evolution of Japan came a military tradition which proved of great importance in the world into which in the nineteenth century Japan was hurried. In the preceding chapter we sketched the history of the emergence of the military class and of its control of the nation through a form of feudalism. For centuries the actual power was in the hands of the military aristocracy operating through a feudal system.

As we suggested in the previous chapter, this had important consequences for modern Japan. When, in the nineteenth century, Japan opened her doors to the West, she was thrust into contact with a civilization in which the military tradition was also strong. In Western Europe the military class had once been feudally organized and still bore traces of that ancestry. Japan was, therefore, somewhat prepared for her new relationships. In this she differed decidedly from China, where the scholar class was in control and the soldier was, in theory, despised. Possessed of such a background, Japan found it congenial to her spirit to perpetuate and strengthen her armed forces. She had merely to adopt the military tools of the West.

To be sure, Japan had had little experience on the sea and presumably would be handicapped in becoming a naval power. The martial tradition facilitated the creation of armed fleets, but always the latter were ancillary to the army. The army was first in plans for conquest and defense. Jealousy developed between the two armed services, but in general the navy was made to subserve the purposes of the army.

The Japanese had, too, what they deemed a record of invincibility. Never in historic times had their islands been successfully invaded. The ancestors of the Japanese must have come as conquerors, but their arrival is lost in the mists of legend. Since the islands have been the dwelling of the Japanese no would-be invader had ever effected a continuing foothold. The Mongols were the most serious menace, and the memory of their defeat fed Japanese confidence. Hideyoshi failed in his design to conquer China, but that was not through any signal defeat of the Japanese on the field of battle. Nor back of the several Japanese evacuations of parts of Korea which they had occupied was there any acknowledgment of military disaster. To be sure, during the invasion of their land by Hideyoshi, the Koreans inflicted serious blows on Japanese transports. The Japanese armies too, failed in their attempt to conquer China and were withdrawn from Korea. However, the Japanese memory was one of the rout in which the Korean armies had fled. The evacuation of the Japanese forces came in consequence of the death of Hideyoshi and not from spectacular military weakness.

This record of military prowess must be attributed in large part to the favored geographic position of the islands. Her island position was of immense advantage to Japan. Never had she been compelled to face, on fairly equal terms, a major military or naval power. The sea was in the way. However, other major island groups of the Far East were mastered in whole or in part by invaders. The Philippines yielded to the Spaniards and then to the Americans and the Japanese. Indians and then Portuguese and Dutch had built empires in the East Indies. Not without reason could the Japanese ascribe their independence to their valor and military skill. They also professed to see in it evidence of the continuing protection of the gods and of the imperial ancestors.

That tradition and that confidence contributed to the undertaking, late in the nineteenth and in the twentieth century, of adventures on the continent. For these their pre-nineteenth century record offered the Japanese no such assurance of striking and enduring victory. Their territorial holdings on the continent had been limited to the southern part of Korea, just across the channel from Japan. Even here there was no permanent incorporation into the Japanese life and realms.

The Beginning of Continental Imperialism

There was, moreover, a tradition which invited to continental ambitions. Since almost the dawn of their history Japanese had from time to time invaded Korea and for longer or shorter periods had held territories there. Once, under Hideyoshi, as we have just reminded ourselves, there was the attempt to use Korea as a highway for the conquest of China.

In the nineteenth and twentieth centuries these ambitions were renewed. Even before the end of the Tokugawa, two young men were executed as traitors who put down in writing their dream of a Japan dominant in the Far East. Japan's forehandedness in adopting Western industry and weapons before the rest of the Far East gave her an advantage and permitted a success far greater than she had earlier achieved. It was in Korea that her ambitions for continental empire found their earliest expression. Korea was the first part of the continent annexed and became the point of approach to further conquests.

The Stratification of Japanese Society

A striking feature of the social organization of Japan was its stratification. At the very lowest level were the *Eta.* How they originally came by this status we do not certainly know. They may have been descendants of aborigines or of foreign immigrants. It may be that their despised position was due to their occupations and eventually to the fact that they were butchers and leather-workers, and that these occupations in a land which under Buddhist tutelage professed to look askance at the taking of life—in spite of the inconsistency of these scruples with the honor paid the soldier—were held in ill repute. It is possible that they were of diverse origin. Prostitutes, entertainers, diviners, undertakers, and caretakers of tombs were in the rank of the socially ostracized. The tillers of the soil were another class, although it was possible for farmers to gain admission to higher groups. Artisans were also somewhat distinct. Merchants were regarded as inferior. They were held to be unproductive and it was thought that they would do anything to make money. In the latter half of the nineteenth century Japan entered a world in which commerce and finance counted for much with an heredity which held the merchant in contempt and which did not exact of him high standards of probity. It is no wonder that in the new age Japanese businessmen were regarded by Westerners as untrustworthy. Yet many Japanese shopkeepers were the soul of honesty. So, too, some of the merchants succeeded in obtaining entrance into the *samurai,* by purchasing for themselves or their sons adoption into a family of that class. The members of the military class, whether *samurai* or *daimyo,* were peculiarly privileged. *Ronin,* "wave men," were a special kind of *samurai,* those who for one reason or another had lost their lords and were masterless. Some of them had abandoned their lords because the latter had insufficient income to support them. From the Forty-Seven *Ronin,* famous for having revenged the death of their master, an aura of the romantic and heroic gathered about the name. They had taken the law into their own hands and had assassinated the high official who, they believed, had been responsible for the death of their lord. Having accomplished their purpose, they gave themselves up to justice. But the nation canonized them. In the nineteenth and twentieth centuries this *ronin* tradition seemed to justify violence, and especially the assassination of officials who, to those who did the deed, appeared to be enemies of the country. Often popular opinion esteemed them patriots, even though misguided, and constrained the courts to deal gently with them. Higher than the military class were the court nobility about the Emperor, the *kuge*. Although impoverished by the *Bakufu*, they outranked the *samurai* and the *daimyo* and preserved a humanistic, nonmilitary tradition. Class distinctions were much more marked and less fluid than in China.

The Family

As in China, the family counted for much. Indeed, Chinese teaching and example had much to do with the exaltation of the family. In Japan as in China the family and not the personal name came first, a convention which seems to symbolize the contrast with the more individualistic Occident. Family solidarity was of great importance. Marriage was practically universal and was not by the will of the bride and groom but through the decision of the heads of the family. On important matters concerning the children, the senior and influential members of the family must be consulted. The line must be continued. If sons were lacking, adoption was resorted to. Some who became distinguished were not born into the family whose name they bore but entered it through adoption. The family felt obliged to look after its members. It provided the equivalent of what in the modern West is known as old-age assistance and unemployment insurance. The individualism of the nineteenth century Occident would have been the rankest heresy. Filial piety, the respect and the duty of the child to its parents, was marked, as it was in China. Honors were paid to the spirits of the ancestors. In contrast with China, however, loyalty to one's feudal lord might take precedence over obligations even to one's immediate kin. The family and the traditions and attitudes associated with it persisted into the twentieth century.

Women

Women were subordinate to men. This had not always been true. By the middle of the nineteenth century, however, it had been so long accepted that it seemed part of the established order. A wife was even more subject to her husband than in China. She was required to be obedient to her spouse and to be self-effacing and faithful. Her husband might be guilty of habitual infidelity to her, yet she must not complain. Prostitution was professionalized. The *geisha*, highly trained courtesans expert in entertaining men, constituted a well-recognized occupation.

In better Japanese homes, especially of the higher classes, the women were not without great influence. The wife managed the household. She had a marked effect upon the character of her children, and reverence was owed by them to her as well as to the father.

The training of the girl for prospective wifehood and motherhood was carried on by the mother or supervised by her. It included courtesy, the direction of the home, the preparation of food, the care of the clothing of the family and of the furnishings, the decoration of the house, and the arrangement of furniture, pictures, and flowers.

The Clan

What the Westerner rather loosely called the clan was of importance in feudal Japan. The name is something of a misnomer, for no family tie or descent from a common ancestor provided the bond which held the group together. The clan was made up of the *daimyo* and his retainers. It was an important political and social unit. For centuries the clans played an important role in Japanese life. They continued to do so after the coming of the Westerner in force. The kind of group spirit represented by the clans continued even after the latter had disappeared and has been important in recent Japan.

Japanese Courtesy and the Aesthetic Side of Japanese Life

The Japanese were and are noted for their love of beauty and their appreciation of the aesthetic. This may have been in part because of the physical charm of their country, with its mountains, its streams, its forests, its flowers, and its Inland Sea studded with islands near which so much of their culture developed. Whatever the cause, the fact was and is of great importance in Japanese life.

The love of beauty and the attendant sensitiveness displayed themselves in a variety of ways.

One of these was courtesy. By training and tradition the Japanese were and are a polite people. Individuals, especially when conquerors among a subject folk, may be crudely arrogant and cruel, but in Japan itself thoughtful courtesy has seemed the rule. Good manners have been a fine art among the upper classes, but they have been by no means absent among the lowly. With Japanese courtesy has gone a degree of formality and reserve which was and is often misunderstood by the Occidental. It has often been regarded as a mask behind which to hide deceit. It has been, rather, a convention and a protective shield for an extreme sensitiveness.

Related to courtesy and sensibilities that were unusually acute was what is often termed "face." In common with the Chinese, and, indeed, with most peoples East and West, the Japanese set great store on their dignity. Any derogation to it, especially by rudeness or by studied or unconscious lack of *finesse*, may be a mortal offense. The way in which a deed is performed may be as important as the deed itself. Appearances must be preserved, and self-respect and the outward form of the regard of one's fellows must be maintained.

Art in its many forms was cultivated. Although architecture owed a debt to the Chinese, the Japanese placed the mark of their own genius upon the forms derived from the continent. This, too, was true of painting, of sculpture, of ceramics, and of various skilled handicrafts. The *No* drama, in its studied simplicity, was primarily a Japanese product. Japanese gardens had their Chinese prototypes, but had been modified by the use of native materials and plants to meet local ideas and scenes. The tea ceremony was developed under the influence of Zen Buddhism, with its emphasis upon frugality and restraint. It was originally a gathering of friends, regulated by strict etiquette, centering around the drinking of tea and the discussion of the qualities of some object of art, a poem, or an arrangement of flowers. Later it became more elaborate. The arranging of flowers was also a fine art. The swords which were a badge of the *samurai* and were universally carried by members of that class were the object of much skilled workmanship. Lacquer, cloisonne, and damascene were highly developed. Except music, there were few phases of art in which the Japanese did not register major achievements.

The Japanese enjoyed many features of their physical surroundings. In their art they made much of Fujiyama. That famous mountain was, too, the goal of innumerable pilgrimages. Cherry blossoms were prized, and their coming was the occasion of festive parties. Autumn colors brought their thrill. There were excursions for viewing the moonlight. Some insects were kept caged for their songs.

Much of this love of beauty goes back to the earliest historic times. As far in the past as our own records enable us to probe, the Japanese associated divinity with flowers, rocks, sun, moon, and tempests. In this they seemed to have joy and gratitude as well as awe. There was an element of *naïveté* about the simple pleasure of the Japanese in nature which appears to hark back to the childhood of the race.

In the attitude toward nature was an undercurrent of sadness. The fleeting beauty of the cherry blossoms was a symbol of the transitoriness of human life. The falling of autumn leaves brought poignant reminder of the fast approach of death. In this minor note the Japanese had much in common with the Chinese. Both seem to have had the common human awareness of mortality and change accentuated by Buddhism with its teaching of the impermanence of all things. Yet the minor key appears to have been more pronounced in Japan than in China.

The sentimentality of the Japanese was a pronounced national trait. It was in strange contrast with the stress placed on the military virtues of stoic heroism and endurance.

Religion

The characteristics of the Japanese came out markedly in their religious life. The Japanese were responsive to foreign influences. Buddhism became one of their chief religions. Confucianism was widely studied and honored and had a profound effect upon morals and politics. For a time, until the state deemed it a menace and strove to extirpate it, Christianity made rapid headway. The Japanese, for all their adoption of foreign faiths, refused to abandon their past. Shinto persisted, the primitive native faith cherished in a sophisticated age. Moreover, the lack of originality was seen in the failure of the Japanese genius to produce a really new high religion or a major system of philosophy. Yet here, as in so much else of their culture, the Japanese made their own selection from what came from abroad and placed their stamp upon that which they accepted. From China came Confucianism, but Taoism, although prominent in China, did not exist as a distinct cult in Japan. Much of Chinese popular religion, with its special forms of animism, its tutelary deities of soil and of the cities, and its pantheon, was not copied by Japan. Many Chinese beliefs and practices had their effect, but the religion of the Japanese masses was not a reproduction of that of China. In Buddhism the Japanese genius brought new sects or schools into existence.

Shinto went through more than one phase. It was first the original faith of the Japanese, a quite unorganized religion. Then it was modified by the introduction of Chinese culture. The growth in the position of the Emperor and the imperial family which followed acquaintance with Chinese political ideas gave to the cult of the putative ancestress of the Emperor, the Sun Goddess, the leading position over the various other clan cults. With the popularity of Buddhism, it seemed that Shinto was on the way to extinction, absorbed by Buddhism under the convenient theory that the Shinto deities were appearances of the members of the Buddhist pantheon. Under the Tokugawa, especially in the eighteenth century, a revival of Shinto took place. The attempt was made to purge Shinto of its Buddhist accretions, to separate it and restore it. Schools or sects which obtained followings among the masses arose in Shinto. One which flourished in the twentieth century, *Tenri-kyo*, began in 1838 through a vision by which the founder, a woman, was healed of an illness.

Shinto preserved many of its primitive qualities. Its conception of what constituted an object of honor was very vague. The term *kami* was applied not only to what the Westerner would call gods, but also to any object or being which begot a sense of mystery and evoked awe. The line between men and gods was not closely drawn, and princes and heroes might be *kami*. Shinto was in part the worship of spirits. It included the reverence paid to the ancestors of the imperial house. Its most sacred place was Ise, the center of the cult of the Sun Goddess. Its moral content was slight. It had formal, ceremonial lustrations. Its temples were of simple construction and are supposed to perpetuate, more nearly than any other structures, the lines of early Japanese buildings. A straw rope marked off the hallowed spot of ground or object. Pieces of paper or cloth on a pole of wood or bamboo might give notice of a sacred place. A portal, or *tori-i,* stood at the entrance of every sanctuary, composed of two quadrangular beams of wood or stone supported by two round pillars. In the shrine was no image, only symbols of the deity. Here were made offerings of food and drink. There was a priesthood in charge of the shrines and the ceremonies. Prayers might be read, and formal dances celebrated. Charms, spells, and divination were utilized.

It is interesting and characteristic of Japan that, although so primitive a faith, Shinto persisted in the face of the much higher systems, Buddhism and Confucianism. It survives today, in spite of the coming from the West of a science which views its basic myths as untenable historically and a product of the childhood of the nation. Until soon after 1945 it flourished and was a potent reenforcement of intense nationalism. Because of it, patriotism was more ardently religious than in any other major country. Japan was, so Shinto taught, the land of the gods. Shinto nourished national exclusiveness and delusions of national grandeur.

Buddhism has been so frequently mentioned in the preceding chapter, and its course and schools so sufficiently recorded, that we need not take the space here to describe it. To do so would entail needless repetition. Although somewhat decayed under the Tokugawa, it continued to hold an important place in Japanese life. It was more vigorous and less moribund than in China. It encouraged some forms of art and architecture. It promoted kindness and a sensitiveness to beauty. In earlier centuries it had been the vehicle for much of civilization. Its shrines, monasteries, and places of pilgrimage remained prominent. Its conceptions of the future life entered into Japanese popular belief and folklore. It did not, however, do much to check war or militarism. Nor did it ensure chastity. Indeed, in some districts phallicism and an attendant promiscuity at festival times persisted.

Confucianism was less a religion in Japan than in China. Confucian temples were not, as in the Middle Kingdom, a feature of every administrative division. The Emperor of Japan did not officiate at elaborate and stately sacrifices to Heaven and Earth as did the Emperor of China. Nor did Kyoto have an imposing Temple of Heaven as did Peking. These ceremonies and ceremonial buildings so prominent in China and associated with Confucianism were not part of the Japanese religious picture. It was as ethics and philosophy that Confucianism had its primary effects. Here its influence was very profound. Even in these phases, however, Confucian teachings were modified by the Japanese scene. For instance, as we have already suggested, filial piety, while prominent, was not accorded quite so exalted a status as in China, and loyalty to one's feudal lord, so outstanding in Japan, was lacking in a China from which feudalism had disappeared. In addition to its effect upon ethics and philosophy, the influence of Confucianism was seen in the reverence for ancestors and the ancestral cult. What foreigners rather loosely term ancestor worship appears to have been present in Japan before the introduction of Chinese culture. The latter reenforced it. The cult of ancestors was much older in China than Confucius, but Confucius helped to conserve it, and it was through Confucianism as well as the example of China that the Chinese ceremonies in honor of the family's progenitors contributed to Japanese thought and practice.

Taoism affected Japanese thought and magic, but did not exist as a separate cult.

Festivals, many of them of religious origin and some of them containing features from more than one religion, added variety and picturesqueness to life and helped to keep alive awareness of the unseen world. As in China, the New Year season was a great occasion, with honors to the ancestors and worship of the gods.

There was, too, a daily household religion, centering around the "god shelf."

Bushido

Here probably some mention should be made of *bushido*. *Bushido* was not a religion. It was the manners and ethics of the warrior class. It had a long history and showed various stages of development. Under the Tokugawa, in the seventeenth and eighteenth centuries, it was elaborated by philosophers. In time it ceased to be identified exclusively with the warriors. Not all warriors lived up to it. Many who were not warriors were influenced by it. It was the outgrowth of many antecedents. Shinto, Confucianism, and Buddhism, especially Zen Buddhism, contributed to it. Under it a cardinal virtue was loyalty and obedience to one's superior. It inculcated dignity, calmness of manner, and quietness in speech. Probably to this background must be assigned in part the inarticulateness of the Japanese. To this day the Japanese distrust fluency, prize the sparing use of words, and conduct some of their ceremonies in silence. They believe themselves handicapped by this trait in international conferences and are, therefore, reluctant to enter into them. *Bushido* had rules for every act in social intercourse, including conversation, fencing, and salutations. It had a prescribed ritual for suicide. As a set of ideals its effect was marked, even after the influx of Western culture.

Language, Literature, and Scholarship

Enough has been said in the preceding chapter of the development of language, literature, and scholarship to allow us here to pass over them with only brief mention. We have seen that in spite of the basic dissimilarity of the Japanese and Chinese languages, the Japanese adopted the Chinese written character, studied Chinese literature, and did much of their writing in Chinese.

It is possible that from the ensuing disjunction between ideas and their normal medium of expression came another characteristic of the Japanese—a vagueness, a blurring of the meaning of words, an inarticulateness, and a seeming lack of candor. Or this congeries of characteristics may go back to the pre-Chinese language of the land. Whatever its source, here was another group of qualities common among the Japanese. Certainly many terms and phrases were employed without giving them a precise definition. Unquestionably, too, the Japanese were at times indefinite, seemed evasive and unwilling to speak their minds, and left much of their meaning to be inferred, with the possibility of misunderstanding. As in other phases of her cultural importations, Japan made adaptations in the method of writing. The Chinese characters were retained, but phonetic writing by means of *kana*, abbreviated Chinese characters, was devised. This was probably by an evolutionary process, although tradition declares it to have been the invention of Kobo Daishi, the Japanese introducer and founder of the *Shingon* school of Buddhism. A sign was thus devised for each Japanese sound or syllable. Much of the writing and printing used a combination of Chinese characters and the *kana*.

The employment of *kana* did not relieve the Japanese school child or scholar from the arduous task of memorizing the Chinese characters and learning to use them correctly. The influx of a vocabulary in Chinese added to the problem of achieving literacy. To master the vehicle of the written language and even the oral expression of ideas was no easy assignment.

Japanese literature was varied. It included the several branches known in China. It embraced as well some forms of poetry distinctively Japanese, especially brief verses. In contrast with the Indians and Occidentals but like the Chinese, the Japanese developed no epic poetry. They had no Iliad or Mahabharata. Although the Japanese did not accord to the scholar the high post of honor enjoyed by him in China, they inculcated respect for the teacher and held in esteem the man of letters.

The Chinese pseudo-science of *yin* and *yang* and of the related *fêng shui*, or "wind and water," with its devices, through geomancy, of determining lucky and unlucky sites for buildings and tombs, was carried over to Japan, but was not as prominent as in China.

Economic Life

By the beginning of the nineteenth century, Japan had long possessed a multiform economic life. Basic, as in almost every land, was agriculture. Since very early days industries, all of them in the handicraft stage, had been in existence. Craftsmen were important, if lowly. Although the upper classes affected contempt for them, under the enforced Tokugawa peace merchants were increasingly prominent. Yedo was by far the largest of the cities of Tokugawa days, but there were others of importance. Fishermen provided, then as now, a large proportion of the food for the population of the country.

The peasant cultivators of the soil constituted the most numerous element of the population. Some of them were in comfortable circumstances, but for the majority life was hard. Most of them were renters, not owners of the soil they tilled. Rents were high and taxes were heavy. The burden of the corvée, the labor requisitioned of peasants and their horses, was severe. There was a landowning userer class whose members loaned money to peasants at high rates. The cultivated land was excessively atomized into small parcels. Sometimes peasants, in angry desperation, broke into open revolt. Many of them fled to the cities. The agrarian problem which plagued the administrators of Japan in the twentieth century was not new.

In spite of its hardships, rural life had its charms. Many a rural village could boast an able and public-spirited elder who promoted its welfare—perhaps through an irrigation system or a school. Possibly a priest or a priestess from a hermitage or cherished shrine ministered to the physical as well as the spiritual needs of the villagers and, in return, was revered and fed by them. Festivals gave variety to life.

Summary

In the second half of the nineteenth century, this culture of Japan, the product of so many centuries of evolution and now, for two centuries, kept all but hermetically sealed against contact with any other except that of China, was to be thrust into the rapidly moving current of world affairs.

For this abrupt change, the Tokugawa had given, unwittingly and quite unintentionally, an admirable preparation. The country was more nearly united than it had ever been. It had become accustomed to submission to a highly centralized administration. To be sure, the Tokugawa were to be demoted, the *Bakufu* was to be abolished, and a new administrative structure was to be created. However, the land, although still divided under the Tokugawa into feudal fiefs, was more nearly accustomed to regimentation under the last two and a half centuries of the Shogunate than it had been under the earlier feudalism, and especially under the weak years of the later Ashikaga. The western fiefs were jealous of the Tokugawa, but when they succeeded in seizing the reins, they had under them a nation more ready to act as a unit in a turbulent world and in face of an aggressive West than it had ever been. Fortunately, too, there was at hand the imperial institution, accepted since the dim beginnings of the realm, a center and symbol of unity, with a tradition of dignity and of noninterference in direct administration which made its effectiveness largely independent of any particular occupant of the throne.

Japan was much better fitted to deal with the new age than was her huge neighbor. Both were in the hands of a regime which was decrepit. In China, the stucture of the state was such that the decay of the ruling dynasty was a handicap. In Japan, the Tokugawa *Bakufu* was a kind of chrysalis which allowed the gestation of a new Japan. When the encasing shell was shattered by the coming of the Westerner, the life within was strangely ready for the environment into which it was so rudely thrust.

The life of this Japan when it emerged into the modern world was both responsive to its external environment and tenacious of its past. In many ways it was not creative, but its political structure was unique. It centered about an Emperor whose ancestors had been on the throne since the earliest dawn of known history. He was the fountain of all authority and maintained a punctilious court, surrounded by the civil nobility, the *kuge*. The tradition had long been established that the real power should be held by those who in the rough and tumble of competition had demonstrated their ability to exercise it. For several centuries the land had been actually ruled by the military class organized feudally under the *Bakufu*. Since the seventeenth century the Tokugawa family had provided the *Shogun*, the head of the *Bakufu*, and had been dominant. However, by the middle of the nineteenth century, in the long peace maintained by the Tokugawa, feudalism was in decay.

Japanese society was stratified, with the Emperor at the top, followed by the court nobility, and with the military tradition very strong. Merchants were a despised but a growing force. The family was prominent. Women were held in a subordinate status. Most of the art forms were originally from China, but the Japanese, highly sensitive to beauty, had developed them in their own way. In religion Shinto, the primitive cult, persisted, but Buddhism was very strong. Confucianism had a profound effect upon philosophy and ethics. Under the Tokugawa *Bushido* flowered as the standard of conduct primarily for the members of the military class but also with influence upon other elements of the population. Literature and language were under great debt to China. Economic life was diversified, but the peasants, who formed its foundation, were suffering from a variety of ills. Here, too, as in the political sphere, the land was ripe for change.

BIBLIOGRAPHY

For Brief Reference

G. B. Sansom, *Japan: A Short Cultural History* (New York, 1943).

For More Extended Study

M. Anesaki, *History of Japanese Religion* (London, 1930).
L. Binyon, *Painting in the Far East* (London, 1923).
H. Borton, S. Elisséeff, E. O. Reischauer, *A Selected List of Books and Articles on Japan, in English, French, and German* (Washington, 1940).
B. H. Chamberlain, *Things Japanese* (Kobe, sixth edition, 1939).
E. F. Fenollosa, *Epochs in Chinese and Japanese Art* (New York, 1921).
S. L. Gulick, *The Evolution of the Japanese* (New York, 1905).
W. Gundert, *Die japanische Literatur* (Wildpark-Potsdam, 1929).
L. Hearn, *Japan, an Attempt at Interpretation* (New York, 1904).
D. C. Holtom, *National Faith of Japan: A Study in Modern Shintō* (London, 1938).
E. Honjo, *The Social and Economic History of Japan* (Kyoto, 1935).
G. Kato, *A Study of Shintō* (Tokyo, 1926).
H. Minamoto, *An Illustrated History of Japanese Art* (Kyoto, 1935).
I. Nitobe, *Bushidō, the Soul of Japan* (New York, 1905).
S. Ninomiya, *An Inquiry into the Origin, Development, and Present Situation of the Eta* (in *The Transactions of the Asiatic Society of Japan*, 1933).
K. Okakura, *The Book of Tea* (New York, 1912).
C. H. Page, *Japanese Poetry* (Boston, 1923).
A. L. Sadler, *Chanoyu, or The Tea Philosophy of Japan* (Honolulu, 1929).
D. T. Suzuki, *Zen Buddhism and Its Influence on Japanese Culture* (Kyoto, 1938).
L. Warner, *The Craft of the Japanese Sculptor* (New York, 1936).

Chapter VIII. THE LESSER LANDS

Tibet, Sinkiang, Mongolia, Korea, Eastern Siberia, Indo-China, Siam (Thailand), Burma, Ceylon, the Malay Peninsula, the East Indies, and the Philippines to the early part of the nineteenth century

IN THE PRECEDING CHAPTERS we have covered, even though of necessity cursorily, India and the major lands of the Far East, China and Japan, to the eve of the revolutionary changes brought by the nineteenth century expansion of the Occident. There remain a number of countries and sections which have not played outstanding roles in the history of the Far East but which have been and are part of the scene and which no well-rounded survey of that region can omit. The only general tie which binds them together is geographic. With one exception, Ceylon, they are all in the Far East. Ceylon is included because of its geographic relationship to India and southeastern Asia. A number of the lands covered in this chapter were influenced by India through Buddhism or Hinduism or both. They are here grouped for the convenience of the author and the reader and not because of any community of race or culture. We will here tell their story, although in a much condensed form, from the beginning to the fresh access of contact with the expanding Occident which came in the nineteenth century.

Tibet

First we must say a word concerning Tibet, although it need be little more than a word. Still technically a part of China, Tibet is really a separate land. In race, culture, and history, as well as in geography, it is distinct from its overlord.

Because of its unfavorable geography—a high inland plateau on much of which the struggle for a bare existence engrosses the energies of the inhabitants—Tibet developed no high civilization comparable to that of India or China. Lying between India and China, it received cultural contributions from both lands. During the period of the T'ang dynasty, in the seventh century, a strong kingdom arose in Tibet. During much of the T'ang, Tibetan invasions periodically troubled the Chinese. On one occasion the T'ang capital, Ch'angan, was taken by Tibetans.

It was in the seventh century, under a powerful ruler of the Tibetan kingdom, that Buddhism entered in force. In time, notably in the eighth century, a special form of Buddhism developed in Tibet, in part by adaptation to the preceding shamanistic cults. From the color of the garb worn by its monks it was known as the Red sect. The Buddhist monks, or lamas, depended for their power largely upon the supposed potency of their incantations. The monasteries became very strong. Eventually they dominated the country and the land was ruled by them. Since the Red sect eschewed celibacy, the headship of the monasteries became hereditary.

Attempts at reform were made, to bring the monks to conformity with the orthodox Buddhist rules of celibacy and poverty. Not until the fourteenth century, however, did these meet with continuing and widespread success. In that century there arose, through the initiative of a remarkable religious enthusiast, the Yellow sect whose lamas assumed the regulation vows. Early in the fifteenth century a monastery of the Yellow sect was established at Lhasa which became the headquarters of the movement. Succession in the headship of each of the various Yellow monasteries was not by heredity, as with the Red sect, but by the principle of transmigration. Each division and lamasary was supposed to have as its patron a *bodhisattva* or a *buddha* who was reincarnated in the successive abbots. On the death of one of these leaders, search was made for the child in whom the *bodhisattva* had been reborn. Distinguishing marks were set up by which he could be recognized.

Khubilai Khan became interested in Tibetan lamaism and favored it. The Ming Emperors also supported the lamas and showed honor to the Dalai Lama, the ruling monk at Lhasa. They established relations with Nepal and brought that state, bordering Tibet and India, to acknowledge Chinese suzerainty. Presumably they did this because it seemed to them the best way to keep Tibet at peace and under their influence. The Ch'ing dynasty followed much the same policy. The K'ang Hsi Emperor, indeed, extended his rule over the country. In a dispute over the succession to the Dalai Lama-ship there was danger that the candidate of Mongols opposed to K'ang Hsi would attain the post. The K'ang Hsi Emperor intervened, in 1720 his forces entered Lhasa as victors, his candidate was enthroned, and he appointed commissioners to direct affairs, established a garrison in the city, and posted troops at strategic points on the road to China. Tibet thus became a part of the Chinese Empire and in theory and usually in actuality has remained so to this day. During the Ch'ien Lung period, late in the eighteenth century, the connection was threatened by an invasion of the Gurkhas, from India. However, the Ch'ien Lung Emperor sent an army which, in spite of the vast distances from its base and the inhospitable terrain, drove back the Gurkhas and, indeed, brought Nepal to acknowledge the suzerainty of the Ch'ing.

The first waves of the spreading European tide which reached the Far East left Tibet comparatively untouched. It is not certain that European travelers of the fourteenth century reached the country. In the seventeenth and eighteenth centuries Jesuits and in the eighteenth century Capuchins, Roman Catholic missionaries, made their way into the land. In 1774 and again in 1783 the British sent from India a representative. Geography, however, was against any extensive penetration by Europeans.

At the dawn of the nineteenth century most of the Tibetans were under the overlordship of the Ch'ing. Buddhism with its many lamaseries was dominant, and the heads of its organizations were also the lords temporal of the country. The Yellow sect was the more prominent, but the Red sect survived, divided into a number of subsects. There was a secular nobility. Traders were a distinct class. Peasants formed the bulk of the scanty population. The monasteries of the Yellow sect, by drawing numbers of the men into a celibate, economically nonproductive life, seem to have been a brake on the population. Commerce was maintained with the more prosperous neighboring lands. Imported tea, mixed with the butter of the country, was a staple item for food and drink.

Sinkiang

Sinkiang, the region north of Tibet through which ran the traditional overland trade routes between China and the West, can be dealt with even more briefly than Tibet. The history of the region is very complex and is not fully known. Sinkiang was the source of invasion after invasion of China Proper. Kingdoms and empires were set up, only to vanish. From time to time the stronger dynasties which governed China extended their rule to part or all of the land. Merchants plied the roads and settled in the cities. As a result of these varied contacts, the population was a mixture. Much of the land was an unpeopled, arid waste. Oases, however, through which ran the caravan routes, were well settled. In A.D. 1800 the Ch'ing dynasty was in political control. The land had seen several religions enter from the west along the convenient corridors. Buddhism, Manicheanism, and Christianity had each won extensive followings, only to wane. In the nineteenth century, Islam was dominant.

Mongolia

Mongolia burst into prominence in Far Eastern and world history under the genius of Jenghiz Khan. Long before his day, during the favoring rainy climate which accompanied the last ice age and made at least part of Mongolia well watered, stone age man had established settlements. Later, but still before Jenghiz Khan, Mongolia had been part of that reservoir from which, from time to time, issued invaders who sought to master the fertile valleys of China and against whom the Chinese built and maintained the Great Wall.

After the collapse of the Mongol Empire and the expulsion of the Mongols from China Proper, Mongolia did not immediately lapse into a state of powerlessness. More than once the reconquest of China was attempted.

However, as a military force the Mongols were increasingly decrepit. One cause of the decay is said to have been the growth of Lamaistic Buddhism. This had spread from Tibet. Thousands of Mongol boys were drawn into the celibate ranks of the Yellow sect and so became neither fathers nor warriors.

Buddhism did not completely master the country. Among a people dependent for livelihood upon their herds, it could not enforce its prohibition against the taking of animal life. Nor did it eliminate the shamanism which preceded it. The latter existed side by side with the former. The Mongols were divided, as, except under Jenghiz Khan and his early descendants, they had been from time immemorial. It is not surprising that the powerful Ch'ing dynasty succeeded in reducing them to submission and incorporating them into its empire.

Korea (Chosen)

We must pause a little longer on Korea, or, as the Japanese call it from a designation long accepted by the Koreans, Chosen. Korea has played a larger part in the Far East of the nineteenth and twentieth centuries than has Tibet, Sinkiang, or Mongolia and we need historical background to understand it.

As in most countries, the population of Korea was and is of mixed origin. Where all the ingredients came from we do not know. We are not even sure what they all were. At the dawn of the time when records give us some information about the land, the peoples in the north were somewhat distinct from those in the south. The northerners were akin to those in Manchuria and Mongolia. The southerners were more like the inhabitants of the neighboring southern Japan. To these were added, during the period of the Chou dynasty, immigrants from China.

It is with Chinese colonies that what appears to be authentic history begins. By the time the Chou dynasty had about half run its course, there existed in northern Korea and southern Manchuria a state ruled by the family of Ki and tracing its ancestry to a Chinese. Under the Ch'in dynasty the number of Chinese migrants to Korea increased, probably through political malcontents and merchants. The advent of the Han dynasty meant the augmentation of the Chinese contingents. Some of these drove out the last of the Ki monarchs. Under the Emperor Han Wu Ti the expanding frontiers of China were stretched to include the northern part of Korea. It is here that the Japanese excavations mentioned in the third chapter have uncovered the remains of a wealthy Chinese community. Obviously through these contacts Chinese culture was being carried to the peninsula. Korea was being brought within the cultural zone of China.

By the close of the first century before Christ the rule of the Han in Korea had come to an end and the peninsula was divided among three states, Koguryu in the north and in southern Manchuria, Pakche in the southwest, and Silla in the east. In the extreme south, Japanese influence was strong. Cultural relations with China were still maintained and Chinese civilization remained potent. Here, as in Japan a little later, Chinese characters were introduced and became the medium for writing.

For about seven centuries the three states continued, with shifting boundaries. They were often at war with one another. The political influence of both China and Japan was felt. On at least one occasion, in the fifth century after Christ, a Japanese invasion threatened the existence of one of the states. In the sixth century, in spite of Japanese opposition, Silla conquered the Nippon-influenced southern part of the peninsula.

During the long period of division in China between the Han and the Sui dynasty, there was no strong China to attempt to enforce its will on its neighbors. With the achievement of unity under the

Sui Chinese political expansion was renewed. The downfall of the second Emperor of that dynasty, Yang Ti, was in part because of the exhaustion of his forces in the vain endeavor to conquer Korea.

The more powerful and longer lived T'ang succeeded where the Sui had failed. Silla sought the aid of the T'ang against Koguryu and Pakche. In spite of the intervention of the Japanese, these two foes were crushed. The T'ang annexed southern Manchuria and part of northern Korea and was acknowledged suzerain by Silla. An attempt of the latter to escape from this vassalage led to a severe defeat at the hands of the Chinese. Silla continued to be among those subordinate states who drew their culture from the T'ang. Koreans went to Ch'ang-an to study. Thousands entered T'ang China as merchants and sailors. They conducted much of the commerce between China and Japan and were engaged in the coastal shipping. Many were brought in as slaves. Some Koreans entered the service of the Chinese. It was a Korean commander who led a Chinese army on one of the most notable military exploits of the T'ang, on the extraordinarily difficult march across the Pamirs into the northwestern fringes of India. Numbers of Koreans, returning from China, became officials and scholars in their home land.

From China came not only the culture of that land, but also Buddhism. In the great period of its prosperity in China, the period of division and the early part of the T'ang, Buddhism almost inevitably spread to Korea, closely tied to China as it was by geography and history. Chinese monks were active. Many Koreans, monks, studied in China or made the long pilgrimage to India and, returning, strengthened the faith in their native land. As in China and Japan, Buddhism proved the vehicle and inspiration of art. In morals and philosophy it also brought enrichment to the life of the country.

In the days of the decline of the T'ang dynasty, the realm of Silla also disintegrated. Shortly after the final downfall of the T'ang, a leader who claimed to have sprung from the royal house of Koguryu led a revolt which placed a new dynasty, that of Wang, in control of Korea. Until 1392, or for more than four and a half centuries, the land was governed by this ruling house.

Under the Wang dynasty Korea continued a vassal of China. It acknowledged successively the suzerainty of more than one of the houses which reigned in the northern part of that Empire. It was invaded by the Khitan, who displaced the Sung in North China. It allied itself to the Juchên, who wrested North China from the

Khitan. Korea, in turn, became part of the Mongol Empire and was required to provide a large part of the personnel and equipment of the huge expeditions that Khubilai Khan directed against Japan.

As the collapse of the T'ang in China had been followed by the end of the rule of Silla in Korea, so the expulsion of the Mongols from China and the replacing of the Yüan by the Ming soon had as a sequel the demise of the Wang dynasty. The commander-in-chief of the Wang forces, who was also the father-in-law of the king, deposed his son-in-law and inaugurated a new dynasty. He is known by his title of Yi Tai-jo, and the dynasty which he founded was that of Yi (in Chinese, Li). The Yi dynasty survived all the vicissitudes of the following centuries and endured until, in 1910, the Japanese annexed the peninsula.

Under the Yi Korea was still a vassal of China, first of the Ming and then of the Ch'ing. Vassalage did not entail administration of Korea's internal affairs by the Chinese. As in a number of other states which bordered China and which acknowledged the suzerainty of the Emperor who reigned in Peking, the relationship was without exact parallel in Occidental practice and law. Its basic principle was as much cultural and commercial as political. The vassals were, from the Chinese standpoint, barbarians and through accepting the subordinate status were engaged in the process of conforming to Chinese culture. Since, from the dominant Chinese theory, there could be only one true civilization and all men were bound to recognize the position of the legitimate head of mankind, the Son of Heaven, the rulers of the tributary states sought authorization of their position from the Emperor. This status involved for the Yi monarchs, among other things, accepting titles and sending periodical tribute-bearing embassies to Peking. It also entailed the adoption of the Chinese calendar. In return for tribute, the Chinese Emperors gave valuable presents. The embassies were the occasion for commerce. The penetration of Chinese culture proceeded apace.

Relations, unfortunately not so peaceful, were had with Japan. Under the later years of the Ashikaga *Bakufu* Japanese pirates repeatedly raided the coasts of Korea. In 1420 Korean and Japanese forces clashed on Tsushima, an island in the strait that separates Korea from Japan. At the close of the sixteenth century came the most serious of the Japanese invasions before the end of the nineteenth century. This, as will be recalled from the sixth chapter, was initiated and directed by Hideyoshi in his ambitious plan for the conquest of China. The

Korean armies were defeated and dispersed with an enormous loss of life, and the capital, Seoul, was taken. Yet guerrillas harassed the Japanese forces, and the latter deemed it wise to withdraw to the southern coast. Moreover, Korean craft, known as tortoise boats, attacked the clumsy Japanese transports and impeded communications between the Japanese armies and their home base.

After the final Japanese evacuation, a limited commerce was maintained between the two countries through the southern port of Fusan, and on the accession of each *Shogun* a congratulatory mission was sent by Korea. The relations, however, were by no means as close as those maintained with China.

Because of the intimate ties, and the impression made by the power and civilization of that Empire, Korean culture was in large part patterned after that of China. The Confucian classics were the standard study of the educated. On the model of China, a civil service was erected and its members were recruited by means of competitive literary examinations. Art, including architecture, was inspired by Chinese examples. At Seoul the chief buildings were reminiscent of those of Peking, although erected on a much smaller scale. Buddhism, popular in Korea during its heyday in China, shared the decline which it suffered in China after the T'ang. Indeed, it became rather more decrepit than in China.

Korean culture was not the exact reproduction of that of China. There was a native garb. Popular religion, of a rather primitive type and not particularly vigorous, was different. Although Chinese characters were used by the scholars, an alphabet was invented for writing the vernacular. Yet the Koreans did not show as much enterprise in adapting the imported culture to their genius as did the Japanese. Less numerous and geographically more closely tied to China than were their island neighbors, the Koreans were more inclined to conform to the ways of the Middle Kingdom.

Until the nineteenth century Korea had almost no contact with the Occident. In the days when it flourished in Japan, Christianity seems to have made a few converts. From the close of the eighteenth century Roman Catholic Christianity, although often persecuted severely, had a continuous existence in the land. More intimate relations with the West did not come until later than in China and Japan.

Like the two great adjacent realms, Korea entered upon the nineteenth century, with its enhanced irruption of the Occident and the ensuing difficult adjustments, under a decadent regime. The Yi dynasty, like the Ch'ing dynasty and the Tokugawa *Bakufu*, had seen its best days. However, much less resilience was displayed in facing the issues produced by the novel situation than in the other two lands. As we are to see in a later chapter, disaster and the sacrifice of independence became the price of incompetence.

Eastern Siberia

Eastern Siberia did not come significantly into the Far Eastern scene until the seventeenth century. Climatically it was forbidding. The few scattered tribes which inhabited it were primitives or in culture not far removed from the primitives. The Manchus, who in the days of their strength considered part of it as in their sphere of influence, were but slightly interested in it. China Proper, with its wealth and its dense population, was the center of their concern.

It was with the Russian eastward advance that eastern Siberia began to attract attention, and it was that advance which, down into the present century, gave the region its chief significance. The Russians were using it as a bridge and a point of approach by which to seek to extend their control over more salubrious lands. They made, too, beginnings toward the development of the natural resources of the area. Until the nineteenth century these were mainly limited to the fur trade.

The Russian eastward advance began late in the fifteenth century, not far from the time that the Portuguese were opening the sea route to the Indies. It was partly under the direction of the state whose capital was at Moscow and whose rulers were soon to consider themselves the heirs of the Christian Byzantine Empire.

Not until the close of the sixteenth century did the Russian expansion east of the Urals assume large proportions. Then Cossacks, sturdy frontiersmen, led the way and were followed by peasants who began to till the great plains of Siberia. In the first half of the seventeenth century, when the initial permanent English settlements were being established on the eastern seaboard of America, Cossacks reached the northeast shore of Asia. By the close of the seventeenth century continuing colonies had arisen on Kamchatka. About the middle of that century a Russian force penetrated to the Amur.

Here the Russians came into conflict with the Ch'ing armies. The Russians were defeated. In 1689 a treaty between the representatives of the Ch'ing and the Czar was signed at Nerchinsk, the earliest between China and a European power. With supplementary agreements, until 1858 it was to regulate the intercourse between the two empires. In spite of the desire of the Russians to control the Amur as a channel for trade, the Treaty of Nerchinsk fixed the boundary at the edge of the watershed north of that river except for a slight compromise in favor of the Russians. From the Russian post at Kiakhta, south of Lake Baikal, commerce with China was carried on, the Russians sending furs and various European commodities and the Chinese silk, tea, cotton cloth, porcelain, and other Far Eastern products.

Russian enterprise, part of it private and part of it official, extended the Czar's domains in northeastern Asia. The island of Sakhalin was placed upon the Muscovite map. Kamchatka was conquered. Some of the Kurile Islands were explored. Repeated though futile attempts were made to inaugurate commerce with Tokugawa Japan. A slight clash occurred between Japanese and Russians on one of the Kuriles in which the latter were worsted. Russian posts were founded across Bering Strait in Alaska. However, little colonization was effected. The thinly occupied Russian possessions were traversed by trappers, hunters, fur traders, missionaries, and adventurers and were used for a place of exile for convicts. Their importance was mainly in the future.

Tongking, Annam, and Champa

Tongking and Annam, south of China Proper and east of the mountain range which juts southward from the highlands of Yünnan and separates the east coast of Indo-China from the valley of the Mekong, by geography have been on the borders of China and have also felt Indian influence. From time to time under the more powerful of the dynasties which ruled in China they were partly or entirely within the Chinese Empire. So far to the south were they, however, that they were often independent or in the category of tributary states.

A brief survey of these Chinese occupations will serve to show how Tongking and Annam were politically both in and out of the Chinese Empire and so were on the southern fringes of the Chinese cultural zone. Near the close of the third century before Christ that first of the great Chinese conquerors, Ch'in Shih Huang Ti, incorporated what we know as Tongking and part of Annam into his domains. The ruling people who had mastered the region before the coming of Shih Huang Ti's armies were of Thai stock and thus were related to some of the strains which entered into the composition of the Chinese. With the collapse of the Ch'in dynasty, the region escaped from the Chinese yoke. Not until approximately a century later, near the close of the second century before Christ, did it again become part of the Chinese realm. This was in the Han Wu Ti era, when the Chinese boundaries were extended even more widely than under the Ch'in. While brought to acknowledge Chinese rule, these southern marches were allowed to remain under their own chieftains and to retain their own customs. During the reign of Wang Mang, which, it will be recalled, separated the Earlier Han from the Later Han dynasty, Tongking slipped away from the Chinese rule and became the refuge of some of the partisans of the Han, now unwelcome in China. When, as the Later Han, the Liu family was restored to the throne of China, Tongking and Annam were reconquered. The land now became Sinicized. Chinese letters, schools, social customs, and political institutions gradually became dominant. Chinese culture was especially potent among the upper classes. In the centuries between the Han and the Sui, when China was divided, Tongking and Annam were usually subject to one of the houses which ruled in the Yangtze Valley. In the sixth century they were brought under the Sui. They were among the domains of the Sui's long-lived successor, the T'ang dynasty. In the weakness of China which accompanied the decline and downfall of the T'ang, Annam gained its independence. A series of princely families governed the land, but continued the tradition of Chinese culture. In the last quarter of the thirteenth century three Mongol expeditions penetrated Annam. On the field of battle they were victorious. However, the climate proved their undoing and their rule was ephemeral. Early in the fifteenth century, the Yung Lo Emperor, the third monarch of the Ming dynasty, conquered Annam, but after death had withdrawn his strong hand a revolt reestablished the independence of the region. Chinese culture was retained, and tribute-bearing embassies were sent to Peking. During the Ch'ien Lung period, the Ch'ing dynasty intervened in the politics of Annam and the rulers accepted investiture from Peking and became tributary. Chinese administrative control was, however, not restored. Annam was one of those satellites of the Middle Kingdom which retained its autonomy but recognized the superior dignity of the Son of Heaven who reigned in Peking.

With political independence went something of cultural independence. In the latter part of the fourteenth century the Annamese developed a less difficult form of writing than the Chinese characters. A national literature written in it began to appear. In art, too, a native style arose.

South of the Annamese, but still on the coast east of the central mountain chain, were the Chams. In language they were related to the Malays. In the early part of the Christian era the Chams had only a primitive culture and were said to have made their living by fishing and hunting and not to have known agriculture. When Annam was being conquered by the Han, the Chams did not submit and, because of their distance from China, were let alone.

While in political institutions, social philosophy, and written language and literature Tongking and Annam had become largely assimilated to China, in religion and much of the accompanying art India was potent. The ports were frequented by Indian merchants. In some of them Indian colonies sprang up. Hinduism and Buddhism were introduced. Eventually the latter prevailed. Indian religious art, with its temples and sculpture, entered and was adopted.

Indian influence, largely from the south of that land, was especially marked among the Chams. Sanskrit became the official language. Not far from the close of the second century after Christ the kingdom of Champa was founded. This state had as its capital first the city of Lin-yi or Simhapura and then the city of Indrapura, some distance south of the present Hué. In Indrapura the ruins of the many buildings which once gave the place architectural glory are predominantly in Indian style. Under Indian tutelage the Chams became civilized. From marts on their indented coast commerce flourished, with China on the one hand and with India, Arabia, and Persia on the other. Under some rulers of the T'ang and the Sung dynasties the Cham monarchs sent tribute embassies to the court of China. The Chams developed an art which, while predominantly of Indian elements, showed the effects of the relations with China.

In the thirteenth century Champa was for a time incorporated in the Cambodian Empire. Between Annam and Champa, occupying, as they did, adjacent portions of the coast, intermittent warfare existed. In the fifteenth century most of Champa was conquered and annexed by Annam and in the seventeenth century the remaining southernmost province of Champa was incorporated in the Annamese Empire. The Chams were either largely exterminated or were driven back into the mountains. The monuments of Cham architecture were left in ruins. The Emperor of Annam was now dominant over the region south of the Chinese province of Kwangtung and east of the mountain chain which separated the east coast from the Mekong Valley.

In the Annamese realms contacts with Europeans before the close of the eighteenth century were almost entirely confined to merchants and to the efforts of Roman Catholic missionaries to plant their faith. The merchants were Portuguese, then Dutch and English, and latterly French. The missionaries were so far successful that they prepared the way for a large growth of their church in the nineteenth and twentieth centuries and provided, although in the earlier stages not by deliberate policy, the footholds and the excuse for the extension of French political power over the region.

At the dawn of the nineteenth century Annamite culture was dominant east of the mountains. It showed the effect of the long contacts with China. Chinese literature was prized and studied. Side by side with Chinese literature was a vernacular literature, distinct, and written in the indigenous script. As in China, officialdom was in two wings, civil and military. The family was the basic social institution. An easygoing Buddhism, a modified and corrupt Taoism, Confucianism reenforcing a native ancestral worship, and the cults of many local deities with a strong admixture of animism provided the religion of the land. Much skill was shown in agriculture, in building dikes and canals, and in reclaiming waste land. As in China, the village was a self-governing unit, the foundation of the superimposed hierarchical administrative system of the central government.

Cambodia

In the valley of the Mekong, to the west of Annam and Champa, arose what was once a powerful and wealthy state, the Kingdom of Cambodia.

On the fertile plains along the lower reaches of the Mekong River dwelt, at the dawn of history, peoples of Malay (or Indonesian) and Khmer stocks. To this early population, at the mouth of the Mekong, came Indians, largely traders, and settlements, partly Indian and partly of native folk, came into being. Within the first six centuries after Christ two kingdoms affected by Indian culture arose. For their monarchs Indian descent was claimed.

About the middle of the sixth century after Christ, the two kingdoms were united. However, it was not until the beginning of the ninth century that enduring union was effected. It was then that the Cambodian Empire was founded.

Late in the ninth century a great burst of energy began to make itself felt in Cambodia. Through it there was begun the erection of a vast capital, the city of Anghor. The ruins of this city, Anghor Thom, and of the adjacent huge temple, Anghor Vat, begun in the twelfth century, are among the architectural wonders of the Far East.

In the architecture and sculpture of this vast expanse of buildings, Indian influence predominated. It was Hindu rather than Buddhist. However, Buddhism was present and had some effect. There were contacts as well with China. They, too, left an impress, although not nearly so marked as in Annam.

Invasions plagued Cambodia and eventually reduced the realm to a shadow of its former power and magnificence. The Chams pressed in from the east. At various intervals over centuries came the Siamese and the Annamese. Anghor was abandoned and was covered by jungle.

The causes for the decline of the formerly strong Cambodia as for its earlier rise to brilliance are complicated and perhaps obscure. It has been suggested that in the migrations of the Indians whose leadership helped to create the Cambodian state only the more sturdy and ambitious had the imagination and initiative to leave home and possessed the stamina to survive in the new environment, that these handed down their qualities to posterity, and that this process of biological selection was in part accountable for the Cambodian Empire and building. As this stock decayed or disappeared, so this theory would declare, the land easily fell a prey to its neighbors. It seems clear that the proximate causes were the dissatisfaction of the masses under the burden of taxation required to maintain the great Anghor buildings, new religious developments, and foreign invasions.

Beginning in the sixteenth century, Europeans began to arrive. Late in the sixteenth and early in the seventeenth century the Cambodians sought and received some Spanish assistance through Manila against the Siamese. Merchants and Roman Catholic missionaries came. In the last quarter of the eighteenth century, through a French missionary as intermediary, French aid was given to an aspirant for the throne of Cochin-China. He was successful and later became the ruler of all Annam. The tradition of French interest which was thus created paved the way for the French conquest in the nineteenth century.

The culture of Cambodia was quite different from that of Annam. To be sure, in both lands Indian elements were strong. In both, Hinduism and Buddhism powerfully shaped the religious life and, of the two, Buddhism prevailed, although Hinduism was the earlier and persisted. Both Mahayana and Hinayana Buddhism entered, but the latter became more potent. As in Siam, the monks taught the young to read. However, Chinese culture was less influential in Cambodia than in Annam. Much of pre-Indian and pre-Chinese animism remained. Basically, too, differences existed between the pre-Indian and pre-Chinese customs of the Khmers and of those of the peoples of Annam. The Khmer language was also distinct. Sanskrit and Pali, although basically different from it, added to its vocabulary. Physically the Cambodian Khmers were larger than the Annamese and Siamese.

Thailand (Siam)

When we first begin to catch authentic glimpses of the valley of the Menam, it, unlike the lower courses of the Mekong, was peopled by Mons. To it, as to Cambodia, came Hindu settlers and Hindu culture. Not far from the second century after Christ a Buddhist state was formed there. In the tenth or eleventh century the Khmers, civilized and a little later predominantly Buddhist, moved into the valley and established a kingdom. In the eleventh century the southern kingdom was annexed to the Cambodian Empire.

In the twelfth and thirteenth centuries the Thai peoples began a movement southward from what are now Yünnan and its border areas. The Mongol conquest seems to have been either the impelling cause or contributory to it. Some of the Thai, as we are to see in a moment, entered Burma and there are known as the Shans. Others came down the Menam. Various states including the Khmer kingdoms were extinguished. In the upper part of the Menam Valley the Thai established the Kingdom of Chiengmai. In the middle of the fourteenth century some of the Thai founded a kingdom which became dominant over the other Thai states of the lower part of the valley of the Menam and which took the name of Siam (from the word Shan). The capital was at Ayuthia. The Thai had moved south into the Malay Peninsula, and at least part of that area acknowledged the suzerainty of Siam. Siam carried on wars against Cambodia, to the great damage of the latter, and controlled a portion of the Malay Peninsula later incorporated into Burma. Wars between Siam and Chiengmai were chronic and from time to time the latter was subordinate to the southern kingdom. In the fifteenth and sixteenth centuries, invaders from Burma and Pegu repeatedly attacked the country. In the sixteenth century they succeeded in capturing Ayuthia and bringing the country into subjection. Some time later, the Siamese regained their independence under a great conqueror. In the eighteenth century the Burmese again invaded Siam. This time (1767) they destroyed Ayuthia. A Siamese general restored the kingdom, with Bangkok as the capital. When this general went insane and was put to death, one of his subordinates became monarch and founded a dynasty, the Chakkri, which continued into the twentieth century. The Thai remained dominant. It was from the Thai that in the twentieth century the country was given the official name, Thailand. This was soon abandoned for the earlier name, Siam, but still associated with the Thai.

Siam maintained friendly relations with China. Tribute embassies were sent to Peking. The Chinese administrative system had marked effect upon that of Siam.

In the sixteenth century the Portuguese established a number of trading posts. Roman Catholic missionaries arrived. Later came the Dutch and the English, as traders.

In culture the Siamese were influenced by both India and China. In religion they were largely Hinayana Buddhists, and very loyally so. The boys were educated in the Buddhist temples and each layman was supposed to spend time as a monk. Yet Hinduism persisted and Brahmans took part in some public ceremonies. In the thirteenth century a form of writing was devised for Siamese. From China came craftsmen who introduced their industrial arts. Chinese merchants, too, were prominent.

Burma

Because of its geographic location, it was to be expected that Burma would receive much of its early culture from India. As they developed shipping, the merchant adventurers of southern India were attracted by the Burmese coast and the fertile lower valleys of the Irrawaddy, the Sittang, and the Salween.

The Indian merchants found the land occupied by a variety of peoples. On the west coast, known as Arakan, were Tibeto-Burmese. On Tenasserim, the east coast, stretching part way down the Malay Peninsula, were Mons. Branches of the Thai family, known as Shans, were in the northern uplands of the north and northeast and in the upper portions of the valleys of the Irrawaddy and the Salween.

Early, although just when we do not know, there were trade

contacts between Burma and China Proper by way of the land route from the Yünnan plateau.

Before the third century after Christ Indian colonies had been established at various points on the coast. Here the Indians inaugurated states which they and their descendants ruled. They brought a higher culture and introduced the art of writing. In due time came Buddhism, of the Mahayana type.

A major center of culture and political life eventually arose at Pagan, some distance up the Irrawaddy. Here, in the eleventh century after Christ, the able Anawrata became the founder of a dynasty which for about two centuries headed the most powerful state in Burma. Anawrata extended his kingdom to Arakan and Tenasserim and into the Shan territories. One of his armies even fought its way into what later was called Yünnan. Under him Hinayana Buddhism became dominant. Into a form of writing adapted to Burmese, translations of Buddhist texts were made. With Hinayana Buddhism, art contacts were strengthened with southern India and especially with Ceylon, where that form of the faith was strong. Pagan became embellished with great buildings. An embassy was sent to the Sung court.

In the latter part of the thirteenth century the royal line of Anawrata went to pieces. Incompetent monarchs were on the throne. They clashed with the Mongols. Mongol armies swept into the country. They captured and looted Pagan. They extended over much of Burma the suzerainty of the Grand Khan. After the expulsion of the Mongols from the Middle Kingdom, some of the local princes received commissions from the Emperors of China.

Still greater damage to the rule of Pagan was done by the Shan. The tremendous southward movement of the Shan which in the thirteenth century was marked by the establishment of a state in the valley of the Brahmaputra and the Thai kingdoms in Siam swamped Burma.

Following the destruction of Pagan and the abandonment of the site, until the sixteenth century no one kingdom united Burma. Various states, some of them Shan and some Burmese, governed parts of the country. In at least one of the Shan principalities the blood of the dynasty which had once reigned in Pagan coursed in the veins of the ruling house. Ava, north of Pagan, became the capital of what was usually the most prominent of these states. War was frequent between it and a state in Lower Burma which had its headquarters in Pegu. Another state was at Toungoo, on the Sittang River. There was also a state in Arakan. In Arakan in the fifteenth century Islam became strong, although Buddhism still prevailed.

Arakan was the home of bold seamen. In the seventeenth and eighteenth centuries Portuguese joined with the Arakanese in developing a sea power which preyed upon commerce in the Bay of Bengal. In the second half of the seventeenth century Aurangzeb's viceroy in Bengal captured Chittagong, the main stronghold of Arakan, and greatly reduced the power of the sea-rovers. Arakan lapsed into civil strife.

The creation of a united kingdom in Burma was not the work of the Shan. It was the achievement of Burmese whose seat was first at Toungoo. In the first half of the sixteenth century Toungoo was the strongest state in Burma. In the second half of the sixteenth century a ruler of its royal house obtained the assistance of Portuguese mercenaries. They possessed firearms, until then not used in Burma. This equipment proved of marked advantage. However, Portuguese adventurers were also in the service of Arakan and Siam, with whom this Burmese prince waged war, and these states were not overcome. In the second half of the sixteenth century Bayinnaung, who reigned from Toungoo and then from Pegu, made himself master of most of Burma except Arakan. He also invaded Siam and captured Ayuthia. After his death Siam regained its independence and Burma fell into civil strife. The most powerful of the resulting states had its capital at Ava. In the middle of the eighteenth century another conqueror, Alaungpaya, united much of Burma and founded a dynasty which reigned eventually from Ava, until the completion of the British conquest in 1885.

In the course of the Manchu conquest of China a representative of the Ming took refuge in Burma and Chinese freebooters ravaged the border. The Manchus sent an army into Burma. In the second half of the eighteenth century a war between China and Burma was followed by the enrollment of Burma among the states which acknowledged the suzerainty of the Emperor of China and periodically sent tribute-bearing missions to Peking.

The renewed wave of European expansion which began in the fifteenth century brought to Burma the Portuguese and then the Dutch, the English, and the French. Free-lance Portuguese played a picturesque part in the sixteenth century politics of the country. Not until the nineteenth century, however, did that conquest begin which eventually brought all of Burma into the British Empire.

At the outset of the nineteenth century, most of Burma was under the rule of the somewhat decrepit royal house which had its seat at Ava. The valleys were inhabited by civilized folk whose religion was Hinayana Buddhism. In the hills and mountains which flanked the valleys were other peoples of various ethnic groups, primitive and near-primitive in culture. The civilized Burmese were deeply indebted to India and, because of the Hinayana Buddhist tradition, to Ceylon. Sanskrit and Pali were long familiar languages to the educated. There was also an indigenous literature in the vernacular. China had less effect on Burma than upon Annam, Cambodia, or Siam. However, there were Chinese in the land, largely merchants and artisans.

Ceylon

Ceylon, as a quick glance at the map will show, lies southwest of Burma and directly south of India. Indeed, it is connected with India physically by Adam's Bridge, a series of sandbars, some of them above and some slightly below the surface of the strait which separates the island from the mainland. Ceylon is about 272 miles long and 137 miles wide and is about five-sixths the size of Ireland. From its low coast there rises a high interior, with the most lofty peak extending beyond the eight thousand foot level. Because of the mountainous character of the interior, none of the streams are navigable beyond their lower reaches. The largest of the rivers empties into the best harbor of the island, Trincomalee, on the east coast. Trincomalee is, moreover, one of the finest harbors in the world and because of its commanding position is of great strategic importance for the control of the approach to India and the Far East.

The history of Ceylon of which we have fairly authentic records stretches over more than two millenniums. Of what are supposed to be its earlier population, akin, probably, to some of the most primitive peoples in Malaya, only a scant four or five thousand remain. In the latter part of the sixth century before Christ there came invaders of Aryan blood, possibly from the northeastern shores of India. They and their successors multiplied. Today the bulk of the population is made up of Sinhalese, more than half of them of the varieties on the lowlands and the remainder of the highlands. Between the two, differences exist which give rise to jealousies and friction. Both lowlanders and highlanders speak Sinhalese, an Aryan tongue related to Pali, the language of the early Buddhist classics.

Buddhism reached Ceylon at least as early as the third century before Christ and became, as it remains, the prevailing religion of the island. It is of the Hinayana branch of the faith and forms a cultural tie with Burma and Thailand, where Hinayana Buddhism is also dominant. In the course of the centuries invaders and immigrants arrived from the south of India and brought to the population a Tamil element which in numerical strength became second only to the dominant Sinhalese.

Sometime during the history of the island extensive irrigation works were built for an arid section. They were allowed to lapse, but their ruins testify to the enterprise and ability of those who constructed them.

Because of its strategic importance on the oceanic trade routes of Southern Asia, Ceylon was from early times frequented by merchants from various lands. As we saw in our fourth chapter, in the Ming dynasty China claimed at least part of Ceylon as a tributary country. Largely through foreign commerce there entered a Moslem element whose descendants today constitute about four per cent of the population.

The European era of Ceylon began with the Portuguese invasion in the early sixteenth century. When they arrived the Portuguese found the island divided into several states. They made themselves masters of a large part but not all of the island. Under them thousands of converts, chiefly from the lower social strata, were won to Roman Catholic Christianity, the basis of the fairly extensive Roman Catholic element of today.

In the seventeenth century the Dutch displaced the Portuguese. They, too, ruled part but not all of the island. They gave to their portions a much more systematic and methodical administration than had the Portuguese. They stimulated trade. Their Roman-Dutch law left a permanent deposit in the legal structure of the island. Their descendants, most of them with a strong admixture of native blood, today are known as the Burghers. They number not far from twenty-five thousand and have long been important in the clerical staff of the regime maintained by the English.

During the Napoleonic Wars Holland, then under French control, was supplanted in Ceylon by Great Britain. It was in 1795 and 1796 that the British conquest of the island was effected. Here, as in India, the East India Company was the agent. The transfer of power was made with very little bloodshed. However, the harsh administration of the Company early provoked a serious rebellion, and in 1798 the island was removed from the control of the Company and was made a crown colony. In the year that the Napoleonic Wars came to an end, the English completed the conquest of Ceylon and thenceforth ruled it all, as the Portuguese and the Dutch had not succeeded in doing. In the settlement which followed the Napoleonic Wars, Ceylon was left in British hands.

The Malay Peninsula

Because of its geographic location, the Malay Peninsula has an importance all out of proportion to its size. It commands the shortest sea route from India, Western Asia, and Europe to most of the Far East. The possession of strategic points on its coast, especially near its southern tip, has been the ambition of those peoples who have sought the mastery of the sea approaches to the east of Asia.

At the dawn of recorded history, when we first begin to obtain clear glimpses of the peninsula, the bulk of the population was of Malay stock. There were also darker folk of more primitive culture who might be classed as aborigines. The Malays, like so many other peoples, are of mixed origin. Their origin is a matter of dispute, but those in the Malay Peninsula seem to be Mongolian with a dash of Caucasian blood. They developed no advanced indigenous culture, but borrowed from other races.

In the early centuries of the Christian era, Indians, bent on commerce, settled near the southern end of the peninsula. They brought with them their culture, including Hinduism. Later came Buddhism. For most of the time from at least the seventh and eighth centuries into the twelfth century after Christ a kingdom, Sri Vishaya, with its center in Sumatra, controlled the Straits of Malacca, including part and perhaps occasionally all of the Malay Peninsula. In the fourteenth century the Javanese kingdom whose capital was at Madjapahit obtained mastery of the lower part of the Malay Peninsula. Sri Vishaya and Madjapahit were of Indian culture and under them Indian civilization was dominant.

In the early part of the fifteenth century the naval expeditions sent by the third Emperor of the Ming dynasty acquired for a brief time an important political position for the Chinese and gave an impetus to Chinese commerce.

More enduring was the influence of the Arabs. For centuries the Arabs had been coming as merchants to the Far East. With the decay of the Madjapahit Empire their influence increased in the Malay Peninsula as well as in the East Indies. By the close of the fourteenth century, they had obtained possession of Malacca, a strategic post on the strait of that name. In the course of the fifteenth century, Islam made rapid headway in the Malay Peninsula and in the adjacent archipelago. Numbers of the local principalities adopted that faith. The progress of Islam seems to have been due in part to commercial contacts with the Arabs, in part to the weakening of the states which had represented Hinduism and Buddhism, and in part to aggressive missionary efforts by the Moslem Arabs, especially by the Sayyids, who claimed descent from Mohammed himself. By the end of the fifteenth century, Malacca, now Moslem, was the leading port in that part of the world and a center for the spread of the faith of the Prophet.

The coming of the Europeans in the sixteenth century brought a change. European political and commercial power became important. However, except among a minority, European culture did not supplant its predecessors. In 1511 Albuquerque, the outstanding builder of the Portuguese Empire in Southern Asia, captured Malacca. Malacca now became the chief center of Portuguese power in the Far East. From it the lucrative spice trade with the East Indies was controlled. In 1641 the rising Dutch power took Malacca. This success helped to assure them the monopoly of East Indian commerce. During the Napoleonic Wars, Holland, as a satellite of France, was embroiled with the English. In 1795 the latter seized Malacca. In the general settlement which followed the defeat of Napoleon the port was restored to the Dutch. Sir Thomas Stamford Raffles, dreamer and administrator, whose vision called for a greatly enlarged British domain in that region, in 1819 purchased Singapore from the Sultan of Johore. Singapore, with its better harbor, soon eclipsed Malacca, and in 1824 the Dutch exchanged the latter for a British post on Sumatra.

The East Indies

The Malay Peninsula is closely associated with the East Indies. The two are separated only by the Straits of Malacca and the one partly commands the sea routes to the other.

The East Indies are very extensive. They embrace hundreds of islands. Their population is varied. Some of it is Papuan and very dark. Some of it is Negroid. A very little is Australoid, related to the primitives of Australia. Much of it is Malay, but the Malays are divided into many groups. In the Malays, especially those on the west, are infusions of Mongoloid blood.

Civilization seems first to have come to the East Indies through merchants from India. Not far from the beginning of the Christian era Indian settlements were in existence on both Sumatra and Java. States grew up under Indian influence, perhaps with rulers of Indian descent. As early as the first century after Christ the kingdom of Sri Vishaya (or Shrivijaya), which a few paragraphs above we noted in connection with the Malay Peninsula, seems to have been in existence on Sumatra. Toward the end of the seventh century it became the outstanding state in that island. It appears to have had its strength in its command of much of the commerce of the East Indies. In the eleventh century it was subdued by a fleet from a southern Indian state, but after about a generation it regained its independence and soon was more powerful than ever. It had as vassals its former masters of southern India and at least part of Ceylon. It controlled the Malay Peninsula and about half of Java. Under its protection were trading posts in a number of other islands of the East Indies and in Hainan and Formosa. Buddhist by faith, in the eighth century it built in Java the Buddhist Borobudur, now the most famous ruin in that island.

In the eleventh century a ruling house brought much of the eastern part of Java under its sway. In the thirteenth century there arose in eastern Java, with its capital at Singosari, a state whose apex was reached in the thirteenth century. The Javanese kingdom eclipsed Sri Vishaya and took away much of its commercial empire. Hinduism rather than Buddhism prevailed in most of Java, especially since the reigning families of eastern Java were long of the former faith. Not until the latter part of the thirteenth century did Buddhism become dominant in eastern Java. Even then Hinduism continued in Java. The island of Bali, just to the east of Java, jealously conserved its Hinduism and has done so to this day.

In the fourteenth century the kingdom of Madjapahit (or Modjopahit), also centered on Java, succeeded to much of the territory once held by the Singosari state. Madjapahit was the name of its capital, a city not far from Singosari, and the founder of its might was a son-in-law of the last monarch of Singosari. Madjapahit at first joined forces with the Mongol expedition which arrived in the last decade of the thirteenth century and helped it to destroy a rival which had overthrown Singosari. This rival having been eliminated, Madjapahit turned against the Mongols and made good its resistance. By the end of the fourteenth century Madjapahit had destroyed the remnant of Sri Vishaya and held part of the Malay Peninsula and posts in the East Indies as far north as the Philippines. Like its predecessors, the empire of Madjapahit was primarily commercial. In the fifteenth centurn it rapidly declined.

One of the factors in the decay of Madjapahit seems to have been the Chinese naval expeditions sent under the third emperor of the Ming dynasty. However, the heirs of Madjapahit power were not the Chinese but the Moslems. In the fifteenth century Moslem traders and rulers became dominant. In the civilized areas, except Bali, Islam supplanted Hinduism and Buddhism. It became the faith of most of the princes. As they turned Moslem, the princes threw off the yoke of the non-Moslem Madjapahit rulers. The populace followed the example of their masters and adopted Islam. So rapidly did Islam spread that among the majority it remained superficial. Many customs and beliefs survived from the centuries of animism, Hinduism, and Buddhism.

The Portuguese arrived in the East Indies in what for them was a fortunate time. No great kingdom was there to dispute with them a share in the spice trade which had lured them to the East. The Chinese had not established their rule. Islam and the Arab power were represented by a number of principalities, none of them extensive. Their capture of Malacca (1511) near the initial stages of their enterprise in the South and East of Asia gave the Portuguese a striking advantage, for Malacca was then the most strategic port for the East Indian commerce. The Portuguese set up fortified posts in a number of places in the East Indies, but, as in India, did not attempt large territorial conquests. Commerce and not empire was their motive.

Missionaries of the Roman Catholic Church, from the great revival in that body in the sixteenth century, took advantage of Portuguese contacts to plant their faith. Here as in India Xavier was the chief of the pioneers. However, Roman Catholic Christianity made no such headway as had Islam. Where adopted, it usually remained the religion of the minority.

After nearly a century, the Portuguese were all but supplanted by the rising Dutch power. The island of Amboyna, in the "Spice Islands," was taken by the Dutch in 1605. The Dutch seizure of Malacca (1641) gave the Hollanders the supremacy in the East Indian trade which the possession of that port had accorded successively to the Moslems and the Portuguese. The Portuguese retained slight territorial footholds, but the Dutch were dominant.

Dutch power was threatened by the English. For a brief time at the beginning of the seventeenth century merchants of the two nations cooperated. Inevitably, however, the two clashed. The English all but withdrew, concentrating on other parts of the East, principally India.

Dutch enterprise was through their East India Company. Since its purpose was primarily commercial, it did not stress either territorial conquest or assimilation to Dutch culture. Yet there was some of both of these. Eventually the Dutch established headquarters at Batavia, near the western end of Java. Most of Java came under their rule, through local princes who paid tribute. Alliances were negotiated with some others of the native rulers. Dutch military and naval assistance was requited by trade. In several of the Spice Islands territory was acquired. Dutch Calvinistic Christianity was also propagated. The East India Company subsidized missionaries and a state church came into being to which Dutch residents, the population of mixed Dutch and native stocks, and native converts belonged. Dutch Christianity made the most gains in the Moluccas, for here Islam had not so preempted the field as in Java. Some accessions, too, were from among the Roman Catholics. In Java, Islam, always especially resistant to Christianity, remained the faith of all but a very few of the natives.

For many years the commerce of the East Indies proved highly lucrative to the Dutch. The East India Company officially had a monopoly of it. It sought profits rather than the welfare of the natives. Somewhat ruthlessly it exacted tribute in the form of commodities which could be sold. However, in the areas which it controlled, it helped to maintain order, for this was advantageous to it. It also introduced coffee and sugar. These crops proved rewarding to the stockholders. They also added to the prosperity of the islands.

By the latter part of the eighteenth century the regime of the Dutch East India Company had run its course. Mismanagement at home and in the Indies and peculation by the Company's servants had burdened the Company with debt. In 1798, under the innovating government set up as the result of the occupation by the revolutionary French, the state took over the assets and liabilities and abolished the Company.

The British conquest in 1811, as an incident of the Napoleonic Wars, served further to mark the end of an era. Although, as a result of the Congress of Vienna, the British handed back to the Dutch their East Indian seizures, the few years of British administration were a break in the continuity of Dutch rule. It was a new age into which the East Indies, again under the Dutch, were ushered in the second decade of the nineteenth century. That story we are to recount in a later chapter.

The Philippine Islands

The Philippine Islands are really part of the East Indies. From the standpoint of physical geography they belong with them. Until the infusion of European blood brought by the Spanish conquest, racially the Philippines were largely East Indian. The bulk of their population was Malay, of several tribes and languages. In the hills were Negritos, akin to those found elsewhere in the East Indies. In the fifteenth century, as in much of the rest of the East Indies, Islam was making its way rapidly in the Philippines. Indeed, by the middle of the sixteenth century it had become dominant in the southern part, among those whom the Spaniards, carrying over the name which they had used for Moslems at home, dubbed Moros. What gave to the Philippines their distinctive place and made them an entity was the Spanish conquest and their prolonged subjection to acculturation by the Spaniards.

Before the coming of the Spaniards, as we have hinted, the Philippines were backward in civilization as compared with most of the rest of the Far East. Some influences had come from India, via the East Indies, and from China. However, the strongholds of Indian culture were in the southeastern islands of the East Indies and in the southern part of Indo-China, and the Philippines were on the northern extremity of the archipelago. The Chinese were as yet not aggressive in migrating overseas or, except for the brief efforts under the Yung Lo Emperor, in building either a commercial or a political oceanic empire. Moslem Arab culture had only recently arrived in force. The Filipinos were still but partly removed from the primitive stages of culture. To be sure, they had houses, used some of the metals, had terraced fields, and employed irrigation. In addition to Arabic in the Moslem south, they had systems of writing for some of their languages. Firearms had recently come in from the Arabs. However, except for the Moros and for half-forgotten remnants of Hinduism and Buddhism, the Filipinos were largely animists. They had no elaborate political organization and no unified government.

The Spanish conquest and prolonged occupation brought the

majority of the Filipinos within the zone of European culture. Because of the Spaniards, the Philippines were more affected by Occidental civilization than was any other Far Eastern land before the middle of the nineteenth century.

The contact of the Philippines with Spain began in 1521 when Ferdinand Magellan, in the famous voyage which effected the first navigation of the globe, touched at the islands and sought to claim for the Spanish crown those which he found. He had been looking for the Moluccas, in an effort to break into the monopoly which the Portuguese had acquired of the spice trade with Europe. It was because he sailed too far north that he reached the Philippines. In a local war in which he joined to gain recognition of Spanish authority, Magellan was killed. Only two ships of the five with which he began his expedition reached the Moluccas, and only one succeeded in pursuing its way around the Cape of Good Hope to Spain.

Spain made several efforts to enter the door which had been opened by Magellan. Not far from the time of that voyage the conquest of Mexico had been begun by Cortez, and the western coast of Mexico proved an advantageous point of departure for ships to the Far East. In 1525, 1526, 1527, and 1542, expeditions were sent toward the Far East, the first two from Spain and the last two from the convenient Mexico. The second of the four failed to reach its goal, and the other three ran afoul of the Portuguese, who regarded the Spaniards as interlopers in a region which they claimed had been allotted them by the Pope. Moreover, Spain, by the Treaty of Saragossa, in 1529, agreed to a demarcation line which placed the Philippines as well as the Moluccas well within the Portuguese zone.

In 1564 came the expedition which began the effective Spanish occupation. Led by Legaspi, it sailed from Mexico in 1564. Cebu, where Magellan had lost his life, was captured. Very soon, in 1571, Manila, already a flourishing port, was taken from its Moslem ruler and was made the capital of the colony.

By 1576, or within little more than a decade after Legaspi first landed, the Spaniards had conquered the larger part of the islands. The political and tribal divisions of the Filipinos favored their success. The mountainous interiors and the Moros in the south held out, but in general the non-Moslem coastal peoples submitted.

Until the nineteenth century the Philippines were more a religious than a commercial outpost of Spain. One of the purposes of the Spanish occupation was the conversion of the Filipinos to the Roman

Catholic faith. Beginning with Magellan, efforts were made to attain this end. Missionaries came with Legaspi and were followed by others. They were of several religious orders. A hierarchy was created for the islands. The missionaries did not confine themselves to Manila, but scattered through the provinces. Where necessary, they were protected by soldiers. However, little force was employed to effect conversions. Except where Islam had gained a foothold, the docile Filipinos, being of faiths which offer but slight resistance to higher religions, quickly conformed to the wish of their new masters and accepted baptism. Before many years the majority had become professing Christians. Only in the outlying districts and in the mountains did paganism survive. Under the direction of the priests, churches were erected. The church building with its tower was usually the most prominent structure in the village. Religious literature was prepared in the vernaculars. Most of such education as the islands possessed was through the Church. To the clergy, too, were due improvements in agriculture. The Moros held to their Islam, but elsewhere, even in the mountains, Christianity progressively gained.

From the Philippines, moreover, Spanish Roman Catholic missionaries went to other parts of the Far East. They made their way to China, Formosa, Japan, and Indo-China, and in China and Indo-China established continuing enterprises.

Commercially the Philippines were of little importance to Spain. They were halfway around the world from that country. The approach via Africa was in the hands of the Portuguese. The most feasible route was across the Pacific to Mexico, over Mexico, and then through the Caribbean and across the Atlantic. The Spanish Government, too, closely directed the commerce of its colonies and was opposed to much intercourse with its distant possession. The trans-Pacific trade was limited to an annual exchange, usually through one galleon.

Some commerce existed between the Philippines and other parts of the Far East. In this the Chinese were prominent. The Chinese arrived in such large numbers that the Spaniards were alarmed and from time to time dealt with what they believed to be a menace by the simple though cruel expedient of a massacre. Yet, after a brief pause, the Chinese continued to come.

Under Spanish rule the Philippines prospered. To be sure, they were governed paternalistically, both by Church and state. The Filipinos were not admitted to the leading posts and were kept in subordinate positions. In spite of the benevolent Laws of the Indies which ostensibly sought the spiritual and material welfare of the wards of the Spanish crown, there was much exploitation of the Filipinos by the civil and ecclesiastical authorities. Yet the Filipinos were probably as well off as were any people of the Far East in their day. The Spaniards protected them from foreign invasion and prevented extensive civil strife. The occasional revolts were usually promptly suppressed. Population increased.

The Philippines were partly assimilated to European culture. Under Spanish tutelage they became the only Christian and Europeanized nation of the Far East.

Summary

This chapter has had to deal with a wide variety of countries and peoples. All played minor roles in Far Eastern history. None developed a strikingly original advanced culture. They were borrowers, chiefly from China and India and latterly, to a less extent, from Europe. Yet several attained a high degree of civilization and made modifications in the imported culture. This series of sketches, even though brief, has been necessary if the volume is to achieve its purpose of assisting in a well-rounded understanding of the Far East of the present day.

BIBLIOGRAPHY

D. P. Barrows, *History of the Philippines* (Chicago, 1924).
C. Bell, *Tibet: Past and Present* (Oxford, 1924).
F. A. Golder, *Russian Expansion on the Pacific, 1641–1850* (Cleveland, 1914).
R. Grousset, *Histoire de l'Extrême-Orient* (2 vols., Paris, 1929).
G. E. Harvey, *History of Burma* (London, 1925).
H. B. Hulbert, *History of Korea* (2 vols., 1905).
O. Lattimore, *Inner Asian Frontiers of China* (Oxford University Press, 1940).
J. H. Longford, *The Story of Korea* (London, 1911).
A. Vandenbosch, *The Dutch East Indies* (Grand Rapids, 1933).
B. H. M. Vlekke, *Nusantara: A History of the East Indian Archipelago* (Cambridge, 1943).
W. A. R. Wood, *History of Siam, from the Earliest Times to the Year 1781* (London, 1926).
G. Cœdès, *Les États Hindouisés d'Indochine et d'Indonésie* (Paris, 1948).
K. P. Landon, *Southeast Asia. Crossroads of Religions* (Chicago, 1947).

INDIA AND THE FAR EAST IN REVOLUTION

Chapter IX. INTRODUCTION TO CHANGE

THUS FAR we have concerned ourselves with the geography, the history, and the culture of India and the Far East before the revolutionary changes produced by the coming of the Occident.

As we have seen in the earlier chapters, Western peoples had long been coming to India and the Far East. Before the time of Christ the Greeks had reached India. Greek culture left its impress upon that land, notably on the art of Buddhism. Through Buddhist iconography Hellenistic art in more or less modified forms had its effects in China and Japan. During post-Alexandrian and Roman days there was commerce between the eastern Mediterranean world and India and China. In the thirteenth and fourteenth centuries Western Europeans, both merchants and missionaries, made their way to India and China. For a time in the fourteenth and fifteenth centuries direct contacts between Western Europe on the one hand and India and China on the other ceased. At the close of the fifteenth and during the sixteenth century Western Europeans once more reached India and the Far East, this time in greater numbers than in earlier times. They inaugurated and maintained commercial contacts and established territorial footholds and throughout the sixteenth and seventeenth centuries were a force to be reckoned with. However, except for their effect upon Japan and their conquests in the Philippines and the East Indies they were of minor importance. The major streams of Indian and Far Eastern politics and culture were but little affected.

Toward the close of the eighteenth century and particularly in the nineteenth and twentieth centuries the impact of the Occident was greatly intensified. In the eighteenth century the increase of Occidental might was experienced chiefly in the land nearest to Europe, India. In the nineteenth century the power of the West began to make itself felt in augmented fashion in the Far East. Because of geographic propinquity, this it did first in Burma and southeastern

Asia. Before the middle of the nineteenth century China had begun to feel the force of the new tide and had been compelled to make concessions to it. In the second half of the century Japan and Korea, still more remote from Europe, were constrained to open their doors to the West. By the beginning of the twentieth century the West was dominant in India and the Far East, and adjustment to it and its culture was working revolutionary changes throughout that vast area.

Some of the causes of the rapid increase in the impact of the Occident are fairly obvious. The industrial revolution and the immense growth in commerce, wealth, and power which accrued to the Occident from the adoption and development of new mechanical appliances were clearly of major importance. The rapid growth of factories impelled their possessors to ransack the world for markets and raw materials. The improvement of communications through the steamship, the railway, the electric telegraph, the telephone, and latterly the radio and the airplane facilitated travel and commerce. Its monopoly of the new machines gave the Occident an enormous advantage in both the economic and the political field. Equipped with these new appliances, the armies and navies of the West could make short work of the opposition of peoples who did not possess them. Moreover, the nineteenth century was one of comparative peace in the Occident. After the many storms of the seventeenth and eighteenth centuries, between the close of the Napoleonic Wars in 1815 and the outbreak of World War I in 1914 no general conflict and no prolonged war between any of the major powers troubled Europe. Wars there were, to be sure, but none of the extent of those in the preceding two centuries. Europe had leisure to accumulate wealth and to grow in population. Europe and peoples of European stock were set free to dominate the world. Accompanying the political and economic expansion of Europe in the Far East was religious expansion. The nineteenth and twentieth centuries witnessed a Christian missionary movement from Europe and the United States unequaled in the history of religion. Thousands of missionaries, Roman Catholic and Protestant, inspired and impelled by a great revival of Christianity, carried their faith to India and the Far East and at a number of points, in education, medicine, and other forms of philanthropy, as well as religion, touched the cultures of the south and east of Asia.

As we hinted in our second chapter, beyond these causes of the increase of European influence which were there for all to see were others that were basic, but more intangible and of such a nature as to escape exact determination or precise measurement. Why was it that European and especially Western European peoples should be the ones to give rise to the machine and to modern science and should, even before the beginning of the machine age, set themselves to exploring the world? Is the answer to be found in race, in climate, in geography, in resources of mine, field, and forest, in the Graeco-Roman heritage, in religion, or in a combination of two or more of these factors? We do not certainly know. Perhaps we cannot know. Yet it would be extremely important to be able to determine the causes of the phenomenon. If we had the correct reply we would be better able to forecast the future. It might then be possible to tell whether the dominance of European peoples, which is a matter of only one or at most four centuries, is to continue or whether it is transient. We would also be in a better position to foresee the future of the peoples of India and the Far East. For at least the moment, however, we lack the necessary information, and the interpretation of the mystery is hidden from our eyes.

Whatever the causes, irruption of the Occident into India and the Far East occurred. In magnitude and extent it was without precedent in Far Eastern history, as, indeed, in all history.

In the impact of the Occident upon India and the Far East, Great Britain led the way. This was partly because of the position which she had won in the seventeenth and eighteenth centuries and especially during the Napoleonic Wars, and partly because she was the pioneer in the industrial revolution and long had almost a monopoly of the new machines. France was a poor second, the Dutch expanded their holdings, and in the north the Russians were extremely active. From across the Pacific came the Americans. They played an increasingly prominent role and in the mid-1940's became the dominant maritime power in the Pacific. Australia and New Zealand had to be reckoned with in the southwestern Pacific, but somewhat tardily.

As in the rest of the world, the reenforcement of the invasion of the West was followed by striking changes. India and the Far East were brought under the partial or complete political control of Western peoples. Occidental commerce and the products of Occidental factories flooded the region. Japan, which suffered less from the compromise of its independence than any other Far Eastern power, except possibly Thailand, and which regained its full political independence earlier than did any other, was the first to be thoroughly industrialized after the Western pattern. Impressed by the power of the West and envying the might and the wealth of that favored region, the peoples of India and the Far East began to adopt various phases of the culture of the Occident. Since it was the material and technological side of the might of the West which most impressed them, it was the machines and the intellectual processes which seemingly led to the machines that India and the Far East were most eager to acquire. Railways, factories, and telegraph and telephone lines were built. Where a degree of political independence remained, armies and navies equipped after the fashion of the West were developed. The kinds of science and education that the nineteenth and twentieth century Occident displayed were copied, sometimes under indigenous initiative, sometimes under the guidance and at the instance of Western overlords. Modifications were made in the political structures to bring the governments more or less into conformity with Occidental precedents. More slowly but basically, changes began to appear in the family, in various other social institutions, and in religious and ethical concepts and systems. A gigantic revolution, or, rather, a series of revolutions, was under way which eventually affected all phases of life.

The domination of the West was facilitated and the revolution was accentuated by a singular coincidence of political and cultural weakness in the major lands of the region in the nineteenth century. In India the Mogul Empire, the largest which India had thus far known, was disintegrating. In China the Ch'ing dynasty was manifestly in its twilight and Chinese culture was ceasing to be creative. In Japan the Tokugawa *Bakufu* had enforced an internal peace which could only issue in the demise of the regime which had imposed it. India and the Far East were too weak to offer effective resistance to the aggressive Occident. The access of vigor in the West was paralleled by decrepitude in the south and east of Asia. It was an unusual combination of circumstances which produced the changes of the nineteenth and twentieth centuries.

By the close of the first quarter of the twentieth century, the political and economic supremacy of the Occident was passing. Presumably the Occident could not permanently retain the monopoly of the mechanical appliances and the types of knowledge which had done so much to assure it the mastery of the rest of the world. Especially would the civilized peoples of India and the Far East be likely to break it. The peoples of the East were never happy over Western domination. Although some of them, perforce, were passive, others, and these included the most numerous, ardently desired to be rid of the Occidental yoke. They resented the Occidental air of superiority and envied the higher standard of living of the West, flaunted before their eyes, as it was, by the Occidental enclaves in the Orient. The passing of white supremacy was hastened by wars most of which had their rise in the West and which devastated much of Europe, weakening its power. What in many ways was civil strife in the Occident greatly reduced the ability of the West to impose its will upon other peoples and regions, particularly in lands so remote from it and so populous and highly civilized as the Far East. The challenge to the Occident first came from Japan. In the course of the first half of the twentieth century it spread to other peoples. When the century was in mid course the political and economic hegemony of the Occident was being rapidly liquidated.

The passing of Western imperialism in India and the Far East did not end the revolution. It was only by adopting much of the culture of the Occident that political power of Occidental peoples could be ousted. India and the Far East could acquire their political independence only at the cost of the partial loss of their cultural independence. The Westernization of the civilizations of the region continued.

It is this story which we are to summarize more in detail in the subsequent chapters. We will arrange those chapters largely in the sequence of the coming and progress of the revolution. We will begin with India, where the white man's penetration was first felt and was earliest completed. We will go on to the lands of southeastern Asia and the adjacent island world. We will then make our way to the Chinese Empire. From there we will move on to Japan. We will eventually tell how Japan sought to oust the white man from the Far East and to substitute its rule for his and will recount the steps the white man took to deal with Japan and the reaction of Far Eastern peoples in the vast struggle which ensued. In the process we may gain some inkling as to how far Western supremacy was to be maintained.

Chapter X. SUBJECT INDIA

The British conquest and administration: the beginning of emancipation

AS WE TURN to the second main section of our story of the Far East under the impact of the Occident in the nineteenth and twentieth centuries, we come first of all to India. Here the conquest by the West was begun and completed earlier than elsewhere in the region. Here the recession of the Occidental wave first began. We must, then, commence with India as we did in the initial major stage of our pilgrimage.

The outstanding feature of Indian history in the second half of the eighteenth and the first half of the nineteenth centuries was the British conquest. In the second half of the nineteenth century the predominating factor in Indian development was the British administration of the country and the progressive introduction, largely under British direction, of Western education and Occidental machines and conceptions of law and government. The most striking characteristic of Indian history in the first half of the twentieth century was the growth of Indian nationalism and the rapid increase of Indian self-government. Throughout all the decades, Western culture in its various phases was permeating Indian life and was bringing with it striking changes.

The British Conquest

One of the most amazing movements in human history was the British conquest of India. Great Britain, with a population only a fraction of that of India, of an utterly different culture, and thousands of miles away, brought under its dominion a larger proportion of Indian territory and peoples than had ever before acknowledged a single rule. This it did, not by a land invasion through the northwest passes, as had the earlier major conquerors, but from the sea. The larger proportion of the British forces came by way of the long water route around the Cape of Good Hope, for the Suez Canal was not completed until 1869, and the conquest had then been practically accomplished. In other words, in terms of distance, at the time it was subduing India, Great Britain was halfway around the world. Moreover, the conquest was begun and was far along toward completion before the industrial revolution had more than commenced to equip Great Britain with the appliances which presumably would have been of advantage in such an enterprise. More amazing still, the English did not originally contemplate making themselves masters of the land. They first came to India as merchants. The conquest was inaugurated and carried through under the English East India Company, which was primarily a commercial corporation having as its object profits for its shareholders and which found wars and administration expensive burdens. To be sure, some of the great leaders in the reduction of India dreamed in terms of empire, but at the outset no one foresaw the extent which the British domains would attain. If the British Empire in India did not exactly grow up in a fit of absence of mind, as some would have us believe, at least at the beginning no one consciously planned it. Nowhere else in the entire range of the experience of mankind is there a parallel which in magnitude equals the British achievement.

The reason for the phenomenon of the British conquest is to be found largely in the divided state of India in the second half of the eighteenth century. The Mogul Empire had passed its peak and was in rapid and irreparable decline. No central authority existed which could accord protection to foreign merchants or effectively resist encroachments by aliens. India, never fully united, was losing such political integration as it possessed. The English felt constrained to protect their trading establishments against annoying local princes. They were faced with European rivals, notably the French, with whom they were chronically at war in several other parts of the world. The French were seeking to curb the English and were enlisting in their behalf some of the Indian rulers. The English, to safeguard their factories, as their trading centers were called, found themselves under the necessity of going to war, now against some prince who misused them, and now against the French. In the course of the wars they met with successes and came into possession of territories taken from their foes. These territories they were constrained to administer. They also deemed it imperative to protect these territories against Indian and foreign foes. Thus they were led into further wars. Since, in general, these were followed by additional acquisitions of territory, the English came into control of larger and larger domains the borders of which, in turn, must be defended. Eventually the conquest had to be carried to the natural frontiers of India, for as long as any of the land was held by unfriendly or jealous princes the British rule would not be secure. In their military operations the English were immeasurably aided by the divisions of the country. They found allies among the Indian princes. Their armies were predominantly Indian in personnel, sepoys, although officered by Europeans and drilled and armed in Occidental fashion. The actual British forces brought from the British Isles were comparatively small.

Although weakness brought by division and the palsied state of the Mogul dynasty account in large part for the British conquest, these were not the sole factors. Portuguese, Dutch, and French were confronted by the same India, but did not gain more than limited footholds. Much must be ascribed to the ambition and ability of the English and especially to a succession of extraordinarily able leaders.

The history and means of the British conquest were reflected in the subsequent political map of the land. The country was eventually divided into three types of units—(1) British India, under the direct administration of the British *raj*, (2) the native states, some of them former allies of the English, who retained their own lines of rulers, but whose foreign relations were in British hands and whose internal affairs were conducted under varying degrees of British supervision, and (3) a few surviving enclaves, none of them large, held by the Portuguese and the French.

From these generalizations we must move on to the main outlines of the story of the British conquest.

In the middle of the eighteenth century the three main centers of British power were Bombay, Madras, and Calcutta. It was from these that the British domains were chiefly extended. The first operations were from Madras, with Calcutta as a fairly close second.

The preliminary measures in the British conquest of India issued directly from conflicts between the French and the English which had their rise and center in Europe. In 1740 the War of the Austrian Succession broke out. England and France were on opposite sides. The struggle extended to the French and British posts in India. In Dupleix, the Governor in their principal post, Pondichery, the French possessed an able and ambitious representative. In the course of the war a French fleet, well led, captured Madras, the chief British stronghold on the southeast coast. Madras was restored to Great Britain by the peace that concluded the European war.

The coming of peace in Europe did not end the struggle in India. Dupleix dreamed of building in India a French Empire. As a step toward this end he espoused the cause of claimants in disputed successions in native states. The English felt that such an extension of French power would be inimical to their trade and opposed it. Resistance took the form in part of support to rivals of the French protegees. The French made spectacular gains in the Deccan but were weakened by English strength in the Carnatic, on the southeast coast. In 1754 Dupleix was recalled by his home authorities.

Yet the struggle in India between the French and the English continued. It was given added momentum by the Seven Years War (1756–1763) in Europe and the contest for empire in America which had led to the outbreak of hostilities (1755) on the Franco-British border in that distant land. In India the conflict spread to Bengal. There both the French and the English had factories. The British center was Calcutta. In 1756 the youthful new Nawab, or Governor of Bengal, theoretically a Mogul official but practically independent, conceived an animosity against the English, and attacked and took Calcutta. His captives were thrown into the "black hole," or military jail in the fallen Fort William, and after a night in the hot, confined room only a small minority of those who had been imprisoned survived. When news of the disaster reached the English at Madras a force was sent to retrieve the British fortunes. Calcutta was regained; the French center in Bengal, as a potential source of aid to the Nawab, was seized; and on June 23, 1757, the Nawab was overwhelmingly defeated at the Battle of Plassey. The English did not immediately assume the administration of Bengal, but they placed in the post of Nawab a claimant friendly to themselves. From him they obtained concessions in Bengal which foreshadowed the wider extension of their power in that region. This Nawab in turn fell out with the English, and in a decisive battle in 1764 they defeated him, the Wazir of Oudh, and the Mogul Emperor.

The commander of the British forces at the Battle of Plassey and the founder of British rule in Bengal was Robert Clive (1725–1774). Clive was the first of the great founders of the British Empire in India. He was of a good Shropshire family, had proved unruly in school, and at the age of eighteen had been sent to seek his fortune in India as a "writer" or clerk in the civil service of the East India Company. He was first assigned to Madras. Energetic and extraordinarily able, Clive early rose to prominence in the wars in southern India. Here his success as a commander presaged his triumphs in Bengal. He had three periods in India. The third and last of them was from 1765 to 1767, when as Governor in Bengal for the East India Company he obtained the financial administration of much of Bengal, Bihar, and Orissa for the East India Company and reformed the Company's administration. The Company exercised authority in Bengal, Bihar, and Orissa not in its own name but theoretically as Diwan of the Mogul Emperors. Inevitably Clive made many enemies. On his return to England these attacked him and his conduct of Indian affairs. He made no attempt to placate them but added fuel to their ire by advocating the drastic measure which did not come for two generations, the taking over of the British possessions in India by the crown. Disheartened, Clive died by his own hand when he was still short of fifty years of age.

The second of the great builders of the British empire in India was Warren Hastings (1732–1818). A scion of an old Oxfordshire family which had fallen into poverty, like Clive he went out to India in his late teens as a "writer" in the service of the East India Company. By 1771 he had so far advanced that he was made Governor in Bengal. As Governor Hastings carried through important reforms which were urgently needed and the necessity for some of which arose from the additional functions the Company had undertaken as a result of its victory on the field of battle. As one consequence of the reforms the Company in fact became responsible for the whole civil administration of Bengal. The East India Company was more and more a territorial power. The changes put through by Hastings also included alterations in the judicial procedure, with a better graduated system of courts. From 1774 to 1785 Hastings was titular Governor-General of all the company's possessions in India. A unified administration was in process of development.

The years of Hastings' leadership in India were marked by further wars and additional conquests. In the west the British power at Bombay had already become involved in a conflict with the mighty Mahratta Confederacy which in the seventeenth and eighteenth centuries had become a military force of primary importance. In the first war between the English and the Mahrattas, which ended in 1782, the English made progress, but by no means crushed their adversaries. In the south the most active enemy of the English was Hyder Ali, of Mysore. Hyder Ali's son, Tipu, perpetuated the contest.

When he returned to England Hastings, like Clive, was faced with the attacks of his foes among his own countrymen. An impeachment of Hastings gave rise to one of the most famous trials in English history. The hearings were before the House of Lords and dragged out for seven years, from 1788 to 1795. Hastings bore himself with the same undaunted courage he had displayed in India, and that in spite of the fact that some of the most notable orators of the day, including the great Burke, were ranged against him. He was acquitted, but the costs of his defense had eaten up his fortune and, although his name was cleared, further public employment for him was out of the question. The long evening of his life was spent quietly, surrounded by devoted friends, at his ancestral home.

Under Lord Cornwallis, who was Governor-General from 1786 to 1793, great advance was made toward ruling India, not for the profit of the East India Company and its servants, but for the benefit of the people of the land. Cornwallis was a man of incorruptible honesty and with a desire for the public good. His defeat in America at the hands of Washington had not shaken the confidence of his friends in his character. Unlike his predecessors in high office in India, he had not come up through the Company's service but had been appointed to carry out improvements desired by the reformers at home. Thanks in part to the Evangelical Awakening and its able representatives in Parliament and in the Company, a movement was under way, already foreshadowed by Hastings, to rule in India through men of integrity and with the welfare of India as a main object. India had been a land in which, under the East India Company, fortunes could be quickly amassed by those coming out from the British Isles, often by means which to a later age seemed reprehensible. A rising public conscience in Great Britain was demanding that India should not be selfishly exploited. Under Lord Cornwallis improvements in administration were continued or inaugurated which went far toward the attainment of that ideal. Cornwallis's term of office also saw a continuation of the struggle of the English with Tipu, Sultan of Mysore, and with the Mahrattas.

The wars which accompanied the French Revolution and which culminated in the long struggle of the English with Napoleon brought a renewed French threat to the growing British power in India. As we hinted a few paragraphs above, even before the French Revolution

French intrigues against the English had long been a feature of Indian life. It was French activities at the courts of native princes which had been a continuing factor in provoking the East India Company to its conquests. The Company felt that it must meet fire with fire. Napoleon's expedition to Egypt and the Near East seemed a major menace. The English rose to the occasion, and the era of the French Revolution and Napoleon brought the reduction of French power in India to a point where it was no longer a danger. French stations on the way to India, the Isle of France and Bourbon, were taken by the English. The Dutch, then subject to the French, were expelled from Ceylon and British rule was established in that island. While, by the settlements of 1814 and 1815 which ended the Napoleonic Wars, the French were allowed to retain a foothold in India, they agreed to maintain there no troops and to erect no fortresses. French rivalry was eliminated.

During the wars of the French Revolution and Napoleon, British domains in India were being rapidly extended. In 1798 there arrived in India Richard Wellesley, Earl of Mornington and eventually Marquis Wellesley, older brother of the still more famous Arthur Wellesley, the later Duke of Wellington. As Governor-General, Wellesley laid down the guiding principle that the British must be the dominant power in India and that native princes could retain the insignia of sovereignty only by surrendering the substance of their independence. Wellesley was, moreover, a man of marked ability who made substantial strides toward rendering this policy effective. Tipu was eliminated. Part of Tipu's territory was annexed by the English, but Mysore was allowed to continue as a state, with diminished boundaries, under another ruling line and under the protection of the Company. A war with the Mahrattas led to a defeat of the latter. As an incident of the Mahratta wars, British control was established over Delhi, the traditional seat of the Mogul Dynasty. The English were succeeding to the Mogul heritage. In addition to the conquests made during the years of his rule, Wellesley, an excellent administrator, achieved improvements in the machinery of government. Among these was the establishment of a college at Fort William, in Calcutta, for training young men from Britain for service in India. Wellesley found the scattered beginnings of a British territorial rule in India. In his approximately seven years in the land (1798–1805) he built what was in effect the British Empire of India.

During most of the remainder of the Napoleonic period, or from

1807 to 1813, Lord Minto was Governor-General. His task was to consolidate the conquests made under Wellesley.

Lord Minto was followed by Lord Moira, better known as the Marquis of Hastings. Lord Moira was Governor-General from 1814 to 1823. Under him was fought a war with the martial Gurkhas, who were ruling in Nepal. Under him, too, was waged the final war with the Mahrattas. The resistance of those vigorous opponents of the British *raj* was at last broken. It was in Lord Moira's time, moreover, that the legal fiction was ended by which the East India Company acted as an agent of the *fainéant* Mogul Emperor. The Mogul line continued, but Moira declined to acknowledge its supremacy over the Company's dominions.

In succeeding decades, down into the middle of the 1850's, additional conquests further expanded the British borders. British possessions were extended into the Punjab and Sind, both in the northwest, and a war was fought with the Afghans. In the opposite direction, two wars in Burma brought much of that country under the British flag. By 1857 the English were clearly masters in India. Much of the land was ruled through the East India Company. Such of the native princes as continued in their hereditary states did so on British sufferance. Territorially, except for some details, the British Empire in India had been completed.

The Mutiny

Now, when the British achievement had apparently reached the climax of its success, came, in 1857 and 1858, a violent upheaval which for the moment threatened all that had been attained. There was a mutiny of a large body of the sepoys, or native troops, which was accompanied in some areas by uprisings of the population and of a few of the princes. Here was an explosive effort to be rid of the English and all their works. Mutinies there had been before among the native forces of the East India Company. None of them, however, for magnitude could match what by common consent has been termed the Mutiny.

The causes of the Mutiny were many. There was restlessness over the rapid extension of British rule. The prohibition by the English of some accepted Hindu customs, such as *suttee*, or the immolation of widows on the funeral pyres of their husbands, and female infanticide, brought discontent to many. The subordination of the Brahmans to the criminal law aggrieved others. Numbers of landowners, especially Moslems, were unhappy over the regulations imposed by the Company. The gulf between the English rulers and the Indians in race, color, customs, and religion was deep and was a source of discontent. Various actions and policies of the government had given rise to unrest, especially in the Bengal army and its affiliated forces. The proportion of European troops, the core of the army, had been reduced, partly because of the need for troops in current wars in Persia and China and partly because some had been sent to newly acquired territories in India. The immediate occasion of the outbreak was the offense taken at a new type of cartridge which had been issued. It was reported to be greased with the fat of beef or of swine which had to be bitten by the soldier before it could be used, thus involving ceremonial defilement, the one to the Hindus and the other to the Moslems.

The Mutiny was chiefly in the Ganges Valley. It did not have any serious extension into the administrative areas, which centered in Madras and Bombay. Scores of Europeans, soldiers and civilians, were killed, and some of the native Christians. It took reenforcements of European troops and months of hard fighting to restore British authority. In general, however, the masses of the population remained passive and the vast majority of the native princes were either friendly to the English or neutral. British rule had been challenged, but now was planted more firmly than ever.

Transfer to the Crown

One consequence of the shock given by the Mutiny was the end of the Mogul Empire. That regime had long been little more than a legal fiction, but the last to bear the title of Emperor had been compromised by his attitude during the outbreak and was banished to Burma. The final survivor of the non-British lines which might lay historical claim to the rule of all India had been removed from the scene.

Another result was the termination of the anomaly of the rule of the British Indian Empire by the East India Company. In 1858 the British political interests in India were placed directly under the crown. For many years there had been those who advocated this step. It took the shock of the Mutiny to precipitate decisive action.

Nearly two decades later, in 1877, the further action was taken of proclaiming Queen Victoria Empress of India. The formal ceremony was staged at a huge and colorful durbar on a ridge overlooking

Delhi, with its memories of Mogul might. Thus the British crown became, in a sense, the successor of the last of the great Indian dynasties, and that personal element was given to British rule which was in accordance with Indian tradition. The Queen-Empress reigned over a larger proportion of India than had even the greatest of the Moguls or had ever monarch of any dynasty before her.

Progressive Westernization

We need not detail the progress of administrative changes under the crown. Some of the main features of the British contribution to India during these years must claim our attention, however, for it was through the British contacts that the Occident chiefly impinged upon India and worked changes in Indian life.

One of the marked channels through which Western influence flowed into India was education. In the days of the Company's control and before the Mutiny and the transfer to the crown, the main principles of the British educational system in India had been laid down. Two theories had contended for the mastery. The one, championed by European Orientalists, would have made much of Indian languages and learning but would have added Western sciences to them. The other, having as its outstanding advocates a Scotch missionary, Alexander Duff, and the famous historian, Thomas Babington Macauley, who in 1835 as head of the Committee on Public Instruction presented a memorandum which carried great weight, wished education to be through English as a medium of instruction and the content to be English literature and Western learning. It was the latter program which prevailed. The government set up a system of schools from primary grades through the universities. Some of these it conducted directly with teachers who had official status. Others were maintained locally but under government supervision. Still others, many of them conducted by Christian missions, received "grants-in-aid" from the state and were also under government inspection and conformed to standards set up by the government. In general the schools trained Indians for employment under the government and for professions, notably law, connected with the British regime. They produced an oversupply and the resulting unemployment was one of the elements which later contributed to dissatisfaction with British rule. Built on the foundations of an English prototype, the educational system was one of the most potent forces for the Westernization of the land. English became the one language spoken by all the educated. Even when, late in the nineteenth and in the twentieth centuries, the Indian National Congress met to denounce the English and all their works it was constrained by this fact to do so through the medium of the English tongue.

Stress was laid upon secondary and higher education. Primary education, notably that in the vernacular, while by no means entirely lacking, lagged behind. The emphasis upon English was by no means uniform throughout the country, but English had commercial value, since it led to employment in commerce, transportation, and government. Increasingly the more ambitious students went to Great Britain to complete their education. Education was primarily for boys. In accordance with Indian tradition, schools for women were relatively few.

A marked feature of government policy was the persistent effort to prevent starvation. Undernourishment was chronic among many of India's millions. From time to time acute famine killed thousands and even millions. The failure of the monsoon in a particular area, a flood, or some other natural disaster would tragically reduce the already narrow margin of subsistence. The British *raj* was not the first government in India to fight famine. Some of its predecessors had done so. Yet none had contended with it on so extensive a scale, or, on the whole, so successfully, and that against the rising odds of a rapidly growing population. Irrigation ditches, some of them serving large areas, were constructed, and waste lands were reclaimed, notably in the arid and semiarid Punjab. The development of railways facilitated the transportation of grain from regions of plenty to those of dearth. Agrarian legislation which was mainly in the interest of the cultivators assisted the peasants. Cooperative credit societies helped to free the farmer from the usurious interest rates of the professional moneylender. Research developed better strains of existing crops and more efficient methods of agriculture. These improvements were only in their beginnings but they were attempts at meeting some of the fundamental causes. When, in spite of all efforts, famine came, as it sometimes did, the government gave relief, earlier in return for work done, usually on irrigation projects to prevent future famines, but latterly gratuitously to those who could not work or for whom no work could be provided.

Some attempt, too, was made, in part by the governments, native and British, to improve the public health. Several of the diseases which had been all but excluded from the Occident of the late nineteenth century, such as bubonic plague and cholera, were chronic in India. To these were added such scourges as tuberculosis, malaria, the dysenteries, and, from time to time, influenza. The extreme poverty and undernourishment of the masses combined with the absence of even the most elementary sanitary precautions to exact a heavy toll of life. Compared with the magnitude of the task, no very great advance was registered. Yet something was done. Hospitals were opened in many of the towns and cities, and here and there in the countryside as well as in the towns were dispensaries. In several of the cities pure drinking water was introduced and improved methods were installed for disposing of the sewage. Vaccination and inoculation were furthered.

It must be added that those who fought the age-long evils of famine and disease were confronted by a most discouraging increase of population. The *pax Britannica* removed the chronic plague of internal war. Strenuous effort reduced the frequency of famine. Public health measures met some of the disease. Once these traditional restraints on population were weakened, the census figures jumped at an appalling rate. In 1881 the total was 253,000,000. In 1921 it was 319,000,000. In 1931 it was 352,800,000. In 1941 it reached the astounding figure of 388,800,000. The issues brought by this expansion, particularly when it is recalled that India was predominantly rural and possessed few large cities, scarcely need comment.

The British occupation was followed by the growth of modern methods of transportation. Railways were built, chiefly with British capital. At first construction was by private companies guaranteed by the state. It was in this fashion that the main trunk lines were built. In 1870 the policy of developing railways by the state was adopted. Much of the privately owned mileage was acquired. By the mid-1920's nearly three-fourths of the mileage was in state hands and about two-fifths was managed by the government. An extensive post office system was also developed by the state. The post office had as adjuncts savings banks and a life insurance department. The telegraph was introduced and extended, largely by the government, and telephones were installed.

British India was given a sound financial structure. The currency was on the silver standard, and it was silver which circulated in the basic coins. This seems to have been by the choice of Indian public opinion, for attempts by the government to introduce gold coins proved unsuccessful. Efforts to tie the rupee (the standard unit of currency) to the English pound long failed of complete success, although by 1914, as measured by the pound sterling, based upon gold, the rupee had become comparatively stable. Indeed, in 1914, the rupee was legally fixed at a value of sixteen pence and became a token coin. As against the pound, the exchange rate of the rupee fluctuated greatly during and immediately after World War I. In 1926 Indian currency was placed on a gold bullion foundation and the rupee was given a value of one shilling and six pence. The public debt, measured in terms of the size of the country and by similar obligations of other lands, was not large, and even after the increase attributable to the costs incurred in World War I the major part of it had been acquired in constructing public works of a productive character, such as railroads and irrigation projects. Until World War I most of the debt was held in Great Britain. After that time a rapidly increasing proportion was held in India.

To India was given a structure of courts which ensured even-handed justice. A high standard of judicial impartiality and of legal competence was developed. Codes of law were framed. In some of its phases the law was based upon the English tradition, notably the common law, and on precedents derived elsewhere in the Occident, such as the French penal code. Trial by jury was introduced, although in a modified and restricted form. Yet much of the native law was retained, especially the family law. Even this, however, was modified from time to time, as, for instance, the innovation permitting the remarriage of a widow without forfeiture of all her rights to the property of her former husband and the raising of the age of attaining one's majority and of the age of marriage.

To hold and defend India only a comparatively small army was maintained. When in 1858 the government was transferred from the East India Company to the crown, the Company had only slightly over 15,000 European troops in its service. Toward the close of the nineteenth century the British forces totaled a little less than 75,000 and the native troops a little above 150,000. During World War I, more than 1,215,000 men were recruited in India and sent overseas in the support of the British cause. After the war the Indian army was reorganized, but its strength was only about 204,000, of which two-thirds was Indian and one-third British. The larger part of this small force was in the northwest, to protect the land in that traditional highway of the earlier great invasions.

As we suggested a few pages back, politically India fell into three categories. One was the remnant of the Portuguese and French possessions. These comprised only a very small percentage of the area and population of the country and were of no particular importance. Second were the native states. These embraced more than a third of the area but only a little more than a fifth of the population of the land. The largest were the size of some of the more important European kingdoms. The most extensive were Kashmir, in the northwest, and Hyderabad, in the Deccan. The heads of some of the native states were extremely wealthy. Others of the native states were very small, only a few square miles in extent. Numbers were in the interior. Still others were on the northern frontiers. The degree of control exercised by the British overlords varied from state to state. Relations were based partly upon treaties, partly upon precedent, and partly upon the varying policies of Viceroys and changing administrations. Even the most important of the princes had at court a representative of the British government, usually termed a resident. Foreign affairs were entirely in British hands. In case of flagrant misgovernment the British paramount power could step in and put things to rights, if necessary, deposing the ruler and placing another prince in his stead. Yet the English respected the prerogatives of the princes and, after the conquest had been completed, did not seek to annex their domains. Existing native states were preserved. When British rule had once been thoroughly established, the native princes were loyal. In World War I they rallied to the support of the British Empire. In the course of time they came to esteem the British *raj* as the mainstay of their position, especially against the programs of the extreme nationalists. Some of the native states were very backward. Others, notably Mysore, Travancore, and Baroda, had very progressive administrations.

The third and the largest political division was what was known as British India. This was directly under British rule.

The administrative system developed for British India was fairly complex. After the control of the East India Company was terminated, there was created in England a structure composed of a Secretary of State for India, a Council of India, and the India Office, with professionally expert officials. In India there was a kind of hierarchy, with the Governor-General, later termed the Viceroy, at the top. British India was divided into a number of provinces, of which Bengal, Bombay, and Madras, as the original centers of the British occupation, were the chief. At the head of each province was a governor. The Viceroy and the Governors of Bengal, Bombay, and Madras were appointed by the crown, of course on the recommendation of the government in power in Great Britain. By an act of Parliament in 1861 which sought further to set affairs in India in order in light of the lessons of the Mutiny, the Viceroy was given an executive council which was in effect a kind of cabinet and which for legislative purposes was enlarged by appointed members, of whom some were non-official. At the same time the councils of the governors of the main provinces were given advisory powers in legislative matters. The final authority remained with the government in Great Britain.

The provinces were in turn divided into districts. Of these there were at one time 273. Each district was headed by an official called a collector or deputy commissioner and district magistrate. Over three or more districts was a commissioner. Underneath the Viceroy, his council, and the provincial governors were the members of what was known as the Indian Civil Service, about one thousand in number. For many decades the Indian Civil Service was recruited from Great Britain through competitive examinations of youths in their early twenties. Because of its high traditions, prestige, and powers, and the ample salaries and retiring allowances attached to it, the Indian Civil Service attracted a high type of man, hard working, honest, intelligent, and forceful. There were a number of other services under the government, most of the ranking posts of which long went to men from the British Isles. The majority of the lower posts were filled by Indians. In the twentieth century, especially after 1914, as we are to see, the higher positions also began rapidly to be filled by Indians. In general, particularly as the nineteenth century wore on toward its close, the members of the Indian bureaucracy, notably those in the upper ranks, were more and more actuated by ideals of public service and of financial integrity. This was true of British colonial officialdom, and, indeed, of most European colonial officialdom in that period. Kipling, himself from an Indian background, gave the attitude poetic expression in his *White Man's Burden*. The atmosphere of official circles was in striking contrast with that a century or a century and a half earlier, when even the average employee of the East India Company might hope to acquire a fortune after a few years in the East and by methods which would not bear the scrutiny of public opinion of the later, more conscientious age.

Their Indian Empire was for the British by no means an entirely unrequited burden. Whether the advantages outweighed the costs it would be difficult to determine. On the credit side of the ledger were a number of items, some of them important. During the nineteenth century and on into the early years of the twentieth century India afforded large markets for the products of British factories. Cotton goods from Lancashire entered in quantity, in part supplanting the cloth made by hand in village industries. Equipment for the Indian railways and for other Western innovations came at first chiefly from Great Britain. English investors, too, found in India a profitable and secure outlet for their surplus capital. Railways and other public works were built largely by funds borrowed from the British. Throughout the nineteenth century Great Britain kept India as a market for its manufactures, an outlet for its capital, and a source of raw materials. Many thousands from the British Isles found an occupation in India, in the army, in one of the many branches of government service, in private enterprises, or as roving adventurers. In World War I India provided the British Empire with hundreds of thousands of troops which were of substantial aid, especially in the Near East. Against these advantages must be set other items, notably the proportion of the cost of the British fleet, undetermined, but essential to the safeguarding of the sea routes to India, and the cost of the wars in which the prize of India was one of the stakes. The balance sheet is not easily struck.

British government and administration were by no means the only channels through which Western influences entered India. The extensive commerce, both with Great Britain and with other Western lands, was important. Thousands of Christian missionaries, Roman Catholic and Protestant, came not only from the British Isles but also from various countries of the Continent of Europe and from the United States and some of the British Dominions. As the nineteenth century progressed, the numbers of missionaries markedly increased. They served all classes of the population. The accessions to Christianity came chiefly from the depressed classes and from the primitive or near-primitive tribes. There were relatively few baptisms among the middle and upper classes. The caste structure and the hold of Hinduism and Islam were too strong to permit many formal conversions. Yet through their schools and other contacts Christian missionaries influenced more or less profoundly thousands from the upper social strata. Their effects were seen in varying degrees upon all levels of the population.

The revolutionary effects of the impact of nineteenth and

twentieth century Occidental civilization were not always so immediately apparent in India as in the great lands of the Far East. To preserve her political independence Japan had felt herself constrained to adopt much of the machinery and the outward trappings of Western culture. She began the period with huge cities, and under the impulse of the new conditions her urban centers grew apace. Since cities quickly responded to the new currents of civilization entering from the Occident, superficially Japan's Westernization proceeded rapidly. In contrast, India had few large cities and in proportion to the total population they did not show a significant increase. India remained as she had traditionally been, a land of rural villages. Since as a rule rural communities are more conservative than cities, change proceeded more slowly in India than in Japan. In the nineteenth century Chinese life was much less affected by the Occident than was India. That was in part because until almost the close of the century China succeeded largely in preserving her aloofness. She jealously guarded and maintained both her political and her cultural independence. At the turn of the century, however, she found her political integrity gravely menaced by the advancing Occident. At the end of the nineteenth and in the twentieth centuries a revolution began which included all phases of life and which proved more drastic than did the changes in India. Moreover, India, by the very fact of her subjection to British rule, was more passive and, under the protective *pax Britannica* which guarded her from civil war and foreign aggression, was able to continue her old life with fewer alterations than was either Japan or China.

Yet the differences in the rate of Westernization between India on the one hand and China and Japan on the other were probably more apparent than real.

Outwardly, to be sure, the façade of Indian life remained largely intact. Hinduism and its associated social structure of caste, so basic in Indian culture, continued, seemingly unimpaired except in details. The striking combination of tolerant flexibility and intolerant intransigence which Hinduism presented permitted the incorporation of many ideas from the Occident without yielding on essential issues. Under the impact of Western ideas, movements arose from Hinduism or within it, among them the Brahmo Samaj, which incorporated much from Christianity, and the Arya Samaj, which was vigorously Hindu. Theosophy, with Occidental as well as Indian leadership, was an eclectic combination of Indian and foreign ideas. Islam retained its hold. By its nature, it, too, was unyielding. The masses of its adherents responded less quickly to Western education than did the middle and upper Hindu castes and so were less markedly affected by the Occident. Even the numerically minor religious bodies, such as the Sikhs, the Jains, and the Parsees, were tenacious of their inherited beliefs. It is true that in all of these religious bodies movements appeared under the impact from the West, and especially Christianity, which strove to revitalize them, but there was no extensive renunciation of these cults. It was only from animism and from the debased and animistic tincture of Hinduism of the primitive tribes and the depressed classes that mass departure from the ancestral religions took place. These were chiefly to Christianity. Since religion was dominant in India to a degree it did not attain in most lands of the Far East, in the twentieth century the life of India seemed more nearly intact than did that of China and Japan.

Behind this façade, however, the acids of modernity were at work. Some thoughtful Christian observers, biased no doubt, but well informed and honest, declared that Hinduism had become a hollow shell. Many Hindus, educated in schools of a Western type and familiar with the Occidental scientific attitude, lost all religious faith. Outwardly they remained Hindus, but they held to Hinduism not because it was true but because it was Indian. The education given by the British Government, so predominantly Western and familiarizing the Indians trained in it with Occidental literature and thought, could not help but prove corrosive to basic Indian patterns. Since this education was the road to the prestige, the power, and the wealth which ambitious men desire, most of India's leaders had subjected themselves to it. The universal use of English by the educated, even when they employed it to berate the British *raj*, was an indication of how far the Occident had permeated India. Although the industrialization of India had not progressed as far as that of Japan, and although political and religious revolution was not as spectacular as in China, in the infiltration of Western ideas among the educated the Occident may have penetrated life in India quite as basically as in these other two lands. It may be significant that the overwhelming majority of the Indians of the twentieth century who influenced their country most profoundly, while proud of their native heritage, were in large part products of Occidental education. Thus Rabindranath Tagore, poet, mystic, and saint, was from a family which had long been prominent in the Brahmo Samaj and had come out of a circle of intellectuals who had been reared in Western as well as Indian culture. Gandhi, outstanding in the nationalist movement, had been educated in England. Indeed, in the ardor of these men for Mother India there was something almost nostalgic for an older India which they could not fully embody.

We need to note the movements for the emancipation of women from their traditionally subordinate and secluded status. They affected profoundly only a relative few. To a large extent they were due to contact with Christianity and were clearly not indigenous. Yet schools for girls were appearing and congresses of Indian women were being held.

The Movement toward Emancipation

The revolution brought by the West was strikingly apparent in India in the movement toward emancipation from British rule. This movement made its appearance in the nineteenth century, but it had its rapid growth in the twentieth century. Although having in it much which was distinctly Indian in its background, the trend toward independence, so rapid and pronounced in the twentieth century, was in large degree an outgrowth of contact with the Occident and particularly of the British tutelage.

The Occidental source of a large proportion of this drive toward emancipation from the Westerner becomes apparent through a number of facts. The leaders were chiefly men who had come up through the educational system established by the English. Many of them, indeed, had received part of their education in Great Britain itself. Contact with the nationalism which was so outstanding a feature of the nineteenth and twentieth century Occident contributed to the development of nationalism in India. The systems of transportation and communication which had been built on British initiative and under British direction helped to weld the country together and to give it a sense of unity. Although two of the native vernaculars were close rivals and were favored by ardent patriots, the English language, introduced and taught by the conqueror, was the one medium of speech and writing most familiar to all educated Indians and helped to make possible a united front against the British masters. Never before had so much of India been brought together and administered as a whole as by the English. India had formerly been a geographic expression and, with limitations, a cultural whole. British rule made it for the first time a political entity. The *pax Britannica* and the

British tolerance, the latter not complete but greater than that of most other powers which have governed subject peoples, made possible the continued agitation through which the nationalistic movement spread. Moreover, the British attitude of aloofness, at times haughty, which rendered the British overlords almost a distinct caste, and a caste which in background and temper was always alien and never Indian, proved irritating to the Indians, especially to the Brahmans, who had been accustomed to the position of social leadership. The English were feared, and at times respected, but were not loved. Then, too, the familiarity with English literature brought by the British educational system acquainted educated Indians with ideals of liberty. The overproduction of those prepared for service in the government by the schools subsidized by the British *raj* led to unemployment and discontent. Moreover, the English extended local self-government in India and in so doing prepared the way for a larger participation of Indians in the administration of the country and gave training in it. From time immemorial the Indian rural village had had much of self-government. The English utilized this machinery to assist in famine relief, in education, and in dispensing justice. They also developed rural boards for the maintenance of roads and the assumption of other community functions. In the towns they encouraged plans for a greater share by the inhabitants in local affairs. They sought to do this according to English models. While in this they did not meet with entire success, they accomplished some training. In these and other ways British occupation and administration prepared the way for their own elimination. Contacts with the Occident were a major cause of the nationalist agitation.

The emancipation of India from the British rule proceeded rapidly in the twentieth century and had more than one phase.

Progress toward Economic Autonomy

An important aspect was the development of modern industry in India and the progressive freeing of Indian economic life from British domination. This would probably have come in the normal course of events, for Great Britain could not hope to retain indefinitely the monopoly of modern machines and factories. It was hastened by World War I. The participation in the equipping of the troops of the British Empire in that conflict stimulated the growth of Indian industry. In 1919 India was accorded the privilege of fixing her own tariffs. She used it in part to encourage her industries, even against British manufacturers. In the 1920's, partly as a reaction from the stimulus given by the war, while the number of laborers in the factories slightly increased, their proportion to the total population declined. The system of imperial preference, adopted in 1927 to encourage intraempire trade and to assist British manufacturers, worked against Indian industry. The protests of Indian industrialists were of no avail. Moreover, the world-wide economic depression which had its onset in the United States in 1929 was accompanied by repercussions in India. Since India's chief exports were raw materials and the demand for these declined sharply after 1929, Indian economy, particularly agriculture, suffered severely. Under these circumstances, industry could not prosper, even though tariff measures taken to relieve the government's embarrassed finances might give encouragement. Still, in the 1920's and 1930's Indian industry grew, but not as rapidly as some patriots desired. By 1940 India was eighth in the world in magnitude as an industrial power.

The chief of the new industries in India, as in so many countries in the initial stages of the industrial revolution, was the spinning and weaving of cotton. The Lancashire mills suffered in the competition and the import of British cottons sharply declined. From supplying approximately two-thirds of India's imports, as she did on the eve of 1914, by 1940 Great Britain sank to being the source of only about a quarter of the imports of her Indian Empire. Japanese goods, particularly low-priced cotton textiles, began to enter in quantities, for in Japan, too, the industrial revolution first expressed itself on a large scale in the manufacture of cotton. Manned by cheap labor, as were the Indian mills, and increasingly efficient, Japanese mills could undersell the Indian products in their home markets. It was only as India took tariff measures to protect her factories against the Japanese commercial invasion that the Japanese flood could be stemmed. These measures, it may be added, made the Japanese unhappy and adjustments were effected which, in the nature of a compromise, permitted a market, although a somewhat restricted one, for the cottons from the Land of the Rising Sun. Secondary to the cotton factories, but important, were jute mills, mostly in Bengal. Great iron and steel works were also erected by the Tata family, Parsees, at Jamshedpur in the northeast to take advantage of the huge deposits of ore in that region. In these various enterprises British capital had a share, but more and more of the capital was Indian. Although she was beginning to make the machines of the Occident her own, India was far from an industrialized country. She had a few large cities, but in proportion to the general rise in population these had grown but little if at all. She remained primarily rural and agricultural.

Coming Political Autonomy

More spectacular than progress toward economic independence were the steps toward political autonomy. The steps were taken largely in response to agitation by Indians who had had a Western type of education. The average Indian student was voluble in English, bitterly critical of the British rule and rulers, and smarting under what he deemed the lack of liberty accorded his country and the exploitation of the land by the British overlords. He was hypersensitive and quick to take offense at any slight, fancied or real, to his native land. He was inordinately proud of Indian culture, though he might know far less of it than had his fathers, and was disdainful of much which came from the West, even when he utilized it.

The British rulers were disposed to accord Indians an increasing share in the government of the land and even eventually to give to India within the British Empire the kind of autonomous dominion status enjoyed by Canada, Australia, New Zealand, and South Africa. However, they did not move as rapidly as the extremists among the Indian nationalists desired. Usually they gave the impression of grudging reluctance, of making concessions in the effort to allay agitation. Measured by decades, the Indian advance toward self-government achieved with British cooperation was rapid. Never was it fast enough to satisfy the Indian radicals. Britain would on the one hand take measures to increase Indian participation. On the other she would forcibly suppress the expressions of discontent with her unwillingness to go further.

Part of the British failure to meet the full demands of the radicals must be ascribed to conservatism and to the desire to maintain the British position. Part of it, however, arose from an awareness of the basic divisions in the land which, the British firmly believed, would bring disastrous civil war if full independence or even dominion status were granted at once. Much of it, too, came from a sense of obligation of the ruling power to the various elements in the country and the resolution to see justice done to all.

The divisions within India were obvious, at least to all impartial observers. Chief among them was the gulf between Moslems and Hindus. Friction between the two communities was chronic and repeatedly broke out in open riots. Moslems, although in the decided minority, had been accustomed in pre-British days to rule much of the land. They would not tamely submit to being governed by the Hindu majority. From time to time efforts were made to compose the differences between Hindus and Moslems and to present a united front against the English. The body which carried the main brunt of the movement for self-government, the Indian National Congress, numbered some Moslems in its membership, but it was predominantly Hindu and as a rule the bulk of the Moslems held aloof from it. Nor were the Hindus united. Many of them could not follow the Congress party and wished to pursue more slowly the road to autonomy. Then, too, there were the untouchables, the sixth or so of the population who were below the Hindu caste structure. They were divided and not vocal, oppressed and exploited by their caste neighbors. The English rulers felt a responsibility for them. In an attempt to increase the numerical strength of the Hindus and to promote Indian solidarity, some of the nationalist leaders wooed them, but, at least by the 1940's, with only slight success. The native states presented a problem. The ardent nationalist might consider them an anachronism, but they could not be lightly disregarded or quickly eliminated. The British Government believed itself in duty bound to see that the native princes had justice, especially since the relations of some of the strongest of the states with the British *raj* were based upon solemn treaties. The English could honestly offer these divisions as obstacles to the early granting of all the demands of the more intransigent nationalists. The attainment of a united autonomous government for India offered almost as great difficulties as would the achievement of a politically united Europe. The goal might be eminently desirable, but no facile solution for reaching it at any early time was discernible—at least not to most British eyes.

The main advances toward the goal must be outlined. The detailed story would be very confusing, but the chief stages can be fairly clearly narrated.

The first steps toward a united government for India were taken under the East India Company, with its administrative structure of a Governor-General and subordinate governors. After the Mutiny, with its challenge to British rule, the act of Parliament of 1861 prepared the way for further integration of Indian administration and for a slight participation in legislation by Indians who were not members of the bureaucracy.

Among those who had been affected by Western ideas, there came into being, in 1885, after several preliminary groups and gatherings, what was termed the Indian National Congress. At the outset it desired that elected representatives be placed on the legislative councils which the government was beginning to institute to assist its executive officers in some of the provinces, that the system of councils be extended, that examinations be held in India as well as in England for recruiting members to the Indian Civil Service, and that military expenditure be limited. In other words, the Congress was asking for larger Indian participation in government, but by patterns, such as elected representation, largely derived from the West. The Congress met annually. Its membership was chiefly Hindu, although it included some Moslems and, in its early years, a few Europeans. The Hindu membership included many who were affected by Western liberalism and others, conservatives, who wished to hold to the old ways against Western modifications. Partly in response to the demands of the Congress, the British government, in 1892, adopted, in a very limited form, the principle of election to some of the seats on the Viceroy's council and the provincial councils.

As time passed, numbers of the nationalists became more extreme and anti-foreign, but, not altogether logically, utilized the Occidental device of the press and journalism to disseminate their views. Some of the opposition first took the form of violent criticism of the measures that the government was taking to check the bubonic plague.

In 1905 radical nationalism began to assume even more violent aspects. The Japanese victory over Russia in that year inspired many Indians with the hope that the Occidental tide was beginning to be rolled back from Asia. As an administrative measure, the government had split Bengal into two parts and had given the Moslems numerical predominance in the eastern portion. This aroused vigorous criticism from Hindus, and a boycott was declared against foreign goods. The press operated by the Hindu extremists was stridently bitter and underground conspiracies flourished, partly among the students, for the use of terror against Europeans in general and British officials in particular. There were assassinations. In the course of the next four or five years the agitation spread to other parts of India, and here and there riots broke out. The Indian National Congress supported the boycott and demanded *swaraj*, "self-government." To the moderates in the Congress *swaraj* ment full parliamentary government. To the extremists it connoted complete independence from Great Britain.

The British government responded by suppressing the disorders on the one hand and by making concessions on the other. In November 1908, fifty years after the assumption of the direct government of India by the crown, the King-Emperor announced in principle the extension of representative institutions. In December 1909, detailed constitutional changes were promulgated which are usually associated with the names of the Secretary of State for India, Lord Morley, and of the Viceroy, the Earl of Minto. The Morley-Minto reforms enlarged the legislative councils of the Viceroy and the provincial governors by additional elected members, chosen in such fashion as to ensure a voice of more classes and groups. It was still only limited upper classes who were included. The councils, too, were given slightly enlarged powers, but powers which were largely confined to criticism and offering suggestions. The measures satisfied some of the moderates for the time being, but were far from acceptable to the extremists.

In 1911 the King-Emperor George V and his consort came to India and held a huge durbar at Delhi. In a sense this was a gesture meant to satisfy Indian susceptibilities by having the monarch appear in person to demonstrate the importance attached by his government to India and to personalize, in Indian fashion, his rule. The fact that the King-Emperor held the durbar at Delhi, the ancient Mogul capital, helped to associate his authority with Indian tradition. He announced, too, the removal of the capital from Calcutta, a British creation, to Delhi, which was again an attempt to mollify Indian pride.

World War I and its aftermath speeded the movement toward self-government. The Indian National Congress had grown in strength and influence. Its outstanding leader was now Mohandas K. Gandhi. Gandhi, born in 1869 of an Indian family of the Vaishya caste and of official traditions, had been educated for the law in England. Soon after he had begun practice in India, he was called, in 1893, to South Africa on professional business. There he espoused the cause of his fellow-Indians in their opposition to the measures which were being taken to discourage Asiatic immigration and to limit the rights of Asiatic residents. In South Africa he worked out the principle and some of the methods of nonviolent or passive resistance which he was later to apply on a large scale in India. In 1914, when a commission, appointed in part because of the agitation he led, recommended the removal of some of the worst abuses he had opposed, he felt that victory had so far been won that he could leave. He was on his way home when World War I broke out. He offered his services to the British as an ambulance driver and was accepted, but ill health compelled his return to a warmer climate and he left England for India in December 1914. In India he aided in recruiting for the British forces, hoping that by voluntarily offering their help to Britain in her hour of need, Indians would eliminate distrust and win the repeal of the law by which they had been forbidden to carry arms. In India Gandhi quickly became outstanding in the nationalist cause. Deeply religious and ascetic, he made a profound appeal to the Hindu spirit. Although affected by Christianity, he remained primarily a Hindu in faith and practice. He came to have more influence in India than any other man of his generation. Popular acclaim attached to him the title of *Mahatma*, "great spirit." He was undoubtedly a saint after the Hindu pattern. He was also an extremely astute politician. To him the two roles were not inconsistent or mutually exclusive, but were integral parts of a whole. It was into the Indian National Congress, in reality a party and predominantly Hindu, that he fitted.

In the meantime Moslems, alarmed by the possibility of Hindu dominance in an India controlled by the Congress, had formed, in 1905, the Moslem League. The new political machinery of Indian nationalism was following the ancient religious alignments.

There were other nationalistic organizations which were in the nature of parties, but the two most influential were the ones we have stressed, the Indian National Congress and the Moslem League.

In the course of World War I events moved rapidly toward a greater degree of home rule for India. In 1916 Mrs. Besant, of the Theosophical Society, launched a Home Rule League which produced so much excitement that she was forbidden to enter Bombay and the Central Provinces, and in Madras she was restricted. Late in 1916 the Indian National Congress and the Moslem League appeared to have agreed upon a scheme of reform. Several of the Indians elected members of the Legislative Council made suggestions looking toward a parliament for the entire country and legislative assemblies for the various provinces. A British group of students of politics, the Round Table, suggested that Indians have a more responsible share in the government.

Yielding in part to this agitation, the British government appointed a royal commission. In due course a report was issued, bearing the names of Montagu-Chelmsford, from the Secretary of State for India and the Viceroy. Montagu had already (August 1917) declared that the policy of the government was the increasing association of Indians in every branch of administration and the gradual development of representative institutions. In 1919 the Montagu-Chelmsford Report was implemented by an act of Parliament. In general, the act of 1919 largely increased the participation of Indians, chosen by election, in the national and provincial governments, but did not go as far in this direction as was desired by the Congress. In the national government the Viceroy was assisted by an executive council, three of whose seven members were Indians. This council was a kind of cabinet but was not responsible, as were cabinets in Great Britain, to the legislature. The legislature consisted of two houses, a council of state and a legislative assembly. Of the council's membership of sixty, twenty-six were appointed and thirty-four were elected. Of the assembly membership, slightly more than two-thirds were elected and the rest appointed. The elected members were apportioned communally, or by the natural groups of India, such as Hindus, Moslems, Sikhs, and landlords. The legislative assembly could debate and pass bills, but the Viceroy could overrule its decisions. In every provincial government there were to be, under the act, a governor, an executive council, and a body of ministers responsible, in the British fashion, to the legislative council. Thirty per cent of the membership of each legislative council were appointed and the remainder elected. The franchise was limited by high property qualifications. Representation, as in the national legislature, was communal. In the provinces what was called dyarchy was made the rule. Under dyarchy some powers, such as health, education, and local government, were transferred to the legislative councils. Others, such as justice, police, and revenue, were reserved to the governors. The governor could veto any act of the legislative council.

The reforms of 1919 failed to satisfy the extreme nationalists. Especially were the latter critical of the dyarchy with its reservation of so many important functions to British officials. The dissidents, with Gandhi as the outstanding figure, were in control of the Indian National Congress. Following the procedures which Gandhi had developed in South Africa, the Congress organized protests in the form of boycotts and nonviolent demonstrations. Symbols and banner-cries were employed to enlist and arouse the masses. Here and there riots broke out. The government replied by the Rowlatt acts of 1919 and vigorous measures to suppress agitation. In April 1919, at Amritsar, riots were put down by troops and several hundred Indians were killed or wounded. The Amritsar incident poured fuel on the flame of popular discontent, and noncooperation spread. When, however, it led to violence, Gandhi called it off.

In 1920 and 1921 the Hindu nationalists made common cause with some of the Moslems who were protesting against the indignity offered, as they believed, to the Khalif of Islam, the Sultan of Turkey, by the British postwar settlements. This Hindu-Moslem *rapprochement* was disrupted, however, in part by a fanatical Moslem movement, that of the Moplahs, in southern India, which sought to compel the conversion of Hindus to Islam and in the process killed both Hindus and Europeans.

Political controversy continued, with boycotts and nonviolence engineered by the Indian National Congress under the leadership of Gandhi. From time to time, to enforce a point with the British or with his own followers, Gandhi would embark upon a fast which he would not break until his end seemed attained. Gandhi, too, in an attempt to revive village industries and thus relieve some of the dire poverty of India, advocated the use of homespun as against factory-made yarns and cloths, and set the example by busying himself with the spinning wheel and wearing its products.

Since the act of 1919 had provided for a review of its results at the end of a decade, in 1927 a commission bearing the name of its head, Simon, was appointed to visit India and to make recommendations. The nationalists took umbrage because they were not represented on it. In 1929 the decision was reached to hold a series of round table conferences in London, with both Indian and British representation, to go afresh into the issues at stake. In 1929, too, the Viceroy announced for the government that the goal of India's progress, as the British envisaged it, was dominion status. Dominion status had a few years earlier been precisely defined by the Statute of Westminster, so that it was clear what this promise entailed. The Indian National Congress did not participate in the first Round Table Conference, but instead launched a new campaign of civil disobedience. Gandhi attended the second Round Table Conference, held in 1932. From the third conference, convened in 1935, came the basis for a new act, that of 1935.

The act of 1935 contemplated a federal union for India which should embrace both the existing provinces of British India and the native states. This part of the act did not come into operation, for the conditions laid down for its fulfilment were not met by the states. The states were unhappy because the proposed constitution curtailed some of their privileges, while the Congress was opposed because it believed an alliance would ensue between the English and the conservative elements represented by the states which would saddle India with reactionary rule. In 1939 the large majority of India's princes rejected a proposed plan for bringing them into a federal structure. However, some provisions of the act of 1935 were carried out. The act gave to the provinces responsible government, making the councils of ministers dependent on the provincial legislatures. The first elections were held in 1937. The Indian National Congress obtained control of the legislatures in eight of the eleven provinces. The act of 1935 abolished dyarchy in the provinces, but retained it in the national government. To the Viceroy were reserved control over defense and foreign affairs and any action which he might deem necessary for the maintenance of public order and the public credit. These reservations were criticized severely by the Indian extremists.

The 1930's saw other developments. The Indian share in the bureaucracy was increasing. More and more the Indian Civil Service was being recruited from Indians. India no longer held out the promise of a lifetime career to ambitious young Englishmen. The Indian National Congress was moving toward the demand for full independence rather than dominion status. Moslems were agitating for the Pakistan scheme, by which those portions of India in which they were in the majority should be segregated as autonomous units with themselves in control. Obviously this would not be acceptable to the Hindus who dominated the Congress. Among the untouchables there were movements toward the removal of their age-old disabilities. Some of the nationalist Hindus, with Gandhi as an outstanding leader, were seeking, on their side, to remove these disabilities, partly from a sense of justice and partly, it must be confessed, from the desire to swell the Hindu majority by incorporating the untouchables into Hinduism. Women were taking part in Indian affairs. Newspapers were becoming familiar. In the Congress, Gandhi was still outstanding, but there was coming to the fore a younger man, Jawaharlal Nehru. Nehru was born in 1889 in a wealthy Brahman family. He was educated in aristocratic fashion in England and on his return to India shared for a time the luxurious life of his class. He then was seized with a passion to help the masses, became active in the Congress, and suffered imprisonment for his political activities. Highly intelligent, sensitive, forceful, and extremely able, Nehru inclined toward Socialism but was far from being a Communist. Religion, at least in the historic sense, had largely faded out of his life. In this he was unlike Gandhi, but resembled many of the young intellectuals. Nationalism and social reform were his inspiration.

Summary

This, then, was the situation on the eve of the world war that broke out in 1939. British rule, achieved in the eighteenth and nineteenth centuries, was passing. Rapid progress has been made in self-government. Yet it was not rapid enough to satisfy the Indian National Congress. The demands of that body kept ahead of what the British government was willing to concede. India was still divided. In spite of the effort of the Congress to extend its operations to the native states, the latter persisted and were not incorporated in the administrative or legislative structure of British India. The gulf between Moslems and Hindus, between the Moslem League and the Congress, was as deep as ever, and perhaps was deepening. The untouchables were beginning to move, and their outstanding leader declared that Hinduism had nothing for them but chains. It was an India in ferment, still maintaining the British tie, but with that tie weakening, which entered the new world struggle. To developments in India during that struggle, as in the Far East, we are to come in a later chapter.

Before we pause, however, to take up the lands which belong more specifically to the Far East, we must note that in spite of all her unhealed divisions, India was, for the first time in her long history, becoming a self-conscious national unity. Measured by years, progress toward that goal might be slow. Seen against the perspective of decades, it was rapid. Much suffering might lie ahead. The vision of unity might never be fully realized, but, in light of the obstacles, the advance had been little short of amazing. It was due primarily to what had come through contact with the Occident and especially to the contributions of the British rule. It would not have been possible, however, but for qualities inherent in the Indians themselves.

BIBLIOGRAPHY

For Brief Reference

V. A. Smith, *The Oxford History of India* (Oxford, 1920).

For More Extended Study

V. Anstey, *The Economic Development of India* (London, 1929).
D. H. Buchanan, *The Development of Capitalistic Enterprise in India* (New York, 1934).
The Cambridge History of India, Volumes V and VI.
V. Chirol, *India* (London, 1926).
J. Cumming, *Modern India* (Oxford University Press, 1932).
J. Cumming, *Political India. 1832–1932* (Oxford University Press, 1932).
Economic Problems of Modern India, edited by R. Mukerjee (2 vols., London, 1939–41).
Mahatma Gandhi. His Own Story. Edited by C. F. Andrews (New York, 1931), and *Mahatma Gandhi at Work. His Own Story Continued.* Edited by C. F. Andrews (New York, 1931), or M. K. Gandhi, *The Story of My Experiments with Truth* (2 vols., Ahmedabad, 1927–1929).
J. H. Kelman, *Labour in India. A Study of the Conditions of Indian Women under Modern Industry* (London, 1923).
A. Lyall, *The Rise and Expansion of the British Dominion in India* (London, 1910).
J. Matthai, *Village Government in India* (London, 1910).
Toward Freedom. The Autobiography of Jawaharlal Nehru (New York, 1941).
C. N. Vakil and others, *Growth of Trade and Industry in Modern India* (New York, 1931).

Chapter XI. WHITE RULE IN THE LESSER LANDS

Ceylon, Burma, Thailand (Siam), the Malay Peninsula and Singapore, Indo-China, the East Indies (Portuguese, British, and Dutch), and the Philippine Islands

As WE PURSUE OUR WAY EASTWARD, following the course of the renewed and enhanced impact of the Occident in the nineteenth and twentieth centuries, we come to a series of comparatively small states and of scattered peoples in the southeast of Asia and on the southeast fringes of Asia. Like the much larger India, all of these but Siam (now called Thailand) lost their political independence to the all powerful Westerner. All of them had their cultures and economy modified by the impact of the West.

Ceylon

First we come to Ceylon, which, like India, is not strictly speaking in the Far East and therefore cannot command much of our space, but which, also like India, is so on the near periphery of the Far East that we must pay it some attention.

In the eighth chapter we noted that, as a result of the Napoleonic wars, Ceylon passed into British hands. It was ruled as a crown colony and was not incorporated with India. In spite of its proximity to the latter, its dominant religion was Buddhism and by historical tradition, while related, it was distinct.

Under the British administration great prosperity came to Ceylon and Western civilization permeated the island more deeply even than under the nearly three centuries of Portuguese and Dutch occupation. Agriculture was extensively developed. Coffee culture was first entered upon and by the middle of the nineteenth century coffee was the main export. However, in the third quarter of the century a fungus which attacked the leaves of the coffee plants wrought havoc with that product. Tea raising thereupon became the main enterprise of the plantations. Rubber was later introduced and became second only to tea. Derivatives from the cocoanut tree, notably copra, cocoanut oil, and cocoanuts were also important. Cinnamon, cacao, cardamon, and a few other tropical products found their place among the exports. Population rapidly increased. In 1857 it was said to have been 1,700,000. In 1927 it was 5,115,000. Schools of a Western type were introduced, some of them by Christian missionaries. Especially in the course of the twentieth century the British rulers made decided progress, as in India, in sharing the government with the peoples of the land. Jealousies between the different racial and social groups complicated the political situation and became important factors in the development of self-government.

Burma

The nineteenth century influx of Western civilization into Burma came primarily through British contacts.

Before the nineteenth century Western influences had entered Burma by way of the Portuguese, the Dutch, and the English. All had been represented on the coast. At the dawn of the nineteenth century the English, through their East India Company, had a very limited trade with Burma, chiefly through the port of Rangoon.

The extension of British political control over Burma was made in three stages. It began as a result of friction between the growing territorial power of the English East India Company and the youthful vigor of a new dynasty in Burma. About the middle of the eighteenth century Alaungpaya began a march of conquest which made him master of much of Burma. In this he was aided by the English and his major rival was supported by the French. However, he obtained numbers of French cannon and artillerymen and with this potent assistance was able to defeat his enemies and partly to repel the Chinese invasion of 1769. Under Alaungpaya's son Bodawpaya (1782–1819) the new Burmese Empire attained its greatest extent. From its capital, Ava, it reached from Tenasserim in the southeast to Assam in the northwest. Its path was marked by great destruction of life. In Assam the Burmese are said to have reduced the population by half in the nine years 1816–1824. The monarchs deemed themselves all powerful and regarded the English with vast contempt. Since the domains of the East India Company and of the Burmese Empire bordered and the East India Company was engaged in territorial expansion, a clash was all but inevitable. War came in 1824. The Burmese were roundly defeated, although not without considerable cost to the English in life and treasure. In 1826 a peace was signed by which Burma agreed to enter into a treaty of commerce with Britain, to accept a British Resident at Ava, to renounce claim to certain disputed sections of India, and to cede the coastal provinces of Arakan and Tenasserim. This brought Great Britain into Burma.

Friction between the Burmese and the English was only temporarily allayed. In 1852 war broke out again. Once more the Burmese were defeated, this time more easily than before. In consequence, the province of Pegu, in Lower Burma, was annexed.

In the years which followed, the English regarded what remained of the Burmese realms as only semi-independent and as holding a status somewhat similar to that of the native states of India. One of the last monarchs of the dynasty endeavored to obtained recognition of Burmese full independence by various Western powers, but with only partial success.

At length, in 1885, Britain determined to take over what was left of autonomous Burma. She was moved to this step in part by the French threat to the region. In the 1880's France was building an empire in Indo-China, and in Africa and the islands of the Pacific a contest was on between some of the leading powers to obtain whatever territories remained uncontrolled by the Occident. France was actively engaged in intrigues to bring Upper Burma within her orbit. While the ostensible cause of British action and her third Burmese war was the misbehavior of the Burmese regime, an underlying factor was the desire to forestall the French. The war was brief. Mandalay, the capital, was taken, the Burmese monarch was captured and exiled to India, and his realms were annexed. In the ensuing decade British authority was extended into adjacent territory, notably the Chin hills and the Shan states, which had never submitted to the Burmese dynasty. The shadowy Chinese suzerainty represented by decennial missions to Peking bearing what the Chinese regarded as tribute were professedly to be continued, but in 1896 were abandoned by the British officials. Anglo-French rivalry did not die, but was now on the borders of Burma. All Burma had been incorporated into the British Empire.

Under British rule Burma prospered and for several decades was only slightly troubled by either internal disturbances or external politics. The mechanical appliances of Western civilization were introduced and were widely adopted. Hundreds of miles of railways were constructed. Steamboats manufactured in Scotland plied the principal waterways. Schools partially after Western models were encouraged, and a university of Occidental type was placed at their apex. Canals were dug. Hundreds of miles of telegraph wires were strung. A Western form of postal service was developed. Electrical appliances were brought in. Rice cultivation flourished and provided the country's leading export. Petroleum was discovered and exploited. Exports of timber became a source of wealth. Some of the land's mineral resources, in addition to petroleum, were utilized. In foreign trade rice and petroleum were of chief value. Western civilization was making its way also through Christian missions. Superficially Westernization was proceeding apace.

Yet Western culture was a foreign importation and much of the economic prosperity was through non-Burmese channels. The capital was chiefly Indian and British, with the Chinese also fairly important. Much of the labor was performed by Indian coolies. Hundreds of thousands of Indians came to the land, many of them as seasonal workers, birds of passage, and others as presumably permanent residents. By 1942 the number of Chinese was not far from a quarter of a million. Most of them were merchants and artisans. Both Indians and Chinese remained unassimilated enclaves, retaining for the most part their own languages and customs, and that in spite of the fact that most of the Chinese also spoke Burmese. The Burmese clung tenaciously to their hereditary dress and manners. They might avail themselves of the mechanical appliances brought in by the Westerner, but they wished to remain spiritually aloof. Christianity achieved its chief gains, not among the Burmese, but in the non-Burmese tribes which had long been in the land, notably the Karens. Industry was but slightly developed. The land remained a source of foodstuffs and raw materials. If they were intended for factories, the latter were sent out of the land to be processed.

Because of the historical accident that the British conquest had been effected from India as an incident to the British expansion in that land, under British rule Burma was long closely tied to its huge neighbor. Until 1935 Burma was administered by the English as part of India. Even after Burma had been separated politically from India, more than half of her exports went to that land. It was from India, as we suggested in the last paragraph, that much of the labor for the expansion of Burma's economic life was acquired.

Burmese nationalism did not awake until about the time of the Russo-Japanese War. It did not become pronounced until after World War I. It had a rapid growth in the 1920's and 1930's. As in India, nationalism was largely directed against the British overlords. It sought to emphasize Burmese traditions and regarded the inherited Buddhism as an integral part of the nation's past.

As in India, so in Burma, the British masters moved toward associating Burmese with themselves in the government. Indeed, since until 1937 Burma was administered as part of India, the various measures taken to increase Indian participation in government applied also to Burma. Thus both the Minto-Morley Reforms of 1909 and the Montagu-Chelmsford measures of 1919 were extended to Burma. For a time, to be sure, Burma was not included in the reforms of 1919, but Burmese agitation worked a reversal of the original decision and in 1921 Burma was brought into conformity with the other provinces of the Indian empire. Burmese participation in government was thus appreciably increased. Indeed, a certain advance was made over India. Eighty per cent of the members of the legislative council were elected as against seventy per cent in the other provinces, and the forest department was among those "transferred" to Burmese control, an important concession in a land where timber export was of large dimensions.

At the time of the Simon Commission (1927–1928) the Burmese nationalist leaders advocated divorce from India. In 1931 a special round table conference on Burma met in London, and the British government announced its purpose to leave to the people of Burma the decision as to whether they should be separated from India. Something of an impasse followed, for the Burmese electorate appeared to oppose the step on the terms offered by the British. However, in 1935 the English consummated the division and gave Burma a constitution. Under this document Burma was accorded some of the powers of a self-governing dominion within the British Empire. Technically, however, it remained a crown colony. The Governor, appointed by the crown, had large powers. There was created a bicameral legislature to which membership was elective. Certain minorities, notably the Karens and the Indians, were guaranteed representation.

Under the new constitution Burmese political activity and consciousness grew apace. Radicals demanded even more autonomy. Burmese nationalist sentiment, moreover, broke out in riots against the Indians. Burma, from being a placid land with little internal agitation or unrest, as it had been in the opening years of the twentieth century, was seething with nationalism and with the demands of the Burmese leaders for control over the racial minorities and with marked restiveness under what remained of British rule.

Mention must be made in passing of the Andaman and Nicobar Islands. The summits of submerged mountains stretching southward from Burma, they have but a small population. From the third quarter of the nineteenth century until the Japanese occupation in 1942 they were continuously under British rule.

Thailand (Siam)

It was under something of a handicap that Siam, or Thailand as for a time it preferred to be called, approached the end of the eighteenth century and the new age. In the second half of the century it had suffered from invasions by the Burmese, led by a new and vigorous dynasty. Ayuthia, the capital, was taken and razed. With that destruction much of what European culture had entered in the sixteenth and seventeenth centuries perished.

However, after the disasters of these years came a partial reversal of fortune. A general of mixed Chinese and Siamese stock defeated the Burmese and fixed the capital at Bangkok, where it remained. It was lower on the Menam than Ayuthia and became a convenient port. It also prospered because of its command of the fertile delta of the Menam, the wealthiest portion of the land. This general was disposed of by his ministers, presumably because of growing eccentricities, and was succeeded by another general, Chakkri, the first of a dynasty which still (1945) reigns. The continued decay of the Burmese royal line and the defeat of Burma by the British in the 1820's freed the Siamese from the chronic threat from that quarter.

Siam early felt the accentuated pressure from the Occident which came in the nineteenth century. The substitution of the English for the Dutch in the Malay Peninsula as a result of the Napoleonic Wars brought a more aggressive European neighbor on the southern borders. In 1826, the year of the conclusion of the first Anglo-Burmese war, an Anglo-Chinese treaty was concluded. In 1855 a treaty with Britain provided for extraterritoriality and fixed tariffs, port dues, and land revenues. In 1833 a treaty was signed with the United States. In the second quarter of the nineteenth century there came a strengthening of Roman Catholic missionary effort, under a French society, from the low ebb to which it had fallen at the close of the eighteenth century, and the beginning of resident Protestant missionary enterprise, largely from the United States.

It was not until the middle of the nineteenth century that the penetration of Siam by Western culture became marked. In 1851 there ascended the throne King Mongkut (known as Rama IV), who tended to favor Western culture. His important formative years, from 1824 to 1851, Mongkut had spent in a Buddhist monastery, in an enforced retirement as an unsuccessful aspirant for the crown. He had employed this long seclusion to make himself something of a scholar in things Occidental and Siamese, an accomplishment of which he was inordinately proud. He had studied English and Latin with Protestant and Roman Catholic missionaries respectively, and knew a little of Pali and Sanskrit, languages useful for the reading of works on Buddhism. As a monarch he had idiosyncrasies which annoyed or amused Occidental observers, but he employed a number of Westerners, largely from countries from which he had little to fear politically, reorganized the army and navy, inaugurated a mint and a new type of coinage, furthered the teaching of Western languages, built a few structures in European style, and encouraged Western commerce and the coming of merchants from the Occident by signing treaties that accorded Westerners extraterritorial privileges under the supervision of their consuls.

The policy of introducing features of Western culture was continued by Mongkut's son and successor, Chulalongkorn (Rama V). For a time before his accession Chulalongkorn had been under an English tutor. He was only sixteen when his father's death (1868) brought him to power and he reigned for more than four decades, until his own demise in 1910. Like his father, he was a mixture of national traditions and Western ways. He was devoted to the pleasures of his large entourage of wives, concubines, and children, was physically indolent, and, especially in his later years, suffered from ill health which was not improved by his use of drugs. Yet he had intelligence, dignity, and charm, and wished to rule as the beneficent father of his people. He traveled outside his own realms, sent young Siamese to the West to study, partially reorganized the government, utilized Occidental advisers, abolished slavery, furthered public works and education, and modified the administration of justice. During his reign the French and the English relaxed their extraterritorial jurisdiction over their subjects. He created a cabinet and attempted to have its members set up budgets for their respective departments. Yet he was often guilty of personal extravagances. He created a hierarchy of provincial officials recruited largely from members of the royal family and by this act of centralization enhanced the power of the throne and broke up much of the administrative disunity from which the land had suffered. He accomplished his changes in the face of conservative opposition and inertia fostered by a tropical climate. He went far toward putting the country in a position to hold its own in the modern world.

Chulalongkorn's successor (Vajiravudh, better known as Rama VI) had been educated abroad, had expensive habits, and his gifts were more artistic and literary than administrative. In spite of his extravagance, progress was made in the Westernization of the land, the wealth of the country increased, and, after World War I, further steps were taken to remove the extraterritoriality and the regulation of the tariff by foreign treaties which were deemed an infringement on the country's sovereign rights. However, his death (1925) found the finances of the land in bad condition.

The next occupant of the throne was a younger brother of his predecessor who also had had part of his education in Europe. He was quiet and conscientious and sought to bring about an improvement by a drastic cut in expenses through dismissing many officials and through an increase in revenues. He also expressed his purpose to grant a constitution after Occidental precedent.

In 1932 the movement toward a constitutional monarchy was accelerated by a revolt. The leaders were largely junior officials and army officers who had been educated in Europe. For the most part they were not of the old aristocracy. The King bowed to the seemingly inevitable. The movement could not be called one by the people, for the masses were not participants. It was, rather, the effort of new men to gain power from those who had formerly held it. Late in 1932 a constitution was promulgated. Further difficulties followed. Factional strife developed. In 1935 the King, then abroad, abdicated and announced his purpose of residing thereafter in England. His nephew, a minor, at that time in Switzerland, was proclaimed his successor, but there was a general feeling that the Chakkri dynasty was nearing its end. The ferment of Western ideas was working. Accusations were heard that some of the leaders were infected with communism. New men were coming to the fore, largely from families not previously in power, and mainly with an Occidental type of education.

Yet for the masses life went as before. Buddhism was still the religion of the land. The overwhelming majority lived very much as had their ancestors. Christian missions, while influential in the field of education, had won comparatively few converts, an indication that the basic structure of culture had not disintegrated. Nationalism which, among other symptoms, insisted upon the name Thailand, had its chief expression among the vocal educated minority. Some attempts were made to improve agriculture by cooperatives and the scientific fighting of pests, but these were only in their early stages. Much of the Westernization of the land was accomplished not by Siamese but by foreigners, either those in official employment or missionaries.

That Thailand had been permitted to continue her career as an independent state while her neighbors were being brought into political subjection to Western powers was not due primarily to the skill of her rulers but, rather, to the jealousies between the Occidental nations who might otherwise have absorbed her. She had the good fortune to lie between domains acquired by the English and the French. Either empire might have been glad to annex her but each knew that the other would not permit it. To be sure, Siam lost some of her territories to the French and the English. The French, in their expansion in what became their portion of Indo-China, took border territory to which the Siamese laid claim. In 1893 France brought armed pressure on Siam with the demand that the latter evacuate all territory east of the Mekong. The resulting treaty fully satisfied neither, for it granted more to France than the Siamese desired and still left two former Cambodian provinces, to which the French laid claim, in Siamese hands. In the fore part of the twentieth century Thai-French relations were generally amicable, and new treaties eased some of the former tensions. However, rising Thai nationalism brought restiveness and prepared the way for the developments which occurred after France had been weakened in World War II. The English made gains at the expense of Siam both in the Malay Peninsula and on the Burmese-Siamese border. In 1896, to allay the friction over their respective ambitions in this part of the world, Britain and France entered into a convention with each other in which they guaranteed the neutrality of the Menam basin. Since most of the foreign trade of Siam was then in British hands, the agreement in effect preserved this to Great Britain and so was to the latter's advantage.

In the second half of the nineteenth and especially in the twentieth century a growing problem was presented to Siam by an influx of Chinese. The Chinese immigration became particularly marked after 1850 and mounted in later decades. By 1940 not far from two and a half million Chinese of pure or mixed blood were living in the country. They were approximately a sixth of the population. They were industrious and many of them acquired wealth. They dominated the internal trade. Their secret societies became powerful. The Chinese issue was accentuated by the nationalism of the twentieth century. After the Revolution of 1911 in China and the founding of the Chinese Republic, Chinese in Siam became more self-conscious. Siamese patriots sought to regain such of the economic control of the country as had passed into Chinese hands. They placed restrictions on immigration, palpably directed against the Chinese, and sought to extend the control of the government over the schools which the Chinese maintained for their children.

As, in the twentieth century, Japan became an increasing factor in the east of Asia, some fear of her growing power arose in Thailand. However, Japan's victory over Russia in 1904–1905 produced a regard for the Land of the Rising Sun as a leader among Asiatic peoples in their ambition to be freed from white supremacy. Moreover, Japan proved willing to relinquish her extraterritorial rights on the completion of the revision of Thailand's codes of law. During and after World War I and especially after the world-wide depression of 1929 and the depreciation of the Japanese yen, the sale of Japanese goods, particularly cottons, markedly increased. In 1933 Thailand was the sole member nation of the League of Nations which declined to join in the vote of censure by that body of Japan's actions in Manchuria. For this position Japan was grateful, and the friendship between the two countries deepened. The English began to be alarmed and from time to time were disturbed by the report that Thailand was to permit Japan to build a canal across the Malay Peninsula at Kra. The practicability and utility of the project were dubious, but the rumors died hard.

In 1940, on the eve of the Japanese occupation, Thailand was fairly prosperous. It had a population of approximately fifteen millions, a total which was probably about twice that of the beginning of the century. That population was very unevenly distributed. The economy of the country was largely based upon rice. Indeed, rice was a main article of export, for more than enough was grown to supply the country's needs. Population was, therefore, densest where rice could be best grown and that was primarily in the fertile delta of the Menam. There was also reliance upon fishing as another major source of food. Quantities of teak were exported. Under the direction of a modern forestry department, conservation of the forests was instituted and a revenue obtained for the government. Industrialization had scarcely begun. The country lacked several of the raw materials essential to any large development of manufactures. Overpopulation had not yet become a problem and the standard of living was higher than in some other Far Eastern lands. Much of the life of the country centered around the capital, Bangkok. Hinayana Buddhism remained the faith of the overwhelming majority. The monarchs of the second half of the nineteenth century sought to reform and revivify it and in the twentieth century it became more consciously associated with Thai nationalism.

Here, then, in Thailand, was a country whose culture was continuous with a long past, but which was being progressively and rapidly modified by contacts with the Occident. Thanks chiefly to the accident of its geographic position between the British and the French spheres of influence, it preserved its political independence. Of this its leaders were proud. To this picture the Japanese irruption to be recorded in a later chapter brought a sudden change.

The Malay Peninsula and Singapore

As we saw in an earlier chapter, it was chiefly in consequence of the Napoleonic Wars that the English entered upon a prolonged development of the Malay Peninsula. They came in through their East India Company. Shortly before the Napoleonic Wars, in 1786, the East India Company, the British instrument of trade and expansion in India and the Far East, acquired the island of Penang by purchase from the local sultan. In 1795, soon after the occupation of Holland by the French in the course of the wars which arose out of the Revolution, the English took from the Dutch Malacca, long the principal center of Western commerce and power in that region. In 1818, following the reestablishment of peace in Europe, Malacca was restored to the Dutch, but in 1824 it again came into British possession in exchange for posts in Sumatra.

More than to any other one man, the British position in the Malay Peninsula was due to Sir Thomas Stamford Raffles. Raffles was a youth of modest ancestry to whom the expansion of British power in the south of Asia provided both the opportunity and the incentive for a career. In the changes brought by the Napoleonic Wars he saw a breath-taking opening for the growth of British power and commerce in the east of Asia. It was he who was mainly responsible for the British seizure of the former Dutch possessions in the East Indies. For a time he was in charge of the administration of Java. There he governed with conspicuous success. He dreamed of making Java the center of a vast British eastern insular empire and establishing close relations with Japan, then all but hermetically sealed against the European world. When, through the retrocession to the Dutch of their East Indian territories in the post-Napoleonic settlement, that dream seemed to be denied, Raffles did not completely despair. He acquired for the East India Company the island of Singapore, at that time apparently without commercial or political significance. He saw in its geographic position a strategic counter to the revived Dutch power, reenforcement to the East India Company's trade with China, and a stepping stone to further British expansion in that part of the world. Accordingly, in 1819 Raffles took possession of Singapore and there began the development of the port which became the keystone to British power in that region. He was a far-seeing administrator. He made of Singapore a free port, thus greatly stimulating its growth. He formulated a code of laws designed to meet the needs of the mixed population of the cosmopolitan city. He promoted the education of Chinese and Malay youth.

By steps which were gradual and were not part of a comprehensive design, British control was extended over such of the peninsula as was not under Burmese or Siamese jurisdiction.

At the time of the Japanese occupation, in 1942, politically and administratively the area under British jurisdiction was divided into three unequal parts.

First there were the Straits Settlements. These were made up of a number of scattered territories, some islands and islets and some bits of the mainland. The chief components were Singapore, Malacca, Penang, Province Wellesley (on the mainland), and what was known as the Dindings, a region not far south of Penang. The Straits Settlements had been administered in connection with India until 1867, when they became a distinct crown colony.

Second there were the Federated Malay States. These constituted a block of territory, mainly in the heart of the peninsula. In the latter part of the nineteenth century the English found it expedient to extend their control over the Malay sultans, rulers who exercised sovereignty over states of varying size. This seemed to be necessary, partly because of the friction that had broken out between the Malays and Chinese immigrants. Treaties were entered into between the

British government and the various sultans, somewhat after the pattern of the native states of India, and, also partly according to that precedent, British Residents were placed with the sultans to represent British interests and to see that good government was maintained. In 1896, for better supervision of the administration, a Federation was formed which drew into itself four of the native states. For a number of years the power of the central administration of the Federation increased and the position of the sultans became more and more divorced from active government. The sultans were assured of ample revenues and of the honors attached to their titles, but the actual power was exercised by the Resident-General (later called Chief Secretary) and a civil service centering at the Federation's capital, Kuala Lumpur. In the 1920's a movement began which sought to restore more authority to the sultans and their governments and Residents. Decentralization encountered opposition from Europeans and Chinese and was carried only part way. The Chief Secretaryship was abolished (1935) but there remained a Federal Secretary, and for the High Commissioner, who was also Governor of the Straits Settlements, more direct supervision was now entailed. With the great economic development in the last quarter of the nineteenth and the first four decades of the twentieth centuries, the Federated Malay States tended to become more and more an economic unit which invited unified political administration.

The third political division was made up of the Unfederated Malay States. These were five in number. One, Johore, occupied the southern tip of the peninsula. The other four were in the north and were separated from Johore by the Federated Malay States. Technically the five states were independent and bound to the British Empire by treaties. However, in all matters but those touching Islam and Malay customs they were constrained by treaty to follow the counsel of British advisers. Malays had a greater share in government than in the Federated Malay States. Moreover, except for Johore, the Unfederated States were more backward economically than the Federated. In the two on the northeast the mining and agricultural development which was so striking in the rest of the area had scarcely begun, even in 1941. This meant that except in Johore Chinese and Indian immigrants were not so prominent as in the Straits Settlements and the Federated States.

Under the *pax Britannica* the Malay Peninsula and Singapore enjoyed great and growing prosperity. Mines were developed. Much of the land, especially on the west coast, was cleared of its tropical forests and put under cultivation. The mining was chiefly of tin. In 1938 the area produced twenty-nine per cent of the world's output of that metal. It may be added that an additional fourteen per cent came from the Netherlands Indies, ten per cent from Thailand and French Indo-China, and eight per cent from China. The United States was the world's chief user of tin, taking in 1938 approximately a third of the whole. A variety of tropical plants were raised. The coconut was important. Rice was the staple grain. With the coming of the automobile in the twentieth century as a major form of transportation rubber forged ahead. By 1938 about ninety per cent of the world's supply of rubber was from southeastern Asia and the East Indies. Of this more than half was exported through British Malaya and about two-fifths was grown in the area. The United States, with its extensive use of the automobile, bought approximately half of the world's production. This great development in the Malay Peninsula was, accordingly, closely tied to the economy of the United States. The Malay Peninsula and Singapore and the British financial interests which centered there depended in large part upon the American market, and the United States would find itself embarrassed if it were suddenly cut off, as it was in 1942, from this source of materials so important to its industry and life.

The prosperity and order which were the fruit of British rule attracted many immigrants to the Malay Peninsula and Singapore. By 1940 immigration had attained such proportions that Malays, who had been predominant numerically as well as politically at the beginning of the nineteenth century, constituted only about two-fifths of the total population of slightly over five millions.

One large element was from India. Most of this came in the form of labor, mainly for the rubber estates. In earlier years it was chiefly recruited under contract. Later this practice declined and nonindentured, voluntary labor became prominent. In 1931 Indians totaled a little more than six hundred thousand, or about fourteen per cent of the population. As, in the twentieth century, Indian nationalism increased, it interested itself in the lot of the Indians in Malaya. It brought pressure to correct abuses and exploitation, evils which a growing British conscience was already seeking to abate.

The overwhelming majority of the immigrants were Chinese. For centuries Chinese had been coming to the peninsula. However, the opportunity and demand for labor which developed in the later decades of the nineteenth century and in the twentieth century brought a vast increase. The Chinese were mainly from the two southern coast provinces, Kwangtung and Fukien. Until 1914, when that system was abolished, a large proportion of the coolies were recruited on the indenture plan. In 1931 Chinese were approximately thirty-nine per cent or nearly two-fifths of the population. The majority thought of themselves as temporary residents and left their wives and children in China. As time passed an increasing number became permanently domiciled. They were hard-working and frugal and many of them acquired wealth. The marked economic development of the Malay Peninsula in the half century or more before 1942 was due primarily to them and to the British. With the growth of Chinese nationalism in the twentieth century, especially after the coming of the Chinese Republic (1911), the Chinese in Malaya became very much interested in the politics of the mother country. Indeed, the Kuomintang, the dominant party in China, drew some of its financial support from them. Schools using the Chinese language helped to keep alive Chinese culture and loyalty to the homeland.

Another source of immigration was Malays from the Netherlands East Indies. In 1931 they numbered about seven per cent of the total population. In Johore they were nearly a quarter of the whole. They tended to merge readily with the older Malay stock.

In the course of their occupation, the English had done much for the Malay Peninsula. Under them wealth and population had multiplied. Order had been established and the former piracy and internal strife had been stamped out. Health services had reduced disease. Systems of schools had been developed, notably in the twentieth century. Little had been accomplished in the development of self-government or of democratic institutions. Except for a very small minority, the Malays were not politically minded and were content with British administration. Most of the Chinese and Indians, the other large elements of the population, thought of themselves as temporary residents and did not identify themselves with the region. By 1941, however, an increasing proportion of Chinese had been born there. Some of them, with a modern Western education, were restive and were asking for a larger share in the civil service. Yet most of the civil service was recruited from British subjects of European birth. The area was mainly passive, administered by a minority of British origin.

Because of the strategic importance of Singapore, both on the trade route to the Far East and in the defense of the Malay Peninsula,

New Zealand, after World War I Great Britain built
and air base on that island which was practically com-
8. It was the most important and formidable maintained
Empire in the Far East. It was designed against possible
he sea, but, as the events of 1942 proved, was singularly
om the land. No serious menace had been anticipated by
that re...

The year 1941 dawned with a prosperous and quiet Malay Peninsula, somewhat annoyed by the darkening clouds in the north, but feeling secure behind the ramparts of the British fleet and of the Singapore naval base. As a region it was not united, whether culturally, politically, or racially. The only integrating factors were geography and British rule or overlordship. Indeed, because of the Chinese and Indian immigration, there was less of unity than at the dawn of the nineteenth century. The region was far from being a nation.

The French in Indo-China

North of the Malay Peninsula and east of Thailand was a region made up of what had historically been Cambodia, Cochin-China, Champa, Annam, Tongking, and Laos. It contained a medley of peoples and was not united culturally. In Annam and Tongking, to the east of the mountainous backbone of the area, civilization had a strongly Chinese tinge. Over long intervals northern portions of this eastern coastal region had been a part of the Chinese Empire. To the west of the mountains, especially in the lower reaches of the valley of the Mekong, Indian cultural influences had been dominant. In the upper reaches of the Mekong Valley much of primitive culture persisted. In the eighteenth century most of the area was ruled by Annamite princes.

Into this region came French rule, largely in the second half of the nineteenth century, bringing with it Western civilization and imposing an incomplete and decidedly superficial unity.

French political rule came in the wake of French Roman Catholic missions. It was not strongly pro-Roman Catholic. Indeed, during the latter part of its course it conformed to the pattern of the Third Republic and was often anticlerical. Yet the bulk of the Roman Catholic missionaries were French citizens and that fact constituted the grounds for the intervention which eventually issued in conquest.

French interest began in the seventeenth century, especially through a Jesuit who stimulated the formation of the Society of Foreign Missions of Paris and directed its attention to Cochin-China. It was the emissaries of this society who constituted the majority of the Roman Catholic missionaries in the nineteenth and twentieth centuries. In the eighteenth century some of the French commercial ambitions were directed toward Cochin-China and Annam. In the 1780's, on the eve of the fall of the Old Regime in France, a French missionary bishop, hoping to obtain favor for his faith, espoused the cause of an Annamite claimant to power in the southern part of the country. Indeed, Louis XVI entered into a treaty with the prince engaging to give aid. Although the French government did not carry out its agreement, assistance came from French volunteers. Partly through their support, the prince established himself. He became known as the Emperor Gialong, extended his rule over all of the Annamite peoples, and reduced Cambodia and Laos to vassalage. He was not particularly friendly to Christianity and even countenanced persecutions of the faith. However, he did not press them.

Succeeding reigns were marked by recurring and at times intense persecution. In the 1850's the anti-Christian measures became particularly severe, presumably because of fear of Western aggression fanned by the pressure of the Occident upon China, and especially by the Anglo-French war on China in the later years of that decade. In 1858, because of attacks on French and Spanish missionaries, France and Spain sent forces to compel respect for their citizens. France played the larger and more persistent part in the expedition.

In pursuance of the steps then undertaken, France conquered the three eastern provinces of Cochin-China, and in 1863 the Annamite Emperor was constrained to sign a treaty which recognized the French title to that area and promised an indemnity.

In the ensuing five years French control was extended over the three western provinces of Cochin-China, a protectorate was set up over the neighboring Cambodia, and the Mekong was explored. For a time after the defeat of France in Europe in the Franco-Prussian War, French prestige was low and expansion paused. Then, in 1873, a French officer with a contingent of troops made himself master of the delta of the Red River in Tongking. He was killed in a skirmish and the higher French authorities, hesitating to take advantage of his gains, made a peace (1874) with the Annamite court which in reality surrendered his conquests. The Red River was opened and French sovereignty in Cochin-China was confirmed, but the promised indemnity of a few years before was waived. The Annamite government recognized a kind of French protectorate by agreeing to conform its foreign policy to that of France. Yet Annam still acknowledged a loose vassalage to China. Difficulties continued in Tongking. Bandits made life in the delta insecure. China sent troops, ostensibly to deal with the bandits, but in fact to oppose the French. In 1883 and 1884 French forces took the delta and forced the Emperor of Annam to accept the French protectorate. Friction with the Chinese followed, with an undeclared Franco-Chinese war. Peking felt itself compelled to yield. In 1893 Laos was nominally occupied. French authority had now been theoretically recognized in most of the region.

There followed the difficult problem of devising and enforcing effective French control. It was complicated by lack of agreement between the French civil and military officials, by banditry along the Chinese frontier, and by a lack of consistency in the utilization of the traditional Annamese officialdom. In 1887 all of the territory under French control was brought together administratively with a Governor-General and a council at the head. Cochin-China continued to be a French colony and Cambodia and Annam-Tongking protectorates. The courts of justice and the finances were gradually reorganized. Successive heads of the French administration took varying attitudes toward the inherited native institutions. Some would preserve them. Others would weaken them. The trend was in the direction of replacing the old officialdom with direct control through French officials. In general the French had followed in their nineteenth century colonial administration the policy of assimilation. The peoples of the colonial possessions were so far as possible to become French in language and in customs. In Indo-China, in spite of the efforts of some of the Governors-General to further a different program, few of the French officials acquired the native tongues sufficiently to feel at home in their use. In World War I several scores of thousands of Annamites were sent to Europe as soldiers and laborers. Following the war, some effort was made at decentralization and toward increased participation by natives in the government. There were halting steps toward representative assemblies. Natives were permitted to qualify for administrative posts without having acquired naturalization as French citizens. In the 1930's a Paris-educated Emperor sought to bring about a reorganization of his court on Western patterns and to promote education. By gradual steps the share of the natives in the government was being increased. Slowly old institutions, such as the commune and the inherited mandarinate built on Chinese traditions, disintegrated or were modified. French citizenship was granted to French-speaking natives for distinguished service. The degree of the assimilation to French procedures and French courts varied from section to section.

In proportion to the population Christianity made greater numerical progress in French Indo-China than in any other land in eastern or southeastern Asia except Ceylon. In the 1930's Christians numbered more than one and a third millions, or more than five per cent of the population. These Christians were almost entirely Roman Catholics. Protestantism was negligible. The prosperity of the Christian missions antedated the nineteenth century and French rule. In spite of the persecutions of the fore part of the nineteenth century and the lukewarmness and at times anticlerical policy of the French administration, the growth continued. Most of the missionaries were French. The Society of Foreign Missions of Paris and associated women's organizations provided the majority of the foreign staff. By 1940 considerable progress had been registered in the creation not only of a native priesthood but also of an indigenous episcopate.

The French occupation was followed by economic developments which were to be expected from contact with an industrialized Occident. Mining became important. The rich deposits of coal, largely anthracite and chiefly in Tongking, were exploited. Encouraged by the presence of coal, several industries were developed on the Red River delta. Tin and zinc became important articles of export. Rubber plantations were established.

At the same time the region's chief agricultural product continued, as in the past, to be rice. Fertile lowlands, especially the rich deltas of the Mekong and Red Rivers, were mainly devoted to rice culture. Rice was the staple food. It was also a major export. Fishing, too, was prominent as a source of food.

As in the Malay Peninsula, so in French Indo-China, there was an influx of immigrants from India and China. Indians and Chinese, however, did not constitute so large a proportion of the population as in the Malay States. In French Indo-China most of the Indians were moneylenders. The Chinese came not so much as coolies, although many of them were laborers on the plantations, but as landowning farmers and, particularly, as merchants and bankers. Some of them had long been in the region, but their numbers greatly increased in the nineteenth and twentieth centuries. They tended to hold themselves aloof from the natives and, indeed, to view them with disdain.

Under French rule, although it had been in existence even in Cochin-China for less than one long lifetime, population mounted. The French built hundreds of miles of railways and roads. Through dikes and canals they reclaimed additional rich soil in the deltas. They developed schools, even though for only a small proportion of the population. They undertook archaeological studies and excavations. However, they did not weld the diverse peoples of the area into a nation. Great diversities persisted in language, in race, and in culture. Such unity as existed was largely artificial, imposed first by the Annamite and then by the French conquest and administration. Here and there, in 1940, were beginnings of nationalism, but only among small educated minorities.

The East Indies (Portuguese, British, and Dutch)

To the south and east of southeastern Asia stretched a vast island world which Europeans somewhat loosely designated as the East Indies. It was the home of many peoples who at the dawn of the nineteenth century and throughout the ensuing century and a half represented several different types of culture. The larger proportion of the peoples were of Malay stock. In New Guinea and some of the adjacent islands there were Papuans. The languages were chiefly of the Malay family and a kind of common pidgin Malay was understood throughout the majority of the islands. In religion the most populous of the islands, Java, held to Islam, which was superimposed upon remnants of the earlier Hinduism and Buddhism and of a still earlier animism. Hinduism survived on Bali, immediately east of Java. Islam was found along the coast of some of the other islands. Many of the peoples, especially in the interior, were animists and of a primitive culture. By the beginning of the nineteenth century, under Dutch rule Protestant Christianity had gained footholds. Roman Catholic Christianity was to be found chiefly in the Portuguese territories.

By the beginning of the nineteenth century, through the wave of expansion which had begun in the fifteenth century, Europeans had acquired territorial possessions and had begun to affect the culture of the East Indies. Europeanization had proceeded furthest in the northernmost group, the Philippines, which had been under Spanish rule since the sixteenth century. The Dutch had largely succeeded to the Portuguese, but the latter still clung to remnants of their former holdings. The Dutch had their headquarters on Java, but were also dominant in some of the smaller islands, especially in the Moluccas or Spice Islands, once the chief lure to European commerce. The English had, temporarily as it proved, taken over the Dutch territories as an incident of the Napoleonic Wars. The English East India Company also had a foothold on Sumatra, acquired by direct settlement rather than through the Dutch.

In the course of the nineteenth century Westerners greatly extended their power in Indonesia. By 1940 all of the region had been brought at least nominally under their control. In most of the region that control was actual and effective. Accompanying it came Occidental culture and the transformation brought by the impact of the Western world.

In our necessarily condensed survey of the region we will speak first of the Portuguese, next of the English, then, briefly, of the German, then of the Dutch, and finally, and under a separate section, of the American activities in the area.

The Portuguese in the East Indies

At the beginning of the nineteenth century the once extensive Portuguese holdings in the East Indies had dwindled to the eastern end of Timor and some neighboring smaller islands. Boundary disputes between the Portuguese and the Dutch were chronic. In 1859 a treaty between the two countries adjusted some of these, partly through the purchase by the Dutch of Portuguese claims to several islands north of Timor. Additional treaties in the 1890's and the first decade of the twentieth century reached further agreement on the points at issue. The Portuguese retained the eastern end of Timor.

The English in the East Indies

In the latter part of the seventeenth and in the eighteenth century the chief European rival of the Dutch was not the Portuguese but the English. Each people had an East India Company through which it was extending its trade. In the seventeenth century the English East India Company acquired a foothold on Sumatra which it did not relinquish until 1824. During the Napoleonic Wars, as we said a few paragraphs earlier, the English, at war with the French, occupied the Dutch possessions in the East Indies, for the Netherlands had become part of the Napoleonic Empire. The British occupation, achieved by way of India, was from 1811 to 1818. The energetic and able Raffles, in charge of the British administration, carried out many changes in the government and brought rebellious native princes to submission. When, to his great disappointment, the Dutch rule was restored, it was, as we have seen, largely his vision and resolution which laid the foundations for British dominance in the Malay Peninsula. The Dutch eventually acquiesced in an arrangement which virtually gave them a free hand in Sumatra in return for the surrender of their ambitions in the Malay Peninsula.

Yet the British succeeded in establishing themselves in some other portions of the East Indies. In 1941 they had holdings on the northwestern shores of Borneo and in the eastern half of New Guinea. They also had small islands south of Java and Sumatra.

In the eighteenth century the English East India Company established a trading station on Labuan, an island off the northwest coast of Borneo. The project failed and the post was abandoned. However, in the 1840's Labuan was again taken over. Early in the twentieth century, for administrative purposes it was placed under the Governor of the Straits Settlements. Brunei, under British protection since the 1880's, was a sultanate on the mainland of Borneo to which Labuan and much else that later passed into British hands once belonged. In its sadly shrunken state it technically maintained its independence, but with British permission.

Sarawak, on the northwest coast of Borneo, also theoretically independent and a British protectorate, had back of its existence a tale of daring adventure and able administration. It was the creation of Sir James Brooke (1803–1868) who first went to the East in the service of the English East India Company. In the 1830's, moved in part by a desire to spread civilization in the area, he headed an expedition, fitted out at his own expense, to Borneo. Through armed assistance to one of the local rulers in suppressing an insurrection, he obtained the title of Rajah of Sarawak. In the area, with the support of British ships of war and for a time with British appointment as Governor of Labuan and Consul-General of Borneo, he put down piracy, prepared a code of laws, and developed commerce. In 1863 the British government recognized Sarawak as independent and in 1888 in return for assurance of protection took its foreign affairs under its control. Sir James Brooke was succeeded as Rajah by his nephew and the latter in turn by a son. The borders of the state were gradually enlarged and there was marked development in public works, education, public health, forestry, and commerce.

On the northern tip of Borneo was British North Borneo. This came into being as a political entity in the last quarter of the nineteenth century and was chiefly the creation of the British North Borneo Company. It was administered by the company and was under British protection. In the twentieth century rubber plantations brought it prosperity. Both here and in Sarawak Chinese immigrants were attracted and by their industry assisted in the economic development.

In the 1880's, that decade of scramble for territory by rival imperialist European powers, the southeastern portion of the huge island of New Guinea passed under British "protection" and became known as Papua. It was eventually placed under Australia as a colonial possession of that commonwealth. In the 1880's the northeastern portion of New Guinea was made a German protectorate. As a result of World War I it was given to Australia, but as a mandate under the League of Nations.

Several hundred miles south of Sumatra was the small group known as the Keeling or Cocos or Cocos-Keeling Islands. In the first half of the nineteenth century they were settled by the Ross family. It retained title to them, but eventually they were placed under the Straits Settlements. So, too, to the Straits Settlements belonged Christmas Island, south of Java, the peak of a submerged mountain, valuable for its deposits of phosphates and British since the last quarter of the nineteenth century. In most of these British East Indian possessions Christian missionaries, chiefly Anglican, were to be found, with schools, hospitals, and churches.

The Dutch in the East Indies

The major part of the East Indies passed under Dutch control and became known as the Netherlands East Indies.

At the time of the restoration of Dutch rule, in 1819, the conquest was far from being completed. Although the majority of the population were probably under Dutch supervision, the larger part of the area had still to be subdued. Java and the small adjoining island of Madura were in Dutch hands but much of the control was exercised indirectly. The Moluccas were largely Dutch possessions. The Dutch had footholds on several other islands, including Sumatra, Celebes, and Borneo. Yet the archipelago as a whole was far from being Dutch territory.

In the nineteenth and twentieth centuries the Dutch greatly extended their rule. In 1825 they faced a rebellion in Java which was not finally mastered until 1830, and then at no little expense in life and treasure. That experience ended serious Javanese resistance and was followed by the reduction of the area on the island left under native princes to a small portion in the center. The Dutch now administered most of the island directly. In Sumatra the coastal areas were fairly rapidly conquered. Some of the native princes were deposed and direct Dutch administration enforced. Others of the princes were permitted to retain their titles and something of their power, but with Dutch supervision. The interior of Sumatra was much slower to yield. It was not until the first decade of the twentieth century that the last of the interior peoples submitted. That same decade, too, saw the resistance of the northernmost sultanate in Sumatra overcome. The most stubborn opposition was from the tribes and rulers who were Moslem by faith.

Borneo also presented a perplexing problem. Through their use of steamboats the Dutch found the reduction of the chronic piracy on the neighboring seas comparatively easy, although annoying. The stout resistance presented on the west coast of Borneo by the Chinese colonies, long established and sturdy in their independence, was crushed, but only in the 1880's after nearly three-quarters of a century of intermittent effort. The combination of adverse terrain and climate made the penetration of the interior of Borneo peculiarly difficult. The Dutch slowly pushed their borders inland, but in 1941 there were still areas to be explored and, presumably, tribes which had so far never seen a white face.

Parts of the island of Celebes proved resistant. Not until 1910, after numerous intermittent wars, were the last of the Moslem sultanates subjugated. In the interior the animistic primitive tribes were protected by their mountains, but the Dutch officials gradually extended their authority over them.

In the densely populated Bali, Hindu in religion and culture, a revolt flared out as late as 1908. The Moluccas, smaller in area and long under Dutch influence, did not prove especially obdurate. New Guinea, with its dense tropical forests, its rugged mountains, and its primitive peoples, was not, even in 1941, fully brought within the circle of Dutch cultural influence. Here and there on the coast were centers of Dutch authority and settlement. The enterprising Chinese merchants had footholds. But most of the region was still as untouched by European civilization as when the first Portuguese and Dutch ships came in sight of its coasts.

Administratively the Dutch possessions were divided between Java and the adjacent Madura on the one hand, the center of Dutch rule and containing more than half the population, and, on the other, the Outer Provinces, namely all the rest of the area.

The Napoleonic Wars were more than an interlude in the Dutch story in the East Indies. They made both possible and necessary a revolution in Dutch colonial administration. Developments in the eighteenth century had been rendering the Netherlands East India Company an anachronism. Like its British counterpart in India, to protect its trade the Company had felt itself constrained to become entangled in the local political situation. It had gone to war with some of the native princes and had reduced them to vassalage. It preferred to rule through them rather than to establish its own direct administration, but it became a political overlord. The frequent wars entailed by the conquest proved a heavy drain on the Company's treasury. Wars with Great Britain in the last quarter of the eighteenth century brought further embarrassments. Added to these adversities were poor management and growing breaches in the Company's trade monopoly, both by the English and Arabs and by the Dutch themselves. In 1798 the Company was dissolved—anticipating the fate of its English rival by more than half a century. When, after the Napoleonic storm, Dutch rule was restored, the Company was a matter of history. The Dutch possessions were placed under the direct control of the home government.

For a time after the revival of Dutch rule, the policy of the administration was to encourage the entrance of private free enterprise. This procedure was but haltingly pursued. The rebellions in Java which tested out the mettle of the renewed Dutch administration brought heavy drains to the exchequer. The revolts were suppressed, but only at considerable cost. Moreover, Holland itself went through difficult times financially after the establishment of peace in Europe. There was an insistent demand that the East Indies be made to pay.

The urgent clamor for profit led to the adoption by the Dutch in the East Indies of what was known as the culture system. Instead of collecting its revenue in kind, namely, in the rice which was the chief crop but which was of little value to it, the government required the cultivators to devote a portion of their time and land to the raising of such crops as it might direct and which it could sell in Europe. In theory this would consume about one-fifth of the peasants' time as against the two-fifths which it took to grow the rice demanded under the old form of taxation. It seemed to promise for the Indonesians a lightening of their burdens and the assurance of an easier and more prosperous life. In practice the culture system had the opposite result. For a time it seems to have led to an increase in population and prosperity for the Indonesians. However, later it was marked by the ruthless exploitation of the masses. The Javanese were required to spend so much time and energy in producing crops for the state that they had too little for their own crops. The soil became badly exhausted. To be sure, the system brought enormous profits to the Dutch government, but it was at the cost of the welfare of the Indonesians. Corrupt officials, both native and Dutch, seized the opportunity to wrest gains for themselves at the price of the sufferings of the tillers of the soil.

Against the abuses of the culture system the Dutch conscience eventually registered effective protest. The age was one of growing benevolence in much of European colonial administration and of treatment of dependent peoples. In the early part of the nineteenth century the British government set itself against the slave trade and abolished Negro slavery within its empire. The 1860's saw the end of Negro slavery in the United States. In the latter half of the century, utilizing the language of the poet laureate of British imperialism, Rudyard Kipling, many were speaking of the colonial administration of non-European peoples as "the white man's burden." The movement was furthered by the religious awakenings which were stirring the British Isles, the United States, and Holland. Under these circumstances the voices raised against the iniquities of the culture system found a ready hearing. Reform began in 1848 and was carried further in the 1850's under the insistence of a clergyman who as a pastor in Batavia had seen the situation at first hand and who became a member of the States General. It received additional powerful assistance from a stirring novel written by a conscientious Dutch colonial official. By an agrarian law passed in 1870 the struggle was largely won. Of the two chief crops grown under the culture system, the forced cultivation of sugar ended by 1890 and that of coffee in 1915. The abandonment of the system, it must be added, was due to the fact that it had ceased to be profitable as well as to the injustices it entailed.

After the abandonment of the culture system, the development of the economy of the Netherlands East Indies became increasingly dependent upon private enterprise. The government became an arbiter and a protector of the natives from exploitation rather than a participant in business.

With the dawn of the twentieth century, what was known as the ethical policy became prominent. By this was meant the moral obligation of the Dutch administration to further the welfare of the Indonesians and to take steps toward self-government by the natives. It was due to a large degree to the Christian parties in the Netherlands which were the outcome of religious awakenings. It was aided by the rise of socialist parties. The Christian parties also insisted upon a colonial policy favorable to Christian missions. In general the program of the colonial administration in the twentieth century sought the preservation of native customs and institutions and the increasing participation of the Indonesians in the government. Liberals among the Dutch talked of the ideal as being an autonomous state which, while remaining within the Dutch Empire, would do so on the basis of equality with the Netherlands. As a rule, the Dutch did not speak of independence for the Indies. Holland had come to be intimately involved in the life of its huge overseas possession. Thousands of the Dutch depended for their livelihood upon the connection. Severing the tie which bound the Indies to the Netherlands would have meant a grave economic crisis for the latter.

In pursuance of the policies developed in the nineteenth and twentieth centuries, the trend was toward greater participation by the native populations in the central government of the Indies and toward self-government in local units. Movement in that direction was hastened by the rise of Indonesian nationalism. Nationalism was particularly marked among the educated Javanese—those, in other words, who had been most closely in touch with Occidental currents of thought and were aware of what was taking place elsewhere in the Orient. Nationalism began to be vocal in the first decade of the twentieth century and became more intense after World War I. The period was one of a "rising tide of color" against white domination in many parts of the globe which was accentuated by the Wilsonian stress upon the self-determination of peoples. At times in the 1920's the nationalist agitation broke out in open revolts in Java and Sumatra. After the Japanese advance in Manchuria in the 1930's it subsided, partly because of the fear of Japan and partly because of repressive measures by the Dutch authorities.

Partly because of their settled policy and partly under pressure from the nationalists, in 1916 the Dutch created the Volksraad, a kind of East Indian parliament. At first its functions were advisory to the Governor-General. Later, after 1927, it had legislative powers. Its chairman and about one-third of its members were appointed. Approximately two-thirds were elected. Half its members were Indonesians, a little less than half Europeans, and the remainder "alien Asiatic," generally Chinese and Arabs. The administration was mainly through a civil service. The higher ranks of the civil service were filled by Dutchmen, carefully trained in Holland in the languages, customs, and institutions of the Indies. The lower grades of the civil service were increasingly recruited from the natives. In 1941 the latter made up about six-sevenths of the whole.

Part, too, of the twentieth century program was the decentralization of government, the development of local self-government to handle local affairs. This seemed especially important in an area as vast as that of the Netherlands East Indies and made up of so many tribes and peoples on such different cultural levels. Decentralization and local autonomy were furthered by a policy which was much older than the twentieth century, that of "indirect" and "semi-indirect" rule through native princes and states.

The Dutch preserved native customs and laws where these did not run diametrically counter to Occidental conceptions of morals and justice.

It seemed fantastic to hope that at any early time the Netherlands Indies would attain the status of a united, independent nation. The historic and cultural differences were too great to make that goal quickly a reality. Such unity as existed was chiefly that given by the Dutch administration. Yet within the structure of that administration something of cohesion was being attained.

Prominent as a corollary of the Dutch occupation was the spread of Christianity. Before the nineteenth century this was primarily under the supervision and with the assistance of the East India Company. Through that means there came into being a state church, Protestant and Calvinist. In the nineteenth and twentieth centuries the spread was chiefly through missionary agencies supported by popular subscriptions from Europe. In the nineteenth century these were mostly Protestant. The majority of them were Dutch but an important minority were German. In the twentieth century Protestant missions continued to grow, but Roman Catholic enterprises had an even greater proportionate extension. In 1941, Christians totaled more than two millions, of whom approximately four-fifths were Protestants and one-fifth Roman Catholics. This was a little more than three per cent of the entire population. Territorially, the Christians were unevenly distributed. They were chiefly from animistic folk. That meant that only a very small fraction were from the Moslems. Since Java, where two-thirds of the population of the Netherlands East Indies lived, was overwhelmingly Moslem, only a few of the non-European Christians were on that island. The Christians were mainly in certain sections of Celebes, in the Moluccas, and in Sumatra. Nearly a fifth of the Christians were Bataks, a vigorous folk in Sumatra, formerly part Moslem and part animist. It was a race between Islam and Christianity as to which should capture the animists. Christianity was making rapid progress. With it went schools, literature, and, increasingly in the Protestant bodies, ecclesiastical self-government.

The economic development in the nineteenth and especially the twentieth century was very striking. Under Dutch leadership the resources of the islands were increasingly utilized, and the export and import trade took on large dimensions. The growth was stimulated by the opening of the Suez Canal, the great improvements in transportation brought by steam, and the demand for the products of the islands created by the industrialization and multiplication of population in the Occident which were witnessed by the second half of the nineteenth century and the twentieth century. In 1938 British India, with six times the population, had only two times as much foreign commerce as did the Netherlands East Indies.

Much of the East Indies wealth was from the cultivation of the soil. Wherever that soil was of volcanic origin and could have sufficient water, and both conditions existed over much of the area, it produced abundantly. Rice was the principal food crop. Through it the population, which increased amazingly, notably in Java, was able to feed itself. In the twentieth century, rubber was the main export crop. In 1940 more was grown than even in British Malaya. Most of it was from Sumatra, especially the east coast. Sugar was long a major export and in 1941 ranked next to rubber as a plantation export. It constituted about one-twentieth of the world's total export of sugar. Tea was almost as important as sugar. Copra, coffee, agave, and sisal fiber were also prominent. The islands had a virtual monopoly of the world's supply of quinine and pepper and produced three-fourths of the world's kapok fiber. From the islands, notably Sumatra and Borneo, came a great quantity of petroleum, although, in 1940, only about one-twentieth of the amount that flowed from the wells of the United

States. In the production of tin the Netherlands Indies ranked second to the Malay Peninsula and in 1940 supplied twenty-eight per cent of the world's total.

In the nineteenth century the Dutch preserved a complete monopoly of the trade of the islands. In the twentieth century they became somewhat more tolerant of merchants and investors from other nations, but the administration still favored Dutch companies. In 1940 about two-thirds of the private capital invested was Dutch, but not far from one-tenth was held by local Chinese, a little more than a tenth was British, about seven per cent was from the United States, and Belgian, French, German, and Japanese interests were also represented. British capital was chiefly in rubber plantations and petroleum, and American capital was largely in petroleum. The United States was an important market. In 1939 it took a fifth of the exports and thereby displaced the Netherlands as the islands' best customer. From the Netherlands East Indies the United States obtained the overwhelming proportion of its supplies of such tropical products as quinine, pepper, tapioca, kapok, sago, palm oil, and tobacco leaf for cigar wrappers. In 1929 it bought about a sixth and in 1940 about a third of its rubber from the Indies. In 1939 over a fourth of its tea came from that source. In 1940 about a fifth of its tin was from East Indian ores. The United States had much the same share in the East Indian imports—in 1940 a little less than a fourth. As might be expected, American sales were chiefly machinery. For the British Empire the trade of the Netherlands East Indies was important. India, Singapore, Hongkong, Australia, New Zealand, and especially the British Isles shared in it. To the Chinese the Netherlands East Indies were significant, not so much in commerce as for an outlet for emigration. In 1940, Chinese residents numbered approximately 1,430,000. Some of these were descendants of Chinese who had come to the islands many generations earlier. About a third were first-generation immigrants.

In the 1930's imports from Japan had a rapid growth and presented a problem. Japan, by this time highly industrialized and through cheap labor, efficiency, and government assistance able to sell goods at a much lower price than the Occident, took advantage of the world-wide depression to capture much of the Netherlands East Indian market. Partly through her low costs of production and partly by devaluing the yen, Japan was able to sell at prices more nearly within the reach of the Indonesians than were those for similar goods of Western origin. By adopting the principle of licenses and quotas for imports, the East Indian government sought to curb the Japanese trend. Although she remained the chief source of imports, Japan watched her share fall from about one-third in 1934 to about a fourth in 1937. As a result of her war with China which began in 1937, Japan's proportion of East Indian imports continued to decline. During the depression years competition between Dutch and Japanese shipping became acute. The Japanese were reaching toward the Netherlands East Indies as the great prize in the southern seas and were beginning to be formidable. Since in their own domains the Japanese were lacking in petroleum and since mineral oil was becoming essential, the Japanese sought assurance of a supply from the rich fields of the Indies. Through negotiations with the Dutch the Japanese endeavored to obtain more favorable treatment in both the exports and the imports of the East Indies and by 1941 were broadly hinting at their ambitions in the region. Economically, then, Holland, the United States, the British Empire, China, and Japan all had important stakes in the Netherlands East Indies which none of them would lightly surrender.

In 1941 the wealth of the Netherlands East Indies was chiefly in its fields, its forests, its oil wells, and its tin mines. Industrialization had barely begun. In the years immediately preceding 1941 efforts at it had been made. These were partly because of the growing pressure of population and partly because of the threat of World War II. The fear that the latter might cut off the Indies from Holland and its factories led to attempts to step up the rate of industrialization. These efforts had only commenced to take effect when the storm of war broke over the islands.

One of the most urgent problems brought by Dutch rule was the great increase in population. This was especially acute in Java and Madura. When, after the Napoleonic Wars, the Dutch resumed possession, the population of these two islands was about four and a half millions. By the middle of the century it was about ten millions. At the close of the century it was about twenty-eight and a third millions. In 1930, the year of the latest complete census report, it had risen to nearly forty-one millions. This meant a population of about eight hundred a square mile, said to be the densest in the world for an area as large as Java. About nine-tenths of this total was rural and only about one-tenth urban. The increase was due at least in part to the peace and medical and public health services brought by Dutch rule. The Dutch sought to relieve the pressure by encouraging the Javanese to migrate to less thickly settled portions of the archipelago, especially to Sumatra, Borneo, and Celebes. By 1930, however, only about one and a third millions of Javanese were living outside their island. In the Outer Provinces, that is, the islands other than Java and Madura, the population was unevenly distributed. In little Bali it was very crowded. In many other sections it was sparse. Although the Outer Provinces embraced the overwhelming majority of the land area of the Dutch portion of the archipelago, in 1930 they had only a third of the population. In other words, in 1930 the total population of the Dutch possessions was about sixty millions, of whom scarcely twenty millions lived outside of Java and Madura.

In 1941 the East Indies, aside from the Philippines, were mostly in Dutch hands. The Portuguese and the British enclaves were relatively small, both in area and in population. Dutch rule had Java as its heart. Here lived two-thirds of the population. The Dutch had extended their authority over the vast area embraced in what they called the Outer Provinces. From the easternmost of their boundaries to the westernmost the distance was greater than that from New York to San Francisco, and from the extreme north to the extreme south the mileage was about that between Minneapolis and New Orleans. The only unity that bound the region together was Dutch administration. To be sure, the bulk of the peoples were of Malay stock, but there were great variations in culture and speech. Except for the Dutch, there had never been an all-embracing political unity. Slowly the Dutch were introducing inclusive self-government, but this had only barely begun. The peoples were comparatively passive, divided into many tribes and numbers of them still under their hereditary princes. Nationalism had not attained the dimensions that it had assumed in India or even in Burma and Ceylon. The region was not a nation. Yet it was rich in natural resources, and under the impact of the Occident and Dutch direction increasing use was being made of them and prosperity was mounting.

The Philippine Islands

As we saw in an earlier chapter, the Philippine Islands are a part of the Malay Archipelago. Except for the admixture of European blood brought by the prolonged Spanish occupation and by the briefer American one, racially they are akin to the rest of the archipelago. The dominant stock is Malay, divided into many tribes and languages.

Negritos, presumably survivors of an earlier population and akin to remnants found elsewhere to the south, are in some of the hills. Chinese have filtered in, as in so much of southeastern Asia and the rest of the Malay Archipelago. Before the advent of the Spaniards, Islam entered and made converts, notably in the island of Mindanao and in the Sulu Archipelago. These Moslems are known as Moros, a name which reflects the Spanish designation of the Moslems of the Iberian Peninsula.

The Spanish conquest of the sixteenth century resulted in a more extensive penetration of the Philippines by European culture than was to be found in any similarly large area in the east of Asia until the nineteenth and twentieth centuries. Indeed, it is doubtful whether even in 1941 any other equally numerous body of peoples in the Far East had so nearly conformed to Western civilization. The penetration by Occidental culture was due especially to the Spanish Roman Catholic missionaries. They had won to the Christian faith the overwhelming majority of the population. Through the nineteenth century the religious orders, the friars as their members were commonly called, continued prominent in the life of the islands. They owned many of the best lands. They filled the higher posts in the Church. They controlled most of the education, including higher education. In the hills were tribes which were still pagan, and in the south were the Moros, warlike and chronically a challenge to Spanish authority. Aside from these minorities, at the dawn of the nineteenth century the islands were professedly Christian and Roman Catholic.

Until late in the nineteenth century change came slowly to the Philippines. The Napoleonic Wars and the independence of Mexico removed the connecting link through which much of the somewhat attenuated intercourse with Spain had been conducted. The government monopoly of commerce with Europe ceased. Private enterprise entered. By hesitant steps, in the first half of the nineteenth century the islands were opened to the commerce of other Western peoples. The digging of the Suez Canal and the development of steam shipping brought closer contact with the Occident. In the 1860's beginnings of a public school system were instituted. A Filipino middle class emerged.

Through the more direct contacts with Europe, ideas from the modern West began to seep in. Some Filipino youths went abroad to study. Prominent among them was the Chinese mestizo, José Rizal y Mercado.

Out of these contacts came Filipino nationalism which sought the relaxation of the control of the friars and various economic and political reforms. For his activities in organizing and promoting the nationalist agitation, Rizal was arrested and executed (1896), thereby becoming the national hero of the new regime which followed the American occupation. Rizal's death did not end the nationalist movement. Revolt broke out. Its leader, Aguinaldo, made a temporary peace with the Spaniards and went to the safe confines of British Hongkong.

It was at this juncture that the United States appeared actively upon the scene. Events quickly ensued which brought in a new and transforming era. On May 1, 1898, Commodore Dewey defeated the Spanish fleet in Manila Bay. Annexation followed. It was accomplished in face of much opposition in the United States. The treaty of peace which had annexation as one of its provisions scraped through the Senate with only one vote to spare. Yet vigorous Theodore Roosevelt and Henry Cabot Lodge, rising leaders in the dominant Republican Party, were eager advocates of the step, and even before the outbreak of war with Spain were trying to set the stage in such fashion as to bring it about. William McKinley, then President, after much searching of heart, came to the conviction that the Filipinos could not be restored to Spain, turned over to France or Germany, or given their immediate independence, for which, in his judgment, they were unfit, but that the United States must take all the islands, and, to quote his words, "educate the Filipinos, and uplift and civilize and Christianize (sic) them, and . . . do the very best we could by them." The die was cast. Territorially the United States had become a Far Eastern power.

No sooner was the United States in the Philippines than it set about to fulfill the benevolent purpose which McKinley had avowed. The age was one of an Occidental imperialism which professed as an object the welfare of dependent peoples. A large proportion of thoughtful Americans had opposed the annexation and, when that measure became law, insisted that it have as its goal the independence of the islands. Indeed, during the struggle in the Senate over the ratification of the treaty, a motion to promise the Filipinos their ultimate independence was defeated only by the deciding vote of the Vice President. Restored to the islands by Americans in an effort to annoy the Spaniards, Aguinaldo headed a prolonged resistance which now regarded the United States as the enemy of Filipino freedom. Led by

Aguinaldo, in the interval between Dewey's attack and the ratification of the treaty of peace, Filipino patriots had set up a republic. Guerrilla warfare followed. It was not until 1901 that Aguinaldo was captured, and only in 1902 was the last armed resistance quelled. However, without waiting for the final submission of the malcontents, the Americans entered enthusiastically upon their self-appointed task.

To tell even in full outline the story of American policy and achievement would prolong these pages unduly. We can here give only the highlights. Prominent was the rapid development of a system of public education. Even before the army had given place to civilian government, numbers of public schools were established. Civilian administration was followed by the coming of hundreds of teachers from the United States. By the middle of 1902 nearly a thousand of them were in service. English was made the basis of instruction. Before long a system had been set up from the primary village school through the university. It was a kind of lay missionary effort which covered the islands and sought not only instruction in the usual subjects of Occidental learning, but also the inculcation of the American spirit. Filipinos were rapidly trained to fill the thousands of teaching posts in the new structure. As the numbers of qualified Filipinos increased, the American personnel was reduced. Beginning in the 1920's, over a million pupils were enrolled, or more than a third of the population of school age. Attempts were made to fit the curricula to the needs of the students. Trade schools and secondary schools increased and colleges for various professions were organized. Athletics of the American type, including the inevitable baseball, were fostered. The problem of disease and public health was vigorously attacked, first by army physicians and then by civilians. Cholera, smallpox, malaria, and tuberculosis were serious and bubonic plague threatened. By efficient measures the death rate was reduced and Filipino medical and nursing professions were encouraged. A program of public works was developed, with the construction of thousands of miles of roads and the building of many bridges. The mileage of railways was augmented. The administration of justice was reorganized and new codes of laws were formulated. Steps were taken to bring Western control and civilization to the primitive tribes in the mountains. The Moros were subdued, their piracy was suppressed, and disarmament was eventually enforced.

Great changes in the economic life of the Philippines followed the American occupation. Extensive stretches of territory owned by the religious orders, the so-called friars' lands, were purchased and then sold in small parcels to Filipino peasants. For ten years after the annexation, in pursuance of a provision in the treaty of cession which forbade discriminatory legislation for that period against non-Americans engaged in commerce in the islands, the Philippines were kept outside the American tariff wall. In 1909, when the decade expired, the Congress of the United States brought the islands within that wall, with free trade between them and the United States. This step tied the economy of the Philippines to that of the United States. American capital poured in. By 1935 the total private investments from the United States were said to be approximately two hundred million dollars. This, however, was only about one per cent of the total foreign investments of the United States. Part of this was in public utilities, part in banks, part in transportation, part in general merchandising, and much in plantations. The population was engaged mainly in agriculture. Rice was the major crop. Sugar, tobacco, hemp, and coconuts were raised, largely for the American market. Mining was not particularly important. Gold was the mineral most extensively extracted. Industrialization had barely begun, and such as existed was chiefly in connection with agriculture—mainly sugar and rice mills. Population rapidly increased—from about seven and a half millions in 1903 to not far from ten and a third millions in 1918, and to approximately seventeen millions in 1941. Yet it was not nearly as dense as that of Java or Japan. By 1941 space for the overflow was being found in the scantily settled portions of the island of Mindanao.

Religiously, the twentieth century brought important developments. The majority of the population remained with the Roman Catholic Church. However, an extensive schism occurred in connection with the revolutionary movement early in the century. The nationalists asked that the monopoly of the episcopal office by Spaniards be ended and that Filipinos be appointed as bishops. To this Rome would not assent and there came into being the independent Catholic Church of the Philippines, headed by a Filipino, Aglipay. Protestantism entered through missionaries from the United States and had a rapid growth. The Roman Catholic Church partly adjusted itself to the new order by bringing in clergy from the United States. Later it greatly increased the proportion of natives in its clergy and filled most of the episcopal posts with Filipinos.

Most spectacular of all the changes wrought under the American occupation was the encouragement of self-government, with the introduction of representative institutions of the Anglo-Saxon type, and, eventually, the granting of a large degree of autonomy under the form of a Commonwealth and the promise of complete independence in 1946. At the outset the government was by the military. In 1901 civil government was inaugurated. This was under the Civil Commission, usually known as the Philippine Commission. William Howard Taft, later President and then Chief Justice of the United States, was the first head of the Commission and Civil Governor, or, better, Governor-General. Taft proved a generous administrator, with a marked desire for the welfare of the Filipinos. In 1907 a striking step was taken toward self-government. The Philippine Assembly was elected and convened. The Philippine Commission, now made up of five Americans and four Filipinos, all appointed by the President of the United States, became the upper house of a bicameral legislature. The Taft policies remained in force until 1913, when his party, the Republican, gave place to the Democratic Party in Washington. In general the attempt had been to move forward from a regime in which Filipinos assisted an American administration to one in which Americans assisted a Filipino administration.

The coming to power of the Democrats, headed by President Woodrow Wilson, brought a stepping up of the movement toward Filipino autonomy. By tradition the Democratic Party had been opposed to the annexation of the islands and in favor of their independence. Francis Burton Harrison was appointed Governor-General and had as his settled policy the transfer of authority to the Filipinos. Filipinos were given a majority on the Philippine Commission, and thus had control of both houses of the legislature. Many Americans were removed from office and were replaced by Filipinos. Numbers of Americans resident in the islands critized the new policy and believed that they saw a deterioration in the quality of the government. In 1916 the Congress of the United States passed what was known as the Jones Bill. It stated that the purpose of the people of the United States had "always been" to recognize the independence of the Philippines "as soon as a stable government can be established therein." It also provided for an elective Philippine Senate as well as the previously existing elective House of Representatives.

When, in 1921, the Republicans recovered control of the government of the United States, they sent to the Philippines an investigating commission which recommended against the immediate granting of independence and advised greater authority for the American administration. Leonard Wood, a military man who had previously had experience in the islands, was appointed Governor-General. He reversed many of the attitudes of his predecessor. He brought in a firm and efficient regime. For this he was respected by many of the Filipinos and was lauded by the American residents. He was a high-minded and honest executive who had the welfare of the Filipinos at heart, but distrusted their capacity for early self-government and wished the United States to retain the islands as a vantage point in developing its trade in the Far East.

The Filipino agitation for independence continued. The vocal elements of the population seemed overwhelmingly to favor it. To this and to the sentiment in the United States in support of independence as a moral right was added the pressure of economic interests which wished to protect American industries, especially those of sugar, dairying, cottonseed oil, and cordage manufacturers, and of organized labor. These sought, by their independence, to place the islands outside the tariff wall and subject to the immigration restrictions of the United States. A combination of the various factors brought about, in the closing days of the administration of President Hoover, and over the veto of that executive, the passage of what was called the Hare-Hawes-Cutting Act. This law provided for the independence of the Philippines, but placed as a condition the acceptance of the plan by a referendum in the islands. The Philippine Legislature, disliking some features of the bill, rejected it. In 1934 another act, bearing the name of Tydings-McDuffie, was passed by the Congress. This proved acceptable to the Filipinos. Under its provisions they drafted a constitution and in 1935 set up the Commonwealth of the Philippines. Certain powers were reserved to the United States. Washington was represented by a High Commissioner who was a liaison official. Arrangements were specified by the act for placing the islands gradually outside the tariff barriers of the United States. The processes outlined by the Tydings-McDuffie act by which this was to be accomplished threatened a serious dislocation of Philippine economy, but steps were soon taken to revise and ease the procedure. Full political independence was scheduled for July 1946. It was proposed that for the protection of the islands the latter be perpetually neutralized by international agreement. The Commonwealth had as its outstanding features a republican form of government, a president elected for a term of six years, and an elected unicameral legislature. The first President was Manuel Quezon. He was re-elected in 1941.

Scarcely had the Commonwealth been established when the Japanese became a growing source of apprehension. Before it had come into being they had moved fully into Manchuria. Only two years after the Commonwealth was inaugurated they began the long war with China. Japanese activities in Davao were a source of fear. General Douglas MacArthur was engaged to organize an army and to place the islands in a state of defense. Darkening war clouds gave little opportunity for adequate testing of the Commonwealth regime.

BIBLIOGRAPHY

There is no single volume which covers adequately the areas which have been the subject of this chapter. It is, therefore, necessary to give a list of separate books for the respective countries. For those readers to whom these may not be available, the brief references in such works as *The Encyclopædia Britannica* and the *Statesmen's Yearbook* will be found of value.

J. L. Christian, *Modern Burma* (Berkeley, 1942).
Virginia Thompson, *Thailand. The New Siam* (New York, 1941).
K. P. Landon, *Siam in Transition* (Chicago, 1939).
M. Landon, *Anna and the King of Siam* (New York, 1944).
L. A. Mills, *British Rule in Eastern Asia* (Minneapolis, 1942).
R. O. Winstedt, Editor, *Malaya* (London, 1923).
Virginia Thompson, *French Indo-China* (New York, 1937).
R. Kennedy, *The Ageless Indies* (New York, 1942).
A. Vandenbosch, *The Dutch East Indies* (Berkeley, 1942).
J. H. Boake, *The Structure of Netherlands Indian Economy* (New York, 1942).
J. R. Hayden, *The Philippines: A Study in National Development* (New York, 1902).
W. C. Forbes, *The Philippine Islands* (Boston, 1928).
C. Porter, *Crisis in the Philippines* (New York, 1942).

Chapter XII. THE TWILIGHT OF THE OLD CHINA

China in the first stages of the heightened impact of the Occident: from the eve of the first war with Great Britain (1838) to the beginning of her cultural revolution (1895)

IT WAS NOT UNTIL nearly the middle of the nineteenth century that the increased pressure from the Occident began to make itself markedly felt in China. This was much later than in India and somewhat later than in Burma, the Malay Peninsula, and the East Indies. China resisted. Proud of her civilization and disdainful of the Western "barbarians," she attempted to preserve both her political and her cultural independence. As a result she was forced for a time to compromise the one and in the end saved herself only by sacrificing the other.

The experience was for China an entirely new one. Heretofore her invaders had been clearly inferior to her in culture. Now they were in some important respects her superiors. Always conquerors had come by the land and her traditional defenses had been landward and not seaward. In the nineteenth and twentieth centuries most of the danger was from ocean-borne enemies. These enemies had powerful, centralized governments, while China's administration, because of the nature of the problems with which it dealt, was to a high degree decentralized, and so was ill prepared to face the new type of foe.

Moreover, as we have noted in earlier chapters, when the increased pressure from the Occident came, China was peculiarly unprepared to meet it. She was ruled by a decrepit alien dynasty, the Manchus. In contrast with a West which was pulsing with new life and equipped with fresh inventions, in China little that was novel was being accomplished: the rate of creativity had slowed down. China was ripe for change, but was poorly prepared to meet the foreigners who forced it on her. It is not strange that she nearly lost her independence and that she floundered for several generations in an attempt at adjustment.

The heightened pressure of the Occident began to be perceptible about the year 1838. For slightly over fifty years China endeavored to hold the Occident at arm's length. Under duress she entered into treaty relations with Western powers and grudgingly set her doors ajar to the foreigner. Haltingly she began to adopt some of the appliances of the Occident. This she did especially in the area of armaments. Then, in 1894 and 1895, she was drawn into a war with Japan. That doughty neighbor had employed the preceding three decades to equip herself with Occidental machines. Armed with these, she quickly overcame China.

For the Chinese the emotional shock was severe. They had viewed the Japanese with vast contempt as a people who had derived from the Middle Kingdom such civilization as they possessed. To be defeated by them was a bitter experience. The more far-seeing Chinese became convinced that only by doing as Japan had done, adopting much from the Occident, could they hope to preserve the existence of the Empire. Before the transformation could be more than begun, China was threatened by partition by Western powers and helplessly stood by while Russia and Japan fought on her soil with a portion of her Empire as the prize. These experiences provided an additional impetus toward change. Following 1895, therefore, a cultural revolution commenced in China which for magnitude and thoroughness was unequaled in the long history of that land. The period down to 1895 makes a natural division in our story. The era of transformation which began in that year constitutes another obvious chapter. It is, then, to the slightly more than half a century between the years 1838 and 1895 that we now address ourselves.

The British Pressure

It was through Great Britain that the accentuated pressure from the Occident first came. This was to be expected. Britain led in the industrial revolution. She had become the leading commercial power in the south and east of Asia. She was conquering India and Burma and had established herself at Singapore and on the Malay Peninsula. She was augmenting her commerce with China. In 1834 the monopoly which the East India Company had enjoyed in British trade with China was terminated. Commerce with the Empire was thrown open to all British merchants. The step was inevitably followed by greater pressure on China and by friction.

The conflict was one of civilizations. The English, as representatives of the Occident, viewed international intercourse from a position diametrically opposite to that of the Chinese. The Chinese esteemed their civilization as normal and regarded as barbarians all those who did not conform to it. They held as axiomatic the conviction that all men should be subordinate to their Emperor. Diplomatic intercourse on the basis of the reciprocally recognized sovereignty and legal equality of independent nation states was quite alien to all their conceptions. Their judicial procedures differed radically from those of the English. They were disposed to hold a group, such as a family or a village, responsible for the deeds of each its members and to consider an accused person guilty until he could prove his innocence. The English felt that guilt for a particular offense was lodged legally and solely in the individual and that the burden of proof in establishing guilt must be placed upon the accusers.

Under these circumstances the growing pressure of British trade could not but give rise to friction. The English were restive under the restrictions on commerce and official intercourse imposed by the Chinese. The close limitation of trade to one port, Canton; the annoying regulations of the life in the "factories" to which foreigners were confined; the arbitrary customs duties and harbor dues; the monopolistic powers of the *Co-hong*, the group of Chinese merchants through whom commerce must be conducted; the refusal of the Chinese to enter into diplomatic relations and the insistence of the Chinese that Western consuls were only head merchants; and the methods of trial and punishment applied to foreign offenders against Chinese law—all these became increasingly annoying to the English, as to other Europeans, and in time were deemed by them intolerable.

The First Anglo-Chinese War, 1839–1842

The issue between the English and the Chinese became joined over the question of opium. Opium had long been an item in the imports to China. Latterly it had risen in volume. Much of it came from India. In the years after the termination of the East India Company's monopoly of the British trade with China the amount coming in by British ships increased enormously. The Chinese government was very unhappy over the situation, partly because of the effects of the drug upon the population, and partly because the traffic was supposed to be draining the Empire of its silver. Action was therefore taken to enforce the prohibition of the importation of opium which in theory had long been the policy of the state. In 1839 there arrived in Canton a special commissioner with the assignment of ending the traffic. He proved very vigorous. He compelled the foreign merchants to surrender their stocks of the drug for summary destruction and to give bond not again to import the commodity. He achieved this result by the virtual imprisonment of the entire foreign community. The English, aggrieved, withdrew, first to Macao and then to Hongkong. The latter was at that time an almost uninhabited island.

Clashes between the British and Chinese armed forces followed. British operations were chiefly naval and directed against various ports south of the Yangtze. From time to time they were suspended to allow negotiations. The Chinese did not consent to come to terms until the English had captured Chinkiang, thus cutting a main line of communication between Peking and the south, and had threatened an attack on Nanking.

A treaty followed (1842) which bore the name of Nanking. Its outstanding provisions were (1) the opening of the ports of Canton, Amoy, Foochow, Ningpo, and Shanghai to the residence and commerce of British subjects; (2) the cession of the island of Hongkong to Great Britain; (3) the placing of intercourse between British and Chinese officials on the basis of equality; (4) the establishment and publication by the Chinese of a "fair and regular" tariff on exports and imports; (5) the termination of the *Co-hong;* (6) the payment by China of an indemnity for the opium destroyed by the energetic commissioner, for debts owed by members of the *Co-hong* to British subjects, and for British war expenses. In 1843 a supplementary treaty settled upon a tariff schedule, fixed further regulations for commerce, and set up the principle of extraterritoriality.

The British treaty was followed by others with several of the Western powers. Notable was one with the United States (1844) which elaborated the extraterritoriality agreed upon by the Chinese and English. In the same year the French obtained a treaty and an imperial decree which granted partial toleration to Roman Catholic Christianity. In 1845 a decree extended these privileges to Protestants and in 1846 an edict confirmed the toleration of Roman Catholicism and promised to restore to the Roman Catholics some of the churches that had been confiscated in the preceding century or earlier.

Interim

These treaties were followed by an uneasy truce. To the Chinese they seemed to have granted too much. To Westerners, especially to the English, they appeared to have obtained too little. The American and French treaties provided for their revision at the end of ten years. After 1852 the English, under the most-favored-nation clause, pressed for the review of their treaty of 1842, with the granting of added privileges to foreigners. In these demands they were joined by the Americans and the French.

The Second War between China and Western Powers, 1856–1860

Friction followed. In 1856 hostilities again broke out, this time over a comparatively minor incident. At first the war was between the English and the Chinese. Soon the French joined the English, finding a *casus belli* in the execution of a French missionary by the Chinese authorities. There was delay in pressing the war, due in part to the preoccupation of the English by the Mutiny in India. In 1857, however, Canton was captured. The Chinese still proved obdurate, and the British and French fleets carried the war to the north. They captured the forts commanding the entrance to Tientsin and so threatened Peking. The Emperor thereupon bowed to necessity and treaties were negotiated (1858) with Great Britain, France, Russia, and the United States.

The texts of the treaties of 1858 provided for the exchange of ratifications in Peking. When, in 1859, the British, French, and American ministers arrived off the coast for this purpose, they found that the Chinese authorities, intent upon preserving the fiction of the superiority of the Empire over Western states, were insisting that the route be followed which was customarily that of the tribute-bearing embassies from subordinate princes in the Far East. To this the British and French envoys would not accede and the war was renewed. Peking was taken. In retaliation for the violation of a flag of truce, the imperial summer palace was destroyed. Supplementary conventions, signed in Peking in 1860, made additions to the treaties of 1858.

The Terms of the Treaties of 1858–1860

The most significant terms of the treaties of 1858 and 1860 were as follows: (1) eleven additional ports were opened for foreign trade and residence—reaching from Newchwang (in Manchuria) in the north to Hankow on the west and to Swatow in the south; (2) Western merchantmen were given permission to ply the Yangtze River;

(3) the residence of foreign envoys and their staffs in Peking was conceded; (4) foreigners, if equipped with proper passports, might travel anywhere in the interior; (5) Christians, both Chinese and foreign, might propagate their faith and Chinese might accept and practice Christianity; (6) Roman Catholic religious and benevolent establishments confiscated during the past century and a half were to be restored and French missionaries might rent and purchase land in the provinces outside the treaty ports and erect buildings on them; (7) regulations governing extraterritoriality were elaborated; (8) a bit of the mainland opposite Hongkong was ceded Great Britain; (9) indemnities were to be paid; and (10) the opium traffic was legalized. In addition, in 1858 China ceded to Russia its territory north of the Amur and in 1860 Russia was given full title to the territory east of the Ussuri. This afforded Russia opportunity to construct an important port at Vladivostok.

Significance of the Treaties of 1842–1844 and 1858–1860

Until 1943 the treaties of 1842–1844 and 1858–1860 remained the chief legal basis of intercourse between China and the Occident.

The Chinese were never fully content with them and eventually attached to them the adjective "unequal," for they granted to Westerners in China privileges that were not accorded to Chinese in the Occident. Of the provisions to which the Chinese objected, the conventional tariff and extraterritoriality were outstanding. By the conventional tariff (that is, a tariff fixed by treaties and conventions) China surrendered the right to determine her own customs duties. From the foreign standpoint this was not unreasonable and promised to allay friction. Western merchants had long objected to what they deemed the arbitrary tariffs set by the Chinese, to their secrecy, and to the unpredictable fashion in which they were altered by Chinese officials. A published set of tariffs agreed upon by reciprocal negotiation seemed to them eminently fair and clearly desirable. The Chinese, however, resented the procedure as a derogation to their sovereignty. Extraterritoriality also had as an object the easing of the conflicts which were chronic because of the subjection of foreigners to Chinese laws and courts. In criminal matters it placed foreigners, when defendants, under the laws and officials of their respective governments and, when plaintiffs, gave representatives of their governments opportunity to see that justice was done in the Chinese courts in which the cases were heard. Extraterritoriality insured to foreigners a security which they craved and freed Chinese officials from some of the annoyances which were theirs in pretreaty days when foreigners proved intractable. Yet similar privileges were not conceded Chinese in Western lands. Chinese felt themselves to be branded as barbarians and inferiors —a status peculiarly galling to a people who had long esteemed themselves the most civilized of mankind. Moreover, extraterritoriality led to serious abuses which were only slowly corrected. Not all the powers provided for adequate jurisdiction over their citizens in China and lawlessness resulted before which the Chinese authorities were powerless.

As we shall see, it was not until the 1920's that the Chinese unshackled themselves from the conventional tariff, and it was 1943 before the major Western powers with whom (aside from Russia) China had chiefly to do, Great Britain and the United States, relinquished their extraterritorial privileges.

On the basis of the treaties of 1842–1844 and 1856–60 there came into being a pattern of intercourse between the Occident and China and a manner of life of Westerners in China which were peculiar to the Middle Kingdom. Elsewhere in the Orient, as in China, Occidentals considered themselves superior and lived their own social life and on a higher economic standard than the masses about them. Extraterritoriality and conventional tariffs were also to be found in other countries in the Far East, notably in Japan and Siam. Yet in elaborateness and in many of its phases the position of Occidentals in China was unique.

There was Hongkong. Under its status as a British crown colony, this island, almost barren when the English took it over, became the site of a thriving city (officially Victoria but commonly known as Hongkong) and one of the great ports of the world. Most of its population was Chinese, but the rulers were British. It became a center of banking and of transhipping and a formidable rival of the ancient and more populous Canton.

The "treaty ports" became centers of an exotic life. In several of them "concessions" arose, places of foreign residence and business and, under a development from extraterritoriality, virtually independent of Chinese control, foreign-dominated enclaves in the heart of China's main entrepots of foreign trade. Most of the concessions were granted separately to individual nations. At least two, labeled "international," were held jointly by two or more powers.

The outstanding example was Shanghai. In 1842 Shanghai was a seemingly unimportant walled town. It had a good geographic position, for although the Whangpoo (Huangpu), the stream on which it was situated, was small, the port was the one of those opened in the first two sets of treaties which best commanded the entrance to the fertile and wealthy Yangtze Valley. At Shanghai, outside the walled city, there were delimited, in the 1840's, a British settlement and a French concession. There was added an American settlement and the British and American sections were united and constituted the International Settlement. The International Settlement was governed by a municipal council, elected by the foreign taxpayers and long predominantly British. Until well along in the twentieth century the Chinese, although the overwhelming majority of the population, were not represented on this council. The situation of Shanghai near the mouth of the Yangtze and the security given by foreign protection against domestic disturbances in the neighborhood eventually made the International Settlement the financial and commercial heart of China. Particularly important sets of concessions also existed at Tientsin and Hankow, but there were as well similar areas in several other ports.

In the 1850's and 1860's the collection of tariff duties provided for in the treaties passed into the hands of foreigners. Because of a local rebellion, in 1853 and 1854 the Chinese machinery for this function broke down and, by an arrangement between the consuls and the local Chinese official, a Westerner was appointed to undertake the task. The device proved so satisfactory that it was soon extended to other ports. There arose the Imperial Maritime Customs service. It owed much of its development to a remarkable Irishman, Robert Hart, who long headed it as Inspector-General. Its members were employees of the Chinese government, but its outstanding posts were held by Occidentals. These were from several nationalities, but with the British more numerous than any other. The personnel was honest and efficient. Through it not only were the tariff dues collected, but an imperial postal service was also begun and the coasts and some of the rivers were equipped with lighthouses and buoys.

The overseas trade was primarily in the hands of foreigners. Until the twentieth century was well on its way the English predominated in it. Foreign banks, notably the (British) Hongkong and Shanghai Banking Corporation, dominated the financial side of commerce. Great business houses had their branches in the ports. Foreign steamers, mainly British, plied the coastal waters and the Yangtze as far as Chungking. Foreign gunboats patrolled the Yangtze and its main tributaries.

In the ports foreigners were dominant. They were especially privileged and lived their lives largely apart from the Chinese. Few of the merchant community troubled themselves to acquire the Chinese language or to learn much of Chinese history or culture. As a kind of *lingua franca* there was "pidgin English," a language whose structure resembled Chinese but most of whose vocabulary was from English sources. The missionaries, the customs employees, and a few of the consuls and merchants learned Chinese, but the bulk of the foreigners knew little of the real China.

Foreign Trade

Foreign trade did not immediately assume large proportions or work basic changes in the structure of Chinese life. It grew but slowly. In the two decades between 1865 and 1885 it increased only about a fifth. Between 1885 and 1894 it nearly doubled, but was still, when compared with the size of the country, very small. The chief exports were luxuries and semiluxuries—silk and tea. The main imports were cotton goods, mostly from British factories, and opium.

Christian Missionaries

A penetration of China by Western culture in the years between 1838 and 1894 greater than that wrought by commerce was through Christian missionaries. By the treaties of 1858 missionaries, along with other citizens of the treaty powers, were given the legal privilege of traveling anywhere in the Empire. By these treaties, moreover, they were accorded the right to propagate their faith and Chinese were given permission to accept it. Missionaries traversed the Empire more widely than did merchants. In contrast with the merchants, who, by the treaties, had their residence for the most part confined to the "open" ports, many of the missionaries acquired property and inaugurated continuing stations in the interior. The ideas which they spread acted more directly upon institutions and ideals fundamental to Chinese culture than did those brought by merchants. The hostility of missionaries to the rites in honor of ancestors threatened the traditional Chinese family. The opposition to the sacrifices in connection with the Confucian cult struck at the basis of the state and of education. Here was a force which, if extensively applied, would work revolutionary changes in the life of the Empire.

In the nineteenth century, and especially after 1838, the number of Christian missionaries rapidly multiplied. At the opening of the century Christianity seemed to be faced with slow extinction. It was represented by a minute Russian contingent in Peking and by small Roman Catholic minorities in Peking and the provinces. Reinforcements to Roman Catholic missionary staffs were being curtailed by the stringent anti-Christian measures of the Chinese government and by the Wars of Napoleon in Europe. Even before the close of the Napoleonic Wars and before the first treaties missionaries were on the increase. In 1807 came the first Protestant missionary, Robert Morrison. He was followed by others. A series of revivals was making Protestantism more aggressively missionary than at any previous period in its history. After 1815 came a resurgence of Roman Catholic missionary activity. Both Protestants and Roman Catholics saw in China a challenge and an opportunity. After the events of the 1840's, with their partial toleration of Christianity, both Roman Catholics and Protestants augmented their representatives. The treaties of 1858 and 1860 still further opened the doors and eager missionaries flocked to enter them.

Roman Catholics had an advantage over Protestants. They had been in the Empire since the sixteenth century and had Christians in practically all the provinces. Their orders and societies already in China added to their staffs and several new organizations commenced operations. The Jesuits, who had led in the missions of the sixteenth, seventeenth, and eighteenth centuries but whose society had been suspended by Papal order late in the eighteenth century, were reconstituted and reentered the Empire. In point of territory covered, the chief Roman Catholic organizations active in China were the Congregation of the Mission (Lazarists), the Society of Jesus (Jesuits), the Society of Foreign Missions of Paris, the Order of Brothers Minor (Franciscans), and the Congregation of the Immaculate Heart of Mary, with headquarters at Scheutveld, in Belgium. Missionaries were almost entirely from the Continent of Europe, the majority of them French.

Protestants sent in missionaries more rapidly than did Roman Catholics, and by 1895 their staffs outnumbered those of the latter. The overwhelming majority were from the British Isles and the United States—more from the former, as was natural in view of the British predominance in foreign trade. The Protestant missionaries translated the Bible into Chinese and began the winning of converts and the organization of churches. They broadcast the Christian message by the oral word and the printed page. They introduced Western medicine and opened schools in which Western subjects were taught. They were the outstanding pioneers in the development of a medical profession which used Occidental techniques and in Western forms of education, especially of secondary and higher grades.

By 1895 Christian missionaries numbered not far from twenty-five hundred, of whom approximately two-thirds were Protestants. Christians totaled about two-thirds of a million. Of these about five-sixths were Roman Catholics. Compared with the area and population of China, these numbers were not particularly impressive. However, they were scattered among all the provinces and most of the outlying dependencies, they represented a striking increase, and they were forerunners of a still more extensive growth and a rapidly rising influence upon the country as a whole. The dominant classes feared and disliked them and popular feeling against them often ran high. Riots and persecutions punctuated the Christian advance, ample evidence that here was a revolutionary force which adherents of the old order rightly regarded as a powerful leaven which would go far toward remaking the culture of the land.

The disintegration of the inherited Chinese culture would have occurred under the impact of the West had never a missionary come to China. The break would probably have come about the time that it did. Missionaries furthered the collapse but probably did not hasten it. When once the old culture had begun to disappear, as it did after 1895, Christian missions became primarily a constructive rather than a destructive force. They were potent in building positive and helpful elements into the new culture.

The Rebellions of the Third Quarter of the Nineteenth Century

The defeats at the hands of the Western powers gave staggering blows to the decrepit Manchu dynasty. The blows were augmented by native rebellions. Since the latter part of the eighteenth century the ruling house had been going downhill. No dynasty in China had ever been permanent. The Manchus had now held the reins of government for two centuries and had clearly reached and passed their zenith. For a time it looked as though the combination of attacks from without and within would bring an early demise to the imperial line from the north.

The most formidable of the uprisings, the T'ai P'ing Rebellion, was in part the direct result of the impact of the West. It had as its central figure Hung Hsiu-ch'üan. Hung was a village teacher, like so many of his kind an unsuccessful aspirant in the civil service examinations. Through chance contact with a Chinese Protestant Christian, he had come into possession of pamphlets outlining the Christian faith. In them he thought he found the explanation of visions which had been his in the course of a severe illness. Through them he felt himself commissioned to propagate what he there found. Later he had other contacts with Protestant missionaries. As a result of the activity of himself and his first followers there arose, in the 1840's and 1850's, chiefly in the mountainous southern province of Kwangsi, a socio-religious movement which honored the Bible and some customs and beliefs of Christian provenance. It early assumed political aspects and ambitions and essayed to supplant the Manchus with a new dynasty, to be known as T'ai P'ing, or "Great Peace," and with Hung as the first Emperor. Its armies marched northward to the Yangtze, and moved down that stream to Nanking (1854). There a capital was set up. The movement was in part a peasant uprising, one of a long succession which have punctuated Chinese history. It also incorporated a few ideas from the Occident and was the first formidable, although unintelligent and crude, effort to reorganize the Empire to take advantage of what was filtering in from the West. The T'ai P'ing movement was weak in organizing and administrative ability. For a decade it kept in turmoil the populous and erstwhile wealthy lower portion of the valley of the Yangtze. It was not suppressed until 1865 and then only by Chinese who had rallied to the support of the Manchus and by the aid of a force led by foreigners. The outstanding Chinese organizer and leader of the imperial armies was Tsêng Kuo-fan, and his chief subordinate was Li Hung-chang. Both were scholar-administrators, products of the traditional classical education and examination system. The foreign-officered "Ever Victorious Army" was organized by an American, Frederick T. Ward, later deified by the Chinese, and, after his death and a brief tenure by another alien, was led on to the eventual suppression of the rebellion by the British Charles George Gordon. The T'ai P'ing uprising was crushed, but remnants of the defeated forces fled abroad and contributed to the agitation which in the next century overthrew the Manchus and set up the Republic.

The other rebellions need not detain us. Among them was one

in the southwest. There was also one, mainly of Moslems, in the northwest. The latter for a time mastered much of Sinkiang. It was suppressed by a Chinese general whose feat, as a military achievement, was remarkable.

The Manchus Gain a Reprieve

The combination of foreign wars and internal rebellions was the most serious threat the Manchu dynasty had faced since the seventeenth century. Moreover, in the nineteenth century none of its Emperors rose above mediocrity and during much of the second half of the century the throne was occupied by minors.

However, the dynasty obtained a new lease on life which carried it into the twentieth century. This reprieve was due in part to the assistance of able Chinese and in part to a remarkable woman, the Empress Dowager, Tz'ŭ Hsi. Tz'ŭ Hsi is probably more correctly known as the Empress Hsiao-ch'in, but this name is seldom used by Westerners. She also had as a nickname "Old Buddha."

It was Chinese who were mainly responsible for suppressing the rebellions. The most prominent of these, Tsêng Kuo-fan, was the outstanding Chinese statesman of the third quarter of the century. Presumably they were moved by the fear of the chaos which would have ensued had the rebels triumphed and by the loyalty of the minister to his prince inculcated by traditional Chinese ethics.

Tz'ŭ Hsi had a spectacular career. She was from the Manchu nobility and was chosen as a concubine for the Emperor who reigned in the 1850's. She had the good fortune to bear that monarch his son and heir. Her imperial spouse fled from the foreign armies in 1860 and died, away from the capital, in 1861. Through vigorous, prompt, and astute action she became coregent during the minority of her son and by her forcefulness quite dominated the other regent and the court. Her son died soon after he attained his majority, leaving no issue. Setting precedent at nought, Tz'ŭ Hsi had chosen as his successor a child who is usually known by the name of his reign period, Kuang Hsü. She controlled the government during the Kuang Hsü Emperor's minority and, with the exception of a brief interval, continued to do so until her death in 1908.

Tz'ŭ Hsi was more vigorous than any Emperor the Manchus had produced since Ch'ien Lung. She had overweening ambition, love of power, and great physical vitality. She knew well the strength and weakness of the more prominent Chinese and Manchus of her day and by her tact and skill was able to use them for her purposes. She had a fairly good knowledge of Chinese literature, and was interested in music, art, and the theater. Probably she prolonged the life of the crumbling dynasty. Yet she was often guilty of vacillation and indecision, she was a lover of money, she was superstitious, she made many costly errors, and probably she never comprehended the significance of the new forces brought by the West with which the Empire had to reckon.

Halting Beginnings of Adjustment

It is partly because of the blindness of Tz'ŭ Hsi and of those about her that China was slow in adapting herself to the irrupting Occident. In this way precious years were lost. Her smaller neighbor, Japan, was utilizing the closing decades of the century to equip herself with the machinery and learning of the West. Thus armed, the island empire was in a position to defeat China and to wrest from her her traditional leadership in the Far East. While Japan was making the remarkable adjustment which we are to chronicle in the next chapter, China was exerting herself to hold the West at arm's length and to remain as little altered as possible by the enforced contacts.

In a sense this was not surprising. China had been the teacher of her neighbors, not their pupil. To be sure, much of her culture had come from the outside, but most of the foreign contributions had been made centuries earlier. For nearly a thousand years China's civilization had been ingrowing and had become more and more static. Developments there had been, but their rate of emergence had been slowing down since the T'ang and Sung dynasties. The scholar-official class which dominated the Empire was recruited through an educational system which stifled original thought and which bred adherence to the *status quo*. The *literati*, as Westerners dubbed them, were inordinately proud of Chinese culture and had a stake in keeping things as they were. Any changes would threaten their position and their livelihood. Moreover, the West had not come to China in a fashion to commend its ways to her. It had forced itself on her at the mouth of the cannon. Educated Chinese could scarcely be blamed for rating the intruders as barbarians—clever and aggressive, perhaps, but no less crude and at best merely semicivilized. It was only an occasional far-sighted Chinese who perceived that whether they liked it or not he and his fellow-countrymen must learn from the Occident if they were to preserve their independence and the position of their Empire as a great power.

Some few there were who saw more or less clearly the handwriting on the wall. Through them occasional innovations were made, albeit haltingly.

One of the most striking and discerning attempts to prepare China for her inevitable entrance into the world created by the Occident was an ambitious project for educating Chinese youth in the West. This was due to the imagination and initiative of Yung Wing. Yung Wing as a lad from a humble home attended one of the first schools opened by Protestant missionaries. Through an American teacher in that school he had gone to the United States and had graduated at Yale, the first Chinese to become an alumnus of an American college. Through what he had seen in his years in America, Yung Wing had become convinced of both the advantage and the necessity of adjustment by China to the Occident. Among his plans for bringing this about was a project for sending Chinese boys to the United States for a Western education. In the 1870's one hundred and twenty youths were, accordingly, dispatched to America, there to be educated at the expense of their government. Conservative alarm at the rapidity of their Americanization terminated the educational mission before more than a few had completed their preparation. On their return to China, the boys were looked at askance for their Western equipment. However, several of them later had an important share in helping their native land to acquire Western appliances.

There were other foreshadowings of change. The China Merchants Steam Navigation Company was organized, under the leadership of Western-trained Chinese, and won a considerable portion of the coastal and river shipping. The beginnings of railway construction were to be seen in the north. The telegraph was introduced and under contract with the government a line was built which connected Peking with Tientsin and Shanghai. Some application of modern Western methods was made to the mining of coal. A few arsenals of Western type were constructed, and steps were taken to build a modern navy and to drill and equip an army after Occidental patterns. The central government instituted a school for the training of men for foreign diplomatic service.

Yet until 1894 life went on much as it had before the first wars with the Occident. The structure of government and the educational and examination system which supported it were unaltered. Family customs and even the economic life were as they had been. Only small minorities, and these mainly in the coastal provinces and in the treaty ports, were being substantially affected.

The Growth of Diplomatic Intercourse with the West

As a result of the treaties, and especially of the second group of treaties, regular diplomatic relations with the West were inaugurated.

At first this was largely a one-way movement. Foreign consuls were appointed to the treaty ports and the ministers of the treaty powers established residences in Peking.

It was only by slow and hesitant steps that the Chinese reciprocated. The first Chinese embassy to the Western capitals was headed by an American, Anson Burlingame. Burlingame had come to China as Minister from the United States. Affable and sympathetic with the Chinese and with the difficulties of their government, he won the confidence of some of the leading officials. When, in 1867, he was about to resign his post and return to America, the Chinese authorities suggested that he go as their ambassador to the United States and Europe. Both Robert Hart, of the Imperial Maritime Customs, and William H. Seward, Secretary of State of the United States, had been urging upon the Chinese the advisability of establishing legations in Western capitals. The treaties were due for revision in 1868 and foreign merchants were prepared to urge that they be still further liberalized and that the privileges which they promised be more faithfully accorded. The Chinese wished to counteract this agitation and also hoped to forestall pressure to develop the Empire after Western precedents by building railways and telegraph lines and opening mines. Burlingame seemed an admirable representative to effect their desires. A Manchu and a Chinese were appointed as colleagues.

The embassy went first to the United States. Burlingame, sanguine and an orator, in public addresses waxed optimistic over the prospect of the early welcome of Chinese to Christianity and Western culture. In 1868 a treaty between China and the United States was signed at Washington which provided for the integrity of China (a phrase later to be prominent in American Far Eastern policy), for the encouragement of the immigration of Chinese laborers to the United States, for reciprocity in the liberty to propagate religion, to attend the schools of either country, and in residence and travel, and for freedom from interference by Americans in the development of

China. The provisions of immediate practical significance were those relating to Chinese immigration—then desired by Californians—and the American promise not to press China to adopt Western ways and machinery—a reassurance welcomed by Chinese officialdom. In Britain the promise was obtained from the government that it would not apply unfriendly pressure inconsistent with the independence of China. The mission proceeded to several capitals of the Continent of Europe, but was practically terminated by the death of Burlingame, of pneumonia, in St. Petersburg.

Here was an attempt, by an American idealist, to safeguard the independence and territorial integrity of China, a policy to which the United States government became more and more committed as the decades passed.

It was some years after Burlingame's death before China established resident legations in the West. The first was in London, in 1877, and others followed in Washington and on the Continent of Europe.

The Chinese authorities were reluctant to allow an imperial audience to the foreign envoys resident in Peking. To do so would be tantamount to an admission of the equality of Occidental monarchs with the Emperor. An excuse was found for delay. In the 1860's and again in the late 1870's, in the 1880's, and in the early 1890's the reigning Emperor was a minor. Not until he attained his majority would the Chinese government consent to a formal audience. One was obtained in the 1870's and another in 1894, but only after much pressure, and then under circumstances which none too subtly suggested that the foreign powers were still in the category of tributary states.

The Continued Pressure of Western Powers

Between 1860 and 1894 no major gains of foreign powers were made at the expense of China. In the south, as we saw in the last chapter, Great Britain annexed Upper Burma, thus acquiring title to a state tributory to China, and France extended her authority in Annam, Tongking, and Cambodia, also in territory which was within the sphere of Chinese influence. However, in these regions there was little or no effective Chinese control. In 1887 China formally ceded Macao to Portugal, but that small peninsula had been really part of the Portuguese Empire since the sixteenth century. In the Far West, Russia acquired a portion of Ili. All of these foreign gains were on the periphery of the Empire, and, except in the case of Macao and the hostilities with France, did not affect China Proper.

Nor was there a thoroughgoing revision of the foreign treaties. In 1876 the Chefoo Convention, with Great Britain, occasioned by the murder of a British consular official on the borders between Yünnan and Burma, opened new ports to foreign trade and granted a few other concessions, but there was nothing comparable to the treaties of 1842–1844 and 1858–1860. China was given a reprieve which did not terminate until 1894.

Chinese Emigration

The Chinese were migrating. The vast increase in population during the preceding century had brought an unprecedented pressure upon the means of subsistence and this was showing itself in part in an outward movement of Chinese. Much of the emigration was in a form of contract labor which was little better than slavery. By 1880 the worst abuses had been checked by agreements between China and the powers or by unilateral action of individual powers. Much emigration was voluntary. In places the influx of Chinese brought alarm, an alarm which stiffened into regulation or prohibition of what threatened to be an inundation of cheap labor from a bottomless reservoir.

Acute fear was felt and drastic action was taken in the United States. Originally, as we saw a few paragraphs above, Chinese were welcomed to the West Coast, especially to California, as badly needed labor. Chinese did much of the rough work in the rapid opening of the new country and were used extensively in the building and maintenance of railroads. The Burlingame treaty of 1868 with its provision for freedom of immigration was welcomed in some quarters. However, opposition began to develop, particularly from organized labor in California, and pressure was brought on the Congress to put an end to the influx of Chinese. There were, too, anti-Chinese riots in some of the Western states. In 1878 the Congress enacted legislation which would have meant the exclusion of the Chinese. This was vetoed by President Hayes on the ground that it was in violation of the treaty of 1868. A commission was sent to China to seek a modification of that treaty. The Chinese government acquiesced (1880), but only in the regulation, limitation, or suspension of Chinese immigration and not to its prohibition. In 1882 the Congress passed a bill to suspend Chinese immigration for twenty years, but this met a presidential veto on the ground that it was virtually exclusion. The term was then shortened (1882) to ten years. The naturalization of Chinese was also forbidden. More drastic exclusion laws were placed on the statute book in 1888 and 1892. In 1894 China agreed to the full prohibition of laborers for ten years. The act of 1888 was renewed in 1902 and was extended to the island possessions of the United States. In 1904 the exclusion was made perpetual. Resentment against the American restrictions developed in China, especially after 1900, but it was powerless.

Summary

In the little over a half century after 1838 the doors of China were partially forced open to the West. At the mouth of the cannon the Occident, led by Great Britain, obtained treaties which allowed foreign residence and commerce, established diplomatic relations, and legalized the propagation of Christianity. These treaties were wrung from a reluctant China. So far as she was able, China held herself aloof and clung to her ancient culture. In 1894 that culture was substantially as it had been before the advent of the Westerner.

In 1894 began a sudden change which was to issue in a thoroughgoing revolution. The immediate occasion was pressure from Japan. While China had been seeking to go on unmodified by the Occident, Japan had been avidly adopting Western appliances. To that story we must now turn.

BIBLIOGRAPHY

For Brief Reference

H. M. Vinacke, *A History of the Far East in Modern Times* (New York, 4th ed., 1941), Chaps. 2, 3.

For More Detailed Study

M. F. Coolidge, *Chinese Immigration* (New York, 1909).

T. Dennett, *Americans in Eastern Asia* (New York, 1922).

W. J. Hail, *Tsêng Kuo-fan and the Taiping Rebellion* (New Haven, 1927).

A. W. Hummel, *Eminent Chinese of the Ch'ing Period* (Washington, 2 vols., 1943, 1944).

K. S. Latourette, *A History of Christian Missions in China* (New York, 1929).

H. B. Morse, *The International Relations of the Chinese Empire*. Vol. I, *The Period of Conflict, 1834–1860* (London, 1910). Vol. II, *The Period of Submission, 1861–1893* (London, 1913).

F. W. Williams, *Anson Burlingame and the First Chinese Mission to Foreign Powers* (New York, 1912).

Yung Wing, *My Life in China and America* (New York, 1909).

Chapter XIII. EMERGENT JAPAN, 1853–1893

Japan reopens her doors and her transformation begins

THE RENEWED PRESSURE of the West was even later in making itself felt in Japan than in China. It will be remembered that until the middle of the nineteenth century Japan was more nearly sealed against the Occident than was China. The one port, Nagasaki, through which foreign trade was permitted was closed to all except the Dutch and they were under more rigid restrictions than were the foreigners in the one partially opened port in China, Canton. Roman Catholic Christianity survived in Japan, as in China, from an earlier period of prosperity, but in Japan it had been driven completely into hiding, no missionaries were able to enter, and there were no Japanese priests, whereas in China a few foreign missionaries continued to serve their flocks and to train Chinese priests. It was not until 1853 and the famous coming of Commodore Perry that the first dent was made on Japanese isolation. Not before 1858 were treaties granted which conceded as much as did the treaties wrung from China in the previous decade.

Yet, while starting later than in China, in Japan the Occidental invasion was much earlier in producing change. By 1894 what seemed superficially to have been a remarkable revolution had taken place. The Shogunate had been swept aside, feudalism had been abolished, a military reorganization had been effected, and a constitution patterned after Western precedents had been promulgated. Western forms of education had been adapted, railways had been built, the beginnings of a navy and a merchant marine had been constructed, and the industrial revolution was making rapid headway.

The reasons for the greater rapidity of the changes in Japan are not far to seek. Conditions in Japan were ripe for change. The internal peace imposed by the Tokugawa had weakened the military class. The years of peace had encouraged the growth of great cities, a money economy, and a moneyed class, and so had prepared the way for capitalism and the industrial revolution. The peasantry was in straitened circumstances through an unsound agrarian system, a source of continuing rural problems. There were those who were advocating expansion on the Continent, foreshadowings of the later growth of empire. A school of historical scholarship was showing the Bakufu to be a comparatively late development and to have usurped part of the earlier prerogatives of the Emperor. Rivals of the Tokugawa, notably the western fiefs of Satsuma and Choshu, were prepared to take advantage of any opportunity to displace that family and put themselves in control of the state. Unlike China, Japan had a tradition of going to school to other peoples. Her civilization had come chiefly from China. She had continued to learn from that Empire. When they were convinced that there was much that they could profitably acquire from the Occident, the Japanese were eager to be at it. Japan was much smaller than China, both in area and in population, and so was more quickly moved.

Moreover, the changes in Japan, while seemingly revolutionary, actually left the basic structure of Japanese culture but little altered. The revolution was by no means as thoroughgoing as that which came in China after 1895. Such fundamental institutions as those of the Emperor and the family remained substantially intact. The military tradition was strengthened rather than weakened. Among the leaders of the new Japan were representatives of ancient families as well as men who had come up from the ranks. As, centuries before, Japan in taking over the culture of China had made it conform to the existing patterns of Japanese life, so now, in adopting Western civilization, Japan did not allow it to displace her time-honored culture but constrained it to fit into and in some cases to strengthen what had come down from her past. Outwardly, by 1894 Japan's main cities seemed in process of being Occidentalized. Actually the Westernization was compelled to subserve traditional vested interests. There were changes, but these were slow, superficial, or consisted in fresh emphasis upon old ideals.

The four decades between Perry and the War of 1894–1895 with China were employed chiefly in internal alterations and developments. Yet the foundations were being laid for the phenomenal expansion that marked the half century after 1894. The building of the huge overseas Japanese Empire represented no revolutionary innovation. It arose from movements which could be traced to pre-1894 years and even to pre-Perry times.

Precursors to Perry

The advent of Perry was not the first attempt to open Japan. The American expedition owed its success in part to movements which had begun long before. In the eighteenth century several Russian ships had touched at Japanese ports. In 1804 a Russian mission came to Nagasaki, bringing back shipwrecked Japanese sailors, but was repulsed. Early in the nineteenth century American and British traders endeavored to establish commercial relations. In 1808 a British man-of-war entered the harbor of Nagasaki. The development of whaling in the early nineteenth century brought many ships from the Occident to Japanese waters. Many of these sought to obtain wood, water, and provisions from the islands, but in vain. Some were shipwrecked on the Japanese coast and their crews, after being confined, were sent out of the country through Nagasaki on Dutch or Chinese vessels. In 1837 the American ship *Morrison* attempted to repatriate some Japanese fishermen who had been driven offshore by adverse winds, had drifted to the northwest coast of America, had been conveyed to England and thence to Macao, and whose plight had appealed to philanthropic Americans who also had a canny eye for the supposedly lucrative trade of Japan. When it reached Japan the *Morrison* was fired upon and left without accomplishing its purpose.

The United States became especially interested in access to Japan. American whalers were numerous. In the 1840's the occupation of the Oregon Country and the acquisition of California gave the United States a long frontage on the Pacific and increased her interest in the Far East. American ships were more and more frequenting the Pacific and not unnaturally desired access to Japanese ports, if for no other reason than for refueling and reprovisioning. Several abortive plans were made by the United States to establish diplomatic relations with Japan. In the 1840's two ships, commanded by Commodore Biddle, were sent to the Bay of Yedo, but their request for the inauguration of trade was denied.

It was clear that Japan could not long maintain her isolation. The partial opening of China in the 1840's, the Russian advance from the north, and the certainty of increased and successful pressure on China rendered the traditional aloofness of the Land of the Rising Sun an impossible anachronism. Here and there in Japan were those who were more or less dimly aware of the situation. Through the Dutch some eager Japanese minds were obtaining information about the

Occident. Through that same convenient peek hole on the outside world, Tokugawa officialdom was learning of the augmented penetration of the Far East by the Occident. It was obvious that before many years the doors of Japan would have to be opened. The only question was precisely when and by whom. The English seemed the most probable leaders, for they were the chief trading nation and had forced the doors of China. Russia was also a possibility, for her boundaries in the Far East were being advanced, mainly at the cost of China.

The Coming of Perry

It was probably fortunate for Japan that she yielded to the United States rather than to Great Britain or Russia. The United States then had no territorial ambitions in the east of Asia—although some individual Americans wished her to have them—and was less bluntly aggressive than were the other two powers.

It was, moreover, significant that the United States should be the means of opening Japan. The act was a prophecy of the growing part which the United States was to have in Far Eastern affairs and foreshadowed the armed clash with the Occident which was to come nearly a century later in which the United States was to bear so large a part of the load of meeting the Japanese menace.

Instructions for the American expedition were first issued in 1851, but the plans were not carried through until two years later and then on an enlarged scale and under the command of another officer, Commodore Matthew Calbraith Perry.

Commodore Perry was provided with a squadron of four ships and made careful preparations for his task. He sailed into the Bay of Yedo in July 1853. He declined to go to Nagasaki or to be treated in any such humiliating fashion as had been the custom of the Japanese with the Dutch. The President's letter to the Emperor was delivered to prominent Japanese officials and Perry sailed away, leaving word that he would return within a year to receive the Japanese answer. In the interim the President's request for a treaty provoked sharp discussion among the *daimyo* and the coasts were put in a state of defense. However, peaceful counsels prevailed and the *Shogun* decided to grant the American request. Perry was back in February 1854, his return hastened by a Russian demand through Nagasaki for commercial relations. He came with an enlarged force and an impressive array of presents designed to demonstrate the mechanical skill of the West. On March 31, 1854, a treaty was signed. It was not a general treaty of commerce but provided, rather, for a very limited intercourse. It stipulated the opening of two ports for wood, provisions, water, and coal, the appointment of an American consul, care for shipwrecked Americans, and trade under Japanese regulations. It also had a most-favored-nation clause. In contrast with the treaties with China, it contained neither a conventional tariff nor extraterritoriality.

Perry's success was due in part to the impressiveness of his expedition, in part to the threat of force made in so veiled a form that the Japanese could accede without the disgrace of yielding to superior armaments, in part to Perry's tact and firmness, and in part to the clear vision of a few informed Japanese who saw that isolation could not long be maintained, particularly in view of the Russian and British advances.

Similar treaties soon followed with Great Britain, Russia, and the Netherlands. The British treaty opened Nagasaki and the Russian document introduced extraterritoriality. The treaties were negotiated and signed by the *Bakufu*. The Emperor's approval was requested and obtained.

The Commercial Treaties of 1858

The pioneer successes in obtaining more comprehensive commercial treaties with Japan were also achieved by an American, this time Townsend Harris. Harris was the first American consul. He had been a merchant in New York City and while there had been active in politics. After the death of his mother he left his business and wandered rather extensively in the Far East. His appointment as consul came through his political connections, but proved much more opportune than did most of the consular and diplomatic payments of political debts.

Harris was stationed at Shimoda, one of the two ports opened by the Perry treaty. As a port Shimoda had little to offer and Harris's life there was lonely and difficult. For months he and his interpreter were the only foreigners. He gradually won the confidence of the officials. His task was rendered less difficult by the War of 1856–1860 between China on the one hand and Great Britain and France on the other. The strong possibility that the successful powers would turn their arms against Japan could be used as a potent argument for granting concessions voluntarily to a nation which was not an active combatant. Russia, too, was a menace, for she was taking advantage of China's weakness to acquire territory at the latter's expense.

In 1857 Harris obtained a convention which granted Americans the right of residence at Shimoda and Hakodate, the two open ports of the Perry document, the privilege of obtaining supplies at Nagasaki, and extraterritoriality in criminal cases. The year 1857 also saw conventions signed by Japan with the Netherlands and Russia.

Harris now made his way to Yedo, was installed officially in a residence, and was formally received in audience by the *Shogun*. Here he was breaking new ground, for not since the Empire had been finally sealed against the West had such concessions been made.

Harris used his sojourn at Yedo to obtain (1858) a commercial treaty for his government. This stipulated, among other things, the reciprocal right to place a diplomatic representative at the capital and consuls at the open ports, the opening of additional ports, extraterritoriality in civil as well as criminal cases, a conventional tariff, the prohibition of the importation of opium, freedom of Americans to practice their religion, the most-favored-nation clause, and the right of revision after July 4, 1872, on one year's notice by either government.

The treaty was not acquired without difficulties. Powerful interests opposed the further opening of the country. They brought influence to bear upon the Imperial court at Kyoto, and the Emperor declined the approval asked by the *Shogun*. Harris had thought that in dealing with the *Shogun* he was in touch with the supreme authority in the land. He now learned his mistake. However, the news that China had succumbed and had negotiated the treaties of Tientsin (1858) sent a shiver of fear through Tokugawa officialdom. Harris argued that it would be advisable to agree to a treaty before the victorious English and French could deal with Japan as they had dealt with the Middle Kingdom. The treaty was, accordingly, signed.

The Harris treaty became a pattern for others and formed the basis of Japan's relations with Western powers until the drastic revision given in the 1890's. Dutch, British, Russian, and French treaties followed in quick succession and, except for a reduction of the tariff on cotton and woolen goods in the British document—natural in view of the character of British exports to the East—without substantial departure from the American prototype.

It must be noted that under the treaties of 1858 the privileges which foreigners enjoyed in Japan were more limited than those which the treaties of that year accorded them in China. Aliens could not, as in China, travel outside the treaty ports. Nor did they have the right to propagate Christianity. Japan was still less effectively opened to the West than was China.

In 1866 a convention was entered into with Britain, France, the United States, and Holland which reduced the tariff to a general five per cent.

The Meiji Restoration

The signing of the treaties did not finally assure the opening of Japan. They had been negotiated by the *Bakufu* with the approval of the Emperor. The high officials of the *Shogun*, in Yedo and in touch with foreign events, saw the necessity of yielding to friendly pressure from abroad before it became unfriendly. The Imperial court, in inland Kyoto, and out of close contact with the world beyond the shores of Japan, could not appreciate the significance of current happenings and became the center of those who wished to preserve the Empire's isolation. Enemies of the Tokugawa took advantage of the situation to embarrass their heretofore successful rival. Eventually they were able to oust the Tokugawa and in doing so brought the *Bakufu* to an end and professed to have terminated the dual form of government.

It was not to be expected that Japan would readily abandon the isolation which had been part of her national tradition for over two centuries. There were, moreover, enemies of the *Bakufu* who were quite prepared to join the antiforeign forces in the hope of ending that form of government or of weakening the Tokugawa. The opposition was made up of a number of elements, not all of them in accord with one another. There were the court nobles, the *kuge*, descendants of the ancient civil aristocracy, who traditionally resented the dominance of the military and hoped, by restoring the direct rule of the Emperor, to enhance their own power and prestige, long since eclipsed. There were branches of the Tokugawa who were not in harmony with the foreign policy of the ministers of the *Shogun*. It may be, too, that the earlier historical studies which centered about one of these branches and which had shown the Emperor to have been originally the sole ruler and the *Bakufu* an innovation had influenced their views. Several of the feudatories, chiefly in the south and west, had never been content with Tokugawa supremacy. Prominent among them were Satsuma and Choshu. Many of the *ronin*, masterless *samurai*, also were violently antiforeign and attached themselves to the Imperial cause.

The expressions of antiforeignism and of opposition to the treaties and to the Tokugawa took a variety of forms. There was insistence that the Emperor be given back his direct administrative functions as they had been exercised before the days of the Shogunate. There was reemphasis upon Shinto as contrasted with Buddhism, and Shinto would exalt the Emperor and the Imperial ancestors. A slogan spread through much of Japan—"Honor the Emperor, expel the barbarians." There was physical violence to the persons of aliens. Patriotic *samurai* gave expression to their feelings by assaulting individual foreigners. Between 1859 and 1865 the British legation was twice attacked, the British and American legations were burned, and twelve foreigners lost their lives. All this was a natural precursor to the hatred for things Western which became so prominent and aggressive in the 1930's and 1940's. The *Shogun* did what he could to afford protection, and the British and French governments stationed troops at Yokohama to guard their nationals.

In 1862 an Englishman was slain for what the Japanese interpreted as an insult to the *Daimyo* of Satsuma. In retaliation a British squadron went to Kagoshima, a Satsuma port, and, in the ensuing friction, heavily bombarded the forts (1863).

In 1863 the Emperor ordered the country closed to foreigners. This command the *Shogun* would not carry out, for his officers were aware of the quick use of force with which the powers would meet any such attempt. However, the *Daimyo* of Choshu took matters into his own hands. His territories commanded the Straits of Shimonoseki, the narrows between Kyushu and the Main Island through which much of the foreign shipping passed. In the summer of 1863 his ships and forts fired on several foreign vessels. Within a few days an American warship and a French squadron had bombarded the forts and the following year a joint British, French, Dutch, and American expedition silenced the Choshu batteries and destroyed their guns. The *Shogun*, not willing that Choshu should become too independent, assumed the responsibility for its action and paid an indemnity. There was delay in making full payment. Led by the British envoy, the British, French, and Dutch joined in a naval demonstration off Osaka with the intention of impressing the Emperor, and obtained the long-denied imperial approval of the treaties. Incidentally, in 1883 the United States returned to Japan its share of the indemnity.

The position of the *Shogun* was becoming more and more difficult. In 1867 a lad of fourteen, Mutsuhito, better known by his reign name as the Meiji Emperor, came to the imperial throne. Pressure was brought on the *Shogun* and he resigned. Late in the year (1867) the Emperor accepted the return of that official's administrative powers but ordered him for the time being to continue the defense of the Empire and the conduct of foreign affairs. Early in 1868 anti-Tokugawa elements staged a palace revolution, obtained control of the Emperor, and inspired an imperial decree which abolished the office of *Shogun* and commanded the *Shogun* to surrender his lands and revenues. To this the *Shogun* was not disposed supinely to submit. He marched on Kyoto, determined to remove the anti-Tokugawa imperial counsellors. He was defeated and gave up the hopeless struggle. However, some of his followers continued the civil war and were not reduced until late in 1868.

A revolution had occurred. The device by which the military had ruled Japan since the days of Yoritomo, over seven and a half centuries before, had been abolished. Theoretically the "Meiji Restoration" had brought the Emperor again to full power. Actually the Emperor did not openly direct the government. What really had happened was the substitution for the Tokugawa as the controlling power in the state of a coalition of anti-Tokugawa western feudatories. Even before the institution of the Shogunate the Emperor had been a figurehead directed by ministers who acted in his name. This practice continued. The Meiji Emperor proved able and had an important share in the stirring events of his long reign. However, he was influential in part because he was sufficiently astute to conform to the role to which tradition assigned him and to allow his ministers to assume responsibility for his acts.

The Tokugawa had been removed from the dominant position which had long been theirs. Yet they were not destroyed. It was characteristic of Japan that the head of the family continued to be held in honor and was ranked high among the nobility created by the new regime. Moreover, the two and a half centuries of Tokugawa rule had left a deep and lasting impression on the nation. The Tokugawa and their immediate predecessors, Nobunaga and Hideyoshi, had found a divided people, torn by civil strife. They had welded the land together and the Tokugawa had carefully regulated and regimented it. To the new regime this unity and regimentation were of great advantage. Because of it the government could direct the transformation which followed. Indeed, the approach to totalitarianism which marked the 1930's and 1940's had been in preparation under the Tokugawa Shogunate.

Now was speeded up the adoption of Western culture which had been haltingly begun under the last years of the Tokugawa. Every phase of Japanese life was ultimately affected. The change was engineered from the top. This was in contrast with China, where the ruling classes were setting themselves against innovation and where the revolution, when it eventually broke, was chiefly from the bottom, that is to say, led mainly by new men who came up from the masses. In Japan the leadership was taken chiefly by *samurai* and a few of the *kuge*. They effected the changes without destroying the major features of the inherited political, social, and ideological structure of the nation.

Political Changes, 1867–1894

The Meiji Restoration was followed by a reorganization of the government. The process was to continue past 1894, and, indeed, has never been terminated. Yet by 1894 the framework of what was to continue into the 1940's had been constructed. It was within that framework or behind it as a facade that later alterations were to be effected.

Outwardly the changes were impressive. To a large degree they were real as well as apparent. Yet it is highly important to note that, as in the days more than a thousand years earlier when Chinese political institutions were adopted, so now when lessons were being learned from the Occident the importations were fitted into existing Japanese patterns. The imperial institution was preserved and its honor emphasized, and many of the old families continued to be powerful. The situation was very different from that in China after the downfall of the Manchus (1912), for there a basic revolution occurred by which a fairly clean sweep was made of the inherited machinery of the central administration and a successor was developed only slowly and with much pain.

One of the striking innovations was the reversal of the attitude of the Emperor and the western feudatories toward isolation. Relations with Western powers were accepted and the government expressed its purpose to observe the treaty commitments made by the

Shogun. Indeed, in 1868 several of the *daimyo*, including Choshu and Satsuma, previously bitterly antiforeign, memorialized the throne in support of foreign relations and of the reception of foreign envoys after the manner in vogue in the Occident.

This surprising *volte face* was due to a number of factors. Among them was the circumstance that the former opposition now had the responsibility and found isolation untenable. There was also the demonstration of the superior force of the West presented in convincing form to Satsuma and Choshu in the bombardments of Kagoshima and the Shimonoseki forts. The foreigner might not be liked, but obviously he must be accepted and Japan must learn from him how to meet him with his own weapons. Then, too, several of the younger *samurai* attached to the western fiefs had become persuaded of the necessity of learning from the Occident and had helped to reverse the attitude of their feudal superiors. Some of these young men we shall meet along the way.

We shall later return to the course of foreign relations. However, if we are to understand the changes which took place we must note that the administration was now committed to intercourse with the West and was disposed to learn from the Occident. It recognized that for better or for worse it had been ushered into a new world and that the Empire would be wise if it acquired from that world whatever would enable it to enhance its prosperity and power. The majority of the thoughtful Japanese who took this attitude did not cease to be patriotic, nor did they wish to discard Japan's inherited culture. Rather they would adopt whatever would help Japan to be a major force in the new age and would fit in with what had come to them from their ancestors in such fashion as to emphasize features that they deemed of the essence of Japan's historic soul.

Antiforeignism did not immediately die out. Murderous attacks on aliens by ardent patriots continued into the new regime. Notable among these was the assault by two *samurai* on the retinue of the British Minister while the latter was on his way for audience with the Emperor. The prompt punishment of the guilty and an imperial edict decreeing the death penalty for such outrages made clear the policy of the government.

The added emphasis upon the Emperor was central in the new regime. To be sure, the Emperor was to act through his ministers and must not too actively or publicly take the initiative. Yet his descent from ages eternal through a divine ancestry and his own divinity were stressed. Everything was to be done in his name. In contrast with the innocuous if theoretically revered desuetude which had been his place under the Tokugawa, the Emperor was now to be magnified. Loyalty to him was the touchstone of patriotism. Any disrespect to him, as the Japanese defined disrespect, was the major crime. It was not just disrespect. It was both high treason and sacrilege.

The Meiji Emperor fitted admirably into the enhanced role of the crown. As a lad his tutors had accustomed him to Spartan discipline. He came to the throne at the tender age of fourteen, young enough to adapt himself to the new age. He was hard working, intelligent, and tactful, and wisely influenced policy in such a manner that it seems impossible to determine accurately what originated with him and what with his ministers. He lived through the decades of the great transition and the title of his reign is that of an era.

The new regime was dominated by some of the court nobles (*kuge*) and by the southern feudatories—Satsuma, Choshu, Hizen, and Tosa. When the new navy was built, Satsuma men were in control of it, and Choshu's was long the major voice in the new army.

The new masters felt their way toward administrative reorganization but did not hesitate at drastic measures when these seemed advisable. At first there was an attempt to revive the structure of pre-*Bakufu* days. However, a resurrection of an ancient system obviously could not meet the need.

In 1868 the young Emperor read a brief statement to his officials which has been called a "Charter Oath." Its phrases were capable of various translations and interpretations but it became the document to which the later structural changes looked back for their authority. It clearly sided with the reformers. Mixed with reaffirmations of the Empire and of principles formerly derived from China, it seemed to promise deliberative assemblies, decisions based upon public opinion (or, according to another translation, impartial discussion), and the search for wisdom and ability throughout the world.

There was still a sharp division of opinion among the articulate groups as to how far Westernization should proceed. Some wished no accommodation to Occidental ways. Others would go far in adopting the culture of Europe.

In the experimental period the latter so far won out as to obtain assemblies which seemed to foreshadow a Parliament. Moreover, the Emperor moved his residence from Kyoto, with its memories of imperial impotence, to Yedo, the seat of the *Shogun* and, as such, the capital from which the actual administration had been conducted. Yedo was renamed Tokyo, "Eastern Capital."

The End of Feudalism

Under the new conditions and with the abolition of the *Bakufu,* feudalism was rapidly becoming an anachronism. It had been decaying under the long peace brought by the Tokugawa. Memorials to the throne, asking for the abolition of feudalism, began to come in. In 1869 the four feudatories of the southwest, Choshu, Satsuma, Hizen, and Tosa, which had led in the Restoration, set the example of offering their possessions and their men to the Emperor with the purpose of strengthening the centralized rule by the crown and of ending the internal divisions brought by feudalism. The vast majority of the other *daimyo* followed with similar offers.

This remarkable movement was due in part to enthusiasm for the Emperor and his revived power. It came also through pressure from the reformers. Then, too, in many of the fiefs the actual administration had long been in the hands of the retainers rather than the *daimyo.* Moreover, the *daimyo* were appointed governors of their former estates and were assigned one-tenth of their former revenues, while the costs of local government formerly borne by them and the pensions of the *samurai* were to be paid out of taxes and were no longer to be met by the feudal lords. In 1871 an imperial decree ordered the end of feudalism. For a time pensions were given the ex-*daimyo* and ex-*samurai.* Since the cost proved a heavy burden on the national exchequer, in 1873 commutation of these was begun by the payment of a lump sum. In 1876 commutation was made compulsory.

The end of feudalism meant the termination of a system which had begun a thousand years or more before. The attitudes engendered in so long a history could not be quickly erased by fiat, even though that were issued by a divine Emperor. Yet financially and to a certain extent socially most of the *daimyo* and *samurai* suffered. The *samurai* especially were uprooted from their accustomed privileged status.

In general the abolition of feudalism was of advantage to the peasant farmers. Under feudalism the peasants had been bound to the soil and were subject to galling imposts. Step by step many of the hereditary restrictions were withdrawn. Taxes in rice were replaced by taxes in money. Land was revalued and the form of land tenure was altered.

The New Army

A highly significant sequel of the end of feudalism was a change in the character of the army. No longer was the army exclusively from the *samurai*. Indeed, in 1872, the year after the decree ending feudalism, came the beginnings of conscription. In the preceding decade there had been experiments in recruiting militia from the peasantry. Now a nation-wide plan was instituted of building the army from men of all ranks of society. This meant a nation in arms. It also meant that in time the ex-clansmen who for a while controlled the new army would be supplanted by leaders of lowly origin. For decades Choshu was potent in the army, but eventually it was displaced.

Passing Social Distinctions

Related to the legal erasure of feudalism and the beginning of universal military service was the removal of some of the former social distinctions. All *samurai* were required (1876) to lay aside their swords, long the insignia of their rank. The distinction between the court nobility, or *kuge*, and the military was canceled and the two groups were merged in one nobility. The hereditary dishonor imposed upon the *eta* or *hinin* was abolished.

The legal actions decreeing these changes could be taken, but popular attitudes were stubborn and in practice the distinctions tended to persist. The *kuge* still had prestige. The *eta* continued to live in distinct quarters and to be poverty-stricken and despised.

New Political Institutions

Fairly rapidly political institutions were introduced which in part had Western prototypes. A civil bureaucracy was organized. This first found a model and precedent in the reforms of the seventh and eighth centuries, when Chinese institutions were being introduced. It also showed the influence of Occidental systems. At the outset the bureaucracy was largely recruited from the *samurai*, but no one was allowed to hold office in the fief in which he had been born, and recruitment through competitive civil service examinations became the method of admission to the service.

Preparation for a Constitution and a Parliament

Among those who were learning from the West there came, notably in the 1880's, an uncritical enthusiasm for Occidental culture and a swift adoption of many of the outward trappings of Western civilization. This was in no small degree due to the desire to be rid of extraterritoriality and the conventional tariff, regarded as badges of inferiority, and to be admitted to the family of nations on the basis of full equality.

One change which these lovers of the Occident advocated was the introduction of parliamentary institutions. A Parliament had seemed to be foreshadowed in the Charter Oath. Various attempts at assemblies were made, but did not prove satisfactory. Late in 1877 the demand increased and in 1878 a plan for local assemblies was announced. In 1881 the government promised that in 1890 a National Assembly would be convened and a constitution would be granted.

In preparation for this drastic step Ito, one of the younger statesmen, a former *samurai* of Choshu, who had come to the fore in the transition, was sent to the West to study the constitutions in use there. On his return to Japan he became head of a commission to draft the document. Ito, it may be added, had as a youth become convinced of the necessity of opening the country and learning from the Occident. In 1863 he and four others braved the edicts which still made it a capital offense to go abroad and went to London. When Choshu became embroiled with the powers, Ito hurried home to persuade his superiors of the folly of their attitude. In doing this he came into grave peril, but after the Meiji Restoration and the frank acceptance of the West, he rapidly rose in the government.

Ito was impressed with the institutions of Germany and felt that the conditions in that country more nearly approximated those of Japan than did those in any other major country in the West. In the 1880's he remade the cabinet to a form corresponding somewhat with that in Germany. As a preliminary to the creation of an upper house of Parliament he reorganized the nobility. He included in it the ancient court nobility (*kuge*) and former members of the upper ranks of the military class. New men who had emerged in the Restoration were also added to it.

The prospect of a Parliament accentuated the impulse toward the development of political parties. However, their course was not particularly promising for the future of such endeavors.

Armed Opposition

All these rapid changes were not without opposition. In 1877 it took the form of revolt in Satsuma. Several causes gave rise to the rebellion. There was dissatisfaction over depriving the ex-*samurai* of their swords and creating an army on the basis of universal service. Many of the ex-*samurai* were also unhappy over what seemed to them a supine policy toward Korea. Korea had declined to enter into friendly relations with the new regime in Japan, and Japanese missions sent to reopen them were rebuffed. A strong war party advocated vigorous punitive measures. More moderate counsels prevailed. In 1875 a Japanese ship was fired on by the Koreans. The Japanese government did not declare war but contented itself with taking a leaf out of its experience with Commodore Perry and sent a strong naval and military expedition which, without breaking the peace, obtained a treaty (1876). This document recognized Korea as independent. To the war party that seemed derogatory to Japan's dignity. Korea was tributary to China and for Japan to regard her as independent appeared to put her on an equality with Japan and so to place Japan in the category of states inferior to China. Moreover, many of the ex-*samurai* were indignant over the forced commutation of their pensions.

The discontent found a leader in Saigo. Imposing in person, able, the embodiment of the ideals of the *samurai*, Saigo had trained some of the youth of his class in the martial exercises of the past. The revolt did not have the support of all of Satsuma. The ex-*daimyo* of Satsuma opposed it and the head of the imperial ministry was from Satsuma.

Against the ex-*samurai* uprising the government brought the new conscript army. The latter was easily the victor. True to the traditions of his class, Saigo, wounded, asked a friend to cut off his head that it might not come into the possession of the enemy. The friend complied and escaped with the gory trophy.

The Japanese Constitution

In 1889 the commission headed by Ito had completed the framing of the constitution and the document was promulgated. The constitution was the gift of the Emperor, not the work of a popularly elected assembly. Coming as it did from the divine Emperor, it had about it an aura of sanctity. When, in the 1930's and 1940's, pressure was brought on the then Emperor to alter it, he could plead that, since it was the deed of his grandfather, any tampering with it would be unfilial, a major offense on his part, especially since the grandfather was the revered Meiji Emperor. In its wording, therefore, the constitution was not changed until after 1945.

In general the constitution took as its model the corresponding document of Bavaria, but with important modifications to meet the situation peculiar to Japan. It first spoke of the Emperor. He was declared to be sacred and inviolable, in a line which had been "unbroken from ages eternal." He was the source of all authority and combined in himself all sovereignty. His was the supreme command of the army and navy. With him rested the declaration of war and the making of peace. He was to sanction all laws and to order them promulgated and executed. He was to convoke and prorogue the Parliament (or Diet), and when that body was not sitting he could issue ordinances which had the force of law. In practice these various functions were performed through his ministers. These ministers were not, as in Great Britain, responsible to Parliament. That body could embarrass them and impede their program. They were, however, responsible to the Emperor. Their choice was determined by many factors. Various groups which existed or arose apart from the constitution, although not necessarily in contradiction to it, had a voice in the decision.

In some ways the position of the Emperor was not unlike that of the King of England. In both countries the government was in the name of the monarch. The monarch was the fountain of power, but he must not openly make decisions and his ministers must assume responsibility for his acts. Yet in very important ways the Emperor of Japan differed from the King of England. The succession was not, as in England, fixed by act of Parliament. The Emperor was not subject to Parliament. He did not rule "by the grace of God." He himself was divine and was of divine ancestry.

The rights of the Emperor's subjects were also defined by the constitution. All Japanese were eligible for office. Subject to regulations placed by law they could change their place of abode and exercise freedom of speech, public assembly, writing, association, and religion. Their houses were exempt from search. They could not be arrested except according to law and could be tried only by legally appointed judges. Their property was inviolate and they had the right of petition. Superficially this section somewhat resembled a Bill of Rights. However, the rights were distinctly limited by the regulations and procedures authorized in the limiting phrase, "all according to law."

Subjects had duties, including the payment of taxes and military service. These, too, were to be defined by law and not to be levied through the whim of individual officials.

The imperial Parliament or Diet (the two names have been used interchangeably by Japanese writing in English) was to consist of two chambers, the House of Peers and the House of Representatives. The former was composed of members of the imperial family and of the two higher ranks of the nobility, of representatives elected by their peers from the three lower ranks of nobility, of certain imperial appointees, and of some of the highest taxpayers chosen by their fellows. The first three groups were life members. The last two had seven-year terms. The lower house was purely elective. At the outset a fairly high property qualification was placed upon the franchise. As time passed the base was greatly broadened. Parliament was to be convened at least annually and its sessions were to last for a minimum of three months. Special sessions might be convoked. Members of Parliament were to have freedom from arrest and freedom of speech. No law could be passed without the consent of Parliament, and Parliament could initiate legislation. No new tax could be levied without the authorization of Parliament, and the annual budget must have its approval. However, Parliament's financial competence did not extend to the expenditures of the Imperial Household. If Parliament declined to pass a budget, that of the preceding year was to be repeated. The Emperor could veto any and all legislation. Parliament could put questions to the several cabinet members. Parliament might address the crown and could use this privilege virtually to impeach a cabinet minister.

It will be noted that the Parliament of Japan did not have as large powers as the British Parliament. It did not have such extensive control of the purse. The cabinet was not so closely dependent on Parliament as was that of Britain. However, the constitution was so drafted as to allow flexibility in the development of parliamentary institutions. The power of Parliament over administration might be increased. There was nothing in the document to prevent the emergence of a cabinet entirely responsible to Parliament. In practice, too, the place of Parliament might be greatly reduced. Yet Parliament could not be completely dispensed with without violating the constitution.

There was a Privy Council appointed by the Emperor and to be used by him for personal consultation.

Extraconstitutional Institutions and Practices

Outside the constitution, but not in violation of it, institutions and practices arose which became important.

Long the most powerful of these was the *Genro* or Elder Statesmen. The *Genro* were some of the leaders in the reorganization of the Empire. The majority were *samurai* of Satsuma and Choshu. The institution was in conformity with Japanese tradition, by which the oldest members of the family were consulted on matters of importance, and by which the actual power was often exercised by others than those to whom it was formally entrusted. The *Genro* were particularly influential in the closing decades of the nineteenth and the opening years of the twentieth centuries. As the original circle was depleted by death it was only partially recruited. The last of the *Genro*, a late addition, Prince Saionji, survived into the stirring and stormy changes of the 1930's. With his passing the institution vanished.

One of the most important practices was that by which the army and navy could control the formation of cabinets. In the 1890's, under the favoring atmosphere of a war with China, it was ruled by an ordinance issued through the Privy Council that the Minister of the Navy must be a high-ranking naval officer and the Minister of the Army a high army officer. At first these were limited to the active list. Later they might include also those on the reserve lists. Moreover, in 1889 it was ordered that the Ministers of War and Navy might have direct access to the Emperor. No one could serve in these positions without the consent of the inner circle in the respective services. That meant that the army and the navy could, if so minded, prevent the formation of a cabinet and could see that the holders of the other portfolios were at least partly to their mind. At times this control was exercised more drastically than at others. Moreover, this position, with other factors, made the armed services largely independent of civilian control. The traditional dual government, with its sharp distinction between the military and the civil authorities, was in effect revived and perpetuated. As in feudal days, the military were largely distinct from civil officials. At times Parliament, through its partial control of the purse, could exercise a restraining influence, but the military tended to seek the dominance which had been that of their class under the *Bakufu*.

The Inauguration of Parliamentary Institutions

The first years of Parliament proved stormy. They were marked chiefly by a struggle between the cabinet and the political parties. The political parties became active, and there was a strong demand that the cabinet be made responsible to the lower house. The first House of Representatives had a majority opposed to the government. The budget became the chief bone of contention. In the second Parliament the government attempted to obtain the election of its candidates and to this end did not hesitate to employ bribery, intimidation, and even violence. Yet again it could command only a minority in the lower house. The upper house as a rule sided with the government. Ito, the chief framer of the constitution, felt himself obliged to take the premiership, but even he found the task difficult. He made compromises on the budget, but the opposition shifted to other policies. The third House of Representatives was also at variance with the ministry. It was only the war with China which brought a temporary lull in the struggle.

Changes in Religion

Religious movements paralleled the reorganization of the political structure of the nation and in the main bolstered the enhanced emphasis upon the Emperor.

The most widely influential was the revival and strengthening of Shinto. This reenforced the position of the Emperor and nourished the already intense patriotism of his subjects. It will be recalled that Shinto was an outgrowth of the primitive religion of Japan and antedated the advent of Chinese culture. From China and Korea had come Buddhism and from China Confucianism and some Taoist conceptions. Confucianism did not take the guise of a formal cult as it did in China, but its literature was extensively studied and it was very influential, especially among the educated. Buddhism was powerful and had been so for centuries. Confucianism and Buddhism continued into the new era, but with diminished prestige. Confucianism still was potent in ethics. Buddhism was virtually disestablished by a decree of 1871. Between 1867 and 1872 there was even active persecution of Buddhism. The long existing union of Buddhism and Shinto was abrogated and prohibited. Many Buddhist temples were destroyed. Buddhist ceremonies in the imperial palace were estopped and members of the imperial family were commanded to leave Buddhist orders. Yet the great Buddhist sects or schools remained wealthy and their ideals and teachings were important in the life of the nation. Buddhism was much more vigorous than in contemporary China or Korea. However, under the new regime Shinto was stressed by the government.

Shinto was divided into two main branches. On the one hand was what was called sect Shinto. This was made up of a number of movements, several of which attracted a wide following. Some of the strongest of these were of eighteenth and nineteenth century origin. On the other hand was state Shinto. The government declared that sect Shinto was in the category of religion and supervised it, with Buddhism, through the Department of Religion. State Shinto it classed as distinct from sect Shinto, as purely patriotic and not a religion, and placed it in charge of a separate bureau. Remnants of a cult which combined Shinto with Buddhism, assimilating the former to the latter, were eliminated. Shinto was exalted and its uniqueness inculcated. State Shinto stressed the imperial shrines at Ise, the imperial house and its ancestors, and the national heroes. It made much of the myths of the divine origin of the imperial family and of the nation itself. While the educated might know them to be myths, they were taught as historical fact. The shrines of state Shinto were multiplied and attendance on them was eventually made compulsory for school children. An especially important sanctuary was erected in 1869 in Tokyo to those who had died in war in recent Japanese history and was given the name "the Nation-protecting Shrine." The centers of state Shinto were frequented by both soldiers and civilians.

Whether state Shinto should be classed as a religion was a matter of debate among foreign scholars. Unquestionably, however, it inculcated a devotion to the Emperor more widespread and intense than Japan had thus far known. It provided the emotional and mystical basis for the fevered nationalism of the 1930's and 1940's with its fanatical conviction of the invincibility of Japan, of the superiority of the Japanese and their culture, and of the mission of Japan in Eastern Asia and the world as a whole.

The revival of Shinto was typically Japanese. It had begun under the later years of the Tokugawa. It was an example of the fashion in which the revolution which followed the Meiji Restoration was in part a return to Japan's past. As centuries earlier the introduction of Chinese culture had been used to enhance the position of the imperial clan and of a few noble families rather than to weaken them, so now Occidental culture was adopted in such a manner that the basic features distinctive of Japanese national life were emphasized rather than discarded.

Less influential in the life of the nation as a whole than the reinvigoration of Shinto was the growth of Christianity. Yet that faith, so long proscribed, had a rapid increase in numbers and an even more remarkable advance in its effect upon the country.

It was late in the 1850's before Christian missionaries could establish themselves in the land, and then it was only in the open ports. Nor was it then possible to do much to win converts.

To the intense surprise of the missionaries, it was discovered that in the hills back of Nagasaki, in a region where it had been especially strong in the sixteenth century, Christianity had survived. In spite of the persistent effort of the Tokugawa to eradicate every trace of the hated and feared foreign religion, Christian teaching, prayers, and baptism had been secretly perpetuated in a constituency several thousand strong. The disclosure of the hidden Christians was followed by a renewal of persecution, but not in the extreme forms of the seventeenth century. Many of the Christians joined themselves to the church of their fathers. Many others held aloof.

In contrast with the sixteenth century, when Christian missionary activity was entirely by Roman Catholics, missionaries now came from the Roman Catholic, Russian Orthodox, and Protestant communions. There were many more Protestant than Roman Catholic missionaries. The large majority of the Protestants were from the United States and most of the Roman Catholics were from France. Protestantism grew more rapidly than either of the other two main branches of the Church and eventually outnumbered them both. It had its strength chiefly in the cities and among the ex-*samurai* and educated classes. That was partly because the educated were susceptible to Western influences and because many of them had acquired something of their Occidental education through the missionaries.

Anti-Christian edict boards were removed early in the 1870's. This was not done out of any change in the inner temper of the rulers. The latter were no more tolerant in principle than before. It was because they were seeking a revision of the treaties to eliminate extraterritoriality and the conventional tariff and admit Japan to the family of nations on the basis of full equality. Since Christianity seemed to them the religion of the West and since persecution had already brought protests from the powers, on the ground of national expediency the Japanese authorities were prepared to cease active obstructionist tactics.

The numerical growth of Christianity dated from this time. It was particularly rapid in the 1880's, a decade when the enthusiasm for things Occidental was marked. There was even an influential non-Christian publicist, previously anti-Christian; who in that decade advocated that in order to gain prestige in the Occident Japan should become officially Christian. During the revulsion of feeling which followed in the 1890's with something of an antiforeign sentiment, the increase slowed down. In 1894 Christians were less than one-half of one per cent of the population.

However, Christians exerted an influence much greater than their numbers would have led one to expect. Particularly in philanthropy, in social and moral reform, in education, and in creating an international outlook they were potent. Buddhism copied and adapted some of the methods of the churches. The supranational nature of Christianity was in contrast with the intense and narrow nationalism nurtured by Shinto. Yet open conflict was largely avoided in the two decades that preceded 1894.

It was characteristic of the strength of Japanese nationalism that Japanese Christians were eager to achieve ecclesiastical independence of the foreign missionary and to place a Japanese stamp upon the faith which had come to them from the Occident.

Intellectual Changes

In no way was the revolution which followed the opening of the country more striking than in the field of education. Even before the Meiji Restoration eager students were beginning to go to Europe and America, although surreptitiously and contrary to law. On their return to Japan many of them became leaders in the transition. After the transformation had begun, hundreds followed in their wake. Japan literally went to school to the West.

Moreover, the Japanese worked out an educational system on Western models. In 1872 a law was passed which became the basis for universal compulsory primary education. From the primary schools the system pyramided upward through secondary schools to universities. In addition to the government system, private schools were created, some of them maintained by Christian missions, others of them purely secular. Teachers were imported from abroad. The curricula were combinations of Western and Japanese subjects. Chinese characters continued to be employed. Western science and technical subjects were studied. Occidental languages were taught, notably English.

For some reason, the Japanese were not fluent in Western languages. Most Japanese found them easier to read than to speak and few acquired a good vernacular use of English. This may have been because the Japanese distrusted volubility. The lack of oral facility in foreign tongues is said to have contributed to the Japanese reluctance to join in international conferences with Western peoples. Most of their best men were so awkward in the spoken use of Western languages that they felt themselves at a disadvantage in gatherings where these were official.

Thousands of books were translated from Western languages into Japanese. These included scientific works and volumes of history, political science, drama, and fiction. With their eagerness to keep abreast of the times, the Japanese put into their own language the books that were currently most influential in the West. Fresh combinations of the convenient Chinese characters were devised to express the new ideas which were pouring in.

Newspapers appeared and multiplied. Various periodicals were inaugurated. For the masses a journalistic style was developed which was simple and approached the vernacular. The new ideas were being brought to the man in the street. The government felt itself driven to place curbs on the press. In 1875 a press law was promulgated, and from time to time newspapers were suspended and editors imprisoned.

In the waves of popularity of things Western, new movements in thought in the West quickly made themselves felt in Japan. Yet basically the Japanese mind was but slightly altered. Some individuals were greatly changed, but the rank and file of the nation, while adopting the tools of the West, thought in much the same ethical, spiritual, and social terms as had their ancestors. The adoption of things Western was due to patriotic pride and a desire not to be weak or backward as a nation. Western learning was made to subserve historic Japanese ideals and to strengthen the country.

Economic Changes

Very striking in the years of change was the adoption of the mechanical appliances of the Occident. The industrial revolution was brought to Japan. Factories were erected, railways and telegraph lines were built, steamships were constructed, foreign trade grew, and currency and banking were developed according to Western patterns.

The government took the lead. This was in accord with the general character of the revolution, for in most realms the changes were directed by the state. Moreover, it was in part due to the fact that very little capital had been accumulated in private hands in Tokugawa times and that few of the existing men of wealth were willing to take the risks entailed in inaugurating the new enterprises. Then, too, the state alone had the credit necessary to borrow the foreign capital which was required.

In accomplishing the economic revolution the state made extensive use of existing private concerns. It developed model industries and then turned them over at low prices to some of the great financial houses. As a result, certain families acquired an outstanding place in industry, commerce, and banking. Of these the wealthiest and most powerful were the Mitsui. Next were the Mitsubishi. These two family concerns, together with two of much smaller dimensions, Sumitomo and Yasuda, came to be known as the *Zaibatsu*. As we saw in an earlier chapter, the Mitsui claimed descent from the ancient and highly aristocratic Fujiwara, but in Tokugawa times they had become commoners that they might engage in trade in banking. They were organized as a family, but, in accord with characteristic Japanese tradition, the actual management was in the hands of men not of Mitsui blood. The Mitsubishi had also come down from the days of the Tokugawa. In general, the *Zaibatsu* were a kind of business department of the state, not using their wealth primarily for themselves. They drew into their service the flower of the nation's business ability.

True to its intense nationalism, the government was averse to borrowing more from abroad than seemed imperative, for loans from foreigners might mean foreign control and so jeopardize the jealously cherished national autonomy.

From the same desire to strengthen the nation as against foreign powers, those industries were stressed which would assist the army and navy and which would compete with foreign products at home or abroad. Arsenals, foundries, and shipyards were built. Mines were opened. Cotton mills, paper mills, chemical works, and factories for producing glass and cement were erected. By 1890 over two hundred steam factories were in existence. It was not until after 1895, however, that the most striking industrial developments occurred.

The first railway, between Tokyo and Yokohama, was built by the state in 1872. The state also promoted other railways and constructed them directly or through companies which it aided. Later privately owned lines predominated for a time, but eventually the railways were nationalized. The state also built telegraph lines and in 1886 consolidated them with the postal service under a joint bureau. It was the government which introduced the telephone—in 1877.

The first steamships were mostly owned by foreigners, but before long steamers were being built and owned in Japan. Here again the government gave assistance through companies which it subsidized.

Before 1894 foreign commerce was not impressive. Not until after 1887 did it exceed fifty million dollars a year. It then grew more rapidly, partly because of active supervision by the state and partly because of the rise of modern industry. Only after 1894 did foreign trade begin to assume really large dimensions. In the first few decades after Perry, commerce chiefly passed through the hands of foreign middlemen. Fairly early, however, the foreigner was eliminated or subordinated.

In the Meiji period the currency was thoroughly reorganized. In feudal days many kinds of money had circulated and each *daimyo* felt at liberty to issue his own paper. After the Meiji Restoration the currency was nationalized and made uniform. Partly following the example of the United States, the decimal notation was introduced and a system of national banks and paper currency was inaugurated. At first both gold and silver were used, but the country was quickly drained of its gold. This was because at the coming of Perry the ratio between the two metals had been one to four. Since the ratio in the West was then one to fifteen or sixteen, foreign speculators, by buying up the gold with their cheaper silver, soon took most of the yellow metal out of the land and the country was left practically on a silver basis. Not until after 1895 was the currency put on gold. Before many years (1881) the banking system was drastically modified by the creation of a central institution, the Bank of Japan. To assist in foreign trade and foreign exchange, a secondary institution later the Yokohama Specie Bank, was organized. Through the latter foreign commerce was for a time taken over by the state and a specie reserve was gathered. The power to issue notes was removed from the older national banks and was restricted to the Bank of Japan. Postal savings banks were introduced.

Laws and Courts

The Japanese were stimulated to reorganize their laws and courts by the desire to be freed from extraterritoriality. Extraterritoriality was to them a galling badge of national inferiority, but before the Western powers would agree to its abolition and to the extension of Japanese laws and courts to their nationals, Japan would have to satisfy them that the latter would be dealt with justly as that word was understood in the Occident. A new civil code was compiled after Western models. The code of commercial law took that of Germany for its pattern, and the criminal code followed French precedents. In 1890 the codes finally received imperial approval. Judges, specially trained, were appointed to serve for life or for good behavior. Not until late in the 1890's was the entire civil code promulgated. The code of civil procedure went into effect in 1892. The commercial code was not put into force until 1899.

Treaty Revision

Not long after the codes went into full operation, the Japanese obtained their desire in the decision of the powers to surrender extraterritoriality. At the same time the powers agreed to grant Japan tariff autonomy. However, these concessions came only after long agitation and repeated negotiations. Before they were finally achieved the Japanese patience had been worn thin.

In 1872 the question of the revision of treaties of 1858 might, according to those documents, be raised. Accordingly, in that year a mission, headed by Iwakura, a former *kuge*, was sent to the West for that purpose. The United States proved willing to alter its treaty in the direction desired by the Japanese. However, the modification was not consummated, for the Japanese wished a general conference of the powers, to be held in Europe, to effect the revision in all the documents, and to that procedure the United States would not agree. The Iwakura Mission was followed by the establishment of continuing Japanese legations in several of the capitals of the Occident.

In 1878 the United States agreed to the Japanese regulation of tariffs and coasting trade, but the treaty was not to go into effect until the other powers took similar action, and in that there was delay.

In the 1880's, after the revision of the criminal code, the Japanese government again sought the removal of extraterritoriality. Repeated conferences were held with the representatives of the powers. In general the United States proved friendly, but the powers stipulated that foreign judges should sit in Japanese courts until 1903 and, although acceding to an increase in the tariff, still insisted upon fixing it by treaty. To these restrictions the Japanese would not assent.

Japan now pursued the policy of negotiating separately with individual foreign governments. In 1889 Mexico, which had few nationals in Japan and but little commerce with that country, entered into a treaty on the principle of tariff autonomy, no extraterritoriality, and reciprocal freedom of travel, trade, and residence. In 1889, soon after the constitution was proclaimed, several of the powers agreed to a modification of the conventional tariff and of extraterritoriality. This, however, was less than public opinion in Japan demanded and Okuma, the minister who had conducted the negotiations, was seriously wounded by a bomb thrown by a patriotic ex-*samurai.*

When conversations with the powers were again reopened, they were first of all pushed with Great Britain, the country which had the largest stake in trade and the most resident citizens. In 1894 Great Britain consented to a revision which provided for the end of consular jurisdiction and foreign settlements in 1899, for an increase in the tariff, and for reciprocal rights of travel, residence, commerce, and religion. The United States soon followed, but took the further step of omitting a conventional tariff. Other powers fell into line. Extraterritoriality came to an end in 1899. It must be noted that these changes, while obtained in the year of the outbreak of the Sino-Japanese war, were not conceded because of the Japanese success in that conflict. Great Britain, the key power, had agreed to them before the outbreak of hostilities. Nor was full tariff autonomy gained until later. Japan was only slowly being admitted to the family of nations as defined by the West.

Japan Prepares to Enlarge Her Empire

In the years before 1894 Japan was preparing for the great expansion of her empire which was achieved in the half-century after that year. Indeed, by 1894 she had begun the acquisition of territory.

Even in her years of seclusion Japan had had those who urged a vigorous Continental policy. The eastward march of Russia awakened fears and ambitions. Late in the eighteenth century there was proposed the acquisition of Kamchatka and Sakhalin. In the 1850's Yoshida Shoin sought to go abroad to study Western civilization that he might use it to strengthen Japan. He failed to leave the country and for an abortive attempt to overthrow the *Bakufu*, in 1859, was executed. In the meantime he had advocated the seizure of Formosa, Korea, part of Manchuria, Sakhalin, Kamchatka, and the Philippines, and wished the Empire to acquire features of Occidental civilization to chastise the foreigners. Among his pupils were Ito, the framer of the constitution, and Yamagata, who was the chief creator of the new Japanese army. By no means all the leading men of the Empire were committed to his program, but he represented a strain of opinion which was to become dominant in later years, notably in the 1930's and 1940's.

In building her new army and navy Japan was acquiring tools which might be used in implementing a policy of expansion. That was not her sole purpose in bringing them into being. In emerging into a world which already relied largely on force, Japan felt that she must arm in self-defense. However, in equipping herself in this fashion, she was drilling the younger generation in a confident and ambitious patriotism which could be called to support foreign conquest.

The army, as we have said, was largely the work of Yamagata. He was an ex-*samurai* of Choshu and had his opportunity through the triumph of the Western fiefs over the Tokugawa. With several others, he was sent to the West in 1870, soon after the Meiji Restoration, to study Occidental military organization and methods. Foreign military experts were obtained to aid in the formation of the new conscript army. At first France was the chief source. However, Prussian precedent, given prestige by the decisive victory in the Franco-Prussian War, was the example to which the army chiefs turned for guidance. Yamagata, a strong militarist by conviction and an advocate of a vigorous Continental program, did much to shape the ideals of the officers. He became, too, prominent in politics and in that position helped to influence the policy of the Empire.

The navy found its model in the fleet that dominated the high seas in the nineteenth century, that of Great Britain. British naval officers were employed to assist the organization. In the navy, as we have noted, former clansmen from Satsuma were mainly in control.

In the growing army and navy Japan had instruments to support the territorial ambitions which many of her leaders cherished.

Expansion Begins

It was not long after the Meiji Restoration that the policy of territorial expansion began to be implemented. This did not imply a definite schedule unanimously adopted and consistently followed. There was much of opportunism and the leaders were far from being in complete agreement. However, that acquisition of territories was begun which in the twentieth century swelled to such portentous proportions.

The island of Yezo was early brought more fully within imperial administration. Under the Tokugawa it had been in the domains of one of the *daimyo*, but its population was predominantly of the aboriginal Ainu and very few Japanese were to be found there. Japanese settlement and the economic development of the island were now encouraged. Administratively Yezo was called the *Hokkaido*, or Northern Sea Circuit. American experts were employed to assist in the planning for what in effect was a frontier region.

The government was eager to acquire both Sakhalin and the Kuriles, strategically located off the northern borders. Here Russian rivalry proved an obstacle. Under the Japanese-Russian treaty of 1858 Sakhalin was declared the joint possession of the two empires. Later the Shogunate proposed a division with the fiftieth parallel of latitude as the boundary, but no agreement was reached. In 1875 Japan surrendered her claims to the island in return for the withdrawal of Russian claims to the Kuriles. Japan now became the acknowledged owner of that chain of islands.

In 1878 the Bonin Islands, a desolate group in the Pacific with potential strategic importance, were annexed.

The Ryukyu Islands presented a somewhat anomalous picture. Their inhabitants were related to the Japanese by blood and language. For more than two centuries they had been considered part of the fief of Satsuma, for they had been subdued by the *daimyo* of that feudatory. Yet they had been paying "tribute" to China for a still longer time, they had their own ruler, and their prince had entered into treaty relations with some of the Western powers. In the early 1870's Japan cut the Gordian knot by exacting redress for the murder on Formosa of some inhabitants of the Ryukyus who had been shipwrecked on that island. Formosa was then part of China, and Japan, by demanding satisfaction for the Ryukyuans, claimed the latter as her subjects. China both denied Japan's authority in the Ryukyus and disclaimed responsibility for the Formosans. Japan thereupon (1874) sent a punitive expedition to Formosa and occupied a part of that island until China paid an indemnity. Japan also persuaded the Prince or King of the Ryukyu Islands to surrender his treaties with Western nations and to accept the rule of Tokyo. China was still unreconciled and declined to agree to a suggested division of the group between herself and Japan. Japan, however, persisted and retained possession of all the Ryukyus.

The Korean Issue Commits Japan to Continental Expansion

In view of Japan's long historic interests in the peninsula, and in view of the expansionist sentiment among so many of the influential men in the Empire, it was all but inevitable that a strong Korean policy should be pursued. Even though the government did not take at once the drastic action demanded by Saigo and his followers, it was not disposed to look on inactively while Korea was being drawn into the whirl of world politics. In the early centuries of her history Japan had been potent in southern Korea. On the eve of Tokugawa exclusion, Hideyoshi had engineered a large-scale invasion of the land as a preliminary step in his grandiose project for the conquest of China. Beginning early in the seventeenth century and continuing into the fore part of the nineteenth century, Korea had sent "tribute" to Japan as well as to China.

In the new day brought by the nineteenth century enhancement of Occidental interest in the Far East, Korea was peculiarly important geographically. Jutting out as it did from the mainland of East Asia, the peninsula commanded the approach from the sea to North China, Manchuria, and eastern Siberia. In the hands of a strong hostile power it would prove "a dagger pointed at the heart of Japan." France and the United States made gestures toward opening intercourse with the country. French Roman Catholic missionaries and Korean Roman Catholics encountered repeated and severe persecution. Russia proved a greater menace, for, through its annexations from China on the east coast of Asia in 1858 and 1860, the Czar had pushed his boundaries to the border of Korea and needed control of that land to ensure access by sea to his East Asiatic domains. China was fully as deeply involved. Periodically she had controlled much of Korea, culturally Korea owed more to the Chinese than to any other people, and under the Manchu dynasty fairly close tributary relations bound Korea to the Middle Kingdom. In the first half of the nineteenth century Korea was more nearly an appendage of China than of Japan. China would not be disposed supinely to surrender her interests in the land.

In the decades when competition for Korea was being intensified, that land had the misfortune to be in the hands of weak and shortsighted rulers. Officialdom was trained in the Confucian classics, but in the nineteenth century the result was even more sterile than in China under the decadent Manchus. There seems to have been little of ability and still less of insight into the significance of the new forces operating in the world. Those in power were determined to preserve Korea's isolation. China and Japan might yield but not they.

Led by the isolationists, the Korean government treated with contumely the new regime in Japan which had accepted the opening of that country to the West. The administration set up by the Meiji Restoration attempted friendly relations with Seoul, but its advances were rejected. Shortly thereafter three commissioners were sent from Japan to investigate conditions in the Hermit Kingdom and reported that the machinations of Russia and China were such that measures should be taken to preserve the peninsula's independence. Seoul refused to accept missions proffered from Tokyo. In 1873 China disclaimed to a Japanese envoy responsibility for Korea's actions and declared that the little kingdom, although her vassal, had the power to make peace or war. It must be added that the traditional Chinese conception of what was involved in a tributary status did not fit into the Occidental picture of that relationship. In 1874 Korea agreed to receive an envoy from Japan and to send one in return, but when the official arrived he was refused audience. In 1875 a Japanese gunboat, engaged in the provocative act of surveying the entrance to the river that led to Seoul, was fired upon. The persistent rebuffs to Japan were understandable, for Korean experience was not such as to inspire confidence in the disinterestedness of the island Empire. Here was, from the Korean standpoint, a threat more ominous than that of Russia or China. Might not Japan renew the devastations wrought by Hideyoshi's armies?

There were Japanese, as we saw a few pages earlier, who wished to emulate Hideyoshi's exploits. However, milder counsels prevailed. Consciously adopting the procedure of Perry, as we have said, Japan sent a small armed expedition to Korea which asked for a treaty but gave Seoul time for consideration. The answer was favorable and in 1876 a treaty of commerce was signed. This was the first document of the kind to which Korea had agreed. The independence of Korea was acknowledged, presumably an indirect way of denying China's claim to suzerainty, ports were opened, and, contrary to the freedom from that system which Japan was asking of the West, extraterritorial privileges were accorded that Empire.

In 1882 the United States obtained, partly through Chinese channels, a treaty with Korea. In the same year a treaty between Korea and Great Britain was negotiated. Treaties followed with Germany, Russia, Italy, and France.

There now ensued a struggle in Korea between those willing to learn from the Occident and those who advocated holding to the old ways. In general those desiring change saw in Japan a precedent for what they wished to see happen in Korea and were supported by Tokyo. The conservatives were inclined to be pro-Chinese. The situation was complicated by rivalries between palace factions.

In 1882, in consequence of the friction, a mob attacked the palace and the Japanese legation. Several Japanese were killed. China, as the suzerain, acted promptly to restore order. Japan, after the precedent of Western measures on similar occasions in the Far East, exacted an indemnity (of which she later remitted the larger part), a mission of apology, new privileges for her merchants, and the right to place a garrison in Seoul. She insisted upon dealing with Korea directly, as an independent state, and not through China.

China now began to take a more positive policy in an attempt to draw Korea more pronouncedly within her orbit. In Tientsin was one of China's ablest statesmen of the latter part of the nineteenth century, Li Hung-chang. Li sent to Seoul as Chinese resident Yüan Shih-k'ai, years later, in 1912–1916, President of the Chinese Republic. He sought to have organized a Korean customs service which would be closely associated with that of China.

In 1884 violence again broke out. While China was preoccupied with her troubles with France over Indo-China, the Korean progressives attempted to seize control from the pro-Chinese conservatives. The King called upon the Japanese for protection. There resulted a clash between Chinese and Japanese troops, and several Japanese were killed. The Japanese thereupon made demands to which the Koreans quickly acceded—an indemnity, punishment of the guilty, and a mission of apology. Ito was sent to China to conduct with Li Hung-chang the negotiations which had been made necessary by the involvement of the troops of both Empires. In 1885 a Sino-Japanese convention was signed by which the two countries agreed to withdraw their troops from Korea. Neither was to lend officers to drill the Korean army. If, later, internal disorder were to call for dispatching armed forces, neither would send them without notifying the other. China apologized for the attack on the Japanese legation by the Chinese.

The nine years that followed were uneasy ones in Korea. Western powers became involved. Plans were made to provide American and Russian instructors for the Korean army. Britain, chronically fearful of the Russian bear, took alarm at Russian advances and from 1885 to 1887 occupied Port Hamilton, off the southern tip of the peninsula.

However, the main rivalry was between China and Japan. War between the two had become all but inevitable.

Indeed, Japan had entered upon a policy which, like a Greek tragedy, led her logically and almost unavoidably into the expansion which became so striking in the 1930's and 1940's. After the events of the 1880's no Japanese cabinet could have withdrawn from Korea and survived. Participation in Korean affairs entailed war with China and then with Russia. The war with China brought Japan temporarily into Manchuria and the conflict with Russia led her irrevocably into that region. Once in possession of a foothold in Manchuria, Japan would feel constrained eventually to oust her rivals, China and Russia, from these fertile provinces. Since Manchuria was predominantly Chinese in population and awakened Chinese nationalism would not willingly surrender the region, the occupation of Manchuria could not but lead Japan to seek so to control China as to prevent recurring Chinese attempts to rejoin Manchuria to China Proper. The conquest of China could hardly fail to embroil Japan with Western powers, notably Great Britain and the United States. Japan would then believe herself called to move against British and American possessions in the Far East, including Hongkong, British Malaya, and the Philippines. In a land as intensely patriotic as Japan any withdrawal from the path thus marked out would be, in the long run, fatal to any group who made themselves responsible for it. How, step by step, this tragedy unfolded we are to see in later chapters.

Summary

The second half of the nineteenth century witnessed a startling set of changes in Japan. From an isolation more nearly complete than that of China, Japan, after a few years of hesitation, moved out boldly into the modern world created by the expansion of the Occident. While China was trying to maintain her traditional cultural integrity by holding the West at arm's length, Japan was apparently becoming Occidentalized. Political, economic, and intellectual life was being made over to conform, at least in part, to Western patterns. Japan had begun the adoption of the industrial and scientific processes of the West. She had introduced compulsory primary education and had developed secondary and higher education modeled on the precedent of Europe and America. She had created medical and engineering professions in accordance with Western patterns. She had inaugurated factories, railways, telegraphs, and a merchant marine. For business purposes she was adopting structures fashioned after Occidental architecture and in army, navy, and much of government and trade used Western dress. To be sure, the process of Westernization had only begun. So far Japanese seemed to be imitators and not originators. Only later, as the steps taken led to further achievements, was creative originality displayed. Yet in the brief span of the four decades since Perry the alterations had been breath-taking. The Western world was amazed and looked on with patronizing approval, mixed with self-satisfaction, at the aptness of Japan as a pupil.

There were relatively few who discerned that the traditional spirit and basic institutions of Japan had been intensified rather than weakened. Japanese nationalism, strengthened by the long isolation and internal peace of the Tokugawa, was both responsible for the change and reenforced by it. It was to create a strong Japan which could face the Western powers on the basis of equality that the leaders of the "transformation" undertook their task. In the process nationalism was augmented. The Emperor, as the center, symbol, and inspiration of the Japanese spirit, was made more prominent. Shinto, means and channel of Japanese patriotism, was revived. A policy of expansion was begun which, short of an overwhelming defeat, would embrace at least all of East Asia and possibly more. Japan was the first large nation of Asia wholeheartedly to adopt the machines and the scientific techniques of the nineteenth century Occident. In doing so she became the leader of the Far East. She also entered upon a path which, if pursued successfully, would make her its master.

BIBLIOGRAPHY

For Brief Reference

H. M. Vinacke, *A History of the Far East in Modern Times* (New York, 4th ed., 1941), chaps. 4, 5, 6.

For More Detailed Study

G. C. Allen, *Modern Japan and Its Problems* (New York, 1927).
M. E. Cosenza, *The Complete Journal of Townsend Harris* (New York, 1930).
T. Dennett, *Americans in Eastern Asia* (New York, 1922).

J. H. Gubbins, *The Making of Modern Japan* (London, 1922).
D. C. Holtom, *Modern Japan and Shinto Nationalism* (Chicago, 1943).
W. W. McLaren, *A Political History of Japan during the Meiji Era, 1867–1912* (New York, 1916).
E. H. Norman, *Japan's Emergence as a Modern State. Political and Economic Problems of the Meiji Period* (New York, 1940).
S. Okuma, *Fifty Years of New Japan* (2 vols., London, 1910).
G. Sansom, *The Western World and Japan* (New York, 1949).
P. J. Treat, *Diplomatic Relations between the United States and Japan, 1853–1895* (2 vols., Stanford, 1932).
C. Yanaga, *Japan Since Perry* (New York, 1949).

Chapter XIV. CHANGING CHINA, 1894–1930

The transformation of China has its inception and makes progress

IN THE MID 1890's began a series of events which issued in a profoundly altered Far East. They were associated with the heightened impact of the Occident and with the expansion of Japan, equipped with the machines and techniques of the Occident. They centered about China. This was natural, for China was the most populous of the Far Eastern lands and had long dominated the region politically and culturally. Of the occurrences the most momentous was the transformation of China. This was far more thoroughgoing than that of Japan. Every phase of Chinese life, political, economic, intellectual, social, moral, and religious, was strikingly affected. A revolution ensued far more fundamental and sweeping than that which was taking place contemporaneously in India. Indeed, for magnitude it was unequaled in any other people in all human history. Although there were earlier foreshadowings, it may be said to have begun about 1895. It did not end quickly. At present (1951) it may be said to be only in mid course. What the outcome will be no one ought confidently to predict.

It is to this story of the transformation of China under the pressure of the impinging culture of the Occident that we now turn. In telling it we shall be compelled from time to time to concern ourselves with the general international situation in the Far East and, occasionally, in Europe, for the two interacted on each other. The changes in China were precipitated by the developments in the international situation, and the international situation was in part determined by internal events in China.

The Chinese-Japanese War of 1894–1895

The transformation of China was due to the long-continued pressure of the Occident. It began on an impressive scale and at a rapid pace immediately after a defeat administered by Japan in 1894–1895.

It was clear that either Japan or China would have to withdraw from Korea. The dual vassalage of Korea to her two great neighbors which had existed in earlier centuries could not be maintained under the new conditions. Both powers were determined to increase their authority in the peninsula. This could not but issue in an armed clash.

The occasion for the outbreak of war was an uprising in Korea which both powers endeavored to suppress. The rebellion was that of the Tonk-haks, a nationalistic and anti-Christian religious cult. Korea asked aid of China to put down the revolt. China sent troops and, as in duty bound, notified Japan of her action. The Japanese also sent armed forces. The uprising had been suppressed before the arrival of the contingent of either China or Japan.

Friction between Japan and China over Korea was intensified. China continued to declare that Korea was tributary to her. Japan demanded that China acknowledge Korea to be independent, a status which Japan had recognized in her treaty with the peninsula in 1876. Japan, in at least partial contradiction to her insistence that Korea was independent, undertook to promote administrative and financial reorganization in that land. This was unquestionably needed and Japan said that her commercial interests in the country and her geographic propinquity made the step imperative. When Japan proposed joint action of herself and China to carry through the reforms, the latter Empire declined to interfere with the internal administration of Korea. The Korean government accepted the program that Japan presented. Since this meant a severe blow for the conservative pro-Chinese factions, China sought to block the Japanese move. Several Western diplomats attempted mediation, but in vain. The Korean government requested Japan to withdraw her troops. To this Japan countered with a demand that barracks be provided for her forces and that the Chinese troops be sent home. Korea declined to comply. The Japanese thereupon seized the King and obtained a decree abrogating the treaty with China and asking Japan to expel the Chinese forces.

Open hostilities broke out in July 1894, when the Japanese fired on Chinese warships and on a British merchant ship which was transporting reenforcements for the Chinese troops in Korea. Formal declarations of war followed.

The war was of brief duration. Although the Chinese had a modern fleet, it had been hamstrung by corruption which reached to the Empress Dowager herself. The Chinese sea power fell an easy victim to the Japanese. The Chinese armies, only partially equipped with modern weapons, were quickly expelled from Korea. Japan and Korea entered into an alliance to attain this end, but the fighting was done by the willing Japanese. The Japanese moved on into Manchuria and captured, among other places, the naval base of Port Arthur, on the Liaotung Peninsula. They also took the naval base of Weihaiwei, on the Shantung promontory. They now commanded the sea approaches to North China and were in a position to move on to Peking. Japan had demonstrated to an astonished world the military and naval strength which she had won through her adoption of Western appliances and methods.

The Chinese, humiliated but still haughty, were forced to sue for peace with a people whom they had regarded with vast contempt. After futile preliminary essays, they sent the great Li Hung-chang himself to Japan. There he met, among others, Ito. It is interesting that each delegation had an American adviser. One of the Japanese superpatriots of the kind who figured so spectacularly in important crises in the nineteenth and twentieth centuries attempted to take the life of Li and wounded him. The Japanese authorities, in apology, somewhat mitigated their severe demands.

As finally agreed upon, the treaty, known by the name of Shimonoseki, where it was negotiated, was drastic enough. By it China recognized the independence of Korea, thus ending the suzerain-vassal relations to which Japan objected. She also ceded to Japan the Liaotung Peninsula, Formosa, and the Pescadores. She agreed to pay an indemnity and to open four new treaty ports to Japan. These latter, under the most-favored-nation clauses, were thus likewise opened to Western treaty powers. She was also to enter into a new treaty of commerce with Japan and to concede to the latter most-favored-nation status.

Some of the Western powers were aggrieved by Japan's gains in Manchuria. Three of them—Germany, Russia, and Russia's ally, France—counseled Japan to relinquish her claim on the Liaotung Peninsula, on the ground that her ownership of that strategic tongue of land would be a menace to Peking and to the independence of Korea. Japan, seeing back of this "advice" a thinly veiled threat and being in no position as yet to defy it, acquiesced, but on condition of an additional indemnity. At the same time China declined to promise not to cede the returned territory to a third power. Japan did not forget the humiliating concession wrung from her, but bided her time until a favorable opportunity should come to recoup what she regarded as wrongfully taken from her.

The Threatened Partition of China

A spectacular sequel of the Chino-Japanese War was the threatened partition of the loser. The conflict had revealed the weakness of that realm. The age was one of Western imperialism. In the preceding decade European powers had divided much of Africa among themselves. They had reached out into the islands of the Pacific and were picking up bits of hitherto unclaimed territory wherever it could be found. It now seemed to them clear that China was helpless, and each felt that if it did not obtain a slice of the Chinese melon its rivals would crowd it out entirely. The action of Japan in acquiring portions of the Chinese Empire precipitated the scramble. The struggle for China took a number of forms.

There was competition to lend money to China to pay her indemnity to Japan. To meet her obligation China had to borrow from abroad. She seemed good security and loans might entail political and economic concessions. The Russians won the privilege of advancing the first installment—made on the security of the maritime customs—and in it were to have the assistance of French bankers. Great Britain and Germany thereupon insisted that China borrow from the (British) Hongkong and Shanghai Banking Corporation and the Deutsche-Asiatische Bank. This China did in 1896 and 1898 and gave as security the customs revenue and the salt tax and *likin* (a tax on internal trade) in part of the Yangtze Valley.

In 1895, through conventions with France, China agreed to a modification of her Annamese boundary. Some territory thus passed to Annam, which in effect meant to France. China also opened three new treaty ports on the Sino-Annamese border, agreed that if mines were developed in the three southern provinces, Yünnan, Kwangsi, and Kwangtung, French manufacturers and engineers would be given priority in according assistance, and made provision for the building of some railways in that region.

Great Britain, then a rival of France in empire-building, saw in these advances a threat to her interests in Burma and southwest China. In 1896 she obtained an understanding with France. In 1897 she persuaded China to agree to a "rectification" of her boundary with the British possessions on the south and to the opening to commerce of the West River and of ports on that stream, to promise not to cede to a third power certain portions of the frontier without British consent, to give assurances that when railways in Yünnan were built they would connect with British roads in Burma, and to concede additional trading privileges.

In 1895 Germany, embarked under its young Kaiser on overseas empire-building, asked China for a coaling station. Undaunted by Peking's refusal, Berlin directed its ambitions toward Kiaochow Bay, an excellent harbor on the southern coast of Shantung. Russia also had designs on this strategic post. In November 1897, two German Roman Catholic missionaries were murdered in Shantung. In this outrage Germany saw her opportunity. She seized Kiaochow, exacted a heavy indemnity, and in 1898 obtained a ninety-nine-year lease to the bay and some adjacent territory. With the lease went the permission to build two railways in the province and the promise that if foreign assistance were ever needed in Shantung in capital, personnel, or materials Germans would be given the priority. Germany soon undertook the development of a model port at Tsingtao, on Kiaochow Bay.

A few days after Germany had obtained Kiaochow Russia was granted a twenty-five-year lease on the tip of that Liaotung Peninsula which had so recently been retrieved from Japan. On it were Talienwan (better known to foreigners as Dalny and later as Dairen) and Port Arthur. Talienwan was developed into the most important entrepot to Manchuria, and Port Arthur was strengthened as a fortified naval base.

Great Britain was greatly disturbed by these events. They seemed to foreshadow the acquisition of huge portions of China by her rivals. Her chief interest in China was commercial. For several decades she had had the largest share in China's overseas trade. For the sake of her trade she wished China to remain intact and under a government at least outwardly friendly to her. If other Western powers obtained slices of China they would seek to monopolize them to the detriment of British commerce and capital. She therefore deplored the scramble but felt herself constrained to join in it and, if possible, to seize the lion's share in any division of the Manchu empire. In 1898 she obtained a lease on Weihaiwei "for so long a period as Port Arthur shall remain in the possession of Russia." She did this with the consent of Japan, whose troops were still occupying the Shantung port, and with a promise to Berlin that she would not build a railway into the interior in competition with German interests. She also (in 1898) was given a ninety-nine-year lease to such of the Kowloon Peninsula, on the mainland opposite Hongkong, as had not been ceded her in 1860.

In that same year France obtained a ninety-nine-year lease to Kwangchowwan, a bay on the south coast of Kwangtung.

In 1899 Italy, seeking a naval station in Chêkiang, was successfully rebuffed.

These several leaseholds could conceivably be the beginnings of partition. As a further step in that direction, some of the leases were reenforced by nonalienation agreements. By them China promised not to cede—technically, "alienate"—to a third power a particular portion of her territory. By thinly veiled implication the power having such an agreement possessed a special interest in the prescribed territory which might eventually form the basis of annexation. In 1897 France gained from China a promise that the island of Hainan would never be ceded to a third power. In the following year similar assurance was given her for the provinces bordering on Indo-China. In 1898 Great Britain obtained a promise that China would not alienate to another power any of the provinces adjoining the Yangtze. Thus she staked out her claim to the wealthiest portion of China. When, also in 1898, Japan sought a corresponding promise for Fukien, China informed her that she would not alienate any part of that province to any power (which, of course, included Japan). This had the effect of a snub to Tokyo.

Another guise taken by the competition for China was concessions for the construction of railways. They, too, might form the basis for territorial claims in case actual partition came. Late in 1896, Russia formed a secret alliance with China against Japan. This included provision for the construction of a railroad across northern Manchuria. It was to be known as the Chinese Eastern Railway and was really a branch of the Trans-Siberian road. The latter followed the all-Russian route on the north bank of the Amur, but the distance from the West to the East was considerably shortened by the Chinese Eastern, as a glance at the map will show. China also promised to seek only from Russian banks any loans which might be needed for the construction of some other trunk roads north of the Great Wall. Li Hung-chang, who negotiated the agreement, hoped by it to obtain a makeweight against Japan. The lease of the tip of the Liaotung Peninsula to Russia, in 1898, included the privilege of building a railroad southward from the Chinese Eastern to Talienwan and Port Arthur. We have already noted the permission to the Germans to build in Shantung and the special position granted the French in the southwest. In 1896, 1897, 1898, and 1899 France obtained special concessions for railways in this area. The most important was for one from Tongking into Yünnan. This, when built, opened a fairly large region to French enterprise. The British acquired the predominant financial position in the railroad between Mukden and Peking, thus edging into the Russian sphere. They and the Germans were given (1899) a concession for a line between Tientsin and the Yangtze. The Germans were to build the northern and the British the southern section. In 1898 the Belgians, with Russian and French support and the backing of French capital, signed a contract for a loan toward a proposed road from Peking to Hankow. Americans acquired, in 1898, a concession for the southern extension of this line from Hankow to Canton. However, the Belgians bought a controlling interest in the American company and the Chinese, alarmed by this threatened domination by the Belgians and French of the main trunk road from north to south, repurchased the grant. In 1898 the British signed preliminary agreements for roads from Shanghai to Nanking and from Shanghai to Hangchow. They attempted to safeguard their hold on the Yangtze Valley by an agreement with Germany (1898) for reciprocal respect for each other's spheres and by one with Russia (1899) whereby they were not to seek to build roads north of the Great Wall and Russia was to refrain from similar enterprises in the Yangtze Valley. In 1898 and 1899 an Anglo-Italian company was given concessions for mines and railways in Shansi and Honan, the Russo-Chinese Bank was granted a concession, later transferred to a French syndicate, for a road between T'aiyüanfu the capital of Shansi, and the Peking-Hankow line, and a Franco-Belgian syndicate was accorded one for a road to parallel the Yellow River.

The British, who were dominant in the Imperial Maritime Customs service, attempted to ensure a continuation of that position by a promise from Peking (1898) that the Inspector General should be British so long as their trade remained greater than that of any other nation.

In several of the ports special bits of land, "concessions," were demanded by and granted to a number of the powers.

The United States Seeks to Ensure the Open Door

Of the major Occidental powers the United States was the only one which made no attempt to gain exclusive privileges in China. Into the reasons for this attitude we need not attempt to go—except to say that it was not necessarily because of a superior moral standard.

However, the United States was far from being unconcerned with the developments in the Middle Kingdom. By her war with Spain and her acquisition of the Philippines, during these very years the United States had become an Asiatic power and had acquired a territorial stake in the Far East. Indeed, in the 1890's no other Occidental power had come into possession of so much land in that region. Nor had Japan, with all of its annexations as a result of the Chino-Japanese War, done so. In addition the United States, by annexing Hawaii, had obtained an important stepping stone toward the Far East. Americans had long been lured by the apparent promise of the Far Eastern and especially the China market. They and their government were not disposed to sit by idly while China was partitioned among earth-hungry European nations.

The action taken by the United States was neither particularly vigorous nor immediately successful. It did, however, commit her to a course which, if pursued, would involve her very deeply in Far Eastern affairs. It was the logic of this course which in 1941 drew her into the second world war of the twentieth century.

The program followed in the 1890's was known as the "open door policy" and was associated with the name of the then Secretary of State, John Hay. In a real sense it was not new. It was the principle on which the United States had long operated in the Far East and in most of the rest of the world. It meant that the United States asked for its citizens equal opportunity with those of all other nations. It was, too, the principle on which the English had acted in China until the competition of other Western powers had induced them reluctantly to depart from it. Mr. Hay took his mild but momentous step partly at the instance of a British subject, although not at the suggestion of the British Government. In September 1899, after most of the leaseholds and other special concessions had been acquired by the European powers, Hay instructed the American ambassadors to Great Britain, Germany, and Russia, and in November 1899, the American minister to Japan and the American ambassadors to Italy and France, to attempt to obtain from the governments of these countries assurances (1) that they would not interfere with any treaty port or any vested interest within any so-called "sphere of interest" or leased territory that they held in China; (2) that the Chinese treaty tariff would apply to all merchandise shipped into such ports within these "spheres of interest," no matter to what nationality it belonged, and that the duties would be collected by the Chinese government; (3) that no higher harbor dues should be exacted from vessels of another nation entering ports in the "spheres of interest," and no higher charges be made on railroads within the "spheres" than on merchandise belonging to the citizens of the power which had the "sphere." In some respects Hay did not fully hold to the "open door" of equal opportunity. For instance, he recognized the existence of "spheres of interest" and he said nothing about preferential treatment to investors of capital.

Even these requests met with a lukewarm reception. Great Britain assented but with reservations respecting the leased territory of Kowloon. Russia agreed, but ignored the reference to harbor dues and railway rates. France and Germany approved but, as had Great Britain and Russia, on the condition that the other powers do so. Only Japan and Italy concurred without reservations.

The real significance of the Hay action was that through it the United States committed herself to a policy in the Far East of equal opportunity for all nations. Unless she were to withdraw from the position so taken, the United States might find herself forced to implement it by the use of armed force. She alone of the powers had made herself responsible for the policy. By pursuing it she assumed major obligations which embroiled her ever more deeply in the politics of the Far East.

The Wave of Change Begins to Mount

The catastrophes in their foreign relations which began in 1894 stirred many of the Chinese to action. In general there were two trends, one almost the exact opposite of the other. Numbers of far-seeing Chinese were keenly aware that the Occident could no longer be held at arm's length. If China were to maintain her political independence, so they declared, she must put her house in order, eliminate the corruption and inefficiency in her administration, and take over some features of Western civilization. On the other hand were those who would expel the foreigner and resume the isolation which had been the imperial policy before the pressure had become so acute. The reformers first had their way. The reactionaries then took charge. After they had brought the Empire even closer to the brink of ruin, the forces of change once more gained the ascendancy.

Following the war with Japan, numbers of societies sprang up which had as their purpose the reform of the Empire. Their existence was indicative of the fashion in which the revolution in China was eventually wrought. It came primarily by action from below rather than, as in Japan, through direction from the top. Since most officials had a stake in the old order, they clung to it and viewed with alarm proposals for modifications, for these might break their rice bowls. In the governing classes were a few who were willing to step out and take the lead. Among these was a prominent viceroy, Chang Chih-tung, whose book *Learn* advocated the adoption of some of the methods of the West lest the Empire forfeit its independence as India, Annam, and Egypt had done. The little volume had an enormous circulation.

Among those of lowlier rank who labored for fundamental alterations was Sun Yat-sen. In the first half of the twentieth century he was to influence his people more than any other of his contemporaries. In the 1890's Sun was known within only a small circle. His fame and influence were to come later, but it was in the closing years of the old century that he began his career as a professional revolutionist. Sun Yat-sen, or Sun Wên as he was also called, was born, the son of a farmer, in 1866, in a village on the delta of the West River about forty miles from Canton. The family was poor and in later years Sun bluntly declared that he was "a coolie and the son of a coolie." He was from that sturdy peasant stock which for long has been the backbone of China. An elder brother sought his fortune in Hawaii, as did many another from the crowded, sea-bordering region around Canton. Prospering, in the dutiful Chinese manner he sent for the younger brother and put him to school. The lad was placed in an institution maintained by an English mission. Here, at an impressionable age, he was given an introduction to Western learning, the English language, and the Christian religion. After approximately three years he was returned by his brother to his home village. There he gave evidence of the new ideas contracted in Hawaii by denouncing idolatry. To give point to his criticism he defaced images in the village temple. Forced by this sacrilege to leave the ancestral scene, he took refuge in Hongkong. Here he again attended foreign schools and here he was baptized. Later he studied Western medicine in Canton and Hongkong. In 1892 he received his certificate in medicine and surgery. For a time he practiced in Macao and Canton. However, he was convinced of the need of remaking China. This, he believed, entailed ridding the Empire of its Manchu rulers. The national disgrace of the defeat by Japan led him and a few like-minded Chinese to plot the seizure of the offices of the provincial government in Canton. The conspiracy was discovered (1895) and Sun fled the country. He became a roving agitator, stirring Chinese outside the Empire to support the revolution for which he continued to plan.

More immediately prominent was K'ang Yu-wei. Like Sun, K'ang was a native of Kwangtung. Unlike Sun, his training was purely Chinese. With that background, however, he had developed a social and political radicalism which envisioned the eventual erasure of national boundaries, the popular election of officials, the abolition of the family, and the assignment to public institutions of the rearing of children and the care of the aged. He would not insist upon the precipitate attainment of these ideals but would begin with much more moderate measures.

The reformers included many more than the ones we have singled out for mention. They had no one recognized leader nor were they organized in any two or three well-articulated groups. They were, moreover, only a small minority. The weight of tradition was against them. The tide had begun to flow in their direction, but they could not expect at once to have their full way.

For a brief time the surge of change seemed about to carry all before it. In the summer of 1898 the young Emperor, whom we know best by the name of his reign period, Kuang Hsü, moved with it. During what were later known as the hundred days of reform, in June, July, August, and September of 1898, edict after edict came out with his support. At the time they seemed drastic, but compared with what was to be witnessed later they were moderate. They included provision for the modification of the civil service and military examinations, the inauguration of a system of schools culminating in a university in which both Chinese and Western learning were to be studied, the encouragement of railway building, military and naval reform, and the abolition of numbers of sinecure offices.

The Kuang Hsü Emperor was not the man to carry through successfully even the first stages of a revolution. He was intelligent, but he had no direct knowledge of the world outside the palace, he was unskilled in administration, as a politician he was immature, he was lacking in vigour in both character and body, and he had been reared under the shadow of the domineering and forceful Tz'ŭ Hsi. Most of his advisers, including the one on whom he placed chief reliance, K'ang Yu-wei, were quite unschooled in statecraft. He and they could scarcely be expected to ride out the inevitable storm.

The First Wave of Reaction

Dissatisfaction with the young Emperor's edicts was great among the influential classes. Added to the settled dislike of change that is usually characteristic of those who profit by the social order of which they are a part was the alarm of those whose livelihood was threatened.

The antagonism was given powerful support and leadership by no less a person than Tz'ŭ Hsi. In spite of her astuteness in the manipulation of the elements in the political structure with which she was familiar, the Empress Dowager seemed blind to the significance of the forces in the Western world which were impinging upon China. As was natural in one who had suffered from them in her young womanhood in the war with Great Britain and France, she disliked Occidentals and things foreign. She believed what she wished to believe, that they could still be kept at arm's length and that the Chinese state and Chinese society could be conserved without basic adjustments. The Emperor, aware of the attitude of Tz'ŭ Hsi and those about her, attempted to forestall interference by her. In this he was thwarted by the official to whom he committed the task, Yüan Shih-k'ai. Thus goaded, the Empress Dowager acted promptly. She suddenly and dramatically resumed control of the government. The Emperor was constrained to sign an edict saying that he had asked her to assume the burdens which she had earlier laid down and that she had graciously consented. For a time his life was in peril. He was henceforth kept to what in effect was confinement, impotent and the butt of thinly veiled contempt and galling indignities at the hands of the palace eunuchs. Most of the reform edicts of the summer were annulled. Some of the reformers were executed. Others, including K'ang Yu-wei, took refuge abroad.

The Boxer Outbreak

The spasm of reaction against compromise with the Occident culminated in what is often termed the Boxer Rebellion. The designation "rebellion" is something of a misnomer, for the uprising was not directed against the government. Indeed, one of its slogans was: "Protect the Dynasty." It was antiforeign and was an attempt to purge the realm of Westerners and Western influence. Although the repercussions were felt through most of the Empire, violence was most acute in the northeast, for a time in Shantung until it was suppressed by the governor, Yüan Shih-k'ai, but chiefly in the provinces of Chihli and Shansi, in Manchuria, and in Inner Mongolia. Here railway building, a visible symbol of the foreigner, was most active; here Christians, especially Roman Catholics, who had imbibed the foreigners' religion, were the most numerous; and here, if one includes Shantung, were the majority of the leaseholds recently acquired by European powers.

The origin of the movement was mixed. It was partly spontaneous popular opposition to foreigners and their ways expressing itself under a traditional form of societies with religious features which offered the protection of magic against Western bullets. It was partly in the support of violently antiforeign officials, largely Manchus. It was partly in local militia which the Empress Dowager ordered to be put in readiness for the defense of the country. To some degree it was through troops which had been summoned to Peking for the defense of the capital, when an Italian demand early in 1899 for the lease of a bay in Chêkiang had brought fear of a foreign attack. The militia and antiforeign societies attracted the ruder elements, some of them brigands, and many who had been thrown out of normal occupations by a drought-induced famine. The name adopted by several of the groups, "Righteous Harmony Fists," together with the gymnastic exercises practiced, won for the entire movement from foreigners the sobriquet of Boxer.

It was late in 1899 that the Boxer movement began to assume menacing proportions. Chinese Christians, regarded by fire-eating antiforeign agitators as "secondary devils," accessories to the hated aliens, were being attacked in Shantung. Under pressure from the powers, the antiforeign governor of the province was removed and Yüan Shih-k'ai was appointed in his stead. Yüan made short work of the Boxers. However, before he had the province fairly in hand, in the closing days of the year an English missionary was killed. By the summer of 1900 Chinese Christians were being slaughtered in Chihli. Late in May a party of railway engineers and their families south of Peking were attacked as they were trying to make their way to the coast.

Alarmed, the diplomatic corps in Peking obtained for the protection of the legations a few hundred marines from the foreign ships of war stationed off the coast. Boxer bands, taking this as proof positive that the foreign invasion had begun, cut the railway between Tientsin and Peking. The legations asked for additional guards. An international force of a little over two thousand started from Tientsin.

A few days later the foreign admirals, the Americans abstaining, seized the forts which commanded the river approach to Tientsin, thus to ensure access to that city for the safeguarding of foreigners there and in Peking. The Boxers interpreted this as an act of war. So did the extremists at court. The diplomatic corps and all foreigners were ordered to leave Peking for the coast within twenty-four hours. While the advisability of compliance was being debated, the German minister was murdered while on his way to the Tsungli Yamen (the Foreign Office). This tragedy was regarded as the probable fate of the others if they left the frail security of the legations for the uncertainty of the road and served to terminate the debate about the wisdom of obeying the command of the Chinese government. All the foreigners gathered either in the legations which, fortunately, were in a fairly compact group, or in one of the Roman Catholic churches. There, too, assembled many of the Chinese Christians, who without the foreigners' protection would undoubtedly have been massacred. Here siege was stood until the middle of August. An international force then fought its way through from Peking and relieved the beleaguered.

In the meantime the attacks on foreigners and Chinese Christians outside Peking were being pressed by the Boxers and the war party. Scores of foreigners, mostly missionaries, as the most exposed, and thousands of Chinese Christians were done to death.

Opinions at court were divided. The Empress Dowager wavered between the extremists and the moderates. Had counsels been unanimous the legations might not have held out and the loss of foreign life would have been much greater. In effect the Empress Dowager declared war against the world. She ordered that wherever in the Empire a foreigner was found he be killed. Courageous officials, reputedly two Chinese ministers, succeeded in altering the telegrams before they were sent out so that for "kill" they read "protect."

Moreover, outside Peking both Chinese in high places and foreigners strove to keep hostilities localized and to prevent a real war between China and the powers. The great viceroys, Chinese, among them the aged Li Hung-chang, and some of the provincial governors, including a Manchu and Yüan Shih-k'ai, declared the Boxers to be a rebellion and not the act of the lawful government. They sought, therefore, to maintain order but made it clear that they could not and would not do so if foreign armies were landed in the provinces under their control or if an attack were made on the imperial family. Foreign commanders were quite willing to respect this policy. Most of the loss of life and destruction of property was, accordingly, as we said a few paragraphs above, confined to the northeast.

When the foreign relief expedition reached Peking, the court, headed by the Empress Dowager, precipitately fled. Tz'ŭ Hsi insisted upon taking with her the luckless Emperor, but, before leaving, had his favorite concubine thrown down a well: even in distress, her dislike and contempt for the unfortunate ruler were not forgotten. Additional foreign forces came, notably Germans, and, under the guise of hunting down and extirpating the Boxers and of punitive expeditions to cities and communities in which foreigners had been ill-treated, instituted a reign of terror. Several of the powers expanded their existing concessions in Tientsin or obtained new ones. Russia sent large contingents to Manchuria, already partly her sphere of influence. It seemed that this fertile, virgin region would be abstracted from the Empire and added to those areas north of the Amur and east of the Ussuri which a generation earlier, in another hour of China's distress, Russia had detached from the Manchu realm.

Compared with the world wars of the twentieth century and with the civil strife and the Japanese invasions of China in the first half of that century, the Boxer outbreak was a minor event. In the relatively peaceful world of the turn of the century, however, it seemed to be of major proportions.

The Boxer Settlement

Although when contrasted with the huge disasters of the ensuing half century the loss of life for both Chinese and foreigners was almost infinitesimal, the consequences of the Boxer year for China were momentous.

First of all was the settlement with the powers. It was clear that some Western governments might take advantage of China's weakness and of the Boxer attacks on foreigners to carry further the partition of the country which had been foreshadowed by the leases and spheres of influence of the preceding three or four years.

From this fate China was saved partly by the attitude of the United States but chiefly by the preoccupation and jealousies of European governments. In 1900 John Hay was still the American Secretary of State. He quickly realized the peril to the open door policy—in which his notes of the preceding year had been able to gain at best only lukewarm acquiescence. On July 3, 1900, while the allied force was assembling for the relief of the Peking legations, he sent out a circular note which declared it the policy of the United States to act concurrently with other powers, to protect American lives, property, and other legitimate interests, and "to seek a solution which may bring about permanent safety and peace to China, preserve Chinese territorial and administrative entity, protect all rights guaranteed to friendly powers by treaty and international law, and safeguard for the world the principle of equal and impartial trade with all parts of the Chinese Empire." The main significance of the note was not its immediate effect, for that was not particularly impressive, but the declaration of purpose to "preserve Chinese territorial and administrative entity." This was new. It was a logical implication of the open door policy, but it had not before been concretely expressed by the United States government. It was a phrase which was to become part of the American interpretation of the open door policy and was to reappear, with slight modifications, at critical junctures and in crucial documents. It was another step toward the undertaking by the United States of grave responsibilities which were to entangle her ever more deeply in the affairs of the Far East. In November 1900, Hay, in something of a deviation from his avowed procedure, attempted to obtain a naval base and a territorial concession on the coast of Fukien.

Fortunately for China and the United States, for the moment European powers were too engrossed elsewhere to undertake the carving up of China. Great Britain was involved in war with the Boers. Diplomatic maneuvers in Europe were more concerned with the balance of power in that continent and elsewhere in Asia than with China and for the time accrued to the advantage of that unhappy Empire. In October 1900, an Anglo-German declaration was issued in support of the open door and the territorial integrity of China, but this was clearly dictated by a desire to adjust the conflicting interests of the signatories rather than to conform to the precedent set by the United States. Nor were Great Britain and Germany willing to become embroiled with Russia by including Manchuria in their definition of the China whose territorial integrity was to be respected.

In spite of jealousies and partly because of them the powers entered jointly into negotiations with the Chinese. On September 7, 1901, the final agreement was signed in the form of a protocol. Its chief provisions were (1) an official apology to Germany, through a special envoy, for the murder of her minister and the erection by China of a monument in his honor on the scene of his death; (2) punishment, by the Chinese, of the officials chiefly responsible for the atrocities (by agreeing to the infliction of these by the Chinese authorities rather than by foreign officials, something of face was preserved for China); (3) the suspension by imperial edict of the official examinations for five years in towns where foreigners had been killed or harshly treated; (4) apology for the murder of the chancellor of the Japanese legation; (5) the erection by China of expiatory monuments in foreign cemeteries which had been desecrated; (6) the prohibition for at least two years of arms and ammunition and of all material employed exclusively in their manufacture; (7) the payment of an indemnity of 450,000,000 taels (in United States currency, $333,900,000), in thirty-nine annual installments; (8) the setting aside of the legation quarter in Peking in such fashion that it could be easily defended, the exclusion from it of Chinese residents and police, and the permission to each of the powers to maintain there a permanent guard; (9) the razing of the forts at the mouth of the river leading to Tientsin, that free communication might be maintained between Peking and the sea; (10) the occupation by the powers of certain strategic points, including Tientsin, also to ensure such communication; (11) the posting by the Chinese government in all district towns of edicts designed to prevent antiforeign activities; (12) assent to negotiations for the modification of treaties of commerce and navigation between China and the powers; (13) the improvement of the river channels leading to Tientsin and Shanghai; and (14) the transformation of the Tsungli Yamen (Foreign Office) into a Ministry of Foreign Affairs (Wai Wu Pu) which would take rank above the other ministries and so give greater dignity to intercourse with foreign governments.

China emerged from the Boxer experience with a greatly enhanced debt, added humiliation, and, in effect, the position of a subject nation. The foreign legations were an armed fortress in her capital, and contingents of foreign troops were stationed there and at Tientsin to keep open the route to the sea and so to prevent the recurrence of such a siege as the summer of 1900 had witnessed. For the next quarter of a century foreigners, and especially Westerners, assumed, even though usually almost unconsciously, the attitude of conquerors in a vassal country. It was a situation which could not but be galling to a proud people.

We must also note that the United States, along with other powers, maintained armed forces in Tientsin and Peking. While her contingents were not large, they entailed commitments such as had never been undertaken by her for so long a time in any other land outside the Western hemisphere. Her citizens and few if any of her statesmen were aware of the full implications of what was happening. It was to be decades before the logical corollaries revealed themselves.

We must also record the fact that the United States early agreed to return to China such portions of her share of the Boxer indemnity as were not required to meet the expenses of her part in the suppression and indemnification of the uprising. The refunding, however, was in such fashion that the sums released were employed for the education of Chinese youth, largely in the United States.

A Russo-Japanese War in the Offing

Still more was to follow for China. A succession of events ensued which was also to engage Japan and deeply to concern the Occident. Indeed, more than any other which had thus far transpired in the Far East it was to have violent repercussions in the West. Although we are placing it in a chapter on China and although the war in which the conflict culminated was fought on Chinese soil and had grave consequences for that country, the controversy over Manchuria which followed the Boxer outbreak profoundly stirred the Far East and India, engaged the attention of much of Europe and America, and was part of a chain of events which contributed to the world war of the 1930's and 1940's. It therefore belongs not alone to the history of China but also to that of the entire Far East and the world.

As we saw a few paragraphs earlier, late in the 1890's Russia was moving rapidly into Manchuria. The resources of the land were comparatively undeveloped, for the region was but sparsely settled by the peoples who regarded it as their traditional home and the Chinese had not as yet moved into it in large numbers. In soil, minerals, and forests it was potentially a rich prize. By her leasehold on the tip of the Liaotung Peninsula and the railways which she was building, Russia was acquiring a strategic position from which it would be hard to dislodge her. Her activities in Manchuria were part of the vast expansion of her territories in Asia which had been in progress for several centuries. Earlier in the second half of the nineteenth century she had acquired territory north of the Amur and east of the Ussuri. She had finished the Trans-Siberian Railway, thus obtaining steam communication between her main seat in Europe and her holdings in the Far East. Her railroad enterprises in Manchuria were in effect a continuation of that line. Russian ambitions in the east of Asia were far-reaching. The influential classes in Russia were not unanimous in their Far Eastern program for the Czar's empire, but the trend of the more daring was to claim as a Russian sphere everything north of the Great Wall, which meant not only Manchuria but also all of Mongolia.

The Boxer troubles gave to Russia what to the more aggressive among her ruling groups seemed a golden opportunity. The disturbances were violent in the southern part of Manchuria, where Chinese were the majority of the population. Russia sent in thousands of troops, ostensibly to restore order. Next to Japan, Russia provided the largest contingent in the force which in the summer of 1900 marched to the relief of the Peking legations. Her share of the Boxer indemnity was greater than that of any other power. Once ensconced in Manchuria, Russia was clearly reluctant to withdraw.

Moreover, Russia extended her ambitions to Korea. There she came in conflict with the Japanese. Japan, having fought the war with China over Korea and having been jockeyed out of the Liaotung Peninsula by Russia, France, and Germany, was not disposed to be expelled from Korea. Thanks to an aggressive representative, in 1895 Japan overplayed her hand. With the encouragement of the Japanese minister, a group of Japanese and Koreans broke into the royal apartments in Seoul, killed the Queen, whom the Japanese regarded as an obstacle, and terrorized the King into appointing pro-Japanese officials. A few months later, in February 1896, the King and the Crown Prince took refuge in the Russian legation and remained there until the following February. In 1896 Japan deemed it wise to acknowledge the Russian position in Korea by an agreement with the Czar's government. In 1897 Russian interests in Korea were pushed. In the course of the year, incidentally, the King of Korea assumed the title of Emperor, presumably to place himself on a par with the monarchs of China and Japan, a step to which the powers gave their consent. In 1898 another Russo-Japanese agreement over Korea was signed in which Russia promised not to obstruct the development of the commercial and industrial relations between Japan and Korea. This Japan was doing very rapidly. However, Russian and Japanese ambitions in the peninsula continued to clash. As was to be expected, the Russians became especially strong in the northern part of Korea, near the Manchurian border. There they held timber concessions which, in 1903, they began actively to develop.

In Great Britain Russia had a traditional opponent to her expansionist ambitions. It was to check Russia in her southward advance toward the Mediterranean that Britain had fought in the Crimean War. Through the second half of the nineteenth century she was fearful that the Russian annexations east of the Caspian and the development of railways in that region spelled danger for India by way of the northwest frontier. In the Russian southward movement in Manchuria and Korea Great Britain saw a threat to her position in the Far East.

Faced with the common menace of Russia, Great Britain and Japan came together in January 1902, in the Anglo-Japanese Alliance. The British authorities endeavored to persuade Germany to join the pact, but the Kaiser was unwilling. Influential Japanese had been divided as to whether their country should align herself with Russia or Great Britain. Some had strongly favored Russian friendship and hoped for a partition, in agreement with Russia, of Korea, Manchuria, and North China. However, the pro-British elements won.

In the treaty of alliance the independence and territorial integrity of China and Korea and the open door in these countries for the commerce and industry of all nations were declared to be the purpose of the engagement. The signatories disavowed aggressive tendencies in either country, but British concern was said to relate principally to China and Japanese mainly to Korea. It was to be admissible for either power to take such measures as might be indispensable to safeguard its interests if they were threatened by any other power or by disturbances arising in China or Korea. In case either party, in the course of the defense of its interests, became involved in war with another power, the other party to the alliance was to remain neutral and was to seek to prevent any other power from joining in the hostilities against its ally. If, however, an additional power or powers joined in the war against the ally, the other ally would come to the assistance of its partner and would conduct the war in common and make peace in mutual agreement with it. The duration of the alliance was to be five years. Japan had thus won the support of the mightiest naval power and had been accepted as an ally of one of the greatest of Occidental states. By the demonstration of her prowess in her war with China Japan had made herself a force with which to reckon, even if somewhat condescendingly, in the struggles among the nations of the West.

Great Britain and the United States were already seeking to bring about the withdrawal of Russian troops from Manchuria and to check the increase in the special privileges which Russia was acquiring in that region. Russia was making fresh demands on China, and Great Britain and Japan were endeavoring by pressure on China to prevent them from being granted. The United States, by requesting the opening of additional ports in Manchuria, was attempting to keep that region from becoming an exclusive Russian preserve.

In Russia a group centering about the Ministry of Finance wished for peaceful economic penetration of the Far East but opposed steps that might lead to war. On the other hand, interests associated with the Ministry of War wished a more aggressive policy and the construction of strategic railways. The Czar, in general, backed the latter.

The Russo-Japanese War

Japan continued to press Russia for an agreement. She was prepared to make concessions and even proposed that a line be drawn across northern Korea, the territory to the north being left a Russian and that to the south a Japanese sphere. Russia pursued her usual tactics of delay. Japan thereupon (February 8, 1904) severed diplomatic relations and the following day attacked and defeated a Russian fleet off Port Arthur. A war was on between Russia and Japan whose full consequences have not even yet been seen.

Into the details of the war we need not go. The fighting was entirely in the Far East, chiefly in Manchuria and the adjacent seas. Russia could not bring her huge resources to bear, for she was handicapped by having to fight in a region at a vast distance from the centers of her population and industry. Her one effective connection was the Trans-Siberian Railway. That had been recently completed and was mostly single track. It was therefore of limited capacity. Japan was near at hand and early obtained the mastery of the intervening waters which enabled her to ship troops and supplies at will. Her industrial development of the preceding decades, her military tradition, and her Westernized armies stood her in good stead. Japan took Dairen and, after a bitterly contested siege, Port Arthur, the Russian stronghold on the Liaotung Peninsula. The remnant of the Russian Far Eastern fleet which had been caged in Port Arthur attempted to escape, but its ships were either destroyed or badly damaged. The Russians, stubbornly contesting the ground, were slowly pushed back in southern Manchuria. After the long voyage around the Cape of Good Hope, for, because of the Anglo-Japanese Alliance, it could not take the shorter course through the British-controlled Straits of Gibraltar and Suez Canal, the Russian Baltic fleet was all but annihilated (May 27 and 28, 1905) in the Sea of Japan. Japan was still in possession of the sea lanes to the land front.

Peace followed late in the summer of 1905. In Russia, taking advantage of the defeats suffered by the Czar's forces and the weaknesses and ineptitude of the imperial regime thus revealed, revolutionists were engaging the attention of the administration. Japan's resources were badly strained. Both St. Petersburg and Tokyo were ready to negotiate.

The good offices which brought representatives of the belligerents together were from President Theodore Roosevelt. In the struggle the sympathies of Americans had been solidly with Japan. It was in the United States and Great Britain that Japan floated the loans which enabled her to prosecute the war. Roosevelt embarked, with his characteristic zest, in the game of world politics. He favored Japan, although latterly with misgivings as he began to fear the advantage victory would give the Japanese in the Far East. It was on his initiative that the conference was arranged. It was held in the United States, at Portsmouth, New Hampshire.

The Treaty of Portsmouth

The resultant treaty was signed (September 5, 1905) at Portsmouth and bore the name of that quiet New England town. The terms were, in the main, favorable to Japan as the palpable victor, but Russia obtained concessions that made the document unpopular with the Tokyo populace.

The main terms of the treaty which had continuing importance were: (1) the promise of both Japan and Russia to evacuate Manchuria except for the leasehold on the Liaotung Peninsula and to restore the exclusive administration of China in the area; (2) the declaration that neither power had in Manchuria any territorial advantages or preferential or exclusive concessions which impaired Chinese sovereignty or were inconsistent with the principle of equal opportunity for all nations; (3) the promise of both powers not to obstruct any measures common to all countries which China might take to develop the commerce and industry of Manchuria; (4) subject to the consent of China, the transfer by Russia to Japan of its lease to Port Arthur, Dairen, and the adjacent portion of the Liaotung Peninsula and her railway properties in Manchuria south of a specified point about halfway between Harbin and Mukden; (5) the engagement by both parties to develop their railways in Manchuria solely for industrial and commercial and in no way for strategic purposes; (6) the transfer by Russia to Japan of the southern part of the island of Sakhalin and an undertaking to grant fishing rights to Japanese along the coasts of her possessions in the Japan, Okhotsk, and Behring Seas. Japan was not given all of Sakhalin nor was she accorded any indemnity.

Concomitants and Immediate Sequels of the Russo-Japanese War

Associated with the Russo-Japanese War were developments of importance for much of the Far East. In April 1904, Great Britain and France signed the *entente cordiale* by which the two countries drew together against the rising power of Germany, a stage in the alignment of the European states which was to affect international politics in the Far East. In 1904, moreover, still fearing Russia, Great Britain sent to Tibet a military mission headed by Sir Francis Younghusband. The expedition, after a little fighting, made its way to Lhasa and there obtained an Anglo-Tibetan convention which clearly placed Tibet within the British sphere of influence. By it Tibet undertook to remove all armaments and forts which might impede free communication between the British frontier and Lhasa, and, except with British permission, not to cede or lease to any foreign power any Tibetan territory, nor admit a representative of any foreign power to Tibet, nor grant to any foreign power any concession for railways, telegraphs, mining, or other rights, nor to pledge any of her revenues to a foreign power. China, not unnaturally, questioned an arrangement which affected one of her dependencies, but it was not until 1906 that in an Anglo-Chinese convention Great Britain agreed that the term "foreign power" in the Anglo-Tibetan agreement did not include China and that she would not annex any Tibetan territory nor interfere in the administration of Tibet.

While the Russo-Japanese War was still in progress, in August 1905, the Anglo-Japanese Alliance was renewed. This time it was to run for ten years and India and all Eastern Asia were included within the scope of the territory in which Britain and Japan undertook to maintain each other's interests. Great Britain was chiefly concerned for India and Europe, but she was prepared to aid Japan in the Far East proper in case another nation were to join Russia in attempting to dislodge Japan from her holdings in that region. The British and the Japanese stars seemed to be in the ascendant.

In December 1905, China, in an agreement with Japan, assented to the transfer of the Russian holdings as provided in the Treaty of Portsmouth. China also agreed to open several additional towns and cities in Manchuria to foreign residence and trade. She acquiesced in the maintenance by Japan of the railway which the latter empire had built, as a military line, between the Korean border and Mukden, thus allowing a connecting road between the railway system in Korea and the rail facilities which Japan had acquired from Russia. It was alleged that at the same time secret agreements were made between China and Japan which enlarged Japanese control in Manchuria. Among the promises which Peking is said then to have given to Japan was the assurance that until the South Manchurian Railway (as the system belonging to the Japanese was denominated) had been turned over to her, China would construct no lines which would parallel that road or seriously compete with it. It was the violation of this undertaking which the Japanese gave as one reason for their military activities in Manchuria in 1931 and 1932.

To administer the holdings thus acquired in Manchuria, Japan organized the South Manchuria Railway Company and the Government-General of Kwantung. Kwantung meant literally "east of the barrier," namely, the customs post near the eastern end of the Great Wall, and was an alternative name for the southern province of Manchuria. It was also a name for the Japanese holdings in that province. To the South Manchuria Railway Company were entrusted not only the railways, but also water transportation, the operation of mines, the sale of goods carried on the railway, business relating to the land and buildings attached to the railway, and other economic functions. The South Manchuria Railway Company, in other words, although in theory jointly Chinese and Japanese, was in fact a Japanese government enterprise with monopolistic powers over most of the Japanese economic holdings in the region. The Government-General had at its head a Governor-General who was appointed directly by the Emperor of Japan and was to be either a general or a lieutenant general. The South Manchuria Railway Company was to be subordinate to him and he was to have charge of the troops within his jurisdiction and was to conduct all negotiations with the Chinese provincial authorities. The Japanese army, having won the war against Russia, was determined to retain its hold on what had been gained. From this precedent and organization there arose what in time became almost a distinct branch of the Japanese forces, the Kwantung army. The

Kwantung army was later to have an active and prominent role in Japanese expansion both in Manchuria and in the Far East in general.

Growing American Involvement in Manchuria

In the events leading up to the Russo-Japanese War, in the war itself, in the negotiation of the peace, and in the immediate aftermath of the struggle the United States participated in a manner which was indicative of the interest of her government in the Far East and was a further step to even greater involvement in the affairs of that section of the globe. When, after the Boxer outbreak, Russia was clearly reluctant to withdraw her troops from Manchuria and seemed to threaten to absorb the region, the United States, as we hinted a few pages earlier, endeavored to persuade the Russians to evacuate the area and in the new commercial treaty with China (1903) had a provision inserted for the opening to foreign trade of Antung and Mukden in the southern province of Manchuria. She was thus seeking to promote the open door. High American officials believed that in this American interests were in accord with those of Japan and Great Britain. In the war, as we said a few paragraphs back, the sympathies of the people and government of the United States were almost wholly with Japan. It was highly significant that the President of the United States took the lead in bringing the belligerents to the peace table and that the treaty was framed on American soil. The United States was thus sharing in the affairs of East Asia as she had never done in those of the European continent. Precedent was being strengthened for an American role in the one which tradition emphatically discouraged in the other.

The Russo-Japanese War was still in progress when another American move was made, this time by a private citizen. E. H. Harriman was then building a railway empire in the United States. In the summer of 1905 he negotiated an agreement with Ito and the Japanese Premier whereby he was to provide the capital for rebuilding the South Manchuria Railway. The project proved abortive, but it had interesting possibilities of American control of the line.

In 1906 there came to Manchuria as American Consul-General at Mukden the vivid, ambitious Willard Straight. Only five years out of university, he had the vision and energy of youth, combined with persuasive charm. He wished to extend American influence in the

Far East. He hoped to effect this and to preserve the open door by increasing American investments in China. He labored assiduously to check the growth of Japanese monopolistic control in Manchuria. When, in 1908, he returned to the United States as acting head of the newly created Far Eastern Division of the Department of State, he found his views in substantial accord with what was soon to become a general policy of the United States government under the vernacular designation of "dollar diplomacy." In his later years as President, Theodore Roosevelt had been deeply concerned over the growing friction between the United States and Japan, of which we are to say more in the next chapter, and sought to allay it by entering into agreements with Tokyo which would soothe the latter's irritation. However, under President Taft, Straight had an administration more to his mind. Joint international loans were to be made to China to assist her development. In 1909 Harriman and Straight, the latter not now a government official, sought to buy the Russian interest in the Chinese Eastern Railway (the portion of the Manchurian railways still in Russian hands) and to use this as a leverage to purchase the South Manchuria Railway. Harriman's death brought the project to a sudden end.

Later in 1909 Knox, then American Secretary of State, proposed that, to annul special interests in Manchuria, the railways be neutralized. Early in 1910 Russia, Japan, and Great Britain rejected the plan. Presumably the American project was a contributing factor to a Russo-Japanese convention (July 4, 1910) which further cemented an understanding reached in 1907 by which the two governments agreed to respect the *status quo* in Manchuria and to communicate with each other if that were menaced. American activity in behalf of the open door was increasing, but it was palpably driving together the former enemies in their resolution to conserve their respective interests.

The Russo-Japanese War had, then, been an occasion for augmented American activity in Far Eastern affairs. This had been in the attempt to preserve the open door with its corollary, the administrative and territorial integrity of China. Occasionally the United States had seemed to waver slightly, but in the main her purpose was clear. She would seek to cooperate with those powers who would work toward that end. If a power, once apparently friendly to that policy, were, because of its changing interest, to run counter to it, its relations with the United States would become strained. Because of this Japan was increasingly the opponent. She became much more so than any other power or group of powers.

Other Long-range Sequels of the Russo-Japanese War

From the vantage of the wisdom that comes after the event it is now obvious that the Russo-Japanese War made almost inevitable continuing friction in Manchuria. Three strong governments could not have administrative rights in the same area without collision. The railways opened up the land to settlement and Chinese poured in. As nationalism increased, the Chinese more and more regarded the region as an integral part of their domains and would not tolerate the thought of its separation from the rest of the country. Through the Chinese Eastern Railway Russia still had holdings in the north. The Japanese, having expended blood and treasure while China stood by idly and watched the war fought on her soil, were not disposed to surrender what they had obtained at such cost. Moreover, Japan was growing in wealth and population and found in Manchuria an outlet for part of her energy. Her interests were in charge of her army, and the latter thought in terms of guns rather than diplomacy. There was no room for three powers in Manchuria. Two of them would eventually have to get out. In the process force would almost certainly be invoked.

Another and even wider repercussion of the Russo-Japanese War was the accentuation in much of Asia of feeling against the domination of the Occidental. For four centuries, in spite of occasional minor reverses, Europeans had been extending their power over the non-European races of the world. Against that there had always been resentment. Contact with the exaggerated nineteenth century nationalism of Europe had stimulated an incipient nationalism among some of the peoples of the Far East and had further inflamed the opposition to white rule. This was usually most acute among those who had had a Western type of education and who, through it, were aware of what was taking place outside their own immediate neighborhood. Because of the uniform success of European arms, especially in the nineteenth century, resistance had seemed hopeless. Now Japan had fought one of the largest and most imperialistic of the Western powers and had won. This spelled hope. In several countries, notably in India, unrest against Occidental rule mounted. The Japanese, too, were encouraged to think of themselves as champions of the Asiatics. As we are to see in a later chapter, it was a role they were to press in the 1940's.

The Progress of Internal Change in China: Chiefly Political

In China the failure of the Boxer outbreak to oust the foreigner, followed by the further subjection of China to the powers and the humiliation of having helplessly to watch Japan and Russia contend on Chinese soil for the control of territory which had once been Chinese, greatly stimulated the pace of the political and cultural revolution. The consciousness of impotence was given added poignancy by the knowledge that neutral powers had felt China to be so incapable of defending herself that they must make arrangements among themselves for the ostensible respect of her independence and territorial integrity.

We must first carry through the story of the political transformation, together with some of the accompanying modifications in China's foreign relations. We will then take up, under the main phases of culture, the other developments in the reshaping of China's life. We tell our story in this order, not because it occurred in that fashion, but in an attempt to simplify a complex and confusing era in China's history. All aspects of Chinese civilization were being altered at the same time. Each set of changes was interacting on every other. We can better understand what was taking place, however, if we seek to disentangle the several strands, political, intellectual, religious, economic, and social, and to carry each down to 1931. Then fresh events in the international sphere brought further complications. The political side of our story is no more important than the others, but it is the one to which attention was most frequently called, and the others went on within the framework provided by it. We must again stress what we said at the outset of this chapter. A revolution was now in progress such as China had never before known. It was on a larger scale than any the world had ever seen in any one nation, even in the colossal world-wide changes of the twentieth century.

For a time the Manchus sought to guide the revolution. It is conceivable that had the dynasty produced outstanding leadership it would have succeeded in retaining its hold on the helm. However, its sands were fast running out and it produced no one of sufficient stature to reverse or even greatly to delay their course. Since the later years of the eighteenth century the dynasty had clearly been in decline. Had traditional patterns been followed, it would eventually have been displaced by a rebellion and the successful leader of the revolt would have founded another dynasty which would have perpetuated, with unessential modifications, the laws and the framework of administration of its predecessors. This, however, was not to be. Indeed, it was impossible.

The Empress Dowager, now in her late sixties but still vigorous and domineering, endeavored to adjust herself to the new conditions. Presumably she had no more love for the Westerners than when she was ordering their extermination. However, even she was not so blind but that she knew that she must dissemble her true feelings and must seem to like what she could not remove. After the return of the court from its flight she made a point of receiving in friendly fashion the ladies of the legations.

After 1901 there came, with imperial sanction, changes which made those authorized by the Kuang Hsü Emperor in 1898 seem very mild. The reorganization of defense was projected and in part carried through. In effecting the modernization of China's forces Yüan Shih-k'ai was the outstanding general. For a decade or so after 1911 the army built up under his command was an important factor in Chinese politics. It was the army and not the navy which was strengthened. The latter was almost entirely neglected. Remarkable progress was registered in eliminating the domestic growth as well as the importation of opium. In 1902 the intermarriage of Manchus and Chinese was permitted and an order was given that promising Manchu youths be selected and sent abroad for study.

The most far-reaching of the innovations were those in education. Steps were taken to develop a graduated system of government schools in which Western as well as Chinese subjects should be taught. A ministry of education was created. In 1905 the existing civil service examinations based upon the Chinese classics were abolished. The acres of examination stalls in the provincial capitals in which some of the more important of these had been given were dismantled and were turned to other uses.

To the intellectual and ideological significance of these drastic measures in education we will recur in later pages. Here we must note that politically they were of primary importance. Since early in the Han dynasty the Chinese state had been built upon the principles of Confucianism. For stability and successful operation it depended upon a public opinion which accepted Confucianism as the standard for life and upon a body of officialdom thoroughly committed to Confucianism and well grounded in Confucian principles. The civil service examinations and the education that led up to them had been an integral part of the political structure. They, too, went back to the Han dynasty. Increasingly they had been based upon Confucianism. Now they had been wiped out and the educational system was being remodeled in such fashion that for most students in the new schools the Confucian classics would not be accorded chief place. The political question was whether the Confucian state could long survive the change. Even more fundamental was the threat to the basic convictions and assumptions which underlay Chinese civilization. If these were not to be stressed in the schools, would the oncoming generations adhere to them or even know them? They could still be inculcated through the home and through inherited social institutions. However, in the alteration in the educational program one of their chief bulwarks had been weakened. The foundation not only of the state but also of traditional Chinese culture was being undermined.

From the shifting political scene two prominent figures were almost simultaneously removed. In 1908 Tz'ŭ Hsi and the Kuang Hsü Emperor died within a few hours of each other. Gossip inevitably connected the two events and suggested that either the Empress Dowager had made sure that her long-time prisoner should not survive her or that the palace eunuchs who had helped to make his life miserable feared his vengeance once she was withdrawn and saw to it that he accompanied her to the imperial shades. Probably neither should be held accountable, but simply a strange coincidence.

The Emperor who succeeded to the throne was only an infant. The title of his reign period was Hsüan T'ung. He himself was often known to foreigners as Pu-yi. He will reappear from time to time in our story, always as a somewhat pathetic figure. Those of his family in whose hands was the conduct of the government during his minority had even less force and political wisdom than had the dead Emperor and Empress Dowager. They were clearly incompetent to save the dynasty.

Moreover, the new reign was confronted with almost impossible difficulties. Peking was still a center of contending international jealousies and pressures, and the regent and his advisers had to steer a course which called for the greatest astuteness. Financially the government was hard pressed and currency reform was an urgent necessity. Much of the Empire, especially the south and the Yangtze Valley, was honeycombed with secret revolutionary societies.

In the twilight of the Ch'ing attempts were made to placate the reformers by introducing the Western machinery of representative government. A commission was sent to the Occident to study the political institutions in use there. A written constitution was promised. Provincial assemblies were inaugurated in 1909 and a national assembly was convened in 1910. They were to have been followed by a parliament. Membership in these bodies was largely by election, although by a very limited franchise. Had there been wiser and stronger leadership at the top, China might conceivably have been transformed by peaceful processes into a constitutional monarchy of an Occidental type.

The Beginning of the Republic

The requisite leadership was not forthcoming. Instead, the dynasty was swept aside. With it went the Chinese monarchy which in its ideals and forms dated from before the time of Christ. In place of their ancient and accustomed system the Chinese embarked upon the perilous experiment of a republic. The venture was highly dangerous because it was without precedent in the history of the country and the Chinese were without experience with the kinds of institutions on a national scale which the West associated with a republic. In their village and clan organization they had been accustomed to something akin to what the Occident meant by democracy. There was, too, a long-accepted principle that government should be by the worthy and not depend primarily on heredity. This was good Confucian doctrine. If Confucius himself fell short of its full implications and held to the legitimacy of hereditary princes, Mencius, also revered by the orthodox, had seemed to make the voice of the people the voice of God. Although China had long been ruled by a succession of family dynasties, in theory each of these held the throne by the mandate of Heaven, and in case of prolonged incompetence and misgovernment Heaven would withdraw its decree. No orderly method of shifting from one ruling line to another had been worked out. The change had always come through rebellion and civil strife. Popular unrest had been recognized as a warning that Heaven was not happy with the reigning house and, if the latter did not mend its ways, would abandon it. Moreover, through the civil service examinations a way had been gradually developed in which those who, regardless of birth, were best equipped in the basic principles of

Chinese—namely, Confucian—civilization were enabled to come to the attention of the state. Through those chosen from among that group was the actual administration of the imperial government.

This was not what the West meant by democracy. The machinery for making the popular will known and effective was very different from that evolved in the Occident. The successful domestication of Western democratic republican institutions in China could be only by a long and painful process of trial and error. So far as China had the temper of a democracy short cuts under autocratic direction, whether of an individual or a group, would fail. Only gradually and through the efforts of many, both locally and nationally, would machinery be developed and experience be acquired for a democratic republic. Here lay much of the reason for the internal disorder of the ensuing decades.

China stumbled upon her career as a republic. It was much more the weakness of the Ch'ing dynasty and the decrepitude of the old order than the skill of the revolutionists which brought the experiment at the particular time that it began. Quite unintentionally, moreover, joint Western financial aid to China contributed to the initial explosion. For several years revolutionary societies had existed, proscribed, but plotting. Locally there was agitation for greater control by the provinces of mines and railways and resentment against foreign loans made by the central government for the development of these projects. In May 1911, after long negotiations in which shifting Occidental international politics were important, a four-power group, which included American interests, signed a loan with Peking for the development of railways in portions of the valley of the Yangtze, and an imperial decree announced that all privately financed railroads were to be taken over by the national administration and that henceforth all trunk lines were to be built and managed by it. This led to unrest which first broke out in Szechwan. The discovery, through the premature explosion of a bomb, of a revolutionary plot in Hankow led to an insurrection in Wuchang on October 10, 1911. The latter event, the "double tenth" (the tenth day of the tenth month), is officially celebrated as the birthday of the Republic. Li Yüan-hung, an officer in the imperial army at Wuchang, was compelled to assume the leadership of the local revolutionary forces. A republic was proclaimed. Similar uprisings occurred in numbers of other cities. However, there was very little fighting.

To quell the revolt, the imperial court, in a panic, called on Yüan Shih-k'ai. Yüan, as we saw a few paragraphs above, had been in command of what was supposed to be China's best army, equipped and drilled after the Western fashion. During the first few weeks of the new reign he had been given high posts at Peking. However, his part in the *coup d'état* of 1898 had not been forgotten. The regent was the brother of the Kuang Hsü Emperor and presumably had never forgiven what he regarded as Yüan's betrayal of that hapless monarch. Probably for this reason, Yüan had been dismissed, under the face-saving excuse that an affection of the leg incapacitated him. Now the one hope of the dying dynasty seemed to be Yüan and his army. He was frantically summoned to take command. Had he acted promptly and vigorously, as he could had he so wished, he would probably have enabled the dynasty to weather that particular crisis. Had he done so, it would only have been to stave off the inevitable. As it was, he dallied and the revolutionary movement gathered momentum. After delay, presumably to be able to exact his own terms, he yielded to the entreaties of the court. He was appointed premier and was given the most ample powers. Indeed, in actuality if not in open word, the court threw itself upon his mercy. He was able to maintain the authority of the Manchus in most of the north, and especially the northeast, for it was there that his army was based. He moved southward rather deliberately and recovered Hankow and Hanyang.

In the meantime a provisional national organization for the Republic was being set up. Headquarters were established at the old southern capital, Nanking, memorable more recently as the seat of the mid-nineteenth century challenge to the Manchus, the T'ai P'ing movement. The choice for Provisional President fell upon Sun Yat-sen. At the time of the October outbreak, Sun was in the United States, still organizing the overseas Chinese against precisely such a day. Summoned by the revolutionists, he returned to China, was greeted with an ovation, and on December 29, 1911, was elected by a council at Nanking as Provisional President of the Republic. Three days later, on January 1, 1912, he was inaugurated in Western style, taking an oath of office.

In the meantime, negotiations between the revolutionists and imperialists were in progress. The latter were straitened financially as in other ways. Foreign interests were chary of making loans to a palpably shaky regime. Mongolia and part of Sinkiang seemed about to break loose from the now palsied Manchu empire and to be drawn into the Russian orbit. Danger appeared of Japanese intervention.

On February 12, 1912, the six-year-old Emperor abdicated. In the decree issued in his name, sovereignty was vested in the people and Yüan Shih-k'ai was appointed to organize a republic. The Emperor was to retain his title for life, was to receive a large annuity, and was to have the use of a palace. Manchus, Moslems, Mongols, and Tibetans were assured their titles and property and equality with the Chinese. By prearrangement, Sun Yat-sen resigned (February 13) and the council at Nanking elected Yüan as Provisional President (February 14). Thus national unity was reestablished and, with a minimum of civil strife, China set out upon the untried road of a republic. Recognition was accorded by the complacent powers. Outwardly the auspices were favorable.

In this almost casual fashion, seemingly with only a slight jar, China abandoned the Confucian monarchy to which she had been accustomed for at least two thousand years. It is not surprising that the comparative peacefulness of the immediate transition was deceptive and that decades of disorder followed.

For about fifteen years, into 1926, the course was downward. The authority of the central government declined. As earlier after the collapse of a dynasty, rival military leaders arose and multiplied, war lords contending for power. Had precedent been followed, one of them would eventually have eliminated the others and founded a new ruling line. Yüan, indeed, tried it. However, the idea of a republic was too deeply implanted, a convenient slogan for Yüan's opponents. He failed. Beginning with 1926 the party triumphed which had Sun Yat-sen as its tutelary spirit and which, in theory, was committed to republican principles. Disunion continued, but was lessened. Significantly, too, the most persistent division was not between monarchists and republicans, for the former faded out, but between differing degrees of radicalism in the adoption and adaptation of social and political theories from the Occident. In 1945 the conflict had not yet been resolved.

To the main outlines of this story we are now to turn, interrupting it from time to time to note the relations with other nations. The two strands, domestic and foreign, were so closely intertwined that, so far as this is possible, they must be followed concurrently.

China under Yüan Shih K'ai (1912–1916)

The ease with which outward differences between Yüan Shih-k'ai and the revolutionists had been composed was only a brief precursor to more troubled days. Those who had brought about the revolution were dominant in the Parliament. The most powerful group of these was in the Kuomintang, the National People's Party, organized in the summer of 1912. Under the provisional constitution under which the Republic was operating, the authority of the President was greatly restricted, and the Kuomintang determined to keep it so. Yüan controlled the strongest army in the country but temporized for the time being. Sun Yat-sen, busied with the congenial task of elaborating grandiose plans for railway development, was cooperative.

However, against the opposition of the Kuomintang, Yüan concluded (1913) a large loan with a financial consortium in which were represented bankers of five powers, Great Britain, France, Russia, Germany, and Japan. The security was the salt tax, an ancient form of Chinese revenue. The American group had pulled out when President Wilson, a few days after his inauguration, withdrew the support of the United States government on the ground that the terms of the loan compromised the administrative independence of China. Thus supplied with the sinews of war and assured of a certain degree of moral support by the five governments whose financial interests were involved, Yüan felt himself in a position to take action against the radicals. He placed a number of his own men in important military posts in the Yangtze Valley and the south. Open revolt came in the summer of 1913. Yüan promptly and ruthlessly suppressed it. Sun Yat-sen, who had sympathized with it and was accused of diverting to it funds earmarked for railways, took refuge in Japan.

Yüan thereupon obtained the adoption of those portions of what was optimistically termed the permanent constitution which had to do with the selection of the President and had himself placed in that office. Thus he ceased to be simply the provisional head of the government. In November 1913, he dismissed the Kuomintang members of Parliament and the following January rid himself of the rump Parliament which remained. He now seemed to be in effective and dictatorial control. Li Yüan-hung, a hero of the early days of the revolution, was elected Vice-President.

In 1915 Yüan Shih-k'ai felt himself powerful enough to take a further step and reestablish the monarchy with himself as Emperor. He first went through the form of taking a nation-wide referendum among the vocal classes. This was so conducted that the return was deceptively favorable. The monarchy was to be restored on January 1, 1916. Japan, reenforced by Great Britain, Russia, and France, allies in the world war then in progress, counseled delay. In December 1915, rebellion broke out in Yünnan and spread to other provinces. Yielding to pressure, Yüan postponed the coronation and then re-instated the republic.

However, Yüan's enemies, now thoroughly aroused and heartened by their successes, refused any longer to tolerate as head of the state the repentant President. Yüan, broken in health and by chagrin over his humiliating loss of face, died (June 6, 1916) before his enemies could effect his removal.

Now that Yüan was conveniently taken away by death, Li Yüan-hung, as Vice-President, automatically became President. The radicals were disposed to accept him. He further won them by restoring the constitution of 1912 and recalling the Parliament that had been dissolved by Yüan. As the dominant element in Parliament, the Kuomintang was again in a position to make itself felt. Ostensibly the country was once more united. However, the group representing the elements that had supported Yüan Shih-k'ai, including the army which he had trained, was still potent. Again the calm was only the lull before the renewal of the domestic storm.

The Revolution and Tibet and Mongolia

While Yüan Shih-k'ai was making his four and a half year bid for power, developments were concurrently in progress in the international scene which still further complicated the situation for China.

In the first stages of the Republic, Tibet and Outer Mongolia, two of the dependencies which had been brought into the Empire by the Manchus, loosened the ties that bound them to the government in Peking. The republican administration insisted that Tibet was still a part of China. However, by the end of 1912 Chinese troops were expelled from all but the fringes of the land. The British attempted to bring about a tripartite settlement between themselves, the Chinese, and the Tibetans, but the Chinese would not assent to the proposed agreement. In 1914 Great Britain reached an accord whereby the portion of Tibet which adjoined India was to be autonomous, although still technically a part of China.

On the eve of the Revolution the Chinese had been strengthening their hold on Mongolia. Chinese settlers pushed forward into the grasslands of Inner Mongolia, bringing more of them under the plow. Other Chinese, many of them traders, went into Outer Mongolia. Chinese officials attempted to tax the Mongols and to require of them military service. Much discontent arose, partly over the exactions of Chinese traders, moneylenders, and officials. The Mongols sought help from Russia.

At the first news of the Revolution, Outer Mongolia declared its independence. Russia welcomed the step, but disavowed territorial ambitions in the region and suggested that, while direct Chinese rule should cease, Chinese suzerainty be retained. Indeed, in 1912 Russia formally recognized the autonomy of Outer Mongolia. In the year 1913 China, perforce, entered into an agreement with Russia whereby, in return for recognition of her suzerainty, she accepted the autonomy of Outer Mongolia and the special privileges which Russians enjoyed in the region.

China in the First Months of World War I

The Republic had been in existence less than three years when it found itself a pawn in a world war.

The outbreak of that struggle in the summer of 1914 presented to Japan what seemed to her a most fortunate opportunity. Europe was in internecine strife and could pay little attention to its holdings in the Far East, on the far periphery of its interests. Here was a chance to gain at the expense of the Occident.

At the inception of the war in Europe, the Chinese government, realizing something of its peril as a weak neutral and with enclaves of the belligerents within its borders, asked that hostilities be kept out of its territories and waters and the foreign leaseholds within its domains. It also declared its neutrality. Peking requested the good offices of the United States in obtaining from the belligerents their promise to respect this request. China thus sought the aid of the United States in what proved to be a further step toward American commitments in the Far East. Washington did not undertake all that Peking had desired, but it did make some effort to induce the belligerents to assent to the Chinese notes. None of the warring powers would comply, except Germany, and she only tardily and because she stood to gain by the measure and not to lose. The others clearly hoped to see Germany ousted from China.

Before many days Japan entered the war. This she did under the convenient cloak provided by the Anglo-Japanese Alliance. She "advised" Germany to withdraw her armed vessels from Japanese and Chinese waters and to hand over to Japan her leased territory of Kiaochow, in the province of Shantung, "without condition or compensation . . . with a view to eventual restoration of the same to China." Japan could plead not only her alliance with Great Britain but also an *entente* with France and treaties with Russia, the absence of similar agreements with Germany, and the memory of Berlin's part in easing Japan out of the Liaotung Peninsula in 1895. In Japan there were those who favored the German cause, but the weight of sentiment was with the Allies. Later in August 1914, since Germany had not responded, Japan declared war.

Japan thereupon proceeded to take Kiaochow. She had already advised China not to go to war or to allow Germany to recede Kiaochow. In moving against Kiaochow, Japan violated China's neutrality by dispatching her attacking forces across Chinese territory and treating with great harshness the Chinese who were unfortunate enough to be in their path. China protested, and then, following the precedent of the Russo-Japanese War, defined a war zone. The Japanese, however, did not consider themselves bound by either. Nor did Great Britain, although she had entered the European war ostensibly because of the violation of Belgian neutrality, formally object to the action of her Far Eastern ally. Indeed, a small British contingent cooperated with the Japanese attack. Early in November 1914, the Japanese overcame the German resistance and captured Tsingtao, the port for Kiaochow.

The Twenty-One Demands and Other Japanese Activities in China

Although, in August 1914, Okuma, the Premier of Japan, emphatically declared that his government had "no ulterior motive, no desire to secure more territory, no thought of depriving China or other peoples of anything which they now possess," in January 1915, less than six months later, Japan presented China with a set of demands which sought to bring all of that vast land under Japanese control and within the effective orbit of the Japanese Empire.

These demands were twenty-one in number and were arranged in five groups. Group one had to do with Shantung. China was to agree to any disposition which Japan might arrange with Germany of the latter's former rights in Shantung. She was to promise not to alienate "to a third power" any territory in that province or along her coast—a provision which would mark that territory out as a Japanese sphere of influence, for it was a phrase by which such spheres had been set aside by European powers in the period of the threatened partition of China late in the 1890's. China was also to grant Japan permission to build an important railway in the province and to open certain key cities and towns in Shantung as treaty ports. Group two of the demands dealt with southern Manchuria and eastern Inner Mongolia. China was to assent to the extension of the lease on Port Arthur and Dairen from the twenty-five years originally specified to ninety-nine years and similarly to extend Japan's control of her railways in southern Manchuria. Anywhere in these regions Japanese subjects were to be allowed to reside or travel and to lease or own land—a treaty right which China had not accorded aliens in China Proper. Moreover, China was not to employ political, financial, or military advisers in the region without the consent of Japan or to grant to citizens of any third power the privilege of building railways in the area without Japanese permission. The third group provided for transforming into a joint Chino-Japanese enterprise the Hanyehping Company, located in central China and the largest iron works in the Republic. By group four China was to undertake "not to cede or lease to a third power any harbor or bay or island" along her coast. This in effect would have made all China a Japanese sphere of influence. Group five was even more sweeping. China was to employ Japanese "advisers in political, financial, and military affairs"; she was to grant to Japanese hospitals, churches, and schools the right to own land in the interior and to Japanese missionaries, presumably Buddhist, the privilege of missionary propaganda; in "important places" police were to be "jointly administered by Japanese and Chinese" or numerous Japanese were to be employed; China was to buy from Japan fifty per cent or more of her munitions of war or establish an arsenal to be jointly worked by Chinese and Japanese; the right of constructing some important railway lines in the Yangtze Valley (presumably the sphere of interest of Japan's ally, Great Britain) was to be given to the Japanese; and before borrowing capital "to work mines, build railways, and construct harbor works (including dockyards) in the province of Fukien" China was to consult Japan.

The effect of these demands, if granted in full, would have been to reduce China to a protectorate of Japan. It was frequently said by the apologists of Japan that more was asked than was expected. However, in view of Japan's actions in the 1930's and 1940's, the Twenty-One Demands merely foreshadowed what the extremists in Japan desired.

It is not surprising that Japan enjoined upon the Chinese government secrecy as to the content and even the existence of the demands. Nor is it remarkable that secrecy could not be maintained. As the demands leaked out they brought consternation and indignation in China and the articulate elements rallied to the support of the government.

Of the larger Western powers, only the United States was in a position to protest. The Allies were engrossed in their life and death struggle with Germany. Even the United States became occupied with the *Lusitania* crisis. Washington somewhat cautiously remonstrated with Japan and later notified both Tokyo and Peking that it could not "recognize any agreement or undertaking which has been entered into or which may be entered into between the Governments of Japan and China impairing the treaty rights of the United States and its citizens in China, the political or territorial integrity of the Republic of China, or the international policy relative to China commonly known as the Open Door policy." In sending this note the United States was clearly within its legal rights. It was also holding to its principles reiterated again and again since the closing years of the nineteenth century. It was the one major third power to place a *caveat* against Japan's action. Moreover, additional precedent was provided for further efforts to restrain Japan and especially for the Stimson Doctrine of 1932 to which we are to come in a future chapter. Yet the United States was neither in the mood nor the position to use armed force.

Although unable herself to contest in battle the issue raised by Japan and without a friend who was prepared to fight for her, China came off remarkably well. She assented to the demands in the first three groups, but with important modifications in her favor. Group four was met by a presidential mandate which directed that no portion of China's coast should be ceded or leased to any power—and this, of course, included Japan. As to the ominous fifth group, Japan said that its contents were "postponed for later negotiation," but China stated that she had no intention of giving any foreign nation a foothold on the coast of Fukien. Even such concessions as their government had made were viewed by patriotic Chinese as obtained under duress and not binding.

In 1916 Japan attempted further to extend and consolidate her position in Manchuria and eastern Inner Mongolia. To this end she took advantage of a clash between Chinese and Japanese troops on the Manchurian-Mongolian border, disregarding the fact that her forces were where they had no legal right to be.

Early in 1917, moreover, as the German pressure on the Allies was intensified through a renewal of unrestricted submarine warfare, Japan obtained secret assurances from Great Britain, France, and Russia of their support at the peace table of her claim to the former German holdings in Shantung. In return, Japan sent a naval force to the Mediterranean to assist the Allies. Japan was also to be backed in her request for the German islands north of the equator—which she had taken early in the war. She, too, was to encourage China to break diplomatic relations with Germany. In other words, in their life and death struggle, the chief Allies, to bolster their cause, were clandestinely selling out China to Japan to make sure of the latter's support.

World War I Brings Further Complications

China was drawn still further into the maelstrom of the world war. In 1916 France began recruiting Chinese laborers for noncombatant service behind the lines in the West. In 1917 Great Britain adopted a similar procedure. Scores of thousands of Chinese coolies, accordingly, served in the Occident, most of them in northern France.

In 1917 China became a belligerent on the side of the Allies. When, in February of that year, President Wilson severed America's diplomatic relations with Germany, he suggested to other neutral powers that they do likewise. The following month China, partly in response to pressure from the American Minister in Peking, followed Washington's example.

The additional step of formal belligerency, apparently logical, entailed internal discord. It was taken in August 1917, but not before it had led to a breach in the frail semblance of unity which the Chinese government presented to the world. The division was not so much over entry into the war as it was over which branch of the government should take the initiative in the decision. The head of the faction representing the Yüan Shih-k'ai tradition was Tuan Ch'i-jui. Tuan was Premier. Tension between him and Parliament, where the Kuomintang was the strongest element, was already acute. Tuan carried on the negotiations with the Allies. He brought pressure upon Parliament to pass the war measure which he favored. Parliament resented what it deemed an effort to dragoon it. Constrained by parliamentary wrath, Li Yüan-hung, the President, dismissed Tuan Ch'i-jui. The latter's supporters, military men with their center at the adjacent Tientsin, declared the independence of several of the northern provinces. For a time Li stood firm, but neither he nor Parliament had an effective military force to maintain their hold on Peking. Li called to his aid Chang Hsün, a military man not committed to the Tuan Ch'i-jui clique, who had an army conveniently astride the railway between Nanking and Peking. Chang Hsün responded, came with his forces to Peking, and advised that Parliament be dismissed. Li had no recourse but compliance. Thereupon Chang Hsün astonished the nation and the world by declaring the restoration of the Ch'ing dynasty. He seems to have taken this startling decision from a sense of loyalty—inculcated by traditional Chinese ethics—of a minister to his prince. However, the Tuan Ch'i-jui group were no more prepared to brook the boy Emperor and his entourage than they were Parliament. They marched on Peking and before the middle of July had taken it. Chang Hsün sought sanctuary in the hospitable Dutch Legation. The boy Emperor retired again to the quiet seclusion of his palace. Li Yüan-hung, suffering from immense loss of face, refused longer to carry the thankless burden of the presidency and found haven in the foreign concessions of Tientsin. Tuan Ch'i-jui once more became Premier and an obedient Parliament summoned by his supporters chose for President an ex-official of the old regime, the elderly and harmless Hsü Shih-ch'ang. China was officially in the war, but the members of what claimed to be the legitimate Parliament, disgruntled and irate, set up a rival administration at Canton.

China, thus divided, could play neither an active nor a glorious part in the war. She both lost and profited by her participation. Partly as a result of her belligerency, she fell further under the influence of Japan. The Tuan Ch'i-jui clique, in control in Peking, seemed complacent to mounting Japanese authority. A "war participation board" was constituted with a Japanese adviser. This and an "arms contract" were ominously reminiscent of the fifth group of the Twenty-One Demands. Extensive loans were made by Japan to China, on the security of railways, mines, forests, telegraphs, taxes, and bonds.

While these ultimately proved uncollectible, at the time they appeared to presage the kind of control by Japan which earlier loans had seemed to secure to European powers.

Moreover, through the Lansing-Ishii agreement the United States appeared to have softened in her attitude toward Japan's activities in China. Now that the United States and Japan were associated in the war against the Central Powers, it was only common prudence to attempt to compose the differences which had brought strain upon their relations. The European Allies had been unhappy over the manner in which Japan was obtaining an economic strangle hold on China and were attempting to persuade the United States once more to participate in the consortium for joint loans to China. In the autumn of 1917 came American reentrance into that financial group. Ishii, sent to Washington to obtain better relations for Japan with the United States government, endeavored to induce the latter to recognize his nation's "paramount interest" in China as akin to that which the United States had in Mexico. To this the American Secretary of State, Lansing, would not assent. He countered with a proposal that a joint Japanese-American declaration be issued to respect the open door and the territorial integrity of China. This was not acceptable to Ishii. A compromise was agreed upon by which Tokyo and Washington expressed themselves as opposed to the acquisition by any government of "any special rights or privileges which would affect the independence or territorial integrity of China, or would deny to the subjects or citizens of any country the full enjoyment of equal opportunity in the commerce and industry of China," but prefaced this with an acknowledgment "that territorial propinquity creates special relations between countries" and with a statement that the government of the United States, accordingly, recognized "that Japan has special interests in China, particularly in that part to which her possessions are contiguous." This seemed on its face to be a surrender of the United States to Japan and was so interpreted by some circles in Japan and China. However, in a secret protocol Ishii assented to Lansing's stipulation that the war should not be used to upset the *status quo* in China. Moreover, by reconstituting the four-power financial consortium of France, Great Britain, Japan, and herself the United States hoped to check Japanese unilateral expansion in China by means of loans.

On the positive side, by her entry into the war China registered some distinct gains. The Allies agreed, with certain exceptions, to the suspension for five years of payments by her on the Boxer Indemnity. China took over German concessions in Tientsin and Hankow and the Austro-Hungarian concession in Tientsin. France and Britain had welcomed China into the war as a means of driving German merchants and German commercial competition out of China. This they accomplished for the time being, but their temporary advantage was probably their ultimate loss. A breach had been made in the solid front of European special privileges in China—an advantage which China was to pursue. The collapse of Russia and the Russian Revolution in 1917 led, as we shall see in the next chapter, to the occupation of eastern Siberia by Japanese, Americans, and some of the European Allies. This entailed control of the Russian road in Manchuria, the Chinese Eastern Railway. Japan sought possession of the line as she did of eastern Siberia and was checkmated there as in the latter by the United States. An interallied commission with an American at its head operated the Chinese Eastern Railway until 1922. China was represented and for a time after 1920 had the chief hand in the management. China, moreover, was, as a belligerent on the side of the Allies, represented at the peace conference at the close of the war. This gave her an opportunity to make her voice heard in the post war settlement.

China at the Peace Conference

At the peace conference at Paris, China ably made her case. She had a delegation which officially spoke for both her governments which claimed legality—the one at Peking and that at Canton.

The leaders of the delegation demanded not only the retrocession to China of the former German properties in Shantung but also the abrogation of the Chino-Japanese treaties of 1915 which grew out of the Twenty-One Demands and of the Chino-Japanese agreements of 1918 which had brought further limitations on China. In general, the Americans were favorable and even labored to obtain China's desires in Shantung. However, the European Allies, bound by their secret treaties of 1917 with Japan and themselves seeking portions of former German overseas possessions, were in no position to thwart Tokyo. The Shantung properties were awarded to Japan, but the latter's representatives declared it to be the policy of their government to hand back to China the debated territories, retaining only the economic privileges granted to Germany in Shantung and the right to establish a settlement at Tsingtao. Japan was to keep her word, although under strong pressure. This was at the Washington Conference of 1921-1922, of which we are to say more in the following chapter.

The Shantung settlement was intensely unpopular among the articulate classes in China. Because of it China declined to sign the Treaty of Versailles. An anti-Japanese boycott swept across the country. Students were especially vociferous.

By refusing to agree to the Treaty of Versailles, China by no means sacrificed the advantages obtained by participating in the war. She gained membership in the League of Nations through the general treaty with Austria, to which the Covenant of the League was also attached, but from which the objectionable Shantung provisions were absent. She made a separate treaty with Germany. The latter agreed to the surrender of all her special privileges in China, including extraterritoriality. Moreover, in the treaties with the new states in Europe which arose out of the war no provision was made for extraterritoriality. China was thus obtaining partial emancipation from restrictions upon her sovereignty.

The Progressive Deterioration of China's National Government

After the division between the Parliament and Tuan Ch'i-jui and the departure of Li Yüan-hung, China's internal affairs went politically from bad to worse. This was probably to be expected. China's abandonment of her hereditary imperial structure and her lack of experience with republican institutions spelled difficulty. The traditional local and provincial semi-autonomy with the minimum control from the national capital also assisted centrifugal forces. The precedent of civil war at the fall of a dynasty was confirmed with rival aspirants for power fighting one another. The disorder made for unemployment. The armies of the rival war lords were thronged by those thrown out of their regular occupations. Most of the armies were poorly disciplined and were as much a scourge to the civilians as were the multitudinous bandits. Civil strife and banditry threw still more below the poverty line and further swelled the ranks of those who took to fighting or robbery in preference to starvation. Here was a vicious circle which for the moment could not be broken.

The details of the next few years are confusing in the extreme. Fortunately they are not essential to an understanding of the later China and so need not here be recounted. We must, however, mention a few of the major incidents and figures of the nine years which followed 1917, for they lead directly to the succeeding period.

In 1921 Sun Yat-sen was elected head of the government at Canton which claimed to represent China. He maintained himself there precariously. He was a revolutionist and not an administrator and in the latter capacity failed as signally as he succeeded in the former. From the nucleus at Canton was to come the reunification of the country on the basis of his ideals, but not until after death had removed him from his ineptitudes as the head of a government and made it possible to canonize him as the patron saint and the rallying point of the progressives.

The Peking government became progressively weaker. In 1920 a combination of war lords drove out of Peking the group which had centered about Tuan Ch'i-jui. It was badly discredited by its willingness to truckle to the Japanese. One of those who joined in the act of expulsion was Chang Tso-lin, the master of Manchuria. Chang Tso-lin, soft in voice and scholarly in appearance, was one of the most vigorous and ruthless of the tribe of war lords. In 1922 he was worsted at Peking and withdrew to Manchuria. Wu P'ei-fu, the rival who had defeated him, sought the reunification of the nation by recalling Li Yüan-hung to the Presidency together with the Parliament which had been elected in 1913 and which had been dismissed first by Yüan Shih-k'ai and then, in 1917, at the behest of Chang Hsün. Wu P'ei-fu was something of a scholar of the old school and won grudging respect from many by having more of idealism than the majority of his competitors. Wu's hope was that since Li Yüan-hung and the Parliament of 1913 had been the government last recognized by most of the country, they would be able to heal the divisions. This dream proved illusory. After about a year, in 1923, Li Yüan-hung, discouraged, withdrew again to the somnolent security of the foreign concessions in Tientsin. A successor obtained election by the brazen use of heavy bribes, but the following year was forced out. Civil strife seemed to reappear with the coming of each spring. Tuan Ch'i-jui for a while came back as Provisional Chief Executive (not President), but in 1926 even he retired. Only a rapidly shifting cabinet kept up the fiction of a central government in Peking. Chang Tso-lin, Wu P'ei-fu, and Fêng Yü-hsiang were the major military figures in the north. Fêng Yü-hsiang was of rude peasant stock, huge of frame and forthright. He had become a Christian and for a time gained fame by the fashion in which he disciplined his troops into freedom from most of the usual camp vices and from preying on the countryside.

The Reunification of China under the Kuomintang

Reunification began to be apparent in 1926 and was eventually achieved under the Kuomintang, the party of Sun Yat-sen.

Sun Yat-sen died March 12, 1925, while in Peking conferring with Chang Tso-lin and Wu P'ei-fu in an endeavor to bring the country together. In 1923 he had called to his assistance Russian advisers, Communists. He himself was not a Communist, but he was disposed to accept aid wherever he could obtain it. Under the counsel of the Russians the Kuomintang was reshaped somewhat after the pattern of the party in Russia. Sun Yat-sen, deceased, was accorded a position akin to that of Lenin in Russia as the national hero and center of cohesion. Weekly memorial services before his picture were instituted in the schools and in community after community. His last will and testament, directed to the nation, was formally and regularly read in public as a means of inculcating his ideals. A book of which he was the author, the *San Min Chu I*, or the *Three People's Principles*, was made the textbook for the state, the design on which the nation was to be organized. The three principles can be succinctly summarized as the people's government (namely, government by the people and for the people), the people's livelihood (or an adequate standard of living for all), and the people's nationalism (freedom from control by foreign nations). Sun Yat-sen was said to envisage a period of tutelage under the domination of one party, but to have regarded this as only a stage to a fully democratic regime. A military academy was set up at Whampoa, near Canton, in which officers were trained for the armies of the Kuomintang and in the party's program. The Communist agitators organized unions of laborers and peasants. Foreign imperialism was denounced and all forms of capitalism, including landlordism, were anathema. Although Russians were influential and Communists were within the structure of the Kuomintang, by no means all the members of the party were committed to them. The marriage was one of convenience and proved temporary.

In the summer of 1926 the Kuomintang armies started from Canton on a northward advance. This for a time was like a triumphal progress. The armies were preceded and accompanied by propaganda which painted rosy pictures of a new order. The Communists seemed dominant and the path of the armies was marked by anti-capitalist and anti-imperialist agitation and action. The young general in command of the armies, Chiang Kai-shek, was able and vigorous. Chiang, born in 1887 of sturdy stock in the province of Chekiang not far from Ningpo, had early adopted revolutionary principles. In the days of the Ch'ing dynasty he had deliberately acquired a military education, first in an academy in the north and then in Japan. He was an ardent admirer and a trusted and tested follower of Sun Yat-sen. After a trip to Russia where he had studied the Soviet system sympathetically but without becoming a Communist, he had been commissioned by Sun to organize and head the Whampoa military academy where, as we saw in the preceding paragraph, the officers for the new army were trained. Incidentally, that academy, Chiang's first love, was moved to successive Kuomintang capitals—Nanking and Chungking. Chiang was an ardent patriot, sternly self-disciplined, deeply read in some of China's literature, including not only Confucian classics but also a leading Taoist and an outstanding Legalist, the biographies of some of the great Chinese generals of other ages, some of the Chinese standard works on military tactics, and the writings of Sun Yat-sen.

The country, wearied by the years of pointless civil strife and of the exactions and interminable quarrels of selfish war lords, was in a frame of mind to listen eagerly to the promises of peace and well-being. By the spring of 1927 much of the Yangtze Valley had been mastered and the strategic cities of Wuchang, Hankow, and Shanghai had fallen to the Kuomintang armies.

The approaching unity was early threatened by dissensions within the Kuomintang between the Communists and their opponents. For a time Communism was on top. Students returned from the Sun Yat-sen University, founded in Moscow especially for the indoctrination of Chinese youth. Headquarters of the Kuomintang, set up at Hankow, were in the hands of the left wing. The province of Hunan, through which the armies had moved on the northward advance, was largely controlled by Communists. However, moderate and conservative elements in the Kuomintang were increasingly unhappy over the radical swing. With them sided Chiang Kai-shek. The internal conflict was brought to a head by events connected with the capture of Nanking, in March 1927, by the Kuomintang armies. Extremists took the occasion to accord harsh treatment to foreigners and killed some of them. Foreign gunboats probably saved the lives of many more by a timely barrage under the cover of which survivors escaped. Only the self-restraint of the powers prevented the kind of intervention which had punctuated earlier stages of friction between aliens and Chinese. As it was, five of the major powers presented identical notes of protest to the Kuomintang leaders demanding apology, punishment of the commanders involved, and indemnification for damage done. The United States government stood for a conciliatory policy and the others were prepared to give the moderates in the Kuomintang opportunity to deal with the extremists. The former set up a regime at Nanking in opposition to the one at Hankow. For the moment the northward advance of the Kuomintang halted. By the end of 1927, however, public opinion had turned overwhelmingly against the Communists, the government at Hankow came to an end, and the Russian advisers fled. The anti-Communist elements instituted a stern purge and many radicals, among them hundreds of students, were executed.

Once more fairly well unified through these drastic measures, the Kuomintang pressed its northward campaign. In June 1928, its armies entered Peking. The victory was slightly delayed by a clash with Japanese troops in Tsinan, the capital of Shantung. In the taking of Peking Chang Tso-lin fled with his forces to his special territory, Manchuria. On his retreat he was killed by a bomb dropped on his coach. The Chinese were convinced that the act was by Japanese. Chang Tso-lin was succeeded by his son, Chang Hsüeh-liang. The latter was much more inclined to cooperate with the Kuomintang than his father had been. This contributed, as we are to see in the chapter after next, to the clash with the Japanese which was the first act in the drama that opened in September 1931.

The occupation of Peking assisted the unification of China under the Kuomintang, but did not complete it. Here and there local provincial leaders held out or collaborated only under thinly disguised opposition. Moreover, in 1930 Yen Hsi-shan, governor of the province of Shansi since the early days of the Revolution, and Fêng Yü-hsiang joined in opposition to Chiang Kai-shek. The latter won. Although the center at Hankow had been reduced, Communism remained strong. From 1930 to 1933 Communists were in control in a large land area which comprised portions of the provinces of Kiangsi, Anhui, and Fukien. For a brief span in 1930 they were in possession of the capital of Hunan. They were also strong in sections of Hupeh. Against the Communists Chiang Kai-shek waged relentless war. He was backed by the wealthy elements which were based on the trade and manufactures of Shanghai and the lower reaches of the Yangtze Valley. In 1931 China was much more nearly one than in 1926, but was still far from being a completely united nation. Not only were some of the war lords and the Communists in opposition, but also in large areas banditry was rife.

However, by the summer of 1931 the prospects for a united China were better than they had been since 1915 and in some respects brighter than at any time since the Revolution of 1911. The Kuomintang had an organization whose network covered most of the country. The capital was at Nanking, an ancient city with imperial traditions in the section of China's greatest wealth and where the influence of Western civilization was particularly strong. Here, within the vast area embraced by gray walls erected early in the Ming dynasty, a modern city was rapidly developed. New streets and thoroughfares and numerous government structures were physical testimony to the new life. On an adjacent mountain a massive mausoleum was constructed for Sun Yat-sen and, with great pomp, his body was deposited in it.

Chiang Kai-shek was the strongest figure in the Kuomintang. This he was because of ability and force of character. He also allied himself by marriage with the Soong family. This was already influential and gained in power by its relations with him. The elder Soong, now dead, had as a lad gone to the United States and had there, through the kindness of American friends, acquired a Western education. He returned to China as a missionary, but later, while remaining an earnest Christian, went into business in Shanghai and became wealthy. He gave his children an Occidental education, culminating in colleges and universities in the United States. He was a warm friend of Sun Yat-sen and an ardent supporter of the latter's revolutionary projects. Sun married one of the Soong daughters. Another of the sisters was wooed and won by Chiang Kai-shek. Still another married H. H. Kung, an American-educated Christian descendant of Confucius who became prominent in the new government. A son, T. V. Soong, was the financial wizard of the Kuomintang regime.

In general the Kuomintang attracted the progressive elements who had had an education of an Occidental type. Through them the Westernization of the country and of the government proceeded apace. The driving power was not slavish imitation of the West, but nationalism. It was appropriate that the usual English translation of Kuomintang was the Nationalist Party. Among the articulate elements the sense of nationalism, already strong, was mounting. Although the Kuomintang did not yet control all the Empire, some of the services, including the Maritime Customs, the Salt Gabelle, and the Post

Office, which headed up in the capital, embraced areas which otherwise had not submitted. The Post Office especially was nation-wide.

Democracy was not yet fully achieved. Government was by one party without legally recognized opposition. The Kuomintang itself was largely dependent on propertied elements. Chiang Kai-shek, while not an unregulated dictator, was clearly the strong man upon whom depended much of such unity as the state possessed.

Yet Sun Yat-sen's principles were accepted as standard and through them a fairly cohesive ideology was at the base of the regime. In this China was running true to form. As the Empire had been built upon Confucianism, so the Republic was being constructed on the doctrines set forth by its chief founder, and especially in his *San Min Chu I*. Chiang Kai-shek, too, was appealing to principles of Confucian origin and these were still deeply imbedded in Chinese customs and standards.

Progressive Recovery of Autonomy

In the 1920's China made striking progress toward freeing herself from the restrictions on her full autonomy to which she had been subjected in the course of the preceding two or three generations.

At first sight these gains were amazing, for, as we have seen in the preceding few pages, until 1926 the course of China's internal affairs was progressively toward disintegration.

However, on more sober second thought they were not at all surprising. By World War I a breach had been made in the solid front of Western special privileges in China. The Germans and Austrians had lost their concessions in the cities and their extraterritorial status. The new states in Europe were not accorded extraterritorial privileges. The Russian Revolution seemed to make further for the emancipation of China. In 1919-1921 the Chinese took advantage of the disorder in Russia and Siberia to renew their effective control over Outer Mongolia. In 1920 China suspended the payments on the Boxer indemnity to Russia. In 1919 the Communist regime in Russia offered to negotiate with China on the basis of the renunciation of extraterritoriality and all other special Russian privileges in China, the cancellation of its share of the Boxer indemnity, the return of territory seized under the Czar's regime, and the restoration to China of full control of the Chinese Eastern Railway. From the standpoint of the Soviets the loss of extraterritoriality was no sacrifice, for practically all those affected were refugees, adherents of the Czar, and the Communists would be very glad to see them deprived of such preferential status as was theirs under the old treaties. As to the return of territory and the Chinese Eastern Railway, we shall see in a moment that when it came to action Soviet Russia was quite as unyielding as the Czar's officials had been.

As to the United States, Great Britain, and France, the other major Occidental powers, the period was one in which public sentiment swung somewhat away from imperialism and there was reluctance to impose the will of these countries by force upon non-Occidental peoples. During most of the 1920's, moreover, Japan was less disposed to be aggressive in China than she had been in the previous few years or than she was to be in the 1930's. Under these circumstances, external conditions favored Chinese efforts to annul the compromises of independence that were so galling to sensitive nationalists.

The nationalism which was a chief bulwark of the Kuomintang pressed for the liberation of China from what it dubbed the "unequal treaties." It did this even before the Kuomintang came to power. Since the Three People's Principles included "the People's Nationalism," with full emancipation from alien control, it was to be expected that the party which took these as its slogans would stress treaty revision. The radical wing of the Kuomintang made foreign imperialists a chief object of its wrath. The moderates in that party, while not so extreme in their measures, were no less determined to regain what the Ch'ing dynasty had sacrificed.

In its campaign against foreign privileges and its opposition to foreign aggression Chinese nationalism had at hand as a most annoying weapon mass action, especially through the boycott. This was no innovation in China. The Chinese had long employed group measures against such of their own officials as proved obnoxious. The student leadership in anti-imperialistic agitation was also a continuation of the prominence of the scholar in Chinese society. Chinese traditional methods, therefore, could be and were invoked by the new nationalism. The newspaper and the postal service, Western importations, were employed to reenforce the hereditary methods. The boycott hit foreigners at a peculiarly vulnerable point, their trade, for it was commerce which had drawn the majority of the foreign residents to the Middle Kingdom. Yet the boycott hit both ways. Chinese as well as foreigners suffered from it. Moreover, what were in effect Chinese racketeers often made considerable profit from toll levied on goods which they allowed to slip past the prohibitions.

The gains which the Chinese achieved against the "unequal treaties" were noteworthy. We have already remarked the breach in the wall of extraterritoriality effected through World War I.

The Washington Conference, to which we are to come for fuller treatment in the next chapter, brought China further concessions. The Japanese restored the Shantung properties, although not unconditionally. The major Western powers except Germany and Russia (who were unrepresented at the gathering) promised to respect the sovereignty, the independence, and the territorial and administrative integrity of China, to give China opportunity to develop a stable and effective government, to use their influence to preserve "the principle of equal opportunity for the commerce and industry of all nations throughout the territory of China," to refrain from taking advantage of conditions in China to seek special privileges which would abridge the rights of subjects or citizens of friendly states, and to respect China's rights as a neutral in any war to which she was not a party. Those powers having special postal agencies in China—an infringement on China's postal service—agreed to discontinue them not later than January 1, 1923. This especially hit Japan, for that power had most of the foreign post offices in China. The signatory powers agreed to a revision, through a commission, of duties on imports into China. They also promised the appointment of a commission to study extraterritoriality. Great Britain gave assurances that she would surrender her leasehold on Weihaiwei which had been acquired in the concession-grabbing year of 1898. She completed the restoration in 1930. Japan relented a little on some of her claims to priority in loans and the appointment of advisers in southern Manchuria and Inner Mongolia. She also withdrew completely the objectionable fifth group of the Twenty-One Demands which previously she had merely deferred for further consideration.

Russia so far fulfilled her promise of 1919 that in 1924 she signed an agreement that relinquished Russian extraterritoriality, special Russian concessions, and the Russian portion of the Boxer indemnity. However, Russia reserved a veto on the use of the funds so remitted and set conditions on China's repurchase of the Chinese Eastern Railway.

Other countries followed up the suspension of payments on the Boxer indemnity by conditional permanent remission. In every instance the sums thus released were specifically earmarked for particular purposes—such as the education of Chinese and the purchase in the remitting country of materials for the construction of railways and other public utilities.

As an aftermath of the Washington agreements China regained full control over the fixing of her own tariff rates. Conferences were held in Peking in 1925 and 1926 which sought to solve the problem. In 1928 and 1929 practically all the powers except Japan agreed to China's resumption of tariff autonomy. In 1930 Japan gave her consent, and the Dutch followed later in the year. On February 1, 1929, without waiting for Japanese and Dutch permission, China put into effect a schedule of duties which she herself had fixed. What had been one galling feature of the treaties was thus eliminated.

Many of the "concessions" which China had granted in her cities were also annulled. Some of these had been granted before the 1890's, chiefly to Great Britain. Others dated from 1898 and 1899, the era of the threatened partition of China. Still others, in Tientsin, were the result of the Boxer year. All of them were irritants. Commanding, as they did, China's most important ports and being under alien jurisdiction, they were symbols ever in the eyes of China's nationalists of their country's weakness. The German and Austrian concessions reverted to China in consequence of World War I. The Russian concessions passed into her hands as a sequel to the collapse of the Czarist regime. In the second half of the 1920's the anti-imperialistic ire of China's nationalists was directed chiefly against the British. This was partly because Great Britain had taken the lead in forcing open the doors of China and in negotiating the treaties which the Chinese deemed "unequal." Moreover, Great Britain still had an outstanding position in China's leading port, Shanghai, and in several of the river cities along the Yangtze. The Yangtze Valley, the center of the power of the Kuomintang, was the special sphere of influence of Great Britain. Hongkong, moreover, was still British. Then, too, British citizens often gave the impression of arrogant aloofness which was peculiarly provocative to the Chinese. Communist enmity toward Great Britain was not unwilling to take advantage of the Russian position in the Kuomintang to annoy the British lion.

The anti-British agitation became particularly acute after an incident on May 30, 1925, in the British-dominated International Settlement in Shanghai. A strike had led to a demonstration by students and other sympathizers with the workers. In the ensuing disturbance the police arrested several of the agitators and then, goaded by the attacks of Communists who seemingly wished to provoke them, they fired and killed some in the attacking crowd. In the inflamed state of Chinese opinion, this incident led to an outburst of indignation against British subjects and privileges. A boycott proved costly to British trade. In June 1925, a clash occurred between Chinese and the guardians of Shameen, the foreign settlement in Canton. A further incident arose in 1926 in connection with British shipping on the upper Yangtze.

As, in 1926, the armies of the Kuomintang moved northward from Canton, foreigners, especially British and Americans, were harassed by the expropriation of their properties, local boycotts, and threatening mobs. Kuomintang forces seized the British concessions in Hankow and Kiukiang. In spite of extreme provocation, the defenders of the concessions withheld their fire. The British government, determined to be conciliatory, turned over to Chinese authority the disputed areas. Strong reenforcements to the garrisons in Shanghai helped to prevent a similar fate for the International Settlement and the French Concession in that city. British concessions in Amoy and Chinkiang were voluntarily returned to the Chinese. Belgium also restored her concession at Tientsin. Chinese were admitted to membership in the councils which governed the International Settlements in Shanghai and Amoy, the French Concession in Shanghai, and the British Concession in Tientsin. The Shanghai Mixed Court, which the Consular body had taken over in 1911, was given back to the Chinese. Marked though Chinese advances had been, however, in 1931 the most important of the concessions were still in alien hands.

In freeing herself from extraterritoriality, by 1931 China had a similar record. She had achieved progress, but most of the major powers had not yet surrendered that status for their citizens. Several smaller countries and, of the major powers, Germany and Russia had acquiesced and negotiated treaties from which extraterritoriality was omitted. As other treaties which contained the provision came to their terminal dates, the Chinese government notified the signatories that they would be renewed only on the basis of equality and reciprocity. Several of the governments concerned complied with China's conditions. By the year 1928 slightly over half of the aliens in China were without extraterritorial rights. However, Great Britain, France, Japan, the United States, and a few smaller states had not yet yielded. In December 1929, China announced that by her unilateral action extraterritoriality would be ended on January 1, 1930, but postponed the actual assumption of jurisdiction over the affected foreigners until January 1, 1932. By that date new and unexpected developments in her foreign relations, Japan's actions in Manchuria, still further delayed the proposed step. Eventually, as we are to see in the chapter after next, the United States and Great Britain amicably agreed to the termination of extraterritoriality and China was not under the necessity of disregarding her treaties with them.

Association with Russia did not proceed in the friendly fashion that had been forecast by the Soviet declaration of 1919 and the Russo-Chinese agreement of 1924. In 1921 Soviet troops assisted in setting up in Outer Mongolia a government organized on Communist principles. While by the treaty of 1924 Russia recognized Outer Mongolia as "an integral part of the Republic of China," she conducted direct relations with that dependency and for most practical purposes Outer Mongolia was one of the Union of Soviet Socialist Republics rather than a portion of the Chinese Republic. The attempt (1927) of the Kuomintang to purge its ranks of Communists led to strained relations with Russia. To prevent them from being used as centers of Communist propaganda and plotting, China ordered all Soviet consulates in its territories closed (1927). In Manchuria relations between Chang Tso-lin and Russia became strained in 1923, especially over the theoretical joint control of the Chinese Eastern Railway. They did not greatly improve. In 1929 undeclared war ensued. The Nanking government endeavored to extend its control to Manchuria and to break the hold of Russia on the northern part of that region. This policy was facilitated by the willingness of Chang Hsüeh-liang, the son and successor of Chang Tso-lin, to coöperate. In the summer of 1929 China attempted to take over the administration of the Chinese Eastern Railway. Russia sent an ultimatum demanding a conference on disputed points, the cancellation of Chinese orders regarding the railway, and the release of Russian citizens whom the Chinese had arrested. China countered with another set of demands, and diplomatic connections between the two countries were severed. No formal declaration of war was made, but there were clashes between Soviet troops on the one hand and Chinese and anti-Soviet Russian forces on the other. A Soviet army invaded Manchuria and inflicted such severe defeats on the Chinese that Chang Hsüeh-liang sued for peace. The Russians were content with the restoration of the *status quo* and to this Nanking consented.

The Russo-Chinese conflict had wider repercussions. The United States, through Henry L. Stimson, its Secretary of State, attempted to avert hostilities. The Pact of Paris, better known as the Kellogg Pact, had recently been signed by more than fifty of the governments of the world. The parties to it renounced "war as an instrument of national policy" and promised to use only pacific means in the settlement of disputes. Secretary Stimson drew the attention of China and Russia to their obligations under the pact. His motive seems not to have been active intervention in Far Eastern affairs but a desire to give the pact force and life by implementing it in a specific controversy. At the outset he was supported by several of the other major signatories. Nanking replied reaffirming its willingness to negotiate. Moscow, however, rebuffed in blunt language the American appeal. It resented action from Washington, with which at that time it did not have normal official dealings, and declared that the pact did not give to any state or group of states the function of its protector. The Soviet Foreign Minister believed the United States to be unneutral, since the latter had accorded to the Chinese government diplomatic representation which it had denied to Russia. Secretary Stimson was undoubtedly sincere in his effort to promote peace by invoking the pact. He had, however, strengthened the precedent for vigorous American participation in Far Eastern affairs.

Out of all this summary of her foreign relations in the 1920's, it must be clear that China was making progress in canceling the compromises on her sovereignty and independence which she had suffered in the preceding eighty years. In the offing, however, was the most serious threat she had faced since the Manchu conquest. To this we are to come in the second chapter after this.

The Intellectual Revolution

It has been said that in the five decades after 1895 China was passing simultaneously through five revolutions and that in so doing she was telescoping into half a century the changes which in Europe had required six centuries. In the six hundred years after A.D. 1300 Europe had been politically reconstituted first by the emergence of the absolute monarchies and then by the French Revolution and the democratic revolution; intellectually it had been made over by the Renaissance and the developments of the eighteenth and nineteenth centuries; religiously it had been reshaped by the Reformation; in its economic life it had known the commercial and the industrial revolutions; and in social customs and institutions it had been remolded. China, so it was declared, was passing through five comparable revolutions in approximately the span of one generation.

Like most generalizations, this one is not to be taken with precise literalness. For one thing, the congeries of revolutions had not been completed by the 1940's. Indeed, they seemed only to have begun. Yet the parallel with Europe brings into vivid focus the magnitude and complexities of the changes through which this vast and ancient people was passing.

In the preceding pages of this chapter we have recounted the political transformation to the crucial year of 1931. We now turn to the intellectual changes.

In some respects the intellectual revolution was even more significant than was that in the structure of the state. The educated had traditionally controlled the life of the Empire. They had set its standards. They had been dominant in the government and had been respected as the custodians of the ideals and forms of civilization. The prevailing influence in shaping the intellectuals had been Confucianism. Earlier such rival philosophies as those of Mo Ti and the Legalists had been potent, but these had long since aroused only an antiquarian interest. Later Buddhism had attracted many. It had left a permanent deposit in what became the orthodox interpretation of Confucianism, that of Chu Hsi and his predecessors, but it had long been regarded as heterodox. Taoism held a continuing fascination, and some of its classics, notably the writings of Chuang Tzŭ, were read by numbers of the orthodox. Yet it also was outside the pale. Increasingly the intellectual patterns of the educated had become stereotyped, conventionalized by the elevation of one school to be the exclusive norm for the state and society, and made rigid by forced conformity to the requirements of the civil service examinations. Less and less was anything new emerging. Creativity had slowed down. Now, suddenly, the Chinese mind was released from the molds into which it had been compressed and was exposed to all the multiform intellectual currents of the Occident. The immediate result was a near approach to chaos. That chaos meant disruption for more than the educated. It profoundly affected the state and all of society, for these had traditionally looked to the *literati* for guidance. The intellectual revolution, therefore, was more far-reaching than the political one.

The intellectual revolution was in large part a consequence of the sweeping aside of the traditional educational system and the substitution of one adopted and adapted from the Occident. The abolition of the old examination system in 1905 was one of the most momentous events in modern history. It was a foregone conclusion, but it symbolized an abrupt break, almost like a vast geological fault, in the mental attitudes of a quarter of the human race. The old education did not immediately disappear. Hundreds of thousands of boys were still trained in the ancient classics and in the traditional manner. Yet the incentive, preparation for the civil service examinations through which led the road to social prestige, public office, wealth, and power, had been lost.

Rapidly, when measured by decades or even years, the inherited style of education vanished. In its place came a system of schools that gave the chief place in the curriculum to Occidental subjects. Many of these schools were private. Christian missions were the major pioneers. Yet more and more the national government brought all education under its direction, fixed the curriculum, and set the standards.

The new schools ran from primary grades through secondary institutions to the university. The patterns were those of the Occident. The traditional Chinese characters were taught and ancient Chinese literature was still given a place on the course of study. However, the subjects which proved most attractive and on which greatest emphasis was placed by youth were ones introduced from the West. Geography, history, and mathematics in Occidental categories were taught even in the lower grades. In the secondary and higher schools science and scientific subjects had enormous prestige. This was because, as elsewhere in the non-Occidental world, the wealth and power of the West were attributed to science and to its application to the material aspects of life. Because of the problems presented by the Chinese state and because of the traditional emphasis of the Chinese mind, much attention was paid to the social sciences, but these also were studied in Western categories.

The new system had a mushroom growth but could not quickly be brought to high standards of intellectual achievement. Buildings had to be erected and laboratory equipment and libraries assembled. More difficult still, hundreds of thousands of teachers competent in the imported subjects and methods were needed. Traditions of sound scholarship in the new fields were to be established. Under the novel conditions students often proved assertive, restless, and rebellious. Discipline was difficult to establish and maintain. Progress had to be made in the face of chronic political upheaval, civil war, and foreign aggression. Students were peculiarly sensitive to political and intellectual developments. They were intensely patriotic. They organized boycotts and strikes and engaged in passionate propaganda among the masses. Sometimes these were directed against domestic leaders, and sometimes against foreigners and foreign governments. Financial means, too, were usually very inadequate. The amazing fact was not the superficial character of much of the new education, marked though this often was, but the advance which was registered.

Tens of thousands of Chinese went abroad to study in what was the greatest student migration in the history of mankind. The majority journeyed to Japan, for the distance was shorter and the expense much less than if they had gone to the Occident, and they could there obtain at least a smattering of the desired learning. However, thousands journeyed to the United States and there constituted important contingents in several of the larger universities. Some scattered, too, to the smaller colleges and universities. Other thousands went to the British Isles and the Continent of Europe. After World War I very substantial numbers were in France and Russia, but most of those who studied in the Occident were in English-speaking lands. Many more were in the United States than in any other one country except Japan. Returning to their native land, these students were conveyors of the culture they had acquired abroad. Some of them had been so thoroughly uprooted and had been so Occidentalized that they were of slight use to China but congregated in her chief cities, mainly in Shanghai, and there lived an exotic existence. They tended, too, to group themselves by the countries in which they had studied. However, the overwhelming number were enthusiastically Chinese and the large majority found places in the continuing life of the nation. Many rose to high position in education, the state, and business. Numbers of the army officers had acquired part of their training in Japan—although this by no means necessarily implied that they were pro-Japanese.

The new educational system was for girls as well as boys. Many schools were coeducational. This in itself was a revolution, both intellectually and socially. Heretofore schools had not been for the education of women. Women were homemakers, and their training for that function had been given in the homes by their mothers. Many had been taught to read, but privately. Now education was given them in schools, and very often in association with boys or men. This altered the function and status of women. Moreover, in the schools, whether coeducational or not, members of the opposite sex saw much more of one another than had heretofore been considered proper. This made for profound changes in the relations between the sexes.

It helped to alter the fashion in which marriages were arranged and contributed to modifications in that basic institution of China, the family.

An objective of the new educational ideals of China was literacy and primary education for all. This was new in the history of the Empire. In the nineteenth and twentieth centuries it had become commonplace in the West and in Japan, but it had once been an innovation everywhere. It was deemed essential to a modern state and to an industrial society. In adopting it China was conforming to a world-wide trend.

One means of speeding literacy for all was the Mass Education Movement. This began with James Y. C. Yen, a returned student from the United States. In France, during World War I, Yen, under the auspices of the Young Men's Christian Association, worked out a method for teaching the Chinese laborers serving behind the lines. By helping them acquire the most frequently used Chinese characters he taught many of these coolies to read. Back in China after the war, and at first still in connection with the Young Men's Christian Association, Yen applied this method to the country as a whole. He chose certain of the key cities as demonstration centers and attracted much attention. Later the movement was conducted apart from any one religious organization. Eventually, too, its program was extended beyond mere literacy to the transformation through education of individual units of the community as a whole, and methods were worked out intensively in particular *hsien*.

Partly because of their traditions which set great value upon education, the Chinese of the new day had an almost pathetic confidence in schools as a means of remaking the nation and of saving it from its disunity and its many palpable weaknesses.

A striking feature of the China of the twentieth century was the student class and the new movements which were sweeping across it. The prominence of the students was not new. In this respect China was running true to form. What was novel was the fashion in which the intellectuals, including the students, were being swept into new currents of thought. Increasingly and for centuries, as we saw in our fourth and fifth chapters, the mind of the Chinese scholar had been compressed into a single and very constricting pattern. Scholarship and the *literati* had become extremely conventional and both feared and held in contempt new ideas. Now, by the passing of the old examinations and educational system, that pattern had been shattered.

The Chinese student mind was subjected to stimuli from every quarter. All the intellectual winds of the Occident blew across it, for Chinese were studying in every major country in the West and were there being brought in touch with the many movements and philosophic and social theories of a vital and stormy age. Chinese intellectuals were also rediscovering the many philosophies of the past of their own culture—schools which had long been denounced by the standard Confucianism as heterodox. For numbers the stimulus proved too great. They were like the famous knight who enthusiastically jumped on his horse and rode off in all directions. They were superficial, excitable, dogmatic, and changeable. They were often swept into mass hysteria. Almost always they were burningly patriotic. They were easily stampeded into boycotts—against school authorities, the Japanese, or the British—or into demands that a particular official resign. During the 1920's many became Communists. The fact that the majority were in their teens, in secondary schools or mushroom universities, added to their susceptibility. They displayed a combination of mass suggestibility and rampant individualism. Yet here was unquestionably vigor and life. Chinese youth was on the march.

For many of the students as they approached maturity, the trend was toward what is sometimes known as the New Tide, or, in more conventional Western terminology, the Renaissance. Everything everywhere, whether from the Occident or China's past, was subjected to inquiry. The Chinese student was an animated question mark. Yet there was a sublime confidence in the competence of the human intellect and an unchallenged adoption of the scientific method. There was an intense publishing activity. Textbooks of the new learning poured from the presses by the hundreds of thousands. Reprints and new editions were issued of Chinese works, those of both the hitherto orthodox and unorthodox schools, and of the standard poets. Translations were made of Western literature, ancient and modern. Newspapers multiplied. Many new journals appeared—scholarly or for belles-lettres. Learned organizations arose, some of them as branches of the Academia Sinica, a government-related congeries of groups covering various branches of the natural and social sciences, including history and archaeology. Floods of new writers appeared, many of them radical.

A phase of the New Tide was a literary revolution. Partly because of the initiative of the extraordinarily brilliant and facile Hu Shih, who had been trained in the old style learning in China and in some of the most radical philosophy of the United States, Chinese scholars now began to write in a standard form of the vernacular. Heretofore scholarship had disdained the common tongue. For centuries there had been a vernacular literature, but scholars, if they shared in its composition, usually did so anonymously. Any work of standing in the world of learning must be in the classical style. Now the younger scholars ventured to break with this tradition. The *pai hua*, or "plain speech" of the people, became an accepted literary form. It was a dignified type of Mandarin, the vernacular of the majority of the Chinese. This was fully as significant a change as that which centuries before, in Western Europe, had substituted the vernaculars for Latin as the medium of scholarship and polite letters. Moreover, the step did not, as in Europe, lead to literary division or centrifugal tendencies. In China a form of Mandarin was taught in the new schools as the *kuo yü* or "national language." Even in those extensive districts on the coast from Shanghai southward, where the dialects had been numerous and reciprocally unintelligible, the *kuo yü* was making headway. A standard Mandarin was becoming the linguistic vehicle of the Republic.

It must be noted, however, that the historic Chinese characters were not discarded for a purely phonetic system of writing. Alphabetic and syllabic methods of writing the language were devised, but none of them won wide acceptance. In one important respect this was fortunate. By continuing the use of the characters the Chinese of the new day were able to utilize the vast stores of the literature of their past. While the acquisition of the character was something of a handicap and learning the classical style in which most of the older writings were composed entailed labor, the treasures of earlier centuries were more easily accessible than if the characters had been discarded in current writing.

It was as yet an unanswered question whether the stimulus of the new day would quicken the Chinese mind to fresh and significant creativity. The best of the new intellectuals were undoubtedly able, even brilliant, and could meet on equal terms the finest minds in the contemporary Occident. They were yet to demonstrate, however, that they could be genuinely creative. It was not clear whether they could make of the new Chinese culture an advance over the old or whether their activity would issue in a fortuitous and uninspired combination of remnants of the past with contributions from the Occident.

In the domestic political storms of the latter part of the 1920's, especially with the effort of the Kuomintang to suppress Communism and radicalism among students, and in the darkening international situation in the 1930's, the New Tide ebbed. What the future held in store no one could confidently predict.

Religious Changes

The religious aspect of the revolution was no less important than the political and the intellectual one. Indeed, it may have been the most significant of the three, for it had to do with the ideals and the motivation of individuals and society as a whole. It was basic, especially in a culture which, like that of China, by its Confucian rearing tended to esteem religion as having as a main object the achievement of a perfect human society.

Of Buddhism and Taoism little need be said. Buddhism had been in progressive decay in China since the T'ang dynasty, or for approximately a millennium. It was still far from dead. It helped to mold the ethics of the nation and the conceptions of a future life. There were thousands of Buddhist monks and hundreds of Buddhist nuns. In the twentieth century there were attempts at Buddhist revivals, some of which had scholarly, high-minded leaders, both monks and laity, and which produced a fairly extensive literature. However, the efforts at reinvigoration affected seriously only a few thousands. The general course of Buddhism was downward, accelerated by the political upheavals, the antireligious movements, the general skepticism, and, still more, the secularism of the age.

Taoism was even more moribund than Buddhism. Its core of solid philosophical thought and of profound religious insight and experience was smaller, its organization was weaker, and it had more nearly surrendered to magic and crass superstition. It persisted, partly because of its supposed ability to control the demons and to assist the soul beyond death, partly from inertia, and partly from the appeal of some of its literature to wistful, world-weary spirits.

Nor need we pause long on the popular polytheism and the animism which were so widely spread. They continued and in places flourished. Yet the drift was away from ancient religious practices. Numbers of temples were allowed to fall into ruin and many were converted into barracks or schools. The masses still clung to the traditional belief in demons and kept to ancient ways of fending off these chimeras or of expelling them. The educated, who had historically tended to scorn the popular superstitions but often had shared them, were increasingly emancipated from participation in the hoary thaumaturgical customs.

Here and there were new religious movements. Usually they were syncretistic. That is to say, they sought to combine what their creators deemed the worthy features of the existing major faiths—Buddhism, Taoism, Confucianism, Islam, and Christianity. Without exception, however, they tended to be ephemeral and even at their peak attracted only minorities.

Islam displayed little marked change. As earlier, it was the faith of a substantial minority which was scattered through all the provinces, but was strongest in the northwest and the southwest.

The most startling and significant changes were the decline of Confucianism and the continued rapid growth of Christianity.

Confucianism, as we have repeatedly had occasion to note, provided the ideological foundation on which Chinese culture, including the state and the family, had been chiefly constructed. Since the Han dynasty it had been the official philosophy of the state and had won that position, presumably, because for a much longer time it had been the main current in the stream of Chinese ethics and concepts. It had been closely associated with the monarchy and the time-honored system of education and civil service examinations.

Confucianism had been dealt body blows in the first few years of the twentieth century, first by the sweeping away of the examinations and the ancient educational system, and then by the collapse of the monarchy and the coming of the Republic. The examinations and the old type of schools had been founded upon the Confucian classics. The new kind of school in effect relegated the classics to a minor place. To be sure, the Confucian classics were still included in the curricula. However, students were more attracted to the subjects introduced from the West, partly because these had the glamor of novelty and popularity, and partly because a livelihood was more readily obtained through them. Then, too, Chinese traditional literature was usually more poorly taught than were the newer courses. The instructors were inclined to cling to the pedestrian, mechanical pedagogy in which they had been trained. In practice only a minority of students were attracted to the classics and of these still fewer majored in them. In its fall the monarchy, based as it had been upon Confucianism, threatened to carry its established philosophy with it. The Republic was a Western, non-Confucian importation. There were efforts to maintain the Confucian temples, and Yüan Shih-k'ai revived the ancient sacrifice to Heaven at the winter solstice. However, the upkeep of the temples depended upon the *literati* who had been educated in the old patterns. As their ranks were thinned by death or their interests were diverted, the ceremonies lapsed and the temples fell into disrepair. The revival of the sacrifice to Heaven by Yüan was as fleeting as was his ill-starred effort to renew the monarchy.

The fading of Confucianism from Chinese life was a sobering development of the first magnitude. Chinese culture and Confucianism had been so closely intertwined for more than two thousand years as to be almost inseparable. From the latter were drawn the ideals, the dominant ethical standards, and many of the ceremonies which governed society. Especially were the family and Confucianism closely interdependent. Now that the latter seemed to be disappearing, the rest of traditional Chinese culture, including its criteria of right and wrong, the forces which had created and nourished Chinese character, and the basic institutions, would presumably also crumble. If something better could take their place, the revolution might ultimately prove of advantage. This, however, was clearly not quickly developing. In the meantime, society was imperiled by chaos in what was fundamental.

The disappearance of Confucianism was by no means complete. It might easily be exaggerated. The system had so long been an integral part of Chinese life that it tended to go on even when some of the chief traditional means of perpetuating it had vanished. The family largely persisted and the moral precepts of Confucian provenance which it embodied and inculcated continued except for the few who had been most dislocated by the new currents from the West. The Confucian classics were still read. New editions were issued and reflected a demand. The rising tide of nationalism reenforced much from the heritage of the past which was deemed peculiarly Chinese. Moreover, Confucianism had been so bred in the bone that the Chinese were confident that the salvation of their land from its current ills must be by a revival of morality. In seeking to bring this about they would turn to the principles to which they had been accustomed through the centuries.

A reemphasis upon Confucian standards was notable in the efforts of Chiang Kai-shek. In the late years of the 1920's Chiang became a Christian, and, so far as could be judged, by honest conviction. Yet in his appeals to the nation and to youth there was more of Confucian morality than of distinctively Christian teaching. He sponsored the

New Life Movement. This had as its aim the moral renovation of the nation, in itself a Confucian ideal. It was deeply indebted, especially in its inception, to Christianity, but it contained quite as much if not more that was Confucian than Christian.

It seemed clear that, in spite of the blows dealt it, Confucianism possessed sufficient vitality to survive. Whether it would be a progressively waning force or whether, revivified and modified, it would become the ethical basis of the new China no one could be confident.

In the decades which succeeded 1895 Christianity had a phenomenal growth. This was marked in the numerical increase of the churches. It was even more striking in the rising influence of the faith upon the nation.

The amazing increase in the place of Christianity in the life of China was attributable to a number of factors. One was the mounting size of the missionary body. The Russian Orthodox Church never had more than a small staff in China, but in 1896 or 1897 Roman Catholic missionaries totaled not far from seven hundred and fifty and in 1929 about thirty-four hundred. In 1895 the total Protestant foreign staff was approximately thirteen hundred. In 1925 it was more than eight thousand. Then the anti-Christian movement of the 1920's and especially the anti-imperialistic campaign of the radical elements in the Kuomintang which bore particularly heavily upon British and Americans, from whom were the majority of the Protestant force, led to a reduction in the missionary body. The multiplication of the foreign personnel of the Christian enterprise was due to the continued vigor and the rising missionary interest among the Christians of the Occident and to the conviction that China constituted a peculiarly challenging field. Added to the striking augmentation of the missionary body as a cause of the growth of Christianity were the crumbling of the resistance offered by traditional Chinese culture and the eagerness of many Chinese for the spiritual and moral reenforcement of religion in a time of revolution. The main opposition to Christianity had been offered by the Confucian state and the scholars trained in the Confucian tradition. In 1912 the one disappeared, and long before 1931 the *literati* were a dwindling old guard, no longer recruited by fresh additions and with much less prestige than formerly. Many sensitive spirits, moreover, oppressed by the disintegration of society, appalled by the moral weakness and corruption about them, and profoundly convinced by their Confucian heritage that moral regeneration was necessary if the nation were to find itself, looked to Christianity as a dynamic for such a rebirth. Others, too, became Christians because of the assurance which the faith gave in meeting the recurring crises of life and death. There was, as well, in Christanity that which met other needs and the longings of many eager and hungry Chinese.

Resistance to Christianity did not cease. Skepticism, indifference, and preoccupation with other issues were chronic hindrances to the progress of the faith. Opposition became acute in the 1920's, first in 1922 and then, after a partial lull, in 1926 and 1927. In its new form it attacked Christianity as unscientific, intellectually untenable, and allied with foreign imperialism. Theoretically the criticism on the count of being contrary to science was directed against all religions. In practice the animus was especially anti-Christian. A secularism and religious skepticism already strong were augmented by contact with similar attitudes in the Occident and led to the discounting of Christianity along with other religions. The popularity of Communism also militated against Christianity, for that ideology was openly and actively antireligious.

Because of the factors in its favor and in spite of its opponents, Christianity had a rapid numerical increase. The Roman Catholic form of the faith, chiefly because of the advantages it possessed in a head start of over two centuries, still had many more adherents than did Protestant Christianity, but the latter grew proportionately slightly more rapidly than the former. In 1896 Roman Catholics totaled about half a million and in 1929 were approximately two and a half millions. Protestants in 1898 had about eighty thousand and in 1932 over four hundred and fifty thousand communicants. Were all baptized included, as in the Roman Catholic figures, and not communicants only, the totals for Protestants would have been larger. As it was, they multiplied nearly sixfold in a period in which Roman Catholics increased about fivefold.

The increase in the influence of Christianity was more difficult to measure with any degree of exactness than was the numerical progress. It was, however, even more phenomenal. That of Protestant Christianity was particularly significant. Christian schools, and especially those of Protestants, flourished, notably those of secondary and higher grades. For years they were the chief pioneers in introducing Western education. Until after 1912 and to a certain degree until after 1931, they afforded the best opportunity in China to acquire the now greatly desired Occidental learning. In the 1890's, especially in the few years immediately after 1895 when the hunger for guidance in the ways of the Occident was new and acute, publications issued by the Christian Literature Society, a list which included secular as well as religious subjects, had a circulation of many hundreds of thousands. The Commercial Press, a purely Chinese and entirely secular organization which became the largest publishing house in the country and as such was a leading purveyor of the new knowledge, was inaugurated by men trained in a Protestant mission press. Christian missions, notably those of Protestants, laid the foundations for the new medical and nursing profession and for public health measures. It was in Christian hospitals and medical schools that the pioneers in these fields were prepared. Christian missionaries blazed the trails in modern institutional care for the insane, and in teaching the blind to read and equipping them with useful handicrafts. They led the way in introducing new methods of agriculture and forestry from the West. They fought opium and were active in the relief of the recurring famines.

A surprising number of Christians, quite out of proportion to the statistical strength of the churches and mostly Protestants, were prominent in the higher offices of state under the Republic and were leaders in education. Sun Yat-sen and Chiang Kai-shek were, as we have seen, Christians. So were the Soong family and a number of others in commanding posts. Some of the most honored heads of the new government and private schools were Christians. The position held by Christians was due in part to the fact that Christian missions, notably those of Protestants, by blazing the trails for the new forms of education had provided a very large proportion of those equipped with the new learning and competent to lead in the age into which China was being hurried. It also partly arose from the spiritual and moral dynamic inherent in Christianity which produced the kind of character required by China in the transition. Although many of the Christians who rose to prominence in the state were far from ideal embodiments of it, from their faith they drew much of the idealism, the stamina, the courage, the persistence, and the public spirit which the age of revolution so desperately required if the country were to make its way successfully through the time of chaos.

Less tangible than most of these other results but even more important were the changes wrought in tens of thousands of individuals by the ethical challenge and spiritual power of Christianity. In many these were slight. In others they were so marked as to result in the complete remaking of character. Here was a force being brought into Chinese life at a time when the latter was extremely fluid. It might well become an enduring and a prominent constituent of the culture that was to be.

Moreover, Christianity was rapidly ceasing to be dependent upon foreign support and was becoming firmly rooted in Chinese leadership. A mounting percentage of Roman Catholic nuns, monks, priests, and bishops were Chinese. Protestant churches, schools, and hospitals were more and more headed and staffed by Chinese. Many of these indigenous leaders, both Roman Catholic and Protestant, were of large caliber in devotion and native ability. The transition from foreign to Chinese control had not been completed in 1931, but it was gathering momentum.

Protestants were becoming united. As introduced, that branch of the faith was represented by many denominations and several nationalities. It seemed hopelessly divided. More and more, however, it drew together. Some of the denominations coalesced. The majority of Protestants cooperated in the National Christian Council, constituted in 1922. This in turn was in association with world-wide Protestantism through the International Missionary Council.

When the storm of Japanese invasion broke in the northeast in 1931, Christians, while constituting scarcely one per cent of the population, were much more influential than their numerical strength would have suggested. Christianity was rapidly forging to the fore. It was making a phenomenal growth in a day when the other faiths were either stagnant or declining. In some respects it was the most active religious and moral force in the China of 1931.

Economic Changes

By 1931 the economic phase of the transformation of China had not proceeded as far as had the political, the intellectual, and the religious aspects of that vast movement. Foreign commerce was a mere trickle. In 1921, for instance, China had less than two per cent of the international trade of the world. This was about the same proportion as that of Japan, and the latter Empire had scarcely a seventh of the population of China. It was only half that of India, which had a slightly smaller population. China might potentially be one of the greatest markets of the world but, when its size was taken into consideration, it was still actually among the smallest. In spite of nearly a century of being open to foreign commerce, in 1931 China was economically almost as self-contained as when Great Britain first forced her doors ajar. Modern transportation was only beginning to make headway. To be sure, steamers plied the coastal waters of the Yangtze and its chief tributaries, but they were largely owned and operated by foreigners. Railways had been built, but only Manchuria could be called adequately supplied with them, and there the roads were mostly under either Japanese or Russian direction. There were trunk lines in China Proper from Peking to Hankow and southward from Peking to Shanghai (in both cases the Yangtze had still to be bridged), but the through road from Peking to Canton was uncompleted and the great provinces in the west were still to hear the call of the iron horse. Modern factories had begun to appear, but the majority of them were concentrated in comparatively small areas. The automobile had only commenced to make its appearance. Modern banking was largely dominated by foreign institutions. In other words, the economic revolution had not yet become native to China and had not proceeded very far. Most of the new economic life was still under the direction or control of aliens.

The reasons for the retardation of the economic revolution were to be found partly in the political situation. Before 1895 the Chinese were attempting to hold the Occident at arm's length and adopted only so much of Western ways, including those in the economic realm, as foreigners forced on them. After 1895 the governmental scene was so chaotic that economic development was slowed down. Domestic strife, political upheavals, and disabling uncertainty concerning the future discouraged efforts at the large scale capital investments which would be necessary if China were to be industrialized. Foreigners were made cautious by the chronic civil war, and Chinese either did not have the capital or were unwilling to risk it in costly physical equipment which might be wrecked by next spring's excursions of war lords. The government was too weak and too fluctuating to take the leadership in the economic development of the country which the state had assumed in Japan.

Yet with all this delay, by the year 1931 the economic phase of the revolution had begun and in places and in some aspects of life throughout the nation it was beginning to work profound changes.

Foreign commerce, while slight in comparison with other large nations, was mounting. In 1929, on the eve of the world-wide depression which began in that year, it was, in monetary value, seven times that of 1894. This increase seems larger than it actually was, for the currency in which it was measured displayed marked fluctuations. Moreover, the era after 1894 was one of expansion in international trade the world around, and China's proportion of the commerce of the globe did not grow as rapidly as did the figures in which the trade of the Empire was computed. Yet in terms of the price level in China the advance in foreign trade was considerable. Foreign goods played an increasing part in the daily life of the average Chinese and had to be paid for by exports the production of which affected many.

The character of the imports was altered in the nearly four decades that followed 1894. In the year 1894 cotton goods were first, with opium second. In the year 1931 opium had disappeared from the list of imports and cotton goods had declined to about ten per cent of the total. The decrease in the latter arose from the multiplication of cotton mills in China, to which we are to revert in a moment. In the years immediately preceding 1931 the items which loomed most prominently in the imports were kerosene, foodstuffs, tobacco, and machinery. The kerosene had trebled in quantity since the beginning of the twentieth century. It was used chiefly for lighting and was depended upon for this purpose in a large proportion of the homes of the nation. It was distributed by a nation-wide network of foreign agencies, chiefly those of the Standard Oil Company and the Asiatic Petroleum Company. By affecting the domestic lighting of China's millions it was also modifying the customs which depended upon artificial illumination. The importation of foodstuffs was an indication that China was ceasing to be agriculturally self-sufficient. Much of the tobacco was in the form of cigarettes, the consumption of which had sky-rocketed under an efficient campaign of advertising and had become a national habit. While the imports continued to be mostly manufactured or processed goods, the growing place of machinery among them gave evidence that China was ceasing to rely so exclusively upon the factories of the Occident.

In her exports, China was still showing traces of her traditional role. Tea and silk remained on the list. Yet in the year 1927 tea was only three per cent of the whole and silk between a fifth and a sixth of the total. Chinese tea had been supplanted in the world market by the product of modern plantations and of improved standardization in curing and grading in such lands as Ceylon and Assam. Although in America and Europe Chinese silk was preferred for the finest fabrics, Japanese silk constituted the bulk of the Occident's supply of that commodity. Items which had forged ahead in China's exports were vegetable oils (from the soy bean, sesamum seed, the castor bean, and a tree whose oil was used in varnishes), bean cake, dried vegetables, eggs, furs, hair, timber, and antimony. The exports were chiefly of raw materials, some of them partially processed, but by the year 1931 cotton goods and threads were appearing, the products of modern factories and proof that the industrial revolution had begun to arrive. The gap between imports and exports was filled (for the former regularly exceeded the latter) by remittances from overseas emigrants to their families, loans, and the expenditures of missionaries, tourists, and foreign diplomatic and military establishments. Of these the remittances from emigrants were the most substantial. The prominence of soy beans, coal, and timber in the reports reflects the growing place of Manchuria in China's economy, for these products were chiefly from that region. One set of exports which did not loom large in monetary returns but whose ultimate effect upon other lands might be great was seeds and plants. Hundreds of varieties of plants were sent to Europe and America. The Department of Agriculture of the United States had agents in China who had as their assignment the search for plants which might prove useful. Most of the finds were inconsequential but some, notably the soy bean, became prominent in American agriculture.

The relative shares of foreign countries in China's trade displayed important changes in the nearly forty years after 1894. In 1894 Great Britain was easily first, a position which reflected that nation's early leadership in the industrial revolution and its part in opening the doors of China. By 1931, however, Japan had surpassed Great Britain. Much of the Japanese advance was in Manchuria and so was localized, but Japanese were competing in China Proper, including what was supposed to be the special British preserve, the Yangtze Valley. On the Yangtze River Japanese steamers were pushing British craft for the dominant place the latter had long held, and in Shanghai Japanese cotton mills were far outstripping those financed by British capital. The United States was rapidly moving forward. By 1931 she had passed Great Britain and, if Manchuria be excepted, where Japan enjoyed almost a monopoly of foreign commerce, she was ahead of that Empire. In the total trade of the United States China was far down in order of importance, much below Japan. Yet the fashion in which the United States was augmenting her share of China's commerce was significant, for it meant added American interest in China and growing fear in Japan of the trans-Pacific colossus. The waning place of Great Britain indicated that more and more China was on the periphery of British concern and that British commitments were increasingly elsewhere. Yet in 1931 the British still had more shipping in the China trade than any other people. They probably had a larger capital investment than any other folk, although the Japanese, because of their stake in Manchuria, were pushing them hard for first place. British banking institutions remained the most imposing in the ports, solid and dependable. Hongkong, a British possession although with a predominantly Chinese population, had a unique place in China's trade as a port of call and of transhipment and banking. Other parts of the British Empire, moreover, were sharing in China's commerce. In Shanghai, British leadership, although somewhat shaken, continued. In the administration of the customs service, so important in China's governmental structure, British predominance, while not so marked as formerly, persisted.

In foreign trade the processes were changing. More Chinese firms were taking a direct part in importing goods. The compradore who served as an intermediary between Chinese and foreigners was passing. Through their agents foreign manufacturers were dealing directly with Chinese merchants. Chinese banks were gaining in prominence. The proportion of trade which passed through Hongkong was declining. Increasingly the Chinese were handling their own commerce and were eliminating the foreign, and especially the British, middleman.

Factories and modern machinery were appearing. But for the internal political disorder they would have come more rapidly. In China as in so many other lands the industrial revolution first developed in the manufacture of cotton. China seemed peculiarly adapted to this enterprise. In raw cotton grown she was surpassed only by the United States and India. She had a vast reservoir of cheap and industrious labor. By the year 1928 approximately a quarter of a million Chinese were employed in cotton mills. About half of this cotton manufacture was in Shanghai, partly because so much capital, domestic and imported, had been concentrated in that city under foreign protection. Not far from two-thirds of the cotton mills were owned by Chinese, and most of the remainder were the property of Japanese. Other kinds of plants employing modern machinery included silk filatures, match factories, sugar refineries, breweries, distilleries, and flour mills. Heavy industry was of small dimensions. Clearly the industrialization of China was beginning, but quite as obviously it was only incipient. China possessed enough coal, iron, labor, and potential water power to form the basis of a larger industrialization than any other country in the Far East, but in iron reserves she was far behind the great manufacturing lands of the West and she was almost totally lacking in petroleum. Moreover, China still suffered from a paucity of technical skill. Also important as an obstacle to industrialization was the lack of experience of the Chinese with stock companies. Family loyalties militated against the successes of these devices of Western capitalistic economy, for such loyalty placed a premium upon giving employment to the relatives of the officers of such concerns, even though efficiency and the profits of stockholders suffered.

Old types of economic organization were weakening and new ones emerging. The guilds persisted, but here and there were breaking down or were being supplanted. Labor unions were appearing in some of the centers of modern industry. The Communist wing of the Kuomintang was particularly active, in the mid 1920's, in stimulating the organization of unions of laborers and peasants. Later these declined. Chambers of commerce were attaining prominence.

Currency presented a serious problem. It was complicated and unstable. In 1894 the traditional copper cash were still the chief coins in circulation and the main medium of exchange for small transactions and so for the rank and file of the population. The *tael*, not coined, and varying from locality to locality, was a unit of weight of silver. For larger transactions silver bullion was the medium, with the *tael* as the measure. To these native currencies there had been added, before 1894, silver dollars of several countries, chiefly Mexico. All this was perplexing to the inexperienced and a source of profit to banks and smaller shops which dealt in exchange. After 1894 the confusion was further confounded by the appearance of Chinese-minted silver coins, the major one called the *yüan*, akin to the dollar, and the subsidiary ones supposedly decimals of that unit, but so debased as to be of fluctuating value. Paper money was issued in floods, some of it by banks and some by various units of government. A few kinds of paper, notably those of the (British) Hongkong and Shanghai Banking Corporation, were adequately supported by cash reserves. Others had very slight specie backing or none at all and depreciated rapidly. China continued on the silver basis while most of the rest of the world was on gold.

Prices mounted. This arose partly from the poor character of the currency and partly from a world-wide upward trend. Moreover, in many commodities Chinese prices were decidedly below those of most of the Occident. As China was drawn into the world stream of economic life, they tended to climb toward the level of those in the West. Wages also went up but as a rule did not keep pace with the cost of living. The masses of the Chinese probably suffered from the fact that their country was now part of the world economic scene.

The transportation of China was sharing in the revolution. The railway was entering and after 1894 several thousand miles were built. As we suggested a few paragraphs back, a third or so of the mileage was in Manchuria, and most of the remainder was in the northeastern portion of China Proper in an area bounded by lines drawn from Hangchow on the southeast to Hankow on the southwest and to Kalgan on the north. In the civil wars which succeeded the coming of the Republic, especially those of the 1920's, the railways suffered severely. Rival armies commandeered and misused rolling stock and allowed the roadbeds to deteriorate. Receipts of the lines were appropriated by local war lords with no regard for the bondholders. Yet, given peace, the roads would prosper, for they were extensively patronized. In the 1920's automobiles came into use. Thousands of miles of roads were constructed for them. Most of the new roads had dirt surfaces and became all but impassible after heavy rains. Only a small proportion were given a rock covering and, except for some of the main thoroughfares in the larger cities, almost none were bitulithic. This meant that the transportation of freight by automobile was unusual and that the new vehicle was mainly for passengers. Auto buses multiplied. In many of the cities, especially in the 1920's, streets were widened, or new, broad, straight thoroughfares were built regardless of conflicting buildings. Some of the walls, so characteristic of Chinese cities, were razed and broad streets laid on the foundations. The use of steam craft mounted. These ranged from launches for the smaller streams to substantial coasting vessels, large boats which plied the Yangtze from the eastern end of the gorges to the sea, and ships with peculiarly powerful engines for the dangerous trip through the Yangtze gorges and their rapids. The airplane, too, made its appearance.

Changes in Social Customs and Institutions

The coming of Western ideas and appliances could not but work changes in the inherited customs and social institutions. Moving pictures, most of them produced in the Occident and a large proportion in the United States, familiarized millions with Western life, even though in bizarre and distorted form. The use of kerosene and especially of electric lights in the cities wrought alterations in the night life. The factory, the railway, and the automobile brought people together in new groupings and rendered society more mobile. The newspaper introduced fresh ideas. Schools and modern periodical literature and books broadcast Western conceptions and made for familiarity with Western ways.

Some of the resulting alterations were striking but relatively superficial. They did not quickly or deeply modify basic institutions. Such were the changes in dress. The queues worn by the men were imposed by the Manchus and were regarded as badges of loyalty to these rulers. With the advent of the Republic and the overthrow of the Ch'ing dynasty, these were, therefore, discarded. Many Chinese adopted Western garb. In general, however, native styles of dress persisted and the intensification of nationalism under the Kuomintang led to a swing back toward indigenous costume, especially on the part of those who had most affected Western forms, the intelligentsia and the official classes.

Athletics were being introduced in the schools, with sports involving physical skill and stamina. This transformed the habits of the student class. Formerly such games were considered undignified and the only pace fitting for the scholar was a slow walk. Now physical fitness was admired.

Somewhat more profound in its implications was the transition in etiquette. The old, elaborate forms of politeness in social intercourse were passing, especially among the younger intelligentsia, those who supposedly set the standards for the nation and after whom the nation would eventually pattern. More brusque, direct ways followed.

Still more significant was the changing status of women. Women were demanding and receiving more liberty. They were participating actively in political agitation and maneuvers. They were going to school. As workers in factories and as wage earners they were more independent of their husbands than formerly. Especially in Communist-dominated areas they were working side by side with men. Women laborers in modern factories, girl students, and those women who had passed through modern schools were particularly affected. The binding of feet was being discontinued. This made for greater independence.

The altered position of women was accompanied by new relations between the sexes. Men and women, especially students, were mingling freely on terms of equality in a fashion which would have scandalized the preceding generations.

Associated with the innovations in the association between the sexes was an even more revolutionary change, revolutionary for that fundamental institution of Chinese society, the family. Increasingly young people, particularly students, were making their own marriage arrangements and were not leaving to their parents the choice of a mate. This meant that marriages were supposedly contracted from reciprocal affection and had as their goal the happiness of husband and wife and not the provision of male offspring to carry on the ancestral line. By no means all these matches were successful. When marriages were arranged by the elders for a modern educated son to an old style wife the consequences were also often unhappy. The gap between generations and between those reared in the old manner and those educated in the new was very great. Reverence for and obedience to elders was declining.

In some instances the family itself was being modified. Large families in which members of three or more generations dwelt together in one vast establishment with its series of courtyards were slowly ceasing to be. Young people wished their own distinct menage.

Had these changes quickly affected the majority the consequences would have been chaotic. In many instances they issued in shipwreck. Fortunately for China the more profound alterations proceeded very slowly. For the vast multitudes marrying and giving in marriage were after the manner approved by custom and the family and its loyalties remained intact. Secret societies, long a factor, even though unadvertised, of the Chinese scene, continued powerful. The society affiliations of the leaders had to be known if the politics of the new age were to be understood. In many ways the old order persisted. It was chiefly among relatively small circles in the larger cities, mainly on the coast, that Western ways prevailed. Yet that minority may prove to have been a symptom and a prophecy, a foreshadowing of what was to spread through all of Chinese society.

Summary

This chapter has recorded the beginning of the most extensive and momentous series of changes which China had experienced in all her history. They came as a sequel to the heightened impact of the Occident which had begun in the first half of the nineteenth century. To that invasion of the West, China, proud in her past, her achievements, and her culture, offered resistance for more than half a century. She endeavored to preserve both her political and her cultural integrity. She had not learned, as had Japan, to conserve her political independence and to maintain the basic features of her life through the adoption of some of the aspects of the civilization of the Occident. In the decade beginning in 1894–1895 came a series of blows which left to her Westernization as the only alternative to alien conquest and partition. She was defeated by Japan, whom she had heretofore despised. Some of her strategic ports were seized by Western powers under the euphemism of leaseholds. She was constrained to grant concessions to build railways and to consent to preliminaries to partition in the guise of spheres of influence. In mad reaction the extreme conservatives endeavored to expel the aliens, only to have the foreign yoke more tightly clamped upon the Empire. Soon thereafter, China sat helplessly by while Russia and Japan contended on her soil and had no choice but to consent to the arrangements which the two powers made with each other.

Then began the revolution in full seriousness. The Manchus were swept out and with them the traditional form of government, the Confucian monarchy. A Republic was proclaimed. The immediate result was progressive disintegration of the state, both national and local. However, in the mid-1920's, reintegration began and by 1931 had made marked headway. China was drawn into World War I, but in actual participation remained on the periphery. In spite of Japanese attempts at aggression, in the 1920's she made considerable strides toward canceling the compromises of her independence. She regained some of the leaseholds, extinguished several of the concessions, recovered tariff and full postal autonomy, and was in process of abolishing extraterritoriality. This she was able to do partly because of the division and weakness brought to Europe by war, partly because of the support of the United States, and partly through the resolution of her own nationalists. In her education Confucianism was largely demoted and Western subjects and methods adopted. Religiously Confucianism was greatly weakened. Here was a threat to the ideological basis upon which Chinese culture had rested for at least two millenniums. Christianity made phenomenal gains, but not sufficient as yet to fill the void left by the decline of Confucianism. The economic structure was only beginning to be altered, but the foretaste of industrialization hinted at a revolution in this phase of life. Manners and social institutions were being modified. Even the family, so fundamental to Chinese society, was displaying symptoms of profound change.

In 1931 the revolution was only well under way. No one could foretell how long it would continue or what its outcome would be. Nor could anyone know when comparative stability would be achieved in the life of the state. If progress were at approximately the rate which had been witnessed since 1895, probably at least a half century would elapse before government would be as strong, comprehensive, and effective as under the great Emperors of the eighteenth century or in the major nations of the Occident. Foreign war might retard the process.

Almost automatically the observer compares and contrasts the revolution in China with the contemporary, or nearly contemporary ones in Japan, India, and Russia. In Japan the revolution began earlier, but by 1931, while superficially impressive, was not nearly so sweeping. The Japanese had managed to conserve and even to strengthen the main features of their chief traditional institutions, especially the imperial house and the rule of the military. In India the revolution had not proceeded nearly so far. The protective, inclusive structure of the British *raj* and the conservative forces of religion and caste had operated to retard it. Changes were occurring and disintegration may have gone further than was usually recognized, but if so it was behind a facade which as yet was largely intact. In Russia a revolution which was seemingly as sweeping as that in China had occurred and reintegration and stability had been achieved much more quickly. The new Russia was more powerful and more united than was that of the Czars. Did this imply greater competence on the part of the Russians? Were the Chinese incapable of united, vigorous action? The answer seems to be found in the difference between the geniuses of the two empires. Russia was accustomed to autocracy and regimentation. When the rule of the Communists was substituted for that of the Czars the nation, after brief resistance on the part of minorities, fell obediently into line. China, while under a monarchy, had had a government very much less centralized than that of Russia and responded traditionally to example and moral suasion rather than forceful regimentation. Her reintegration, therefore, would have to come as a result of the loosely coordinated efforts of many individuals and groups. It would be much slower. The end result, however, might be something much more akin to that which the West meant by democracy than was what was seen in Russia.

BIBLIOGRAPHY

For Brief Reference

K. S. Latourette, *The Chinese. Their History and Culture* (New York, 1945), Chap. XII.

For More Detailed Study

J. Arnold, *China. A Commercial and Industrial Handbook* (Washington, 1926).
P. S. Buck, *East Wind, West Wind* (New York, 1930).
J. B. Condliffe, *China To-day—Economic* (Boston, 1932).
H. Croly, *Willard Straight* (New York, 1924).
G. M. Friters, *Outer Mongolia and Its International Relations* (The Johns Hopkins Press, 1949).
A. W. Griswold, *The Far Eastern Policy of the United States* (New York, 1938).
A. N. Holcombe, *The Chinese Revolution* (Harvard University Press, 1930).
S. K. Hornbeck, *Contemporary Politics in the Far East* (New York, 1916).
R. F. Johnston, *Twilight in the Forbidden City* (London, 1934).
P. Joseph, *Foreign Diplomacy in China* (London, 1928).
T. E. La Fargue, *China and the World War* (Stanford, 1937).
K. S. Latourette, *A History of Christian Missions in China* (New York, 1929).
O. Lattimore, *Manchuria, Cradle of Conflict* (New York, 1935).
J. V. A. MacMurray, *Treaties and Agreements with and concerning China* (3 vols., New York, 1921; Washington, 1929).
P. Monroe, *China: A Nation in Evolution* (New York, 1928).
H. B. Morse and H. F. MacNair, *Far Eastern International Relations* (Boston, 1931).
C. S. Peake, *Nationalism and Education in Modern China* (New York, 1932).
R. T. Pollard, *China's Foreign Relations, 1917–1931* (New York, 1933).
J. G. Reid, *The Manchu Abdication and the Powers, 1908–1912* (New York, 1935).
P. S. Reinsch, *An American Diplomat in China* (Garden City, 1922).
C. F. Remer, *Foreign Investments in China* (New York, 1933).
C. F. Remer, *The Foreign Trade of China* (Shanghai, 1926).
E. A. Ross, *The Changing Chinese* (New York, 1911).
L. Sharman, *Sun Yat-sen* (New York, 1934).
A. H. Smith, *China in Convulsion* (2 vols., New York, 1901).
G. N. Steiger, *China and the Occident* (New Haven, 1927).
Sun Yat-sen, *San Min Chu I. The Three Principles of the People.* Translated by F. W. Price, edited by L. T. Chen (Shanghai, 1927).
T'ang Leang-li, *The Inner History of the Chinese Revolution* (London, 1930).
C. W. Young, *The International Relations of Manchuria* (Chicago, 1929).

Chapter XV. JAPAN BECOMES A WORLD POWER, 1894–1930

ONE OF THE MOST AMAZING DEVELOPMENTS of the stirring and stormy epoch which spanned the closing years of the nineteenth century and the first forty-two years of the twentieth century was the forging to the fore of Japan as a world power. Until the mid-nineteenth century Japan had, by her own volition, been all but hermetically sealed from the rest of the world and was resolutely isolationist. In 1895 she had back of her less than a half century of adaptation to the Occident. Now, beginning in 1894-1895, she became first a force to be reckoned with in Far Eastern politics through her defeat of China. Then, less than a decade thereafter, she was taken into alliance with the world's leading maritime nation, Great Britain. Within another five years she successfully challenged a major Western power, Russia, and achieved control over Korea and adjacent portions of Manchuria. In World War I she further strengthened her hold on the continent. It was only through the resistance of the United States that she was estopped from acquiring large additional holdings. In consequence of that war she obtained strategic islands in the Pacific and was given a permanent seat on the Council of the League of Nations, thus becoming the first non-Occidental nation to be admitted to the inner circle of the Western powers. In 1931, pursuing her expansion, Japan embarked upon a course of conquest which for a time made her mistress of Manchuria, much of China Proper, the Philippines, the East Indies, Indo-China, and Burma. Since the events of 1931 were a prelude to the second world war of the century and to a conflict which marked an epoch in the history of the Far East and India, we have reserved them for a separate chapter. In the present chapter we will trace the story of Japan from the war with China, in 1894-1895, through the year 1930 and to the eve of the fateful September 1931.

The chapter division is in part artificial. The story, like most history, is continuous. Japan's expansion, as we saw earlier, began before 1894. It went on by leaps rather than by gradual, regular movement. The chief stages make convenient headings for the author and student.

Although we are here centering upon Japan, we must never forget that that empire was only part of a larger whole. In the preceding chapter we narrated the Chinese segment of the story of the years between 1894 and 1931. Increasingly, moreover, the Far East, including Japan, was carried into the stream of world events, and developments in the Occident strongly influenced the course both of Japan and of her near neighbors.

The expansion of Japan was in part territorial. It was more than that. It was also economic and cultural. During the four and a half decades between the defeat of China in 1895 and the enlargement of her adventure on the continent, Japan grew enormously in population, industry, and commerce, and impressed her culture upon her dependent territories. Within Japan, moreover, there was a pulsing life with striking shifts in ideas and government. The transformation which the coming of Perry had inaugurated continued and with varied manifestations. Yet, with all the changes the pre-Meiji Japan survived in its essence and, in some of its features, strengthened. As in the coming of Chinese culture centuries earlier, so now the influx of alien ideas and institutions wrought alterations which superficially were striking but which basically reenforced fundamental features of the nation's life.

We shall first concern ourselves with an account of Japan's relations with other countries. Then we shall turn to the changes within the islands. Yet here, too, the arrangement, while convenient, does violence to the on-going stream of events. Foreign relations and domestic affairs were part and parcel of the one story and continuously interacted.

The Causes of Japanese Expansion

To those upon whom it bore heavily, Japan's expansion appeared the result of a sinister program devised early and carried through with preternatural resolution and persistence. That it entailed aggression on neighbors was clear. It was also obvious that it followed a fairly consistent pattern. There had been those Japanese who, even before 1894, had advocated extensive expansion. Thus the Dark Ocean Society and the Black Dragon Society, composed of supernationalists, dreamed of making Japan dominant in at least the East of Asia. As time passed, hyperpatriotic societies of a somewhat similar kind multiplied. Several of them were composed of former army men. Numbers of the leaders in the army also advocated a bold and aggressive foreign policy and labored to achieve it.

However, to see in the amazing growth of the Japanese territorial and economic empire the work only of a minority of extreme chauvinists is greatly to misunderstand it. That enlargement was the consequence of many factors. Japan was a vigorous nation, rapidly mounting in population and wealth. The first land in the Far East to be industrialized through the adoption of Occidental science and machinery and in an advantageous geographic position which enabled her to command the sea approaches to the east of Asia, whether for commerce or for war, Japan quickly acquired a preeminence in the new Far East which was at once economic, intellectual, and political. Increasingly her ships plied the China Sea and the waters of the Yangtze and its tributaries. Indeed, her merchant craft became familiar visitors in the ports of the entire world and in the 1930's she was exceeded in the gross tonnage of her merchant marine only by Great Britain and the United States. Her manufactures, notably her cotton goods, were widely sold in the Far East and made their appearance elsewhere in the world. To her schools flocked thousands of students from China, there to acquire the new learning for which the youth of that changing land were hungry, and which could be obtained in Japan at smaller expense if less thoroughly than through the more costly pilgrimage to the West. Politically Japan became, especially after her war with Russia, the outstanding nation of Asia. Thanks in large degree to industrialization and commerce, Japan's wealth, although much behind that of the most powerful Occidental nations, was being augmented. The population of the islands was also multiplying. Between 1872 and 1894 it had risen from approximately thirty-five millions to slightly over forty-one millions. In 1930 it was between sixty-four and sixty-five millions.

This nation, with its abounding life and mounting riches and population, need not have turned to territorial expansion. Had it been content with peaceful industry and commerce, it might more greatly have added to its wealth. Eventually the colossal armaments and wars to which the ambitions and energies of Japan were diverted in an effort to extend the empire first retarded advance in the standard of living and then wrought impoverishment. It was a combination of the long military tradition of the nation, pride, and the officers of the army and the navy, especially of the army, who, because of their profession, thought in terms of conquest, which led this vigorous and growing Japan upon her perilous imperial venture.

We must also recall that the world into which Japan emerged from her seclusion was one in which colonial empires were being won by leading Western powers through either the threat or the actual use of armed might. In the nineteenth century the major Western countries, notably Great Britain, the United States, France, Russia, and Germany, were acquiring vast additional territories. The competitive scramble for leaseholds, concessions, and spheres of influence in China in the 1890's brought the imperialistic struggle close to the shores of Japan. The acquisition by the United States in 1898 of Hawaii, in which Japanese were the largest single element in the population, and of the Philippines, only a short distance south of the Japanese-held Formosa, could be interpreted by the fearful and the militarists as a further threat. When she set out to build an overseas empire Japan was but conforming to the pattern of the times.

The Japanese were a proud and sensitive folk. To them, theirs was the land of the gods. They were the first Oriental nation to win admission to the hitherto exclusive circle of the great powers of the Occident. That admission was grudging and somewhat supercilious. This attitude the Japanese resented. To employ the psychological jargon of the day, the Japanese presented a combination of a superiority and an inferiority complex. Each interacted on the other. Because of their sense of being a superior race headed by a descendant of the gods, the chauvinists among the Japanese felt it the right of the nation to rule other peoples. Yet there was a consciousness of being late arrivals in the society of the dominant Occident. Slights, fancied or real, on their national dignity by Western governments and peoples were, accordingly, magnified and met with hot resentment. They would show the Occident their might and would expel the arrogant white man from the Far East.

Moreover, Japan's first essays at expansion through the application of armed force were peculiarly successful and were a temptation to further imperialism. The war with China in 1894–1895 brought quick victory, the rich island of Formosa, and added voice in Korea. The war with Russia, ten years later, while straining the nation's resources to the utmost, ended in victory and was followed by control of additional territory. Participation in World War I did not prove particularly taxing and was rewarded by fresh increments of land. It is not surprising that Japanese militarists, thus encouraged, regarded empire-building as feasible and that public opinion esteemed Japanese arms invincible.

While territorial empire was not essential to her prosperity and the dream of it ultimately led Japan to frustration and disaster, the reasons for her course are fairly obvious.

An added feature, and one that lent itself to popular propaganda both for internal and external consumption, was the increase in population. This led to a demand for more land. The argument was specious. Here was a population about half that of the United States crowded into an area approximately the size of the state of California. Because of the mountainous character of the islands, only about a fifth of the surface could be brought under cultivation and in 1931 only about fifteen per cent was thus employed. Much of the remainder could be utilized for forests and could thus be a source of the wood needed for building and other purposes, but it was useless for the production of food. Japan's population was four times as dense as that of China and twice as dense as that of India. The rate of growth was progressively mounting. Late in the 1920's about a million were being added each year. As one observer succinctly put it, there were being added a million more individuals each year, each of whom wanted more things.

Emigration was not the solution, for most of the sparsely settled and desirable land of the world had been preempted by the white man, and, as in the United States, Canada, and Australia, barriers had been erected by him against the influx of peoples from the Orient. Some effort was made to find an outlet in Manchuria, still comparatively unoccupied, but there the Japanese farmer found a harsh climate, a standard of living lower than his own among competing Chinese and Korean peasants, and most of the best land already taken. Even had room abroad been discovered for a few millions, that would not have solved the problem for most of the millions who remained at home. If experience in Europe with emigration to the United States was a safe precedent, the birth rate, or at least the difference between the birth and death rates, would have jumped to take up the slack and the tension between population and land would not have been appreciably relieved. The obvious solution was industrialization. Japanese labor could be turned to the manufacture of goods which could be sold abroad in exchange for what the Japanese wished. If this solution were to be successful, there must be access to foreign markets and sources of raw materials. In peacetime raw materials would not be a serious obstacle if the Japanese could pay for them, for most peoples would be willing to sell. Markets, however, were not always so accessible, for tariffs could easily be imposed if Japanese goods became serious competitors of domestic products. It was on the plea of more land for emigration, a secure source of raw materials and capital investment, and markets, that propaganda rang the changes on the necessity of expansion. Both national prestige and economic necessity were invoked for a program of imperialism.

Japan's opportunity for expansion, particularly on the continent, might prove temporary. Traditionally China and not Japan had been the great power in the Far East. Delay in making her adjustment to the Occident and the prolonged internal disorder that followed the beginning of the adaptation had demoted China from that position. In the meantime, Japan, quicker in accommodating herself to the Occident, had moved to the fore. Many Japanese saw the danger of a powerful China and were resolved to hold the hegemony in East Asia. Others despised China for her weakness but were intent on exploiting her. Whether China would be able to assert herself and resume her ancient position was one of the questions only the future could answer. There were Westerners, long expert in Far Eastern affairs, who believed that Japan's prominence was in large part due to transient circumstances and that, even apart from military defeat, Japan could not maintain her preeminence in the western Pacific or as a first class power.

It would be a narrow vision, however, which could see Japan's bid for empire merely as a national or a Japanese phenomenon. Here was both a symbol and a symptom of something far more extensive and significant. For four hundred years, and especially during the nineteenth century, European peoples had been expanding in both territory and wealth. They had become dominant throughout the earth. They had seemed to owe this position to the possession of certain techniques and the machines which arose from those techniques. Non-Occidental peoples were both resentful and jealous. Increasingly they hoped, by acquiring the methods and appliances developed in the West, to throw off the yoke of the white man and to equal him in wealth and power. The Japanese were the first of the non-Occidental peoples to equip themselves in fairly thorough fashion with the science and machinery of the West and to challenge the supremacy of Europeans. Their success or failure might constitute precedent for the other non-Occidental peoples.

The First Stages in the Territorial Expansion of Japan

The steps by which Japan added to her empire between 1894 and 1931 have been in part recounted in the preceding chapter. Those which have there been covered need here be given in only brief summary. Those which have not been treated will require more extended notice. We had best proceed chronologically, both because this was the fashion in which the steps were taken and because some sense of the growth of the Empire can in that way be best conveyed.

In the chapter before the last we saw that Japan began her expansion shortly after the Meiji Restoration. Yezo was early brought more closely under the imperial administration. In 1875 Japan obtained full title to the Kuriles, the long chain of rocky islands reaching northward from Yezo to Kamchatka. Climate and terrain were unfavorable to settlement, but the islands were of major strategic importance in controlling the sea approaches to the eastern shores of Siberia. In 1878 the Bonin group was annexed, a group of no economic or commercial importance but, if in other than Japanese hands, a potential threat to the eastern shores and the main cities of Japan. In the 1870's Japan also extended her control over the Ryukyu Islands, and that in spite of the protests of China. In the 1880's, as we noted, Japan became active in Korean affairs and took measures the logic of which drew her ever more deeply into the continent and led to the events of the 1930's and 1940's.

Formosa (Taiwan)

As partial reward for her defeat of China in 1894–1895 Japan acquired, through the treaty of Shimonoseki, Formosa, or Taiwan as the Chinese and Japanese called it, and the Pescadores, a small group near the southwest coast of Formosa and naturally going with that island.

Here we must note that in the succeeding half century Japan developed the resources of Formosa greatly to her own advantage. The population was overwhelmingly Chinese, but in the mountains were remnants of pre-Chinese peoples of primitive culture. The Chinese element was comparatively recent, most of it dating back no earlier than the seventeenth century. It was made up of contingents from the adjacent mainland, partly Hakkas and partly other Chinese stocks. Under Japanese rule the population more than doubled, chiefly by an excess of births over deaths. In 1930 it was more than four and a half millions and in 1939 it was approximately five and three-quarters millions. Of these, in 1938 only about a hundred and fifty thousand were aborigines and about three hundred thousand Japanese. The remainder were Chinese. The Japanese did not permit further Chinese immigration, except of seasonal laborers and merchants. Yet in density the population about equaled that of Japan Proper. Formosa was predominantly agricultural. Through the policy of the Japanese administration, the main crops were rice and sugar. Under Japanese rule, rice, the chief crop, more than doubled in volume, and about half was exported to Japan Proper. The output of sugar was almost entirely the work of the Japanese authorities. The increase in both rice and sugar was in consequence of the desire of the Japanese government to make the empire self-sufficient in its food supply. Most of such industry as existed was for the preparation of various foods for the market and hence was closely related to agriculture. Japan reduced the use of opium and furthered education. In more than one way the lot of the average Chinese on Formosa improved. Health conditions were better and there were more opportunities for education. However, in the latter the Formosans did not fare as well as did the Japanese on the island and wages were much below those in Japan Proper. After 1919 the government sought more and more to assimilate the Formosans, and knowledge of the Japanese language became essential to all who worked for the rulers. The peoples of Formosa were comparatively passive. Initial resistance through a phantom "republic" soon after annexation was speedily suppressed, occasional uprisings among the aborigines were curbed, and a movement for greater participation by the Chinese in government did not attain formidable dimensions. In the 1940's Formosa became a strategic base for the great southward Japanese expansion in the fore part of that decade.

Territories Acquired from Russia

Ten years after the treaty of Shimonoseki, in 1905, by the treaty of Portsmouth which terminated the Russo-Japanese War, Japan acquired the Russian leaseholds and the Russian rights in the railways of southern Manchuria and also full title to the southern part of the island of Sakhalin. In the second half of the nineteenth century Japan for a time had laid claim to the island, but had surrendered her interest there in exchange for a corresponding relinquishment by the Russians of their claim to the Kuriles. Japan now reentered the island.

In the last chapter we recorded the main outlines of the process by which, during the next few years, Japan developed her interests in Manchuria. These were, as we also saw in that chapter, enlarged and confirmed by the concessions wrung from China through the first group of the Twenty-One Demands.

Korea (Chosen)

The Russo-Japanese War was accompanied and followed by the incorporation of Korea, or Chosen as the Japanese called it, within the Japanese Empire. Japan's war with Russia had arisen directly out of the clash over Korea. Japan now sought to make her hold upon the peninsula so secure that it could never again be seriously threatened. At the outset of the war, the Japanese Emperor had declared that the separate existence of Korea was essential to the safety of his realm. This, of course, was with the Russian menace in mind. A few days later, in February 1904, Korea, in exchange for the promise of the security of her imperial family and the integrity and independence of her land, became an ally of Japan and agreed to heed the advice of the latter in administrative matters. While nominally an ally and indedependent, Korea was now in fact a subordinate protectorate. The Japanese armies were followed by merchants, laborers, and *ronin* who exploited the privileged position of Japan to their own private profit and aroused the deep resentment of many Koreans. Within the next few months Japanese control was rapidly extended. Advisers nominated by Japan were given authoritative posts in foreign relations and finance. The postal, telegraph, and telephone systems were taken over. Fishing rights along the coast were granted to Japanese. Valuable lands were seized. Japanese began to flood the land with morphine. The ruling house and most of the leading officials of Korea were hopelessly inept and corrupt and no Western power was disposed to come to their rescue. The British government believed that Korea must fall under the control of Japan and in the renewal of the Anglo-Japanese Alliance in 1905 formally recognized Japanese supremacy in the peninsula. The United States government, although alarmed at the growing power of Japan and seeing in it a possible threat to the Philippines, was not disposed to aggravate its deteriorating relations with that empire in supporting the forlorn hope of Korean independence. In

November 1905, Ito was sent to Korea. Employing the threat of superior force, he obtained the transfer to Japan of all foreign relations. He then became Resident-General. The attempt was made to rule through a distinct indigenous government in much the fashion that Great Britain supervised the native states in India. Yet less liberty was left to Korea than to the chief Indian native states: Japanese advisers directed the major departments of the government. In 1905 a frantic appeal by the Korean Emperor was sent to President Roosevelt to intervene, and in 1907 recourse was had to the international conference then meeting at The Hague. The latter step precipitated the Japanese demand for the abdication of the Emperor in favor of the Crown Prince, a feeble-minded puppet. For a time Japan persevered in the attempt to govern through a Korean ruling house. All along extremists among her military men had labored for direct annexation. Assassinations by Korean patriots, among them that of Ito (1909), although the latter was no longer Resident-General, played into their hands. In 1910 the final step was taken. The Korean Emperor abdicated, and his realm was formally annexed.

In the decades following annexation Japan steadily pursued her policy of assimilating Korea and its inhabitants. She met little organized resistance. The leadership in the old order had been too decrepit to head any effective opposition. Japanese police were usually efficient in preventing incipient unrest from becoming formidable. In 1919, under the stimulus of the hopes aroused by World War I and President Wilson's advocacy of the self-determination of peoples, a rebellion broke out in which some of the Christian minority were prominent. However, it was quickly suppressed. Students who made their way to the Occident cherished hopes of national independence, and here and there, under other flags, chiefly in China and the United States, were small groups of Korean revolutionaries who labored for freedom. Yet their efforts were pathetically futile.

The Japanese achievement in Korea was of mixed quality. Critics complained that Korean peasants were losing their land to large Japanese concerns and that tenantry was increasing. They pointed to the better school facilities provided for the children of Japanese residents than for Koreans. They called attention to the fact that the standard of living was so much lower in Korea than in Japan that laborers were flocking to the great cities of the islands, although there they could have only the lowest wages and were predominantly in the humblest types of unskilled occupations. They could also point to conditions under which, while Korea raised large quantities of rice, few of the farmers who produced it could afford to eat it. Instead, the producers sold it, much of it was shipped to Japan, and the cultivators were under the necessity of eating the cheaper millet, barley, and wheat. On the other hand, Japanese noted with pride that the value of agricultural products had more than doubled in a quarter of a century of Japanese administration; that afforestation had been undertaken by the government on a large scale and that the existing forests were scientifically managed; that the government had encouraged new crops, such as the sugar beet and American strains of cotton; that manufactures, although still not extensive, had multiplied; that railways had been built; that strict measures had been taken against the use of opium and morphine; that much had been done to promote public health; and that in the twenty years between 1911 and 1931 the attendance at schools had increased more than sixfold. To be sure, much of the development of Korea had been for the benefit of Japan. The Japanese were seeking to utilize the resources of their dependencies in such fashion as would aid imperial economy and the homeland. Yet they could insist that Korea was also profiting. Part of the problem in Korea, as it was in Japan Proper and in Formosa, in Java and in India, was the rapid increase in population. In 1911 it had been a little over thirteen millions. In 1935 it was nearly twenty-three millions. In other words, it had almost doubled in a quarter of a century. In a land such as Korea, which was overwhelmingly agricultural and did not possess the natural resources for extensive industrialization, this meant distress. Some relief was had through emigration, chiefly to the adjacent sections of Manchuria and to Japan. The growth seems to have been due in large part to the order and better health brought by Japanese rule. However, it complicated the situation for both Koreans and Japanese.

A Balance Sheet of Japan's Gains and Losses from Her Colonies

It is highly doubtful whether Japan's colonial ventures were paying investments. On the credit side was the near monopoly by Japan of their trade, her control of their economy, her use of them as sources of raw materials and as outlets for her manufactures, and the fact that no tariff barriers between her and them impeded the flow of goods. On the debit side was the initial cost in blood and treasure of the wars through which they had been acquired, the fact that their budgets, over the long course of years, required balancing from the imperial treasury, and their failure to provide an outlet for any but the merest fraction of Japan's growing population. Certainly as far as the government exchequer was concerned, the colonies were liabilities and not assets.

Japanese Gains from World War I

To Japan the outbreak of World War I in 1914 afforded what seemed a golden opportunity. Europe was now engaged in internecine strife and could not extend its holdings in the Far East. Indeed, rival European powers, bidding for Japanese support in their deadly struggle, eventually made concessions that could not have been extracted from them in time of peace. While Japan became a belligerent, she was fortunate in associating herself with the side which proved victorious. She did not need to expend much energy in actual warfare. Her fighting was confined to the Far East and the Pacific. Here the Germans were easily and quickly eliminated. Nor did the Siberian adventure, which we are to narrate a few pages below, entail the use of large forces. Such territories and other holdings as were acquired in World War I were obtained at very slight cost. Moreover, Japan became a source of manufactured goods. In industry and especially in shipbuilding she enjoyed a remarkable expansion. She sold heavily to the Allies. With the proceeds she built up balances of exchange and gold and became a creditor as well as a debtor nation. She was distinctly better off after than before the war.

As we saw in the preceding chapter, Japan greatly augmented her influence in China. There she also acquired the former German leaseholds and railways in Shantung. While in 1922 she returned these to China, she retained important interests in the province.

Out of the war Japan also obtained the German-owned islands north of the equator. These included the Marshalls, the Carolines (subdivided in turn into the Palau, Yap, Truk, and Ponape groups), and the Marianas, except Guam, which had been American property since 1898. They were held as a mandate of the League of Nations and in theory were not to be fortified. Their economic value was slight, for their populations and areas were small and their products were chiefly agricultural. Yet one of the Palaus had large phosphate deposits, of marked value to Japan. Moreover, the mandated islands were of enormous strategic importance. They constituted a shield against possible hostile approach to Japan Proper from the south and east and could become important stepping stones for further southern adventures. The value to both functions was vividly and, to the United States and the British and Dutch Empires, tragically apparent in the 1940's.

Japan Is Balked

Although Japan made gains in World War I quite out of proportion to their cost to her, she found herself foiled in some of her attempts to profit from the conflict. Much although by no means all of her frustration was attributable to the United States. It was the United States which gave most support to China in the latter's resistance to the Twenty-One Demands. It was largely through the pressure of American public opinion, exerted at the Washington Conference in 1921–1922, that Japan felt herself constrained to restore to China the former German properties in Shantung.

Moreover, it was chiefly through the United States that, during the weakness of Russia which came in consequence of the war, Japan was prevented from annexing the northern half of Sakhalin and the portions of Siberia bordering on the Amur River and the Pacific Ocean, and from acquiring Russian interests in the Chinese Eastern Railway. These holdings were tempting to Japan. Japan had long coveted all of Sakhalin. Control of the Chinese Eastern would all but complete her domination of the rail transportation of Manchuria and with it the full mastery of the economic life of the region. If she could take eastern Siberia she would be mistress of the east coast of Asia from the southern tip of Korea to the Arctic.

As early as January 1918, the Japanese government hinted that it would be glad to occupy Vladivostok and operate the railways which had their terminus in that port. Great Britain seemed willing, but the United States was stoutly opposed.

In 1916 Japan, in return for war supplies, had obtained from Russia in a secret treaty consent to take over part of the Chinese Eastern Railway, and in May 1918 she signed agreements with China for join military and naval action "against the common enemy." The Russian Revolution in 1917 was followed by confused fighting in the Russian Far East between rival factions, ostensibly between Bolshevik and anti-Bolshevik or White forces. One of the White leaders had taken refuge in Manchuria. In July 1918, on the pretext that the peace of the region was threatened by possible attempts of Reds and Germans to enter the area in pursuit of their prey, Japan sent troops into northern Manchuria, and that in spite of the protest of Washington. It must also be added that the United States would not acquiesce in the efforts of the Chinese to take over full administration of the Chinese Eastern Railway. The United States government solved the dilemma by an arrangement for the operation of the line by an interallied board headed by a distinguished American engineer. The road was thereby kept from falling into the hands of Japan, for with Japanese armed forces in the area the control by China, even though technically recognized, would presumably have been nominal.

The chief Japanese attempt and the main frustration were in eastern Siberia. Here an excuse for intervention was given by the presence of Czecho-Slovaks, captives or deserters from Austrian armies in which they had been constrained to fight, and now seeking to make their way back to Europe to assist in the liberation of their land from the Austrian yoke. These Czecho-Slovaks were reported as being harassed by Bolshevik forces officered by Germans and Austrians. Late in June 1918, the Czecho-Slovaks seized Vladivostok. They were probably never in acute danger from the Germans, but public opinion among the Allies believed them to be threatened. To protect them and military stores, the following month the administration of Vladivostok was taken over by the Allies. President Wilson permitted American participation, reluctantly, because he had become persuaded that only so could the Japanese be prevented from absorbing eastern Siberia. Ostensibly the purpose of the Allied forces was to aid the Czecho-Slovaks, protect Allied material, and encourage Russian efforts at restoring order and self-defense. Intervention in Russian internal affairs was disavowed and respect for Russia's territorial integrity was affirmed. There were small contingents of British troops and of Annamese under French command. The Americans totaled slightly over nine thousand. Japan ultimately sent more than seventy-two thousand men and clearly had the lead. The United States attempted, by diplomatic means, to prevent the Japanese from building up so large a force. The Allies took over the management of the Trans-Siberian Railway.

In Siberia order was slowly restored by the Russians themselves, but under a regime which became a unit of the Union of Soviet Socialist Republics. Various White, anti-Communist leaders put up resistance to the Red tide. Of these the most formidable was Kolchak, who had been an admiral under the Czar. For a time there seemed to be some likelihood that he might extend and consolidate his rule over all Siberia. However, early in 1920 his regime collapsed. In

January 1920, the United States government announced its purpose of withdrawing from Siberia, and on April 1 of that year the last contingent of its troops embarked. The Japanese remained. Only slowly did the Russians succeed in establishing a unified government for eastern Siberia. Eventually they did so under what called itself the Far Eastern Republic of Siberia. In November 1922, this republic was incorporated into the Soviet Union.

In the interval between the departure of the American forces and the extension of the domains of the Union of Soviet Socialist Republics over eastern Siberia, the Japanese maintained their armies in the region. After the fall of Kolchak civil strife continued. Rival bands of Russians fought one another. In the melee some of the Japanese were killed. Early in 1920 a number lost their lives at Nicholaevsk, near the mouth of the Amur. In retaliation Japan occupied the northern half of Sakhalin until reparation should be made. She thus was in possession of the entire island, a position which her extremists had long coveted. The Japanese army, moreover, continued to operate in the maritime province.

However, in November 1922, Japan withdrew from the mainland. This step was presumably facilitated by the airing given the Siberian situation at the Washington Conference and the pressure exerted upon her at that gathering by the United States. In January 1925, after prolonged negotiations, Japan opened regular diplomatic relations with the Soviet government. Communist Russia recognized the validity of the treaty of Portsmouth, conceded, for the time being, fishing rights to the Japanese off the Siberian coast, and granted to Japanese the privilege of developing fifty per cent of the oil of the northern part of Sakhalin. She also extended apologies for the Nicholaevsk affair. Japan promised to evacuate her troops from the northern part of the island. She kept her word and in that year removed the last of her forces from Russian soil.

The Siberian adventure had proved costly to Japan and had won little tangible reward. For the failure to obtain a permanent footing in eastern Siberia several factors were accountable. Among them was the undeviating opposition of the United States. Japan had again been balked, and in part by the American government.

The Partial Frustration of Japan at Paris

At the Paris Peace Conference which arranged the settlement of World War I Japan realized some of her desires. The assignment to her of the German properties in Shantung and of the strategically important islands in the Pacific in part satisfied her ambitions.

However, in attaining these goals she met opposition from the United States. American sympathy was clearly with the Chinese delegation in its demand that the German holdings in Shantung be restored to China. President Wilson, moreover, was unhappy over the necessity of granting the Pacific islands to Japan, even under a mandate. Here his hand was forced by the insistence of Australia and New Zealand on being awarded some others of the German territories in the Pacific. If they were to be appeased, Japan also must have her claims. The secret agreement which she had been able to exact from Great Britain and France in 1917 also aided Japan. President Wilson labored for a different settlement and was as troubled over the Shantung award as over any feature of the Treaty of Versailles. He was chiefly responsible for Japan's promise eventually to return the properties to China. He it was, too, who worked most persistently for the mandate principle and so for restricting Japan's rights in the Pacific islands by trusteeship through the League of Nations rather than awarding the islands in full sovereignty.

Moreover, at Paris Japan was thwarted in an endeavor to obtain recognition of the principle of racial equality. In view especially of the attitude of Occidental peoples toward Orientals and of her sensitiveness over the discrimination against her own nationals in some lands controlled by Westerners, a subject to which we are to revert shortly, the rebuff to this request rankled deeply and long. The Japanese first proposed that an amendment be added to the Covenant of the League of Nations which would state that "the equality of nations being a basic principle of the League of Nations, the High Contracting Parties agree to accord, as soon as possible, to all alien nationals of States members of the League equal and just treatment in every respect, making no distinction, either in law or in fact, on account of their race or nationality." President Wilson and Colonel House assisted the Japanese to prepare the resolution and presumably favored it. However, it was loaded with dynamite. Australia's representative took fright and vigorously opposed it, for his country, thinly settled and intent on achieving and maintaining a high standard of living, was resolved on keeping its soil for the white races and viewed with apprehension the crowded lands of Asia to its north. Moreover, as we are to see a few pages below, the problem of the treatment of the Japanese was acute in the United States, especially in California.

Were President Wilson to throw his full weight for the amendment he might augment the already serious opposition to the ratification of the Covenant in his home constituency. The British leaders opposed the amendment. France and Italy seemed to favor it. The Japanese modified their request and wished to add it to the preamble of the Covenant as "the endorsement of the principle of the equality of nations and just treatment of their nationals." This amendment passed the Commission on the League of Nations which was preparing the Covenant, but by a narrow vote. As chairman, Wilson ruled that since the vote was not unanimous the amendment was lost. The decision seemed clear evidence of the determination of the white nations to maintain their supremacy. It greatly offended the Japanese. They could also point to their part in raising and pressing the issue as evidence of their championship of the cause of the nonwhite peoples against Occidental arrogance and discrimination.

The Washington Conference, 1921–1922

In 1921–1922 there met at Washington an international conference which concerned itself largely with Far Eastern affairs. It came in part as an aftermath of World War I. Although for several years it eased tension in the Pacific and may have postponed a war in that ocean, it drew the United States more deeply than ever into the affairs of the Far East, eventually heightened clashes with Japan over the renewed aggressions of the latter in China which commenced in September 1931, and was one of the steps that brought the United States and Japan to the fateful December 7, 1941.

The Washington Conference met on invitation from the United States. The reasons for convening it were somewhat complex. Ill feeling between the United States and Japan was acute and threatened a war which it was to the clear interest of both powers to avoid. The friction arose in large part from conflicts between the United States and Japan over the east of Asia. Ever since the Russo-Japanese War the United States had been getting in the way of Japanese ambitions in that area. In her role as advocate of the open door and the correlated independence and territorial and administrative integrity of China, the United States had sought to curb Japan in Manchuria, had expressed her apprehension over the Twenty-One Demands, and had balked the realization of Japan's full aims in Shantung. Moreover, American criticism of Japan on these issues had been loud. The United States, too, had forced Japan to be content with a mandate rather than full annexation of the Pacific islands acquired from Germany. She was challenging Japan's full control in Yap, one of the Carolines, which as an important cable center was of value to her, and wished the internationalization of the island. American opposition had contributed to Japanese frustration in eastern Siberia. There was the memory of the race issue at Paris. Then, too, ever since 1906, with varying intensity, Japanese immigration to the United States and the treatment of Japanese on America's west coast had been an irritant. The United States was impeding Japanese expansion whether by the acquisition of territory or by emigration. A race was developing in naval armaments. Japan and the United States were building, and the competition made relations between the two peoples ever more brittle. Great Britain was apprehensive. Although feeling the drain of the late world war, she felt herself impelled to keep her fleet up at least to the level of that of the United States. She was bound by the Anglo-Japanese Alliance. That pact was due to expire in July 1921, and there were many reasons for its continuation. Yet, in a war between Japan and the United States, the tie might conceivably draw Britain into the conflict. This possibility was sufficient to make Canada emphatic in resisting renewal, for Anglo-American belligerency would presumably embroil her with her huge neighbor on the south. Would not a general agreement for the preservation of peace in the Far East and the Pacific in which Great Britain, Japan, the United States, and other interested governments would join be a desirable substitute for the Anglo-Japanese Alliance? An added incentive was the fact that leaders of the Republican Party, then in power, having thwarted American participation in the League of Nations, were not averse to a procedure which might demonstrate their ability to settle international issues without having recourse to that instrument.

The Washington Conference met on Armistice Day, November 11, 1921. It was officially described as having as its assignment the limitation of armaments and Pacific and Far Eastern problems. Invitations to the gathering had been sent to Great Britain, France, Italy, and Japan, for these, together with the host, were the principal allied and associated powers of the late world war. In addition, China, Belgium, the Netherlands, and Portugal had been asked to confer on Pacific and Far Eastern issues. Of these, the last three had sought invitations. Russia was conspicuously not among those invited, for her Communist regime was still something of an international pariah. Japan had delayed acceptance and finally agreed to be represented only with the stipulation that "problems such as are of sole concern to certain particular powers or such matters that may be regarded accomplished facts should be scrupulously avoided." By this Japan obviously meant to exclude from the agenda the Twenty-One Demands, Shantung, Siberia, and Yap. She was serving warning that the conference must not review her recent actions and gains, for she was clearly apprehensive that the United States, with her known antagonisms to her, would attempt to use this gathering at her capital to coerce her. Yet she could scarcely refuse to come, for if she did a war might be precipitated in which she might find Great Britain as well as the United States arrayed against her. American diplomacy had again placed her in a most embarrassing position.

The gathering was really two. The five powers, the United States, Great Britain, Japan, France, and Italy, met on naval disarmament, and in parallel fashion all nine powers conferred on the Pacific and the Far East. Secretary of State Hughes startled both the delegates and the world by offering at the initial business session, on November 12 (the preceding day had been devoted to ceremonial), a drastic plan for naval disarmament. By it all building of capital ships was to be abandoned, certain ships already in use or under construction were to be scrapped by the United States, Great Britain, and Japan, the capital ship tonnage was to be taken as the measurement for the strength of the navies, a proportionate allowance of auxiliary combatant ships was to be prescribed, and regard was to be had for the existing naval strength of the powers concerned. The eventual strength of the three navies, those of Great Britain, the United States, and Japan, was to be in the ratio of 5-5-3. The powers all quickly subscribed "in principle" to the proposal, but the Japanese delegation held out for modifications which would have given to their navy a slightly larger proportion—in the ratio of 10-10-7 rather than 10-10-6. They eventually yielded. Replacements for Italy and France were set at the ratio of 1.75 each as against the 5-5-3 of the other three powers.

A corollary of the limitation of naval armaments was the fortification of islands in the Pacific. Japan insisted that if she were to consent to a navy smaller than those of Great Britain and the United States she must be assured against the construction of naval bases which would enable either of these powers to employ its superior naval force against her. Accordingly, the three governments agreed that they would construct no new fortifications or bases in their island possessions in the

Pacific. For the United States, such advanced positions as the Philippines, Guam, and the Aleutians were included in this self-denying ordinance. However, Hawaii and islands adjacent to the Panama Canal Zone, Alaska, and her west coast were exempted. Great Britain was not to arm Hongkong or others of her islands east of the one hundred and tenth meridian. Since Singapore was west of that line she might there construct a naval base. Moreover, islands adjacent to Canada, Australia, and New Zealand might be fortified. Japan was not to fortify the Kuriles, the Bonins, the Ryukyu group, Amami-Oshima (between the Ryukyu islands and Kyushu), Formosa, or the Pescadores.

This provision meant that, under the existing state of naval skill and equipment, Japan was left practically impregnable in the western Pacific. Presumably she could be successfully attacked only by naval forces three or four times as strong as her own. Even the combined fleets of Great Britain and the United States as fixed by the agreement would scarcely be strong enough to essay such an adventure.

On the other hand, the agreement protected the British Empire and the United States from attack from Japan, for by surrendering the privilege of arming insular possessions and mandated groups outside her home islands Japan was estopped from being a serious threat to Australia, New Zealand, Canada, British Malaya, Hawaii, the American mainland, or, to a certain extent, the Philippines. By the permission granted to fortify Singapore and Hawaii, the British Empire and the United States respectively could erect formidable bastions against potential Japanese aggression on their domains. Each of the three powers was presumably made secure from attack, the United States and the British Empire from Japan and Japan from either of the other two nations. These safeguards continued during the life of the pact. It was only after the agreement was ended that Japan became a serious menace to the others.

The provisions for limitation of naval armament and of fortifications in the Pacific islands were incorporated in a five-power treaty signed by the British Empire, the United States, Japan, Italy, and France. The document was to remain in force until December 31, 1936, and in case none of the contracting powers gave notice two years before that date of its intention to withdraw, it was to continue to be binding until two years from the time at which notice of termination should be given by one of the parties to it.

A further supplementary treaty among the five powers made

certain limitations on the submarine and prohibited the use of noxious gases in time of war. To this no terminal date was set.

The Anglo-Japanese Alliance presented a problem. The Japanese feared that without it they would be isolated and subject to a possible Anglo-American combination. Great Britain tended to favor it because of the partial control it gave her over Japan's actions. Australia wished it as a protection against Japan. Canada and the United States were against it. There was a suggestion that the United States become a third party to the alliance. Secretary Hughes, for the United States, wanted something akin to the Root-Takahira Agreement, signed in 1908, by which Japan and the United States "firmly resolved reciprocally to respect the territorial possessions belonging to each other" in Eastern Asia and the Pacific Ocean and declared themselves for the existing *status quo*, the open door in China, and the independence and integrity of that country. The resulting treaty was a combination and modification of the varied desires. The Anglo-Japanese Alliance was not renewed. In place of it there was signed a four-power treaty whereby the United States, the British Empire, France, and Japan agreed "to respect their rights in relation to their insular possessions and insular dominions in the region of the Pacific Ocean"; that if a controversy developed between any of them arising from any Pacific question and involving their rights which was not satisfactorily settled by diplomacy they would invite the other parties to a conference for consideration and adjustment; and that if any of the rights embraced in the treaty were threatened by the aggressive action of any other power, the parties to the treaty would "communicate with one another fully and frankly in order to arrive at an understanding as to the most efficient measures to be taken, jointly or separately, to meet the exigencies of the particular situation." The treaty was to remain in force for ten years and then was to continue subject to the right of any of the signatories to terminate it upon twelve months' notice.

The four-power treaty was supplemented by two declarations, also by the four powers. One of these, to meet a request of the United States, stated that the treaty was not to be deemed "an assent on the part of the United States of America to the mandates" and should "not preclude agreements between the United States of America and the Mandatory Powers respectively in relation to the mandated islands." This referred especially to the Japanese-American controversy over the island of Yap. That issue, fortunately, was amicably settled in February 1922 by a treaty between the United States and

Japan by which the interests of American nationals in the former German islands were guaranteed. The other of the supplements was to satisfy Japan. It exempted from the "insular possessions and insular dominions" of that treaty the homeland of Japan and included, so far as it applied to Japan, only the southern portion of Sakhalin, Formosa, the Pescadores, and the islands under Japanese mandate.

The United States government was determined to use the Washington Conference to check the Japanese advance in China. In the preceding chapter we have seen the result. Japan, by arrangement with China, returned the Shantung properties; she relented slightly on some phases of her claims in southern Manchuria; she formally abandoned the fifth group of the Twenty-One Demands; and she joined in the omnibus nine-power treaty which had to do with China and which was subscribed to by the United States, Belgium, the British Empire (including Great Britain, Canada, Australia, New Zealand, and India), China, France, Italy, the Netherlands, Portugal and herself, by which the signatories agreed "to respect the sovereignty, the independence, and the territorial and administrative integrity of China; to provide the fullest and most unembarrassed opportunity to China to develop and maintain for herself an effective and stable government; to use their influence for the purpose of effectually establishing and maintaining the principle of equal opportunity for the commerce and industry of all nations throughout the territory of China; to refrain from taking advantage of conditions in China in order to seek special rights or privileges which would abridge the rights of subjects or citizens of friendly states, and from countenancing action inimical to the security of such states." Japan had bound herself to as strong a statement as the United States had yet devised for safeguarding China.

The United States also extracted from the Japanese a disclaimer of designs on Russian territory and an avowal of a purpose soon to withdraw Japanese troops from Siberia and the northern part of Sakhalin.

For the time being the Washington Conference eased the tension in the Far East, and notably between Japan and China and the United States and Japan. However, the settlement, like most international arrangements, was based upon the good faith of the signatories. From the naval standpoint, Japan was left almost impregnable in her own islands and in complete command of the coast of China. If she would abide by her pledged word, all would be well. If she were to disregard it and turn aggressor, checking her would be a long and costly process.

Moreover, through the Washington Conference the United States had assumed greater initiative and weightier responsibilities in the Far East than ever before. By calling the conference, she had taken a leadership in the affairs of that part of the world which was in logical consequence of earlier policies but was greater than it had yet been. While she had, on paper, undertaken no more responsibility for peace in the Far East and for checking Japan than had other signatories to the treaties and was under no written obligation to defend China or any other portion of the Far East, in effect she had put herself in the forefront of maintaining the *status quo* and would presumably bear the chief burden, aside from China and possibly Russia, in opposing any renewal of the Japanese advance in the Far East and the western Pacific. A growing nation such as Japan, confronted with the economic situation she had to meet, and with powerful military elements which dreamed in terms of armed force and expansion, would probably be again a problem to her neighbors.

It was ominous for the future that, while at the London Naval Conference of 1930 Japan acquiesced in a compromise which only slightly raised her proportionate ratio of ships, the Japanese navy and army felt deeply aggrieved. Moreover, on December 29, 1934, Japan gave, as she was entitled to do under the Washington treaty which limited armaments, notice that, two years hence, she would not be bound by its restrictions. This freed, beginning with January 1, 1937, all the signatories from their obligations under that agreement. Naval competition and the arming of the Pacific islands might again begin.

Japan and the Continent of Asia between 1922 and 1931

From nearly a decade after the Washington Conference Japan seemed to have forsworn aggression. She withdrew her troops from Siberia and the Russian part of Sakhalin. In China she exercised great self-restraint. As we saw in the last chapter, the 1920's were a time of growing and rampant Chinese nationalism. By agitation, boycotts, and riots the Chinese were striving for emancipation from the "unequal treaties" and to rid themselves of the restrictions on their territories and sovereignty to which their rulers had consented in the preceding eighty or ninety years. Japanese as well as British subjects suffered from the unrest and violence following the incident of May 30, 1925. Indeed, the trouble which culminated in the shooting on that day had broken out in a Japanese-owned mill. In the northward advance from Canton of the armies of the Kuomintang Japanese were roughly handled. In the attacks on foreigners in Nanking in March, 1927, the Japanese consulate was looted and the consul and some other Japanese were wounded. In April of that year Japanese were attacked and injured in their concessions in Hankow. In all these incidents the Japanese did not retaliate in the vigorous fashion that might have been anticipated. To be sure, as Kuomintang armies neared Shantung on their way to Peking, first in 1927 and then in 1928, Japan sent forces to that province, for there her financial stake was considerable and her subjects were numerous. When, in May 1928, the Nationalists entered Tsinan, the capital of Shantung, they clashed with the Japanese. The latter were left in control of the city, but an angry boycott swept China and hit the Japanese at their most vulnerable point, their trade. Yet in May 1929, in consequence of a Sino-Japanese agreement reached a few weeks earlier, the Japanese troops were withdrawn from Tsinan. Moreover, Japan fulfilled both the portions of the nine-power treaty of Washington which had to do with her rights in China and her agreement with China which had been consummated at Washington. She returned the Shantung properties, she discontinued her post offices in the Republic, and, somewhat reluctantly and tardily, she consented to the resumption of tariff autonomy by China. This last step was peculiarly difficult for her, since her neighbor might thereafter raise her duties on foreign manufactures and thus place restrictions upon what was potentially a chief outlet for the products of Japan's factories.

Japan did not fully yield her position in China. Like Great Britain, the United States, and some of the other powers with interests in China, she did not relinquish extraterritoriality. She continued to develop her holdings in Manchuria. In the main, the Japanese and the Chinese ruler of Manchuria, Chang Tso-lin, managed to keep the peace with each other, but Chang Tso-lin's violent and somewhat mysterious death (June 1928) was believed by many Chinese to have been the work of Japanese. Japan was still firmly entrenched in southern Manchuria. Sooner or later the issue of final control in that region of rich natural resources would inevitably be joined. The growing nationalism of China would insist that the Republic be paramount, and the Japanese would not tamely submit to ejection or subordination.

The reasons for the comparative leniency of Japan in China in the 1920's as contrasted with the preceding and the succeeding decade were to be found both outside and inside Japan. The era was one in which democracy and liberalism seemed triumphant. In World War I the democracies had won. In international relations the idealism of which President Wilson had been the chief spokesman was given lip service. Japan, sensitive to the currents of world opinion, responded and partly conformed. In Japan itself, as we are to see a few pages below, political liberalism appeared to be making progress. The franchise was being broadened and the power of Parliament was advancing. For the moment the armed services were partly in eclipse. The mild policy toward China was consistent with the domestic scene.

Friction over Japanese Emigration, Especially with the United States

One form of tension between Japan and some of her neighbors around the Pacific remained chronic, even during the 1920's with their lull in the advance of Japan's imperial boundaries. That was the resistance to any influx of Japanese emigrants and discrimination in some lands against those who were admitted. Friction was particularly marked with the United States. It entered again and again into the relations between the two nations. During the quarter of a century before 1931 it was never completely absent. On occasion it was so acute as to threaten war. At other times it was less noticeable. Yet never after 1906 did it entirely disappear. The Japanese were more chronically aware of it than were the rank and file of Americans, but periodically it forced itself upon the attention of the entire United States.

The conflict over Japanese migration was, unfortunately, to be expected. Japan's population was growing and must find outlets. Most of the increase was cared for in the mounting industrialization and foreign trade of Japan Proper. The surplus largely found employment in factories, in service to the urban population, and in shipping. Yet some sought in emigration escape from the pressure for subsistence. A few tens of thousands went to Formosa, Korea, and Manchuria. However, among the farmers in these lands the standard of living was even lower than in Japan, and relatively few of the Japanese migrants made as good a living by tilling the soil as they could have done at home. Most of the Japanese in these regions were in government employ in the army or as clerks or officials or were in business or one of the professions. Emigration would naturally flow to lands where standards of living were higher than in Japan. These countries were occupied by Occidentals. Hawaii had proved very attractive, even before its annexation by the United States, and Japanese had come to form the largest single racial element in the islands. The west coast of the United States and Canada, sparsely settled, looked inviting. So, too, did Australia and some of the South American states. Yet in all of these regions restrictions were sooner or later placed upon the ingress of Japanese.

In the United States, after brief flare-ups in the 1890's and 1900, the friction first became really serious in 1905. This, unfortunately, was about the time that the official attitude of the United States toward Japan's activities in the Far East changed from friendliness to antagonism. The two sources of irritation—conflict in East Asia and tension over Japanese immigration to the United States—reenforced each other.

Emigration from Japan was not well under way until after 1894 and in point of numbers was never extensive. It had, naturally, been impossible during the days of Japan's self-imposed isolation. After the opening of the country the movement of Japanese abroad was long numerically not large, and much of this was not for permanent residence but for commerce and temporary study. Between 1868 and 1884 only a few more than 15,000 passports were issued, and presumably most of these were for transient residence abroad. The number of passports given then began to rise, but in 1895 it first exceeded 20,000 in any one year. By 1927 the Japanese living outside the Empire were officially said to total 676,262. Of these, 250,423, or nearly 37 per cent, were in China; 140,709, or nearly 21 per cent, were on the mainland of the United States; 129,387, or 19 per cent, were in Hawaii; 65,189, or nearly 10 per cent, were in Brazil; 21,155, or 3 per cent, were in Canada; 15,207, or 2.2 per cent, were in Peru; 12,101, or 1.17 per cent, were in South Asia; 11,288, or 1.6 per cent, were in the Philippines; and 30,803, or 5.3 per cent, were in other countries. A larger proportion of the whole, 41.3 per cent, were living under the American flag—in continental United States, Hawaii, and the Philippines—than under any other foreign standard, not even excepting that of China.

The issue of immigration first arose between the governments of Japan and the United States in connection with Hawaii. The planters, largely from the United States, required labor for the estates which were the chief source of the island's wealth. Following the example of the United States, in 1887 and 1888 the Hawaiian legislature enacted measures to stop the immigration of Chinese. As a substitute, the planters turned to Japan and between 1885 and 1894 nearly thirty thousand Japanese were brought in. In 1900 Hawaii had slightly over sixty-one thousand Japanese. This was approximately forty per cent of the total population, more than twice the size of any other racial group. The Hawaiian government, alarmed by the influx, in 1897 refused admission and sent back to Japan over a thousand would-be immigrants. The Japanese government protested and sent a cruiser to demand indemnification. This action spurred annexation by the United States, a step which was consummated in 1898. Japan protested the bringing of the islands under the American flag, and thus strengthened the resolution of Congress to carry through the measure which made Hawaii American soil. Under pressure from the United States, before annexation, Hawaii paid Japan an indemnity of $75,000 and Japan withdrew her opposition (December 22, 1897) to the extension of American sovereignty to the islands. Thereafter the percentage of Japanese in the total population did not greatly vary. It was slightly over forty-one per cent in 1910 and by 1930 had sunk to approximately thirty-eight per cent. However, the sex and age composition of the Japanese contingent had altered. In 1900 men were almost four times as numerous as women and there were few children. Thirty years later males were only about fifteen per cent more numerous than females and children and youths had increased. Many Japanese had returned to their native land. Until 1908 numbers went to the mainland of the United States. A decreasing proportion were laborers on the sugar plantations. More and more were attracted into other occupations and their economic status improved.

It was because of Japanese on the mainland of the United States that the conflict over their immigration became the most severe. Before 1890 Japanese immigration to the continental United States had been meager. By the census of 1890 only slightly more than two thousand Japanese were counted as residents. In the following decade, 1891–1900, not far from thirty thousand were admitted. In the succeeding decade, slightly less than fifty-five thousand arrived directly from Japan. An unknown total came to the mainland from Hawaii. In 1920, the census reported 111,010 Japanese in the continental United States. Of these, 27.2 per cent had been born in the United States and were, therefore, under the fourteenth amendment, American citizens. In 1930 Japanese numbered 138,834. The overwhelming majority were in the three Pacific Coast states, Washington, Oregon, and California. In 1930 California had 97,456, or more than two-thirds of the whole. Even in California Japanese were only a small percentage of the total population, 2.1 per cent in 1920 and 1.7 per cent in 1930. In that state, however, they were concentrated chiefly in certain districts and occupations. Although many were in the cities as shopkeepers and in various trades, more were in the rural districts, largely growing vegetables and small fruits. Most of their farms were under thirty acres in size and were intensively cultivated. The Japanese were hard working and thrifty and, accordingly, prospered.

As, in the second half of the nineteenth century, agitation had arisen and centered in California which led to the exclusion of Chinese immigration, so now, in the fore part of the twentieth century, also in that state, a movement against the Japanese sprang up and quickly became virulent. In 1901 the California legislature memorialized Congress to place restrictions on the immigration of Japanese. It was in 1905 that the agitation first became fervid. In that year the legislatures of California, Idaho, Montana, and Nevada petitioned Congress to curtail the immigration of Japanese laborers. Labor interests organized the Japanese and Korean Exclusion League, with the purpose of extending the Chinese exclusion laws to these two nationalities. The San Francisco Board of Education determined to segregate Chinese and Japanese children in a separate school. Action was delayed, but in 1906 the step was actually taken. President Theodore Roosevelt, with his customary vigor, opposed the proposed exclusion and was embarrassed by the inconsistency of the advocacy by the United States of the open door and equality of opportunity in the Far East and the discrimination against Orientals in America. The Japanese press seethed with indignation over the act of the school board, and the Japanese ambassador formally protested it as a patent violation of the treaty of 1894 between his government and that of the United States. In December 1906, President Roosevelt, in a message to Congress, denounced the segregation order as a "wicked absurdity," advocated naturalization for the Japanese, and declared that he would, if necessary, employ the army to protect the Japanese in California from violence. His message mollified Tokyo but stirred up a hornets' nest in San Francisco. The President called the Mayor and the offending Board of Education to the White House and prevailed upon them to rescind the order, but only in return for his promise to end the immigration of Japanese laborers. The following year he obtained from Congress legislation which allowed him to stop the influx of Japanese from Hawaii to the mainland. Executive proclamation also closed it from Canada and Mexico.

Washington now sought from Tokyo a reciprocal labor exclusion treaty. Tokyo demurred and in place of it (February 1907) promised to continue its policy of granting no passports for the mainland of the United States to skilled or unskilled laborers except such as sought to resume a formerly acquired residence, to join a parent, wife, or child, or to assume active control of a previously acquired interest in a farming enterprise. In 1907 and 1908 an arrangement was worked out with Japan whereby the latter agreed to place this restriction on passports issued to Japanese on the condition, to which the President assented by "executive agreement," that the United States would not enact exclusion. In 1911 a new treaty of commerce and navigation was negotiated and ratified in place of the one of 1894. In the 1911 document no permission was given the United States, as had been done in that of 1894, to adopt exclusion laws, but the Japanese government attached to the treaty a declaration that it would continue to limit the emigration of laborers to the United States. This was what came to be known as the Gentlemen's Agreement. Tokyo also by its own action extended to Hawaii its refusal of passports and more greatly restricted those issued for Mexico. So far was the Gentlemen's Agreement carried out that during the fifteen years during which it operated only 16,096 more Japanese entered the United States than left it, and most of them were women. Indeed, more men left than entered and the net increase of women was 38,833.

The influx of women brought uneasiness to Californians. Many of the newcomers were "picture brides," married by proxy to Japanese in America before leaving their homeland. Since the earlier immigrants had been overwhelmingly men, the women tended to reduce the disparity in the proportion of the sexes and to increase the birth rate of American-born Japanese. To allay American agitation, in 1920 the Japanese government, at the instance of the United States government, voluntarily ceased issuing passports to "picture brides."

In spite of the Gentlemen's Agreement friction continued. In 1913 the legislature of California, in consequence of prolonged agitation by pressure groups, passed a law which prohibited to aliens ineligible to citizenship the acquisition of title to land in the state. This was clearly directed against Japanese. Public opinion in Japan was aroused, Washington was deeply concerned, but the measure was enacted and signed by the Governor, even though Secretary of State Bryan made a special trip to the west coast in an attempt to prevent the action. In 1920 the people of California through direct vote under the initiative withdrew from aliens ineligible to citizenship the right even to lease land. While Washington stoutly maintained against the protest of Tokyo that the legislation was not in violation of the treaty of 1911, the measures gave great offense in Japan.

The year 1924 saw the enactment by Congress of a law which still further wounded Japanese feelings. After World War I American public opinion demanded heightened restrictions on all immigration, especially to forestall a flood from an impoverished Europe. In 1921 those admitted were limited to three per cent of persons of that particular nationality residing in the United States in 1910. In 1924 this was modified to two per cent on the basis of the census of 1890. The well-known purpose was to reduce those coming from Southern and Eastern Europe as against those from Northern and Western Europe, a palpable discrimination although made in such fashion that it could be claimed not to be directed against any one people or group of peoples. In 1924, following a similar device to avoid naming a particular nation, a bill was introduced to prohibit admission to the United States of aliens ineligible to citizenship. Secretary of State Hughes objected on the ground that the measure would again embitter the relations between Japan and the United States which had been improved by the Washington Conference and suggested, instead, that the two per cent quota be applied to Japan. This substitute, if adopted, would permit the admission of not more than two hundred and fifty Japanese a year. The Japanese ambassador, in a letter to Secretary Hughes, declared that entire exclusion would entail "grave consequences." This was seized upon by proponents of the measure in the Senate as a thinly veiled threat. The bill with the exclusion clause was thereupon enacted by an overwhelming vote and, reluctantly, signed by the President. By it the Gentlemen's Agreement was in fact, although not explicitly, abrogated.

The successive actions by California culminating in exclusion by act of the Congress of the entire United States gave offense in Japan and had repercussions far out of proportion to the numbers involved. To a proud people, sensitive over the haughty attitude of Westerners to them and to other Orientals, they appeared wanton insults. The agitators who were responsible for the measures raised the specter of hordes of Asiatics who, if the bars were lowered, would swamp the west coast, depress the standard of living, and eventually drive out the white race from that area. On both sides passion and prejudice were substituted for reason.

In various other countries measures were taken to keep out Japanese, along with other peoples from the Orient. Australia made exclusion effective by a reading test. New Zealand adopted a similar procedure. Canada, following the pattern set by the United States, had a Gentlemen's Agreement which kept Japanese immigration to very small dimensions. Several Latin American countries forbade Asiatic immigration. Brazil and Peru admitted it. By 1931 the former country had 119,740 Japanese and in 1937 had 197,733. Peru's numbers were smaller—20,650 in 1931 and 22,150 in 1937. Brazil welcomed the influx, and not until 1942 did she take steps to prevent a further increase. In 1936 Peru enacted restrictions, but in a general form to avoid giving needless offense.

Although the numbers of Japanese in lands under Occidental control were not large, the struggle over their admission was of outstanding significance. The restrictions on the admission of Japanese were, in general, the same as those applied to all peoples from the east of Asia and India. Lands in which the whites strove to maintain their supremacy in the population and in standards of living were kept all but closed to the folk with whom our story has dealt. In struggling against these barriers Japan could pose as the champion of Orientals against Occidental arrogance. She could take this same attitude when, in the 1940's, she fought to end the colonial rule of Occidentals in southeastern Asia and its adjacent islands. Here were not so much two cultures as two standards of living in conflict. The white man, with high average income, many comforts and luxuries, and ever shortening hours of labor, and struggling for economic security, faced in eastern and southern Asia teeming and swelling populations inured to what seemed to him incredible poverty, low wages, and long hours. Inhabiting, as he did, relatively unoccupied lands and depending upon that fact for his comfort, he was determined to keep out the hordes from Asia who by their competition would swamp him and drag him down to their levels of subsistence. Here were two different worlds now, because of ever improving means of communication, brought into close juxtaposition. Clearly, in a shrinking planet, they could not remain apart. Either the one must be raised to the economic level of the other or the other must sink to the standards of East Asia. In the struggle Japan was a symbol and a self-appointed champion. The pressure of Japanese immigration was only a symptom of a basic maladjustment in global relationships which must sometime be resolved.

General Developments in Japan, 1894–1931

In the nearly four decades intervening between the outbreak of the first of Japan's modern wars with China in 1894 and the renewal of hostilities in 1931, great changes seemed to be in progress in Japan. The Westernization of the country appeared to be proceeding apace. The cities were growing and were taking on Occidental aspects. Industrialization by the machinery and processes of the West was making rapid strides. The education adapted from the Occident was molding the entire nation. Yet basically the revolution did not proceed as rapidly as in China. The fundamental institutions of the country were far less altered. Indeed, in some aspects they were emphasized.

Politics in Japan, 1894–1931

The contradiction between the progress of Westernization and the adherence to inherited institutions and traditions was a feature of political development in the nearly four decades between 1894 and 1931. Under the constitution granted by the Emperor and promulgated in 1889, parliamentary government seemed to be developing. Parliament (often also termed the Diet by Westerners), an importation and adaptation of European representative institutions, appeared to be gaining more and more power. The basis of the franchise by which the lower house was elected was broadened. The lower house struggled to achieve the kind of position held by the House of Commons in the British Isles and to bring under its control the cabinet and so the administration of the Empire. It seemed to be making progress toward this goal, especially in the 1920's.

Yet the Emperor retained the exalted position which had traditionally been his and which had been reemphasized by the Meiji Restoration. To be sure, as a person he could directly have little if any initiative. The government was in his name, but he was bound to act in accordance with the advice of whoever was the real power in the state. This, however, was as it had been with rare intervals for at least a millennium. As had been the case since Yoritomo, moreover, the actual power was largely exercised by the armed services. For a time in the interval between 1894 and 1931 the dominance of the military was challenged. Particularly in the 1920's that challenge seemed to be succeeding and the military to be checked. Yet the army and navy continued to enjoy a special position. The imperial ordinance of 1889 which by implication gave the ministers of war and navy direct access to the Emperor on "military affairs of secrecy and grave importance" without going through the Premier still stood. To it was added, in 1898, at the instance of Prince Yamagata, the main creator of the modern army, another imperial ordinance which limited the appointment of the ministers of war and navy respectively to generals and lieutenant-generals and to admirals and vice-admirals in active service. Since it was very seldom that a man holding one of these ranks would assume office without the consent of his colleagues, this rule in effect gave the high command in the army and navy a veto power over the formation of a cabinet. Clearly no cabinet could be constituted without ministers of war and navy and no incumbent for these posts could be had without the endorsement of the inner circle in the armed services. By their privilege of going straight to the Emperor the ministers of war and navy and, therefore, the armed services could, on occasion, obtain imperial sanction for acts without the concurrence or, indeed, the previous knowledge of their colleagues in the cabinet.

However, in its partial control of the purse Parliament possessed a weapon of no mean strength. Since no new tax could be levied without its consent and the annual budget must have its approval, Parliament could block, if it were so minded, all expansion of the armed services. Yet because, in the event that it failed to pass a budget, the one for the previous year would be repeated, Parliament could not starve out the army and navy.

In addition to the imperial institution and the power of the armed services, continuations from Japan's past, there were other factors which entered into the ebb and flow of politics. There were the Elder Statesmen, the *Genro*, an extraconstitutional group which enjoyed great influence with the Emperor. Although this group was a new development since the Meiji Restoration, it was in accord with the Japanese tradition through which control was exercised in the name of, but not by, the officials who were formally responsible. It was natural, too, in a land in which the elders carried so much weight in family decisions. There were also patriotic organizations. They multiplied in numbers and influence. Some of them were made up of veterans of the armed services. As a rule they were prepared to support the army and navy and were chauvinistic. The civil bureaucracy had to be reckoned with, but, in pursuance of Japanese precedent, was not so potent as the army and navy. The impressive financial, industrial, and commercial power represented by the great capitalistic families, the *Zaibatsu*, could not be ignored.

However, none of these elements in the contest for political control acted as a unit. Not always did the army and the navy agree. Within both the army and the navy there were many rival groups, each seeking power and in ever shifting combinations. For years Satsuma dominated the navy and Choshu the army. They could not always agree as between and among themselves. Moreover, as the twentieth century wore on their control over the armed services passed into other hands. The *Genro* were seldom all of one mind. In Parliament there were several parties, and within each major party there were rival elements. The *Zaibatsu* did not present a solid front. No one individual could speak for all the civil bureaucracy. The force of tradition estopped the Emperor from public personal intervention on his own volition. All was done in his name, but he must be open to counsel and his ministers must take responsibility for his acts. If he were a strong man, behind the scenes he could be effective, but, especially in times of grave national crisis, he must steer a discreet course if he were not to be constrained to retire and make way for someone in the imperial line more amenable to the elements which in the shifting contests for power were for the moment dominant.

The Parliamentary Struggle

For the details of the parliamentary history of Japan there is no room in a summary such as ours must be. The story is bewildering. Yet it is important. In it is the fate of an attempt to acclimatize in Japan representative institutions developed in the Occident and of the aspirations of the minority of Japanese who were attracted by the democracy of the West. If the experience of Japan's past was a fair criterion, the outcome would be quite other than had at first been anticipated. In an earlier chapter we have seen to what unexpected developments the introduction of the Chinese political patterns and ideals had led. Presumably something of the same general nature would follow upon the attempt to graft Western institutions upon the Japanese native stock. The details and even the main outlines, however, could not be forecast. Here we will take the space merely for some of the outstanding incidents and main lines of development in the Japanese government between 1894 and 1931 in the endeavor to operate under the constitution which was so hopefully issued in 1889.

In the chapter before the last we saw that in its initial years

Parliament was distraught and the government handicapped by the efforts of some elements in the lower house to bring the cabinet under the full control of the legislature and to make it responsible, in the sense in which the British cabinet was responsible, to Parliament and especially to the lower house. Ito, the chief architect of the constitution, felt himself under the necessity of attempting to solve the problem by himself accepting the premiership.

In the war with China, the various elements buried their differences. This was only temporary. When peace was restored, the conflict revived. Even before the issuance of the constitution political parties had appeared. They had sprung up in the 1880's, stimulated by the promise of the government (1881) to grant a constitution, and had been anticipatory of a parliament. The leading ones were the Jiyuto, or Liberal Party, rather extreme in its demands for a frame of government representative of the people; the Kaishinto, or Liberal Conservative Party, which had as its head Okuma; and a more conservative group, the Constitutional Imperialists, or Rikken Teiseito. At the outset of the constitutional regime, an effort was made by the dominant elements, largely the Satsuma and Chushu (Sat-Cho) groups who had been prominent since the Meiji Restoration, to carry on the government without reference to the parties. Cabinets, as the conservatives conceived them, were not to be party affairs. To make them such would be a step toward the control of the administration by Parliament. Ito had felt constrained to compromise and as Premier had sought the support of the Jiyuto. The constitution was not operating as he had wished. It seems to have been in partial confession of his failure that he consented to the war with China which was desired by the more intransigent military expansionist elements. During the war Ito, as Premier, led the government. On the coming of peace, the attack on the cabinet by the parties in the lower house was renewed, and, late in the summer of 1896, Ito resigned.

The new ministry was formed by the inclusion of Okuma. Okuma had, early in 1896, formed the Shimpoto, or Progressive party, by adding to the Kaishinto some other elements. The Shimpoto had among its announced purposes the achievement of cabinets responsible to Parliament. Okuma, by the accident of birth, was outside the Sat-Cho combination. He was, however, too able and prominent to be ignored, and his presence was acclaimed as a victory for parliamentary government. However, Okuma found the new combination made up of Sat-Cho men with whom he could not work happily, and after a little more than a year he withdrew. His departure meant the downfall of the cabinet.

Ito now once more essayed the task of forming a cabinet and thus of proving operable the constitution of which he was the main author. In opposition, the Shimpoto and the Jiyuto joined in a new party, the Kenseikai or Constitutionalists. Ito found himself so blocked that he resigned.

Then came what seemed amazing steps. Ito advised the Emperor to call upon the leaders of the Kenseikai to form a cabinet. It looked as though the principle of party government had triumphed and with it control by the lower house. The divergent elements in the Kenseikai could not be held together, and their differences wrecked the ministry. The Kenseikai broke apart. One section retained that name, and the other, the one which had centered around Okuma, eventually re-adopted its former designation of Shimpoto. A ministry led by Yamagata and representing the Sat-Cho and conservative forces and supported by the Kenseikai, now weak in the lower house, did not last long. Thereupon Ito, in a further astonishing step, accepted the leadership of the Kenseikai. He reorganized that party, renamed it the Seiyukai (1900), and upon the downfall of the Yamagata cabinet again became Premier (1900), backed by the Seiyukai. Once more it appeared that the creator of the constitution had conceded the principle of a cabinet responsible to the lower house of the Parliament. Yet Ito, in announcing the organization of the Seiyukai, declared that the Emperor must be free to appoint ministers irrespective of their party affiliations and that, once in office, they should not be the servants of their party. Politics now became a three-cornered struggle, in the main between Ito, the extreme militarists, and the groups that centered about Okuma. This particular Ito cabinet lasted less than a year. In May 1901 it was overthrown.

Upon the resignation of Ito, the militarists came back into power under the premiership of Katsura. Katsura, a Choshu man, had been a leading commander in the army in the war with China. He attempted to stand aloof from any of the political parties but by tact and conciliation managed to remain in power for several years. He it was who concluded the alliance with Great Britain, choosing that association in preference to the one with Russia which might have averted the Russo-Japanese War. He led the country into the war with Russia and saw it safely through that struggle.

The unpopularity of the treaty of Portsmouth proved the undoing of the Katsura ministry. Although Japan had fared very well in that settlement in view of her near exhaustion, public opinion had not appreciated the narrowness of her escape and was angered by the failure to obtain an indemnity from Russia and by the appalling size of the national debt and the mounting burden of taxation. Late in December 1905, Katsura resigned.

He was followed as Premier by Saionji. Saionji was a Fujiwara and hence of the family which, next to the imperial house itself, was the most aristocratic in all Japan. At the time of the Meiji Restoration he was in his late teens. Largely because of his impeccable family associations he early came to prominence. As a young man he studied in France and there had his somewhat liberal proclivities strengthened. He was an associate of Ito and in 1903 became the head of the Seiyukai. Being of the ancient court nobility he was not of the military and not affiliated with the powerful Sa-Cho combination.

Between 1906 and 1913 there were four cabinets in which Saionji and Katsura were alternately Premier. Katsura, although from Choshu, eventually broke with the Sa-Cho leaders and formed a party of his own. The Sat-Cho elements put in a short-lived cabinet.

In 1914, upon the downfall of this ministry, Okuma, now in his middle seventies, became Premier. In spite of his age and his loss of a leg several years before through the attack of a would-be assassin, he displayed great vigor. His appointment again seemed a victory for the principle of party government. It was Okuma who took the nation into the first of the world wars. It was under him, too, that the Twenty-One Demands were made on China. In spite of his supposed liberalism and of his public declaration that Japan desired no more territory and nothing that other peoples possessed, the temptation afforded by the preoccupation of Europe and the expansionist pressure from within the nation proved irresistible, and the Empire entered upon another stage of advance at the expense of its neighbors.

Late in 1916 Okuma's cabinet was forced to give way. Its successor, headed by Terauchi, represented the military elements. It carried the nation through most of World War I, but in September 1918 unrest over the rise of the cost of living, a concomitant of the war, culminated in rice riots, and Terauchi went out of office.

Terauchi was followed as Premier by Hara. This step was hailed as the most considerable yet taken toward cabinet responsibility to the lower house and democratic control of the government. Hara was an untitled commoner. He was also the able head of the Seiyukai, having succeeded the aristocratic Saionji in that position. The Elder Statesmen, consulted as usual in the choice of a new Premier, suggested Saionji for the post. Saionji declined and urged the choice of Hara. Hara accepted only on condition that he be allowed to form a party cabinet, a bitter pill to Yamagata, now one of the three surviving *Genro*. Hara had his way, and his cabinet was composed of Seiyukai men except for two or three, and they were mostly pro-Seiyukai. The age was one in which democracy seemed triumphant in the world, and Japan, sensitive to such trends, responded. The Seiyukai did not have an absolute majority in the lower house, but in 1920 a general election gave Hara that desired position. He was pushing forward measures for the extension of the franchise and for a civil rather than a military head of a colony such as Korea and Formosa when, in November 1921, he fell victim, in the Tokyo railway station, to the dagger of a young assassin. Here was an ominous recurrence of a violence which assumed the name of patriotism, a foreshadowing of even more tragic recourse in the following decade to that means of checking political liberalism. The cabinet outlasted Hara's death, but only by about six months.

Since the parties were weakened by internal dissensions, for about three years nonparty bureaucratic cabinets were in power.

In 1924, however, after a general election, a coalition of the major parties united in forming a cabinet. Here again seemed to be a victory for parliamentary government and a step toward democracy. In 1924 this achievement appeared to be reenforced by a wide extension of the franchise through the adoption of universal manhood suffrage. The proportion of seats in the upper house held by the nobility was also reduced. Following the enlargement of the electorate, numbers of proletarian parties, most of them small, came into being. The swing toward liberal representative institutions was marked. The major party groupings retained a lineal descent from those of the 1880's. The Seiyukai, which through various combinations and names went back to the Jiyuto of those days, was matched by the Minseito which emerged in 1927 through a union of the Kenseikai with an offshoot from the Seiyukai. The Kenseikai, it will be recalled, traced its lineage from the Kaishinto. There had been prevailingly Kenseikai cabinets from 1925 to 1927. Then followed Seiyukai dominance until 1929, when the Minseito came in under Hamaguchi. In November 1930, Hamaguchi was shot in that Tokyo railway station which had proved fatal for Hara. Hamaguchi survived for several months and another member of the Minseito took over as Premier. This brings the story of cabinet changes down into 1931, the year when developments in Manchuria ushered Japan, China, and eventually the entire Far East into a new and stormy era. That era we are reserving for the next chapter.

From the condensed narrative in the preceding paragraphs it will be seen that until 1931 Japan had been making progress, although by halting steps, toward parliamentary government of the kind familiar in Western democracies. That parliamentary structure was as yet rudimentary. It was far from being complete or from being above reproach. Japanese traditional methods of control persisted. The *Genro*, a relatively new but typically Japanese institution, were consulted by the Emperor in the formation of cabinets. The armed services, by their favored position acquired through imperial ordinance, had a continuing voice. From time to time, as in 1894, 1905, and 1914–1919, extreme military and expansionist elements gained the upper hand over the moderates and carried the nation further into foreign imperialistic adventures. Cabinets and governments reflected the varying strength of many elements. In addition to the army and the navy and the *Genro*, the *Zaibatsu* were potent. The Seiyukai tended to represent the landowners and the Mitsui. The Minseito was bound up closely with industrial interests and the Mitsubishi. The parties were by no means perfect. Between the major ones no basic, continuing difference in program existed. There was much of political corruption among their members, for numbers lived by the spoils of office or battened off bribes. When all of these qualifications have been made, however, it must still be said that in the 1920's Japan was moving, even though hesitatingly and as yet far from the goal, toward representative democracy. That it was doing this in a fashion which entailed no abrupt break with Japan's past augured well for the continuation of the process. From this nascent democracy the 1930's witnessed a rapid reverse. This, as we have already suggested, we must recount in the subsequent chapter.

Changes in the Throne

The four decades that succeeded 1904 brought important changes in the occupancy of the throne. In 1912 death removed Mutsuhito, or the Meiji Emperor as he is posthumously and more correctly known. His going was deeply mourned, partly because of his own ability and partly because he symbolized the age of transition in which

Japan emerged from isolation into the stream of world affairs and reorganized her life to meet the new situation. His memory was greatly revered and to him was erected, on the outskirts of Tokyo, what became one of the Empire's outstanding shrines. He was succeeded by Yoshihito. The new reign period was designated Taisho, "Great Righteousness." Yoshihito was increasingly unwell from mental illness, and in 1921 the Crown Prince, Hirohito, became regent. In December 1926, on the death of Yoshihito (the Taisho Emperor), Hirohito became Emperor and the reign period denominated Showa ("Enlightened Peace") began. Before his accession the Showa Emperor had visited the Occident and so was familiar with that region. He showed himself more freely to his subjects than had his predecessors, and his Empress was given public recognition after the manner of Occidental royal consorts. His private family life was supposed to be happy—so far as could be known through the curtain which convention placed between it and the public eye. He was much interested, as a hobby, in marine biology. His personal preferences were probably for a liberalizing of the government and against the extreme militarists and chauvinists. He did not have the force of character or the political acumen and statecraft of the Meiji Emperor. He could not, therefore, have as much weight in national policies as the latter had had. He was doomed to see extremists with whom he was out of sympathy came to power and, in his name, carry the nation upon a disastrous imperialistic adventure.

Economic Developments

THE RAPID GROWTH OF POPULATION

More spectacular than the political changes in Japan in the decades between the first of the modern wars with China and the outbreak of the next test of war with that country, in 1931, were the economic developments. Japan was becoming more populous, more highly industrialized, even more an urban nation, and more prominent in the commerce of the world. National wealth increased. Prosperity, however, was unevenly distributed. The *Zaibatsu* flourished and became even more potent in economic life and in politics. The farmers were hard pressed and the agrarian situation, already acute under the Tokugawa, remained unsolved.

The growth of the population was striking. During the first part of the Tokugawa period, because of the achievement of internal peace and order, the population had risen sharply. In the hundred years or so before the coming of Perry it had remained nearly stationary. It had about reached the capacity of the country under the existing economy and was kept in check by famines, pestilence, and the widely spread practices of abortion and infanticide. At the time when Commodore Perry ushered Japan into a new age it totaled about twenty-seven millions. By 1872 it had increased to approximately thirty-five millions, and in 1894 it was around forty-one millions. In 1930 it was more than sixty-four millions. Whereas in the twenty-two years between 1872 and 1894 it had mounted by slightly over seventeen per cent, in the thirty-six years between 1894 and 1930 it had jumped approximately fifty-six per cent.

This rise in population was by no means exceptional. It was an accompaniment of rapid industrialization. It was not as marked as that of England and Wales in the early nineteenth century when those realms were in the first full tide of industrialization. Indeed, until 1911 the rate of growth in England and Wales was greater than that in Japan. Only after that date did the increase in Great Britain become so retarded that the population seemed to be approaching stability. The population of the United States had grown even more spectacularly, although that was due to immigration, a factor which scarcely operated in Japan, as well as to the excess of births over deaths. That of Western Europe had also multiplied in the nineteenth century. In the 1920's the excess of births over deaths in Japan was higher than that in the United States, Germany, Great Britain, or France, and even than in Italy. This, however, may have been because Japan had been more recently industrialized. In a subsequent stage of industrialization it, like the others, might display a slowing down of the rate of growth. Already, by 1931, the marriage age was becoming later, the fecundity of Japanese women was beginning to decline, and, in spite of its illegality, dissemination of birth control propaganda was commencing. In the meantime, the pressure of population would, as we indicated earlier in this chapter, provide a convenient argument for imperial adventure.

THE PROGRESS OF INDUSTRIALIZATION

The striking rise in the population was associated with the rapid expansion of industry and commerce. This latter, as we saw in the chapter before the last, had begun before 1894. It continued and the country became more and more occupied with manufacturing and trade. This, indeed, was necessary if the increasing numbers of mouths were to be fed and the standard of living was to be advanced.

As was to be expected, textiles occupied the chief place in manufactures. Since the population had to be clothed, they had been prominent before the country had been opened to the West. Japan's traditional experience with silk proved an asset. Her large supply of cheap labor was of assistance. In the textile industries, indeed, approximately four-fifths of the workers were women, and these could be had at even lower wages than could men. Most of the women so employed were from the families of farmers, and their earnings relieved that sorely pressed element of the population.

The growth of the mulberry, the rearing and care of the silk worm, and the production of raw silk were a welcome supplement to the income of the rural districts. In 1928 Japan's production of silk was more than two-thirds of that of the entire world, and, measured in terms of yen, in 1929 silk in all its forms constituted slightly over two-fifths of the nation's exports. Most of the silk shipped abroad was sold in the United States. In 1929 more than four-fifths of the raw silk produced was exported and of this all but 3.3 per cent was sent to the United States. As we are to see in the next chapter, the depression in the United States starting late in 1929 had disastrous effects upon the price of silk and so upon this prominent feature of Japan's economy. The resulting repercussions on the internal and external politics of Japan, as we are also to note, were of great moment to that land and, through it, to the Far East and eventually the entire world.

The manufacture of cotton became the most important occupation of the factories of Japan. The rapid growth of cotton spinning began about the year 1890. It became remarkable during World War I and, after a brief pause in the *post bellum* reaction, continued with occasional slight recessions. In 1931 Japan ranked third among the countries of the world in the consumption of raw cotton. Since she grew little cotton on her own soil, she was forced to import what was needed for her spindles. She obtained it chiefly from the United States and India. In 1929 slightly more came from the latter than from the former source. Most of the cotton yarns exported from Japan's factories went to India and China. Increasingly after 1895 Japan went beyond the spinning of yarns to the weaving of cotton cloths. In 1929 the foreign sale of her cotton yarns brought Japan only about one-fifteenth as much as did that of her cotton fabrics. The latter she sold not only in China and India but also in Asia Minor and Africa. She engaged as well in the production of knitted goods. Of these the larger part were cotton.

The manufacture of woolens was far behind that of silk and cotton. The adoption of Occidental garb made for a demand for woolen cloth, but much of this was imported. However, by the year 1931 the woolen industry was rapidly expanding.

Japan was backward in the production of iron, steel, and machinery. Her deficiency in ore as well as her lack of domestic capital and technical skill militated against it. However, after the Russo-Japanese War and especially because of World War I a stimulus was given the heavy industries.

THE GROWTH OF RAILWAYS

Industrialization after the Occidental pattern was accompanied by rapid expansion in transportation facilities of the kinds employed in the West. Until 1906 more miles of railways were constructed by private companies than by the government. However, in that year the principle of government ownership was established, and in 1906 and 1907 the large majority of the privately owned mileage was bought by the state. Yet private ownership was not entirely extinguished. Most of the local lines which fed the trunk roads remained in private hands, and while they were controlled by the government their construction was encouraged by subsidies. Growth in mileage continued, and earnings made the roads profitable to both the government and the private companies. In contrast with Great Britain and the United States, where considerably less than half the revenue was from passenger traffic and the larger proportion was from freight, in Japan three-fifths of the total income of the railways came from passengers. The electrification of the lines made rapid progress. Electric tramways became features of the main cities.

THE INCREASE IN SHIPPING

Japan even more markedly developed her ocean shipping. Before 1890 foreign steamers had been almost completely eliminated from coastwise shipping. In the 1890's Japanese steamers began to appear regularly in overseas commerce. The wars with China and Russia stimulated shipping, for it was needed for the transportation and supply of the armies. After the Russian conflict Japanese shipping companies greatly expanded their services to other countries. Their vessels became familiar sights in the sea lanes and the great ports of the world. They connected Japan with her overseas possessions and competed in Chinese waters with the hitherto dominant British craft. World War I gave a fresh stimulus to Japan's shipbuilding industry. The demand for tonnage by Japan's allies and the destruction by German submarines combined to press Japan to her capacity to supply the need. With the end of the war a slump occurred. Yet Japan's tonnage continued to mount, although slowly. In 1929 Japan was third in order among the merchant fleets of the world. Only Great Britain and the United States were ahead. They were, however, very far in the lead. The ratios were 100 for Great Britain, 68 for the United States, and 21 for Japan. Increasingly the foreign trade of the country was carried in Japanese bottoms. The officering of Japanese ships by foreigners, a practice in the early Meiji period when technical education was backward, was becoming history and not present reality.

THE AUTOMOBILE AND THE AIRPLANE

Other modern means of transportation were developing. The automobile had no such phenomenal adoption as in the United States, and in 1931 roads which could be used for it between cities were still few. Yet in the cities it was common. So, too, civilian air transport was appearing. By 1931 it was displaying a striking growth.

THE GROWTH OF FOREIGN TRADE

After 1895 and especially beginning with World War I the foreign trade of Japan rose rapidly. Before 1894 its volume was almost negligible. It then increased until the war with Russia. For a short time after that event it fell. During World War I it shot upward. While, with the coming of peace, it suffered a decline, it soon recovered and by 1925 attained new heights. There, in general, it held until after 1929.

In the share of the various countries in Japan's trade the decades after 1895 showed striking changes. In the mid-1890's Japan purchased more from Great Britain than from any other nation. This reflected the predominance of that country in the foreign commerce of the Far East in the second half of the nineteenth century. By 1930, however, the United States had become both the best customer and the chief source of the imports of Japan. In 1930, next to the United States as a market was China. If Manchuria be included in China, the latter country was, after the United States, the main origin of Japan's imports. In 1930, following the United States and China came India, both as a purchaser from Japan and as a seller to that country. Because of Japanese leaseholds and railways in Manchuria, that region was beginning to loom large as both a market and a provider of raw materials, but in 1929 it was still behind the United States, China Proper, and India.

In the imports, as was to be expected, raw materials and machinery were of first importance. Japan was utilizing her labor and skill to meet the problem posed by her growing population and her own limited natural resources by becoming industrialized and selling the products of her factories. This meant that she must buy raw materials abroad and, for the time being until she could develop her own heavy industry, much of the machinery for her industrial plants. In 1929 cotton was by far the largest import. After it came, in the order named, iron and steel, machinery, wool, lumber, beans, bean cake, and wheat. In 1929 the major export was raw silk, followed, at a far distance, by cotton tissues and silk tissues. The importance of raw cotton and machinery explains the prominence of the United States in Japan's imports. The outstanding place of raw silk accounts for the fact that that country was Japan's best customer. Clearly, too, it was Japan's need for raw cotton which gave India so high a rank as a source of imports. It was the outlet which they provided for cotton goods which helped to make India and China so significant in Japan's export trade. Both these great Asiatic lands were much more backward than Japan in adopting the industrial processes of the West and, since the products of Japan's cotton mills could undersell both the native handicrafts and the factories of Lancashire, they found ready purchasers in these countries of low incomes.

It must be noted, however, that Japan's position in foreign trade was still precarious. So large a dependence upon raw silk, a luxury item and in demand chiefly in one country, was unhealthy. Moreover, India and China were fairly certain soon to become more important industrially. When they did so, if they followed the precedent of Great Britain, the United States, and Japan, it would first of all be in textiles. With inexhaustible reservoirs of labor obtainable at even lower wages than those in Japan, they would become exporters rather than importers of cotton yarn and cloth. It would require all of Japan's ingenuity and persistence to develop industries which would provide substitutes for these leading items in the exports which were so essential to the economic well-being of the Empire.

Japan was also developing her domestic markets. As her population rose and the national wealth mounted, more and more internal purchasers were found for what her factories and handicrafts produced.

AGRICULTURE AND FORESTRY

In spite of the growth of manufactures, agriculture was the major single occupation in Japan. Yet farmers were fairly chronically in a serious financial condition. The situation had been bad under the Tokugawa. This was partly because of the system of tenantry and absentee ownership which prevailed for much of the soil. It was also because of the pressure of population, resulting in small tracts and intensive methods of cultivation with much application of human labor. In becoming an industrialized country, Japan chose to develop her manufactures and for this purpose needed cheap food for factory laborers. She did not, therefore, give the tariff protection to agriculture which she might have done had she been chiefly a farming country. Moreover, landlords and peasant proprietors were taxed more heavily in proportion to their incomes than were merchants and manufacturers. The government was favoring the latter. After 1934 the mortgage indebtedness of the farmer rose rapidly. Yet, partly because of the very great need of food for her cities, Japan gave much government assistance to farmers, notably in technical advice and in fighting plant and animal diseases. There was extensive use of fertilizers, partly imported minerals, especially phosphates.

Nor was the farmer's lot uniformly hard. World War I with its urban prosperity brought higher prices for farm products. In Japan, as in most other lands, the postwar years meant agricultural depression. However, some farmers were able to add small comforts to their homes. They were not so badly off as were most of the peasants of China and India.

The main crop was rice. The Japanese preferred it to other grains and as the standard of living rose the proportion of land given to it increased and that to barley, millet, and wheat declined. The cultivation of the mulberry for the rearing of silkworms was a major occupation. As a rule, more than six-sevenths of the rice consumed in Japan Proper was grown on the islands and only about a seventh was imported from the colonies and other countries. Next to rice as a grain crop came barley, then, far behind, wheat. Sweet potatoes, tobacco, and tea also ranked high as agricultural products.

Because of the climate and mountainous terrain, much of Japan was heavily forested. About half the forest area was privately owned, and about half was the property of government, either national or local. Improved care of the forests on scientific principles was a feature of the twentieth century. The demand for wood was great—for charcoal, of which much was used for domestic heating and cooking, for the building of dwellings, since almost all these were of timber, for pulp, for shipbuilding, for telegraph poles, and for railway ties. Japan's needs outstripped domestic production.

FISHERIES

Japanese did not use large amounts of meat or dairy products. However, they consumed enormous quantities of fish. They led the world in fisheries and their catch was about a fourth of that of the entire globe. Steam and motor boats were increasingly employed and many fishermen went great distances in the Pacific to augment their hauls. Much of the catch was canned for export.

GROWTH IN NATIONAL WEALTH

The national income of Japan was growing. Between 1905 and 1924 the aggregate wealth of the land, when measured in yen, about doubled. In the same interval and by the same standard the per capita wealth mounted by more than a third. The increase had been chiefly between 1913 and 1924, as was to be expected from the boom of the years of World War I. It continued after 1924, but probably more slowly.

On September 1, 1923, an earthquake seemed for a time to have dealt a serious blow. It and the fires which followed it destroyed large portions of Tokyo and Yokohama, the chief metropolitan center. Official estimates placed the losses of property at figures which were between five and ten per cent of the wealth of the entire nation and put the number of deaths as approximately one hundred thousand. There followed a period of reconstruction which brought a great demand for labor and stimulated industry. However, it meant additions to the national debt and, like war, stimulated inflation.

In spite of the improvement in wealth of the country as a whole and of the average individual, in both respects Japan lagged behind the United States and the leading lands of Western Europe. In 1928 her per capita income was considerably less than that of Italy, only a little more than a third of that of France, about a third of that of Germany, less than a fourth of that of the United Kingdom, and only about an eighth of that of the United States. Japan was still a poor country. Yet from the economic standpoint she was probably better off than was any other country in the Far East and was certainly in better condition than India.

The increase in wealth and the rising average income of the Japanese were achieved under the handicap of a heavy burden of armaments. In the 1920's Japan was the only nation which was maintaining both a major army and a major navy. The United States and the United Kingdom were carrying great navies, but their armies were not large. France and Italy, and, in the 1930's, Germany and Russia, had huge armies, but their navies were far behind those of Japan. Japan alone, and that in spite of resources much smaller than those of the other powers, was supporting both an army and a navy of formidable dimensions. This endeavor, relatively unproductive, was a serious load upon the economy of the Empire.

The Mounting Prominence of the Zaibatsu

The mounting industrial, commercial, and financial development of the country brought augmented prominence and power to the *Zaibatsu.* The *Zaibatsu,* the family corporations through which much of the economic transition of the forepart of the Meiji era had been accomplished, flourished even more after 1894 and in the twentieth century. They profited enormously by the feverish prosperity of World War I. They expanded their operations in industry, trade, and finance. In their control of capital through their large holdings in banks and insurance companies they were also outstanding.

For the *Zaibatsu* the growth in wealth was accompanied by an increase of influence in politics. As we saw a few pages back, the two strongest of them, Mitsui and Mitsubishi, became associated with the two leading political parties, the former with the Seiyukai and the latter with the Minseito. In the cabinet which was in office in 1924–1925 both the Premier and the Minister of Foreign Affairs were related by marriage to the Mitsubishi interests. Indeed, most of the members of that particular cabinet were directly or indirectly linked with the Mitsubishi. There was a Mitsubishi clique in the imperial household. Saionji, the last of the *Genro,* had Sumitomo connections. Mitsui had Choshu and therefore army associations and Mitsubishi enjoyed relations with Satsuma and the navy. In general the *Zaibatsu* favored the peaceful economic penetration of China which characterized Japan's foreign policy in the 1920's.

Nothing in any country of the Occident quite corresponded to the position of the *Zaibatsu* in Japan. Here was a uniquely Japanese set of institutions, a quite unanticipated outgrowth of the impact of the Occident.

Indebtedness

The Westernization of Japan, the wars in which the Empire was engaged, and other developments in the life of the country entailed an accumulation of debt. Much of this was by the imperial government. Some of it was by local governments. The latter had to expand facilities for education and undertake various public works and social services. Although it was a relatively small item in their total obligations, on occasion the local units of government also subsidized industry. The debt of the imperial government was increased somewhat as a result of the first of the modern wars with China. It was, however, the war with Russia which first sent it sky-rocketing. Until 1917 this was slowly reduced. It then began climbing once more and by 1930 was more than double the high total of 1906. Increasingly the debt was carried by the Japanese themselves. Down to the year 1904, except for the decade of the 1870's, almost all the debt had been floated in the domestic financial market. Japan feared possible compromises of her independence if she were to owe much money to foreigners. The war with Russia forced her to go to foreign bankers. At the close of the Russo-Japanese War slightly more than half the national debt was held abroad. In 1930 only a little more was owed to aliens than in 1906. Most of the additions to the national debt in the 1920's depended upon domestic sources. The mounting wealth of the country and improving banking and investment facilities made this possible.

Religion

Between 1894 and 1931 the spiritual and moral foundations of the life of Japan were somewhat modified. This was in no revolutionary fashion. Such changes as occurred were developments from movements already in progress before the war with China.

A phase of the result of the impact of the West was the continued growth of Christianity. That faith, officially proscribed from early in the seventeenth until well past the middle of the nineteenth century but never completely stamped out, had been reenforced by missionaries from the Occident. To Roman Catholic Christianity, the wing of the faith which had been introduced in the sixteenth century and which had survived the long persecution, had been added the Russian Orthodox Church and several branches of Protestantism. Protestantism, spread chiefly by missionaries from the United States, grew more rapidly than did either the Roman Catholic or the Orthodox Church. The 1890's witnessed a reaction from the phenomenal popularity of Christianity in the 1880's. However, growth did not cease. It only slowed down. After 1900 it again became marked. Between 1900 and 1913 the number of Protestant communicants more than doubled. By 1936 it had again more than doubled and was over two hundred thousand. In the same year Roman Catholics totaled only slightly more than half that number, and the figure then stood at merely twice that of 1895. The Russian Orthodox, a much smaller body, increased but slightly in the twentieth century and suffered severely from the reverses which overtook the mother church in Russia after 1917. The Protestant foreign missionary body outnumbered that of the Roman Catholics, but not as markedly as did the membership.

As will readily be seen, numerically Christianity was almost insignificant. Although proportionately it was increasing more rapidly than was the population, in 1931 its adherents were barely one-half of one per cent of the latter. In both India and China, Christians, although also small minorities, constituted a larger part of the population.

In its influence upon the country, Christianity was far more important than the totals of the communicant rolls of the churches would have given reason to expect. In the 1920's there were careful observers who believed it to be not only more vigorous but also more potent in the life of the nation than any other religion. In stimulating various phases of social reform and service, and in some aspects of education it was having notable results. The observance of Christmas was becoming widespread. Buddhism was paying Christianity the sincere flattery of adopting some of the methods of the churches, especially in religious education, in hymns, in street preaching, in orphanages, in homes for ex-convicts, and in Young Men's Buddhist Associations, counterparts of the Young Men's Christian Associations.

Moreover, Christianity was rapidly taking root in Japanese leadership and support. Increasingly the Protestant churches were becoming independent ecclesiastically of the founding bodies in the Occident, and all churches, whether Protestant, Roman Catholic, or Russian Orthodox, were developing an indigenous ministry or priesthood, were placing Japanese in positions of administrative responsibility, and were supplying funds to meet the budgets of their organizations. Christians, especially Protestants, were largely from the urban middle classes and professional groups, strata from which leadership could be expected to emerge and which were able to accord financial support to the churches.

Buddhism was probably losing ground. Under the Tokugawa, although it was a state religion, it had suffered from competition with Confucianism and the leadership of the nation was progressively more influenced by the great Chinese sage than by the stream of life which had issued from India. Soon after the beginning of the Meiji era Buddhism was deprived of its position as a cult supported by the state. The trend of the life of modern Japan was away from it. The secular temper of the age and the growth of industrial and urban centers tended to usher it out as irrelevant. Yet it remained a strong even though a somewhat diminished feature of the nation's culture. It retained its hold especially in sections which were least touched by the new ways—on the west coast, in rural districts, and in the ancient capital, Kyoto. It had been too long and too intimately intertwined with the life of the country quickly to be left behind. It displayed enough vigor to initiate new methods of reaching and even increasing its constituency. There were revivals of particular strains within Buddhism. Thus after 1900 there was among many a reversion to Nichiren and his strong Buddhistic nationalism. There was also a return to the simple faith and piety associated with Shinran. Thus religious worthies who had flourished centuries earlier remained living realities. Some of the schools of Buddhism undertook to follow emigrants to their new homes, whether on the adjacent continent or in Hawaii and the Americas. Buddhists sent missionaries to attempt to revive the faith in China and Korea. Japanese customs and ideals were still shot through and through with contributions from the religion in which so much of the earlier Japanese civilization had been nurtured.

Shinto flourished. Numbers of the Shinto sects of nineteenth century origin were popular. Among the sects was one which, in the unrest associated with World War I, taught that all Japan was to be destroyed with the exception of one town and that this town was to become the center of a new, theocratic world order. Although it was eventually suppressed by the police, its popularity was an indication of the ferment in the Japanese spirit. State Shinto, whose shrines had government support, was intimately associated with the growing nationalism of the Meiji and post-Meiji period. As was to be expected, it gained from the patriotic fervor evoked by the wars of the era, notably that with Russia. The shrine erected on the outskirts of Tokyo to the Meiji Emperor added to the nationalistic devotion which centered on the imperial house. Associated with this loyalty was the honor paid in the schools to the imperial portrait and the imperial rescript on education. The shrine erected in Tokyo in 1869 to those who had died in war in recent history assumed additional significance after the struggle with China. Here the souls of those who had lost their lives in behalf of the Emperor were supposed to be, revered and potent guardians of the realm. Through Shinto Japan was being nourished in the intense and religious patriotism which came to white heat in the 1930's and 1940's.

To the ordinary member of a rural village community and to many in the cities religion was still what it had been for centuries. Buddhism was a means of insuring salvation in the future life. It was at funerals that the Buddhist priest had his most prominent functions. Buddhism also entered into memorial services for the dead. The monks were more familiar than the laity with the intricacies of their faith. For them the time-honored schools survived and many were learned in the intricacies of Buddhist thought. The masses, however, in communities where Buddhism still counted, knew little or nothing of the subtleties of the schools. For them the simple faith in Amida seemed to assure security in the life to come. The generality of peasants held to both Buddhism and Shinto. To them the latter was chiefly valuable for the protection presumably afforded by it in this life. The ordinary village homes had a Buddhist shrine. Many also had a Shinto center in the form of a small plain box. There might as well be a picture of the Emperor and Empress and of the god of the crops. Many a house had images of Shinto deities. Wayside stones were revered as having religious significance. The water god was held to reside in springs and streams. Witches were believed to bring curses upon those in their disfavor. For healing of disease recourse was often had to both men and women who were thought to be potent in prayer. Charms were widely employed. Thus ancient beliefs and practices existed in the midst of a Japan which was supposed to be modern.

Education

Fully as effective as the organized religions in shaping the new Japan was the educational system. The universal primary education outlined early in the 1870's became an accomplished fact. All children were supposed to enter school at the age of six and to continue there through the lower primary course of six years' duration. Beyond the lower was the higher primary, of two or three years. With very few exceptions the requirement of attendance was carried through. This meant that the overwhelming majority of Japanese became literate. The subjects in the primary grades included arithmetic, geography, science, drawing, singing, gymnastics, and Japanese language and history. In the higher primary years vocational subjects were added. Because of the difficulties imposed by the retention of the Chinese characters, even though these were somewhat reduced by the use of the syllabic signs, the *kana*, literacy might leave much to be desired. Some, indeed, might relapse into a near-illiteracy. Yet enough retained the ability to read to provide a vast public for the newspapers. Moreover, the national system of education, enforced throughout Japan, tended to erase local loyalties and local and regional dialects and to weld national unity. In feudal days provincial dialects differed so greatly as in some instances to be almost reciprocally unintelligible. Loyalty, too, was more to the *daimyo* than to the Emperor. The national system of primary education promoted uniformity in the spoken language and inculcated loyalty to the state as personified in the Emperor. Although the schools were theoretically nonreligious in the sense that no instruction was given in any one of the existing organized cults, they made powerfully for patriotism. The Imperial Rescript on Education, issued in 1890, enjoined, in brief form, loyalty to the state and the imperial house and the ethical code long esteemed by Japanese and embracing much of the traditional Confucianism. It was held in great honor and at stated times was read to each assembled school with decorous ceremony. School children, too, were taught to revere the shrines of state Shinto and in other ways were drilled in patriotism. The system of primary schools did much to foster the patriotism which became particularly intense in the twentieth century.

From the primary grades a fair number of the pupils went on to secondary schools. In the 1920's about ten per cent of the girls and about eight per cent of the boys who graduated from the lower years pursued secondary education. Many attended normal schools, preparing to be teachers in the primary grades. Others enrolled in technical and vocational schools. The larger number found their way to what were known as middle schools, in which a broad course was offered in history, geography, natural and physical science, mathematics, Japanese, ethics, and English. English was the foreign language most widely studied and demanded much of the students' time. In some of the courses for girls instruction was offered in various branches connected with the making of a home and the rearing of children. Indeed, a diploma from such a school was almost a prerequisite for marriage for girls of the urban middle classes. The secondary school course was five years for boys and four years for girls, but for the latter it might be extended by a year.

Beyond the secondary schools were higher technical schools and universities. Of the universities the ones in highest repute were those which were known in English as imperial, notably the one in Tokyo. There were also many private universities.

Competition in education was extreme. In a land as thickly populated as Japan the struggle for existence was intense. Education was a road to employment and achievement in business, the professions, or government posts. Graduation with distinction, and especially from the more famous schools and universities, was an open door to a decent if modest livelihood and possibly to outstanding success. The goal of the ambitious youth was admission to one of the more desirable schools. This meant hard work, for enrolments were limited and only the best, as evidenced by scholastic records, were chosen.

A phase of education, extremely important from the standpoint of national policy, was that given by the army and navy. All able-bodied males, except those who were the sole support of their families, were required to have training in either the army or the navy and were subject to active duty in emergencies from the age of seventeen to that of forty. Students in certain schools could defer their service until graduation or the age of twenty-seven. Military drill was also given to young men in the schools. The training through service in the armed forces had a formative influence and tended to inculcate unquestioning patriotism and loyalty to the state. It also bred a frame of mind which regarded war as normal and afforded support to the extreme expansionists who dreamed in terms of conquest and the building of empire. There were schools for officers. Through these, leadership in the armed forces was more and more passing from the Choshu and Satsuma groups who had won it through the Meiji Restoration and the demotion of the Tokugawa. It was increasingly in the hands of commoners. The education of the officers, especially those of the army, was extremely technical and therefore narrow. It was designed to produce good drillmasters, commanders, and strategists. It included little if any knowledge of other countries. It made for chauvinism and the military mind in their most restricted and bigoted forms. Naval officers had a somewhat broader training and, because their profession entailed travel, more knowledge of the world. Through the system of required service in the armed forces, the military tradition of the country, already strong, was being intensified. The army and the navy had ceased to be the privilege of the few and were becoming the obligation and the training of the many. The nation was being welded into a mighty fighting force.

Somewhat in the same direction were many of the voluntary patriotic organizations. There were societies of veterans. There were young men's and young women's associations. There were secret, intensely chauvinistic societies. Not all of these had the promotion of patriotism as their chief aim, but all contributed to that end.

Newspapers, Periodicals, Books, and Libraries

In part because of the wide diffusion of education, the Japanese became a reading people. Even the pullers of rickshaws perused newspapers between their fares. The first daily paper appeared in 1872. Others followed, but for years their circulation was limited. By 1930, however, the two largest of the dailies, both issued in the great industrial center, Osaka, each printed more than a million copies in their morning and evening editions, and the two leading papers in Tokyo each had a circulation of more than six hundred and fifty thousand in the morning as well as the evening. In addition to these leading metropolitan papers, over a thousand other dailies were published in cities big and little. The four huge ones already mentioned in Osaka and Tokyo were sold throughout the entire country and together had a sale larger than that of all the others combined. Except for type and typesetting, the machines by which the papers were produced were much like those in the West. The newspapers were influential in molding public opinion and more than once contributed to a shift in cabinets. They were active in promoting athletics and some of them carried on social welfare work and poor relief. They were somewhat less free from state control than their counterparts in the United States or Great Britain, but within limits which were not narrow they were at liberty to print what they wished. Under the press law which operated during more than two decades before 1931 censorship was strict only on articles prejudicial to public order or good morals. The censors were particularly unfriendly to Communism, extreme socialism, and to anything which could be interpreted as disrespectful to the Emperor. In times of national emergency the censorship was, obviously, more exacting than in quiet periods.

In addition to the daily press, there were weekly periodicals. Magazines were numerous, especially those which had women as their clientele. Thousands of books were published, a large proportion of them translations of foreign works but the majority of them original productions in Japanese. They ranged from popular fiction and poetry to abstruse works of scholarship. Most of the books which were standard in Europe or the United States, whether fiction or on government, philosophy, and science, were put into Japanese. The Japanese were responsive to the currents of thought in the Occident. In their indigenous literature, moreover, they reflected trends in the West. Periodicals and books as well as newspapers had to take government censorship into account. Some were suppressed because of alleged indecencies or Communistic leanings. The state was sensitive to what were termed "dangerous thoughts," notably whatever might threaten the existing order.

Libraries abounded. Many of them were public, supported by educational societies or local and prefectural governments, but some were private.

The Study and Application of Science

The adoption of Western learning begun, from Dutch sources, under the Tokugawa was greatly accelerated in the Meiji era and especially in the twentieth century. It was the age of science into which Japan emerged, and if she were to be a great power she must make the scientific method her own. This was true, whether for the armed services, for industry, for agriculture, for forestry, for the fisheries, or for public health and the added comforts of life. The universities paid much attention to science. World War I stimulated scientific research, and various institutes to further it were inaugurated. There was striking growth in the professions of medicine, surgery, and dentistry, all using Occidental knowledge and techniques. Marked progress was made in public health and sanitation. Japanese were beginning to make original contributions to science, including medicine. They were not content with reproducing what had been learned in the Occident.

Language

Through contact with the Occident the language was being modified. This was not as yet in basic structure and grammar. It was, rather, in the coining of expressions for new ideas and objects and in the incorporation of foreign words into the vocabularies of both the learned and the masses. Most of the loan words were from English. In taking them over the Japanese, as was natural, modified the pronunciation. Moreover, many English idioms and sayings were translated and became incorporated into written and spoken Japanese.

Insurance and Cooperatives

Japanese were adopting some of the devices of Occidental origin for security for individuals and companies. Life insurance had a rapid growth, especially after World War I. Much of this was by private companies. Through the post office the government entered into the life insurance business, but, that it might not compete too drastically with private enterprise, for a relatively small gross amount for any one individual. By 1929 almost a fifth of the population were insured through the post office. In the 1920's health insurance was made compulsory for all employees on the lower wage levels in those factories and shops which came under factory and mining legislation. The cost was borne by the government, the employer, and the employee. By 1930 over a million individuals were protected in this fashion. Fire insurance was widely developed, notably after 1895. Many other forms of insurance also came in. Under a Cooperative Societies Law, enacted in 1900, thousands of such organizations came into being for such purposes as credit, purchase, and sale.

Social Work

In other ways care was increasingly being taken to promote the welfare of the masses in the new and complex society brought by the industrial age. The earthquake of 1923 with its train of destitution on a large scale gave a striking impetus to efforts to meet not only the acute but also the chronic needs of Japan. Before that date there had been legislation for the improvement of insanitary housing, for the prevention of tuberculosis, and for employment agencies. World

War I had also stimulated efforts for poor relief, free medical attention, better housing, and the protection of children. In much of this those responsible for the military power of Japan were concerned, for better health and living conditions would make for more able-bodied recruits and higher industrial efficiency. However, purely philanthropic motives also entered. Christian missions and churches and many Buddhist organizations were active in relieving and preventing poverty and suffering.

The Labor Movement

It was to be expected that in a country which was becoming as rapidly industrialized as was Japan, organizations of laborers would appear. By 1931 they had come into existence and had begun to have some influence. However, they were not so prominent as in such lands as Great Britain and the United States. This was in part attributable to the fact that Japan had much more recently embarked upon an industrial career. To some degree it was due to the circumstance that a very large proportion of the factory workers were girls and young women who did not look forward to that occupation as a life work but would soon marry and make homes. It also arose from the attitude of a government which regarded with suspicion all movements which had about them even a suggestion of social radicalism with a Western and especially a Communist taint.

By the 1920's labor unions had begun to appear. Indeed, the first had been organized late in the 1890's, after the war with China. However, in 1925 membership was less than a quarter of a million and by 1929 had not quite reached a third of a million. This was considerably less than a tenth of those in occupations which would be expected to organize and less than seven per cent of those regarded as laborers under the factory law. In 1928 the government ordered the dissolution of unions suspected of leftist tendencies. However, conservative unions survived and the Central Federation of Japanese Labor, which brought many of them together, was the mainstay of the Social Democratic Party. Strikes were by no means rare. In 1907, for instance, a number of these broke out and the use of troops was required to restore order. Subsequent to World War I Japan joined in the International Labor Conference, set up after that conflict, and ratified a number of the conventions which came out of it for the improvement of the conditions of labor.

Radical ideas were especially prevalent in the 1920's among students, particularly the unemployed intellectuals who, coming from poor families, had had a struggle to acquire an education and then found it impossible to obtain a good position. Here and there were youths from the upper classes and Christians who, moved by idealism, became radicals. Some of the radicalism took conventional Occidental forms. In the 1930's it was to assume Japanese garb, as we are to see in the next chapter, and, under the guise of patriotism, was to lead to grave political disorder.

Sports and Recreation

Various Western sports and athletics found a welcome. Of these, baseball, introduced from the United States in the 1870's by American teachers, became especially popular. Japanese also participated in the Olympic Games in such branches as running, jumping, and swimming. They competed in international tennis tournaments. Skiing and certain forms of skating came in. Wrestling, which had a long history in Japan, became increasingly prominent because of its association with military training. Great stadiums for athletics were built in several of the chief cities and universities.

Of the amusements, some of the ancient ones, such as the *No* form of the drama, persisted. The moving pictures introduced from the West achieved popularity. Eventually Japan produced the majority of the films shown, but in 1931 many were still imported.

Western music had a wide vogue. Orchestras and bands appeared. Phonograph records reproducing some of the best Occidental music enjoyed large sales. Much of this development took place in the relatively prosperous 1920's.

Occidental dancing and cafés became the rage, and the old-fashioned *geisha* began to pass. "Jazz" was an accompaniment of this café civilization. This, too, was largely a sequel of World War I and a feature of the 1920's, a decade which in Japan as in so much of the Occident was a fevered aftermath of that struggle.

In the 1920's, moreover, the radio had a rapid adoption and hundreds of thousands of receiving sets were sold to the eager listeners.

Summary

From the standpoint of the casual and even the more thoughtful observer, the nearly four decades which intervened between the first of the modern wars with China and the dramatic outbreak, in 1931, of the second and much more prolonged struggle with that neighbor were marked by striking changes in the life of Japan.

The course of territorial annexation entered upon after the Meiji Restoration was pursued with spectacular results. As before 1894, so after that year, not all Japanese were prepared to follow the ambitions of the most ardent of the expansionists. Many wished to go more slowly or would have the nation content itself with economic rather than political imperialism. The road to empire was followed, not steadily, but with halts and occasional although infrequent retreats. Yet in the brief decades, scarcely a generation, covered by this chapter, Japan acquired Formosa, the adjacent Pescadores, Korea, the southern portion of Sakhalin, a leasehold and railways in southern Manchuria, islands over a vast expanse of the Pacific to the south and east, and for a time appeared about to obtain permanent footholds in Shantung and much of eastern Siberia. From the self-chosen isolation of two and a half centuries, Japan had emerged to win a place as the most aggressive country in the Far East and as one of the half dozen leading powers of the world. She came to 1931 with one of the largest armies and, in size, the third navy of the globe, both thus far undefeated. Presumably she was only at the inception of her growth.

Fully as impressive as the enlargement of the Japanese Empire and the formidable armed forces was the rapid rise of the country as an industrial and commercial power. The adoption of the machinery and the science of the Occident proceeded apace. Factories appeared, great and small, and Japanese shipping became a familiar sight in all the major and many of the minor ports of the world. Modern machinery was still most prominent in cotton textiles, and cottons and silk were the major exports. These were insecure foundations for continuing industrial and commercial growth, but they were being broadened by other and more varied industries.

Japan was advancing strikingly in both population and wealth. Her cities, already large, were becoming larger. In 1931 her greatest metropolitan center had the doubtful distinction of being the third or fourth in size in the world.

Japan was apparently traveling the road toward political democracy. The carefully guarded attempt at constitutional, representative government embodied in the conservative document issued only five years before the outbreak of the initial war with China seemed, in the 1920's, to be headed toward full control by the elected spokesman of the masses of the people of both legislation and administration.

In her educational system and intellectual life, moreover, Japan was apparently becoming increasingly conformed to the Occident.

To those who knew the history of Japan, however, these changes and this avid adoption of things Occidental did not necessarily mean full conformity to the West. The memory of the experience, centuries earlier, with the introduction of Chinese civilization was a restraint upon facile prophecy of a fundamental revolution in the nation's life. The adoption of Chinese civilization had been accomplished in such a manner that the basic institutions of Japan were not eliminated but emphasized. Moreover, from that adoption had issued quite unanticipated and revolutionary developments. The military tradition, potent from the earliest times, had found expansion in the emergence of a warrior class which, under a feudal structure, a development novel to Japan, achieved and maintained dominance as it had never done before. The ancient aristocracy and the imperial house survived, with their nominal importance enhanced by the adopted Chinese ideas. Yet in practice they became subservient to institutions and customs whose emergence no man could have foreseen in the first few generations of the popularity of the civilization of the adjacent continent.

With this precedent before them, the more thoughtful could not but wonder whether a somewhat similar future might now be in store for Japan. Certainly in 1931 more of the basic institutions and traditions had survived the impact of the Occident in Japan than in China. The dignity and nominal power of the Emperor had been enhanced rather than weakened. The military were as potent, although through somewhat different channels, as they had been before the advent of the West. Even the old court nobility, the *kuge*, persisted, and some of their members were prominent in administration to a degree which they had not seen for centuries before the coming of Perry. The tradition was perpetuated that the semblance of power should be conserved in the hands of persons and classes which had legally held it but that actual power should be exercised by those who were able to grasp it. Behind the facade of the Emperor and an imperially granted constitution a struggle for power was in progress. In the 1920's, civilian, democratic elements seemed to be in the ascendant, but the armed services were not roundly defeated. Quite unreconciled and with inward resentment, they were biding their time.

That a revolution would come, as it had after the first stages of the adoption of Chinese culture, was probable. What form or forms it would take no one could know. Clearly, if it had begun it was only in its earliest stages. It was not nearly so far along as was that in China. Although outwardly Japan had been much more prompt in adjusting herself to the Occident than had her huge neighbor, actually she had been more resistant. Or, to put it in another and perhaps more nearly accurate way, Japan had put the new wine of the Occident into existing wineskins. By so doing she had temporarily succeeded in keeping more of the old than had China. China had first refused to accept the new wine. Then, her old wineskins largely destroyed, she had set about creating new to accommodate the fresh ferment. Presumably the Japanese effort would eventually issue in explosions. What then would follow no one could be sure. Japan had adopted the outward trappings and much of the mechanism and learning of the Occident but had refused to accept the ideology which was the motivating power of the Occident. Christians were a small, even though influential minority; socialism was viewed with suspicion; democracy was seemingly making progress but only superficially; Communism was more and more proscribed. Tensions were developing. The future could not but be stormy.

Ominous, too, was the growing and chronic friction with Japan's nearest powerful neighbors. Japan clearly had ambitions in China which that great country, as it found itself, would not tolerate. Russia, becoming stronger under the Communists than she ever had been under the Czars, would not be happy over Japan's aspirations in East Asia. Great Britain and France, although the Far East was on the periphery of their interests, through their possessions in that area stood in Japan's way. The Netherlands East Indies, militarily weak, were also a challenge and a temptation. Clashes with the United States were increasing. More and more the United States was active in the western Pacific and East Asia. Already the two nations had more than once been at the point of war. The chances were in favor of the tension breaking into a gigantic armed conflict. The relative quiet of the 1920's was a prelude to tempest.

BIBLIOGRAPHY

For Brief Reference

No single volume can serve as a reasonably satisfactory well-rounded supplement to this chapter.

For More Detailed Study

R. Benedict, *The Chrysanthemum and the Sword* (Boston, 1946).
R. L. Buell, *The Washington Conference* (New York, 1922).
C. D. Carus and C. L. McNichols, *Japan: Its Resources and Industries* (New York, 1944).
A. J. Grajdanzev, *Formosa Today* (New York, 1942).
A. J. Grajdanzev, *Modern Korea* (New York, 1944).
A. W. Griswold, *The Far Eastern Policy of the United States* (New York, 1938).
Y. Ichihashi, *Japanese in the United States* (Stanford, 1932).
M. D. Kennedy, *The Changing Fabric of Japan* (New York, 1931).
W. W. McLaren, *A Political History of Japan during the Meiji Era 1867–1912* (London, 1916).
H. G. Moulton, *Japan, An Economic and Financial Appraisal* (Washington, 1931).
I. Nitobe, *Japan. Some Phases of Her Problems and Development* (New York, 1931).
I. Nitobe and others, *Western Influences in Modern Japan* (Chicago, 1931).
J. F. Normano and A. Gerbi, *The Japanese in South America* (New York, 1943).
G. Sansom, *The Western World and Japan* (New York, 1949).
P. J. Treat, *Japan and the United States, 1853 . . . 1928* (Stanford, 1928).
C. Yanaga, *Japan Since Perry* (New York, 1949).
T. Yanaihara, *Pacific Islands under Japanese Mandate* (Oxford, 1940).
C. W. Young, *The International Relations of Manchuria* (Chicago, 1929).

Chapter XVI. INTO THE STORM

The Far East and India in the world struggle which had its inception in 1931 and ended in 1945

ON THE NIGHT OF SEPTEMBER 18, 1931, an explosion and shooting were heard on the outskirts of Mukden, in Manchuria. The Japanese alleged that Chinese had blown up a section of the track of the South Manchuria Railway. In retaliation, so they averred, they fired. This "incident" was the first in a succession of events which not only affected Manchuria, but also opened a prolonged struggle between Japan and China and embroiled the rest of the Far East and the entire world. It was, when viewed from the vantage of later years, the real opening of the second of the world wars of the twentieth century. Through that conflict all the Far East and India were profoundly altered. The inheritance from the past was significantly modified. Some movements that had been in progress before 1931 were quickened and some were retarded. What the ultimate consequences would be no man could foresee. It was clear, however, that for many generations not only the Far East and India but also the Occident would show the results. Of the Occident the United States especially was affected and, for weal or for woe, became more deeply involved than ever in the Far East and the western Pacific. Not even through the Mongol conquests had so much of the Far East been so stirred by a single war. The struggle was an outcome of the impact of the West, but never before had so much of the Far East and the Occident been so disturbed by one set of events arising from that impact. It is to this story that we must turn. If we seem to be devoting to it a large proportion of our space, that is not primarily because we are so near the events. We give it so much time chiefly because of its significance for the Far East and the world at large.

The Immediate Background of September 18, 1931

The events of the fateful September night were not accidental. Although the precise form which it would take had not been foretold, for some time the situation in Manchuria had been moving toward a crisis. The virtual condominium of China, Japan, and Russia could not endure. One or another of those powers would sooner or later eliminate the others. Manchuria was fertile in soil, contained valuable forests, and possessed extensive mineral resources. Its southern ports were strategic for the control of the northern part of China Proper as well as Manchuria. So desirable a region could not but be a bone of contention among its three powerful neighbors. Legally the area belonged to China. Because of extensive immigration, mainly in the twentieth century, the population was overwhelmingly Chinese. Chinese nationalists did not call the region Manchuria, as though it were a colony, but the Three Eastern Provinces. They insisted that it was an integral part of the republic. In 1931 the Three Eastern Provinces were ruled by the young Chang Hsüeh-liang, the son of the late Chang Tso-lin. Unlike his father, Chang Hsüeh-liang was disposed to cooperate with the government that the Kuomintang was establishing. This in itself proved irritating to the Japanese, for the Kuomintang was intensely nationalistic and against all foreign encroachments upon China's sovereignty.

In 1929, it will be recalled, Chinese nationalism had attempted, futilely, as it proved, to oust the Russians from the Chinese Eastern Railway. The Chinese were seeking to reduce the Japanese monopoly in southern Manchuria by a projected system of railways which would in part parallel and so compete with the Japanese lines. It was to have an outlet at the newly developing Hulutao, on the Gulf of Liaotung, which would be a rival to Dairen, the chief Japanese port in the region. To this ambitious project the Japanese, not unnaturally, objected. They claimed that it was in violation of a promise given by China after the Russo-Japanese War not to build lines which would compete with the South Manchuria Railway.

The Chinese, moreover, claimed that, since the concessions made concerning the Three Eastern Provinces in consequence of the Twenty-One Demands were extracted from them under duress, they were not binding. In March 1923, not long before the expiration of the original twenty-five-year lease to the Liaotung (Kwantung) territory which Japan had inherited from Russia, they protested the extension of that agreement which had been made in 1915. The Japanese insisted that the treaties and agreements of 1915 were valid and complained bitterly of Chinese attempts to annul them.

There were conflicts over the taxing power in the zone of the

South Manchuria Railway, over the application of the right of the railway to purchase land, and over the Japanese railway guards. The latter often carried their activities outside the railway zone. The Japanese alleged that, as a corollary of extraterritoriality, they had the right to maintain consular police. This the Chinese hotly denied. The Japanese were unhappy over refusals of the Chinese authorities to issue passports to them and over obstacles placed by Chinese officials against the renting of houses and the leasing of land by Japanese. About eight hundred thousand Koreans had moved into Manchuria, mainly into areas adjacent to Korea. The vast majority of them were farmers. They were Japanese subjects and were feared by the Chinese as a vanguard of Japanese penetration. The Chinese sought to prevent the influx and denied to the Koreans, so far as they could, the buying or leasing of land. While some Koreans had become Chinese citizens, the problem of the continued claim of Japan to their allegiance led the Chinese to be slow to grant naturalization. In July 1931, there was conflict between Chinese farmers and Koreans over an irrigation ditch and retaliatory riots in Korea directed against Chinese residents in that country. Moreover, in the summer of 1931 a Japanese military officer was killed in Manchuria by Chinese soldiers, an unforgivable affront to the Japanese army. All these conditions and events added up to create a situation which at any moment might become open war.

As a further contribution to the tinder-box character of the situation in Manchuria was the fact that Japanese control in the region was predominantly in the hands of the Kwantung army. This unit was inclined to go its way, acting on its own initiative regardless of the civil authorities in Japan and even of the general command of the army. It was expansionist in spirit and its temper was brittle. It was not minded to endure tamely the growing restiveness of Chinese nationalism under the Japanese domination.

In 1931 the irritability of the Kwantung army was augmented by a combination of events originating quite outside the Far East. The economic depression which came upon the United States late in 1929 had direct and serious repercussions in Japan. The price of silk, a luxury item, dropped alarmingly. As we saw in the last chapter, on the eve of that event silk constituted two-fifths of Japan's exports and was sold almost entirely in the United States. The thousands of farmers who depended upon the American market were thrown into dire distress. Their sons in the army knew of the suffering at home and communicated their unhappiness to their officers. The Kwantung army endeavored to solve the problem by tightening its grip on Manchuria in the hope of utilizing the rich resources of the region to redress the weakened economic condition in Japan. Once again, as so often before and later, the United States became intimately involved in a crisis in the Far East.

The Creation of Manchukuo

Using the incident of September 18, 1931, as an excuse, the Kwantung army quickly seized the Three Eastern Provinces. Indeed, the Chinese insisted that the incident had been deliberately manufactured by that army and pointed out that the train against which the explosion had allegedly been directed had arrived on time, undelayed by any damage to the track. Most of Chang Hsüeh-liang's troops were south of the Great Wall, and such of them as were in Manchuria were promptly scattered. The chief cities were seized. Armed resistance long continued in the back districts, but the Kwantung army was soon in effective control of the strategic centers.

Early in 1932 the state of Manchukuo appeared. In theory this was independent, a spontaneous creation of the people of Manchuria. The Japanese acclaimed it as a voluntary separatist movement. Actually it was inspired by them. It was preceded by local and provincial organizations. It was in February 1932 that an administrative council was set up for the region and a declaration of independence issued. In March 1932, an organic law was promulgated. At that time, in addition to the Three Eastern Provinces, the adjacent province of Jehol, the easternmost portion of Inner Mongolia, was incorporated in the new state. Jehol, however, was not actually overrun by the Japanese armies until early in 1933. As the head of the new state the Japanese procured the last Emperor of the Ch'ing dynasty of China. A small child when he had succeeded the Kuang Hsü Emperor, he had now reached manhood. In 1924 he had been driven out of the imperial palace in Peking by Fêng Yü-hsiang. After a few days of virtual captivity, he had escaped and taken refuge in the Japanese legation. From there he had moved to a commodious house in the Japanese concession in Tientsin. In going to Manchukuo the ex-Emperor had returned to the land of his ancestors. The Japanese were clearly endeavoring to give the air of legitimacy to the new regime. The new state was, however, safeguarded in the interests of its real creators by an ample supply of Japanese advisers. Technically independent, it was actually a puppet of the Kwantung army.

The rest of China did not tamely submit to the loss of the Three Eastern Provinces and Jehol. It had recourse to the boycott. With an intensity which varied with the condition of relations between the two countries, for the preceding several years the boycott had been applied to Japanese goods, banks, and steamers. It had been stiffened in the summer of 1931, even before the Mukden affair, and was now enforced with rigor.

Friction, moreover, became intense in Shanghai, augmented by lawless elements among both Chinese and Japanese. The Japanese authorities peremptorily demanded that the anti-Japanese boycott associations in Shanghai be dissolved. Although the Chinese municipal authorities eventually promised compliance, Japanese marines supported by the fleet occupied a densely populated part of the city. Fighting ensued and parts of the municipal area were laid waste with a heavy loss of life. Nanking, the Chinese capital, was bombarded (February 1) by Japanese gunboats. Chinese resistance proved formidable and was overcome only after the Japanese had landed heavy reenforcements. It was not until May 1932 that peace was restored.

In all the disorders and clash of armed forces which followed the Mukden incident, there was no formal declaration of war between Japan and China. Diplomatic relations, though strained, were maintained. Here was, from the Occidental standpoint, one more anomaly in Far Eastern international politics.

The Attempt to Apply the Peace Machinery of the Occident

The Japanese actions in Manchuria and then Shanghai were a challenge to the machinery for the maintenance of peace which had been so hopefully constructed by Western liberals in the years following World War I. The League of Nations, the Pact of Paris, and the treaty structure set up by the Washington Conference were all involved. To each of these Japan was a party. Some Japanese might claim, as they did, that their government had not violated its obligations under any of these instruments. They might insist that the Kwantung army had been acting quite within its rights, that Manchukuo had come into being as a purely domestic movement of the people of Manchuria, and, in any event, that Manchuria was not an integral part of China. Their pleas, however, seemed to most of the rest of the world too specious to inspire credence. Eventually all of the machinery was invoked, but without budging Japan from the path chosen for her by the radicals in the Kwantung army.

On September 21, 1931, China formally appealed to the League of Nations and requested immediate action. This meant that the League could not ignore the situation. On that same day the secretariat of the League asked the United States whether she believed the Pact of Paris to be involved. On September 22 the President of the League appealed to Japan and China to refrain from hostilities and withdraw their troops. In the meantime China had urged the United States under the Pact of Paris to take steps to uphold the peace in the Far East. The United States showed herself, although not a member, willing to cooperate with the League but wished to do so in such fashion as would not arouse Japanese sentiment to support the extreme militarists against the more moderate elements in their government. The American Secretary of State, Henry L. Stimson, declined to join in a League commission of investigation, but sent independently, although with the consent of the Japanese Foreign Minister, two Americans to Manchuria to look into the situation.

Japan replied to the League that the use of her troops was solely for the protection of her nationals and their property, that she would withdraw her troops to the railway zone as soon as was consistent with the achievement of that protection, and that she wished to settle by direct negotiation with China the issues involved. She disclaimed any territorial designs in Manchuria. In contrast with the assurances given by the Japanese government, however, the Kwantung army continued its aggressive action. Presumably it had taken the bit in its teeth regardless of what the cabinet and the foreign office might say.

After consultation through the League in October several of the European governments and the United States sent notes to Japan and China calling their attention to their obligations under the Pact of Paris. In November, since the Kwantung army was methodically pursuing its reduction of Manchuria, Stimson made it clear that his government would not object if the League were to apply economic sanctions. He also protested to the Japanese Foreign Minister the continued advance of the Japanese armies. In that same month, at the suggestion of the Japanese government, the League took steps to appoint a neutral commission of inquiry.

In December the Japanese cabinet, largely Minseito in affiliation and by tradition inclined to a mild and conciliatory policy in China, gave way to one in which the Seiyukai was more prominent and which took a more vigorous attitude. The army continued to move ahead in Manchuria.

This combination of circumstances led Secretary Stimson to believe that more forthright action by the United States was needed. On January 7, 1932, he sent identical notes to the governments of China and Japan in which he stated that the United States government "cannot admit the legality of any situation *de facto* nor does it intend to recognize any treaty or agreement entered into between those governments, or agents thereof, which may impair the treaty rights of the United States or its citizens in China, including those which relate to the sovereignty, the independence, or the territorial and administrative integrity of the Republic of China, or to the international policy relative to China, commonly known as the open door policy; and that it does not intend to recognize any situation, treaty, or agreement which may be brought about by means contrary to the covenants and obligations of the Pact of Paris of August 27, 1928, to which treaty both China and Japan, as well as the United States, are parties." This was what became known as the Stimson Doctrine. It was a continuation of the American policy which had been traditional since at least the time of Secretary Hay. Secretary Stimson was simply following consistently in the path of his predecessors. He set the United States again, as had other acts in the past, squarely athwart the ambitions of Japan. One or the other of the powers would have to give ground or a head-on collision would follow. For the time the decision was delayed, for neither country wished war or was ready for it.

Secretary Stimson had hoped for the support of Great Britain. In this he was disappointed. The British government issued a communique which he regarded as a rebuff. It was willing to take at face value the public assertion of the Premier of Japan that his government adhered to the open door policy and would welcome participation and cooperation in Manchurian economic enterprises. Clearly Great Britain was not prepared to go to war to restrain Japan. The English had vividly in mind the recent anti-British agitation in China and were not disposed to put themselves to any great inconvenience to protect that country. Some were inclined to sympathize with the Japanese vigorous reaction to the repeated irritation of anti-Japanese acts. Moreover, the Far East was on the periphery of British interest. British prestige might eventually be involved, but British financial interests in China were so small a part of total British foreign investments that they did not warrant a war. In Manchuria British commercial and financial interests were almost negligible. In its reply to

Secretary Stimson's note the Japanese government took over almost bodily the British argument as it was voiced in the London *Times*. Yet when, a few days after the American note, fighting broke out at Shanghai, a center where British interests were prominent, a British note was sent the Japanese sharply protesting the bombing of a section of the city. At British suggestion Stimson sent a similar representation to Tokyo.

For a time the most vigorous action from the Occident in the developing situation in China was not from Great Britain or even the League, but from the United States. The American fleet, already in maneuvers in the Pacific, was held in Hawaii, poised for possible emergencies. The United States kept closely in touch with the League. When the Premier of Japan suggested that the powers proffer their good offices to stop the fighting in Shanghai, the United States government took the lead in drafting proposals for a settlement which with slight amendments were concurred in by Great Britain, France, and Italy. These the Chinese accepted but the Japanese rejected. The United States now had recourse to the Nine Power Treaty. Secretary Stimson urged upon the British Foreign Minister the timeliness of invoking that instrument and bringing into operation the processes for consultation provided for in the document. To this the British would not assent. Stimson thereupon had recourse to another method. He wrote (February 23, 1932) a long public letter to the chairman of the Foreign Affairs Committee of the Senate of the United States. In this he called attention to the fact that in the Nine Power Treaty the signatories, among them Japan, with full knowledge that the progress of China toward orderly self-government would be slow, had agreed to respect the sovereignty, the independence, and the territorial and administrative integrity of that land. He declared that the treaties entered into at the Washington Conference were interdependent and strongly hinted that, if the Nine Power Treaty were flouted by Japan, the United States would feel herself no longer bound by the limitations imposed upon her by the other treaties in enlarging her navy and fortifying her island possessions in the western Pacific. He suggested that the other governments of the world join in the principle of nonrecognition adopted by the United States the preceding month. The letter was intended to be a note of encouragement to China, a warning to Japan, and a prod to Great Britain and the League of Nations.

Stimulated by the initiative of the United States, in March 1932 the Assembly of the League of Nations, employing the language of Secretary Stimson in his note of January, declared that it was incumbent upon the members of the League "not to recognize any situation, treaty, or agreement which may be brought about by means contrary to the Covenant of the League of Nations or to the Pact of Paris."

The efforts of the United States and of the League were not entirely without success. Through representatives of the neutral powers and Geneva, terms were drawn up for the settlement of the Shanghai affair in which, in May 1932, Japan and China acquiesced. The last of the Japanese invading forces withdrew on May 31. Japan was probably glad to find an honorable way to desist from her operations in and near Shanghai. They had proved more difficult than she had anticipated and for the time being Manchuria was a sufficiently large problem.

However, Japan was adamant on her program in Manchuria. On September 15, 1932, lacking three days of a year from the Mukden incident, she recognized Manchukuo as a distinct country and signed with her a treaty by which the two governments agreed to cooperate in insuring each other's safety. This document, while in the form of an alliance between equal states, was in reality a notice served by Japan to the world that she would brook no interference with what the Kwantung army had accomplished. By forestalling the report of the League's commission of inquiry, Japan, although still a member, was flouting that organization.

The commission of inquiry appointed by the League had in the meantime completed its investigation and prepared its findings. It had been headed by an Englishman, Lord Lytton. On it had been as well an Italian, an American, a Frenchman, and a German. The report had been signed at Peking on September 4, 1932, but it was not published until October 2. It was adverse to either the restoration of the *status quo* or the recognition and maintenance of Manchukuo. It proposed a solution which would respect the interests of China, Japan, and Russia, with a government for Manchuria which would be largely autonomous but which would still be consistent with the sovereignty and administrative integrity of China.

The presentation of the Lytton Commission's report precipitated a long and heated debate in the League. After months of futile effort to effect a settlement, in February 1933 the League, through its Assembly, adopted the report. In taking this action the Assembly virtually backed the Stimson Doctrine. It endorsed observance of the covenant of the League, the Pact of Paris, and the Nine Power Treaty and declared that the members of the League would not recognize the new regime in Manchuria. It called upon Japan to cease her military pressure on China and ordered negotiations for the settlement of the dispute to be carried out under the supervision of the Assembly. Thereupon Japan gave notice of her intention to withdraw from membership in the League. Her formal communication conveying this decision was sent in March 1933.

The Significance of the Manchurian Affair

We have gone so extensively into the Manchurian affair of 1931–1933 because, as we hinted a few pages back, of its enormous consequences for the Far East and the entire world. Japan had defied the instruments which had been devised after World War I to prevent the recurrence of a global cataclysm. She was a member of the League of Nations and a signatory of the Pact of Paris and the Nine Power Treaty. Although some of her nationals, in defending her, argued that she had not violated the last two documents, the Assembly of the League, either directly or by implication, denied flatly the validity of these contentions. Japan had, in effect, snapped her fingers at the League and the United States and had made it clear that she intended to continue the course upon which she had entered.

Japan seemed to have taken the action with impunity. The League did not apply even the mildest of the sanctions prescribed by its covenant. If it had done so it would have had to depend chiefly upon Great Britain, and that power was not minded to undertake the burdens of the war which might ensue. Nor was the United States as yet willing to apply force.

Since Japan seemed to have escaped unpunished, other powers were emboldened to flout the League and the Pact of Paris. Italy was soon to do so in Ethiopia. Thereupon the League once more proved powerless and the Pact of Paris ineffective.

In a very real sense, therefore, the second of the world wars began on that September night in 1931. The shots then fired were the opening of the global conflict. From Mukden the path led to Ethiopia, Munich, the invasion of Poland, and Pearl Harbor. The machinery for peace had been tested in Manchuria and found wanting. Other would-be aggressors were encouraged to set it at nought.

From Manchuria, as we are to see, Japan moved on farther into

China, at first somewhat cautiously, and then into other portions of the Far East.

The sequel to the Mukden incident made it clear for all who had eyes to see that the Far East and the remainder of the world had become inextricably bound into one pattern and that what happened in the one might well be of supreme importance to the other.

Russian, Siberian, and Outer Mongolian Sequels to Mukden

Russia was obviously much concerned with the enhanced position of Japan in Manchuria. The Union of Soviet Socialist Republics was no more disposed to relinquish its hold on the Russian holdings in the Far East than had been the Czar. It had vividly in memory, moreover, the Japanese attempt to take over the region during the stormy days of the Revolution. Autonomous republics, members of the USSR, were developed in part of the area—the territories of the Buriat Mongols immediately to the south and east of Lake Baikal, and of the Yakuts, a Turkish folk, in the vast forbidding frontier which lay largely in the valley of the Lena and stretched northward to the Arctic Ocean. The remainder was organized into administrative territories.

Moreover, although technically still a part of China, Outer Mongolia was much more within the Russian than the Chinese orbit. The Mongolian Peoples Government, which had been set up in 1921, had early established diplomatic relations with the Soviets. To be sure, in her 1924 treaty with China the USSR had recognized Outer Mongolia and had agreed to withdraw her troops from it. This pledge she fulfilled in 1925. Yet in the ensuing years the revolution in Outer Mongolia continued. In 1924 Outer Mongolia was declared a republic. Blows were dealt to the traditional economic and social order. The state and the powerful Buddhist organization were separated. Lands, minerals, forests, and waters were declared nationalized. Power was centralized in a Peoples Assembly. Most of the cattle, the chief wealth of the country, remained concentrated in a few hands, but in 1928 left-wing tendencies seemed to prevail and in the following three or four years progress was made toward collectivism and steps were taken to confiscate the cattle of the Buddhist monasteries and give them to the collectives and the lay cattle breeders. Reaction came, but the new policy adopted in 1932 preserved many socialist features. Obviously in geography and ideology Outer Mongolia's orientation was Russian.

In the 1930's Russia, possibly partly as a protection against Japanese advance and certainly with the utilization of the natural resources of the region as an objective, began the rapid development of her lands on the Pacific. Immigration was encouraged from other parts of Russia, agriculture was fostered, industrialization proceeded apace, and transportation facilities were improved.

Migration to Siberia from European Russia had fallen off the first few years after the Revolution. This was in part because of the distribution of the land in Russia in Europe among the peasants. When, under the stimulus of the government, it mounted once more in the Russian Far East, migration was still small. In 1942 the population was slightly less than three millions in the two Far Eastern territories. Only a minority went into farming. Most of the immigration was engaged in industry and mining and swelled the cities. The climate was adverse to agriculture, for during much of the year the ground was frozen. However, in parts of the region there were fertile arable lands and grain was cultivated. Koreans even raised rice north of Vladivostok. There was a notable Jewish colony. New crops were introduced. The acreage under cultivation was expanded. Collective farms became normal and with them the extensive use of machinery in agriculture.

Industry was pushed. This was partly to form a basis for materials for defense against possible embroilment with the Japanese and thus to make the region independent in time of war of aid from the distant manufacturing portions of Russia. One of the two chief cities was Khabarovsk, near the mouth of the Ussuri where the Trans-Siberian Railway crossed the Amur. In 1939 approximately two hundred thousand in population, Khabarovsk had multiplied nearly fourfold since 1926. Vladivostok, slightly larger in 1939, had almost doubled in the same period. A new industrial city with great steel mills, Komsomolsk, founded in 1932, by the year 1939 had a population of seventy thousand. Between 1926 and 1939 the total urban population of the Russian Far East had trebled. However, the exact degree of the industrialization was not known by the outside world.

Nor was the precise extent of railway building published. A railroad was being constructed to connect the western stretches of the Trans-Siberian line with the sea which would be less vulnerable to Japanese attack than the long line which followed the Russian bank of the Amur and the Ussuri. Highways supplemented railroads and the use of trucks increased. Roads and railways were of especial help in the 1940's when lend-lease aid was going to Russia from the United States. The route across the northern Pacific was a primary supply line to the Soviet Union. For the reception of lend-lease shipping new ports and additional landing quays were developed in the Soviet Far East.

The mineral resources of the region were progressively utilized. By 1938 the annual amounts of coal mined had been stepped up over four times since the Soviets took charge. Between 1928 and 1939 the output of oil from the wells on the Russian portion of Sakhalin multiplied about twenty times. Shipbuilding was furthered. Lumbering in the vast forests of the area was rapidly increased. Fur trapping proved a growing source of foreign exchange. Fisheries were extensive. Education was pushed, and by the 1940's almost all children of suitable age seem to have been in schools. Higher schools, largely technical, were instituted.

Relations with Japan were marked by chronic suspicion and thinly veiled hostility. Occasionally there were open clashes. From time to time concrete sources of friction were removed and temporary agreement was attained.

At the outset of the Mukden incident and Japan's enlarged adventure in Manchuria the Russian attitude was not entirely unfriendly. Russia's relations with the Chinese government had been strained ever since the dominant party, the Kuomintang, had broken with the Chinese Communists, in 1927. The two countries had been engaged in a brief and undeclared war in 1929 over the Chinese Eastern Railway. Presumably Russia, like Great Britain, would not be unwilling to see the Chinese self-assertiveness curbed.

At the same time there was fear that the League might try to direct Japanese animosity against Russia and that Japan, in moving into northern Manchuria, might attempt to go on into Russian territory. The Japanese, moreover, believed Russia to be aiding forces opposed to them in northern Manchuria. However, the Japanese gave assurances that they would control the anti-Soviet White Russians in northern Manchuria and asked permission of Moscow before transporting troops over the Chinese Eastern Railway, in which Russia had an interest. By the end of 1932 Russia and Japan had entered into trade agreements and a peaceful adjustment of difficulties over the latter's fisheries off the Russian coasts. Yet the reestablishment, in December 1932, of diplomatic relations between China and Russia, after the strain of 1927 and 1929, was attended by Japanese criticism. To Tokyo this rapprochement appeared ominous, coming as it did at a time when it was in undeclared war with China and was on the point of breaking with the League of Nations. To Russia, on the other hand, the Lytton Commission seemed to be trying to divert Japanese animosity toward her. Clearly the Japanese advance in Manchuria was adding to the tension between Tokyo and Moscow.

In 1935, the Chinese Eastern Railway ceased to be a bone of contention between Russia and Japan. So long as Russia retained the financial interest and the partial control which she had exercised (except for the period of transition from the Czarist regime to the Soviets) ever since the 1890's when the road had been started at Russian instance, the line would remain a source of irritation. The creation of the Japanese-dominated Manchukuo made the Russian position in the railway critical in the relations between Moscow and Tokyo. Negotiations for the sale of the Russian interests were begun in 1933. They encountered many snags and were not consummated until March 1935. The Chinese government felt aggrieved by this transfer, without its consent, and protested it in notes to several of the Occidental powers.

Boundaries between Manchuria on the one hand and on the other the Russian territories on the north and Outer Mongolia on the west became a source of friction between Russia and Japan. The Japanese, as we shall see in a moment, were pressing westward from Manchuria into Inner Mongolia. Their temper was anti-Russian and anti-Communist. By establishing control over Inner Mongolia they would be outflanking Russia if the latter were to attempt an advance southward into China Proper. They were also feeling out the Russian strength along the long frontier which Manchuria had in common with Russia both in the Siberian provinces and in Outer Mongolia, of which Russia had made herself the protector. Japan claimed that the boundaries were vague and professed a desire for "demarcation." Russia was inclined to insist that the boundaries were clear and would consent only to a "redemarcation." Clashes between Japanese and Russian forces along the border were fairly frequent, especially in 1935, 1936, 1937, 1938, and 1939. In 1936 Stalin, on behalf of Moscow, gave blunt warning that an attack on Outer Mongolia would be considered an act of war against the USSR herself. In 1938 serious fighting occurred near the corner where the Korean, Manchurian, and Russian borders approached one another. The Japanese found the Russians so strong that they were content not to press the contest.

Possibly, too, the increasing involvement in China which began in July 1937 led the Kwantung army not to wish to add Russia to its active enemies.

In 1935 the Kwantung army sought to penetrate Outer Mongolia by demanding the privilege of being officially represented at the latter's capital and of building telegraph lines in the country. Manchukuo and Outer Mongolia also had negotiations over the reciprocal reception of official representatives. Both efforts, however, came to nought. Russia was not minded to countenance the entrance of Japan into Outer Mongolia either directly or through a puppet.

Increasingly the trend in Japan was to regard Russia as the chief menace to the future of the Empire. With that frame of mind went a fear of Communism. In November 1936, Germany and Japan signed an anti-Comintern pact. This seemed to the Soviet government to be directed against it. Clearly it appeared to be a step toward an alliance of potential enemies on the eastern and western borders of Russia. The anti-Comintern pact was purely a marriage of convenience. Germany and Japan, or at least a large proportion of their articulate groups, distrusted and disliked each other. Hitler, who had by then come to power, had expressed openly his contempt for the Japanese. While no love was lost between Japan and Germany, for a time after 1936 the tension between Russia and Japan became more marked. Subsequent to July 1937, when the Chino-Japanese conflict took on a more aggravated form, Russia appeared to be aligning herself with China. In August 1937, China and Russia entered into a nonaggression pact, thereby in part, although not to the extent of an alliance for reciprocal aid, presenting a common front against Japan. Russia took part in the Brussels conference called in November of that year under the Nine Power Treaty of 1922 to consult on the problem posed by Japan's fresh advance in China. This, too, ranged Russia on the side of Japan's critics. While the Brussels conference was still in session, Japan and Italy completed an agreement. Japan was in search of support in the impending showdown with her opponents, and Russia seemed clearly to be in the hostile camp.

However, as the war on the continent spread and was prolonged far beyond the time originally anticipated in Tokyo, Japan's leaders evidently were reluctant to come to an open break with Russia until the China affair should be safely in hand. Trouble with Great Britain and the United States was looming on the horizon. It became the part of wisdom, therefore, to compose the differences with Russia so far as might be and at least for the moment. Moreover, in August 1938, presumably to the vast surprise and consternation of Tokyo, Germany and Russia entered into a nonaggression pact, thereby seeming to deprive Japan of her anticipated ally on Russia's western front. While in 1939 border incidents were still occurring and it was generally thought that Japan was keeping a substantial army in Manchuria to watch Russia, there were those in Japan who believed an understanding with the Soviets to be desirable. In 1941, accordingly, Moscow and Tokyo entered into a nonaggression pact. By this they agreed to respect each other's territorial integrity and to remain neutral if either were attacked by a third state.

The last paragraph somewhat runs ahead of the orderly sequence of our story. We must pause for the time being in the narrative of Russo-Japanese relations and bring down the account of events elsewhere in the Far East. We will then be in a better position to tell of the part which Russia had in the developing scene.

We must round out the picture of Russia in the Far East by recording the fact that in Sinkiang Soviet influence was mounting. The building of a railway in Russian territory skirting the western base of the mountains which separated Sinkiang from Russian soil made for a rapid increase of trade across the border. The Soviet government, moreover, accorded aid to one of the Chinese who was struggling for mastery in Sinkiang, and this assistance helped to give the Russian protegee the victory. Communications with China Proper were so difficult and attenuated that Nanking, with urgent problems nearer by, could do little to assert itself. Sinkiang seemed, although to a lesser extent than Outer Mongolia, to be moving into the Russian orbit.

Japan in Manchuria, 1933–1937

The Kwantung army was not content merely with bringing Manchuria under its control. It sought to develop the area in such fashion that it would meet the economic needs which had been an incentive in the adventure. There were grandiose dreams of so utilizing the resources of Manchuria that the standard of living of Japan would be substantially raised. These were not fulfilled. This was in part because of an overestimate of the early possibilities of the area. It was also because of the enormous costs of the armed services and the wars into which the ambitions of the extremists drew the country. Yet in the course of the years substantial development was seen in the exploitation of the admittedly large natural wealth of the region.

Prerequisite to economic development were political order and stability. Here distinct progress was registered. Gradually armed resistance was reduced. Those whom the Japanese regarded as bandits but whom the Chinese thought of as patriots or irregulars were hunted down. In contrast with the Chang Tso-lin and Chang Hsüeh-liang regime, currency was tied to the yen and became unified and stable, taxes were lowered, the government was placed on a budget and the budget was practically balanced, and security of life and property increased. The sale and use of opium, hitherto a scourge, were markedly restricted. Near the center of the country, at the former Changchun, where the South Manchuria and the Chinese Eastern Railways met, a new capital, Hsinching, modern in buildings and streets, was developed. Manchukuo was given a monarchical form of government and he, commonly known as Pu Yi, who had once been the last Manchu monarch of China became, on March 1, 1934, the first Emperor of the new state under the reign title of Kang Tê. Manchukuo became officially Manchutikuo, or the Manchu Empire. The new regime was inaugurated with great pomp. The young Emperor made a state visit to Japan. Although the overwhelming majority of the population were Chinese by blood, speech, and culture, the Japanese overlords insisted that they were to be known and were to regard themselves as Manchus. The attempt was made to base the new order upon Confucianism, with its respect for the monarch.

Yet, while nominally independent, Manchukuo was kept under careful Japanese supervision and direction. This, as we saw in the last chapter, was characteristic of Japanese colonial administration. Although "Manchus" were nominally in the chief posts, the actual control was in the hands of the Kwantung army. Japanese officials were in key positions, either as advisers or directly. Higher education was discouraged or discontinued. Clearly the "Manchus" were to be kept subordinate to the master people. Being in effective control and having reformed the laws and the courts, the Japanese could afford to go through the gesture of abolishing extraterritorial privileges. This they did in 1935. The standard of living of the farmers was probably higher than south of the Great Wall, but this was due as much to the fact that the country was newly settled and not yet crowded as to Japanese administration.

The puppet character of Manchukuo was evidenced by the slowness with which official recognition was accorded by foreign governments. The Stimson Doctrine and its reenforcement by the League of Nations were effective. Consulates dating from before the creation of the new state were continued by the United States, Great Britain, and some of the other powers, but without granting legality to the new order. In 1934 the Dominican Republic and Salvador formally opened diplomatic relations. In that year, too, the Holy See appointed an Acting Apostolic Delegate. In 1935 a trade agreement was concluded, through Tokyo, with Germany. As was to be anticipated, as a corollary of the anti-Comintern pact, formal recognition was granted by Italy.

For the defense and the economic development of Manchuria old railway lines were extended or completed and new ones were constructed. Several of the new lines were clearly for strategic purposes, directed against possible attack from the north. All, including the former Chinese-owned lines and the Chinese Eastern after its purchase, were placed under the unified administration of the South Manchuria Railway. New highways were built and hundreds of motor buses traversed them. Manchuria was much better suppled with rail and bus transportation than was China south of the Great Wall.

The attempt was made to coordinate the economies of Manchuria and Japan. The former was to supply what the latter lacked. In general this meant that Manchuria was to be a source of raw materials and Japan the industrial center of the structure which was being created in East Asia. As before 1931, so after that year, the soya bean and its derivatives, bean oil and bean cake, were Manchuria's major export. Germany was the chief market for the soya bean and its products. Manchuria had deposits of iron ore, in which Japan was notoriously lacking. In Manchuria, therefore, the iron and steel industry was encouraged. Manchuria was the chief source of Japan's pig iron. The iron works at Anshan were notable. Coal, especially from the vast open pit mines at Fushun, was a prominent item of export. A beginning was made toward distilling the enormous deposits of oil shale and thus toward augmenting the petroleum in which Japan was distressingly short. The resources of the forests were conserved and developed. Increasingly Manchuria's imports came from Japan. Cotton goods led. Iron, steel, machinery, and tools were next. Electrical appliances and vehicles were important. Wheat flour, largely from Japanese mills, and sugar loomed large.

All was not smooth in the economic development of the region.

The formation of Manchukuo brought a sharp falling off of trade with China Proper, especially of exports. This was due to the anti-Japanese boycott in China Proper, to the erection of customs barriers between Manchukuo and the provinces south of the Great Wall, and to China's economic difficulties. Moreover, because of exchange problems and attempts at autarchy, Germany, the major outlet for the soya bean, greatly curtailed her purchases. In the early years of its existence Manchukuo developed a highly adverse balance of trade. This was in some degree due to the loss of export markets in China Proper and Germany. It was also because of an import boom from Japan. In the development of her holdings in her newly acquired puppet ally, Japan sent in large quantities of goods. Japanese immigrants multiplied and were purchasers of the products of the mother country. Substantial amounts of Japanese capital came in, seeking outlet and the high profits promised by the new order.

In an attempt to provide the needed foreign exchange, efforts were made to diversify the agriculture of Manchukuo. The growing of wheat, sugar beets, tobacco, and hemp was fostered, but without much immediate success.

Attempts were made to encourage the immigration of Japanese farmers. It was hoped thus to relieve the congestion of the rural population in the islands. These endeavors met with scant success. The miscarriage was attributable to a variety of factors—among them the severity of the winters, the competition of Chinese and Korean farmers with their lower standards of living, and the circumstance that most of the best lands, particularly in the south, were already occupied by Chinese and those which remained, largely in the north, suffered from a sub-Arctic climate. However, Japanese poured in and settled in the towns and cities. They came as soldiers, officials, technical experts, professional men, and businessmen. They swelled the cities.

Thanks in part to this immigration and in part to the influx of Koreans and Chinese, the population grew. In 1936 it was nearly thirty-four millions and was said to be mounting at the rate of over eight hundred thousand a year.

Manchukuo did not immediately become the golden west and the treasure house which the roseate dreams of Japanese expansionists had envisaged. However, it was being integrated into the economy of the Empire and was part of the larger structure which Japan was erecting. For many individual Japanese it meant wealth. The holdings of the South Manchuria Railway Company were greatly augmented. New aggregations of capital, corresponding to the older units of the *Zaibatsu*, developed.

Japan Extends Her Lines in China

The Japanese army was not satisfied with having brought the Three Eastern Provinces and Jehol under its sway. It reached westward and southward into Inner Mongolia and the provinces in the northeast of China Proper—Hopei, Shansi, and Shantung. Here its penetration was in part by force, in part by obtaining the friendly cooperation of Mongols, and in part through local and provincial Chinese regimes which collaborated more or less willingly or from a sense of prudence.

While the extension of the Japanese conquest was by free choice of the army, it could scarcely be avoided. Once she had occupied Manchuria, Japan had no option but to go on into the remainder of China. The overwhelming majority of the population of Manchuria were Chinese. Chinese nationalism was increasing and would never rest content until the Three Eastern Provinces were integrated fully into China. Japan, therefore, must either retreat from Manchuria, which she would not do, or subdue, eventually, all of China. Indeed, as we pointed out in an earlier chapter, Japan's activities in Korea in the 1880's and 1890's had led her on, almost with the inevitability of a Greek tragedy, to these further adventures.

In Inner Mongolia Japan was able to take advantage of the competition of Mongols with Chinese farmers. Inner Mongolia was largely a marginal region between farming and grazing. The rainfall was slight. In good years much pasture land could be brought under the plow. In cycles of bad years some of it became unprofitable for cultivation. In general the Chinese, pressing northward from overcrowded provinces on the border, were the farmers and the Mongols the herdsmen. Between the two was the chronic enmity which usually maintains between those who live by their flocks and herds and those who cultivate the soil. Prior to 1931 Chinese officials had furthered colonization by their countrymen, and Mongols, by sale, had lost about two-thirds of their lands in Jehol and substantial portions in Chahar and Suiyüan, the provinces into which had been carved much of Inner Mongolia west of Jehol. The Japanese appeared to side with the Mongols and were able to obtain the support of some of the leading men of that race. This was the more willingly given because the Mongol princes and the Lamas might well regard Japan as a bulwark not only against Chinese farmers but also against Russian Communism. The latter was menacing them from Outer Mongolia.

In 1933, after the incorporation of Jehol into Manchukuo, portions of western Manchuria and of northern Jehol were joined to form a new province of the puppet state. Here the Japanese made a bid for the support of the Mongols by safeguarding the grazing lands from further alienation to Chinese settlers, by granting much of local autonomy, and by giving support to the powerful Lama priesthood.

Mongol princes to the west of Jehol used the Japanese menace to extract concessions from Nanking as a price of their support. In 1934 an autonomous government was set up in Inner Mongolia by the Mongols, under a council which had Chinese advisers. In 1933 the Kwantung army began moving westward from Jehol into Chahar and by 1937 was in control of much of the latter province. Some of this was accomplished by fighting which arose, typically, from border incidents in which the Japanese claimed that the others were the aggressors and that they were acting in self-defense. In 1935, as her power in the northeast of China Proper increased, Japan demanded the dissolution of units of the Kuomintang in Chahar and the cessation of Chinese migration into that province. Japanese military and civil "advisers" were appointed to the provincial government.

Concurrently with expansion into Inner Mongolia went the spread of Japanese might into the northeast of China Proper. The Kwantung army could here also plead the necessity of defense. Chang Hsüeh-liang had not been completely eliminated by the overrunning of his home territory, Manchuria. He still had much of his army intact in the southwest of Manchuria proper, in the area of Peking (or Peip'ing, as it was temporarily known). He sought, although in vain, to prevent the incorporation of Jehol into Manchukuo. The Japanese insisted that the government in Hopei be less hostile. The Chinese had the unpleasant alternative of compromise or invasion. The latter was fairly certain of success. Accordingly, they agreed to personnel in the administration of Hopei which would not be unfriendly to Japan. For instance, for Chang Hsüeh-liang an officer less obnoxious to the Japanese was substituted as commander of the Chinese armies. In May 1933, after Japanese forces had advanced to within a few miles of Tientsin and Peking, the contestants entered into an agreement which was known as the Tangku truce. By it they undertook to withdraw their armies from a region in the northeast of Hopei which was slightly north of Peking and Tientsin but which did not include these cities. The Japanese might use airplanes to inspect the region to see whether the agreement had been carried out. They themselves were to remove their army from the area. This provision was partly nullified by the terms of the Boxer Protocol of 1901 under which they might maintain troops immediately to the south, in Peking, Tientsin, and along the railway between those two cities. Order in the demilitarized zone was to be preserved by Chinese police, but they were not to be hostile to the Japanese. Although technically the agreement was observed, the Japanese continued to complain, probably with some basis in fact, that Chinese officials were uncooperative and that anti-Japanese propaganda was rife. The national government at Nanking was endeavoring to maintain control over the area but was encountering difficulty. In November 1933, the Chinese felt constrained to enter into secret arrangements which gave the Japanese significant concessions in the demilitarized zone. In 1934 and 1935 trade, railway traffic, and postal service were opened between China Proper and Manchukuo. This, however, was accomplished without formal recognition of Manchukuo by China. In 1935 the Kwantung army took another forward step by wresting compliance with demands which removed a Chinese army from Hopei, dissolved the units of the Kuomintang in that area, and suppressed anti-Japanese activities.

Late in 1935 the situation became more tense. Reports from Tokyo, presumably inspired, spoke of an impending organization of an "autonomous" government which would include the northeastern provinces of Hopei, Shansi, Shantung, Chahar, and Suiyüan. Presumably the way was being prepared for severing this vast area from the Nanking government and bringing it under Japanese protection. Nanking sought to forestall the move by a reorganization in the northeast which would, in the nature of a compromise, set up regimes less objectionable to the Japanese. There was created the East Hopei Autonomous Council which was dominated by the Japanese. There was also constituted the Hopei-Chahar Political Council which was not quite so palpably under the Japanese. In much of the northeast Japanese goods were entering by thinly veiled smuggling with consequent avoidance of Chinese tariff. The regime in the eastern part of Hopei frankly instituted duties only a fourth of those levied by the national government. The sale of narcotics by Japanese subjects in the northeast also became an ill-concealed scandal.

Japan Seeks to Control All China

Japanese knew that unless they could have in all China a regime or regimes friendly to them friction and continued clashes would be inevitable. In 1933, through their Minister of Foreign Affairs, they sought to establish an Asiatic union comprising China, Japan, and Manchukuo which would pledge, through a definite protocol, close economic and political collaboration. In effect, this could only mean the submission of China to Japan. Chinese nationalism would make it impossible. However, the Japanese were, for the time, undiscouraged and their apparent success in Manchukuo seemed to give them some ground for hope. Throughout the Republic Japanese diplomatic, consular, and military officials strove to win Chinese consent. They particularly sought a reduction of customs duties against Japanese goods and to make an end to the boycott. In 1935 they so far had their way that the Chinese government promulgated an order enjoining its citizens to refrain from discriminatory or provocative acts or speeches against "friendly nations" and prohibiting the forming of any organization "which might be detrimental to international relations." The Chinese government, moreover, punished the publisher of a Shanghai periodical which had issued an article deemed derogatory to the Emperor of Japan and also took steps against the Shanghai censorship bureau for permitting the objectionable words to appear. The heads of the Chinese government might inwardly rage, but they knew that the country was in no position to challenge Japan on the field of battle and hoped that by giving as little offense as possible they could prevent either an open break or full compliance and that in the meantime they could so strengthen the country that it would not be helpless against the aggressor.

Chinese students, in their youthful ardor, were not so patient and temporizing. In 1935 they organized in Peip'ing (Peking), especially against Japan's encroachments in North China. In May of that year delegates from local units from Peip'ing to Canton formed a federation of what were called National Salvation Unions. The Chinese authorities, under pressure from the Japanese and knowing the danger of such agitation to the already inflamed situation, attempted to suppress the movement. Yet, forced on by the rising tide of patriotic fervor, the Chinese government stiffened its attitude toward Japan.

Japan also strove to fend off what she deemed interference from other governments in her China program and was especially virulent against the League of Nations. Since her break with that body she had regarded it and all its works with a hostile eye. The League, flouted and defeated in Manchuria, sought through advisers to aid China to put her house in order and so to be able to stand against Japan. In April 1934, the spokesman for Tokyo's foreign office warned the rest of the world to keep hands off China. He declared that Japanese "consider it only natural that to keep peace and order in the East of Asia we must even act alone on our own responsibility. . . . There is no country but China which is in a position to share with Japan the responsibility of peace in East Asia. . . . Unification of China, preservation of her territorial integrity as well as restoration of order in that country are most ardently desired by Japan. History shows that they can be attained through no other means than awakening and voluntary efforts of China herself. We oppose, therefore, any attempt on the part of China to avail herself of the influence of any other country in order to resist Japan; we also oppose any action taken by China calculated to play one power against another. . . . Supplying China with war aeroplanes, building aerodromes in China, and detailing military and naval instructors or military advisers to China, or contracting a loan to provide funds for political uses, would obviously tend to alienate friendly relations between Japan, China, and other countries. . . . Japan will oppose such projects." Similar warnings were issued through other Japanese officials in succeeding months and years. In 1935, for instance, a program for Chinese monetary reform, thought by Japanese to have been inspired by a British treasury expert, aroused a storm of protest in Tokyo.

To this Japanese attempt at a protectorate of China the Chinese government took tart exception and in 1934, through one or another channel, declared that no state had the right to claim exclusive responsibility for maintaining peace in any part of the world and that the surest guarantee of peace in the Far East was to be found, not in the abstention from friendly collaboration with China by Western powers, but "in the abandonment by Japan of her policy of ruthless imperialism in Asia."

It was clear that Japan was intent upon extending her control over all of China and that the articulate among the Chinese were determined not to submit. A life and death struggle was clearly impending.

Internal Political Developments in China, 1931–1937

While the clouds were darkening on the international horizon, what of internal conditions in China? What progress was being seen in the basic revolutions that were in progress? Would political unity and the building of an industrial basis for power proceed rapidly enough to enable China effectively to resist her well-armed and determined neighbor?

The revolution went on in all its several phases. China was committed to education of a Western type and schools after that pattern increased. The religious faiths longer current in China continued to lose ground, although not so rapidly as in the preceding two or three decades. Christianity mounted in numbers and influence and did not have to face the widely spread organized movement against it which had troubled it in the 1920's. In territories held by the Communists Christianity suffered. The world-wide financial depression which began in the United States in 1929 meant a falling off of funds which had helped to undergird the missions, especially those of Protestants. Yet Christians, notably Protestant Christians, were prominent as they had never been before. The Soong family, one of whose sons was the financial genius of the Kuomintang regime and three of whose daughters were married to outstanding leaders in the party, was ostensibly Christian. Sun Yat-sen, the patron saint of the Nationalist government and whose program was accepted by the Kuomintang as authoritative, had been a Christian from his boyhood to his death. His widow was one of the Soong sisters. Chiang Kai-shek, the dominant figure in the government, married another of the Soong sisters and became a Christian after entering into that alliance. A number of other men, only slightly less prominent in the state, were also of that faith. In other ways Christianity was expanding and its influence had never been so great.

Social customs were still changing. Women were coming to prominence in circles most affected by the Occident, particularly among the Christians, in the student class, and among the workers in the modern factories.

The industrialization of the country continued. That, as heretofore, was largely confined to a few districts, especially the Shanghai area. The construction of railways was pushed. Notable was the completion of the line from Wuchang to Canton. This meant through rail connections between the north and the south, interrupted only by the unbridged Yangtze between Hankow and Wuchang. Thousands of miles of highways were built. Many of these were for the movement of armies. Few of them had more than a dirt surface. However, over them motor traffic was swelling to substantial proportions. Most of this was passenger buses and army vehicles. The condition of the roads did not encourage the transportation of much freight by automobile and private cars were relatively few. The use of the airplane was mounting, and regular services for mail and passengers were inaugurated between several of the chief cities. Many of the cities were becoming Occidental in appearance: streets were widened, some of the ancient protecting walls were torn down, and buildings of Western types were multiplying. As heretofore, these changes were most noticeable on the coast and up the Yangtze, the regions touched earliest and penetrated most extensively by commerce from the Occident and Japan. Yet all the country was progressively in process of change.

Although the revolution continued in all aspects of China's life, the years were dominated by the struggle with Japan and were shadowed by the impending intensification of that contest. It was a life and death combat. For Japan defeat would spell the end of long cherished ambitions and possible recession to the position of a third-class power. For China a full-scale Japanese victory would mean the end of independence, economic and cultural as well as political, and a subservience of indefinite duration. Clearly China was as yet in no position to meet Japan on the field of battle. She lacked a fleet, an adequate air force, a sufficient number of trained officers, and, especially, the industrial equipment to provide the backing requisite for large armies. She was still far from being fully united and could not as yet present a solid front or a well-coordinated resistance against a foreign aggressor. The interval between the beginning of the Japanese attack in 1931 and the spread of the conflict to full-scale proportions in 1937 was marked by attempts to reduce these handicaps and to stall off the inescapable joining of the issue until preparation could be further advanced to meet the full force of the onslaught. However, the conflict was only postponed, and that but slightly.

If Japan were to be effectively resisted, China must, if possible, achieve internal unity. The strongest center of power was the regime dominated by the Kuomintang, with its capital at Nanking and with Chiang Kai-shek as its outstanding leader. It was this government which had the recognition of the powers and of the larger part of

China. Economically it was based upon the rich lower valley of the Yangtze and the wealthiest city in the land, Shanghai. It had the support of most of the substantial elements in the nation. Here and there were those only grudgingly submissive to it or openly resistant. Some of them were survivors of the war lords of the anarchic years which immediately preceded 1926. In the south, notably in Kwangsi, there was a semi-autonomous region with strong leaders who had no love for Chiang Kai-shek. Bandits remained numerous and widespread, a scourge to the countryside. Yet, by a strange anomaly which was characteristic of China, so important a national organ as the post office, while remaining under Nanking, maintained its services over most of the country and carried the mails through bandit lines and into provinces lukewarm to the Kuomintang.

The most serious and persistent opposition to Nanking was by the Communists. After the Kuomintang had purged itself of them (1927), they continued in more than one part of the country. By 1931 they had established their main center in Kiangsi and were reaching over into some of the borders of the adjacent provinces, notably Fukien, Kwangtung, and Hunan. Here they set up a government which was frankly independent of Nanking and opposed to it. Their leaders were familiar with the ideology of Russian Communism. Foreign Communist concepts combined with indigenous aspirations to bring about a peasant movement which in some ways resembled other revolts of underprivileged rural strata which for many centuries had punctuated Chinese history. Wealthy landlords were dispossessed and some of them and such members of their families as could be found were exterminated. Their lands were distributed among the cultivators. There was much of ruthlessness and stark cruelty. Yet in theory the poor were spared and rural reconstruction for the benefit of the masses was undertaken.

What the Communists might have accomplished had they been left undisturbed no one could know. The Nanking government was resolved upon their complete eradication. This meant chronic and bitter fighting. Nanking launched successive armies in five campaigns. By Fabian and semiguerrilla tactics largely in mountainous territory the Communists succeeded for several years in maintaining themselves against overwhelming forces. In the slaughter and the miseries accompanying the prolonged struggle possibly a million lives were lost, largely of noncombatants. Nanking was not content with the negative policy of extermination. It also endeavored to further measures for the improvement of the lot of the peasants which would remove one of the most potent appeals of the Communists.

So far did Nanking succeed that late in 1934 the Red armies felt forced to evacuate their strongholds. They then began a notable march which took them into a new field of activity in the north, with headquarters in Shensi. Here a local Communist movement had prepared the way. The long march, of perhaps six thousand miles, was much of it over incredibly difficult terrain. The migrants moved along the mountainous borders of Kweichow, Yünnan, Szechwan, Tibet, and Kansu, crossing deep canyons and swift rivers. They lost thousands of lives on the journey and at least in some areas left behind them a legacy of hatred. The memorable trek required slightly more than a year. At the end somewhat less than twenty thousand hardy survivors represented all that was left of the hosts which began the journey. The capital was eventually established at Yenan, west of the Yellow River, over a hundred miles south of the Great Wall. The territory controlled was mainly south of the Great Wall in the northern part of Shensi and in the northeastern portion of Kansu. In later years it was to be extended still farther, notably to the east. Communist principles were put into effect and schools were set up for the training of youth in the program of the party.

Chiang Kai-shek was not minded to allow the Communists to remain in peace in their new quarters. He undertook to press the campaign against them. Out of his insistence came one of the most dramatic incidents of these stirring years and, as a sequel, nominal peace between the Kuomintang and the Communists and the presenting of a united front against the Japanese. Chiang had committed to Chang Hsüeh-liang the waging of the anti-Communist war in the northwest. Headquarters were at Hsian. Discontent developed among Chang Hsüeh-liang's troops. This in part arose from fraternizing with the Communists. The latter urged that Chinese cease fighting among themselves and join in resisting the Japanese. Since the campaign against the Communists was not being pushed as vigorously as he had wished, Chiang went to Hsian to investigate. There, in December 1936, he was taken captive by Chang Hsüeh-liang. He was held for nearly two weeks and for a time his life seemed to be in imminent danger. Late in the month he was released. This was accomplished without formal public commitments by Chiang, for he insisted that his jailers were his subordinates and that he would not enter into treaty with them. Yet he had met and consulted with his captors and one of the Communist leaders and presumably had an unwritten understanding with them. Chang Hsüeh-liang is said to have become convinced of the sincerity and high-minded patriotism of his distinguished prisoner from reading the latter's private diaries which had fallen into his hands. He voluntarily returned to Nanking with Chiang. There he was tried and convicted, but although the penalties were soon remitted he was permanently kept in custody. Chiang Kai-shek's captivity and bearing through it had strengthened rather than weakened the generalissimo in the country as a whole. Hostilities against the Communists were suspended and negotiations were followed by ostensible peace. Face had been saved, in varying degrees, on all sides. Distrust between the Kuomintang and the Communists persisted. Each maintained its own armies and government and each pursued its own domestic program. However, active fighting between them ceased and outwardly both were free to turn their attention to the Japanese.

Patriotism was mounting in China and the spirit of resistance to Japan was increasing. Improvements in government, both national and local, were being accomplished, partly because of the progressive adjustment to new conditions and the slow emergence of officials prepared for the new day and partly under pressure from the foreign peril.

Financially China had not yet emerged from the morass. Modern banks were continuing to multiply and efforts were being made to improve the currency and the financial foundations of the government. However, the world-wide economic depression could not but have repercussions. Since China was on the silver basis, the decline of the status of that metal in the world market in the first two years after 1929 brought a rising price level and a fictitious prosperity. When the English pound went off the gold basis and the American dollar was devalued and when, in June 1934, the United States began the extensive buying of silver, the world price rapidly rose, China began to be drained of her stocks, especially through purchase by Japanese, the domestic price of commodities, measured by silver, fell, the economic pinch became acute, bank failures became numerous, foreign trade fell off, and government revenues decreased alarmingly. To remedy the situation, China nationalized her silver, impounding the stocks of that metal, much as the United States had earlier done with gold. The Treasury of the United States began making (1936) substantial purchases of silver from China, thus enabling the latter to accumulate large reserves of foreign exchange. Presumably, however, China was still in too precarious a financial situation to embark upon a full scale war with Japan.

Domestic Developments in Japan, 1931–1937: Political

While the Japanese and especially the Kwantung army were pushing forward a program for bringing all of China into "cooperation" with them—a euphemism which deceived no one except many of the Japanese themselves—in Japan domestic events were paving the way for the foreign adventure which the year 1937 was to usher in on a large scale. This preparation was seen partly in the changing temper of growing elements in the nation, partly in political changes, some of them violent and spectacular in the extreme, and partly in economic developments.

The temper of the nation was changing. For generations the Japanese had been noted for intense patriotism, but in the 1920's the trend of the government and of public opinion had seemed to be toward a milder policy on the adjacent continent and toward genuine cooperation with other nations. There was a disposition to curb the army and to hold the navy to the policy of restricted armaments which had been inaugurated by the Washington Conference. Now the tide of nationalism was rising and patriotic fervor was becoming intense. This tide was to mount still further after 1937, but the mass psychology was now developing which was to characterize almost all of the country subsequent to that fateful year.

To this intensification of nationalism and its corollary, augmented imperialistic adventure, several factors contributed. Among these were the fighting services, especially the army. The army thought in terms of war and conquest. Its officers, intensively educated in the technique of their profession but with little or no broad knowledge of the world, tended to advocate the fanatical enlargement of the Empire by force of arms. Ever since the Meiji Restoration late in the 1860's there had been elements in the army who had wished to lead the nation in an aggressive foreign policy. At the outset the leaders had been from the *samurai*. Back of them, therefore, were certain traditions of gentility, and several of them, in the days in which Japan was emerging from her isolation, acquired a breadth of outlook which made them seek to restrain the extremists. Latterly, as a consequence of universal military conscription and training, men without *samurai* background had come to the fore. They were, in general, narrower, rougher, and more fanatical than those who had preceded them. Some of them lived lives of Spartan simplicity and were admired as patriots, but theirs was a singularly restricted horizon. The younger officers were especially assertive. By younger was meant those who, largely in their forties, were in the middle ranks, such as majors and colonels. The army was by no means a unit. In it were many factions with shifting affiliations. The most cohesive groups seem to have been made up of classmates from particular military academies. Organizations of ex-service men abounded, and were jingoistic and influential. Many patriotic organizations existed, and some were prepared to use violence to obtain their ends. The economic distresses of the times, arising in part from the world-wide depression and in part from the chronic pressure of a growing population on the limited resources of the islands, bred unrest. Many of the malcontents were inclined to place the blame for their plight upon the politicians, the business and industrial structure, and the capitalists. These they associated with Occidental ways and held that Japan had been unjustly dealt with by the Western powers.

Many of the youthful agitators advocated what they called the Showa Restoration. Showa was the name of the current reign period, so that by this designation they seemed to mean something comparable to the revolution wrought by the Meiji Restoration. As to what was included in this there was much hazy verbiage. Devotion to the Emperor was a basic tenet of the agitators. Any hint of derogation to his dignity and divinity was anathematized. Some, apparently, wished to free Japan from her Westernization, for to this they attributed the alleged insults from Occidental peoples and the corruption and self-seeking with which they charged the politicians and the capitalists. They would be rid of the Parliament and the political parties and would give even more authority to the military. Here was a resurgence of the power of the military, traditionally strong, but latterly somewhat curbed by parliamentary institutions imported from the West. It was akin to Fascism and seems to have been reenforced by the tide which was flowing in the West toward totalitarianism. Yet in its manifestations it was purely Japanese. The army issued pamphlets for popular distribution in which it pleaded for augmented national defense and put forward a plan for improving the condition of the masses by reorganizing the state for social and economic justice. Few if any of the extremists wished a return to the isolation of Tokugawa times, but they would expel the Occident from the Far East and build a new order in which Japan would be supreme. Theoretically that new order was to make, for the welfare of the peoples of East Asia, a "coprosperity sphere" in which all would cooperate and whose benefits all would share, but the Japanese were to be the master race. How much was to be included in the Japanese sphere was not precisely defined. Obviously the existing Empire, Manchukuo, and China were embraced in it. Eventually those of more vaulting ambition brought the Philippines, the East Indies, Indo-China, Thailand, and the Malay Peninsula into their program and even cast their eyes upon Burma and India.

A striking and significant phase of the drive toward militarism and imperialism was a series of assassinations. Violence was not new in Japanese politics. The Forty-Seven *Ronin*, renowned in story and on the stage, were national heroes because of their persistent pursuit of vengeance upon him who had disgraced their lord and, once their end had been attained, their mass suicide. In the Meiji era several high officials had been attacked, some with fatal results. In the 1920's, as we saw in the last chapter, a Premier, Hara, had been killed. Now, in the 1930's, these assaults became more numerous. Most of them were by officers in the army. In 1930, as we also said earlier, the head of the Minseito, the Premier, Hamaguchi, was shot by a fanatical youth. The year 1932 was not very far advanced when the manager of the Mitsui and a former minister of finance were killed. In May 1932, the Premier was assassinated by a group of young officers of the army and navy who for a time held Tokyo in terror. The culprits were arrested, but were given a public trial and were permitted to make long harangues in which they voiced their views and denounced the conditions which they deemed evil. The public regarded them as patriots, although possibly misguided, and they were let off with light sentences. In August 1935, a major general, head of the Military Affairs Bureau, was murdered by a lieutenant colonel who pleaded patriotic motives and the desire to redress the impoverishment of the farmers, the political corruption, and the supine acquiescence in the limitation of the navy by international agreements. The assassin was eventually condemned and executed, but it was clear that many of the younger officers sympathized with him.

The most sobering of the deeds of violence was on February 26, 1936. Less than a week previously a general election had been held for members of the lower house of the Parliament. The Seiyukai, which had had a majority, was defeated, the Minseito made considerable gains, and the liberal groups registered even more striking advances. Communism had been discredited or driven underground, but the moderates appeared to be growing in favor with the electorate. Some of the more radical spirits in the army felt that the time had come for action. They were wearied with parliamentary debates. The acquiescence of the government in the continued limitation of the navy through ratification of the treaty arising from the London Naval Conference of 1930 had probably contributed to the assassination of Hamaguchi and still rankled. Parliament had shown a disposition to curb the army's plan for expansion. On February 26, 1936, about fourteen hundred soldiers, led by lieutenants and captains, seized the houses of Parliament, the residence of the Premier, the headquarters of the Tokyo police, and a leading hotel. They went to the homes of several of the high officials and pumped bullets into those whom they held responsible for the state of the nation. The Premier escaped only because the murderers mistook his brother-in-law for him. For four days the insurgents held the buildings they had taken. In a manifesto setting forth their motives, they declared their objective to be the freeing of the country from the Elder Statesmen, the financial magnates, the government officials, and the political parties who had led the nation to the disgrace of the London naval agreement and to strained relations with other powers. The higher command of the army and the navy moved against the rebels. The latter surrendered on the order of the Emperor. Most of them were pardoned, but fifteen of the leaders were tried by secret court-martial and shot.

For a brief time the army seemed to be discredited, but the incident was followed by an augmentation of its power. It did not immediately gain full control. Civilians and moderates still had influence. The ancient court nobility could make its voice heard against a renewal of military government such as the land had known under the *Bakufu*. Saionji, the last survivor of the *Genro*, was a Fujiwara and traditionally a liberal. To be sure, in February 1937, at the suggestion of Saionji, a general became Premier, but in June 1937, on the eve of the enlarged war in China, Konoye, a Fujiwara and president of the upper house, was appointed to head a cabinet.

Economic Developments in Japan, 1931–1937

Between 1931 and 1937 Japanese industry was undergoing significant changes. These led to greater diversification, with more emphasis upon iron, steel, and the chemicals. As was to be expected from the deterioration of the market in the United States, Japan's chief dependence for the sales of that product, raw silk declined. Indeed, then and even more later, many tracts planted to mulberry trees for the feeding of silkworms were converted to other purposes. The older textiles, cotton and silk, lost ground as Japan's chief factory products. In the 1920's they had accounted for over half of the factory employment and just under half of the factory production. In 1935 they embraced only three-tenths of the output and took care of two-fifths of the employment. The recession was due chiefly to the changed place of silk. The manufacture of cottons increased. The foodstuffs trade declined. In 1929 the metal and machinery group of products were about one-fifth of the industrial whole. In 1935 they were more than a fourth. Chemicals also mounted, notably the production of rayon. The manufacture of woolens and rayons, especially of the latter, climbed rapidly. Mining fell off. In other words, Japan's manufactures, her growing reliance for her economic life, were becoming more varied and, presumably, were therefore healthier.

Japan's industries included some huge units and large numbers of small ones. Improved processes were introduced. The small plants which produced goods for the export trade, such as electric lamps, toys, rubber shoes, brushes, and pencils, had a phenomenal expansion. Bicycles, both for domestic use and for export, were manufactured in ever larger quantities. Efficiency markedly increased, but in most of the modern industries still lagged behind Western Europe and the United States. The scope and intensity of regulation by government mounted. The diversification and the stress on heavy industry meant that Japan, partly deliberately and partly by the normal course of evolution, was becoming better equipped for a war economy.

The Outbreak of Large Scale War in China in 1937 and the Attempted Reduction of That Country by Japan

On the night of July 7, 1937, what in itself seemed a minor affair occurred at Lukuchiao on the outskirts of Peking. Shots were exchanged between a Chinese garrison and a Japanese force which was engaged in maneuvers in an area where it had no legal right to be. The general situation was so tense that the incident was immediately recognized as very grave. As on so many other occasions in history, under circumstances where the trend had long been toward an explosion, a major conflict was set off by what would otherwise have been an inconsequential event.

The Japanese army was ready for the emergency and promptly dispatched heavy reenforcements to Hopei. It did this in spite of the fact that the incident appeared about to be settled locally by the withdrawal of the Chinese troops, the punishment of the responsible Chinese officers, and the suppression of anti-Japanese organizations. The Chinese government, believing that the time for appeasement had passed, also sent large additional forces into Hopei. On July 27 the Japanese took Peking. They moved promptly into Chahar, Suiyüan, and Shansi. In Shansi the Japanese met the Communists and found heavy going. The Communist forces, in theory incorporated (August 1937) into those of the nation as the Eighth Route Army, put up a formidable resistance and kept much of Shansi, especially its western portions, from being overrun by the invader.

The Japanese may have hoped to confine the struggle to the north and to bring that area within their sway, as they had Manchuria, without a general war with China. That, however, was not to be. Infuriated Chinese mobs attacked Japanese in a number of cities in the Yangtze Valley. Several Japanese consulates were closed, Japanese subjects were evacuated, and large contingents of warships and troops were sent for the protection of Japanese interests. As in 1931, fighting broke out in and near Shanghai. It was, however, more intense than six years earlier. The Chinese threw their best troops and their scanty air force into the defense. The outcome could not be long in doubt, for the invaders were clearly superior in mechanized equipment, airplanes, and trained officers, and, having undisputed command of the sea, could pour in and maintain whatever reenforcements were needed. Early in November 1937, the Chinese retreat from Shanghai was begun. Nanking was evacuated by the defenders and was entered by the Japanese early in December of that year. The butchery of defenseless prisoners and civilians and the orgy of looting and rape that attended the occupation of the city were notorious.

The Chinese high command moved westward to Hankow and then, after several months, to Chungking. The latter center, at the westward entrance of the gorges of the Yangtze and protected from approach from the lower river by difficult mountain terrain, was deemed safe except by attack from the air. The Japanese controlled most of the railways and the main ports and possessed full mastery of the air, of the waters of the Yangtze from the coast to beyond Hankow, and of much of the land in which they could employ their superior equipment. On October 21, 1938, four days before they took

Hankow, they seized Canton. In November 1938, Yochow, above Hankow, fell to their arms, followed a number of months later, in June 1940, by Ichang, still farther up the Yangtze. In March 1939, the Japanese took Nanchang, the capital of Kiangsi and an important rail junction. In November 1939, Pakhoi, a port southwest of Canton, was seized, and this step was followed by the occupation of Nanning, also in the south, in an attempt to cut off the flow of supplies from French Indo-China into the free portions of China. Having driven the Chinese from the air, the Japanese bombed at will such cities as seemed to them strategic.

The Japanese conceived their military and naval activities in China as not being war on that country. Indeed, the contest was long carried on without a formal declaration of war. Both sides found advantages in their relations with other powers in not taking that step. Japan, rather, proceeded on the theory that she was freeing China from an oppressive and corrupt regime and was making it possible for the Chinese to set up a better one. She wished, obviously, to have governments which, like that in Manchukuo, would cooperate with her. In the areas she controlled various local administrations were created, staffed by Chinese but with Japanese advisers. What was called the Provincial Government of the Republic of China was organized in Peking in December 1937, with elderly, experienced Chinese, hostile to the Kuomintang, as its officials.

The Japanese endeavored to persuade some outstanding Chinese to head a national government which they could recognize as the legitimate one for all China. They brought pressure upon Wu P'ei-fu, one of the most respected of the war lords of an earlier decade and now living in retirement, to undertake the task, but were rebuffed. Finally they obtained Wang Ching-wei. Wang Ching-wei had been an intimate and trusted friend of Sun Yat-sen and had been prominent in the Kuomintang. He had held high office at Chungking. The reasons for his succumbing to the lure of the Japanese must be in part conjectural. They were probably compounded of pique at other Chungking leaders, ambition, vanity, a conviction that China's best course lay in cooperation with the Japanese, and a belief that he was sufficiently skillful in negotiations to handle the Japanese and preserve China's liberties.

On March 30, 1940, what was proclaimed as the return of the national government to Nanking was celebrated with great pomp. Several other figures active in the Nationalist Party came over with

Wang and the form had been gone through of having him elected by what was styled the orthodox Kuomintang. In theory Wang's regime was based upon the platform of Sun Yat-sen, and in its structure it closely resembled that which had previously had its capital at Nanking. Japan recognized it as legitimate and entered into a treaty with it by which each undertook to respect the sovereignty and territories of the other and to adopt reciprocally helpful and friendly political, economic, and cultural measures with "joint defense" against Communistic activities. As her part in carrying out this latter promise, Japan was to keep troops in the north and in Inner Mongolia. Japan promised to relinquish her extraterritorial privileges. Wang's government recognized Manchukuo by signing a treaty with it and Japan in which the parties promised cooperation and respect for one another's sovereignty. As was to be anticipated, the new Nanking administration was eventually recognized by Japan's associates, Germany and Italy, and their satellites, Franco Spain, Rumania, Slovakia, and Croatia. Yet even this was delayed for over a year. Japanese could persuade themselves that they were attaining their aims in achieving a Far Eastern bloc of friendly governments of which they were the center.

Under the fiction of creating a "coprosperity sphere" embracing China, Manchukuo, and herself, Japan began the economic reorganization of the parts of China Proper which were occupied by her forces. Companies in which the Japanese government owned half the capital were set up for the development of north and central China. Chinese mines, railways, telegraphs, telephone, and bus lines, factories, banks, dockyards, and shipping were handed over to Japanese corporations or subsidiaries either by direct expropriation by the puppet governments or under guises whereby the Chinese retained a share in the ownership but the majority control was held by the Japanese.

Moreover, the Japanese insisted that the schools be reorganized to serve the new regime. They had been hotbeds of anti-Japanese propaganda. The new masters saw to it that textbooks were revised in such fashion as to support them and that Japanese was substituted for English as the second language.

The new governments were clearly subservient to the Japanese. Wang Ching-wei was a pitiable object, completely in the hands of the representatives of the all-powerful "ally." He lingered on, ill and impotent, until, in 1944, death intervened to free him from the misery to which his course had led him. Not many men of repute or character had been willing to cooperate with the Japanese, and the puppet regimes were largely corrupt, fully under the thumbs of their Japanese advisers.

Unoccupied China Carries On

In the meantime the Chinese carried on in the regions into which Japanese arms had not penetrated. Hundreds of thousands of Chinese moved west, beyond the Japanese lines. These included a large proportion of the educated, the people of property, and the more influential. They also counted in their number many in the humbler stations of life. The majority made most or all of the journey on foot, carrying their small possessions with them. Schools, colleges, and universities joined the migration. Students and teachers often went together, in groups, taking with them such laboratory and library equipment as could be carried by the inadequate conveyances available. New locations were found in the west, usually in Szechwan, Kweichow, and Yünnan, but sometimes in coastal provinces in villages or cities presumably beyond the reach of the Japanese armies. A fairly large amount of machinery was transported to western China and there set up in new factories to provide as much as possible of industrial backing for resistance to the invader. Attempts were made to achieve progress in education and government even during the dark days of war and to prepare for the time when the enemy would have been expelled and reconstruction would be possible. It was the hope of rebuilding, indeed, which gave to many Chinese the courage and incentive to keep going. During the early years of the retreat to the west, before the prolongation of the war and the tightening of the Japanese blockade had exacted their heavy toll in inflation and dearth of goods, in some directions real advance was registered. Western China now became permeated as never before with the Occidental influences which had heretofore been most prominent on the coast. Highways were built, enrollments in schools mounted, improvements were made in local governments, industrial cooperatives were organized, the growing of the opium poppy was suppressed, natural resources were surveyed, and attempts were made to bring more fully into the Chinese culture circle the non-Chinese peoples on the Tibetan marches.

Outside western China resistance also continued. Guerrillas made the lives of Japanese insecure outside the main cities and fortified centers. Sections of railways were torn up and traffic impeded. Japanese outposts and advance bands were cut off and exterminated. In North China the Communists proved especially effective. Partly with Communist assistance and direction, local administrations were maintained. Indeed, in time striking changes were made in the government and economic life of "free" China in the north. Progress was registered toward democratic forms of organization, and rents and interest rates were reduced. The Japanese laboriously built an elaborate system of defenses, but Chinese opposition continued formidable.

The Prolongation of the War

Both Chinese and Japanese greatly underestimated the length of the war. The Japanese had expected Chinese resistance to collapse after the capture of Nanking or at the latest after the fall of Hankow. Some leading Chinese believed that Japan would be exhausted after a year of fighting and would be compelled to withdraw.

Early in 1940 the struggle had seemed to reach a stalemate. The Japanese could dominate such regions as they could reach with their ships, whether on the coast or the Yangtze below the gorges, and where their mechanized equipment could operate. Beyond that they appeared unable to go. They seemed to be bogged down, unwilling to retire and unable to advance. The Chinese, on the other hand, appeared merely to hold their own and not to have enough strength to expel the invader. The war had become a test of endurance. Presumably, if the Japanese were willing to pay the price in men and material, they could move anywhere in China. The cost, however, would be very heavy. The strain on Japanese economy, already serious, would be increased. The Japanese decided to rely upon the much slower processes of gradual attrition and blockade. They seem to have counted on the Chinese succumbing to exhaustion before their own resources were dangerously reduced.

Growing Complications with Foreign Powers

Conditions in the Occident increasingly made themselves felt in the Far East. They had been to some degree responsible for the Japanese adventure in 1931. The world-wide financial depression had aggravated Japan's economic problem, thereby adding to the incentive to find relief through expansion on the continent, and had preoccupied the West, so that Japan's leaders felt more nearly secure against possible intervention by Occidental powers. In the 1930's the international situation in Europe was rapidly deteriorating. The Axis was being constituted and was proving aggressive. Its opponents appeared to be divided and supine. Japan aligned herself with the Axis. Her Axis companions were not entirely cordial to her plans. Indeed, for some time German officers served as advisers to the armies of the Chinese government. Yet the Axis was also primarily concerned with Europe and could not interfere with Japan. In September 1939, war broke out in Europe and quickly engulfed most of that continent. In the spring of 1940, Holland was occupied by the Germans, France succumbed, and the English, only partly prepared, suffered disaster at Dunkerque, were seeing their cities hammered by the Nazi air force, and were facing the grim possibility of imminent invasion. The Japanese then saw their opportunity to reduce the power of these three leading colonial powers in the Far East and perhaps to eliminate it, supplanting it by their own "new order in Greater East Asia." It was the opportunity for which some of Japan's leaders had long been charging the nation to watch. Russia was to be feared, but the pact with her in April 1941 mitigated the danger of early war with her, and the Soviets were clearly giving their attention chiefly to Europe—which, after all, was their major concern. They became more deeply involved in the West when, in the summer of 1941, Germany launched her attack on them. Clearly the Soviet government would not, while fighting with its back to the wall in Europe, willingly join in a war with Japan in East Asia.

The French could put up no adequate resistance in Indo-China. Presumably the Japanese might have annexed the region outright, but they chose instead to enter into an agreement with the Vichy regime whereby they were permitted to send troops into the area. This enabled them to block another entrance to unoccupied China. Fairly extensive supplies had been going through Tongking, partly by the railway which wound its tortuous way through the mountains to Kunming, and partly by highway.

Japan's share in the imports to the Netherlands East Indies had been increasing and by 1933 was nearly a third of the whole. This was partly because her manufactures, being cheaper, found a ready market in the islands while they were suffering from the world-wide financial depression. The Japanese were casting about for fresh sources of oil to substitute for supplies from the United States, which, as we are to see in a moment, were threatened. In September 1940, taking advantage of the occupation of the Netherlands by the Nazis, they asked larger quotas of oil, rubber, and tin than had previously been theirs, the privilege of more extensive immigration, and concessions to Japanese companies for the exploitation of the resources of the Indies. The Dutch authorities in the islands were adamant, and in June 1941 a joint statement of the two governments made it clear that Japan had not obtained what she wished.

Japan looked with peculiar disfavor upon her former ally, Great Britain. British financial and commercial interests in China were still strong. Through Hongkong, a British possession, much aid went to the fighting Chinese. A highway constructed by the Chinese with great labor across difficult mountain terrain connected Kunming in "free" China with highways and railways in British-held Burma. While as yet the supplies passing over the Burma Road were a mere trickle, the route had possibilities of large development as a counterbalance to the Japanese blockade. Great Britain, too, to Japan's annoyance, advanced credits to the Chungking government. The British were constrained to suffer indignities at the hands of the Japanese which were peculiarly galling to a people who had been accustomed to rule and had once been dominant in the foreign trade of China. They had to consent to the deposit of the funds collected by the Chinese customs service in the area held by the Japanese in the Yokohama Specie Bank rather than in the (British) Hongkong and Shanghai Banking Corporation. The Japanese authorities made stern and sometimes rough demands for the suppression of anti-Japanese activities in the British and French concessions in Tientsin and in the International Settlement in Shanghai, traditionally chiefly British in its control. In August 1937, the car of the British Ambassador to China, although plainly marked, was bombed and machine-gunned by Japanese, and later in the year several British craft were fired on by Japanese air and land forces. British subjects of lesser note were badly handled in China by the Japanese. Some Japanese seemed to delight in insulting the British and thus showing the latter's impotence. The British government lodged protests, but, engrossed in Europe, could not back them by force. In July 1940, it felt constrained, under Japanese pressure, to close the Burma Road for three months. That highway was reopened in October of that year, but not before British prestige had suffered. In August 1940, moreover, the British troops which remained in China were withdrawn. Great Britain wished, even at great cost, to maintain peace in the Pacific, for she had no forces to spare for war in that region. Of this the Japanese were well aware.

Tension between Japan and the United States

As had been the case since 1905 and especially since 1914, it was from the United States that the chief and most effective Occidental opposition was presented to the Japanese imperial program. This was to be expected. The westward march of the United States and her policy in the Pacific and the Far East had committed her to a course which could not but put her athwart the line of advance marked out by Japan's builders of empire. The great majority of the Japanese were deeply reluctant to come to blows with the United States. They feared her might. Many of Japan's leaders hoped to persuade the United States that her best interests lay in cooperation with Japan and not in opposition to her. However, as we have noted earlier, the two governments were pursuing roads, and had been for a generation, which, if followed, could have only one termination, a head-on collision. Unless one or the other or both would swerve or reverse its course, war must be the outcome. The recent refusal of the United States to recognize Manchukuo was ominous, especially since, quite consistently, the Democratic administration of President Franklin D. Roosevelt adhered to it, although it had been formulated in the preceding Republican administration. Stimson, with whose name that policy had been connected, had the ear of President Roosevelt as he had had of President Hoover. Here was an American policy which transcended party lines and was in accord with the long-time trend in the history of the United States.

Clashes with the United States developed early in the enhanced conflict opened by the incident of July 1937. Early in October 1937, President Roosevelt, in a forthright speech in Chicago, summoned "peace-loving nations" to "make a concerted effort in opposition to those violations of treaties . . . which today are creating a state of international anarchy" and declared that war must be quarantined like an epidemic. The United States participated in a committee of the League of Nations which was attempting to deal with the issue posed by Japan. Although palpably greatly weakened by the chain of events which had been set off in September 1931, the League had taken action on the 1937 crisis, but, as was to be expected, had been rebuffed by Japan. Secretary of State Hull came out flatly against Japan's actions in China as contrary to the Nine Power Treaty and the Pact of Paris. The United States shared in a conference convened in Brussels on the invitation of Belgium, in pursuance of the Nine Power

Treaty, to deal with the issues raised by Japan's advance in China. However, the United States was as yet unwilling to resort to force to implement the treaty, and the other powers made it clear that upon her must rest the burden of applying such sanctions as might be devised. American public opinion was overwhelmingly against Japan's China adventure. A boycott against Japanese goods was promoted by an indignant minority. While it led immediately to only a slight decline in the sale of Japanese products, it was portentous. Moreover, friends of China conducted a campaign for "nonparticipation in Japanese aggression" which had as its objective the prevention of the sale to Japan of scrap iron and gasoline, directly used as they were in the war, especially in the bombing of cities from the air.

In some ways the government of the United States was conciliatory and patient with Japan. It encouraged American citizens to move out of the danger zones and within four months nearly five thousand had been so evacuated. On December 12, 1937, the American gunboat *Panay* and three ships belonging to the Standard Oil Company, which were in the Yangtze, off Nanking, for the protection and use of escaping Americans, were bombed and sunk by Japanese planes. The act was clearly deliberate on the part of the officers directly concerned, but was promptly disavowed by the Japanese government. Tokyo apologized and offered full reparation, and many individual Japanese expressed their deep regret and sought to make amends. Washington presented vigorous demands for indemnification but when these were met declared the incident officially closed. In the following March it withdrew from Shanghai the marines who had been sent there in the emergency and, even more significantly, the detachment of infantry which was in Tientsin in accordance with the terms of the Boxer Protocol. The many violations by Japanese of the treaty rights of Americans in China, both in their persons and property, were protested through the usual diplomatic channels, but the United States government was slow to take more positive measures.

Economic considerations, at least in the short range, might have counseled acquiescence in the Japanese program. Americans sold far more to Japan than to China and bought more from Japan than from her neighbor. Many Japanese, counting on these facts, attempted to persuade the American public that its interests would be better served by the New Order in East Asia than by the continuation of the chronic disorder in China. Americans, however, were not convinced and their moral sense was outraged by what they learned of Japanese actions in the great Asiatic republic.

Both American public opinion and the government of the United States gradually stiffened in their attitude and policies toward Japan. Indeed, the government felt more strongly than the general public and moved as rapidly as the rank and file of its constituency would permit. At the end of 1936, through the expiration by Japanese initiative of the treaty signed at the Washington Conference of 1921–1922 which limited naval armaments and the fortification of island bases in the Pacific, the United States was freed to enlarge her defenses in ships and bases. In 1939 and especially in 1940, after the fall of France, the United States began huge additions to her fleet, the building of submarine and air bases on Guam, Midway, and Wake, and the development of facilities in Alaska and the Aleutian Islands. Defenses in Hawaii were strengthened, and several other islands in the Pacific, heretofore only nominally American, were occupied. The United States would not grant recognition to the Wang Ching-wei regime. In July 1939, acting well within her legal rights, the United States formally denounced her commercial treaty with Japan. After the requisite six months, on January 26, 1940, that agreement expired and Washington was free to place such restrictions upon American trade with Japan as seemed to it good. Before that date, in October 1939, the Ambassador to Japan, Joseph C. Grew, in an address in Tokyo, frankly told the public of the state of opinion in the United States and of the fashion in which it was hardening against Japan. In July 1938, the American Department of State began a "moral embargo" by suggesting that manufacturers and exporters of airplanes desist from sending their products to Japan, since these were employed for bombing civilian populations. In December 1939, it broadened its suggestion to embrace oil companies and their aid in the production of the high-quality gasoline used in airplanes. In July 1940, enabled by an act of Congress, President Roosevelt prohibited, except under license, the export of munitions, many items entering into their manufacture, petroleum products, tetraethyl lead, and first quality iron and steel scrap. While the order was couched in terms which did not specifically direct the embargo against Japan and although it was issued ostensibly on the grounds of national defense, its purport in the Far Eastern situation was clear. In December 1940, the list of commodities requiring licenses for export was extended. On July 25, 1941, on command of the President, both Chinese and Japanese assets in the

United States were "frozen." Under these mounting restrictions, the American market as a source of supplies needed by Japan was first progressively narrowed and then practically closed. Aid, moreover, was being accorded China by the United States through Lend-Lease, the Export-Import Bank, and the Reconstruction Finance Corporation.

The government of the United States also made it increasingly obvious that it was opposed to the extension of Japan's power into southeastern Asia and the East Indies in the time of Europe's misfortunes. When, in 1940, Japan, taking advantage of the weakness of France, sent forces to Indo-China, a spokesman for the Department of State declared that his government was unfriendly toward the substitution of Japanese for French authority. The congealing of Japanese assets in the United States followed so closely upon the Japanese occupation of the region that the connection seemed more than a coincidence. Similar British action and the suspension by the Netherlands East Indies of their oil agreement with Japan whereby the latter had obtained some of its urgently needed supplies followed almost immediately upon President Roosevelt's "freezing" order.

The United States, the British Empire, and the Netherlands Are Drawn into the War

It was apparent that Japan on the one hand and the United States, the British Empire, and the Netherlands on the other were rapidly moving toward war. In April 1941, Japan had freed her hands in the north by her neutrality pact with the USSR. The German invasion of Russia made assurance doubly sure that the Soviets would not engage in war with Japan unless the latter were to invade Siberia. Japan was clearly intent on moving south. This had been foreshadowed when, in 1938, she occupied the Paracels Islands, again when, in 1939, she went into Hainan and the Spratley Islands, and especially by her advance into Indo-China in 1940 and her continued pressure on Thailand and the Netherlands East Indies. It was reasonably certain that the United States government would not tolerate, if it could help it, the Japanese seizure of British Malaya or the East Indies. Because of conditions in Europe the burden of resistance to Japan would fall upon the United States. Public opinion in that country was still divided. Washington was convinced of the danger to the United States of the Japanese program, but was hesitating to go beyond the point where a substantial majority would support it. There were those on both sides who still hoped for peace. The Japanese Ambassador to Washington, Nomura, was among them. To assist him a special representative, Kurusu, was sent in November 1941. In August 1941 the suggestion had been offered from Japan that the Premier and President Roosevelt meet to canvass the situation. On November 20, 1941, Japan proposed that she refrain from further advance in southeastern Asia but only on condition that the United States restore commercial relations with her, supply her with a required quantity of oil, cooperate in obtaining from the Netherlands East Indies the goods and commodities needed by both countries, and refrain from aid to China. On November 26, 1941, the United States countered with a note proposing joint agreement on certain basic principles which included those for which she had traditionally stood in the Far East, and also the abolition of excessive trade restrictions as between nations and the nondiscriminatory access by all nations to raw materials. Some at least of these would help to relieve the economic pressure on Japan as well as militate against Japan's policies on the continent. The note went beyond the enunciation of generalities and set forth concrete proposals, among them being a nonaggression agreement among Japan, China, the British Empire, the Soviet Union, Thailand, the Netherlands, and the United States, the complete withdrawal of Japanese troops from China and Indo-China, the recognition of the Chungking government as the sole legitimate regime in China, and the surrender by both the United States and Japan of extraterritorial privileges in China. In return the United States offered to enter into a commercial treaty in which raw silk should be on the free list and made other proposals for the restoration of trade between the two countries. To such a program Japan could not acquiesce without surrendering the position for which she had been fighting since at least July 1937. It was not surprising that she returned (December 7, 1941) an emphatic no, and that this should take the form of a rehearsal of recent history from the Japanese viewpoint, an accusation that the American and British governments had obstructed Japan's measures for "the establishment of a general peace between Japan and China" and that the American government desired "to maintain and strengthen, in coalition with Great Britain and other powers, its dominant position it has hitherto occupied not only in China but in other areas in East Asia," and a statement that Japan considered it "impossible to reach an agreement through further negotiations." This was more than an ultimatum. It closed the door to discussion or even to a reply. Thus the principles of the open door for which the United States had long stood and of the new order in East Asia of which Japan would be the director had come to an unequivocal impasse. Each power deemed the other to have thrown down the gauntlet. Each profoundly, even passionately believed itself to be in the right. The United States was convinced that she was standing for democracy, freedom, and equal opportunity for all peoples against an aggressive nation which was bent on dominating and ruthlessly exploiting for its selfish ends not only all of the Far East but also all of Asia and, ultimately, the entire world. Japan was persuaded that the United States and Great Britain, especially the United States, were bent upon the domination and enslavement of Far Eastern peoples. She had agreed with her propagandists and their verbiage about the liberating of the Far East from Western imperialism and building a new order in which all peoples in Greater East Asia would cooperate in creating a coprosperity sphere in which each would share. She remembered, bitterly, the discrimination against her nationals in the United States, the refusal at Paris to grant the principle of race equality, and the fashion in which the United States had repeatedly blocked her in the Far East. Her official spokesmen were insistent that the British Empire and the United States must be driven out of the Far East and rendered impotent ever to renew their activities in that region. To employ an ancient paradox, an irresistible force had met an immovable body. The result must be for one or the other an inconceivable catastrophe.

By a sudden and daring act Japan opened the war. At the very time when Nomura and Kurusu were delivering the final note to Secretary of State Hull, but probably without their previous knowledge, the Japanese armed forces had launched an attack upon the American fleet in Pearl Harbor and the main airport in Hawaii. By this spectacular stroke, undoubtedly long and carefully prepared, Japan for the time being rendered incapable of effective counterattack the power whom she had most to fear in the Pacific, the United States. That same day the Japanese bombed Guam, important centers in the Philippines, and Singapore, seized the International Settlement in Shanghai, and put forces in the northern part of Malaya. They also moved from Indo-China into Thailand. Tokyo thereupon announced that a state of war existed with Great Britain and the United States. On December 8 Great Britain, the Netherlands East Indies, and the United States, replying, formally declared war on Japan. Australia followed, and six Latin American countries promptly took similar action.

In attacking Pearl Harbor Japan delivered to the American navy the most serious blow it had ever received. Yet in doing so she lost the war. Her act had in one hour united the American people. They had been divided, hesitant, unready psychologically for vigorous participation in the conflict. Had Japan left American territory, including the Philippines, untouched but continued her advance into southeastern Asia and the East Indies, even though Washington declared war to protect the British and Dutch holdings it is probable that public opinion would not have been unanimously mobilized at any early date in its support. By their dramatic and quite unexpected deed the Japanese had rallied the American people instantly and almost solidly behind the administration in the prosecution of the war.

Japan was protected by distance and by the broad expanse of the Pacific Ocean and as yet the United States was only partly prepared. Since war with other members of the Axis almost automatically followed, the United States must fight a war on two fronts and must first of all direct most of her strength to Europe, where Great Britain, standing alone, was hard bested. Indeed, in December 1941, Japan, Germany, and Italy strengthened through a formal alliance the ties which bound them together in the waging of their common war. Yet when once the huge resources of the United States should be fully mobilized, Japan could not fulfill her daring ambition.

It was significant for the Far East as well as for the United States that the latter had been drawn into the second of the world wars of the century by way of the Pacific rather than the Atlantic. It was no accident, but a culmination of a trend which had long been apparent. It was indicative of the fashion in which American participation in Far Eastern affairs had progressively increased. This came partly in consequence of the westward drive of the American frontier, a constant phenomenon since the beginning of the first settlements on the Atlantic seaboard in the seventeenth century. By successive steps the boundaries of the United States had been pushed to the Pacific, then, through Samoa and Hawaii, into the Pacific, and, through the annexation of Guam and the Philippines, into the Far East. Except for Guam and the Philippines, the United States had, deliberately, not acquired territory in the Far East. She was in process of granting the Philippines their independence. Her open door policy was predicated upon equal opportunity for all nations and exclusive privilege to none, not even herself. By insisting upon it and its corrollaries, however, she had been drawn ever more deeply into Far Eastern affairs. Now she was at war with the strongest military and naval power in that region. Although in the British Empire and China she had important associates, either actually or in prospect potent, she must take the main brunt of providing the sea and air forces and the munitions essential to the winning of the war. What this would entail in her future role in the Far East no one could foresee in detail, but it was obvious that through the war she would be, much more even than earlier, a factor to be reckoned with in Far Eastern affairs.

The Astounding Sweep of Japanese Arms

During the first few months of the enlarged war the Japanese made phenomenal advances. Their armed forces had been drilled and equipped for the kind of warfare involved. For at least the time being their resources, in spite of the long hostilities with China, proved sufficient. Japan seemed to have for her program the quick expulsion of the Americans, the British, and the Dutch from the Far East and the western Pacific while the British, including Australia, New Zealand, and Canada, were engrossed in the European war and before the United States could muster her huge might. Presumably, too, she counted on the absorption of the United States in the Atlantic stage of the struggle and the victory of Germany and Italy, then, to her mind, assured: Germany, at the height of her advance, was overrunning much of Russia's most fertile and populous lands. Once safely entrenched in East Asia and the East Indies, Japan could utilize the resources of those regions for long scale, effective resistance and could, at her leisure, complete the reduction of such opposition as remained in China and among peoples of lesser numerical strength. In time, having availed herself of the riches of the Far East, she might even carry the war into the enemies' home bases, take Hawaii, invade the west coast of America, reduce Australia, bring India into her circle, and settle accounts with Russia. Some such design was in the minds of at least several of her leaders and at the outset seemed to have some prospect of achievement.

In the closing days of that fateful December 1941 and in the first half of 1942, Japanese arms were carried so far that many of the leaders and the rank and file of the nation were confirmed in their belief in their invincibility. Hongkong, for not quite a hundred years a British possession and the center of British strength on the China coast, capitulated on Christmas Day, less than three weeks after Pearl Harbor. On that same day the capital of Sarawak, on the west coast of Borneo and a symbol of British power on that island, fell to Japanese prowess. To the bewildered amazement of much of the world, the Japanese moved rapidly down the Malay Peninsula through terrain which it was supposed would hold them for months or years and perhaps prove impassable. Their planes sank two great British battleships and so dealt what, for the time being, was an irreparable blow to British naval strength in the Far East. On February 15, 1942, less than two and a half months after Pearl Harbor, Singapore and its famed naval base surrendered. Thus was the British Empire seemingly erased from southeastern Asia. In January, under two months from Pearl Harbor, the Japanese had established themselves in the Solomon Islands and were threatening the route by which American aid was beginning to be sent to Australia. Guam had already fallen and a few weeks later Wake Island, after an heroic resistance, had followed. The Netherlands East Indies were rapidly reduced. The Dutch forces, never large, had been reenforced by Australian troops, American aircraft, and British, American, and Australian ships. These, however, proved "too little and too late." They put up a brave fight, inflicting heavy punishment on the Japanese, but March saw the capture of Batavia, the capital.

Sporadic resistance elsewhere was soon overcome. Before summer the Japanese were bombing ports in northern Australia and were pushing into New Guinea, presumably with Australia as their ultimate objective. By the middle of March, Japanese forces, driving into Burma from Thailand, had taken Rangoon and were moving north toward Mandalay. By May they had captured Lashio, a Burma terminus of the famous highway to China. They shortly completed the occupation of Burma. The exodus of Indian and Occidental civilians and of the defeated armies from Burma through the difficult mountain and jungle trails to Assam was marked by intense suffering and much loss of life. The Andaman and Nicobar Islands fell. The British Empire was being pushed back to India. The Japanese were also threatening that realm and bombing some of its cities. Here, as we are to see a little later, nationalist agitation was giving anxiety to the troubled British *raj*. The attack on the Philippines which began on the same day as the raid on Pearl Harbor was pressed from several directions. Filipinos and Americans both resisted. The defense was ultimately, except for scattered forces in the hills, driven back to the

Bataan Peninsula and to Corregidor, both near Manila. Bataan capitulated on April 9, but not before the commander, General MacArthur, on orders from Washington, had escaped. He was to renew the battle, with telling effect, from Australia and the south. Corregidor, a stronghold also near Manila, surrendered on May 7, after bitter fighting.

Within six months after she had launched her lightning attack, Japan had all but eliminated Occidental colonial rule from southeastern Asia and the East Indies. Of the vast domains under the control of the West on December 7, 1941, only French Indo-China and Portuguese Timor and Macao remained, and these were held in collaboration with and only by the consent of the Japanese. By midsummer of 1942 Japanese forces had even established themselves on some of the Aleutians and were threatening the mainland of Alaska. A blow had been given to the imperial possessions of the Occident such as had not been known, even in the defeat of Russia in 1904–1905, since the beginning of the expansion of Europe at the close of the fifteenth century. By careful preparation and ingenious new methods of warfare the Japanese had, for the moment, worsted two of the mightiest of the Western nations. It had been demonstrated that by adopting the science and mechanical techniques of the Occident a non-Occidental nation could successfully challenge the West, at least on the periphery of its holdings.

The Continued Tightening of the Japanese Noose about China

To the Chinese the entrance of the United States and the British Empire into the Far Eastern war had as an immediate result not relief but a heightening of their distresses. By her seizure of Hongkong and Burma Japan cut off the two most important remaining doors by which help from the outer world could reach "free" China. The long overland tracks across Sinkiang to Russia were still open, but were of little assistance. The distance and physical difficulties of the route, the preoccupation of Russia with her struggle with Germany, and a natural reluctance to give Japan an excuse for launching an attack on Siberia and thus bringing to the Soviets a two-front war militated against much aid by that road. Air connections were established and developed with India by Chinese and American pilots. However, the route was over some of the most tangled mountain chains in the world and was subject to attack by Japanese aircraft operating from Burma. Eventually more freight was brought in each month by air over this "hump" than had ever been conveyed over the Burma Road, but most of it was for the American air forces which were built up in China. Through her augmented blockade Japan was slowly strangling that republic. The effects were seen in a rapidly mounting inflation and the continued lack of equipment for China's hard-pressed armies.

Japan Attempts to Consolidate and Exploit Her Holdings

The Japanese now set themselves to the task of making secure their hold upon the territories which had come into their possession and of developing their resources in such fashion that effective resistance could be presented to the counterattack which was certain to be launched from the United States once that country could equip itself for the fray. They also kept in mind a long program for "Greater East Asia" in which the entire vast area would be knit into a "coprosperity sphere."

The range of what was denominated Greater East Asia was not given precise official definition. Individual spokesmen differed as to the boundaries. Expediency and the course of events would broaden or constrict the area to be embraced. The Japanese Empire as it existed in 1937, Manchukuo, and the rest of China were certainly to be the core. Southeastern Asia, the Philippines, and the East Indies were also within the circle. Some wished to include northeastern Asia as far as Lake Baikal, and would reach southward and eastward to take in Australia and many of the islands of the Pacific.

To coordinate policy and administer Greater East Asia there was set up by Japan the East Asia Development League. This was to be affiiliated with the Imperial Rule Aid Association. It was to conduct research and frame policy. Later (November 1942) there was created the Greater East Asia Ministry.

Soon after the conquest of the areas taken subsequent to Pearl Harbor, a military administration was devised for each major geographic unit. Over every territorial division a commander, either from the army or the navy, was placed. Under each commander were departments of general affairs, industry, finance, and transportation, and prefectural and branch offices.

In their program the Japanese were systematic, comprehensive, and thorough, and were planning for permanent control.

The Japanese endeavored, as they had in Manchuria and the other parts of China which they had already occupied, to bring into being regimes that would cooperate with them. They had come into the former holdings of Western powers with vigorous assertions that they were freeing the region from the white man's yoke. These promises they went through the form of implementing. Perhaps some of their leaders were sincere in their protestations. In theory Manchukuo and the Wang Ch'ing-wei regime which had been set up before Pearl Harbor were free and sovereign. Japan also proceeded to grant to the Philippines and Burma what she called independence. In former British Malaya and in several centers in the East Indies councils composed of natives were set up and were professedly given consultative powers to the military governments. At least at the outset the Japanese were respecting many of the indigenous customs and institutions.

The Japanese were, however, striving to bring the peoples of Greater East Asia within their own cultural sphere. For Dutch in the East Indies and for English, which was the second language in much of China, the Philippines, and the former British possessions, they were attempting to substitute their own tongue. The use of Japanese was furthered through radio, schools, and newspapers. The Japanese sought to purge all these areas of the ideological influences which had come in from Great Britain, the Netherlands, and the United States. American and British music was to be eradicated by the prohibition of the playing of records which contained it. British and American moving pictures were proscribed and for them were substituted Japanese, Chinese, and native films. The peoples of the East Indies, the Philippines, and southeastern Asia were reminded of their exploitation by their former Occidental rulers. The treatment of Negroes in the United States, the policy of Great Britain in India, and the American exclusion of Chinese were played up as evidence of the contempt and ill treatment of nonwhite peoples by American and British arrogance. In the regular schools and in special institutions inaugurated for the purpose, the Japanese language was taught and instruction given in Japanese history, literature, culture, and ideals. Youth organizations were brought into being in Burma and the Philippines to support the regimes which were instituted and to train promising elements in the rising generation in admiration for Japan and cooperation with her. Attempts were made to use existing religions to strengthen the ties with Japan. A League of Moslems in Greater East Asia was created, even though Islam was almost nonexistent in Japan Proper. Buddhism, already conveniently strong in Japan, was employed to cement in Japanese friendship the predominantly Buddhist peoples of southeastern Asia. Japanese Christians were encouraged to form connections with those of their faith in China, the Philippines, and the East Indies. Political parties which would collaborate with the Japanese were begun.

In the economic sphere efforts were pushed to weave all of the newly acquired empire into an interdependent whole. As will be remembered from our first chapter, Greater East Asia was rich in natural resources. While not possessing as much coal and iron as the United States and Europe, it had large supplies of these minerals. It had vast stores of petroleum, especially in the East Indies and Burma. In natural rubber, quinine, and tin it led the world. It was outstanding in antimony, manganese, bauxite, chromite, copra, teak, hemp, rice and many other minerals and products of the soil. It had a huge population, a matchless reservoir of man power for labor or war. Properly stimulated and directed, Greater East Asia could in time be given a much higher standard of living and increase in importance in the total world scene. For the moment, the resources must be organized for the prosecution of the war. In some of the conquered areas damage had been done to the oil wells, docks, and other physical equipment, either by the former owners to render them useless for the enemy or by the operations of war. These must be repaired or rebuilt as quickly as possible. There were also problems of labor. Existing banking, currency, and business organizations had been upset and must be revamped or replaced. Long range planning was required to realize fully the "coprosperity sphere," but for the moment it must not be allowed to interfere with the more urgent task of winning the war.

In general, during the war years the industrial development of Japan, Manchuria, and the northern part of China Proper was stressed. Korea, previously kept chiefly as a source of raw materials and food, was rapidly industrialized. Here, from the heart of the Empire, would come the manufactures needed for the prosecution of the struggle. Here, in case the periphery of the Empire was lost, a last and possibly effective stand could be made, perhaps for years. Some of the textile machinery from Japanese factories, idle because of the cutting off of part of the prewar export markets, might be transported to the East Indies or the Philippines and set up to supply the local need for cottons. However, shipping was increasingly a problem and as yet not enough raw cotton was grown in these regions to justify an extensive factory development. The newly conquered territories were called upon to furnish food and raw materials, especially petroleum, rubber, iron, and rice. Plans were made for growing cotton in the Philippines and Thailand to take the place of that which had previously come from India and the United States. Long range programs which would issue in improved conditions of the masses must wait upon the still highly doubtful ultimate victory of the imperial forces.

All was not going well in Greater East Asia. The evicted Western powers were beginning to recover from their initial defeats and to regain the ground they had lost. Japanese shipping, essential to full utilization of Greater East Asia, was burdened to supply the huge armies maintained overseas and was being depleted by the attacks of submarines, airplanes, and surface craft. Efforts were made to replace losses by new construction, but until 1945 the outside world could not know how effective these were proving to be. In southeastern Asia and the East Indies the cutting off by war of accustomed markets brought serious dislocation to labor which had previously found employment on rubber, tobacco, and sugar plantations. In "occupied" China the continued resistance of guerrillas and the armies of Chungking and Yenan interfered with agriculture and industry. Labor was forced into channels which would contribute to the war effort. Since, from the Japanese standpoint, the struggle was being waged for the liberation of the subject peoples of East Asia, the prospective beneficiaries must be asked to make sacrifices for the attainment of that end. Paper money issued by the Japanese authorities or the puppet governments generally depreciated in value. Jealousies and dissensions were rife between the navy and the army and between individual officers in both services. Corruption was said to be common in Japanese officialdom. Trade went on across the shifting and blurred boundaries between "unoccupied" and "occupied" China—with the connivance of authorities on both sides. These were conditions which might have existed under the conquering armies of any nation and did not necessarily spell collapse. They did, however, indicate weakness.

Efforts of the Occidental Powers to Offset Japanese Propaganda

Since the Japanese declared that they were fighting to liberate the peoples of East Asia from the tyranny of the Occidental, it became expedient for their enemies to offer tangible evidence that they wished the emancipation of the nations of that region from the subject status and the discriminations under which they had held them. Moreover, progressive elements, especially in the United States, took the occasion to press for the immediate adoption of changes which they had long advocated.

The Netherlands government declared that it had as its purpose a reorganization of its empire by which its colonial holdings would be placed more nearly on an equal and coordinate basis with the Kingdom of the Netherlands. Presumably this would be in continuation of the movement toward self-government which had been in progress for a number of years. Great Britain announced that as soon as possible after the war Burma would be granted the status of a Dominion. The United States made clear its purpose to give the Philippines their independence. In 1943 in new treaties with China Great Britain and the United States relinquished the extraterritorial privileges which had long been a source of irritation. By the repeal (1943) of the exclusion acts against the Chinese and permitting Chinese to be naturalized, the United States removed another cause of ill will.

The Beginning of the Retreat of the Japanese Tide

By the summer of 1942, except for China, the Japanese tide of conquest had reached its high-water mark and was checked. It was soon forced into retreat.

The task which confronted the British Empire and the United States as they addressed themselves to Japan was formidable in the extreme. China was showing the strain of the long war and did so increasingly as the months and years dragged on their exhausting course. Because of the tight Japanese blockade, almost no direct help could be given her. Most of what was flown in over the "hump" had to be concentrated on equipping and maintaining the American air force in that country. Desperately needed trucks and heavy artillery could not be brought in by air but must wait upon the reopening of old roads or the building of new ones. Japan had the advantage given by distance. The broad Pacific separated her home land from the United States, and she was halfway around the world from the British Isles. After her capture of Guam, Singapore, and Java she had possession of all the naval bases in the Far East and presumably could be reached only by fleets operating from far-off centers such as Hawaii, Australia, Ceylon, and India. Should her enemies succeed in penetrating the outer defenses which her new conquests had given her, each mile which brought them nearer to her would be to their disadvantage and to her advantage, for the spaces over which they must operate would be that much broader and those which separated her forces from her home land that much narrower. Moreover, while Japan could concentrate all her energies on the Far East, Great Britain's chief task was in Europe where her very existence was still in peril and the United States had decided that in her efforts priority must be given to the defeat of Germany and Italy. Not until these enemies had been eliminated could the United States and Great Britain devote their energies chiefly to the Pacific and the Far East. Even Australia and New Zealand, put in imminent jeopardy by the rapid and unexpected Japanese conquests, had many of their troops in far-away theaters of war. Great Britain promised that when Germany and Italy had been disposed of, she would throw her full weight into the Far Eastern struggle. However, her resources were not so great as those of America and had been seriously depleted by the war in the Occident. The major part of the burden of defeating Japan would fall upon the United States.

The war against Japan was waged from all directions. The Chinese continued to engage the attention of a large proportion of her army. The American air force which was built up in China constructed air fields from Szechwan to Fukien. From these it operated against Japanese troops, ships, and air fields in China. From them, too, huge American planes bombed industrial centers in Manchuria and the Japanese Islands. Chinese planes, supplied by the United States, also fought against the Japanese in China. Presumably some of Japan's best troops were kept in Manchuria to watch the northern border, either against a possible Russian breach of the neutrality pact or in case the defeat of Russia in the West were to give the Japanese their long-awaited opportunity to acquire eastern Siberia. Attack was prepared from India. In that land a large army was being recruited and trained and strengthened by British contingents. There, too, as a springboard against Japan, the United States sent thousands of troops. In India Chinese, forced out of Burma, were being drilled and equipped by Americans. It was hoped that Japan could be early driven out of the north of Burma and road communication could be established with China. By 1945 this had been in part accomplished. In 1942, 1943, and 1944 there was fighting on the India-Burma borders and early in 1944 the Japanese pushed forward in a land drive which they heralded as a step to free India from British rule. The Japanese encouraged and assisted a radical Indian nationalist leader who, in exile, had sought their help, and talked of an Indian army which they were equipping for the emancipation of its native land. For a time they made progress, but before the year 1944 was over they had been driven back. Moreover, America, Chinese, and British forces pressed into the north of Burma. A pipe line to bring oil to China was constructed across difficult terrain from Assam and a road was being built to connect Assam with Yünnan. British planes bombed Japanese posts in Sumatra and Singapore. It was long, however, before Great Britain could spare from Europe and the Mediterranean a naval force of sufficient size to conduct a large scale offensive across the Bay of Bengal to recover her former holdings. Americans and Canadians, especially the former, pushed the attack from the north. A great highway was built to Alaska, Alaskan centers were fortified, in the summer of 1943 the last of the Japanese were driven from the Aleutians, and the war was carried by both sea and air to the Japanese-owned Kuriles. British and American submarines took heavy toll on Japanese shipping. Australians joined in beating back the Japanese in New Guinea.

However, through the year 1944 the major advances against Japan were by frontal attacks, chiefly American, directly across the Pacific. In May 1942, in the Battle of the Coral Sea, the American navy inflicted a significant defeat upon its Japanese rival. The following month saw an even more striking American naval victory in the Battle of Midway. The former battle kept the Japanese from pressing farther south and severing direct American sea communications with Australia. The outcome of the latter appears to have been determinative against Japanese efforts to force the struggle nearer to Hawaii and the west coast of the United States. In the spring of 1942 a carrier-based American air force raided Tokyo. In the summer of 1942 American forces, by bitter amphibious warfare, won a foothold on Guadalcanal, in the Solomon Islands. In the months which followed their first operations in the Solomons the Americans continued to press north and west. By the spring of 1944 the Americans had gone far toward expelling the last of the Japanese from the island of New Guinea. By that time, moreover, they had pushed forward into the New Britain Archipelago and the Gilbert and Marshall Islands. By the end of 1944 they had taken Saipan, in the Marianas, and were utilizing it as a base from which to bomb Tokyo. They had recaptured Guam and were in process of constructing there a major naval base. They were bombing the Volcano and Bonin groups and several islands in the East Indies. They had bombed important centers on Formosa. In even more spectacular fashion they had landed large forces on the islands of Leyte and Mindoro in the Philippines and had inflicted disastrous defeats upon the Japanese naval forces which were attempting to prevent the invasion and to crush the American fleet.

The Continued Japanese Advance in China

Although, in 1944, Japan was being pushed back from the periphery of her post-Pearl Harbor advances and was suffering from the attrition of her navy and her merchant marine, she continued to press forward in China. Indeed, near the close of 1944 the plight of China seemed more nearly desperate than at any time since the beginning of the Japanese invasion. We saw a few pages back that in consequence of the spread of the Far Eastern war to the British Empire and the United States the immediate situation for China had become worse. By her attack on the British Empire Japan had been able to plug two of the remaining holes, Hongkong and Burma, in the barrier by which she was encircling China. Her capture of the Philippines and the East Indies gave her possession of remaining bases from which blockade runners might have operated or from which planes might have obstructed her naval patrol. Little early aid could be given, therefore, to the beleaguered Chinese armies. Chinese, hoping that the unequivocal entrance of the two greatest naval powers on their side would ease their situation, were deeply disappointed and saw their condition rendered more rather than less difficult.

As her Occidental enemies, especially the United States, began to constrict the newly enlarged borders of her empire and to build air fields in China, Japan augmented her efforts to knock her huge neighbor out of the war. Her purpose seems to have been compounded of several desires. She wished to complete the conquest before effective help could reach the Chinese. This was beginning to come over the "hump." In 1944, the recapture of the northern portions of Burma by the British, Americans, and Chinese appeared imminent and, in consequence, the opening of a road or roads by which additional assistance could be brought in. The American and American-supplied Chinese air forces in China were beginning to be a threat not only to the Japanese in China but also to Japan Proper. Unless the fields on which they were based could be taken, they would increasingly imperil the Japanese at home, on the sea, and in China. The continued destruction of Japanese shipping by American and British air, undersea, and sea forces put in jeopardy the water communications between Japan and her possessions. It became important, therefore, to have, as nearly as might be, through land routes. These could best be obtained by controlling the lines which, with the single break at the Yangtze between Hankow and Wuchang, gave rail connection between Manchuria and Canton. Roads traversable by automobiles stretched southward from that railway into Indo-China and the Malay Peninsula. Japan's traditional dependence had been upon her army rather than her navy. Could the land routes be in its hands, the army could carry on with less support from the navy. The navy, indeed, was proving a broken reed.

In 1944, accordingly, the Japanese army pressed its attack in China. It won victories in Honan. Driving southward from the Yangtze and northward and westward from Kwangtung, it completed its seizure of the railway from Wuchang to Canton, and this in spite of dogged fighting by the Chinese and the attacks of the American and Chinese air forces. It pushed westward along branch lines and threatened Kweiyang and Kunming, vital centers on the land and air arteries from Burma and India. It forced the abandonment of several of the air fields. By the end of the year 1944, the Japan radio claimed that the army had attained its immediate objective and had established land communications from Manchuria to Indo-China. It had bisected China and largely cut off the American air fields in the East from their base of supplies in the West and in India. The Japanese army appeared to be intent on quickly eliminating China from the war and to be making greater progress toward this end than at any time since hostilities had begun. The stalemate which had seemed to exist in 1940 had been broken and Japan was again on the march. Chinese counterattacks forced back the Japanese from a few advanced positions, but at the end of 1944 the position of the Chungking regime was worse than it had been six months earlier.

The Japanese Retreat Is Accelerated

The collapse of Germany in the spring of 1945 enabled the United States and the British Empire to concentrate their efforts on Japan.

By August 1945, Japanese forces were being pushed back, even in China, and Japan Proper was feeling the weight of the American air and naval attack. Americans had cleared most of the Japanese from the Philippines and had taken strategic Iwo in the Volcano group and important Okinawa in the Ryukyu Islands. The Japanese navy had been all but destroyed. Most of the chief cities and many of the smaller cities of Japan Proper had been heavily bombed. The Japanese had been driven out of most of Burma and land communication had been opened between "free" China and India by the Ledo Road. In China the Japanese were being forced back. The British and Australians had gained footholds in Borneo.

The War a Life and Death Struggle

By the middle of 1945, as in December 1941 and in 1937 and 1931, the struggle in the Far East was for vast stakes. Each side announced itself to its constituency and to the world as intent on total victory and the reduction of its enemies to the place where they could no longer be a menace. Leading Japanese insisted that they would construct the Greater East Asia Coprosperity Sphere. This, they declared, entailed so overwhelming the British Empire and the United States that these powers could never again make themselves felt in Far Eastern affairs. Great Britain and the United States, through their official spokesmen, were committed to the "unconditional surrender" of Japan. Late in 1943 Prime Minister Churchill, Generalissimo Chiang Kai-shek, and President Roosevelt met in Cairo and as a result of their conference issued a communique in which they made it clear that they purposed stripping Japan of her conquests, including Formosa, the Pescadores, Manchuria, Korea, and the islands given her in the Pacific by mandate. This would mean reducing her to her dimensions of 1894. In July 1945, at Potsdam, the terms demanded of Japan were made still more sweeping, and included the occupation of that country and the destruction of Japanese war potential. If such aims were persistently maintained the fight would be to a finish, until one or the other belligerent was completely subdued. It seemed clear that it was Japan which was to be overwhelmed.

Japan Surrenders

August 1945, brought startling developments. The war came to a quick conclusion. On the sixth day of that month Americans demonstrated in spectacular fashion the efficacy of an amazing new weapon by dropping an atomic bomb on the Japanese city of Hiroshima. Two days later they dropped a second of these bombs on Nagasaki, with telling effect. On that same day, August 8, Russia, pursuing a course determined upon before the release of the atomic bombs, declared war on Japan. She moved her forces rapidly into Manchuria. On August 10 the Japanese offered to surrender on the basis of the terms offered by the Potsdam declaration. The Allies assented on condition that the Emperor be subject to the orders of the commander of the forces which would occupy Japan. Japan agreed and on August 14 the announcement of Japan's capitulation was made. On September 2 (September 1, by the time in the United States) the text of the surrender was signed by the Japanese and by representatives of the Allies on board an American battleship in the bay of Tokyo. Before that day most of the widely flung Japanese armies had ceased fighting, and occupying forces had already begun to move into Japan. For the first time in recorded history invaders were triumphantly established on the soil of Japan.

The terms of the Potsdam declaration issued by the United States, Great Britain and China on July 27 and later acceded to by Russia were drastic. These included the elimination of those who had led the Japanese into war, the occupation of Japan until Japan's war-making power should be destroyed, the implementing of the Cairo communique, and the limiting of Japanese sovereignty to the islands of Honshu, Hokkaido, Kyushu, Shikoku, and such minor islands as the Allies should determine. Yet the Japanese were promised that they would not be enslaved as a race or destroyed as a nation, that they would be permitted to maintain such industries as would sustain their economy "and permit the exaction of just reparations in kind" but not those which would enable them to rearm for war. The Japanese Government was to promise to "remove all obstacles to the revival and strengthening of democratic tendencies among the Japanese people" and "freedom of speech, of religion and of thought, as well as respect for fundamental human rights," were to be established. The occupying forces were to be withdrawn when these objectives had been attained and there had "been established, in accordance with the freely expressed wish of the Japanese people, a peacefully inclined and responsible government." The surrender of Japanese armed forces was to be unconditional.

It was highly significant that assent to these terms and the surrender were carried out in the name of the Emperor. Moderate elements in Japan had triumphed over the extreme belligerent elements which had precipitated the war. For the moment, at least, the traditional structure of the Japanese state remained intact.

Russia Re-enters China

On August 25, 1945, a Russo-Chinese pact was announced which appeared to unite the United States and Russia in support of the Nationalist government in China and to make for the bridging of the gulf between the Kuomintang and the Communists in that divided land. The pact was made by Moscow with Chungking and not with Yenan. The regime recognized and aided by the United States was the one with which Russia entered into agreement. Russia seemed to have ignored the Chinese Communists and to have left them to fend for themselves. The pact was to run for thirty years and was then to be renewed for an unlimited period unless one of the parties denounced it a year before its expiration. Russia agreed to give military supplies and moral support to the Nationalist government. She promised to withdraw her troops from Manchuria within three months after Japan's formal surrender and she agreed to keep her hands off China's internal affairs and to avoid interference in Sinkiang. In return the Chinese Eastern Railway and the South Manchuria Railway were to be operated jointly by China and Russia, Dairen was to be a free port open to all nations but administered by China, Port Arthur was to be used jointly by Russia and China as a naval base, and China was to recognize the independence of Outer Mongolia if a plebiscite held in that land showed a desire for that status. Russia, however, was to respect the political independence and territorial integrity of Outer Mongolia. This pact was in accord with an agreement earlier made at Yalta between Russia and the United States.

The Enhanced Power of Russia and the United States

The downfall of Japan would obviously enhance the power of Russia in the Far East, but especially would it augment that of the United States. The British and the Dutch would seek to return to their former possessions and Australia and New Zealand would wish a voice in the final settlement, but of the Occidental states the United States was now unquestionably dominant in the air and on the sea in the Far East and was potent on the land. She would undoubtedly retain bases in the Western Pacific and the Far East and would be more active there than at any time before Pearl Harbor.

Internal Developments in China, 1941–1944

As Japan pushed forward her military front at the expense of "free" China, important developments within that land were taking place. They were connected with the military situation but were extremely complex. China was continuing to change, and so rapidly that those, whether Chinese or foreign, who had been out of the country for two or three years found it difficult if not impossible to keep fully abreast of movements and the many currents of public sentiment.

In "occupied" China Japan gave the appearance of granting more power to the Nanking government, that which she deemed the sole legitimate one for the Republic. In 1943 she completed the handing over to Chinese administration of her concessions in five Chinese cities and the British concession in Canton and Tientsin. Italy surrendered to the Chinese her concession in Tientsin, and France turned over to Nanking her similar holdings in Tientsin, Hankow, and Canton. On August 1, 1943, the International Settlement at Amoy was passed to the Chinese and, still more significantly, the International Settlement in Shanghai, long the center and symbol of foreign special privilege, was abolished as a separate administrative area. Steps were taken to restore full Chinese authority in the French concession in the same port. Although Japan did not immediately keep in full her promise to surrender extraterritoriality, she announced in 1943 that she had given to Nanking the right to tax Japanese citizens and their property. Presumably her action was hastened by the surrender by Great Britain and the United States of their extraterritorial privileges. Both Germany and Italy maintained embassies in Nanking. The Japanese also professed to have returned to their "rightful owners" scores of industrial plants in the Yangtze Valley, to be relinquishing some of their monopolies in the fields of production, distribution, and transportation, and to be easing transit restrictions and duties within the "occupied" areas. Many of the actions of Japan might be, in practice, nullified by the close supervision exercised by her officials, but on paper they seemed significant. Thus the Axis on the one hand and the democratic powers on the other were bidding for the support of Chinese public opinion by surrendering remnants of the special privileges won in an earlier day and against which the Chinese had long been protesting. The Japanese, too, were, at least on paper, relaxing some of their more recently acquired control. Presumably when Japan was eventually expelled, the Chinese would not consent to the restoration of the International Settlements and the other foreign concessions to their prewar status. Through the bitter contentions among the foreign powers China was making some gains.

China, both "free" and "occupied," was suffering from inflation. In "free" China prices shot upward and by the middle of 1944 were two and three hundredfold more than in 1937. By the spring of 1945 they had climbed to two thousand times the 1937 figures. Inflation, as in most countries, bore especially heavily on salaried groups, notably teachers, clerks, and government employees. Some farmers benefited by the high prices for their products, and many merchants and some officials found ways of profiting by the distresses of their fellows. In "occupied" China the inflation appears to have been even more acute than in "free" China.

The growing bodies of American forces in "free" China brought problems. The Chungking government, already bearing extremely heavy burdens, provided much of the food for them. These purchases depleted the surrounding countryside of supplies of meat. The gulf between the high standards of living of the Americans and many of the Chinese about them and difficulties in the exchange between currencies gave rise to irritation. Some of the Americans were openly scornful and were palpably impatient with what they regarded as the corruption, inefficiency, and divisions among the Chinese. The Chinese were highly sensitive. Late in 1944 the growing friction issued in an explosion which removed from China the commanding general of the American troops, Stilwell, and gave rise to much criticism of China in the American press.

"Free" China was far from fully united politically, and the growing pressure of the Japanese seemed to accentuate rather than lessen the dissensions. The one-party government of the Kuomintang continued. Against it much plain speaking was directed and the leaders so far yielded that they granted more of representative government. The People's Political Council, a recent creation, became increasingly an organ for the free expression of public opinion. Yet concentration camps were maintained for those deemed dangerous and some liberals, although they were not Communists, were executed. There were factions within the Kuomintang. Among these were some who tended toward what was loosely termed Fascism, but others were moderate. Secret societies and various dissident groups, even in Szechwan, the seat of the national administration, flouted so far as they dared the authority of Chungking. Chiang Kai-shek retained his leadership. Indeed, if anything, it was strengthened. In China, as in other countries, the exigencies of war tended to put more power in the hands of the single executive.

As earlier, the chief division was between the Kuomintang and the Communists. The Communists maintained a representative at Chungking, but the latter kept some of its best troops on the border to watch them. Each had a profound distrust of the other which went back to 1926 and 1927. However, there was little or no open fighting between the two elements. The Communists possessed their own administration, a distinct currency and postal system, and a separate army. They had an iron party discipline, a rigid censorship, secret police, and "traitors' camps," concomitants of their totalitarian regime. In the area which they controlled they were making improvements in the livelihood of the people and were effecting a reorganization of the forms of local government which they claimed were in the direction of democracy. They were also putting up what seemed to be a formidable defense against the Japanese. Yet many, both inside and outside the Kuomintang, feared that if peace were made on their terms the Communists would seek to dominate all China and enforce, perhaps ruthlessly, their ideology. Many were apprehensive, moreover, that Russia would use the Communist regime as a means of extending her influence and perhaps her control. This seemed the more possible since the Communist territory was in the north and, in the event that Russia were to enter the war against Japan or were to take advantage of the defeat of Japan to bring Manchuria within her sphere, the Communist state might enlarge its borders and become either a member of the USSR or closely allied with it. Relative to the Kuomintang, the influence of the Communists was growing.

Under the stress of prolonged war, in some quarters corruption, self-seeking, and inefficiency became notorious. Most of China's armies were poorly fed and clothed and even more poorly equipped with arms and munitions. Some of the troops turned on the countryside and, to obtain provisions, preyed on the rural civilian population until the latter turned against them. Since, until 1945, trucks could neither be brought in nor manufactured, much of the transportation depending on them was breaking down. Other forms of motor fuel than gasoline were in wide use—camphor, charcoal, wood oil, and alcohol.

In spite of the weaknesses advances were being made. By 1944 more than half the children of Szechwan were in school and in "free" China more children were in educational institutions than in all China in 1937. So, too, in "free" China both secondary schools and universities had a larger total enrollment in 1944 than in all China seven years earlier. Many students were suffering from undernourishment and the tuberculosis which that entailed. Thousands were separated from their families. Many were discouraged and listless. All, especially in the higher schools, were handicapped by pitifully inadequate equipment in libraries and laboratories. The paper shortage was acute. Hundreds of students were working with their hands in gardening and other occupations. This was necessary if they were to maintain life and continue at their studies, but it was a radical innovation in the ancient mores by which the scholar despised manual labor. Teachers were suffering, sometimes more than the students. Yet education went on. Model governments were developing in the *hsien*, the basic local administrative units, and the quality of the *hsien* officials was improving. The graft was usually not there but higher, in government contracts. Better roads were being built. There was much reading of newspapers and a general awareness of the main course of events not only in China but also in the rest of the world. Rural and industrial cooperatives were appearing.

Moreover, trends in progress before 1940, 1937, and 1931 were still present and were being accentuated. Nationalism was on the increase. It displayed itself in many ways, partly in anti-Japanese feeling and partly in sharp criticism of the English and of the British record in China and in India. Strong sympathy was felt in some quarters for the aspirations of the Indian Nationalists. The techniques of modern mass education were being employed by both the Kuomintang and the Communists. The radio and dramatics were in use for this purpose, and teams of students were sent out to instruct the rank and file of the population. Women continued to develop a new status with growing emancipation from former restraints and conventions. Increasingly doors were opening to them in government, business, and industry. The old patriarchal family system was continuing on the road to what appeared to be desuetude, the influence of clan elders was waning, and the "small" family was increasing. These changes in the social structure were hastened by the vast migrations from "occupied" to "free" China and the attenuation or complete severance of the previous family roots.

Much of western China was being brought more to accept the

control of the Nationalist government than at any time during the Republic. This was the case in the border regions between China Proper and Tibet. It was also true in Sinkiang. Sinkiang was still semi-autonomous, but it was less under Russian influence than it had been in the 1930's. Moreover, the threat of the Japanese westward advance had tended to make stronger the somewhat weak ties with Chungking. Here and there were developments in roads and industries and awareness of mineral resources which might make the region of more use to China Proper.

Within "occupied" China Japan was having an effect which in 1944 could not be accurately appraised by the outside world. The education given under Japanese direction was undoubtedly having fruitage, but what that was could not be adequately ascertained.

The revolution brought by the impact of the Occident to all phases of the life of China was continuing, and in some of its aspects at an accelerated pace.

Over all was Japanese occupation, either threatened or actual. War and the attendant famine and pestilence took their toll in millions of lives. In her long past China had repeatedly known the agonies of civil war and foreign invasion. The present sufferings were great, but probably not greater than at some earlier periods. Never, however, had they so been combined with such changes in the basic patterns of life.

Internal Developments in Japan, 1937–1944

The intensification of the struggle between China and Japan in 1937 and the involvement of the British Empire, the East Indies, the Philippines, and the United States in active belligerency in the Far East in December 1941 were followed by changes not only in China but also in Japan. Until 1945, because of the curtain which war had interposed, the alterations in the life of Japan could not be as well known as could those which had occurred up to that time. However, some of them could be discerned. In general, whether in the mind of the nation, in politics, in economics, or in other aspects of culture, they were largely a continuation of those which were in process before 1937. Especially were they an intensification of trends which had assumed added prominence after Japan's adventure in Manchuria in the years subsequent to 1931.

In their national psychology the Japanese were showing the effects of prolonged war and of apparent success in empire building.

The feeling was abroad, cultivated by the leaders in the armed forces, that now was the hour of Japan's destiny, and that the years were critical and decisive in the extreme. Patriotism was intense. No one dared openly to question the program of expansion or the sincerity and idealism of the Greater East Asia Coprosperity Sphere with its announced purpose of expelling from the Far East the predatory and arrogant Western powers and the emancipation and welfare of all the peoples of the region through cooperation with the benevolent and beneficent hegemony of Japan. The wrongs inflicted on Japan by the Occident and by the regime of Chiang Kai-shek were stressed. They were now to be rectified. The people of China, exploited by selfish and incompetent rulers, were to be given internal peace and prosperity. In all this Japan was fulfilling her divine mission. She would, moreover, prosper. So ran the official propaganda and so the great rank and file appeared to believe. Those who might feel inner qualms kept them to themselves.

In political life the fighting services, especially the army, were increasingly dominant. That was to be expected in time of war and in view of the Japanese tradition and the persistent drift in the 1930's. As an illustration of the trend was the substitution, in the autumn of 1941, of Tojo, a general, for Konoye, of the ancient court nobility, as Premier. The coming to the fore of rougher, more jingoistic men, chiefly in the army but later in the navy, which had been an alarming feature of the early 1930's, went on. The new leaders displayed growing ruthlessness and increasing contempt for other peoples and for the sanctity of international obligations. Efforts were made to merge existing political parties to enable the nation to present a common front during the crisis. The Imperial Rule Assistance Association was created in an attempt to bring about this political unity. It had as its parliamentary wing the Imperial Rule Assistance Political Society. The endeavor, too, was made to supersede existing labor unions and to consolidate all workers back of the war effort. For this purpose the government sponsored a labor front which, under the control of one of the ministries of state, in November 1940 became the Patriotic Industrial Society.

The more aggressive elements in the armed services did not have their full way. The constitution was continued, with the Parliament and the cabinet provided for in that instrument. Since the constitution had been the gift of the Meiji Emperor, to abrogate it or to amend it would be regarded as disrespect for that revered ruler's memory. That could be done only in the name of the reigning Emperor and the latter was known to be unhappy over the course of the extremists and could plead filial piety as an adequate reason for keeping the document unaltered. The cooperation of the *Zaibatsu*, powerful in finance and industry, was essential to the successful prosecution of the war. They must be enlisted and given a vital stake in the new order. Leading industrialists in Osaka, at the heart of Japan's textile enterprise, felt aggrieved by a trend which placed the emphasis on the manufacture of steel, machinery, and munitions, and which brought constriction on their activities. The army and the navy still had their factions which handicapped unity of action. Here and there strikes occurred. Efforts were put forth to effect coordination of the resources of the Empire in a struggle whose outcome meant either rule or ruin, but the success of that endeavor was not complete. Japan did not become fully totalitarian.

Attempts were made to bring religion more under control by the state. Shrine Shinto, the cult of patriotism, was increasingly stressed, to the embarrassment especially of the Christians. In 1940 the several Christian bodies deemed it necessary, under pressure, to substitute Japanese for foreigners in such executive posts as those of bishops and heads of schools and to cut down on the financial subsidies received from abroad. The trend toward Japanese leadership had long been present, but was now consummated. In 1941, with the knowledge that if they did not act on their own initiative they might be compelled by the government to take the step, the overwhelming majority of the Protestants brought about a union of their various denominations into what was called the Church of Christ in Japan. Later the National Christian Council, originally Protestant, was reconstituted into an organ which would represent both Roman Catholics and Protestants in their dealings with the government. Yet Christianity was not persecuted as such. Indeed, the state sought the assistance of the churches in cementing ties with peoples of Greater East Asia.

The economic life of Japan felt profoundly the effects of the continued and intensified war. Inflation was in part controlled, but there was stern rationing. The quality of both food and clothing deteriorated. The substitutes for the accustomed textiles were notoriously flimsy. With so many men in the army, the demand for rice to feed them increased. Yet agriculture suffered from the cutting off, through the war, of some of the usual foreign supplies of chemical fertilizers. A labor shortage in rural areas arose in part from the absence of many hundreds of thousands in the armed services. To some extent this was compensated by the increased use of machinery in agriculture. Efforts were put forth, too, to augment the production of fertilizer and rice. Rice was available in Indo-China, Thailand, and Burma, but the shortage of shipping made difficult its transportation to Japan. Indeed, it was reported that much of the Burma crop, which in earlier years had been sent to India, rotted because of the cutting off of contact with India by the Japanese conquest and the lack of cargo space to Japan.

As we have suggested, the necessities of war brought greater emphasis on the heavy industries, a trend which had been in progress before 1937. Japan was so lacking in iron ore that this essential metal had to be imported, either from Manchuria or from other parts of East Asia. Before the restrictions placed by the American government, much scrap iron came from the United States. Presumably substitutes were later found in the areas in East Asia under Japanese control.

In 1941, in an attempt at better coordination of the economic life of Japan for the heightened struggle, what was called the New Economic Structure was launched. This applied especially to industry, commerce, banking, and mining. With the cooperation of the existing interests, large cartels, syndicates, and associations were set up to control the various related branches of the nation's life. Presumably they were regarded not as merely for the emergency but as permanent features of the life of the country. They did not supersede the *Zaibatsu* and in many instances were controlled by the latter.

Efforts were made to utilize more effectively the resources of Manchuria. Capital was poured into the region to hasten its development. Indeed, it was this expenditure rather than difficulties over foreign markets which for a time brought stringency to Japan. Through this vigorous program the production of coal, iron, and steel was pushed up. Large hydroelectric power plants were in process of construction and a beginning was made in the distillation of oil shales. Yet the Five Year Plan did not attain its full goals. Coal production was inadequate to meet the demand. The complaint was repeatedly heard that funds were being invested in Manchuria to the immediate detriment of Japan Proper. The outbreak of war in Europe in 1939 cut off the German market, Manchuria's most profitable connection outside the Empire. Hoped-for supplies of capital from the United States did not come. Foreign exchange ran short. Japan, too, was feeling the strain of the war in China. Accordingly, in 1940 the

Five Year Plan was curtailed and the decision was reached that Manchuria should concentrate on the production of coal, iron, steel, and light metals for sale to Japan. Much of the proposed industrialization of the region was delayed.

As the war lengthened its exhausting course Japanese economy increasingly felt the strain and was concentrated more and more on meeting the demands of the conflict. Severe shortages were felt in coal and hydroelectric power. Because of the urgent demand for shipping, partly through the necessity of supplying the huge army overseas, partly to take advantage of Japan's new conquests in southeastern Asia, the Philippines, and the East Indies, and partly to replace the losses through enemy action, shipbuilding was stressed. Many of the new vessels were wooden, and their construction was a drain on the timber resources of the Empire. Aircraft production was, perforce, enlarged. The manufacture of munitions was, obviously, of major importance. The national debt reached astronomical proportions. This, however, was characteristic of the age and was a fairly usual phenomenon among other governments. Most of it was domestically held, so that the service charges remained within the Empire.

In general, the years after 1937 saw an intensification of traditional features of the life of Japan. Loyalty to the nation as personified in the Emperor and as expressed through Shinto was stressed. The military were dominant to a degree which had not been seen since the passing of the *Bakufu*. Society was regimented in a fashion reminiscent of the Tokugawa Shogunate. The industrialization and mechanization of the land through techniques of Western origin were hastened. The war was being waged by weapons and through military organization and tactics of Occidental provenance. In some respects the *Zaibatsu* and the structure of capitalism which were largely a consequence of contact with the West were strengthened. Yet basically some of the outstanding features of the old Japan were augmented rather than weakened.

India after 1939

We must not bring to an end a chapter dealing with the world-wide war in the 1930's and 1940's and its effects upon the Far East without an account of the changes which were brought to India. These were profound. India, it will be recalled, had been making progress toward self-government. This had been by stages spanning several decades but had been accelerated after World War I. The latest step had been taken under an act of Parliament of 1935 which had not yet been fully implemented.

India was slower to feel the force of the storm than were Japan and China. She was not seriously affected until the outbreak of the European phase of the struggle, in September 1939. Then, as a member of the British Empire, she was drawn into active participation. For her the consequences were more striking than were those of the earlier war of the century.

When, on September 3, 1939, Great Britain declared war on Germany, India automatically became a belligerent and on that day the Viceroy, through a proclamation, officially apprised the Indian people of the fact. At the same time an ordinance was promulgated which legalized measures for the prosecution of the war and the maintenance of order. To this end meetings might be prohibited and arrests made without warrants. It was also announced that plans for the federation of India under the act of 1935 would be suspended until the coming of peace.

The attitudes of the articulate elements in India were about what might have been expected. The princes and Moslem leaders were quick to affirm their loyalty and to offer their aid. The Indian National Congress through its Working Committee voiced disapproval of the act of the British government in making India a belligerent without the consent of the Indian people. It expressed itself as against Fascism and Nazism and as opposed to the German invasion of Poland. It declared that if Great Britain were fighting for democracy she should establish full democracy in India and that the Indian people should be accorded the right to frame their own constitution and determine their own policy. It affirmed that "a free and democratic India will gladly associate herself with other free nations for mutual defense against aggression and for economic cooperation." The Moslem League also spoke its mind and insisted that "no declaration regarding the question of constitutional advance for India should be made without the consent and approval of the All-India Moslem League."

In reply, especially to the Congress, the British government, in October 1939, reaffirmed the pledge given in 1929 through the Viceroy to grant India the status of a self-governing dominion and suggested the formation for the duration of the war of a consultative group composed of representatives of all political parties in British India and of the Indian princes, to be summoned by the Viceroy and presided over by him, to associate India in the conduct of the war. This the Congress declared to be unsatisfactory. It called upon the Congress ministries in the various provinces to resign. That they soon did. In some respects the Moslem League was less intransigent and, while asking for further clarification of assurances, expressed satisfaction at the promised reconsideration of the dominion status after the war and the protection of minorities. In March 1940, the Congress, at a plenary session, declared "again that nothing short of complete independence can be accepted by the people of India."

The Moslem League, under the leadership of its president, Mohammed Ali Jinnah, at its annual session of 1940, came out for the establishment of two independent Moslem states (to be known together as Pakistan), the one in the northwest and the other in the northeast, areas in which Moslems were in the majority. To this many prominent Moslems were opposed. Obviously, too, the Congress would resist it as dividing India.

In August 1940, after the fall of France and when the United Kingdom seemed to be in desperate straits, the British government reiterated, in somewhat stronger terms, its promise of dominion status for India after the war. It expressed itself as favoring a purely Indian constitutional assembly to frame a form of government, but declared that it must fulfill the obligations entailed by its long connection and that the calling of such an assembly must wait until the end of the war. This proposal was rejected by both the Congress and the League. Under the stimulus of Gandhi nonviolent demonstrations against participation in the war thereupon ensued.

As a result of civil disobedience thousands of Indians were arrested and kept in confinement. The British *raj* would take no chance of active rebellion while the United Kingdom was fighting with its back to the wall.

In some of the provinces democratic government under the reforms of 1935 continued. In others, after the resignation of the Congress ministries, the British *raj* took over the administration.

Several of the moderate Indians who could not go the full way with either the Moslem League or the Indian National Congress met early in 1941 and suggested that since those two bodies could not compose their differences the Viceroy's Executive Council should be reconstructed, with the transfer to Indians of all portfolios, including those of finance and defense, and with a membership which should be entirely of nonofficial Indians. This proposal the British government at first rejected, giving as a reason that an Executive Council thus constituted would not be really representative and would therefore be unworkable. It strongly hinted that the moderates should give their attention to bringing together the contending factions. However, it was so far attracted by the idea that in July 1941 it enlarged the Viceroy's Executive Council by the appointment of five distinguished nonofficial Indians. This meant that out of a council of twelve, eight were nonofficial Indians. Yet the key portfolios of finance, defense, and the home department (which was responsible for internal order) were retained in the hands of British officials, the Viceroy kept the right of veto, and the body was not responsible to any elected assembly. Of the five Indians appointed none was from the League or the Congress. A National Defense Council, advisory in character, which included Indian members, was also inaugurated. These measures were avowedly only of an *ad interim* character. They worked somewhat better than many Indians had feared, and the release of thousands of the prisoners held for civil disobedience was said to have been in part due to the influence of Indian members in the Viceroy's Executive Council.

Anglo-Japanese belligerency and the rapid advance of the Japanese in December 1941 and in early 1942 brought so grave a threat to India that both the British on the one hand and the League and the Congress on the other were disposed to moderate their recalcitrancy. Yet both the League and the Congress, knowing the critical situation of the British Empire, were inclined to exact a high price for cooperation. Even a group of Indian moderates sent word to Prime Minister Churchill in January 1942 that in their judgment the situation required prompt action toward the transformation of the Viceroy's Executive Council into an all-Indian body representative of the various groups and the restoration of some form of representative popular government in those provinces where the ministries had resigned in criticism of the government's policy. In February 1942, Chiang Kai-shek visited India. He had long been critical of the British because of their record in China and, in spite and perhaps because of the pomp with which he was entertained by British officialdom, his visit did not make him less so. His coming indicated a certain amount of fellow feeling between Chinese and Indians. Both regarded themselves as sufferers from a foreign aggression from which they were struggling for release. Never before, moreover, had these two most numerous peoples of Asia been consciously so near to each other in their political aspirations.

The position of the British government was one of extraordinary difficulty. The British *raj* was ruling over a vast region which never before its advent had been completely brought under one administration. In India were many dissident elements, to each of which the British felt a moral responsibility. The Hindu majority was not fully united. Nor were the Moslems all in accord with the leadership of Jinnah. The historic gulf remained between Moslems and Hindus. Moslems, in the minority, but accustomed, by their history in India, to rule, would have none of the threatened Hindu domination. They feared it under a politically unified and independent India with representative institutions based upon relative numerical strength. The Indian National Congress was insistent upon a free government which would include the entire country. To this not only the Moslems but also the rulers of the native states would not consent on Congress terms. The princes were adamant upon the preservation of their rights as embodied in treaties with the British government. Various other minorities, including the depressed classes, were suspicious of what the caste Hindus, their traditional oppressors, would do once the strong British arm, with its even-handed justice, was removed. In the United States, moreover, radicals were clamoring that if they were asked to support a war waged ostensibly in defense of democracy, self-determination must be granted to India. Britain was compelled to deal with the complex situation in its most urgent form while the frictions were accentuated by the psychology of war and while she herself and her Empire were reeling under the blows of her external enemies and especially while Japan was battering at the very gates of India.

In an attempt to solve the problem, the British government sent Sir Stafford Cripps to India in March 1942. Cripps was a distinguished lawyer and statesman noted for his sympathy with liberal, even radical, views. His appointment seemed auspicious, for presumably he would be friendly to the aspirations of the Indian nationalists and would, because of his record, be welcomed by them. Cripps met with leaders of all the chief groups and had long talks with Gandhi himself. After several days of such conversations the proposals, called a Draft Declaration for Discussion with Indian Leaders, with which the British government had commissioned him, were made public. These declared the British objective to be "the creation of a new Indian Union which shall constitute a Dominion, associated with the United Kingdom and the other Dominions by a common allegiance to the Crown, but equal to them in every respect, in no way subordinate in any aspect of its domestic and external affairs." Immediately upon the cessation of hostilities, steps would be taken to set up in India an elected body charged with the task of framing a new constitution. In it the Indian native states as well as representatives of British India were to participate. A native state might adhere to the new constitution or remain separate, as it might determine. Any province of British India might refuse to join in the new constitution, and to each such nonacceding province the same status would be given, if it so wished, as that of the Union. With the constitution-making body for the Indian Union the British government would sign a treaty for the protection of racial and religious minorities, but it would "not impose any restriction on the power of the Indian Union to decide in the future its relationship to the other member states of the British Commonwealth." This proposal seemed to safeguard the interests of all the groups to which the British felt themselves under treaty and moral obligation. It also assured the Indian Union the right to withdraw from the British Empire and become fully independent if it so desired. The calling of the constitution-making body was to be postponed until after the war. In the meantime the British government would "bear the responsibility for and retain control and direction of the defence of India as part of their world war effort," but the task "must be the responsibility of the Government of India with the cooperation of the peoples of India."

The Cripps proposals came at an unfortunate juncture. The United Kingdom was so obviously in sore straits and British prestige was at so low an ebb that the Indian critics were inclined to be more recalcitrant than in times of British strength. Then, too, Gandhi, wedded to nonviolence and eager to keep India out of the war, was disinclined to an early solution which might bind the Congress to cooperation in the world struggle.

In April 1942, following the presentation of the proposals, replies to them were issued by spokesmen for the seven major articulate groups, including the Congress, the Moslem League, the Indian states, and the depressed classes. Five of these rejected the British offer, although no two of them did so on precisely the same grounds. The Indian states were noncommittal and the nonparty group gave qualified assent.

Both the rejection and the fact that it was on grounds which differed between the various groups were ominous. It meant that the best offer that Great Britain was likely to make for some time was unsatisfactory to India: a vast gulf existed between the British and Indians of almost all classes. It also indicated that India was basically and seemingly irreconcilably still divided within itself. In addition to the historic cleavages between religious groups and between the castes and the depressed, by no means all Hindus supported the Congress nor did all Moslems follow Jinnah. A protest fast by Gandhi against his continued detention did not lessen the bitterness of Indians toward the British. Later, in 1944, conversations between Jinnah and Gandhi in an attempt to find a method of ending the impasse between the Moslems and the Hindus proved unsuccessful.

The antagonisms were more acute and more widespread than had been known at any time since the Mutiny. They may, indeed, have been felt by more Indians than even at that tragic time. The British conservatives were adamant. The attitude of British liberals was one of troubled impotence before the basic inability of the Indians to agree among themselves. If the Indians would unite in saying what they wanted, the British, so many of the liberals declared, would listen and, if the rights of minorities were assured and the sanctity of British treaty arrangements with the Indian states were not endangered, would grant what was asked. Cripps himself, friendly though he had been to Indian aspirations, in the disappointment over the failure of his mission said that until the various Indian groups could learn to arrive at solutions by compromise, the situation was hopeless. Articulate Indians were tending toward unanimity in the demand for the recognition of the right of India to determine her own future and were deeply distrustful of British sincerity. They accused the British of playing off one group against another and were convinced that if the British were to withdraw the nation would be compelled to compose its internal differences. Some more than hinted that it was the responsibility of the British to bring the groups to agreement.

Politically, the problem of India presented aspects which could be satisfactorily solved only slowly if at all. In a region traditionally divided as markedly as was Europe the British *raj* had brought a certain degree of unity. This was aided by the infection of Western nationalism which brought the dream of independence under a single government. True to their own political development, the British had fostered representative democratic institutions based upon their experience. They pursued, too, in accordance with their tradition, the way of compromise between extreme positions. Whether these institutions and methods could be grafted successfully upon the alien Indian stock was as yet uncertain. The traditional frictions between religions and classes seemed deeper and sharper in 1944 than for many years. The British sought to solve the problem by communal representation, namely, that based upon the several groups. Here lay a certain safeguard for minorities. The Congress, overwhelmingly Hindu, felt that its dominance in an independent India would be jeopardized by the communal principle, for it might not, under that arrangement, have a clear majority. It demanded that representation be arranged on the geographic rather than the communal basis, for by this procedure the historic gulfs which militated against Indian unity might be closed and the Congress might hope for a clear majority in the government.

Temporarily, moreover, as we suggested a few pages back, the scene was still further complicated by the Japanese encouragement to an Indian independence army to fight against the British. In Subhas Chandra Bose, an outstanding radical nationalist who had fled the country, they found a leader, and the force was organized from other exiles.

By the summer of 1945 the tension was slightly eased. The defeat of Germany and Japan partly restored the prestige of Great Britain. The British, too, were less fearful and more conciliatory. A large proportion of the political prisoners were progressively released from custody. In June 1945, at the instance of Lord Wavell, the Viceroy, the British offered to reconstitute the Viceroy's Executive Council as a completely representative all-Indian body except for the Viceroy and the War Minister. The coming to power of the Labor Party seemed to promise a milder policy from London. The situation became slightly less difficult.

In unanticipated ways the war was promoting Indian unity. A large Indian army was recruited by voluntary enlistment. It may have totaled two millions or more. It no longer came, as Indian forces under British direction had previously done, from the traditionally military groups such as the Sikhs and the Gurkhas, but was from all classes and areas. It brought together hundreds of thousands from many language areas, from the castes and from the noncaste and depressed groups. To reduce the language difficulties, each recruit was required to learn a simplified Hindustani. In the regiments segregation on caste lines was broken down: the regiments were mixed.

Only in the company was caste observed. It was the general practice to have each company made up of those of the same religious customs and each with its own cook to prepare food as required by caste. In the navy, however, no caste rules were observed and all men ate the same menus prepared by the same cooks and in common messes. The experience in the army and the navy, therefore, would tend to lessen traditional barriers.

The economic situation was such, moreover, that reason and prudence counseled a united India. The location of the minerals of the land was such that, were India to be divided between the suggested Pakistan and a state in which the Hindus were in the large majority, the former would be poor and the latter rich. Moreover, the unified services which the British had developed and under which population had jumped so amazingly would be imperiled and famine might be the lot of the millions who were never far from extreme poverty. It was possible that, given time, a way to genuine political unity would be found under a fully autonomous national government.

It was not only in the political realm that India was feeling the effects of World War II. Many other aspects of life were affected. For instance, the presence of thousands of troops from the United States brought the country into intimate touch with another nation and a different standard of living.

In what might in an inclusive sense be called the economic phases of its life India was showing the impress of the struggle.

One of the most obvious concomitants of the war was economic distress. The Japanese conquest of Burma cut off an important source of food, for much of Burma's export of rice had gone to India. Indeed, after belligerency came between the British Empire and Japan, severe famine broke out in Bengal. The demands of the armed forces in India, British, Indian, and American, made for a shortage in many commodities. Prices rose, as in most countries during war. The placing of Indian economy on a war footing brought many difficult adjustments.

India became increasingly a center for the supply of the fighting forces of the British Empire. The war expansion of Indian industries began in the summer of 1939. In the autumn of 1940 a conference was convened at New Delhi made up of representatives from the various units of the British Empire in the East with the purpose of pooling for the prosecution of the war the resources of that area. As a result the British Supply Mission stepped up the expansion of

Indian production. The British government met the cost. It was said that Indian industries provided nine-tenths of the military equipment of the Indian and Near Eastern armies. This meant the augmentation of the production of iron and steel. The manufacture of heavy munitions was handicapped by dependence on imported machinery, but such items as ordnance, explosives, small arms, medical supplies, uniforms, blankets, and boots could be produced. The United States and Great Britain united in providing equipment, and advisers and technicians were sent from the United States to assist in swelling the output.

India, moreover, became an important American base in the prosecution of the war against Japan. In India, notably Assam, were the terminals from which air communication with China was maintained and from which the campaigns for the expulsion of the Japanese from Burma and the opening of ground routes to China were waged.

One effect of the war was to reverse the debtor-creditor relations of the United Kingdom and India. Traditionally India had been the borrower, and the payments of interest and dividends to British investors had been a source of revenue for the peoples of the British Isles and one of the grounds for the nationalist complaint of the British exploitation of India. Even before the war India had been paying up her borrowings. It was estimated that at one time about £600,000,000 had been owed to private British investors for such constructive enterprises as railways and irrigation works and that before the outbreak of the war in 1939 this had been reduced by about half. There was now a further lowering of the debt. Indeed, the United Kingdom, buying from India, had become the debtor. Its obligations largely took the form of huge credits in London in favor of India. These were "blocked," presumably for the duration of hostilities and until such time as their unlocking would not too greatly disturb British economy. Here was still another cause for irritation on the part of the Indian critics of Britain.

World War II was bringing many and complex problems to India. In general, however, it seemed to be accelerating the achievement of the political and economic autonomy of the country. Whether India would choose to remain within the British Empire as a dominion or whether it would become fully independent was not as yet clear. Nor was it certain whether it would attain autonomy as a united nation or in two or more fragments. The long-time trend was toward the elimination of British direction. This was being quickened by the war and, presumably, would eventually be consummated.

BIBLIOGRAPHY

For Brief Reference

No single volume or periodical adequately covers the ground surveyed in this chapter.

For More Detailed Study

PERIODICALS

Asia (New York, 1917 ff.).
Far Eastern Survey (New York, 1932 ff.).
Pacific Affairs (New York, 1928 ff.).

CHINA

R. W. Barnett, *Economic Shanghai: Hostage to Politics, 1937–1941* (New York, 1941).
T. A. Bisson, *Japan in China* (New York, 1938).
Chiang Kai-shek, *Resistance and Reconstruction. Messages During China's Six Years of War, 1937–1943* (New York, 1943).
China Handbook, 1937–1943 (New York, 1943).
G. M. Friters, *Outer Mongolia and Its International Position* (The Johns Hopkins Press, 1949).
W. Galbraith, *In China Now* (New York, 1941).
F. C. Jones, *Manchuria Since 1931* (Oxford University Press, 1949).
P. M. A. Linebarger, *The China of Chiang K'ai-shek* (Boston, 1941).
M. R. Norins, *Gateway to Asia: Sinkiang* (New York, 1944).
D. N. Rowe, *China among the Powers* (New York, 1945).
E. Snow, *Red Star over China* (New York, 1938).
E. Snow, *The Battle for Asia* (New York, 1941).

JAPAN

G. C. Allen, *Japan: the Hungry Guest* (New York, 1938).
H. Borton, *Japan Since 1931: Its Political and Social Developments* (New York, 1940).
H. Byas, *Government by Assassination* (New York, 1942).
C. D. Carus and G. J. Nichols, *Japan: Its Resources and Industries* (New York, 1944).
J. B. Cohen, *Japan's Economy in War and Reconstruction* (Minneapolis, 1949).
K. W. Colegrove, *Militarism in Japan* (Boston, 1940).
C. B. Fahs, *Government in Japan: Recent Trends in Its Scope and Operation* (New York, 1940).
J. C. Grew, *Ten Years in Japan* (New York, 1944).
D. C. Holtom, *Modern Japan and Shinto Nationalism: A Study of Present-Day Trends in Japanese Religions* (Chicago, 1943).
T. Kase, *Journey to the "Missouri"* (Yale University Press, 1950).

K. L. Mitchell, *Japan's Industrial Strength* (New York, 1942).
E. B. Schumpeter, editor, *The Industrialization of Japan and Manchukuo, 1930–1940. Population, Raw Materials and Industry* (New York, 1940).
G. T. Trewartha, *Japan, A Physical, Cultural & Regional Geography* (University of Wisconsin, 1945).
C. Yanaga, *Japan Since Perry* (New York, 1949).

THE RUSSIAN FAR EAST

W. Mandel, *The Soviet Far East and Central Asia* (New York, 1944).
H. Moore, *A Record of Soviet Far Eastern Relations, 1931–1942* (New York, 1942).
D. J. Dallin, *Soviet Russia and the Far East* (New Haven, 1948).

INDIA

R. Coupland, *The Indian Problem* (New York, 1944).
W. E. Duffett, A. R. Hicks, G. R. Parkin, *India Today. The Background of Indian Nationalism* (New York, 1942).

HOSTILITIES BETWEEN CHINA AND JAPAN

League of Nations. Appeal by the Chinese Government. Report of the Commission of Enquiry (Geneva, 1932).
Loo Pin-fei, *It Is Dark Underground* (New York, 1946).
H. S. Quigley, *Far Eastern War, 1937–1941* (Boston, 1942).

THE UNITED STATES AND THE FAR EAST

T. A. Bisson, *American Policy in the Far East: 1931–1940* (New York, 1939).
A. W. Griswold, *The Far Eastern Policy of the United States* (New York, 1939.
S. R. Smith, *The Manchurian Crisis 1931–1932. A Tragedy in International Relations* (New York, 1948).
H. L. Stimson, *The Far Eastern Crisis, Recollections and Observations* (New York, 1936).
P. Tompkins, *American-Russian Relations in the Far East* (New York, 1949).

Chapter XVII. AFTERMATH AND CONTINUATION OF STORM

THE WORLD-WIDE STORM, the Far Eastern phases of which we described in the preceding chapter, could not but have results important for all mankind. The clock could not be turned back nor the human situation be the same as it was before the tempest broke. The aftermath of storm was especially momentous in India and the Far East. This is not surprising. It was in the Far East that the first rumblings were heard in September 1931. The storm persisted longer in the Far East than in Europe, for Japan held out against the might of the United Nations after Germany collapsed and it was the capitulation of Japan in August 1945, rather than the fall of Germany earlier that year which ostensibly terminated World War II. After a lull, the storm broke out afresh in Korea in the summer of 1950.

Six sequels which were outstanding in the world at large were very striking in the Far East. We shall meet all of them as we pass from country to country. One was the exhaustion, physical and mental, and the economic disruption and impoverishment which were an inevitable aftermath of an upheaval as violent and widespread as was World War II.

A second was revolution. Many of the former patterns of society had been either weakened or destroyed. Millions had endured the sufferings of the war years hoping that they would be followed by peace and opportunity to build a new and better order in which more of the good things of life would be theirs. Hundreds of thousands took the opportunity afforded by the breakdown of the pre-war structure to attempt, often by violence, to obtain what they had longed for. In several countries this brought civil strife and added to the poverty and agony. In most lands it led to sweeping changes in political structures. A vast upheaval was in progress. The masses were on the march.

A third sequel was the decline of Western Europe, including Great Britain, in the world scene. For more than four centuries Western Europeans had been increasingly prominent. They had made themselves masters of most of the globe, and some aspects of their culture had become world-wide. Seen against the perspective of the whole reach of human history, this dominance was a recent phenomenon. Moreover, it could not be permanent. The science, the techniques, and the machines which had helped to make it possible and through which much of it had been accomplished could not remain the exclusive possession of Europeans. They were desired and were being adopted by non-Occidental peoples. As Western Europe lost the monopoly of this knowledge, these processes, and these instruments, its prominence would wane. However, the passing of the hegemony of Western Europe was accelerated by the two world wars of the first half of the twentieth century, for both of these had centered in that region.

The weakening of Western Europe had a consequence which was especially marked in the South and East of Asia—a quickening of the pace of independence of the peoples which had been under the political control of the British, the Dutch, and the French. Ceylon and the sub-continent of India in its two divisions, India and Pakistan, while retaining a connection with the Commonwealth, became independent of Britain. Burma became independent and did not remain in the Commonwealth. Although continuing a special association with the Netherlands, Indonesia moved toward full independence. The French were seemingly being pushed out of Indo-China.

A fourth feature of the post-war years was the heightened importance of the United States and Russia and the tension between these two nations. The decline of Western Europe had left these two colossi facing each other, unbalanced by any third power of comparable dimensions. Each was extending its influence over peoples and lands which it was trying to draw into its orbit as it built up its defenses against the other. Communists, sympathetic with Russia, were to be found in all lands in the South and East of Asia. Russian and American influences were competing, notably in China and Korea. By 1950 most of China had been drawn toward Russia. As a result of its defeat, Japan was in the American sphere.

A fifth characteristic of the years which immediately followed World War II was the effort at world organization through the United Nations. The United Nations took an active part in seeking to compose the conflicts which followed the war in India, Indonesia, and Korea and was a force with which to reckon.

A sixth feature of the years which succeeded the war was the continued emergence of a world culture through the spread of Western civilization. Although politically and in economic realms Western Europe was receding, many phases of the culture of that region were becoming more widely influential. Science in its many manifestations, schools on Western models teaching subjects which had been developed in the Occident, the mechanical appliances of the West, nationalism as a contagion from Europe, Communism, first formulated by Karl Marx, although modified in Russia, democracy as Western Europe understood that term, forms of government which originated in Western Europe, and Christianity introduced and propagated from the Occident, all continued to spread in South and East Asia as well as in most other parts of the non-Occidental world.

India Achieves Independence but Is Still Divided

One of the most important features of the years which immediately followed World War II was the independence of India.

This step was furthered by a change of government in Great Britain. In a general election in July 1945, the Conservatives were defeated and the Labor Party came into power. The Labor government was distinctly favorable to Indian aspirations and undertook steps to enable the Indians to attain them. Various measures were proposed to further the formulation of a structure for India by the Indians. However, these efforts seemed frustrated by divisions among the Indians themselves. The conflict was especially sharp between the Moslem League, headed by Jinnah, which wished a separate Moslem state, and the Congress party, predominantly but not entirely Hindu, which insisted that all India be under one rule. The princes of the native states were also apprehensive over developments which might eliminate them. During 1945, 1946, and the fore part of 1947 repeated clashes occurred between Moslems and Hindus with considerable loss of life.

In February 1947, the Labor government announced that if the Indians could not come to some agreement it would itself cut the Gordian knot and "take the necessary steps to effect the transference of power into responsible hands by a date not later than June, 1948." At the same time the appointment was announced of Lord Mountbatten to succeed Lord Wavell as Viceroy. In July 1947, the Indian Independence Bill was pressed through Parliament. It set up two new dominions, Pakistan and India. Pakistan, a Moslem state, was comprised of two areas seven hundred miles apart, the larger in the northwest and the smaller in the eastern part of Bengal with an adjacent portion of Assam. Karachi was the capital and Mohammed Ali Jinnah, President of the Moslem League, was appointed Governor-General. The Dominion of India comprised the rest of British India. It had its capital at New Delhi and Lord Mountbatten became Governor-General. The new governments were inaugurated on August 15, 1947. Indian independence was now a reality, for dominion status carried with it the right of choice either to remain in the British Commonwealth or fully to withdraw from it.

Independence had as an immediate aftermath intensified fighting between the various religious communities, chiefly between Moslems and Hindus. Forced by Moslems, Hindus and Sikhs migrated eastward into India from the northwest portion of Pakistan. Moslems, constrained by Hindus and Sikhs, moved westward from India into Pakistan. It is said that ten million people were on the march. The unrest spread to other sections of the land. The suffering was acute and tens of thousands perished. By the end of 1947 the disorders had largely subsided and the shifts of population had mostly been completed. However, thirty-five or forty million Moslems were still in India and presumably would stay, as against sixty or sixty-five millions of their faith in Pakistan. Moreover, many Hindus continued in Pakistan. Neither state was either purely Moslem or purely Hindu. Each, especially Pakistan, had millions of displaced persons to absorb. Late in 1947 India and Pakistan reached an agreement on financial and defense issues. Yet relations between the two dominions were chronically uneasy.

The native states constituted a problem for the new dominions. By the end of 1949 most of them had been absorbed by India. Varying arrangements were made with their princes. Several were allowed to continue much as they had been under the British *raj*. The central government conducted their foreign affairs, had charge of defense, and integrated such services as the post office and railways with those of the nation, but the princes were permitted to retain their thrones and local matters were handled through their officials. Over five hundred of the native states were fully absorbed into the national structure. Of these more than two hundred were merged with neighboring provinces or consolidated into areas administered by the national government, and about three hundred were brought together into bigger units.

The two largest of the native states, Hyderabad and Kashmir, proved to be very difficult. The Nizam of Hyderabad (see p. 57) attempted to maintain his independence. Since he was a Moslem, although his subjects were overwhelmingly Hindus, Pakistan supported him and the tension between Pakistan and India was accentuated. In September 1948, an Indian army moved into Hyderabad and, although he protested to the Security Council of the United Nations, the Nizam agreed to an Indian military governorship for his domains. Kashmir presented an even more delicate situation. It lay on the northern frontiers of both Pakistan and India, its ruler, the Maharaja, was a Hindu, and its population was predominantly Moslem. Pakistani tribesmen entered the country and the Maharaja provisionally threw in his lot with India. The two dominions prepared for war, for the prestige of each was involved. But the United Nations intervened and in January 1949, a commission which it appointed succeeded in bringing about a cease-fire agreement. A plebiscite was to be held to determine the choice of the inhabitants for their future political allegiance. Yet tension continued and charges and counter-charges of encroachments on Kashmir were hurled at each other by India and Pakistan. In 1950 neither country had withdrawn its troops from Kashmir.

Communal differences, namely those between the several religious communities, which had been a traditional bar to Indian unity and which had as one expression the separate existence of India and Pakistan, came to an explosive and tragic crisis in the assassination of Mohandas Karamchand Gandhi on January 30, 1948. Gandhi had deeply deplored the communal friction and had devoted much of his energy to its alleviation. He had, for example, championed the underprivileged depressed "outcaste," "untouchable," or "scheduled" classes. Early that month he had used his characteristic method of protest and had undertaken a five day fast because of disturbances in Delhi and had obtained promises for better treatment for the Moslem minority. As he was going to a prayer meeting he was shot by a member of the Mahasabha group, an organization which stood for pure Hinduism and which was critical of Gandhi's efforts to obtain tolerance for non-Hindu elements. Also accused of fomenting the feeling against Moslems which was responsible for Gandhi's death was the Rashtriya Swayamsevak Sangh (National Voluntary Service Association), an intensely Hindu organization which was founded in 1925.

Gandhi's death made a profound impression upon the entire world and especially upon India. He was acclaimed by many of his fellow-countrymen as the most influential Indian since the Buddha and Asoka. Not all Indians agreed with that appraisal. Numbers among those of

Occidental education viewed him somewhat critically, although with respect, and many of the stricter among the Hindus disliked him. Yet his influence among the masses was prodigious. He had caught their imagination and by his slogans, his symbolism, such as his use of the spinning wheel, his insistence upon non-violence and his own practice of it, his fasting, and his demonstration of some of the traditional Hindu religious convictions, he profoundly influenced them. It is probable that by his emphasis upon non-violence he had saved India from violent revolution. His death, too, arising as it did from his protest against communal strife, tended for a time to ease the relations between India and Pakistan. Before his death his share in the active affairs of the Congress party had begun to wane, but men whom he had inspired continued to be outstanding in the government. Notable among them was Jawaharlal Nehru, who became Prime Minister of India. The Deputy Prime Minister, Vallabhbhai Patel, had worked with Gandhi, but was less inclined to conform to his ideals, especially those of non-violence.

The death of Mohammed Ali Jinnah on September 11, 1948, removed the figure that had been as prominent in the Moslem League and in the creation of Pakistan as had Gandhi in the Congress party and the independence of India. He was succeeded as Governor-General by Nazimuddin.

In India the Congress party remained dominant. Indeed, as a political machine controlling the government, it was even more master of the country than it had been before independence. It contained various elements, but a substantial proportion cherished Gandhi's ideals of social and moral reform, village welfare, universal education, and the franchise for all adults. However, by many it was considered to be in need of reorganization and reform. It had achieved its pre-eminence by leading the movement for independence. Now that independence had been won its task was chiefly one of administration. Corruption was said to be showing itself in the ranks and even in higher circles. Its problem was partly one of reorientation. As the governing power it was now blamed for evils which formerly had been laid at the door of the British *raj*.

The Congress party was not without resistance. Communal divisions were still strong. On the extreme right was the chauvinist Hindu Mahasabha. On the left a Socialist group, led by an American-educated Indian, broke away from the Congress and formed a separate party which was critical of the influence of Indian industrialist capitalists in the Congress and the retention of the British tie. It appealed to urban laborers and students and to a slight extent to agrarian workers. Communists were an active but small minority. The Congress-controlled government sought to repress the Communists. Early in 1949 it arrested hundreds of them and a Communist-stimulated railway strike failed.

When independent, India set to work at framing a constitution. This was done through the Constituent Assembly. The document was adopted in November 1949, and came into effect January 26, 1950. In it India was declared to be "a sovereign democratic republic." Officially known as the Union of India or the Indian Union, it was a federation composed of twenty-eight states: namely, the nine formerly autonomous provinces; ten centrally administered provinces; the three princely states of Hyderabad, Kashmir, and Mysore; six unions of princely states; and such territories as the Adaman and Nicobar Islands. There was a central lawmaking body of two houses, the Council of States of 220 members elected by provincial legislatures and the House of the People chosen by adult universal suffrage of both sexes. The head of the state, the President (the first to hold the office was Rajendra Prasad), had powers akin to those of the King of England. The executive authority was located in a ministry headed by the Premier (the first was Jawaharlal Nehru) and responsible, as in Britain, to the lower house of the legislature. The decades of association with the United Kingdom clearly had their effect on the political framework of the new nation and the framers of the Constitution also studied carefully the federal structure of Canada and the United States. The ideal cherished was federation with powers divided between the states and the Union. The latter had more authority than did the national government in Canada or the United States. There was an independent judiciary and the members of the High Courts were appointed by the President. The constitution provided for the abolition of untouchability and forbade child marriage and discrimination on the grounds of religion, race, or sex.

It was in November 1948, that the Constituent Assembly approved the clause in the constitution which formally ended untouchability. Presumably the legal step would be followed only slowly by the alteration of long-standing social practices and the cessation of the customary assigning of despised occupations, such as scavengery, to what would still be popularly regarded as the depressed classes. Yet in 1948 two "untouchables" were high officials of the central government, the one Minister of Labor and the other Minister of Justice, and the latter was married to a Brahman.

Bharat was adopted as an alternative name for India. Hindi was to become the national language after a specified number of years. In the meantime the use of English as the tongue common to all was to continue.

Here was a triumph for democracy as Great Britain, the British Commonwealth, and the United States understood that word. A great Asiatic people had moved into the family of independent democratic nations with a minimum of internal disorder.

The tie with the British Commonwealth was maintained, but in a much attenuated form. As Governor-General, Lord Mountbatten was very successful in helping to guide India through the transition to independence and in smoothing some of the attendant friction. In June 1948, largely at his own instance, he was retired from the office and an Indian, Chakravarti Rajagopalachari, was appointed to succeed him. At conferences of the Prime Ministers of the members of the Commonwealth in October 1948 and April 1949, a formula was worked out which proved acceptable to India by which the latter was fully acknowledged as an independent republic, and yet recognized the King "as the symbol of the free association of [the Commonwealth's] independent member nations, and, as such, the head of the Commonwealth." In the new constitution under which India was to operate after 1949, no legal ties with the Commonwealth were provided. The Indian Republic owed no allegiance to the Crown and the King had no place in its government. Relations with another member of the Commonwealth, the Union of South Africa, were tense because of the long-standing and recently accentuated discrimination against those of Indian descent in that land. Yet India remained within the family which constituted the Commonwealth.

This was also true of Pakistan. As the most populous of the Moslem states it maintained friendly relations with most of the other states of the Islamic world, excepting chiefly its near neighbor, Afghanistan, and supported the Arabs in their protest against the claims of the Jewish state of Israel. But it, too, continued in the Commonwealth.

Pakistan used its Constituent Assembly as its legislative body. In this body the Hindu minority as well as the Moslem majority was represented. In March 1949, the Constituent Assembly declared that its purpose was to create an independent Islamic democracy in which Moslems would "be enabled to live in accordance with the requirements of Islam," but in which non-Moslem minorities would be guaranteed equal civil status, religious freedom, and cultural autonomy. In contrast with India, Pakistan did not attempt to absorb the princely states within its borders, but these were few and relatively small and unimportant. Like India, it had a strong central administration. It did not as quickly draft a constitution as did India and in 1950 still did not have one.

To thousands in India and Pakistan independence brought a sense of emancipation and a great hope. Nationalistic agitation had bred a profound distrust of the English, had held them responsible for many of India's ills, and had accentuated a feeling of frustration which was ascribed to helplessness under foreign rule. British rule had now disappeared. Indians and Pakistanis believed that under their newly acquired freedom they would be able to make progress against the many social and economic ills of their lands. Indians dreamed of universal education, of the alleviation of poverty, and of improving the standard of living by the development of industry. The air in Pakistan was heady with vast schemes for the development of hydro-electric power, coal mines, oil fields, and shipbuilding.

Moreover, independent India aspired to a role in international affairs commensurate with the size of its population, its long history, and its high culture. Its leaders wished to keep the country from becoming embroiled in the struggle between the two Titans, Russia and the United States. While their sympathies were with Britain and America rather than Russia, they believed that it would be possible to create in Asia a bloc of peoples who might hold the balance of power between the U.S.S.R. and the U.S.A.

Indian statesmen held that, as their land had been freed from the imperialistic control by Britain, so the remnants of Western European colonial regimes in Asia should be eliminated. They sought to absorb the remaining Portuguese and French possessions in India itself. They championed the cause of Indonesia against the Dutch. They called a conference of Eastern countries to deal jointly with the Indonesian problem. It met in New Delhi early in 1949. While the resolutions adopted were not as drastic as had been feared in some Occidental quarters, the fact that the gathering had assembled, and under Indian leadership, was significant: India was exerting itself to bring much of Asia together to reduce the power of the Occident in that region. In 1950 India sought to mediate in the conflict in Korea between the United Nations and Russia.

Yet India's internal problems were not solved, and it was by no means certain that they would yield more readily or quickly to independent India than they had to the British *raj*. From the standpoint of the economic well-being of both countries, the political separation of India and Pakistan was artificial and embarrassing to each. Pakistan had little coal or iron and slight industrial capacity. Its chief export was jute, but it did not produce enough of that commodity to exchange for all that it wanted from India and other lands. However, in 1949 it was in the enviable position of exporting more than it imported. India had made a beginning toward industrialization and possessed natural resources sufficient for a large expansion of its manufactures. But India needed foreign capital to speed the development of its industries and feared to allow it to enter lest it be followed by a renewal of alien control. Poverty was acute, a post-war decline in manufactures occurred, the railways had deteriorated, prices mounted as in so much of the rest of the world, and food had to be imported to make up the margin between consumption and domestic crops. The pre-war source of much of this food, the rice surplus of Burma, had been reduced to the vanishing point by the Japanese occupation of that land and the post-war disorders. The wheat of the Punjab, now in the control of Pakistan, was not as readily accessible as it had been before the creation of that state. Imports of food, therefore, had to be obtained from other lands, notably the United States, at prices which were much higher than had prevailed in pre-war days. The continual growth of population brought augmented pressure on food supplies and heightened unemployment. By 1951 the economic condition of Pakistan was better than that of its larger sister state, yet neither could be called prosperous. Moreover, friction between the two countries continued not only over Kashmir, but also over communal riots in East and West Bengal, over the Moslem minority in India, and over the Hindu minority in Pakistan. In April 1950, an agreement was reached, but while it eased the tension, it would not permanently remove it.

It was clear that India was being hurried into a new age in which the whole structure of life would exhibit sweeping changes. In the cities women were giving up the use of the veil. Many families were showing an interest in birth control. Youth was becoming assertive against age, and the relationship between husband and wife was being strengthened at the expense of the historic tie between mother and son. In the villages where lived four-fifths of the population, new tastes were being created by the increased travel through buses and trains and contacts with soldiers returning from the war. Caste lines were weakening. Many among the "depressed" or "outcaste" millions were feeling the new tides and were restless. The joint family system was beginning to crack. In the cities labor unions were multiplying and being grouped in national organizations.

Thus far India and Pakistan had been more successful in their independence than many somber prophets would have believed possible, but in 1951 both states were young and had yet to demonstrate their capacity to solve the long-range problems which confronted them.

Ceylon Becomes a Dominion and Is Prosperous

The Labor Government of the United Kingdom which had given independence to India proceeded in a somewhat similar fashion in Ceylon. In 1944, even before Labor had come into power, a commission had been appointed by the British Crown to visit Ceylon and to propose measures for constitutional changes. In May 1946, a draft constitution was presented to the Crown, late in 1947 the British Parliament passed the Ceylon Independence Bill, and on February 4, 1948, the autonomy of Ceylon became a reality. Ceylon was now a self-governing dominion within the British Commonwealth. Under the constitution which was granted the island, the state was headed by a Governor-General appointed by the Crown and having much more than nominal power. Among other functions, he was to choose half the members of the Parliament, appoint the cabinet, the prime minister, and all judges, serve as Commander-in-Chief, and be exempt from having his acts questioned by any court of law. The Parliament was to be composed of two houses. In the upper house half the members were to be elected by the lower house and half appointed by the Governor-General. Ninety-five of the hundred and one members of the lower house were to be chosen by a restricted electorate and under some circumstances six might be appointed by the Governor-General.

Although Ceylon had become a dominion, it was more closely tied to Great Britain than was India or Pakistan. It did not show a disposition to declare itself a republic. Fear of its huge neighbor, India, heightened by the large Indian minority in the island, tended to bind Ceylon to Britain. Although the defense agreement of November 11, 1947, provided that they should not be used by Britain without Ceylon's consent, the strategic harbor of Trincomalee and the other military facilities of Ceylon were to be at the disposal of the United Kingdom. The island's economy was closely integrated with that of Britain, for it was based upon rubber, tea, and coconuts which were chiefly for use in the United Kingdom, and most of the tea acreage and about half the coconut trees were British-owned. Many Britons, too, were employed by the Ceylonese in government posts. Technically and in part really a dominion, Ceylon remained to a large extent in a colonial position.

In the post-war years Ceylon was prosperous. It had the highest standard of living and the highest literacy rate of any country in Southeast Asia. Unlike Burma, it had not been invaded by the Japanese, and in contrast with India it had not been torn by communal strife. It experienced some difficulty in obtaining rice, the chief item in its diet, but it partly filled the gap by imports of wheat from Australia. After the war the demand for its rubber fell off, but it found compensation in the continued sale of its chief export, tea, and in the rising price of its coconuts.

Communists, both Trotskyites and Stalinists, were strong, but there seemed to be no immediate prospect of their gaining control of the island. Ceylon was moving rapidly toward socialism of the British type, for the state owned the railways, the telephones, the telegraph lines, and the radio, controlled much of the machinery of distribution, and had possession of numbers of factories.

Burma, Independent, Is Torn by Civil Strife

For Burma the years which immediately followed World War II were much more stormy and unhappy than they were for India, Pakistan, or Ceylon. In contrast with these other lands, Burma had been occupied by the Japanese. The fighting which accompanied the Japanese conquest and then the expulsion of the men of Nippon wrought considerable destruction of life and property and still greater disruption in the economy, the governmental structure, and the morals of the population. Dacoity (armed robbery), earlier endemic, was on the increase, and the cultivation of rice which before the war had provided between 3,000,000 and 4,000,000 tons a year for export to India, fell off to a point where it barely supplied the needs of the country.

On May 3, 1945, the Japanese lost Rangoon and soon afterward their rule elsewhere collapsed. The British Governor returned in October of that year and took over control from the military. However, he met demands from Burmese nationalists. The most powerful of the Burmese bodies was the AFO (the Anti-Fascist Organization) later the AFPFL (the Anti-Fascist People's Freedom League), in which Socialists and Communists cooperated, with the Communists in the minority. The leader of the AFPFL was Aung San, whose personal relations were chiefly with the Socialists and who commanded the AFPFL's armed forces.

In May 1945, the British government took a long step toward Burmese independence by promising to assist Burma "to attain a status equal to the dominions and to this country," but stated that this could not be accomplished before December 1948. Many vocal Burmese demanded more rapid steps toward independence, disorder continued, and in December 1946, the Labor government of Britain announced an offer of independence to Burma on the same terms as those given to India. Unrest persisted, and in July 1947, Aung San and several of the ministers were assassinated. However, negotiations for the transfer of the government to the Burmese continued, and in October 1947, a treaty was signed between the United Kingdom and Burma under which Burma was to become independent on January 4, 1948.

The granting of independence was carried through on the agreed date but was followed by intensified and more confused disorder and civil war. Although they were a small minority, the Communists were able to stir up strikes which proved annoying. The AFPFL, the dominant party, developed internal dissensions. The fighting which broke out was complicated by the longstanding friction between the Burmese, the controlling and majority race of the country, and the Karens, the most numerous of the non-Burmese minorities. More destruction of property and life followed. In 1949 the prospects were not bright for early peace for the distraught land. However, in 1950 conditions improved and confidence was expressed that the worst was over. Among other favorable factors, the United States had promised economic help as part of its program to aid underdeveloped lands.

Siam Is a Center of Relative Calm

While her western neighbor, Burma, was torn by civil strife and on her eastern borders Indo-China was upset by the aftermath of the Japanese occupation, Siam remained relatively peaceful. Its capital, Bangkok, was a main port of the growing air traffic which was carrying passengers and mail from Europe and America to East and Southeast Asia and around the world.

In December 1941, Siam had signed a military alliance with the Axis powers and had declared war on Great Britain and the United States. In return, Great Britain declared war on Siam. However, the United States did not do so. After Japan's defeat, therefore, the United States was disposed to be more lenient with Siam than was Great Britain. The latter made a set of fairly sweeping demands on Siam as a price for concluding the war. January 1, 1946, an Anglo-Japanese agreement was signed which officially ended the state of war between the United Kingdom and India on the one hand and Siam on the other. Under its terms, among other provisions, Siam undertook to restore to Great Britain all territories seized from her after December 7, 1941, promised not to build the canal across the Isthmus of Kra to connect the Gulf of Siam with the Indian Ocean without the consent of the United Kingdom, thus removing a long-standing British fear that Singapore would be by-passed, and agreed to make available to Great Britain 1,500,000 tons of surplus rice for export to adjacent rice-consuming countries. Siam was thus placed in Britain's economic sphere of influence. There was friction with France because of the latter's demands that the portions of Laos and Cambodia be returned to her which had been ceded after 1941 under pressure from the Japanese. The conflict was allayed in November 1946, by a Franco-Siamese agreement to refer frontier problems to an international commission, but flared up again in 1948.

In domestic affairs Siam operated under the revised constitution which was adopted in 1946 and which extended the control of the electorate that had been granted by the constitution of 1932. The death of the King (June 9, 1946) through a bullet wound in the head, created a temporary ripple. November 9, 1947, a *coup d'état* brought about a change of ministry. Yet in 1948, 1949, and 1950, in spite of post-war inflation, Siam became increasingly prosperous through mounting exports of rice, tin, and rubber which were purchased mainly by the United States, the rice being bought for China, Japan, and Korea, and the rubber and tin for stock-piling in the United States.

In 1950 Siam was promised funds by the United States to enable it to strengthen itself in a military fashion against possible Communist aggression.

The British Return to the Malay Peninsula and Singapore

The defeat of Japan was followed by the return of the British to their possessions in the Malay Peninsula and Singapore. The resumption of their rule gave the British an opportunity to make changes in their administration. None of these, however, were especially revolutionary. On April 1, 1946, Singapore was separated from the Straits Settlements, and made a distinct colony. In 1948 a legislative council, part of whose membership was elective, came into being. Here the Chinese are in the large majority.

In 1946 the other British territories, comprising the remainder of the Straits Settlements and the various Malay States which had been under British protection, were combined to form the Malayan Union. This was to have a strong central government and a common citizenship, thus making of it one state. However, objection to the plan arose, mainly from Malays who feared that, a minority, they would be submerged by the Chinese and Indians, especially since the Chinese, already almost as numerous as the Malays, had a much larger birth rate than the latter. In 1948, after consultation with a committee representing the Malayan government, the sultans of the Malay states and the United Malays, a new organization, the Federation of Malaya, was substituted for the Malayan Union. Their "rights, powers, and prerogatives" which they had enjoyed before the Japanese occupation, were restored in part to the rulers of nine of the Malay states, but centralization was preserved by a federal citizenship and a strong unifying government with a High Commissioner appointed by the British Crown, a Federal Executive Council, and a Federal Legislative Council. Great Britain retained authority over foreign affairs and defense and the British high commissioner had a veto power over much legislation. Yet the plan envisaged progressive steps toward self-government. By this arrangement, Malays were favored as against the Chinese. Many Chinese were unhappy over what they regarded as discrimination and organized to obtain more constitutional recognition. However, the provision for a common citizenship included Chinese and Indians as well as Malays.

The Communists were very active and in 1948 fomented an insurrection. This seems to have been part of a common program planned for all Southeast Asia at conferences held in Calcutta early in 1948 and it roughly coincided with Communist-inspired violence in Burma and Indonesia. Since the end of World War II the Communists had been attempting to gain control of labor and through it political domination of Malaya. However, the uprising collapsed, partly because of the failure of the Communists to obtain the support of the masses and of labor, and partly because of energetic British military action. In 1950, however, Communist guerrillas were once more active.

Communism was to some degree weakened by the revival of trade and with it renewed economic prosperity. The production and export of rubber and tin, commodities which had been so important a source of the wealth of the region before the war, sharply mounted in 1948. By 1950 the tonnage of shipping which was using Singapore exceeded pre-war totals.

A change was made in the political status of two of the three British holdings on the island of Borneo. In 1946 Sarawak, for years ruled by members of the Brooke family, was transformed into a crown colony. In that year British North Borneo, the creation of the British North Borneo Company, also became a crown colony. Brunei remained a protectorate.

The French Attempt to Restore Their Power in Indo-China

After the defeat of Japan the French undertook vigorous measures to restore their rule in Indo-China. It will be recalled that on the eve of World War II the French portion of Indo-China had consisted of Cochin-China, which legally was a colony, and four protectorates, Cambodia, Annam, Tongking, and Laos. It will also be remembered that during World War II, beginning in 1940, Japan occupied the region, not by direct annexation but through an arrangement entered into with the Vichy government of France. In March 1945, even before the expulsion of the Japanese, the de Gaulle regime had published a plan for a Federal Union of France which would embrace both France and the French colonial possessions and under which French Indo-China would have a federal government, its natives would have citizenship in Indo-China and the French Union, and a state council composed of Indo-Chinese and French would enact legislation.

However, the plan met determined opposition. In July 1945, to the distress of the French, Chinese troops crossed the border into Indo-China, ostensibly to dislodge the Japanese. French anxiety was increased by indigenous movements for independence. Two parties, the Viet Minh, Communists, founded by Ho Chi Minh, and the Viet Nam, the Nationalist Party, which received the "control" of the country from the Japanese in March 1945, cooperated. In September 1945, they declared the independence of Indo-China from France, and the Viet-Nam Republic came into being. It utilized the opportunity given by the Chinese occupation to entrench itself. In January 1946 it held its first election and chose Ho Chi Minh as President. Ho Chi Minh had been a revolutionist since his childhood. Small of stature, soft-voiced, seemingly frail, expert in several languages, at least sympathetic with Communism, he was primarily an Indo-Chinese nationalist. Eventually Ho formed a coalition government in which Communists, Socialists, Democrats, independents, Catholics, and former dignitaries of the imperial court of Annam were included. Under a Franco-Chinese agreement, the Chinese withdrew in the spring of 1945. In March 1946 the French and the Republic of Viet-Nam seemed to have reached an understanding whereby France recognized Viet-Nam as "a free state within the Indo-Chinese federation and the French Union."

But friction continued, chiefly over the future of Cochin-China. Viet-Nam wished to incorporate the latter into its domains, and France proposed that the issue be determined by a plebiscite in Cochin-China. In January 1946 France gave Cambodia autonomy, retaining control of its foreign affairs and defense. In June 1946 France granted Cochin-China independence within the Indo-Chinese Federation and announced that it would leave to a plebiscite the question of the relation to the Viet-Nam Republic. In 1946 fighting broke out between the French and the Viet-Namese. Hostilities continued into 1950. Neither side seemed able to win a clear-cut victory. The French found the struggle costly in life and a severe drain on their weakened treasury. In Indo-China the warfare was disastrous, for economy was disrupted, property was destroyed, and hundreds of thousands died of disease and starvation. By the middle of 1949 the French control was limited to the major cities and a few military posts.

In May 1948 pro-French elements set up a rival Viet-Nam provisional central government which included Cochin-China. To make the new state viable the French called in Bao Dai, the ex-Emperor of Annam, who before and during the war had been a mere figurehead, for a time in 1945 had worked with the Japanese, had abdicated after the defeat of Japan, and after six months in Ho Chi Minh's government had gone into voluntary exile in Paris. At the end of 1949 the scene was still confused and peace not yet achieved.

The political changes were only one phase of the revolution. In French Indo-China, as in so much of the rest of the Far East, profound alterations were occurring in fundamental patterns of society and in ideas. Distress due to the Japanese occupation aggravated by the brief Chinese tenure, brought on a severe famine in Tongking which cost that area at least a million and perhaps as many as four million lives.

In 1950 the Indo-Chinese situation was further complicated by the struggle between the United States and Russia. The regime headed by Ho Chi Minh, which was now better known as Viet Minh and which insisted upon full independence from France, was given official recognition by Russia and its satellites, including the Communist government of China. In February 1950, Viet Minh asked and received recognition by Jugoslavia, an interesting development in view of the antagonism between Russia and Jugoslavia and of the fact that Communist China had not yet established relations with Jugoslavia. The Communist victory in China, by bringing the Moscow-oriented Peking regime to the very borders of Indo-China, gave added strength to the Viet Minh cause. Late in 1950 the French were losing ground.

Partly to strengthen the French-sponsored and Bao Dai-led Viet Nam government, in January 1950, the French National Assembly ratified agreements whereby a larger measure of autonomy was conceded to Viet Nam, Laos, and Cambodia, while still holding these units within the French Union. In January 1950, at a conference in Colombo the British Commonwealth ministers, with the significant exception of India, opposed as that country was to the continuation of European colonial power in Asia, decided to support Bao Dai's regime. Fully as important was the action of the United States. That government welcomed the enlarging of the autonomy of Laos, Cambodia, and Viet Nam, recognized them as independent within the French Union, and raised its consulate-general at Saigon to the rank of a legation. It thereby at once accorded its support to the French program as against Ho Chi Minh and sought to encourage Indo-Chinese independence under non-Russian-orientated regimes. Later in 1950, the United States gave assurance of economic and, if necessary, military aid to the French and the Bao Dai government. In this it was moved by its desire to contain Russian Communism to its existing boundaries, peaceably if possible, but, if not, by armed force.

The Dutch and Independence Clash in Indonesia

In the vast, sprawling archipelago of the East Indies, or, better, Indonesia, the first years after the defeat of Japan were ones of turmoil. They were marked by Indonesian movements for political independence, by dissensions among the Indonesians, by attempts of the Dutch to revive their rule which had been so abruptly and roughly terminated by the Japanese, by fighting, by efforts of other governments and the United Nations to restore the peace, and by prolonged and for a time inconclusive negotiations. Yet, in spite of these complications, by 1950 progress had been achieved toward the establishment of an inclusive political structure, the United States of Indonesia, independent, but in association with the Dutch.

Indonesia, it will be recalled, was made up of hundreds of islands, large and small, and of many peoples. It had never been fully brought together politically. Although the Dutch had given it a nearer approach to unity than it had ever known, much of the territory had come under their rule in the half century before the Japanese invasion and had not been effectively welded together. Two-thirds of the population was on the island of Java and the adjacent smaller Madura, so that here lay the center of the Indonesian problem.

The sudden collapse of the Japanese rule in August 1945, was followed by a confused political hiatus. The Netherlands, freed from German occupation only a few weeks earlier, was in no position to send troops to repatriate the Japanese and to renew Dutch authority and administration. The Southeast Asia Command of the United Nations under Lord Mountbatten did not dispatch a force to take the surrender of the Japanese until late in September 1945, and then it consisted of only a few hundred men, British and Indians. In the meanwhile, on August 17, a group of Indonesians had proclaimed the Republic of Indonesia at Djakarta (Batavia)—also spelled Jakarta—with Achmed Soekarno as President. The four outstanding leaders of the new republic were Soekarno, handsome, genial, and an orator; Sjahrir, unassuming, the brains of the movement; Hatta, the Republic's strong man, and Sjariffoedin, later (1948) executed for his part in a Communist revolt. Soekarno was a Javanese. The last three were born on Sumatra and had been educated in the Netherlands. All four had long been intense nationalists, working for independence from Dutch rule.

The idea of a republic proved popular and the demoralized Japanese would have been unable to check it, even had they been disposed to do so. Indeed, by their propaganda against Western imperialism during their years of occupation they had stimulated the nationalist movement. Here and there the Japanese maintained law and order, but

Indonesians obtained arms from them, either through deliberate transfer by the Japanese or through the capture of the munitions of Japanese troops who had clashed with Indonesian irregulars. Many Indonesian groups strove with one another. Some were political parties, ranging from Communists to orthodox Moslems; some were nationalists; others were individual leaders and aspirants for political power; some had been trained as auxiliaries to the Japanese forces; and many were robbers and bandits. A near approach to anarchy followed in which the moderates among the nationalists struggled to establish some semblance of order.

Under these circumstances continued conflict could probably not have been avoided and negotiations were lengthy and complicated. On December 6, 1942, Queen Wilhelmina had announced as the policy of the Dutch government a plan for "complete partnership of the Netherlands Indies in the Kingdom and complete freedom regarding its internal affairs." The Dutch were prepared to implement this policy, but the leaders of the Republic of Indonesia demanded full independence. The British and Indian forces slowly extended their control over much of Java, but not without fighting. For a time early in 1946 the British used Japanese as auxiliaries. In 1946, Dutch troops arrived in sufficient numbers to permit the British military authorities to turn over to the Netherlands East Indies government the Dutch possessions liberated from the Japanese, but outside the great cities Java and Sumatra were in the hands of Indonesian forces. The last of the British troops left on November 30, 1946. In October 1946, the Dutch and the Indonesians agreed upon a military truce, but it was not fully effective, and intermittent fighting persisted. November 15, 1946, partly through British efforts, an agreement was reached at Linggadjati between the Indonesians and the Dutch which provided for the establishment of the United States of Indonesia. The United States of Indonesia was to be composed of three autonomous states—(1) the Republic of Indonesia, consisting of Java, Sumatra, Madura, and adjacent islands; (2) the Dutch portion of Borneo; and (3) the "Great East," which was to include Celebes, the Moluccas, and the Lesser Sunda Islands. The United States of Indonesia was to be associated with the Netherlands through a Netherlands-Indonesian Union in which each partner was to have equal rank, in which the common tie, indissoluble, would be the reigning sovereign of the Netherlands, and through which there would be cooperation in foreign affairs, finance, and economic and cultural matters. The agreement met the approval of the moderates on each side, but the extremists, both Dutch and Indonesians, denounced it.

Although on March 25, 1947, the Indonesian Republic ratified the Linggadjati agreement, fighting was resumed. Late in April 1947, a revolt against the Republic broke out in West Java. It set up an independent state which asked the Dutch for military protection. This was given by the Dutch. In July 1947, they began military operations, and by late summer the authority of the Republic had been reduced in Java to only about a third of the island. The Republic continued to control most of Sumatra.

In the meantime the Dutch had taken further steps to implement the plan for the United States of Indonesia. In December 1946, they proclaimed the State of East Indonesia. This comprised all the Netherlands East Indies east of Borneo and Java with the exception of the Dutch portion of New Guinea. Yet here the Dutch remained in control and arrested the more active dissidents. On May 12, 1947, West Bornea was proclaimed a self-governing territory within the United States of Indonesia and in August a similar status was accorded to East Borneo. These actions were chiefly under Dutch initiative and without consultation with the Indonesian Republic. This the Republicans regarded as a violation of the November 1946 (Linggadjati) agreement. By the end of 1947 several other states and what were called autonomous areas within Indonesia had come into being sponsored and in part created by the Dutch.

The outside world, especially India, Australia, France, Great Britain, the United States, and Russia, had become much concerned about Indonesian developments. Through its Security Council the United Nations stepped in. On August 1, 1947, it issued a cease-fire order, and late that month appointed a Good Offices Committee, composed of an Australian, a Belgian, and an American, to attempt to effect a peaceful settlement. In January 1948, the Good Offices Committee brought about a military truce between the Dutch and the Republic of Indonesia, and an understanding was reached (known as the Renville Agreement from the name of the American transport on which it was negotiated) which on the whole favored the Dutch. It allowed the latter to retain the territories which they had seized in 1947 subject to a plebiscite which would determine the wishes of the inhabitants of Java, Madura, and Sumatra concerning their eventual political alignment. Dutch sovereignty was to continue in the East Indies until it should be transferred to the projected United States of Indonesia.

In 1948 Russia and the Communists took an active hand. Communists objected to the Renville Agreement as a phase of "American imperialism." Many Indonesians became Communists from nationalistic motives—from dissatisfaction with compromises which the Republic had made with the Dutch. In May Russia and the Republic agreed to exchange consular representatives, but the Netherlands objected on the ground that the act would be in violation of the Renville settlement, and the Republic did not ratify the Russian undertaking. A Communist revolt inspired by a leader from Moscow failed (by the latter part of October 1948), the Communist party was outlawed by the Republic, and the latter made many Communists prisoners.

The Dutch continued with their program of setting up a United States of Indonesia and in March 1948, installed the Provisional Federal Government of the Netherlands East Indies in which eight Dutch-sponsored states joined, assisted by Dutch officials. In these states the Dutch managed to retain much of political and economic control, partly by supporting Indonesian elements which would cooperate with them. The Republic was asked to join but declined. In October 1948, under pressure from the various Dutch-encouraged states, the Dutch assented to the creation of an *ad interim* federal government.

Further fighting between the Dutch and the Republic followed. Negotiations with the Republic of Indonesia over its possible participation were undertaken, but in December 1948, the Dutch announced that these had broken down and that no further discussions with the Republic would be held under the auspices of the Good Offices Committee of the United Nations. The Dutch government thereupon undertook military operations to constrain the Republic to enter the *ad interim* federal government. At the outset the Dutch seemed to succeed, for the chief officials and main centers of the Republic were quickly seized. Yet fighting went on, and, by their precipitous action, continued in spite of a cease-fire order of the Security Council of the United Nations, the Dutch lost the sympathy of much of the world.

Peace came slowly. Late in February 1949, the Dutch government announced its purpose to convene a round-table conference which would include representatives of the Republic to discuss and effect the transfer of its sovereignty in Indonesia to an all-Indonesian administration. In March the United Nations Security Council instructed its Good Offices Committee to reinstall the Republic in its capital but on condition that it cease guerrilla warfare and join in the round-table conference. Preliminary understanding was arrived at between the Republic and the Netherlands, and the conference met at the Hague. The discussions were prolonged, but late in December accord was reached and on December 27, 1949, at a formal ceremony in the Hague the resulting arrangement came into being.

The agreements entered into were between the Dutch on the one hand and the Indonesians on the other. The latter were made up of the representatives of the Republic, who advocated a centralized administration for the whole vast area, and those, from outside the area controlled by the Republic, who wished the comprehensive structure to be federal in its character, with much autonomy in the constituent units. These two groups of Indonesians had seemed to unite on a federal state, the United States of Indonesia, made up of the Republic of Indonesia, which embraced most of Sumatra and about half of Java, and of fifteen other states and "autonomous areas." By the December 1949 agreements, the Netherlands assented to a Charter of the Transfer of Sovereignty whereby it "unconditionally and irrevocably" transferred "complete sovereignty over Indonesia to the Republic of the United States of Indonesia" and recognized that Republic "as an independent and sovereign state." At the same time the Netherlands and the United States of Indonesia joined in a Statute of Union which effectuated "the organized cooperation" between the two countries "on the basis of free will and equality in status of each of the two new partners as an independent and sovereign state." The head of the Union was to be Queen Juliana of the Netherlands and her lawful successors, but the position was purely titular. Disputes and disagreements arising from the Union were to be referred to a Union Court of Arbitration. The chief organ of the Union was to be a conference of ministers, normally made up of three from each partner. It was to meet at least twice a year and was to deal with "subjects lying primarily in the field of foreign relations and defense, and as far as necessary, finance, and also in regard to subjects of an economic and cultural character." The United States of Indonesia took over all the internal debt and a large part of the public debt of Indonesia. Both the Dutch and the United States of Indonesia wished possession of the Dutch portion of New Guinea, but the two agreed to leave the issue to be determined by negotiations which were to be completed within a year. Soekarno became President and Hatta premier of the freshly constituted United States of Indonesia.

The United States of Indonesia had no easy course. Russia and her satellites refused to join in the action of the United Nations

Assembly which welcomed the formation of the new state, thus showing the disapproval of the Kremlin. Before the year 1950 was half out, revolts multiplied. Some were by the Dutch-led Royal Indonesian Army, the traditional Indonesian-Dutch army, recruited largely in the eastern islands, for it resented the severance of the tie with the Netherlands and the proposed incorporation into the army of the United States of Indonesia with a substantial reduction in numbers. The Dutch authorities sought to hasten the cutting of the tie beween the Netherlands and the recalcitrant troops. On the other extreme, the movement to end the federal nature of the United States of Indonesia and to make it a centralized state rapidly gained headway. In protest against the trend, late in April 1950, the South Moluccas, with Amboina as the capital, declared their independence. That action was precipitated by the adherence of the island of Celebes to the Republic of Indonesia. However, on August 15, 1950, the United States of Indonesia was replaced by a new unitary government, the Republic of Indonesia, with ten provinces. National elections were scheduled for August 1951, to choose a Constituent Assembly to draft a constitution for the new body. The Premier, Mohammed Natsir, was an able Sumatran Moslem.

In spite of the recurrent fighting, in some sections of Indonesia economic and cultural recovery was beginning to be seen.

The Philippines Become Fully Independent and Begin Recovery

The defeat of the Japanese in the Philippines in the spring of 1945 and their expulsion from the islands were followed by steps toward reconstruction. In these the Filipinos were assisted by the United States. Order was much more quickly established and recovery was more rapid than in Burma, French Indo-China, or Indonesia. Yet the devastation wrought by the war, first by the Japanese conquest and then by the guerrilla resistance and by the fighting by which the expulsion of the Japanese was accomplished, had destroyed hundreds of millions of dollars' worth of property and had left an aftermath of unrest and lowered morals.

The expulsion of the Japanese was followed by a resumption of the process by which the Philippines were to receive their full independence. In June 1948, the Philippine Congress reassembled, made up of the members who had been elected in November 1941. On July 4, 1946, following the time schedule which had been projected in 1934 by the Tydings-McDuffie Act, the islands became independent. By act of Congress in April, 1946, the United States set up the Philippine War Damage Commission and the Congress voted $400,000,000 for private claims and $120,000,000 for public property destroyed during the war. In addition, $630,000,000 of war surplus property was disposed of to the Philippine Republic at 21.4 per cent of the original cost. In April 1946, the American Congress also passed the Philippine Trade Act, sometimes known as the Bell Act. Accepted by the Philippines in July, this measure provided for free trade between the two countries for eight years, and then the raising of American duties on Filipino imports by five per cent a year for twenty years until, at the end of that time, the Philippines would be completely outside the American tariff wall. The bill also required preferred treatment in the Republic for American capital in the "exploitation" of natural resources. In March 1947, a ninety-nine year agreement was signed with the United States by which the latter was permitted to erect and maintain military and naval bases in the Philippines. An amendment to the constitution of the Philippines (which was ratified in March 1947) gave American citizens parity with Filipinos in specific economic rights. Thus the economy of the Republic remained closely connected with that of the United States and the islands continued under the protection of that country.

In spite of obvious progress toward recovery and reconstruction, the Republic of the Philippines had major difficulties. One of the most striking of these was the Hukbalahap rebellion. In the days of Japanese rule, the "Huks," as they were called, had been the "People's Army Against the Japanese." They were said to be Communist-inspired and led. Their stronghold was in the central part of the island of Luzon. They persisted after the expulsion of the Japanese and advocated land reforms in their area which would favor the poverty-stricken tenants as against the landlords. They wished the collectivization of farmlands. For some time during the Japanese period they controlled several provinces, terrorized landlords, and fought other guerrilla bands, including those which cooperated with the Americans. After the expulsion of the Japanese they resisted the Republic. Fighting was severe and was long indeterminate. In 1948, after the failure of an amnesty offered by the Republic to induce the "Huks" to lay down their arms, full scale force was employed against them and the backbone of their resistance seemed to be broken.

Yet poverty and unrest continued. American private capital was reluctant to enter the Philippines and the vast sums poured in by the

United States government induced inflation and benefited only a minority. In 1951 economic conditions left much to be desired.

However, the Filipino leaders seemed undaunted and sought to win for their country a position of leadership in East and Southeast Asia. In May 1950, under their leadership a conference of several Asian countries was held in the Philippines for the purpose of joint planning to curb Communism. Significantly, India declined to be represented.

Frustration and Disillusionment in China

In China the immediate aftermath of the defeat of the Japanese was deep disappointment. Many of the thoughtful and sensitive Chinese had been buoyed up during their long years of resistance by the confident hope that the expulsion of the Japanese would be followed by a period of "reconstruction" which would mean peace and prosperity. These expectations met bitter disappointment.

The national government which had had its headquarters at Chungking in West China attempted to move into the areas which had been occupied by the Japanese. The capital was reestablished at Nanking and the administrative machinery was restored in much of the territory which had been under Japanese-sponsored and supported officials. However, in many places the changes brought irritation and disillusionment. Some of the officials returning from "free" China tended to view all who had remained in "occupied" China as traitors and collaborators with the Japanese, even when many had continued underground resistance at great cost. In Formosa, taken over after half a century of Japanese administration, the new regime proved rapacious and incompetent and the Formosans were soon more unhappy under it than they had been under Japan. Resistance developed and was met by wholesale arrests.

Manchuria (the Three Eastern Provinces as the Chinese called them) presented an especially knotty problem. It had never been fully integrated with the rest of China. Geographically and by its history it was a distinct section. Although overwhelmingly Chinese, its population was suspicious of fellow Chinese who came from south of the Great Wall. The troops and officials which the National government moved in to take over the administration were mostly from south of the Wall and hence were viewed almost as strangers and resentment flared up against what was regarded as an alien regime. Moreover, in the last weeks of the war the Russians had moved in as part of the campaign to defeat Japan. They were slow in evacuating their forces and as they left they dismantled many of the factories and mines and shipped the machinery to Russia. They disregarded the American declaration that disposition of such Japanese property as was seized by any one of the belligerents should be subject to the decisions of an inter-Allied reparations commission. Then, too, under the agreement made by Russia, Britain, and the United States at Yalta early in 1945 and confirmed by the Sino-Soviet Treaty of Friendship and Alliance of August 25, 1945, Russia had continuing rights in the region: the railways were to be operated jointly by Russia and China, Port Arthur was to be a joint naval base for the two powers, and Dairen, the chief port, was to be open to all nations. The Russians, in possession, placed obstacles in the way of opening Dairen. President Roosevelt had long felt that Russia was entitled to an ice-free port and that this could best be had through Manchuria. He was, therefore, prepared to acquiesce in the Russian desire to regain the privileged position enjoyed in that area before the defeat by Japan in 1904–05. Although under another guise and by different tactics, Communist Russia was continuing and implementing the imperialist ambitions of Czarist Russia. By the Yalta agreements and the pact with China, Outer Mongolia, while technically independent, was now more clearly in the Russian orbit than before.

Still more disappointing to the rank and file of the Chinese was the renewal of open warfare between the National government and the Communists. The National government, dominated by the Kuomintang and with Chiang Kai-shek as its outstanding leader, had long cherished a profound distrust of the Communists, a distrust which went back at least as far as the break with them in 1927. The Communists reciprocated the distrust. Ill-feeling had been aggravated by the long war through which the National government had sought to eliminate the Communists. It will be recalled that in 1934 the Communists had been driven from south of the Yangtze and had established themselves in the North with headquarters at Yenan west of the Yellow River. A truce had been patched up during the Japanese invasion, but it was at best uneasy and armed. The Communists and some non-Communists complained that the National government had held many of its best troops out of the fight against the Japanese and had kept them on the border between the Nationalists and the Communists to watch the latter. Friction was heightened when, after the collapse of Japan, the National government began moving its troops into territory which the Japanese had occupied, especially in the North, near the Communist strongholds.

In its struggle with the Communists the National government suffered from serious handicaps. It was controlled by the Kuomintang. This was ostensibly in accord with the program of Sun Yat-Sen which the Kuomintang took as its guide and which had prescribed a period when the state should be under the direction of one party before the stage when more than one party should share in the government. The Kuomintang had been in power since 1926 and 1927 and had lost much of the idealistic impulse which had earlier characterized it. Before being driven west by the Japanese it had depended for its financial support largely upon business and industrial interests in and near Shanghai. In its Western refuge it had been associated with land-owning groups. These associations made it vulnerable to the Communist propaganda which accused it of alliance with "feudal" and "reactionary" minorities who were "exploiting" the masses. The Kuomintang contained many elements. Some of these were very conservative and wished a return to Confucian standards as a way out of the nation's distress. Dissension among the various factions was chronic and debilitating. Although the Kuomintang and the government contained many men of integrity and ability, possibly more than any other administration which China had had in the twentieth century, it also suffered from corruption, inefficiency, and nepotism. The luxurious scale of living of many in officialdom was in striking contrast with the austerity of the Communists. The government and the Kuomintang were regarded by the masses as responsible for the continued and growing inflation. Inflation was probably inevitable because of the war with Japan, the struggle with the Communists, and the decline in revenue due to the prolonged Japanese invasion with its occupation of much of China and the loss of customs duties incident upon the disruption of foreign trade. Yet in the minds of millions the National government was associated with it. Moreover, the skyrocketing price level and the reliance upon the printing press for money made ever more difficult the payment of officials and the army. The police measures adopted by the government to repress the rising discontent and criticism were also resented. Chiang Kai-shek was unquestionably a strong man, was personally incorruptible, and wished the welfare of the country, but he was accused of being unwilling to bring in new men, of depending too much upon those to whom he had become accustomed, and of being hesitant to try drastic and needed reforms.

The Great American Defeat

The United States had assumed enormous responsibilities in China but before the collapse of Japan was four years old it was forced to the painful recognition of a colossal failure. It was by way of the Pacific that the United States had been drawn into World War II. This, as we have seen in the preceding chapter, was because in its pursuance of its Open Door Policy with its support of the independence and territorial and administrative integrity of China, the United States had opposed Japan's imperialistic adventure in that land. In assisting the Chinese to free themselves from the Japanese the United States had spent billions of dollars and the lives of thousands of its sons. In the course of the war the American government had sought to strengthen the Chinese resistance by endeavoring to compose the differences between the Nationalists and the Communists. In this it had not been successful.

When Japan surrendered the United States continued its activities in China with the purpose of disarming the Japanese forces and seeing that they were repatriated and of aiding the Chinese in achieving internal peace. The first objective was fairly easily accomplished but entailed keeping troops in China for many months. The second proved far more difficult. The government of the United States recognized that China needed nothing so much as internal peace if it were to recover from the exhausting years of invasion and enter upon the road to recovery and prosperity. Yet peace could not be realized unless the gulf between the National government and the Communists could be eliminated. This might be accomplished either by assisting the National government to crush the Communists or by bringing about cooperation between the two.

The first course would have entailed huge expenditures of money and probably of American manpower with intervention, perhaps prolonged, in China's internal affairs. Its outcome would be highly doubtful, for Japan had been unable to conquer the Communists. Indeed, the latter had grown in strength by their resistance to Japan. Moreover, such extensive American military action would arouse the antagonism of the Chinese national spirit, already hyper-sensitive to anything resembling foreign imperialism, and if it accepted American assistance the National government would be branded by many Chinese as a "running dog" of the alien.

The United States in part followed this policy, but not wholeheartedly. It aided in the transportation of the Nationalist forces into North China and Manchuria and gave them substantial assistance. Much of the latter was in arms, aircraft, and surplus property left over after the war. Much was in loans and in relief, partly through UNRRA and partly in special grants for projects to improve the national economy. Some cities, notably Shanghai, were largely kept going by food and raw materials through the United States. In 1949 the total grants and credits to China since the defeat of Japan were estimated as in excess of $2,000,000,000. A great deal of the economic assistance miscarried because of the ineptness of the Americans employed and the corruption and inefficiency of Chinese officials.

The United States might have withdrawn completely and have washed its hands of China, but this would have been a complete reversal of the policy which had brought it to Pearl Harbor and into World War II. It therefore chose the hazardous procedure of seeking to bring the Nationalist government and the Communists together. In view of the prolonged and deep animosities between the Kuomintang and the Communists, this effort was probably foredoomed. At least the odds were heavily against it. Yet it was this which was attempted.

To accomplish the purpose of reconciling the Nationalists and Communists, late in November 1945, President Truman appointed General George C. Marshall as his special representative in China. Marshall seemed admirably qualified for the delicate and arduous task. He had had experience in China in the 1920's, he had been Chief of Staff during some of the most difficult days of World War II, and he was a man of unquestioned integrity and high purpose. In 1946, at his suggestion, Dr. J. Leighton Stuart was appointed United States Ambassador to China. Stuart had spent most of his life in China as a missionary and educator, knew the Chinese intimately, and had the personal friendship and confidence of thousands, some of them in high places.

For a time it appeared that the American effort at conciliation might succeed. Thanks mainly to American assistance, by the early part of 1947 the Nationalist forces appeared to be on the way to success against the Communists. They had control of the larger part of the territory south of the Yellow River and were in possession of most of the chief cities and strategic centers in North China and Manchuria. During 1946 Marshall was able to bring Nationalists and Communists together for conversations and negotiations. In January 1946, a committee made up of a representative of the National government, a representative of the Communists, and General Marshall agreed to a cessation of hostilities and the heads of both sides sent out orders to cease firing on January 13. There was to be an Executive Headquarters in Peiping with representatives of the National government, the Communists, and the United States to supervise the carrying out of the order.

Further hope for a peaceful China seemed to be given by a meeting of the Political Consultative Conference in January 1946. This body was what its name indicated. It had no legal authority to enforce its decisions but was for consultation among the various groups. Its thirty-eight delegates represented the Kuomintang, the Communists, six other parties grouped together in the Democratic League, and the Youth Party, and contained some non-party members. Chiang Kai-shek opened its sessions with the announcement that the National government had decided to grant immediately certain basic democratic rights, among them equal legal status for all political parties, the release of political prisoners, the holding of popular elections, and freedom of speech, person, conscience, assembly, and association. He pledged himself to see that these were carried out. After three weeks of work the Conference unanimously concurred in a program for government organization, national reconstruction, a procedure for calling a National Assembly, the setting up of a State Council with equal representation of Kuomintang and non-Kuomintang elements pending the meeting of the National Assembly, and the merging of the armies of the National government and the Communists, with an accompanying demobilization of the majority of the troops. For the accomplishment of this last a committee of three was set up with Marshall as adviser.

In February 1946, an agreement was reached through the committee of three. Its terms provided for a drastic reduction of the armies of both the National government and the Communists, thus lightening the burden which the land has so long borne for the support of non-productive millions. The forces of the National government and those of the Communists were so to be distributed that they would be integrated into one military structure, with the Communists in the minority in each region. Marshall strongly emphasized the importance of a non-political, national army which would not be the tool of any one faction. The program, accordingly, forbade political parties to carry on activities in the armed services, prohibited soldiers from engaging in politics while on active duty, and declared that no party or individual should employ the army in a contest for power.

The prospect for domestic peace, made so encouraging by these several steps, was early clouded. Some elements in the Kuomintang were unhappy over the decisions of the Political Consultative Conference. Although the non-Kuomintang groups endorsed them, many within the Kuomintang desired their modification. Differences developed between the Communists and some of the Kuomintang over the structure of the government which was to be set up under the proposed new constitution. The right-wing elements in the Kuomintang wished a strong president and a powerful central government. The Communists advocated more decentralization with a higher degree of provincial autonomy and argued for a president with strictly limited authority and the executive power placed in a cabinet which would be responsible to a popularly-elected legislature. The Communists demanded that a larger place be allocated them in the *ad interim* administration before the formulation and inauguration of the "permanent" constitution. The chronic distrust between the two parties heightened the difficulties. Each was jockeying for control.

Moreover, hostilities between the forces of the National government and the armies of the Communists flared up, partly over the movement of Nationalist troops in the effort to extend the government's administration into the North and Manchuria in the wake of the Japanese. Since their forces had led in the North in the resistance to the Japanese, the Communists were reluctant to see the Nationalists return to that region. It was in Manchuria that the major friction first arose. At its request, the Americans assisted the National government in the transportation of its troops to that region. The Communists also moved in, at first mainly in the countryside, while the Nationalists were confined chiefly to the cities. The Nationalists were impeded by the Russian control of Dairen, for the Russians would not permit them to come through that port. While loudly denouncing the continuation of American troops in China, the Russians were slow to evacuate Manchuria. It was not until the spring of 1946 that their armies withdrew. Critics complained that the delay enabled the Communists to move in and that the Russians left behind them the arms taken from the Japanese in such fashion that the Communists could easily avail themselves of them. The Russians continued their control of Dairen and, under the treaty of August 1945, their share in the operation of the railroads.

In April 1946, open war was declared by the Communists on the forces of the National government in Manchuria on the ground that the latter were seeking to drive the Communists from the sections of Manchuria from which the Russians had withdrawn. Warfare also blazed up in Central China and Shantung. The Communists were indignant at the aid given by the United States to the National government and insisted that lend-lease cease and that American armed forces be withdrawn. The Communists also declared that less than one per cent of the relief given through UNRRA was reaching Communist territory and demanded a larger share. In June 1946, Marshall succeeded in inducing the belligerents to agree to a truce of fifteen days, but each side accused the other of violating it, and fighting continued. In spite of attempts of General Marshall and Ambassador Stuart, the fighting spread. In August 1946, President Truman appealed twice to Chiang Kai-shek, expressing his deep concern over the civil strife and strongly hinting that unless peace were achieved the United States might be compelled to alter its program of aid to China. This did not produce the desired result, and further efforts by Marshall and Stuart did not prove any more successful.

In spite of the fighting, the National Assembly to adopt a new constitution convened in Nanking in November 1946. It was hoped that under this constitution the period of tutelage by one party which had been envisioned by Sun Yat-Sen would end, and thus the final stage of democratic multi-party government would be reached. Ominously, however, the Communists and the third parties declined to come, and more than three-fourths of the gathering were from the Kuomintang. Yet the constitution was presented to the General Assembly, debated, and, on December 25, approved.

In January 1947 General Marshall was recalled to Washington, for his mission had obviously failed. He immediately became Secretary of State and in that post continued his deep interest in China. But he had been clearly baffled by the Chinese enigma. Soon after Marshall returned to the United States, the Americans were withdrawn from the executive headquarters of the Committee of Three to which had been assigned the reduction of the Chinese armies and the merging of the forces of the National government and of the Communists. All American marines were brought back from China except the few who were serving as a guard at Tsingtao for the United States Naval Training Group which was instructing Chinese naval personnel.

Yet the government of the United States did not cease its efforts to help bring about a peaceful China. Its Ambassador, Dr. Stuart, continued to urge on the National government, and especially Chiang Kai-shek, the importance of reforms and to suggest specific measures. Some steps were taken by the Chinese in the desired direction, but not enough to meet the situation. Warfare went on, with some victories for the National government but with increasing loss of morale in Nationalist circles. In July 1947, hoping to gain new light on the situation, President Truman appointed General Wedemeyer to go to China and Korea on a fact-finding mission. From his experience in China during World War II Wedemeyer was deemed to be especially competent for such an errand. In a public statement, made late in August 1947, on the eve of his return to the United States, Wedemeyer declared that the National government could regain the confidence of the masses only by removing incompetent and corrupt officials in national, provincial, and local posts and by carrying out drastic, far-reaching political and economic reforms. His report, intended for the guidance of President Truman, was not made public until 1949. It included the recommendation that, at the request of China and after the latter had notified the United States of that request, the United States give material assistance and advisory aid to facilitate China's rehabilitation and economic recovery, but in such fashion as not to infringe on China's sovereignty. It also suggested that the United Nations take immediate action to bring about the cessation of hostilities in Manchuria, and that it place this region under the trusteeship of China, Russia, the United States, Great Britain, and France. The report was not at once released to the public because it was recognized that the National government would consider the suggestion about Manchuria to be an affront and would not accede to it.

In spite of these discouraging circumstances and in part because of them many Americans wished to give substantial assistance to China. In 1948, acting on the suggestion of President Truman but not authorizing the entire sum which he recommended, Congress appropriated $125,000,000 for special grants to the Chinese government and $275,000,000 for economic aid. The agreement with the Chinese government for the expenditure of these funds closely resembled those being made at the same time with governments in Western Europe.

In its various measures in China the United States had taken a more active part in the internal affairs of the land than it had ever done in those of any other friendly state. Throughout its efforts the United States had sought to preserve the independence of China and to assist it in achieving a democratic government as Americans understood that term. It had endeavored to aid the Chinese to help themselves, and it had sought to avoid making China in any sense an American satellite.

However, the United States had alienated most of the groups in China. The members of the Kuomintang and the supporters of the National government believed that the United States had not given them sufficient support to enable them to overcome the Communists. To this the American government replied that in no instance had a defeat of the National government's forces been due to the lack of munitions and that had the advice of Marshall and other American officials been followed the outcome in the struggle with the Communists would have been victory. The Communists believed that the United States had sided with their enemy. Many among the Chinese who supported neither party and who desired nothing so much as peace held that by its aid to the National government the United States had prolonged the war. Individual Americans might still be regarded as friends, but by 1950, in spite of all its vast expenditure of life and treasure since 1941, the United States had lost the sympathy of all groups and was being denounced by the Communists as the tool of aggressive imperialistic capitalism. Moreover, in many quarters the United States was criticized for its efforts to put Japan on its feet economically. It was feared that Japan might renew its ambitions for expansion.

The Communist Triumph

The National Government did not collapse immediately. Here and there efforts at reorganization were made. The National Assembly, chosen under the new constitution, met in Nanking late in March 1948. Its chief function was the election of a President and Vice-President. At first Chiang Kai-shek refused to allow his name to be considered. Eventually he yielded to pressure and was chosen. However, in opposition to the wishes of Chiang, Li Tsung-jen was elected Vice-President.

Progressively the tide of battle between the National government and the Communists was flowing in favor of the latter. The year 1946 saw the military power of the National government reach its peak. The Nationalists cleared much of the North of the Communists. They held most of the main cities and controlled a large proportion of the railway lines in the North. They made advances in Manchuria. They were distinctly superior to the Communists in numbers of men under arms and in equipment. In 1947, however, the tide began to flow the other way. In Manchuria the Communists began to push the Nationalists out of important centers. Mukden fell in 1948 and with it Manchuria, with its potential industrial resources, was lost to the Nationalists. In January 1949 Tiensin and Peiping surrendered to the Communists. The Communists moved southward and in April 1949 crossed the Yangtze and occupied Nanking. The following month Shanghai came into their possession. That summer Hankow, Wuchang, and Hanyang fell. October saw the occupation of Canton, to which the Nationalist government had moved its capital. The Nationalists thereupon shifted their headquarters to Chungking. A few weeks earlier much of the Northwest and Sinkiang had passed into Communist hands. Late in 1949 the Nationalists continued to hold Formosa and much of the West and Southwest, but they were suffering from internal dissensions and recriminations, and the morale of their forces had been shattered. Before the middle of 1950 they had lost all of the mainland and the island of Hainan and were confined to Formosa and a few small nearby islands. Formosa became the final refuge of the National government. Thither flocked those whose convictions or interests were tied with it. There Chiang Kai-shek, once more in open control, rallied his forces, hoping that an early all-out clash between Russia and the United States would enable him to return to power on the mainland. In 1950, under able administrators, Formosa was given a better government than had been hers since the expulsion of the Japanese. The Formosans, however, although Chinese by race, regarded the Nationalists as aliens.

The Nationalist debacle was due to a number of factors. The Kuomintang suffered from fierce internal conflicts; it also had in it much of corruption. Chiang Kai-shek proved unable to cope with the extraordinarily difficult situation. In January 1949 he voluntarily retired from the Presidency, but he retained his position as head of the Kuomintang and remained the most powerful figure in the Nationalist scene. The final blow to the Nationalist cause was the failure to curb the runaway inflation. In a desperate effort to check the deterioration of the currency, in the summer of 1948 the government issued a new currency supposedly supported by gold and, to gain the needed reserves, ordered the surrender of all gold, silver coins, and foreign currency. Within a few weeks the new currency began to go the way of the old. The Nationalists lost whatever shred of public confidence they had retained. Popular support completely disappeared, and the general opinion was that any regime would be preferable to the one which had so lamentably failed.

The only alternatives to the fading National government were disunion and a revival of warlordism and heightened civil strife on the one hand and the Communist party on the other. Several other parties existed, but they were small, and no one of them had the structure or the leadership competent to administer the nation. The Communists aspired to control the entire country. The Communist Party was well organized, highly disciplined through years of resistance to the Nationalists and the Japanese, and led by men who were profoundly convinced of the competence of their program to relieve China's woes. Its outstanding leader was Mao Tzŭ-tung. It was composed of some who were fanatically committed to Communist ideology, of others who saw in the Party an effective means to the social reforms which the Kuomintang had not accomplished, and of still others who for their own advantage wished to associate themselves with the winning side. It was the convinced Communists who controlled the Party. The Chinese Communist Party more and more frankly associated itself with Moscow's policies and lined itself up with the Kremlin in the international scene, denouncing the United States and the Atlantic Pact. The Party set high standards for admission to its ranks. These involved surrender of individual desires and opinions and complete loyalty to the Party's decisions. The feature of the Party's program which had first been prominent was agrarian reform, with the breaking up of the larger holdings and the redistribution of the land among small peasant cultivators. This was not as revolutionary as it seemed at first glance, for few holdings were over five hundred acres and most of the cultivated land was in small tracts farmed by the owners. However, the Communist Party had more far-reaching objectives. It wished the full communization of China. To that end it sought the rejection of Confucian ideals and the dissolution of the traditional family unit with its tight solidarity and its insistence upon the primary allegiance of its members.

The Communist Regime Is Established in China

On October 1, 1949, the Communists proclaimed a national government, "The People's Republic of China." In it they associated various other parties and groups with themselves, but they made sure that only those willing to cooperate with them were given a voice or an office, and they retained the effective control in their own hands. The traditional provinces were preserved as administrative units, but between them and the central government were inaugurated five Administrative Regions. China was divided among them and to each was granted large powers, always subordinate to the central authorities. Peiping, now restored to its earlier name, Peking, was made the capital. Since Peking was much nearer to Russia than Nanking, its choice as against the latter symbolized the orientation toward Russia.

Russia promptly withdrew its recognition of the National government and gave it to the new regime. Moreover, by an agreement which involved Manchuria, Russia provided for the exchange of products with that region. From Manchuria were to go foodstuffs and other raw materials, and Russia was to pay in manufactures.

Most countries outside the Russian sphere were slow to give recognition to the Communist regime. In the summer of 1949 the United States government seemed to have washed its hands of the Nationalists. While still officially recognizing their regime, it frankly expressed its lack of confidence in it. However, it was not as yet prepared to concede even *de facto* status to the Communist government, and its Secretary of State spoke of conditions which must be met before recognition would be given. After a delay, in December 1949, India and Burma recognized the People's Republic and in January 1950, Great Britain and Pakistan followed. However, Peking was slow to establish diplomatic relations with Great Britain. In January 1950, in protest against the seizure of some of its property in Peking, the United States withdrew its consular and diplomatic officers from the mainland. It continued relations with the Nationalist regime and supported its representatives in the United Nations as speaking for China.

The Communists vigorously set about consolidating their rule in China. They did not seek to make China a fully Communist or, indeed, a fully socialist state at once. They recognized that this would require many decades and perhaps longer. They sought to educate the people in the principles of what they called the New Democracy. To this end they had indoctrination courses. Many of these were in the schools, for they insisted that the latter conform to their patterns. By catchy folk dances and songs, by the radio, motion pictures, plays, placards, and posters, they sought to popularize their regime among both students and the masses and to spread the conviction that a new day had dawned in which China would once more win back her self respect, abolish poverty and civil strife, end the remnants of foreign imperialism, and again become powerful. They speeded up the training of technicians, physicians, nurses, and recruits for the government services. In doing so they shortened the courses and sought to enroll larger numbers, so urgent was the need. They reorganized the administration of the schools, insisting that the governing bodies have on them representatives of teachers, students, and servants as well as principals and presidents. They clung to their program of the redistribution of the land but did not push it everywhere. They sought, not without some success, to cope with inflation, and furthered the practice of making salaries payable in grain and of measuring bank deposits in terms of their purchasing power, so that in withdrawing them the depositors could be assured that they would be able to buy as much with their money as when they had put it in. The Communists struggled with the problem of the cities and of industry and wished especially to restore and develop the industrial possibilities of Manchuria. They also purposed bringing Tibet under their control and "liberating" Formosa.

The leaders among the Chinese Communists who loomed most prominently in the public eye were Mao Tzŭ-tung, Chu Teh, and Chou En-lai. Mao Tzŭ-tung, the chairman of the Communist Party, a farmer's son, was born in Hunan Province in 1893, from boyhood had been a revolutionist, in 1921 had helped found the Communist Party of China, and except for a brief interval in 1927 had been its acknowledged head. Chu Teh, born in 1886, the son of a wealthy father, was a trained professional soldier and head of the Communist army. Chou En-lai, the Party's chief expert in foreign affairs and the first Premier of the People's Republic when it was set up in Peking, was born in 1898 in a wealthy family with scholarly and official traditions, had part of his education in France, and from 1924 to 1927 worked in connection with Chiang Kai-shek before the latter broke with the Communists. All three had been through the gruelling years in Yenan.

The Communist officials were hard-working, lived frugally, and were well disciplined. The Communist army was well fed and well paid, and its officers dressed and lived almost as simply as the rank and file. As a rule it did no looting and respected the populace. Here was something new in China's experience—a tightly knit party, led by men who were profoundly, almost fanatically convinced of the truth of their position and that it held the solution for China's woes, and supported by an army which did not prey on the populace. In the territories in which they had been in control longest, the Communists were enforcing their program more and more stringently. Presumably they would expect to do this eventually in the more recently "liberated" areas. To support the structure of their government and the army they levied very heavy taxes. These bore especially hard on farmers, for the latter were required to pay in grain and much of this was used for the cities, cut off as these were from much of their former foreign trade and especially from the supplies which had recently come in through American relief.

What was the attitude of the masses of the Chinese? In general they acquiesced in the triumph and rule of the Communists. Here and there peasant revolts broke out against the heavy taxation and other exactions imposed by the new rulers. There were also armed bands in revolt. In Szechwan a powerful secret society, the Ko Lao Hui, was unreconciled. Many Chinese were discontented or critical. Incorrigible individualists, the Chinese were not easily regimented into a thoroughgoing totalitarian regime. Yet millions were so disillusioned with the Nationalist government and the Kuomintang that they were willing to give the Communists an opportunity, especially since no viable alternative seemed to present itself on a national scale. Certainly no group or element in the foreseeable future gave any hope of successfully competing with the Communists. Thousands, especially among the students, rebounding from inert despair over the post-war disappointments, enthusiastically hailed Communism as promising hope for employment and for the cure of China's ills. They flocked to the training classes in the principles of the new order and to the schools which gave preparation for serving under the new regime. The larger proportion of Chinese idealism enrolled itself under the new banner.

Communist China was orientated toward Russia. It regarded Russia as the leader and the teacher in the New Democracy. The educational system which had been modeled on that of the West now sought its guide in the U.S.S.R. In many schools Russian was given priority over English, long the most-studied foreign language. In propaganda the Moscow line was followed, especially in the villification of the United States. An increasing number of Russians were employed as advisers, and the effort was made to orient China's economy away from the coastal cities and dependence on the West toward the

U.S.S.R. Official propaganda stressed Russian friendship and assistance and the Russian entrance into the war against Japan as the cause of the latter's collapse.

On February 12, 1950, after prolonged negotiations in Moscow, a thirty-year pact of friendship and mutual aid was announced between the U.S.S.R. and the People's Republic of China. It was declared to have as an object the prevention of renewed aggression by Japan either alone or aided by another power. In the event of aggression by Japan, or of another power allied with Japan, on either Russia or China issuing in war, the other would immediately render military or other aid with all means at its disposal. The U.S.S.R. and China covenanted to cooperate with each other in all important international questions touching the mutual interests of the two governments with joint respect for the sovereignty and territorial integrity of both and non-interference in the internal affairs of either. The pact was to run for thirty years and, unless within a year of that time one party notified the other to the contrary, it was to be in force for an additional five years. By further agreements, the U.S.S.R. promised to withdraw its forces from Port Arthur and to return, without compensation, the Changchun Railway in Manchuria when a peace treaty with Japan had been concluded or at the latest by the end of 1952, was to recognize that the administration of Dalny (Dairen) belonged entirely to the People's Republic of China, and was to aid China with credits to the extent of $60,000,000 for five years for the purchase of equipment and other materials from Russia, the credits to bear one per cent interest and to be repaid by raw materials, tea, gold, and American dollars.

By these developments Russia was more potent in the affairs of China than she had ever been.

In contrast and as a corollary, the People's Republic of China regarded the United States as its chief antagonist. Its official propaganda denounced the United States as imperialistic. The planes which the Nationalists on Formosa were using to bombard the cities of the mainland were described as American and as under the direction of American officers. To support the People's Republic of China, Russia insisted that the Nationalists who served in the United Nations as the representatives of China be ousted and the representatives of the People's Republic be substituted for them. When the United Nations, largely because of the United States, refused this demand, in 1950 Russian representatives walked out of almost all the units of that body and absented themselves from them, including the Security Council until Malik's return to it as chairman in August 1950.

Formosa remained a bone of contention. Many Americans wished the United States to give substantial aid to the National government in its refuge on that island. On January 5, 1950, President Truman issued a statement saying that the United States would not give military aid to the Nationalists, that it had no predatory designs on Formosa or any other Chinese territory, and that it had no desire to obtain special rights or privileges or to establish military bases on the island. However, on June 27, 1950, as a result of the Korean affair of which we are to speak in a moment, and presumably under pressure from military advisers who urged that Chinese Communist possession of Formosa would jeopardize American defenses in the Western Pacific, President Truman ordered the fleet of the United States to resist any Communist attack on Formosa and the Pescadores, but also told the Nationalists to cease their air attacks on the mainland. He said that the disposition of Formosa would await a peace treaty with Japan or action by the United Nations. An American fleet at once sailed to give effect to this action by patrolling the straits between Formosa and the mainland. The Nationalists on Formosa assented, but insisted that Formosa was part of the territory of China.

The events of the years which followed the defeat of Japan accelerated the basic revolution in Chinese culture which had been under way for half a century. The traditional order continued to disintegrate. In spite of the efforts of some in the Kuomintang to rejuvenate it, Confucianism was progressively fading, and its decline was being hastened by the outspoken antipathy of the Communists. The dissolution of Confucianism was one of China's basic problems. Indeed, it may well have been its fundamental problem. By it, China was losing the body of principles which had chiefly molded its civilization for two thousand years. Consciously or half-consciously, the Chinese were groping for something to take its place and around which to rebuild their life, individually and collectively. Communism confidently and dogmatically promised to fill the void and to fill it better than Confucianism had ever done. Indeed, the sweep of Communism in China seems in some degree to be ascribable to its claim to meet the hope which Confucianism had nourished: the achievement of an ideal society here and now.

By its triumph, Communism, frankly contemptuous of historic religions although professedly granting religious liberty, accelerated the decay from which Buddhism, Taoism, and other faiths long present in China had been suffering. Christianity seemed to offer the one alternative to Communism. It displayed much vitality. Its adherents had continued to grow in the years of the Japanese invasion, many missionaries remained under the Communists, most Chinese Christians held true to their faith, and in some areas numerous baptisms were reported. Christian churches were springing up and growing independently of foreign aid or leadership. Yet Christians were still a small minority and in places churches and Christian services and other activities suffered under the new order. This was especially true of the Roman Catholics, for their leaders were particularly vocal in their denunciation of Communism.

Clearly the Communists were furthering the revolution in forms of government and in education which had long been in progress. Even if they did not succeed in abolishing the traditional Chinese family, they were adding to the forces which were working against it and were weakening other inherited social patterns and customs. China was still on its troubled march, and no one could accurately predict what the future would be.

Korea, Liberated from Japanese Domination, Is Arbitrarily Divided and Unstable

Conditions in Korea following the defeat of Japan were no less distressing than were those in China. In 1940 a Korean "provisional government" had been brought into existence in Chungking in connection with the Chinese resistance to Japan. In December 1943 a communiqué recorded the determination of President Roosevelt, Prime Minister Churchill, and Generalissimo Chiang Kai-shek at Cairo "that in due course Korea shall become free and independent." At Yalta, in February 1945, it was agreed that there should be a period of trusteeship pending the setting up of a stable regime. However, as part of their joint war effort against Japan, and to disarm and repatriate the Japanese forces there, Russia and the United States divided Korea between them into military zones, the Russian army moving into the area north of the 38th parallel of latitude and the American army occupying the region south of that line. This division persisted and became a major source of weakness and continuing friction. As had been the case from early times, Korea suffered from being a small country on a strategic peninsula between two major powers. For centuries China and Japan had been the rivals. Following the defeat of China by Japan in 1895, Russia and Japan became the contenders. Now, because of the power vacuum left by the defeat of Japan, Russia and the United States glared at each other across an artificial barrier, and Korean hopes of a united, independent nation were frustrated. Each of the two sections was handicapped by the separation. Most of Korea's industry, mineral resources, and hydro-electric power were in the North, while the latter depended upon the South for much of its rice, fish, and other food.

Efforts which proved tragically futile were made to bring the Russians and the Americans to an agreement to end the division. In December 1945, a British-Russian-American conference in Moscow authorized the setting up of a provisional democratic Korean government and a four-power trusteeship under Great Britain, China, Russia, and the United States for a period of five years. To carry out this program a conference of the Russian and American commands was ordered. Attemps of the joint Soviet-American commission to implement this program were accompanied by friction and ended in failure. In October 1946 the Russian members left Seoul and the commission hopelessly broke down.

In the meantime governments were arising in both the North and the South. In the North a party which followed the Communist program led by Koreans trained by Russians was in control and set up what was called the North Korea People's Government. This called for the abolition of tenantry and the free distribution of the land to the farmers and in 1948 was recognized by Russia and Mongolia. In the American zone there were many parties and much disorder. There was also acute physical distress which was only partially relieved by the pouring into the area of hundreds of millions of dollars' worth of supplies by the United States. Late in 1946 a South Korean Legislature assembled under American auspices and in spite of the refusal of both left-wing and right-wing elements to cooperate, the Americans turned over more and more power to the nascent government. However, American advisers continued to assist in various aspects of the section's life, especially in various phases of its economy.

In November 1947, at the instance of the United States and in face of the opposition of Russia, the Assembly of the United Nations created a commission composed of representatives of nine states to go to Korea and assist in the formation of a government for all the country. Since North Korea refused to cooperate, the United Nations' representatives went ahead with elections in South Korea for a constituent assembly. This latter was chosen in May 1948, adopted a constitution, and in June elected as President of the South Korea Republic the conservative Syngman Rhee, who during the Japanese regime had been an absentee agitator for independence. The South Korea regime had no easy time, but in December 1948, it was recognized by the General Assembly of the United Nations as the only legitimate government in Korea, and the United States announced a three-year $300,000,000 aid program. In January 1949, the republic was recognized by the United States, Australia, China, and the Philippines. Early in 1950 it was making progress, although slow and spotty, toward stability and was undertaking a sweeping action to make peasant proprietors of about a million peasant tenants. American economic aid to South Korea continued and on the whole was well administered.

North Korea retaliated for the action of the United Nations by proclaiming in September 1948, the Democratic People's Republic of Korea. This claimed authority over all Korea and had in its cabinet several Koreans from the South. Russia and its satellites, Poland and Mongolia, quickly recognized it.

Thus the separation of the North and the South was accentuated, with a government in each which claimed jurisdiction over the entire peninsula. The withdrawal of their troops by both the Russian and American governments (the latter in July 1949) did not ease the tension. Beginning in the autumn of 1949 there was sporadic fighting along the 38th parallel, the boundary between the North and the South.

THE WORLD IS INVOLVED IN KOREA

June 24, 1950, brought dramatic developments which involved almost the entire world in Korea. The North Koreans, giving as an excuse an alleged attack by South Koreans, surged in force across the 38th parallel, intent upon eliminating the South Korean regime and uniting all the country under the Communist government of the North. They were well equipped with Russian arms, tanks, and planes, and their core had been well trained. The South Korean forces, lightly armed, for promised American equipment had not reached them, were quickly pushed back.

The United Nations was deeply involved, for it was under its auspices that the South Korean government had been set up. On June

25 its Security Council met, with Russia, due to her abstention policy, absent, voted overwhelmingly that firing in Korea cease, and demanded that the North Koreans retire to their side of the 38th parallel. The United States assumed the main burden of supplying land, air, and sea forces to implement the action of the United Nations. On June 27 President Truman put General MacArthur in command of the American forces to repel the North Korean invasion. On that same day the Security Council voted, by a majority of seven to one, for an American resolution endorsing Truman's decision to send military aid. The secretariat of the United Nations also sent out requests to its member states to give armed aid to enforce its commands. Within a few weeks several governments complied.

The struggle became one with Russia and her satellites on the one side and the vast majority of the nations of the world and the United Nations on the other. It was the most severe test which the United Nations had met. the United States appealed to Russia to use her influence to induce the North Koreans to obey the United Nations. Russia in an extensive statement accused the South Koreans of deliberately starting the affray by attacking across the debated 38th parallel, charged the United States with planned aggression in Korea, and declared that the vote of the Security Council had been illegal. India, on the whole friendly to the United Nations, attempted to act as a mediator. As a preliminary to a discussion of terms of peace Russia demanded that the Communist government of China be seated in the United Nations in place of the Nationalists. This the United States rejected, insisting that a preliminary to any discussion of peace, the North Koreans must obey the order of the United Nations and withdraw to the 38th parallel. In August, as we have seen, Malik, representing Russia, returned to the Security Council to assume the chairmanship which then came to Russia by rotation, vehemently attacked the United States, and insisted that the People's Government of China be seated in the Council and that the North Koreans be invited to sit there to discuss peace terms. The representative of the United States was adamant that the Security Council's order of withdrawal of the North Koreans be given first priority.

For the first weeks the fighting went badly for the South Koreans and the United Nations. The United States rushed forces and supplies to the theater of war, but most of them had to be sent across the Pacific. The aid from other members of the United Nations also had to come from long distances. The North Koreans drove on and were penning the United Nations' forces to a small area in the southeast when, by the middle of August, United Nations' reinforcements, chiefly from the United States, began arriving in quantity and began to roll back the North Korean tide.

On September 15, 1950, in a carefully prepared and sudden move the United Nations' forces made a dramatic landing at Inchon, the port of Seoul. By the end of the month they had taken Seoul. They then moved rapidly northward, crossed the 38th parallel, and on October 20 captured Pyongyang, the North Korean capital. By the end of October they had reached the Yalu River, the boundary between Korea and China. For the moment it seemed that the North Korean Communist regime would be eliminated and that the government recognized by the United Nations would rule all the country.

Then, late in October and in November 1950, the Chinese Communists stepped in and the armies of the United Nations were pushed back. Ever since the intervention of the United Nations the preceding June and the action of the United States in preventing them from invading Formosa, the Chinese Communist denunciation of the United States had been mounting and had become shriller. In their propaganda the Chinese Communists ignored the fact that the United Nations was acting in Korea and that several countries had sent contingents. They spoke as though only the United States had intervened and declared that it was the aggressor. They accused the United States of sending its planes across the Yalu and bombing objectives in Manchuria and insisted that the United Nations hear its case and condemn the United States. Late in November Chinese Communist troops in overwhelming force and supported by Russian-made planes moved across the Yalu into Korea and forced the retreat of the armies of the United Nations. Both the People's Government of China and the representatives of the U.S.S.R. insisted that these armies were "volunteers" and thus the fiction that the Chinese Communist regime was not in the war was maintained. Within a few days the Red armies had retaken Pyongyang and had pinned some of the United Nations' men in a coastal pocket in the Northeast. Here was the most striking success that Chinese armies had had against major Western powers since the latter had forced open the door of China more than a hundred years earlier.

Various governments were feverishly attempting to bring hostilities to an end before they could precipitate another world war. Great Britain, while supporting the United Nations in Korea, believed the American action in neutralizing Formosa to have been unwise. Several Asiatic governments, notably that of India, were proposing solutions.

In the meantime strained relations had developed between India and the People's Government of China. In October 1950, the latter sent armed forces into Tibet to "liberate" that country. These troops were succeeding and Peking laid claims to territories on the southern and southeastern borders of Tibet which India regarded as not belonging to that country. It protested Peking's action in Tibet and in replying Peking said that the movements there were of purely internal concern and not subject to discussion with foreign governments. Both India and Pakistan were fearful for their northern borders and possible Communist aggression from that direction. Friendship between India and Communist China perceptibly cooled.

With the consent of the United States, which had stood against admitting the Communist regime as the representative of China in that body, the United Nations invited Peking to send a delegation to present its charges against the United States. Late in November 1950, the delegation came to the headquarters of the United Nations in New York where the Assembly and the Security Council were meeting, and made a bitter verbal attack on the United States. Further difficulties developed. The United States insisted that Peking was now an aggressor in Korea and that its armies be withdrawn from that land before its charges against the United States were heard. Since no agreement was reached on priorities, in mid-December the Peking deputation withdrew.

In December 1950, with the assent of the United States but over the objection of the U.S.S.R. the United Nations set up, at the suggestion of several of its members, a commission to arrange a peaceful settlement of the Korean affair.

In their activities in the international scene the Chinese Communists had the full support of the Kremlin. How far they were the puppet tools of the latter was not clear. Apparently they were firmly convinced that the United States had imperialistic designs on China. They appealed to Chinese nationalist sentiment. The successes of their armies in Tibet and Korea sent a thrill of pride throughout China.

But at the end of December 1950 the lines were being more tightly drawn between the People's Government of China and the United States. The latter showed no disposition to weaken its position on Korea. Nor did it seem disposed to withdraw its objection to the admission of the People's Government to China's seat in the United Nations, to recognize them as the legitimate regime of China, or to conform to their demand that they be a partner in negotiating the peace treaty with Japan. On December 15 President Truman declared a state of national emergency and that same month the United States cut off American imports to China.

The Ryukyu Islands: Okinawa

In 1951 there remained another thorny problem which was an aftermath of war. What should be done with the Ryukyu Islands? Did the announced reduction of Japanese territory to the four main islands and such other islands as the Allies should determine (see p. 628) mean that the Ryukyus would not be included in the post-war Japanese domains? The Ryukyu islanders were not, strictly speaking, Japanese. Yet for centuries the islands had been within the sphere of Japanese influence and since the 1870's they had been formally a part of the Empire.

The problem was complicated by the largest of the group, Okinawa. American forces had taken it during the late war after bitter fighting. In 1951 the United States continued to occupy it. It was fortifying it as an important bastion in its Far Eastern defenses. The inhabitants were not faring well under its rule. What would be the future?

Defeated Japan, Occupied, Faces a Somber Future

The Japan which emerged from World War II was severely handicapped as it entered the grim years of reconstruction. Most of its chief cities had been bombed, with the destruction of much of the physical equipment of its industries. Its normal overseas markets and sources of raw materials had either been taken out of its control or had suffered so severaly from the war and its aftermath that their value to Japan was greatly reduced. Japan was stripped of its holdings in Korea, Manchuria, Formosa, and Sakhalin. The first three had had their economy so disrupted that they were not the outlet for Japan's manufactures or the assets to Japan's industrial structure which they had once been. The fourth was entirely removed from Japan's economic structure. The Kuriles had been assigned to Russia and presumably had been occupied by that power, so that whatever value they had once possessed for Japan's fishing enterprises was either reduced or eliminated. The devastation wrought in China by the Japanese invasion and the succeeding civil strife had deprived Japan of what, if Manchuria is included, had been its chief market in the years immediately preceding World War II. The merchant marine, which had made Japan the third shipping power of the world, had been sunk by enemy action, and the country had thereby been deprived of one of its main sources of revenue and means to foreign commerce. Japan's problem was further accentuated by the fatigue and prolonged strain of the war years and the diversion of the nation's economy to war purposes. The country had been putting forth superhuman efforts to achieve the ambitions of its imperialists, physical exhaustion followed, and such of the machinery, railways, and factories as had escaped bombing had deteriorated. Inflation, already present, was aggravated by the near bankruptcy of the state and the collapse of foreign trade. Population, one of the major problems of pre-war years, mounted rapidly, and there was less food and clothing to supply its needs than before the war. The millions demobilized from the army and navy returned and swelled the ranks of those looking for employment. To them were added millions of civilians who were sent back from Korea, Manchuria, and Formosa. The population also continued to grow by the excess of births over deaths. It remained true, as it had been before the war, that relief for the pressure of population and a possibility of an increase in the standard of living could be found only by exchanging abroad manufactures for food and raw materials. Japan still had more technical skill in industry and commerce than any other country in the Far East, but, as we have suggested, its physical equipment for industry had been reduced, and its normal overseas markets and sources of food had been removed or damaged.

Yet Japan possessed some assets and in at least one important respect it was better off than before the war. As we had hinted, in spite of the damage wrought by the war, it still had the best industrial equipment and more industrial "know how" than any other land in the Far East. The victors permitted Japan to keep its Emperor and much of the structure of government to which it had been accustomed: the nation could go on to reconstruction without having to build completely from the ground up or without having to go through a period of chaos. Morever, the compulsory disarmament of Japan had relieved the country of the unproductive incubus of a huge army and navy, a heavy load which had long burdened the nation. Then, too, the Japanese became aware that ultimately the only sure remedy of over-population was the reduction of the birth rate. It was significant that in 1949 the Diet passed a measure which permitted abortion under some circumstances and which put local governments behind the dissemination of information concerning methods of birth control. In 1950 this was reported to be producing results.

With these handicaps and the partially compensating assets, Japan was clearly entering a major new era of its history. Never before had it been occupied by an alien power. Its effort at empire balked, it had been deprived of all its overseas possessions and was under the tutelage of the victors. The victors would insist upon drastic changes and upon the complete demilitarization of a people which from the dawn of history had cherished a martial tradition. How long the new era would last or what would come out of it no one could foresee. The few years which immediately succeeded defeat and the beginning of occupation were quite too brief a period to enable long-term trends to be discerned. Yet by 1951 the program of the forces of occupation had taken shape and its immediate accomplishments could be described.

The Program and Achievements of the Forces Which Occupied Japan

The occupation of Japan was primarily by the nation which had led in the defeat of the country, the United States. Others of the powers which had shared in the victory sent small contingents, but they were token forces. Dominant in the occupation was the American general, Douglas MacArthur. MacArthur was described as Supreme Commander of the Allied Powers, and the administrative structure of which he was the head was, accordingly, known as SCAP. As a result of the Moscow conference of the Big Three in December 1945, there was created the Far Eastern Commission on which were represented Russia, Great Britain, the United States, China, France, the Netherlands, Canada, Australia, New Zealand, India, and the Philippines. November 17, 1949, Burma and Pakistan were added. The Commission was to have general supervision of SCAP and MacArthur was to act under its direction. The Commission had its seat in Washington. In addition there was set up by the Moscow conference the Allied Council for Japan on which were represented the United States, Russia, China, and Great Britain. It had headquarters in Tokyo, and its chairman was MacArthur.

MacArthur was Supreme Commander of the Allied Powers in fact as well as in name. As not only the titular head but also by far the ablest and most forceful man in the occupying forces, he entered upon his task with enthusiasm and with the purpose of seeing that the Japanese carried through a program of thoroughgoing reorganization and that, so far as possible, Japan be democratized as the United States understood that term. Japan was allowed to retain the Emperor and much of the rest of its inherited structure, but within this framework MacArthur insisted that there be a reorganization of the nation's life. The Japanese government was kept subordinate to SCAP and had to heed the latter's directives. The Emperor was required to call on MacArthur once a week, although the latter never called on the Emperor.

To the surprise of many observers, the Japanese acquiesced in the occupation, and, indeed, thousands welcomed it. They had suffered so terribly from the prolonged war and its merciless regimentation and were so benumbed by the bombings that they greeted the victors with something akin to relief. The leaders who had brought Japan to its grim plight were discredited, and the mass of the nation was prepared to follow the liberals and moderates.

In general SCAP sought to work through the Japanese government and to assist the Japanese in making the changes demanded by the victors, for in theory it recognized that to be enduring the alterations must commend themselves to the Japanese and, so far as possible, proceed from them and be carried out by them. Yet SCAP was convinced that extensive foreign initiative, advice, and assistance were necessary. To this end it assembled a large staff, many of them military and some of them civilian. The personnel of SCAP was overwhelmingly American. Here was an effort, undertaken chiefly by the United States, to remake a major, highly civilized nation. The task was rendered the more difficult by the factors which we enumerated a moment ago. The first few years of the occupation saw drastic measures, but decades would elapse before the outcome could be accurately appraised.

Before the end of 1945, or in other words with four months of Japan's surrender, MacArthur had issued directives ordering the dissolution of the general staffs of the imperial army and navy; the arrest and trial of "war criminals"; the abolition of the Black Dragon Society which was held to have been a spear-point in Japan's imperialistic program; the ending of military censorship; the purging of the school system from all known militarists and imperialists; the legalizing of labor unions; the giving of the franchise to women; the release of political prisoners; the dissolution of the four major *Zaibatsu* family concerns—the Mitsui, Mitsubishi, Sumitomo, Yasuda; the dissolution of the narcotic monopoly; the severance of all diplomatic ties with other countries; the seizure of the war loot which the Japanese had taken from other lands; the abolition of the secret police and the repeal of the repressive laws associated with that police; the discontinuance of state Shinto; the proclamation of freedom of speech, political activities, and religion; and the reform of the tenure of farming land by ending absentee ownership and large estates and by distributing the land among the peasant cultivators.

The years 1945, 1946, and 1947 witnessed the implementation of these directives and the carrying through of other changes. Late in 1945 state Shinto was disestablished, and thereby a blow was struck at the religious roots of Japanese chauvinism. On January 1, 1946, the Emperor issued a rescript in which he formally declared that his divinity was a false conception based on ancient myths and legends and that the associated doctrine that the Japanese people were superior to other races and were destined to rule the world was also untrue. He sought to identify himself with the people and called for unity and hard work. It must be added that although the Emperor had renounced his divine status and often showed himself familiarly to his people, the reverence felt for him and the imperial institution continued. Indeed, in the midst of the threat of national chaos, the Emperor, as the center and symbol of unity, may have become more important than ever.

Also in January 1946, MacArthur directed the Japanese government to dissolve more than a score of military and patriotic organizations which had been associated with Japanese imperialism and to purge from public employment all who had held office in them.

In March 1946, the draft of a new constitution, prepared through proddings by SCAP but presented through the Japanese government, was given to the public. This was done at the "command" of the Emperor and with the "full approval" of MacArthur. The document was approved by the Diet in October 1946, was promulgated by the Emperor over the radio on November 3, 1946, and went into full effect in May 1947. The procedure followed had conformed so far as possible to that prescribed by the constitution of 1889. In many ways the new document was revolutionary. It declared that war, as the sovereign right of the nation, and the threat or use of force were forever renounced as a means of settling international disputes. Land, sea, and air forces, as well as other war potential, were never to be maintained. The right of belligerency of the state was not to be recognized. The position of the Emperor was also basically altered. The Emperor was declared to be "the symbol of the state and of the unity of the people, deriving his position from the will of the people in whom resides sovereign power." In all matters of state, the Emperor must not act except in accord with the advice and approval of the cabinet. The constitution also insisted that it was to be the supreme law of the state and that no imperial rescript contrary to its provisions should have legal force or validity. It thus sought to prevent measures such as those by which the military had been given so large a voice in the pre-1945 government. The constitution contained a bill of rights, modeled in part on that in the constitution of the United States. This included equal rights of husband and wife, marriage by mutual consent (provisions which, if carried out, would radically alter the traditional family system), freedom of thought, conscience, and religion, the prohibition of involuntary servitude and of torture and cruel punishments, and the right of the individual not to be required to testify against himself. The abolishment of state Shinto was confirmed, and the state was forbidden to engage in religious activities or religious education. Peers and the peerage were terminated. Freedom of assembly and association, as well as of press and speech, were to be maintained, and censorship was forbidden. All the people were to have "the right to maintain the minimum standards of wholesome and cultured living." Workers were guaranteed the right to organize and to bargain and act collectively. All were to have the right and the obligation to work. Standards of wages, hours, rest, and other working conditions were to be fixed by law. The Parliament, or Diet, was to be "the highest organ of state power and the sole law-making authority." It was composed of two bodies, the House of Representatives and the House of Councillors, both elected by the people. At the peak of the reorganized judicial system was placed the Supreme Court, whose members were to be appointed by the Cabinet. The Cabinet was responsible to the Diet, and the Premier and a majority of its members were required to be chosen from members of the Diet. Thus, in contrast with the pre-1945 situation in which various other elements contended with the Diet for power, the government was made to rest upon a Diet chosen by universal adult franchise of both men and women and legally given full charge of the affairs of the nation. Amendments to the constitution could be passed by a two-thirds vote of the members of each house, but must be submitted as well to the people. A majority vote of the latter was necessary for ratification.

In the first national elections held after the occupation, about

26,000,000 exercised the privilege of voting and returned to the Diet representatives who were mainly conservative or moderate. The prewar parties had ceased to exist, but their successors largely continued the frame of mind and the trends which they had embodied.

In the summer of 1946 the Diet worked out a revision of the program for agrarian reform which it had passed in December 1945. Under it the share-croppers would become owners of the land which they had cultivated. The government was to buy the land from the owners at a fixed price. Loopholes in the measure made it possible for owners partly to evade the professed purpose of the bill by selling tracts to members of their families, but in the main the legislation effected a wide distribution of the land and to some degree removed one of the most flagrant evils of the old economic order. Here was an agrarian revolution, peaceably accomplished, much more sweeping than that contemplated in Communist China.

In December 1949, the Diet enacted a law which ended the fishing rights of absentee owners and threw open fishing freely to about a million fishermen. This was hailed as being almost as significant as the redistribution of the land. It was especially important because of the large place which fish had in the Japanese menu.

The encouragement given to labor to organize led to the formation of many unions. To deal with the problems presented by the unions a Ministry of Labor was formed in 1946 with full Cabinet status. As a concomitant of the mushrooming of unions, strikes broke out, some of them fomented by Communists. These led to the passage of legislation in 1946 which provided machinery for the arbitration of industrial disputes, forbade strikes by government and municipal employees, and provided a thirty-day delay of proposed strikes by workers in railways and public utilities after the employer or employees had applied for mediation.

In 1946 steps were taken toward the promised dissolution of the *Zaibatsu*. The five largest of the *Zaibatsu* turned over their holdings in the scores of corporations which they controlled to a Holding Company Liquidation Commission in return for government bonds which were not to be sold for ten years. This was an attempt to break up the economic structure which by many had been regarded as closely associated with Japan's imperialistic policies. Yet the problem presented by the *Zaibatsu* was not so easily solved. The industrial and financial structure of the post-Perry Japan had been largely based upon these family organizations and had been oriented to them. Was it possible to effect the economic recovery which the nation so desperately needed if these accustomed patterns with their accumulation of experience and of men skilled in their operation were dissolved? Would they not creep back in other forms? Moreover, if the purpose was to decentralize the business of the country, who in the impoverished land would have the resources to buy the securities which had been sold to the Holding Company Liquidation Commission? In general, the public was very slow to take up the securities. Yet the dissolution was accomplished. In December 1947, two measures were passed which were designed to insure deconcentration and to make effective the anti-monopoly program.

The year 1946 also saw a drastic purging of the educational system of the chauvinistic teaching which had furthered the indoctrination of youth with the imperialistic ideas. On the last day of 1945 the teaching of history, geography, and morals in the schools was suspended, and the textbooks and teacher's manuals which had previously been employed for that purpose were ordered destroyed. In the ensuing months new textbooks were produced, and with their aid, before the end of the year, the teaching of geography and history was authorized. After an examination of some thousands of teachers, several hundred were dismissed for subversive convictions. In 1947 measures were taken to extend the financial responsibility of the state for education and thus to make easier the enforcement of the requirement, continued from pre-war days, of primary education for all children.

An international tribunal was set up to try those who were accused of being responsible for plotting Japan's imperialistic venture. After a prolonged trial which was given wide publicity, in November 1948, a verdict of guilty was handed down for twenty-five men, including former Premier Tojo. Tojo and six others were condemned to death. In spite of an appeal to the Supreme Court of the United States, the sentence was carried out on several before the end of the year. Before the end of 1950, however, a number held as war criminals had been released.

The problem of reparations proved thorny and intricate. Soon after the surrender of Japan a report was made which recommended the removal of much of the industrial equipment which had been built up in the arming of the nation and the prosecution of the war. The country's heavy industry was to be reduced by nine-tenths. This, it was hoped, would be a safeguard against the renewal of Japan's militarism. Yet the measures, so it was urged, should not be carried out in such fashion as to cripple the nation in producing manufactures which could be exchanged for food and other imports essential to the people's livelihood. However, the decision on reparations was deadlocked because of Russian insistence that the removals of equipment from Manchuria and Sakhalin which the Soviet authorities had carried out must be regarded as "war trophies" and not as reparations. The failure to reach agreement on reparations handicapped Japanese recovery, for Japanese industrialists were unwilling to repair or rebuild their plants until they could be assured of what machinery and equipment would be left to them. This delay in turn added to the burdens of the United States, for that country was having to pour millions into Japan to fend off widespread famine. Moreover, to lighten the load which their government was carrying in feeding the country, the Americans wished as rapid a recovery of Japan as was consistent with preventing a resurgence of militarism and imperialism. This meant that they were increasingly reluctant to support extreme demands for reparations.

As will be gathered from the last paragraph, in Japan the United States was confronted not only with the problem of preventing the country from again becoming a military menace and in pressing the democratization of the government, education, and social and economic patterns. It had also to assist the population, exhausted after the long war and handicapped by the drain on its energies and by the physical destruction of its merchant marine and of many of its factories, to bring back its food supply to a level which would cancel the wholesale undernourishment, and to provide the housing made imperative by the bombings of the cities and the vast influx of repatriates from the armed forces and the overseas civilians who had been compelled by the victors to come home. The problems which we outlined in introducing post-war Japan became those of the American forces as well as of the Japanese.

The most serious single economic problem was that of food. Much food was imported. Fortunately, by 1949 the yield of rice in the islands themselves was increasing. Yet it was by no means sufficient to supply all of Japan's needs. Although the per capita ration was increased, government control was still in force and the black markets flourished.

Coal, too, constituted a major headache. The Koreans and the prisoners of war who had been the source of much of the labor in the mines were no longer available. The imports, chiefly of high grade coking coal and anthracite, from Sakhalin, Manchuria, and North China, largely ceased. Gradually, partly under pressure from SCAP upon the government, employment in the mines rose, and with it the output increased.

Inflation plagued the country. During the war years it had become marked. It increased after the cessation of hostilities. Because of the prostrate economy, the exhaustion and destruction of the war, and the cutting off of foreign markets, the government was desperately short of revenues. Moreover, although it was relieved of the burden of war and of the army and navy, the government was charged with the maintenance of the forces of occupation. It also subsidized essential industries, including the mining of coal. To meet the charges against its budget, the government was forced to resort to the printing press for new currency and bonds. Various efforts were put forth to deal with the inflation, largely under prodding by SCAP. Attempts were made to control prices, to reduce the number of government employees, and to increase foreign trade. At first foreign commerce was conducted on an inter-governmental basis. By 1951 private participation in commerce was beginning. Yet the normal Far Eastern markets of Japan were still disrupted by the civil disorders and the exhaustion which were the aftermath of war. In May 1950, some relief was promised by the action of the United Nations Economic Commission for Asia and the Far East which favored the development of trade between Japan and other Asiatic areas. Slowly and partly by substantial aid from the United States which ultimately fell on the American taxpayer recovery was being effected and with it some prospect was being seen of relief from the disorder in the currency.

By 1951 there seemed to be no likelihood of an early full ending of the occupation. It might be reduced and modified, but it bade fair to go on indefinitely in one or another form. In the autumn of 1949 MacArthur praised the progress which the Japanese had made. He also realized the perils of continued occupation, both to Japan and to the American forces. The Japanese were becoming accustomed to lean on SCAP for guidance and on American funds for support. The Japanese tradition of submitting to superiors and of regimentation by a centralized authority which harked back at least to Tokugawa days disposed the Japanese both to submit to SCAP and to expect SCAP to solve their problems. To this also contributed the paternalistic tradition of the land: the head of the family was regarded as responsible for the welfare of the members of the family. This precedent carried over to employees in the modern factories. It also helped to determine the attitude of the Japanese toward SCAP. SCAP, predominantly American, found itself under the seeming necessity of continuing to give directions. It had curbed the liberty of the press which it had advocated. It had intervened in labor disputes and by fiat had prevented or ended some strikes. Here and there corruption was creeping into its ranks. The turn-over in its personnel was rapid. Some members of the occupying armies were a discredit to the United States. Because of the tension between Russia and the United States, no comprehensive peace treaty was in sight. In the Philippines and China fear was expressed that by encouraging recovery in Japan the United States was—even though unwittingly and unintentionally—clearing the road for renewed Japanese aggression.

Certainly by 1951 it was not yet clear that the basic revolution desired by SCAP was really taking place. The defeat and occupation of Japan had given opportunity for the liberal forces to resume and accelerate the advance toward democracy which had been marked in the years immediately following World War I. Sweeping changes had been begun in giving women equality with men, in the family structures, in labor, in education, in the state, in business, in landowning, and fishing. But basic patterns which had characterized Japan from the dawn of history, notably the military tradition, could not easily be eradicated. It was sobering to remember that in the previous periods of revolutionary change, namely that which marked the introduction and adoption of Chinese culture and that which had followed the arrival of Perry, such historic features of Japanese life as the imperial institution and the military tradition had emerged strengthened rather than weakened and that Shinto as a religion connected closely with the imperial house had persisted. While drastic defeat followed by occupation was without precedent in Japan's experience, the record of the past was not encouraging to those who hoped for permanent democratization and demilitarization. Hope was further dampened by the unpleasant fact that the world in which SCAP was attempting its great experiment was one in which armaments were continuing to mount and in which the development of new and terrifying weapons of destruction was threatening the existence of civilization itself. The growth of the United Nations gave encouragement to those who dreamed of a peaceful world, but a race was on between the creation of some form of effective supra-national and international government and the piling up of armaments with the concomitant of mounting tensions. Should the ideal represented by the United Nations succeed, the unprecedented might happen and Japan remain permanently disarmed and increasingly democratic. Should it fail, Japan might be expected eventually to find a way to rearm.

Japan Between the Two Giants

The situation for Japan was further complicated by the conflict between the two giants of the new age, Russia and the United States. Although Russia was represented on the Far Eastern Commission and on the Allied Council for Japan, in Japan the United States was clearly dominant. Some Americans, notably among the military, were disposed to regard Japan as a bastion against Russia and Communism in the Far East. It was a question whether in this respect Japan was not more of a liability than an asset.

On the asset side of the ledger were several factors. In the event of war between the United States and Russia, the Japanese islands would provide a physical base for American forces. Moreover, the Japanese had a traditional fear of Russia which went back to the nineteenth century and which had been confirmed by experience with Russia under the Soviets. In the government which cooperated with SCAP the moderate and conservative elements rather than the radical were in control. Moreover, in the event of a war with Russia, Japan might provide man-power for armies cooperating with the United States in the Far East which would not have to be transported such great distances as would those recruited in America.

Among the liabilities were the precarious economic position of Japan and the dependence upon markets in the neighboring continent. In case the latter were in the hands of Russia or its allies, Japan would be greatly embarrassed. Under these circumstances the United States might be forced to feed and clothe the Japanese, or at least to cover the margin between what was produced in Japan and could be obtained by exchange in trade with friendly countries and what was needed for the maintenance of the populace. That this might prove very burdensome was made abundantly clear by the cost to the American tax-payers of relief to Japan in the post-war years. Then, too, the Japanese might have little stomach for a war in which their cities would be on the front line, vulnerable to air attacks from the continent. They might seek to exact a price for their assistance and might even attempt by bargaining with each of the two contestants to obtain terms profitable to themselves or might endeavor to maintain neutrality. The Japanese might even attempt to take advantage of the struggle between the Titans to regain the place which had been theirs before their defeat. Of great significance, too, was the extensive poverty. It was in such ground that Communism would find ready rootage. Moreover, restlessness under foreign occupation was growing and criticism was rising. Self-respecting and proud, the Japanese would not be content permanently to remain a subject people. In the spring of 1950 the Japanese government, significantly, wished a peace treaty with any nation which would accord it "freedom and equality."

Russia was endeavoring to encourage Communism. At times it was openly critical of SCAP. It sought to indoctrinate with Communism the hundreds of thousands of war prisoners before it returned them to their homes. The Russians delayed the promised repatriation of these prisoners, pleading the lack of shipping, and that in spite of the American offer of enough boats to accomplish the task. They seemed to exact of the prisoners as the price of repatriation conformity to Communism and sought by education to make the conversion genuine. When they finally were permitted to return, many of the prisoners had been convinced by Communist propaganda.

Moreover, Communism was making headway among workers and students. Communists were seeking to control labor unions. Many students, impatient with the slow recovery of their country and the bleak prospect for their own futures, turned to Communism with its rosy promises of Utopia.

In some ways the basic problem of Japan was one of ideology. Before its defeat, Japan had been held together and inspired by a faith which centered about the nation led by the Emperor and by state Shinto and the associated cults of the imperial ancestors and national heroes. That faith had been gravely shaken by the outcome of the war. The abolition of the state support of Shinto and the renunciation by the Emperor of his divinity required by SCAP had dealt it further blows. Reverence for the Emperor persisted, but something of a vacuum had been created. This void was less marked than that left in China by the waning of Confucianism, for loyalty to the imperial house was still strong, some of the sects of Shinto which had never enjoyed state support were vigorous, and the decay of Buddhism had not gone as far as it had in China. Christianity was growing, and the Japanese were more open-minded to its presentation than they had ever been, but Christians were still a small minority, less than one-half of one per cent of the population. Democracy as expounded by Americans was showing progress, but it seemed scarcely adequate to the needs of the Japanese. Communism was making an energetic bid for Japanese allegiance, but only a minority had been won. The future was uncertain.

BIBLIOGRAPHY

IN GENERAL

T. Cole and J. H. Hallowell (editors), *Post-War Governments in the Far East* (Gainesville, Fla., 1947).
F. Hailey, *Half of One World* (New York, 1950).
O. Lattimore, *The Situation in Asia* (Boston, 1949).
Much of the best material for these years is in periodicals. Those specializing on the area which will be found useful are:
Far Eastern Survey (New York, 1932 ff.).
Pacific Affairs (New York, 1928 ff.).
Foreign Affairs (New York, 1923 ff.) which, while not specializing on the Far East, usually has one or more excellent articles on phases of that area in each of its issues and contains excellent critical bibliographies.

INDIA

G. E. Jones, *Tumult in India* (New York, 1948).
J. Nehru, *Independence and After. Speeches, 1946–1949* (New York, 1950).
P. Talbot, *India and Pakistan–Progress Report* (Foreign Policy Association, New York, 1949).

CEYLON

I. Jennings, *the Economy of Ceylon* (Oxford University Press, 1948).

SOUTHEAST ASIA IN GENERAL

L. A. Mills and associates, *The New World of Southeast Asia* (University of Minnesota Press, 1949).

THE FRENCH IN INDO-CHINA

E. Hammer, *Indochina and Viet Nam* (New York, 1949).

INDONESIA

R. Kennedy and P. M. Kattenburg, *Indonesia in Crisis* (Foreign Policy Association, New York, 1948).
C. Wolf, *The Indonesian Story* (New York, 1948).

THE PHILIPPINES

L. K. Rossinger, *The Philippines, Problems of Independence* (Foreign Policy Association, New York, 1948).

CHINA

A. D. Barnett, *Profile of Red China* (Foreign Policy Association, New York, 1950).
J. Belden, *China Shakes the World* (New York, 1949).

J. K. Fairbank, *The United States and China* (Harvard University Press, 1948).

Department of State, *United States Relations with China with Special Reference to the Period 1944–1949* (U. S. Government Printing Office, 1949).

G. E. Winfield, *China, the Land and the People* (New York, 1948).

KOREA

The Department of State, *Korea, 1945–1948. A Report on Political Developments and Economic Resources with Selected Documents* (U. S. Government Printing Office, 1948).

G. M. McCune, in collaboration with A. L. Grey, Jr., *Korea Today* (Harvard University Press, 1950).

JAPAN

Activities of the Far East Commission. Report of the Secretary General February 26, 1946–July 10, 1947 (U. S. Government Printing Office, 1947).

The Far Eastern Commission. Second Report by the Secretary General (U. S. Government Printing Office, 1949).

W. M. Ball, *Japan, Enemy or Ally* (New York, 1949).

J. B. Cohen, *Japan's Economy in War and Reconstruction* (University of Minnesota Press, 1949).

R. A. Fearey, *The Occupation of Japan Second Phase: 1948–50* (New York, 1950).

M. Gayn, *Japan Diary* (New York, 1948).

E. M. Martin, *The Allied Occupation of Japan* (Stanford University Press, 1948).

E. O. Reischauer, *The United States and Japan* (Harvard University Press, 1950).

H. Wakefield, *New Paths for Japan* (Oxford University Press, 1948).

Chapter XVIII. A PAUSE FOR PERSPECTIVE

THE HISTORY OF THE FAR EAST is still being made. Because of the date at which these lines are written we are having to stop in mid flight in some of the most stirring series of events which that region has ever known. Our pause is not at the end of an era. It can scarcely be set off by a period or even by a colon or a comma.

As we conclude this particular account, however, we must glance back quickly over the course we have traversed and attempt to view it from the perspective of the point we have reached.

We have seen, so far as his knowledge enables the historian to trace them, the origins and development of the peoples and cultures of the Far East, with a more condensed account of India. We have watched great civilizations arise. The two central ones were in China and India. Japan and Korea adopted so much from China that culturally they may be regarded as variants of the civilization of that empire, although both, and especially Japan, placed their own stamp on what was received. Much of Indian culture penetrated to southeastern Asia and the East Indies and, through Buddhism, to almost all the Chinese Empire, Korea, and Japan. China put its impress on Tongking, Annam, and border lands on the west and north. Here were vast centers of civilization as mighty as any which the West knew until the nineteenth century, and, especially in the Far East proper, almost as distant from the Occident as though they had been on another planet.

In the thirteenth, fourteenth, fifteenth, sixteenth, seventeenth, and eighteenth centuries came contacts with European peoples. That was through the initiative of the Occident and not of the Far East. In the nineteenth and twentieth centuries these contacts became an irruption from the West. In consequence, the structure of the life of the peoples of the Far East and India was greatly altered. In some aspects of culture the changes became revolutions. An Occident, itself in process of profound and striking transition, was impinging upon the civilizations of the Far East and India. As a result these latter were displaying a double revolution, that brought them by powerful and aggressive aliens, and that which they were sharing with the Occident. Beginning in the 1930's, the Far East was progressively engulfed in a war which, beginning in that region, became world-wide. As a result of the struggle the changes of the preceding generation were accelerated.

It must be noted, however, that the revolutions were not always as basic as the superficial aspects might have led the casual and even the thoughtful observer to believe. The mechanical appliances and the scientific principles and techniques which had been developed in the Occident were being adopted. Through them Japan had been able to overrun much of the Far East, temporarily to expel the Western powers from most of the region, and to make extremely costly their campaign to defeat her. The industrialization, after the Western pattern, of China and India had begun. Educational systems in which Western learning was dominant became normal. Occidental medical science and public health were being adopted. Western forms of transportation, lighting, and communication were more and more coming into use. Political institutions of Occidental provenance had made headway. Several of the smaller groups were accepting Christianity. This was notably the case in the Philippines, among folk of primitive culture in several areas, and among the depressed classes of India. In Japan some of those of the middle and higher social strata most affected by the Occident had become Christian. Yet in most of the lands, both major and smaller, the cores of the ancient civilizations proved very resistant. Indeed, contact with Western nationalism appeared often to reenforce them. The rise and intensification of nationalism constituted the most widespread ideological modification wrought by contact with the Occident. In India Hinduism, Islam, and caste were modified but not abandoned. In Ceylon and Burma the inherited Buddhism seemed to be reviving. In Japan the imperial institution had been preserved. Until 1945 Shinto had been intensified, and the military, after seeing the traditional form of government by which they had controlled the nation swept aside, had come back into power through other means. The fundamental revolution had proceeded further in China than in any other major land. Here the disintegration of some of the institutions through which the basic principles of the inherited culture had been transmitted had been almost complete. Yet even in China the faith which had come from the Occident, Christianity, while having adherents in high position and helping to shape the new culture, was still the professed religion of only a small minority. Everywhere the secularistic spirit and the nationalism of Occidental origin were making a deep and growing impression. Communism was sweeping China and gaining adherents in other lands. Yet it was a recent phenomenon. Democracy as Anglo-Saxons conceived it was also making great strides. Seemingly the real revolutions had only begun. Presumably the succeeding decades would witness much greater changes than those we have recorded. That is prophecy and not history. As students of history we can only note the direction in which the currents appeared to be setting. Precisely the ways in which those currents would shape the Far East no man could know. It was clear, however, that the nineteenth and twentieth centuries had ushered the Far East and India into a new era. That era was without precedent in the extent and character of the alterations which were being wrought in the peoples of this vast area. Its outcome could not fail to have profound significance not only for the populations immediately concerned but also for the entire world.

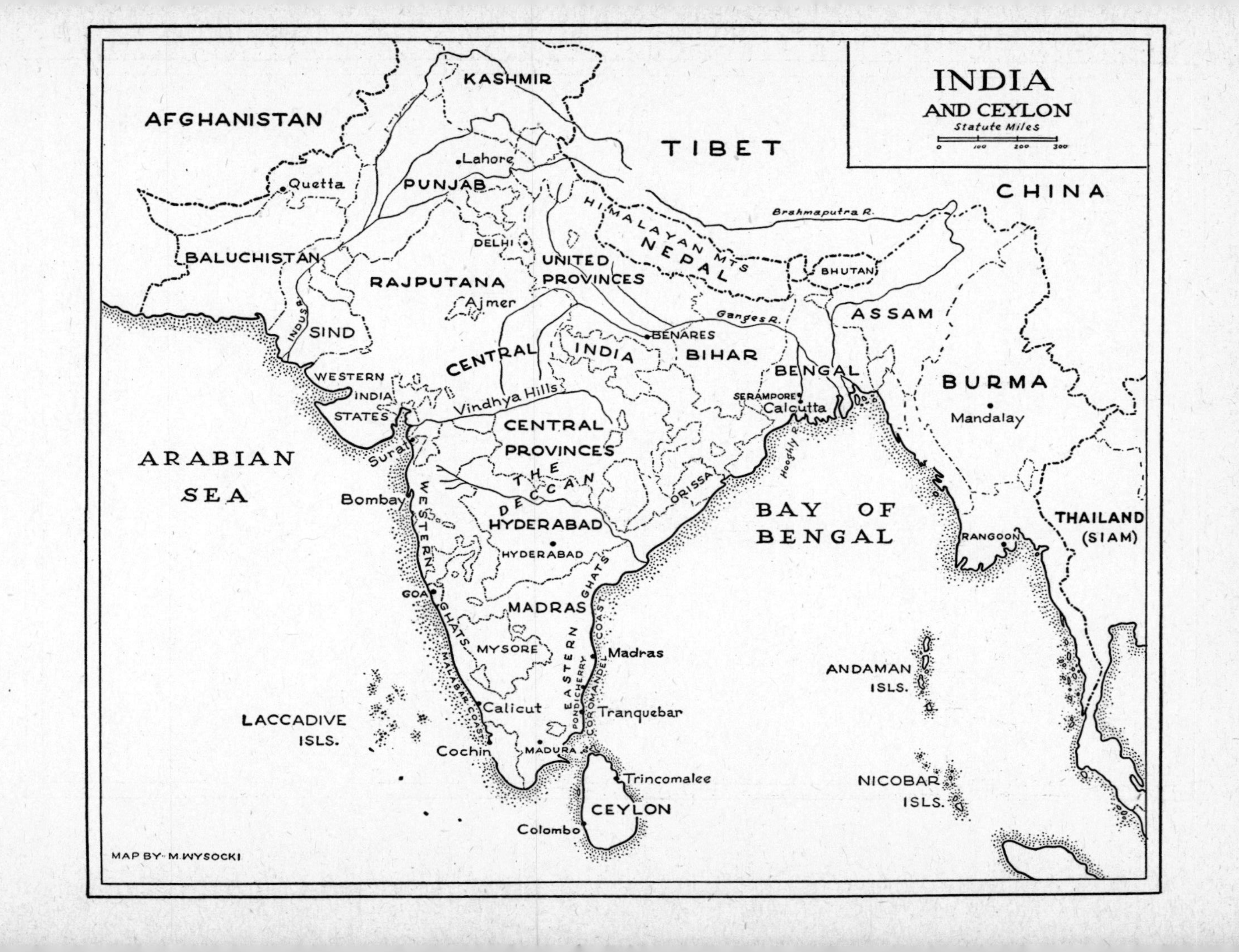
INDIA
AND CEYLON
Statute Miles
0
100
200
300
AFGHANISTAN
KASHMIR
TIBET
CHINA
Quetta
Lahore
PUNJAB
BALUCHISTAN
DELHI
UNITED
PROVINCES
RAJPUTANA
Ajmer
HIMALAYAN MTS
NEPAL
BHUTAN
Brahmaputra R.
Ganges R.
ASSAM
INDUS
SIND
BENARES
CENTRAL
INDIA
BIHAR
BENGAL
BURMA
Mandalay
WESTERN
INDIA
STATES
Vindhya Hills
SERAMPORE
Calcutta
CENTRAL
PROVINCES
Surat
ARABIAN
SEA
THE
DECCAN
Hooghly R.
ORISSA
Bombay
BAY OF
BENGAL
THAILAND
(SIAM)
HYDERABAD
HYDERABAD
RANGOON
WESTERN
GHATS
GOA
MADRAS
EASTERN
GHATS
COROMANDEL COAST
MYSORE
Madras
ANDAMAN
ISLS.
MALABAR COAST
PONDICHERRY
Calicut
Tranquebar
LACCADIVE
ISLS.
Cochin
MADURA
Trincomalee
NICOBAR
ISLS.
CEYLON
Colombo
MAP BY M. WYSOCKI

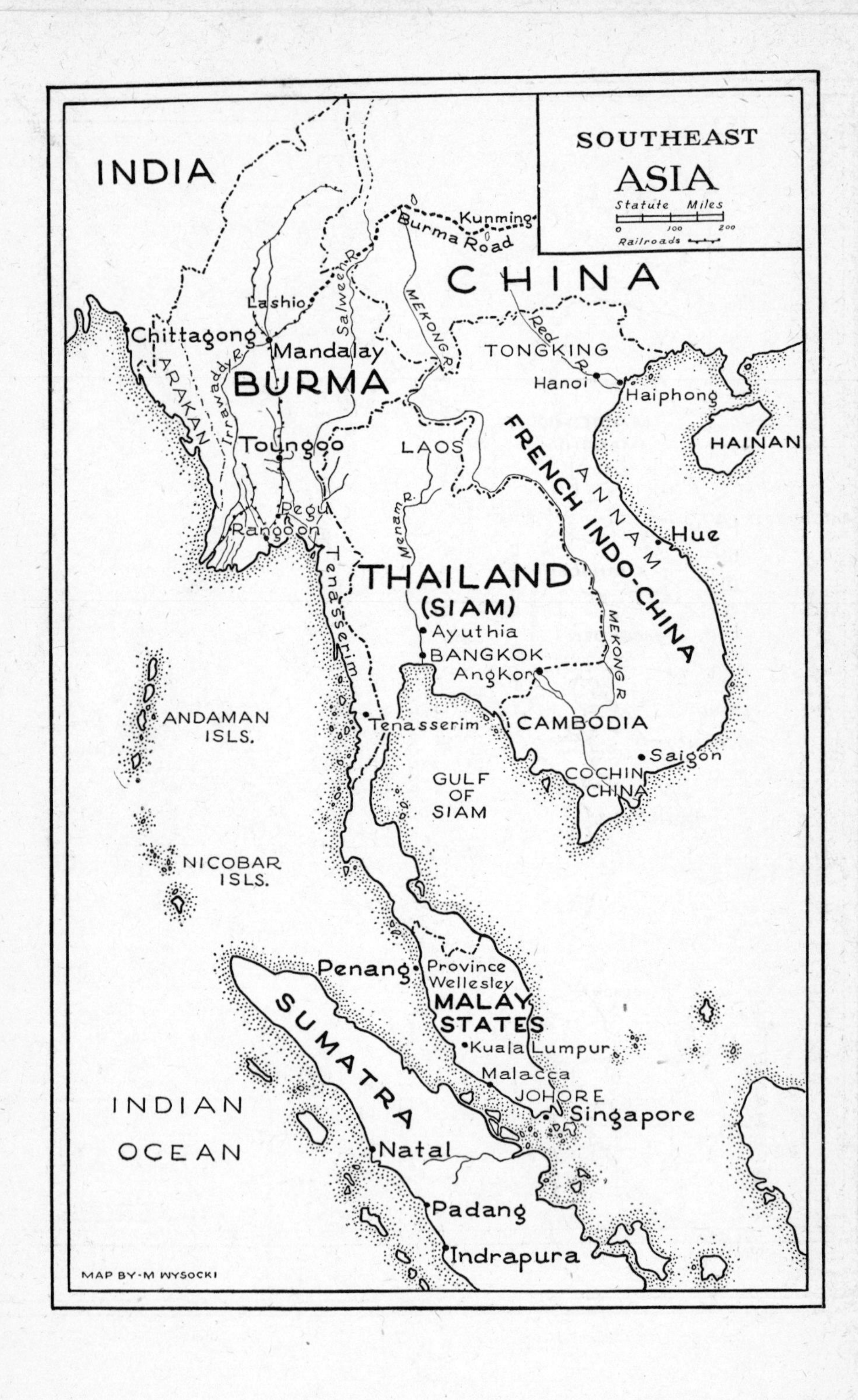
SOUTHEAST
ASIA
Statute Miles
0 100 200
Railroads
INDIA
CHINA
Kunming
Burma Road
Lashio
Salween R.
MEKONG R.
Chittagong
Mandalay
Irrawaddy R.
ARAKAN
BURMA
TONGKING
Red R.
Hanoi
Haiphong
HAINAN
Toungoo
LAOS
FRENCH INDO-CHINA
ANNAM
Menam R.
Pegu
Rangoon
Tenasserim
Hue
THAILAND
(SIAM)
Ayuthia
BANGKOK
Angkor
MEKONG R.
ANDAMAN
ISLS.
Tenasserim
CAMBODIA
Saigon
COCHIN
CHINA
GULF
OF
SIAM
NICOBAR
ISLS.
Penang
Province
Wellesley
MALAY
STATES
SUMATRA
Kuala Lumpur
Malacca
JOHORE
Singapore
INDIAN
OCEAN
Natal
Padang
Indrapura
MAP BY-M WYSOCKI

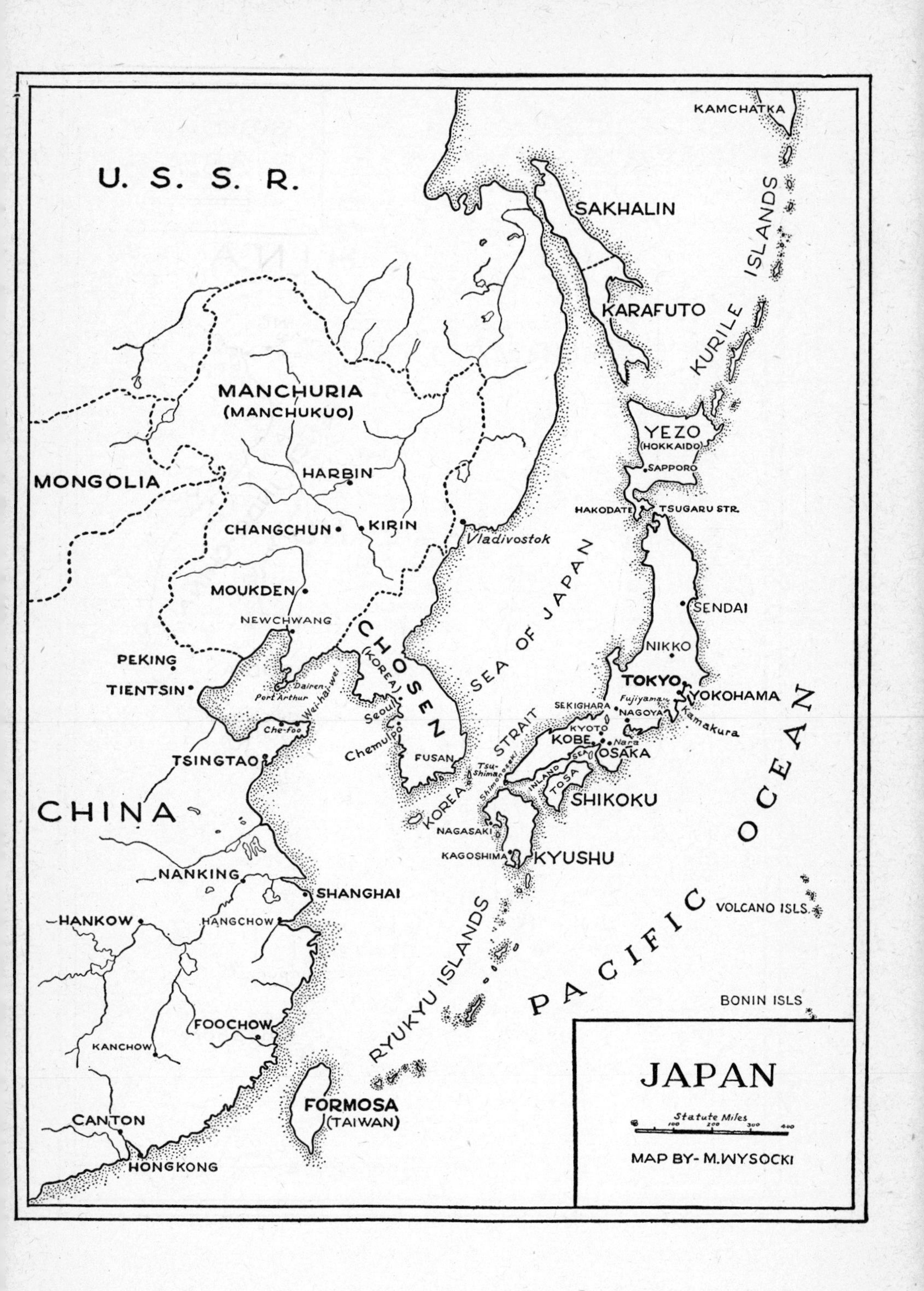
U. S. S. R.
KAMCHATKA
SAKHALIN
KARAFUTO
KURILE ISLANDS
MANCHURIA
(MANCHUKUO)
MONGOLIA
HARBIN
CHANGCHUN
KIRIN
Vladivostok
MOUKDEN
NEWCHWANG
PEKING
TIENTSIN
Dairen
Port Arthur
Wei-hai-wei
Che-foo
CHOSEN
(KOREA)
Seoul
Chemulpo
FUSAN
SEA OF JAPAN
YEZO
(HOKKAIDO)
SAPPORO
HAKODATE
TSUGARU STR.
SENDAI
NIKKO
TOKYO
YOKOHAMA
Fujiyama
Kamakura
SEKIGHARA
NAGOYA
KYOTO
KOBE
Nara
OSAKA
STRAIT
KOREA
Tsu-Shima
Shimonoseki
INLAND SEA
TOSA
SHIKOKU
NAGASAKI
KAGOSHIMA
KYUSHU
TSINGTAO
CHINA
NANKING
SHANGHAI
HANKOW
HANGCHOW
FOOCHOW
KANCHOW
CANTON
HONGKONG
FORMOSA
(TAIWAN)
RYUKYU ISLANDS
PACIFIC OCEAN
VOLCANO ISLS.
BONIN ISLS
JAPAN
Statute Miles
MAP BY- M.WYSOCKI

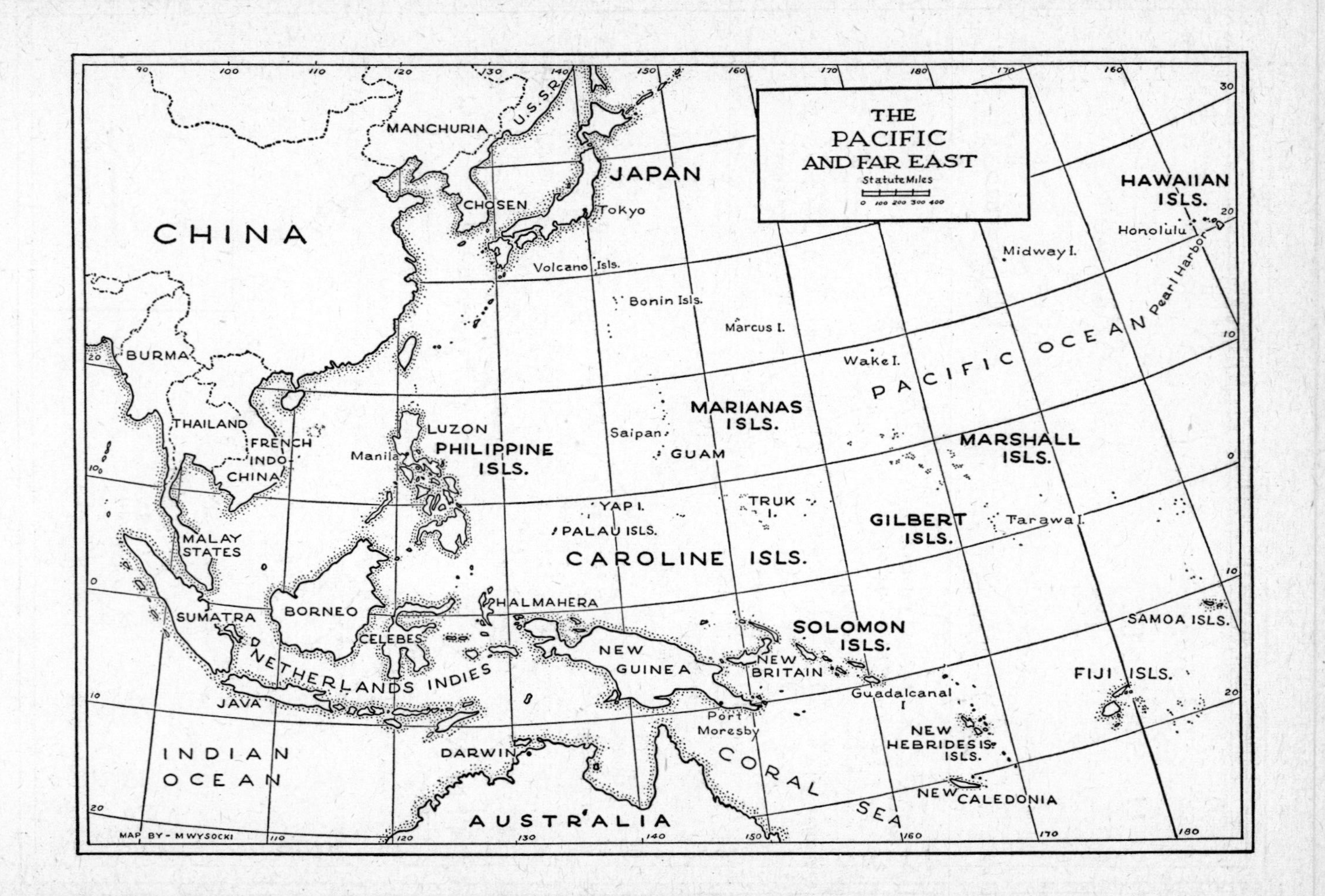
THE
PACIFIC
AND FAR EAST
Statute Miles
0 100 200 300 400
CHINA
MANCHURIA
U.S.S.R.
CHOSEN
JAPAN
Tokyo
Volcano Isls.
Bonin Isls.
Marcus I.
Wake I.
Midway I.
HAWAIIAN ISLS.
Honolulu
Pearl Harbor
PACIFIC OCEAN
BURMA
THAILAND
FRENCH INDO-CHINA
MALAY STATES
LUZON
Manila
PHILIPPINE ISLS.
Saipan
GUAM
MARIANAS ISLS.
MARSHALL ISLS.
YAP I.
PALAU ISLS.
TRUK I.
CAROLINE ISLS.
GILBERT ISLS.
Tarawa I.
SUMATRA
BORNEO
CELEBES
HALMAHERA
NETHERLANDS INDIES
JAVA
NEW GUINEA
NEW BRITAIN
SOLOMON ISLS.
Guadalcanal I.
SAMOA ISLS.
FIJI ISLS.
Port Moresby
NEW HEBRIDES ISLS.
NEW CALEDONIA
DARWIN
INDIAN OCEAN
CORAL SEA
AUSTRALIA
MAP BY - M WYSOCKI

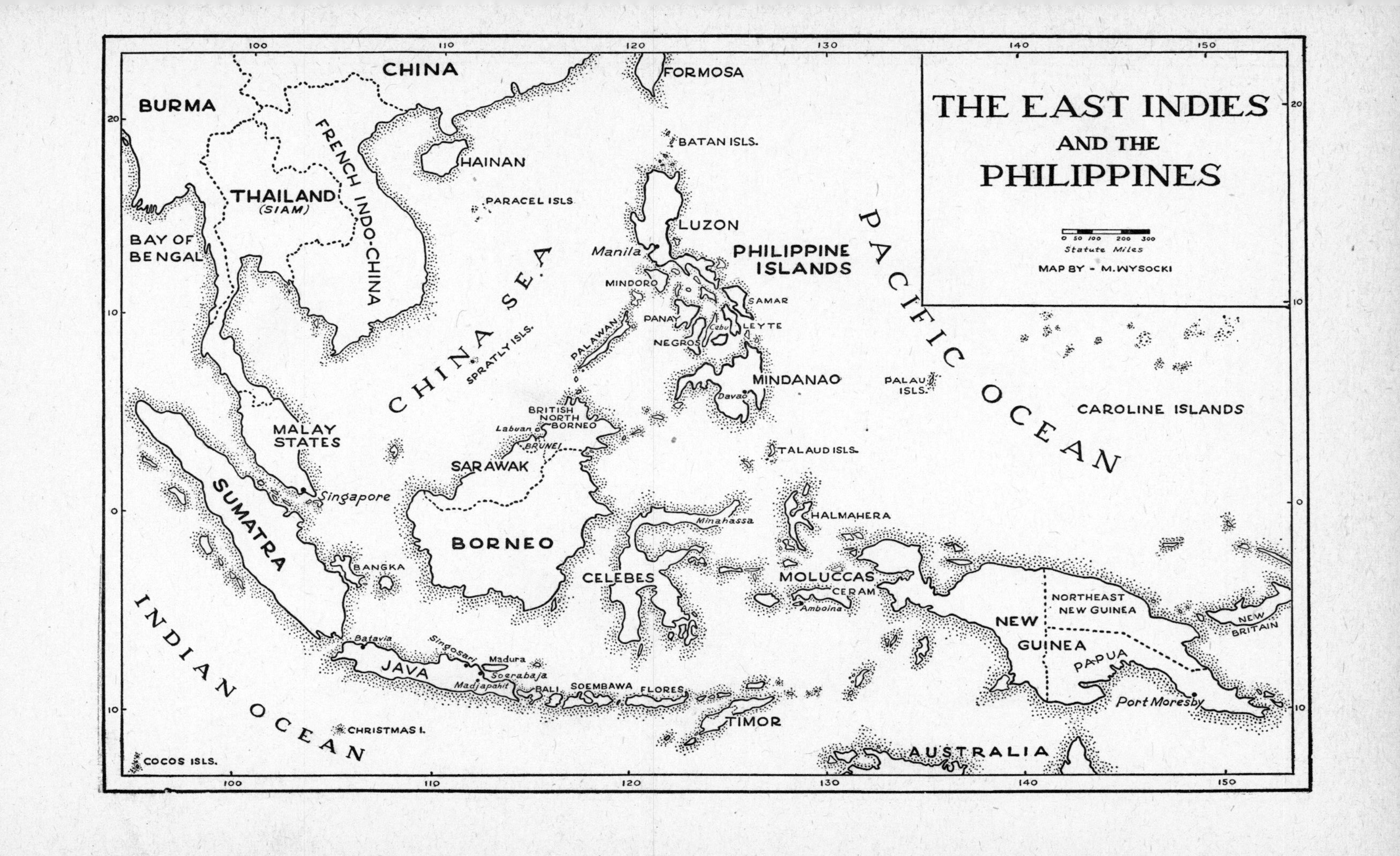
THE EAST INDIES
AND THE
PHILIPPINES
0 50 100 200 300
Statute Miles
MAP BY - M.WYSOCKI
BURMA
CHINA
FORMOSA
HAINAN
THAILAND
(SIAM)
FRENCH INDO-CHINA
BAY OF BENGAL
PARACEL ISLS.
BATAN ISLS.
LUZON
Manila
PHILIPPINE ISLANDS
MINDORO
SAMAR
PANAY
LEYTE
Cebu
NEGROS
PALAWAN
MINDANAO
Davao
PALAU ISLS.
PACIFIC OCEAN
CAROLINE ISLANDS
CHINA SEA
SPRATLY ISLS.
BRITISH NORTH BORNEO
Labuan
BRUNEI
SARAWAK
MALAY STATES
Singapore
TALAUD ISLS.
SUMATRA
BORNEO
HALMAHERA
Minahassa
BANGKA
CELEBES
MOLUCCAS
CERAM
Amboina
NEW GUINEA
NORTHEAST NEW GUINEA
NEW BRITAIN
PAPUA
Port Moresby
INDIAN OCEAN
Batavia
Singosari
Madura
JAVA
Soerabaja
Madjapahit
BALI
SOEMBAWA
FLORES
TIMOR
CHRISTMAS I.
COCOS ISLS.
AUSTRALIA

Akmolinsk
Barnaul
U. S.
Semiplatmsk
TANNU
TUVA
Ulan
Pribalkash
ZUNGARIA
Urga
Ili
Kuldja
GOBI
MONGOLIA
Turfan
Aksu
Hami
DESERT
Kashkar
Tarim R.
INNER
Yarkand
SINKIANG
Lobnor
NINGHSIA
SUIY
MONGOL
Tunhuang
KANSU
NAN SHAN MTS.
K'UNLUN MTS.
ORDOS
KOKONOR
(CHING-HAI)
Lanchow
Wei R.
TIBET
Hsia
SHENS
Han R.
Min R.
SZECHWAN
Agra
NEPAL
Lhasa
HSIK'ANG
Chengtu
Yangtze R.
Chungking
BHUTAN
Allahabad
Patna
KWEICHOW
Kweiyang
Mekong R.
Kunming
Calcutta
YUNNAN
Kwe
INDIA
Red R.
KWANGS
Nann
BURMA
TONGKING
BAY OF
BENGAL
Hanoi
FRENCH INDO CHINA
Pegu
SIAM
MAP BY - M. WYSOCKI

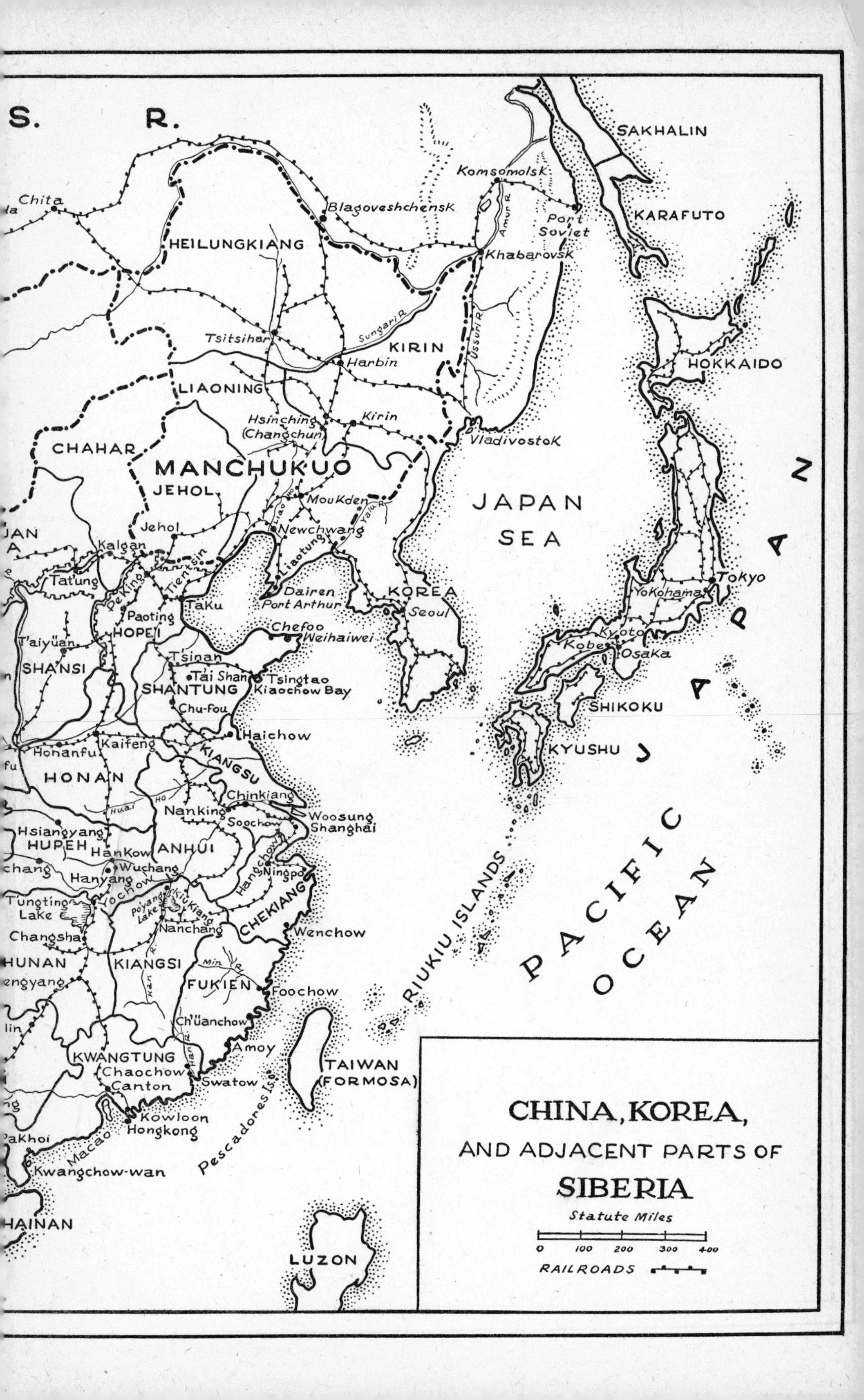
CHINA, KOREA,
AND ADJACENT PARTS OF
SIBERIA
Statute Miles
0 100 200 300 400
RAILROADS
S. R.
SAKHALIN
KARAFUTO
Komsomolsk
Port Soviet
Chita
Blagoveshchensk
Khabarovsk
HEILUNGKIANG
Amur R.
Ussuri R.
Sungari R.
Tsitsihar
KIRIN
Harbin
HOKKAIDO
LIAONING
Hsinching (Changchun)
Kirin
Vladivostok
CHAHAR
MANCHUKUO
JEHOL
Moukden
Yalu R.
Liao Ho
JAPAN SEA
JAPAN
Jehol
Newchwang
Kalgan
Tatung
Peking
Tientsin
Liaotung
Dairen
Port Arthur
KOREA
Seoul
Tokyo
Yokohama
Kyoto
Kobe
Osaka
Taku
Paoting
HOPEI
Chefoo
Weihaiwei
T'aiyüan
SHANSI
Tsinan
Tai Shan
Tsingtao
Kiaochow Bay
SHANTUNG
Chu-fou
SHIKOKU
KYUSHU
Haichow
Honanfu
Kaifeng
KIANGSU
HONAN
Huai
Ho
Chinkiang
Nanking
Soochow
Woosung
Shanghai
Hsiangyang
HUPEH
Hankow
ANHUI
Wuchang
Hanyang
Hangchow
Ningpo
Yochow
Kiukiang
Poyang Lake
Tungting Lake
Nanchang
CHEKIANG
Changsha
Wenchow
PACIFIC OCEAN
RIUKIU ISLANDS
HUNAN
KIANGSI
Min R.
FUKIEN
Foochow
Kan R.
Ch'üanchow
Amoy
Han R.
KWANGTUNG
Chaochow
Canton
Swatow
TAIWAN (FORMOSA)
Kowloon
Hongkong
Macao
Pescadores Is.
Pakhoi
Kwangchow-wan
HAINAN
LUZON

INDEX